ORION'S DOOR

SYMBOLS OF CONSCIOUSNESS & BLUEPRINTS OF CONTROL
- THE STORY OF ORION'S INFLUENCE *OVER* HUMANITY

ORION'S DOOR

**SYMBOLS OF CONSCIOUSNESS & BLUEPRINTS OF CONTROL
- THE STORY OF ORION'S INFLUENCE *OVER* HUMANITY**

NEIL HAGUE

Quester

First published in October 2020 by
Quester Publications

Cover Design: Neil Hague
Orion's Door © 2020

British Library Cataloguing-in Publication Data
A catalogue record for this book is
available from the British Library

ISBN 978-1-8381363-0-7

DEDICATION

For the Earth and *all* of Her Children.

Other books by Neil Hague

Through Ancient Eyes - *Seeing Hidden Dimensions,
Exploring Art & Soul Connections*

Journeys in the Dreamtime - *Keys to Unlocking the Imagination,
Exposing the Untold History of Art*

Kokoro - *The New Jerusalem & the Rise of the True Human Being*

Moon Slayer - *The Return of the Lions of Durga*

Aeon Rising - *Battle for Atlantis Earth*

For more information please visit:

www.neilhague.com
www.neilhaguebooks.com

ACKNOWLEDGEMENTS

*Gratitude and love to the ancient scribes, mystics and teachers of 'all faiths'
who have been persecuted for their work, their passion and their esoteric
knowledge of the universe and the stars.*

I would like to thank several people who, over the years, have been influential
to my work. They are Pierre Sabak, Ellis C Taylor and David Icke.

I am also very grateful to the following people for the research and insight
they have provided over the past decade. They are:

Danny Wilten for his outstanding work surrounding Orion and *'The Mirror
Between Heaven and Earth'*. See his YouTube Channel, and his e-book *Orion in
the Vatican*. I would also like to acknowledge the work of Gary A. David, for
his incredible research on Orion symbolism amongst the Native American
Indian cultures of the South West. (see the bibliography for more details).

I also wish to acknowledge all the authors whose works are briefly quoted or
referred to in the text and in the notes and references.
Especially the following authors scholarly interpretations of various texts,
codices and symbols. They are: John Lash Lamb and Wayne Herschel.

A special mention to various galleries and museums all over the world.
I would like to especially thank, the Metropolitan Museum of Art,
Museo Nacional del Prado and the British Museum.
Gratitude to the various film production companies such as
Paramount Pictures for their inspiring productions.

A special thank you to Wendy for your proofreading skills and friendship.

Also, thanks to Dean at Billion Bites Film for his constant support
and interest in my work.

If inadvertently, I have overlooked anyone, I hope I've quoted from their work
appropriately and that they will accept my gratitude.

Neil Hague

CONTENTS

The door functions as a middle point between the internal world and the external world, between the information within and without – or between those who have been initiated and those who have the gifts of God, but have not yet established a cosmic bridge within themselves.

The cosmic bridge or 'door' becomes a necessary vehicle for people's communication on both sides –
such as the teachers, who are always inside the door, and the students, if not initiated, who are wondering (or wandering) outside the door.

MANTAK CHIA AND TAO HUANG
(THE SECRET TEACHINGS OF THE TAO TE CHING)

You burning sun, O golden mouth of space,
Through which divine imagination speaks
And showers the peace of darkness with its stars,
You burning sun of unconsuming lights,
The honey of all seas and moons and cells,
The consciousness that penetrates all life,
You burning sun who from your flames create
New images of man in joy and peace,
Be present in the dreams of all mankind
So that we know your unity of heart,
Awake the archetypes of doom to soar
On wings that are messages to earth,
And shine the eternal freedom of your smile
On all who in their work reflect your light.

WILLIAM ANDERSON

Opening Orion's Door - Neil Hague 2020

INTRODUCTION

If the doors of perception were cleansed everything would appear to man as it is, Infinite. For man has closed himself up, till he sees all things thro' narrow chinks of his cavern.

WILLIAM BLAKE

I have spent over two decades researching myths and illustrating books that have attempted to convey esoteric truths. The book you are about to read is my 'deepest' to date, and it weaves together various strands found in myths and stories telling of an essential focus on the stars. One particular star system, Orion, seems to have been very important to our ancestors. Its focus is evident in so many archetypes and ancient temples or religions, but more so, it seems to have been a significant focus in esoteric secret societies throughout history. My intention with this book is to collate and present a myriad of connections to Orion and show how much symbolism associated with the Orion constellation has shaped our perception and beliefs.

Orion is not just a star system or constellation. It is an archetype of *giant* proportions, a figure that seems to bring earth nearer to the stars. The book attempts to uncover deeper esoteric connections relating to Orion's influence on humanity and also shows how almost all religious symbolism and many beliefs are underpinned by this constellation. Its presence (along with Sirius) over ancient Egypt (and other ancient cultures further afield) is not a coincidence. Orion offers a significant piece in the 'puzzle' called 'life on earth'. As you will see, it has influenced almost every aspect of human society stretching as far back to the Pyramid-builders and possibly earlier to prehistoric times. The book is no way totally objective in its review of researched material; therefore, some of what you are about to read is purely subjective and open to interpretation, depending on how you perceive religion and cultural habits. However, there are common strands, threads of knowledge, symbolism and ancient narratives, which are undeniably part of an esoteric language connected to Orion, not least teachings associated with hermetic mysticism. I believe Orion is one of several 'stellar' (star) sources that has inspired religions on earth. *He* could be seen as a messianic archetype and presented through layers of symbolism connected to other celestial bodies (planets and suns) and adjacent constellations. Orion seems to hold a special place in the minds of the ancients, through to modern-day magicians, artists, secret societies and movie-makers. The latter will feature hugely throughout the book as I chart a path through esoteric symbolism connected to what I call, *Orion's Door*.

Hidden Knowledge

There are many levels of knowledge connected to Orion and its symbolism, and of course, there are quite a few specialist books focused solely on Orion written over the past decade or so. Some of these works I have considered while writing this book, but in no way is the book you are holding a 'specialist' focus on *one* area. What I attempt here is to delve much more deeply into uncharted esoteric symbolism associated with Orion, while showing how this star system was (and still is) one of the most important focus points for earth's mystery schools throughout the ages. At the highest levels of these elite secret societies are 'off-world' forces which will become clear as I weave my way through the symbolism. It is an enormous subject, one that has never really been covered in one book until now.

Orion is more than a star system; it is a 'multi-dimensional' archetype offering layer upon layer of meaning. The cover image for *Orion's Door* provides insight into the many layers I describe here. The words attributed to the Gnostic teacher, Jesus, in *John* 14:2, 'In my Father's house are many mansions,' is a fitting description for Orion's magnitude and impact on our world. My cover image attempts to convey that message, incorporating hermetic knowledge and celestial regions, stars, sun, planets, moon and mythical figures (such as Prometheus and Pandora), all of which play their part within the narrative. All of these elements, as you will see, 'frame' Orion's presence in the 'house of many mansions'.

Orion's key stars, such as Betelgeuse and Regel, to name but two, were worshipped by the ancients all over the ancient world. The symbolism associated with Orion's stars is in landmarks, megalithic alignments, various logos, and so much of today's military-tech industries. Why? Because Orion (and his connected suns) was, and still is, a key focus for elite power on earth. In ancient times, Orion worship was a global phenomenon, whether in the Americas, or in ancient Egypt. The same gods and myths are the 'blueprints' which seem to have been influential in forming a religious belief. Orion seems to provide a blueprint for our hierarchical structures, not least the pyramid-based civilizations, through to our modern military-industrial complex and political empires. 'Darker' aspects of Orion consciousness, is what I refer to, as the 'Cyber-Grid

Empire', which is of significant importance to an off-world alien force that is forging a 'new world' on Earth. *All* empires, it seems, are governed by Orion's star magic and 'occult knowledge', often held by secret societies stretching back, I believe, to the time of Atlantis. I have termed this strand of occult knowledge (along with a brotherhood that is using 'star magic') - the 'Orion Cult'. As I show in *Part One*, I sense there was an era on earth that could easily have been Orion's Age, a time when giants roamed a very different topology. More so, when you delve deeper, it becomes clear that Orion was more than a giant in Greek myth, *He* was an archetype for bloodlines who claim a heritage to the gods that came to earth in ancient times. Orion symbolism is the ultimate protagonist for all religious stories of 'saviours' and 'heroes' that abound in both Pagan beliefs and Abrahamic faiths alike. But Orion's influence can also be found in the stories of important gods relating to the Hopi, Hindu, Lakota, and Celtic myths and beliefs, stretching back thousands of years. Why did the American Indian Hopi, for example, replicate the Orion constellation on the surface of the Arizona desert? Who was Adam, Osiris, Ptah, Min, Kesil, and the many other deities worshipped by the ancients while measuring Orion's passage across the skies? All of this is looked at in great depth in *Part One*.

The relationship between Orion and the constellations that surround this 'Star Man' is also crucial as they provide religious symbols, cycles, festivals, and 'markers' of the seasons on earth. For example, the Gnostics in all of their expressions throughout history, seem to have understood a deeper connection to Orion and Taurus (the Bull) through their philosophies and teachings. As I show in the book, the relationship between 'Heavenly Adam' (Orion) and the Bull (Taurus/Pleiades) was understood deeply by those who focused on Orion's stars. Orion is key to understanding so much more about the higher cycles and 'celestial clocks' that create what we perceive to be 'reality'. Once the key is grasped the door can be unlocked and the initiate begins to understand the significance of this unique star system. What I have called *Orion's Door*, is a multi-dimensional portal that takes us deeper into knowledge and information beyond its opening in the heavens - in Orion. Book title definition.

Earth Stars & Doorways

In *Part Two*, I travel deeper into Orion's stars and look closer at the connections between science and mythology. Orion's stars and its massive nebulae are crucial to understanding the nature of the 'door'. The title of the book is relevant to Orion's stars which act as portals to other worlds, not least the supposed 'Black Hole' in the centre of the Orion Nebula. I unravel symbolism connected to angels, demons, and various 'darker aspects' of Orion worship, which includes a focus on Saturn, Mars, and the Moon, along with archetypes connected to horned gods and star magic. As I show in *Part Two*, the symbolism connected to Orion worship, seems to include a Science Fiction-like, technocratic New Age, one that focuses the masses on ancient-future gods and the ultimate deity – Artificial Intelligence. The latter part of the book reveals such material, which is essential if we are to understand how Gnostic teachings and a coming technocratic Cyber-Grid Empire are connected.

As the book unfolds, the truth about non-physical realities, our *forgotten* ancient history (myths) and Orion's archetypes, or blueprints, will become clearer, especially in *Part One*. Orion's archetypes continue to shape (or control) human perception. Both the *door* itself, and the *world reality* (illusion) we are all connected to, through our minds, has to be 'expanded on', if we are to be *truly free*. Hopefully, this book will help with the expansion process as we move towards higher states of awareness at this crucial time on earth. The realization that humanity speaks a universal language through music, art and other forms of creativity, reminds us of our deeper connections to *infinite* awareness *beyond* Orion's Door. Higher levels of consciousness accessed through love and our creative imagination are reached by symbolically going *through* Orion's Door, beyond the illusion. But first we have to want to *open* the door. Accessing higher dimensions and higher consciousness comes from our ability to 'see through' the façade of our, too often *crazy*, three-dimensional virtual world. Towards the end of the book, I offer ways to do this and hopefully provide a beacon of light for those who wish to see beyond the day-to-day darkness expressed through our governments obvious abuse of power, mainstream media propoganda and other forms of deception. The book you are about to read will hopefully expand the mind beyond the immediate five senses - the matrix, so to reveal a deeper insight into *who* and *what* we are. On one level, the mission behind this book is to unlock the readers' imagination, to ignite our soul's purpose, and move us into unique worlds where we are *renegade* individual co-creators.

Orion's Door is both a reference book and a penultimate guide to accessing information, which I am sure will take the reader further down the 'rabbit hole' to reveal what dwells *beyond* Orion's stars.

Let me now take you through a myriad of worlds, oral traditions, myths, movies, and symbols as I uncover the esoteric knowledge that beats a path to 'Orion's Door'.

PART ONE

On Earth, as It Is in Heaven

*The Beings who live below say that God is on High;
while the Angels in Heaven, say that God is on Earth.*
ZOHAR.

1
CORRELATIONS & MYSTERIES
'Opening Doors'

Within you is hidden the treasure of treasures.
Oh, know yourself and you shall know the Universe and the Gods!
THE ORACLE - DELPHI

Over the past few years, my research has led me to 'all things' Orion. I have written several books over the past twenty years looking at myth and symbolism associated with the stars. Still, in the book you are about to read, I focus solely on the Orion constellation and its multi-dimensional 'impact' on humanity.

Before I go into considerable depth and focus on the symbolism connected to Orion, it is essential to first weave our way through some fascinating correlations found in cave art, landmarks, temples, and ancient myths. I will also consider symbolism, gods, and untold histories connected to our fascination for one of the most prominent constellations and the stars surrounding Orion. From ancient shamanic skywatchers to more 'advanced' civilisations going back thousands of years, there are untold mysteries and narratives, which point at humanity's relationship with the stars. In this chapter, I want to take a broad view and set the scene for subjects I am going to cover throughout the book. And even though it might seem at times as though I am straying from the subject, I am merely circling multi-layered topics moving towards Orion's influence over life on earth.

Cave Art and Sky Maps

French paleo-astronomer, Chantal Jegues-Wolkiewiez, insists there was a long cultural tradition of 'skywatching' among the people of the Cro-Magnon Age of Europe (30,000-10,000 BCE). For Jegues-Wolkiewiez, original cave art, dated to the Upper Palaeolithic period, seems to have been representations of the stars, not least the region where Orion sits. Taurus, the Pleiades and Orion all seem to have been a common focus point for the cave artists of the Palaeolithic epoch. German researcher Dr. Michael Rappenglueck also arrived at similar conclusions, pointing to the markings

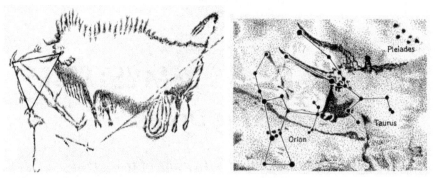

Figure 1: Orion and the bull, Taurus, in Cave art?
(Left) Dead man Lascaux. **(Right)** Constellations of Orion, Taurus and Pleiades juxtaposed on the bull painting.

juxtaposed with the painting of a bull at Lascaux, called 'Dead Man', or the
'Wounded Shaman', which he claims delineates the constellation Taurus
(see figure 1). Orion and Taurus face each other in the heavens and were
possibly used to mark the autumn and spring equinoxes at the time the artwork was created at Lascaux.

In Arabic, the word 'Al Nitak' (the wounded one) and the myths pertaining to the Egyptian god Osiris, who also became the wounded one, all
seem to hint at a connection to Orion's stars. Osiris and a stream of similar
deities will become highly relevant as we proceed through the book. The
'fallen' or 'wounded' figure at Lascaux could be a symbolic image for the
'fallen one', just as Adam, in the biblical sense, was considered the fallen
man, a theme that will become evident as the book progresses.

The earliest known depiction of the constellation Orion, according to Dr.
Rappenglueck, was carved on a piece of a mammoth tusk found in 1979 at
the Geißenklösterle Cave in the Ach Valley of southern Germany. This
32,000-year-old Upper Palaeolithic artifact represents a male figure with
arms and legs outstretched in the same pose as the Orion constellation. The
figure's slim waist with sword, which hangs between the figure's slightly
parted legs, one shorter than the other, appears to confirm this conclusion.
Rappenglueck proposed that the carved image is a depiction of Orion as
the sky hunter (see figure 2). Sculptures of the voluptuous goddess known
as the Venus of Dusseldorf, from the same period, may have also been an
artistic impression of these cycles. Academic Damien Francis Mackey from
the University of Sydney writes in his paper, *So-called Palaeolithic man was
not dumb. Part One: A long cultural tradition of sky watching:*

> *The tablet also has 86 markings on its sides and back, and Rappenglueck notes
> these are the number of days which, when subtracted from a year, equal the aver-*

age number of days of human gestation. That number also matches the days that one of Orion's brightest stars–Betelgeuse–is visible yearly, suggesting early sky-watchers may have connected women's pregnancy with the cycles of the celestial gods. [1]

The Ach Valley portable art also seems to demonstrate how interest in the Orion constellation began at a very early stage in human development, which probably continued to remain important until Neolithic times and beyond, as this book will show.

In Egypt's Western Desert, at the site of a dry lake known as Nabta Playa, a 7,000-year-old megalithic structure was likely built to incorporate particular astronomical alignments featuring the Orion constellation. The southerly line of three stones at Nabta Playa, inside the Calendar Circle, represented the three stars of Orion's Belt. Three other stones inside the calendar circle represented the shoulders and head stars of Orion as they appeared in the sky.[2] What I am highlighting here is an ancient fascination for Orion, along with other important constellations.

Figure 2: A possible 32,000 year-old carved depiction of the sky hunter - Orion.

Other portable artworks used for personal adornment, including red ochre stones, have been unearthed at several archaeological sites in Africa dating back 120,000 years BCE. One particular site, Blombos, is located on South Africa's Southern Cape coastline and has been undergoing archaeological exploration since 1991. Ruth Schuster writing for *Haaretz* in an article called, *The World's Oldest Hashtag: Earliest Known Drawing Found in South African Cave* (2018) said, "For one thing, archaeologists are seriously starting to think that early humans mastered symbolic thinking and the use of symbols a lot earlier than the 40,000-year age given to the earliest art until now." A piece of ochre found at Blombos Cave, featuring symbols, shows lines etched into the stone creating 'X' and 'Y' symbols, which are possible attempts to understand a more profound symbolism linked to our DNA and the blueprint for life. I will have more to say about the X symbolism later in the book.

As Above So Below

There are many facets to the 'Orion mysteries'. The most common focus on the Orion constellation by researchers and authors over the past few decades has been the correlation between Orion's belt stars and various ancient temples on earth. The most obvious are the pyramids at Giza and their apparent alignment with the belt stars of Orion, brought to prominence by Belgium-born engineer Robert Bauval and esoteric writer Adrian Gilbert, in their book *The Orion Mystery* (1994). Other acclaimed writers, such as Graham Hancock and Andrew Collins, have also explored the role of Orion in human consciousness, from its first appearance in the carved art of the Upper Palaeolithic age, through to its place in Orion Correlation Theory.* The Orion Correlation Theory suggests that there is a purposive relationship between the pyramids of the 4th Dynasty on the Giza Plateau

Figure 3: Pyramid Alignments and Orion 'Correlations' all over the ancient world.

and the alignment of three stars comprising Orion's belt. According to these authors, the Great Sphinx constructed c. 10,500 BC (Upper Palaeolithic), and its lion shape is maintained to be a definitive reference to the constellation of Leo, which is connected to Orion, and part of a more profound symbolism I will come back to later in the book. The same circuit-like patterns and alignments of three Pyramids with Orion's belt stars are seen in Mexico (Teotihuacan) and China, Xi'an, so it seems (see figure 3). Some writers and researchers have even shown what appear to be pyramids in similar alignment in the Sedona region of Mars and the Seewarte Seamounts on the floor of the Atlantic Ocean.

This book is in no way offering an argument as to whether the correlations are indeed connected to Orion; at this stage, I am only offering up information that seems to be connected to Orion. Similar alignments can also be seen in the UK at the Neolithic complex, Thornborough Henges, in North Yorkshire (sometimes referred to as the Stonehenge of the North) dating from between 3500 and 2500 BC. As with many ancient Orion (star)

Footnote: The Orion correlation theory (or Giza–Orion correlation theory) posits that there is a correlation between the location of the three largest pyramids of the Giza pyramid complex and Orion's Belt of the constellation Orion and this correlation was intended as such by the original builders of the Giza pyramid complex. The stars of Orion were associated with Osiris, the god of rebirth and afterlife by the ancient Egyptians.

Figure 4: Orion's Belt in what *was* the World Trade Buildings? The position of what was once the World Trade Center in New York, looks remarkably like the position of Orion's belt stars. (Courtesy of Google Earth Map.)

alignments on the earth, they all seem to match the position of Zeta (Alnitak), Epsilon (Alnilam), and Delta (Mintaka) reasonably accurately. As I will explore later in the book, there seems to be macro-cosm-microcosm circuitry running through many of these ancient wonders, which is also connected to more extensive intelligence.

Even what was the World Trade Center in New York, when viewed from an aerial perspective, 'seems' to show the same alignment (see figure 4). I doubt that all this is pure coincidence, and as I will unravel, there seems to be 'off-world' stellar forces connected to Orion, influencing our world.

According to some researchers, like Scott Onstott, Lower Manhattan, including the WTC location and other prominent buildings such as Millennium Hilton and American International Building and 60 Wall Street, all align with the Orion constellation. Onstott also suggests that the Manhattan alignment includes the Statue of Liberty, which is, of course, a representation of Orion's neighbour, Sirius.[3] It is no surprise to me that cities such as New York, Washington, London and Paris, have 'star maps' correlating with prominent buildings and streets. As I showed in my books, Freemasonry is a common reason for such phenomena, and as we shall see later in this book, specific symbols connected to Freemasonry (and off-world forces operating behind the scenes) *are* Orion related symbols. Orion Symbolism (along with Orion's adjacent constellations such as Sirius/Isis, etc.), has played a significant role in creating religious symbolism to dominate our minds over millennia. Many important buildings, through antiquity, seem to have esoteric connections to the stars and other relevant celestial bodies, especially Orion.

The Great Mysteries

The pyramids at Giza have been shown to align with Orion; other constellations show us that some advanced global culture, possibly inspired by advanced 'science', must have existed in the ancient world. Star systems and the astrological symmetry they provide on earth, connected to ancient Egypt, the Hopi, the Aztecs, and other indigenous peoples, tell us something profound about our ancestors. They focused on the stars, especially Orion, for some reason? Whether it was the Egyptians' focus on Osiris, who was a personification of the Orion constellation, or the Hopi's reverence of their version of Osiris – Masau'u – the stars provided a 'message' to the ancients. This message was a promise of an 'afterlife', or a 'return to the source' (the heavens) for our ancient stargazers.

Another aspect to earth's relationship with Orion, evident in the many ancient temple alignments, is that some advanced technology must have been used to build such structures. A knowledge including advanced technologies of some kind must have been utilised to correlate the position of ancient structures with specific stars. The shafts in the great pyramid at Giza, for example, are further evidence that the pyramid-builders purposely fixed their structures on the Pole star, Thubin. Another shaft seems to point to the constellation of Orion at the time the pyramids were being built. Author and engineer Robert Bauval points out in his book *The Orion Mystery*, how the alignment of the three pyramids at Giza seems to correlate with the position of Orion (Osiris) as seen from earth around 10,500 BC. The Sphinx position, according to Bauval, also faces towards the Sun at the Spring Equinox. And above the Sun appears the constellation of Leo. All of these alignments seem to suggest that a higher force or advanced intelligence was at work over 12,000 years ago on earth. Both the pyramids and the Sphinx appear to be the 'markers' for the Age of Leo and the beginning of the Orion cycle, as observed by the ancient Egyptians.

Celestial Alignments

 The great cathedrals of Europe, or what the French physicist and inventor Fulcanelli (real name Jules Louis Gabriel Violle) called 'green argot' (the language of the birds), are steeped in esoteric symbolism. The cathedrals are works of 'high art' that feature correspondences designed and constructed under the guidance of the ancient mystery schools. According to Fulcanelli, in his book *Le Mystère des Cathédrales*, many of these Gothic wonders have 'twin towers', representative of the solar-lunar relationship to Earth. This relationship, known as the 'Alchemical Wedding', shows how the Sun and the Moon 'appear' to be the same size from the surface of the Earth. A subject I will come back to in more detail in a later chapter. The ratio used by astronomers and geometers to calculate this correspondence is 3:11. This ratio translates to 27.3%, which can be observed by noting how long it takes the Moon to orbit the Earth: 27.3 days. At the same time, the Sun's average rotation period of a sunspot cycle is also 27.3 days. It's a 'celestial synchronicity' that seems to defy any natural occurrence on Earth, apart from knowing that the dimensions of the Great Pyramid at Giza also fit within the perfectly constructed Earth-Moon relationship. When geometers have drawn 'moon-to-earth' based on this ratio of 3:11, the resulting geometry is the 'circle squared' (see figure 5). We have to ask the question again, who did build the pyramids? Such a correspondence mathematically would mean that whoever built the Great Pyramid, or pyramids in general, would have also had access to the geometry of the Moon and Sun relationship to Earth.

Megalithic mysteries abound all over Earth, and the Pyramids are not the only magnificent feats of engineering known to man. Despite the magnitude of the Great Pyramid, which is nearly 500 feet high, and consists of six and a half million tons of stone and around two and a half million individual blocks, there are other pyramids and walls of similar size and weight all over the world. At Baalbek in Lebanon, for example, are structures thousands of years old, which include three enormous chunks of stone known as the Trilithon, each weighing more than 800 tons. These had to be moved at least a third of a mile; one of them placed 20 feet up in a wall. The mind boggles! Baalbek is a fascinating place, as it seems to be a location that was once referred to as the 'land of the giants', which again is a subject connected to Orion, as we shall see. One stone monolith discovered in the 1990s at Baalbek weighs around 1242 tons with another well-known stone called the 'Stone of the Pregnant Woman'. Legends say that the monolith is named after a pregnant woman who tricked the people of Baalbek into believing that she knew how to move the giant stone if only they would feed her until she gave birth. Other stories tell of the woman being a Jinn (or genie) who could use magic to make the stones, which isn't something I would rule out. I have heard similar stories in Irish mythology involving the Tuatha Dé Danann (the tribe of gods) performing such magic,

Figure 5: The Circle Squared.
The geometry of two circles (in the diagram above), is exactly the same ratio of our earth and moon: 7920:2160 miles. And the geometry of the pyramid, created out of the earth and moon relationship, is exactly proportionate to the Great Pyramid at Giza.

as I will come to in the next chapter. The use of magic and so-called supernatural forces associated with the gods and stars will become more evident
as I proceed through *Part One* of the book.

Weavers of Reality

Many indigenous cultures, primarily the Native American and Celtic tribes,
used the symbolism of the web as a means to convey the love and power of
what they termed the 'Creator'. The most famous story is the legend of
'Grandmother Spider'; she was considered part of (even a personification
of) the Creator to the ancients. Grandmother Spider, in her various forms,
was said to have 'appeared' out of the centre of creation, to 'weave the web
of the universe'. According to various Amerindian myths, she is a Goddess
whom the 'Great Mystery' chose to weave the original webs of both invisible and physical worlds. Grandmother Spider was said to have made the
'skeletons' or 'blueprints' of connecting circles that hold together the flesh
and realities of *all* life forms.

Symbolic versions of this deity appear in films like *The Matrix*, as represented in the character of the 'Oracle'. The 'matrix' is another name for the
'webs' woven to create reality; therefore, Grandmother Spider, or 'Thinking
Woman' as she is sometimes referred to, was a symbol for the 'infinite possibilities' of creation. She was regarded both as the dreamer and the dream
itself. The Hopi say that the ancient Spider-Woman was the creation of
'Sotuknang' in the First World of 'Tokpela', which seems to be another way
of describing primordial (invisible) worlds that are beyond our human reality. In Gnostic teachings, these worlds are called the Abode of the Aeons, a
topic I will detail later in the book. For the ancients, Spider-Woman was
said to have created powerful twins who took up their positions at each of
the Earth's magnetic poles. One twin travelled the Earth forming solid matter and shaping the topography, while the other filled the Earth with
sounds. The story of the twins is an allegory for ancient understanding of
the Earth being a 'sphere' and how electromagnetic forces shape the world
through sound (vibration). This knowledge was not available to European
scientists before the middle of the 19th Century. The personification of
'energy' in indigenous stories also helps us to understand how forces
shaped other worlds within worlds, from stars through to planets and how
stars such as Orion can affect our reality.

Twin Gods and Blueprints

Two of the essential characters in Native American Navajo mythology, for
example, are twin miracle-performing sons of 'White-Shell Woman', who is
another version of Spider-Woman. The children of this goddess were called

'Monster Slayer' (Alien God Slayer) and 'Tobadzschin' (Bird killer). The twin symbolism can also be seen in the Mayan legends of Hunahpu and Xbalanque, two gods who were supposedly conceived when their mother Xquic spoke through the severed head of their father, Hun Hunahpu. Xquic was the daughter of one of the Lords of Xibalba (the place of fear located in the Orion Constellation). The headless symbolism concerning Orion will become apparent as we progress through the book, so will Orion's connection to Gnostic teachings and 'opposites', duality, and otherworldly doorways (portals) protected by the god twins. The alignments of monuments and temples through correlations discussed so far are all part of an esoteric blueprint on earth connected to the stars. 'White-Shell Woman' is clearly another version of the goddess Venus and the Gnostic Sophia. Venus is known as 'Sukra' in Vedic astrology, and Sukra means 'white', or 'bright' in Sanskrit. The general themes of a goddess giving birth to 'twins' that go on to 'protect' the world from demons (usually a demon bird) is seen in many myths and legends.

The twins, like their father, Hun Hunahpu, are associated with the 'headless' and the netherworlds within Orion. Twin god symbolism also represents the 'opposite ends' of the year (duality) and their fight with forces that emerged from the rift in the Milky Way. In the Gnostic Christian forms, they are the Jesus and John figures, a twin solar force that reigns over the opposite ends of the year (winter and summer). Both are symbolic of the solstice-equinox in a perpetual cycle of life, death and rebirth connected to the same myths. John the Baptist, of course, lost his head, as did also the prophet of the Hopi 'Sun and Fire' clans, Pahana. The headless messenger symbolism is associated with the stars, notably Orion, and the position of the sun and moon concerning the seasons on earth.

In Peru, the mysterious Nazca Lines cover over thirty miles of desert and can be dated to around the second century BC. At Nazca, the ancients scored away the top surface of the land to reveal a lighter subsurface creating many drawings, including a goddess-like figure of a giant spider, a spider monkey, and a hummingbird. Alongside these images are hundreds of other animals, along with birds, runways, zig-zags, and spiral formations. In 2019, over 100 new geoglyphs at Nazca depicting fish, snakes, and humanoids, among other things, were discovered in part by 'artificial intelligence'.[4] On surrounding hillsides many other strange humanoid creatures can be seen, which are symbolic depictions of giants, creator gods and, according to some researchers, there could be actual earth diagrams of specific star constellations. Some of these images certainly look similar to constellations such as Orion, Gemini and Cancer. One particular figure at Nazca, known to the locals as the 'Owl Man' (or El Astronauta), stands 29 metres high on the southern end of Pampa de San Jose. Its arms are interesting, as one points to the star Arcturus, and the other points to the earth. Another is the spider, which is 47 m (154 ft.) in length (see figure 6). I sense the gaint spider image is hugely relevant to the type of extraterrestrials connected to Orion as I will explore later in the book. According to the work of astronomers such as Dr. Phillis Pituga at the Alder Planetarium in Chicago, the Nazca spider is a terrestrial diagram of the giant constellation of Orion. It is interesting to note that the Hopi word for Orion, 'Hotomaqam', is said to mean 'string up' and could relate to the Tripartite on the body of the spider. The spider is also a vampire on one level and its association with the Orion constellation is through the Nephilim, the sons of God and the

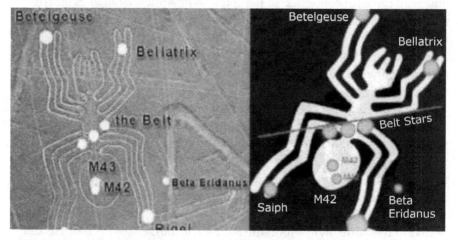

Figure 6: Spiderman-Orion.
Possible alignments between Orion's stars and the giant spider at Nazca in Peru.

daughters of men recorded in the Old Testament. The word Nephilim can be loosely translated as 'giants' and interpreted as 'fallen angels' in some traditional biblical explanations. Other biblical versions, including the *Septuagint, Theodotion, Latin Vulgate, Samaritan Targum, Targum Onkelos,* and *Targum Neofiti*—interpret the word Nephilim to mean 'giants'. As I will come to in the next chapter, I assert that giants (including a now lost technology) were responsible for many megalithic stone sites and other ancient wonders.

The ancient artists that placed the figure of the spider and other similar imagery seem to be telling us something about the connection between the stars and the earth. And like the alignments of various pyramids to the belt stars of Orion, we are instantly reminded of an ancient era on earth, when giants and ancient humans lived on a very different topology. I also wonder if advanced technology was used in this ancient era, or age - a time when all types of extraterrestrials interacted with humanity?

A Once Golden Age

In many ways, these mysterious works of art reflect an advanced understanding of mathematics, astronomy, and symbolism left by a civilization of artists for future generations to comprehend.[5] The Nazca lines are so large they can only be seen in their entirety from 1,000 feet in the air! Why would native people create such images that can only be viewed from these heights? Erich Von Daniken puts forward many theories in his books that relate to ancient spaceship landing bases, some of which could be true. Especially when we consider the Egyptian *Pyramid Texts*, which contain replicate images of flight and aviation.[6] Whatever the case, the image-makers behind projects such as the Nazca Lines, seemed to have a higher dimensional perspective, which could have included humanity's ability to fly in some distant Golden Age. The knowledge that allowed wonders like the Nazca Lines, the Baalbek Trilithon, the Great Pyramid at Giza, Easter Island and other amazing creations, to be built with such precision and scale, I feel, can only correlate with the efforts of an 'advanced race' (possibly connected to extraterrestrial giants) who exercised an advanced science in ancient times.

The ancients across the world described a high-tech Golden Age of human society, although some of it, especially towards the end, was anything but golden. Many myths and stories say the golden age was ended by a high-tech war, along with a series of celestial and geological catastrophes, which caused colossal earth changes through earthquakes, volcanic eruptions, magnetic pole shifts, and tidal waves on a scale we could not begin to imagine today. I have also seen theories of celestial events brought about by the clash of planets creating plasma displays in the skies across the Earth (see figure 7). The work of Hans

Figure 7: Battle of the Planets.
Earth and Mars in action unleashing the 'electromagnetic plasma, the 'thunderbolts of the gods'. © Neil Hague 2012

Hoerbiger in 1913, called *Glacial Kosmogonie*, speculates how the Earth captured another planet, which became our moon. There is more to know about the moon as we shall see later in the book. In the 1940s and 50s, the work of Immanuel Velikovsky connected the 'gods' with the planets and claimed that first Venus, then Mars (in a period 1500-686BC), disturbed the Earth's axis producing worldwide destruction.

Velikovsky's book, *Worlds in Collision* (1950), became a bestseller due to the controversies within its pages. Not least because he proposed that Venus was a comet that caused changes to the Earth and Mars as it settled into its new orbit, some researchers think that a passing planet produced the great rift, or scar, on Mars' surface. Mainstream science is now considering the possibility of life under the surface of Mars after discovering water beneath the planet's south polar ice cap, about 20km (12 miles) across.

The famous image of the 'Squatter Man' found all over the world from America to China, seems to be a Shamanic rendition of what our ancestors

Figure 8: 'Squatter Man' Cave Art found all over the world.

witnessed in the skies at the time of the Venus incident mentioned by Velikovsky (see figure 8).

One of the leading high energy (Plasma Discharge) research scientists in the world, Anthony Peratt, recognized that ancient rock art (petroglyphs, geoglyphs, and pictograms) depicted the same result of what he had seen in the lab. Both Peratt and fellow academic, Anthony van der Sluijs, concluded that most of the rocks used for the petroglyphs had specific characteristics, similar directions with a mountain or hill range shielding those who created the rock art. Did the ancients witness something spectacular in the heavens? I think so, and as I will get into later in the book, the heavenly realms connected to Orion seem to give further credence to this idea.

The Squatter Man image is remarkably like the portable art from the Geißenklösterle Cave in the Ach Valley figure, which makes me wonder if Orion and the Squatter Man were interchangeable in the eyes of the shaman at that time. One of the new finds mentioned earlier at Nazca in Peru also shows a humanoid figure that indeed resembles smaller depictions of the squatter man glyph. If our ancient ancestors witnessed such celestial events, along with the appearance of comets, then it would make sense for such a global phenomenon (a Vela Supernova) seen at the same time 'everywhere'. The Orion figure amongst the stars is also seen everywhere at the same time, which is significant to the logic of why the ancients made such rock art.

According to numerous sources, major upheavals in the ancient world destroyed a global society around 10500 BC. The great flood of biblical proportions, where humanity had to start all over again once the oceans had reshaped the land, is only one such story of such a world-changing event. From biological and geological records, there appears to have been several cataclysmic events from about 12,000 BC to 5000BC, perhaps even later. If you think this is far-fetched, then ponder on today's society for a moment. It may be advanced on one level with power grids, computer systems, and a looming Artificial Intelligent *takeover*, but what would happen to our vast technological society if we were faced today with a global catastrophe that devastated the planet? Within a short period of time, we would be sitting in the technological Stone Age, just as our ancestors experienced when the skies were ripped open, canyons were formed and the oceans rose.

Atlantis and Lemuria (Legends of the First Time)

Atlantis and Lemuria (Mu) were two vast continents said to have been lost to catastrophic global events in the ancient world. Atlantis in the Atlantic, and Lemuria in the Pacific were considered technologically advanced races originating from other planets (the stars). The movies, *Avatar 2* and *Aquaman* (2018), give a feel for the type of advanced civilizations that were lost, leaving behind satellite civilizations. Atlantis, especially, was said to have disappeared under the sea because of terrible cataclysms described earlier, leaving only islands, like the Azores (Atlantic) and Polynesia (Pacific), as remnants of their former scale and glory. Atlantis is said by some to have emerged after the sinking of Lemuria. Others say they disappeared simultaneously, and that's my view also.

The most thorough and outstanding researcher of Lemuria-Mu was Colonel James Churchward, who wrote a series of books (*Books of the Golden Age* and *The Lost Continent of Mu*) in the first half of the 20th century (see figure 9). Churchward visited remote monasteries in Asia and saw the ancient records of the 'Motherland' (Mu), or Lemuria, going back between 12,000 and 70,000 years. He saw how it was the centre of a global empire that included Atlantis.

Figure 9: Colonel James Churchward.

(Public domain / cc)

According to Churchwood (among others affirming similar ideas), the Lemurian races went east to become the Mayans of Central America and the mound-builders of the American continent (more on these in the next chapter). Others went west to become the people of Asia, China and India. Some created colonies in what became Egypt and later, Sumer. All genetic and cultural roads, according to Churchwood, lead back to Lemuria-Mu, the 'Motherland', and an advanced civilisation that existed tens of thousands, possibly hundreds of thousands, of years before today's 'modern' society. In these advanced civilizations, technology was God, just as it is in our current 'global' culture. In many ways, we are 'repeating the past' as we hurtle into a future where both ancient and futuristic worlds will merge. We will eventually realise that the gods of the ancient world are amongst us today in the form of technology, a theme I will come back to in great detail throughout the book.

According to the Egyptian *Edfu* Texts and 'La Mem Ptah' in the *Book of the Dead*, it is thought Osiris (Ptah) Enki (same deity) colonized islands in the Atlantic, possibly the Azores. While Osiris's brother, Set (or Enlil), was said to have attacked Osiris's newfound colony. The Djed pillars (see figure 10) could have been 'weapons' used to protect the colonies of Atlantis and the attacks by forces commanded by Set. Could the pillars have been part of the technology that brought down this advanced civilisation?

The ancient Egyptian era called 'Zep Tep', or the 'First Time', according to researchers Bauval and Gilbert, in their book *The Orion Mystery* (1994), connect Atlantis and Osiris *to* Orion. The 'First Time' was a mythological era rooted to an even earlier advanced civilisation, and another way of describing Mem Ptah. Bauval and Gilbert write:

> *The rule of Osiris on earth was seen as Egypt's happiest and most noble epoch and was believed to have been in the distant abyss of time, long before that which Egyptologists are willing to accept as realistic. When the Egyptians built the pyramids, they were thinking of an important event that related to the First Time; whatever that might have been, we now know it had something to do with the stars and, more particularly, the stars of Orion and the star Sirius - the cosmic lands of the souls.*[7]

Anton Parkes, the author of *Eden* (2013), also claims that the demise of the 'Egyptian Atlantis' called 'La Mem Ptah', could easily have occurred through an internal war amongst brothers and their use of technology, as well as some other simultaneous, deep impact event. One of the reasons why the 'West' is often referred to as the place of death in many indigenous myths and beliefs, is because so much 'death' occurred in the West, in Atlantis, around 12,000 years ago. Deities associated with Saturn, Neptune,

Figure 10: The Djed Technology: Some kind of electromagnetic weapon?

Poseidon, and the Titans, in ancient myths, are all embodiments of the 'death zone' and were considered to be a focus of worship associated with the West. Orion, in Greek myth, was the 'child of the west' and the son of Poseidon, and possibly a symbol of the age that followed the destruction of Atlantis.

What Lies Beneath?

Atlantis was described by the Greek philosopher Plato (427-347BC), but official history dismisses Plato's contention that such a continent existed, even though vast geological evidence seems to support his claims.

The Azores, which some believed were part of Atlantis, lie on the mid-Atlantic ridge, a fracture line that encircles the planet. Both the Azores and the Canary Islands (named after dogs, 'Canine', not canaries) were subject to widespread volcanic activity in the period Plato suggested for the end of Atlantis. Tachylite lava disintegrates in seawater within 15,000 years, and yet it is still found on the seabed around the Azores, confirming recent geological upheavals.

Another piece in the puzzle that was Atlantis concerns the massive number of buildings, temples, and neolithic sites now submerged all over the world. One of the most important finds over the past few decades could be a 'lost city' nine kilometres off the coast of Cabo San Antonio, at the western tip of Cuba. Initially looking for sunken vessels from the Spanish colonial years, Paulina Zelitsky and her husband Paul Weinzweig (with the permission of the Cuban government), discovered a huge underwater megalithic area. The discovery showed what looked like immense monuments, a pyramid, megalithic stones and ancient roads, dating back to what they believed to be around 12000BCE. According to *National Geographic* magazine, the entire story was suppressed. I wonder why? The answer is, of course, discoveries of this kind change our view of history and therefore our present reality. The subject of natural cyclical periods we call 'history', which appear to come and go with the rise and fall of civilisations, all seem to last around 5,000 years. Could the ruins found off the coast of Cuba and other locations be remnants of the ancient civilisation of Atlantis that belonged to a Golden Age?

Atlit Yam, off the coast of Israel in the Mediterranean, is another location where buildings and even skeletons have been found dating back 9000

Figure 11: Sunken Pyramids
The Yonaguni Monument off the coast of Japan: we see submerged Pyramids and man-made structures estimated to be at least 10,000 years old.

years. The Lebanon coast, not far from Byblos, also seems to be another location for submerged monuments. The place is also connected to the alignment of Orion's stars, as I will come to later in the book. Fuxian Lake (the second largest freshwater lake in China), is also another location for a submerged city. Its deepest point is 157 metres, and in 2001, a deep-sea diver discovered a temple structure, eight primary buildings, and a five-story mansion. To this day, the origin/history of this ancient city has yet to be confirmed. Another sunken city is Heracleion dating back to 1200 BC, which is located near to the city of Alexandria off the coast of Egypt. It was found by French underwater archeologist Franck Goddio, in 2000. The number of submerged towns and monuments is staggering once you research the subject. Sunken towns include Olous and Pavlopetri off the coast of Greece, the latter being over five thousand years old. Older finds have been located in the Arabic Gulf of Khambhat dating back four thousand years. Not forgetting the Yonaguni Monument off the coast of Japan, showing us that there was a very different reality on the surface of the earth thousands of years ago (see figure 11). Were some of these locations part of the now sunken global civilizations of Atlantis and Mu? I think the answer is yes.

The Stone Movers & Seafarers
Another theme that seems to connect the enormous cataclysmic changes on earth, ending a Golden Age, is the understanding that advanced civilisa-

tions started at high altitudes. With this came a newfound ability to sow and grow crops in the civilizations that came after the deluge recorded globally. Much symbolism in Egypt, Sumeria, and ancient Greece points towards the notion that the 'gods,' the new founding fathers of the high civilisations emerging after the flood, taught agriculture to the surviving native people in a post-flood world. Deities like Osiris of Egypt and Dagon of the Philistines are but two examples of agricultural deities possibly sent from the stars down to earth. Osiris, as we shall see, was a living god entwined with the star man - Orion. Stars such as Orion, Bootes, and the Ursa Major (Great Bear) were observed by civilisations that used the oceans to navigate their ships from one satellite of Atlantis to other surviving civilisations. One group of Semitic people hardly mentioned in the history books, who looked to their ancestral star connections, are the Phoenicians.

The Phoenicians were an ancient Semitic-speaking Mediterranean civilization that originated in the Levant in the west of the Fertile Crescent (now Lebanon). Traditional historians place the Phoenicians between 1500 and 300 BC, and around 1050 BC, but their ability to write, build ships and populate a vast area, stretching from the Levant to the Atlantic, suggests that their ancestors came from an even more ancient civilisation, possibly Atlantis. It was the Phoenicians who gave us the alphabet used for writing, which became one of the most widely used writing systems, spread by merchants across the Mediterranean world. It is where the roots of the Phoenician alphabet, called the 'Proto-Canaanite alphabet' (the oldest verified alphabet), originates. The alphabet evolved and was assimilated by other cultures, including the Roman alphabet used by Western Civilisation today.

The Phoenicians were dominant in the Mediterranean and probably originated from their homelands in the Gulf of Arabia. The Greek historian, Strabo, believed that the Phoenicians originated from Bahrain.[8] Herodotus also believed that the homeland of the Phoenicians was Bahrain. They were possibly the predecessors of Neolithic warriors that emerged out of the Sahara in what author, Steven Taylor, calls the 'Pre-Fall era' in his excellent book, *The Fall: The Evidence for a Golden Age, 6,000 Years of Insanity, and the Dawning of a New Era* (2005). The Phoenicians were among the greatest traders of their time and owed much of their prosperity to trade. At first, they traded mainly with the Greeks, trading wood, slaves, glass, and powdered Tyrian purple. The Phoenicians' religious practices were similar to their cousins in the Levant (the Canaanites); both groups seemed to have had giants amongst their genetic lines; all remnants of a bygone age. Both the Phoenicians and the biblical merchants worshipped a trinity of deities: El, Baal, and Astarte (Ashtoreth). The Phoenician city of Carthage in North

Africa was the main focus for Tanit (El) and Baal worship. Tanit, a lion-headed goddess, very similar to lion-headed Sekhmet of Egypt, and the lion-headed humanoid image prostrate, are also depictions of the previous-ly-mentioned Jinn. Baal is remarkably identical to Orion also, as we shall see. The Lion Goddess Tanit, in her reversed guise, was called Anat, the demander of 'war and sacrifice', mainly through fire, for the priests of ancient Carthage.

The Carthaginians were notorious for the intensity of their religious beliefs, invading, and using war as part of their beliefs. Besides their repu-tation as merchants, the Carthaginians were also known in the ancient world for their superstition and intense belief in the Jinn, or demons. They imagined themselves living in a world inhabited by supernatural powers, which were mostly malevolent, a theory that would surface through the ancient brotherhoods and sects connected to the Stoics and Gnosticism in Egypt and the Levant. The crucial historical message regarding the Phoenicians was that they formed the basis of an ancient trade federation, which included the Maghadans (Macedonians of Greece), the Leh-Bana (Lebanese) and the Megiddo of Palestine. The latter are the current Syrian people. Authors like Gene D. Matlock, in his book, *The Last Atlantis Book You'll Ever Read* (2001), suggests the Phoenicians were Atlantean, whose secret brotherhood called the Cabeiri, instigated the ancient trade wars between India and Persia.[9] The name 'Cabeiri', or Semitic 'Kabir' (Kabar means 'great' and 'copper'), connects to the mines, trading, metal, money and wealth associated with this ancient elite caste of seafaring traders. It could also relate to an ancient race of gods that were metallic, a subject I will address later in the book. According to Matlock, the Hopi, Yadavas, Afghans and Phoenicians *are* the Cabeiri.[10] The Cabeiri, or Cabiri, are also depicted as enigmatic subterranean deities as well as 'sailors' and according to some historians, they were given a mythic genealogy as sons of Hephaestus and related to the Cyclops. The single eyes of the Cyclops would also connect to Watchers, a subject I will come to shortly. Author Pierre Sabak, in his book, *Holographic Culture* (2018), equates the word sailor with the angelic 'otherworldly' hosts that could easily be connected to the Cabeiri.[11]

I mention the Phoenicians and Cabeiri in this context because of their connection to the Pelasgians, or what Gene Matlock calls the 'Panis', who were believed to be the pre-Indo-European 'first people' of what we now call Greece, centuries before the Hellenization of the Mediterranean. The prehistoric Pelasgians were thought to have possessed secret knowledge of moving stones weighing hundreds of tons across great distances. Harold T. Wilkins, the oft-debunked 19th Century British journalist, known for his books on treasure hunting and pseudo historic claims about Atlantis,

claimed the Lakota also
talked about an ancient seafaring race that had the 'technology' to cut stone and
change sand to solid stone.
How else were global
megalithic rocks moved and
made in the ancient world?
The Phoenicians, Cabeiri, and
the Pelasgian 'elite' were the
'ancestral pirates' that became
the seafaring secret societies
of Europe.

Figure 12: The Universal Cross (of Orion).
(Left) A Lakota perfleche, or bag. **(Right)** The
Teutonic Cross pattée.

The Maltese Cross, or cross pattée, (see figure 12), was essentially a naviga-
tional symbol (due to its eight principal points and four cardinal directions
on one level). Atlantis researcher, George Erikson, calls the Maltese Cross
the 'quintessential symbol of navigation that focused on the stars and the
position of these boats.' Ancient Sailors, whether Atlantic Phoenician or
Pacific Polynesian peoples, would use the locations of particular stars, especially those of the constellation Ursa Major, Polaris, Orion and the
'Southern Cross', to orient the ship in the correct direction. The Phoenician
traders, Egyptians, and the serpent cult of the Nagas from India, may have
first introduced this cross symbol to America thousands of years before
Christianity. The cross mandala painted on Lakota Sioux parfleche (bags)
and ceremonial objects is so similar to the cross pattée that it must have
been either imported or is part of a universal language (see figure 12). I
think the latter. The cross pattée, also used by the Teutonic knights in the
12th Century, was the symbol of the Phoenician Pirates and a symbol for
the 'cross of the churches' that would connect these ancient brotherhoods to
the stars – not least Orion's stars. Some ancient schools connect the words
ORION, INRI and ZION, through Gematria (an alphanumeric code of
assigning a numerical value to a name), a code said to have inspired mystery schools, such as the Knights Templar. The use of 'three' lions, three
suns, swords and a crosses in heraldry, all seem to be focusing on Orion
symbolism, as I will show in a later chapter.

The Teachers of the Harvest

Ahuro Mazadao, the founder of Zoroastrianism and Osiris in Egypt, is
attributed to teaching the Egyptians how to grow crops, specifically corn.
Many myths speak of a divine origin for agriculture and handicrafts.[12] The
maize god, Hun Hunahpu, mentioned earlier in this chapter, was one of the

most important Mayan deities owing to his connection with this vital, staple food. The general themes across the ancient world, of 'pyramid building' and the direct teaching of 'how to live' on a new earth, by celestial deities (possibly extraterrestrials), are common to post-flood advanced civilisations.

The earliest gods associated with agriculture and the harvest, seem to be Adonis (Assyria) to Tammuz (Summer), both are personifications of what seems to have been a Golden Age on Earth. Parvati (Hindu), Osiris (Egyptian), Dagon (Semitic) and Attis (Phrygian), the latter of which turned himself into a tree in myths associated with rebirth and regeneration, are all deities of the harvest. The Roman goddess, Ceres, is where we get the word cereal, and she too, was a fertility harvest goddess. The common theme connected to these deities and the ancient epoch is what Steven Taylor, in his book, *The Fall: The Insanity of the Ego in Human History* (2008), calls the 'unfallen peoples' of the 'Pre-Fall Era'. For hundreds of thousands of years until around 8,000 BC, all human beings lived as hunter-gatherers, and then around this time, beginning in the Middle East, there seemed to be a shift to horticultural activity, growing corn and crops. Animals were domesticated, and more permanent homes were built. Ancient Chinese mythology says that the population grew large and less food was available for 'hunter-gatherer' groups. In simple terms, human beings, over thousands of years, settled down and seemed to focus on worshipping the Earth (goddess), the stars, and the invisible forces in nature. The ancient city of Catal Huyuk in Turkey, discovered by James Mellart in 1952, is a perfect example of the post Atlantean, peaceful, agricultural settlements that flourished between 7000 and 5500 BC. What we have learned from ancient places like Catal Huyuk is that the goddess, and women in general, was revered, unlike later war cultures (centred on the Sahara-Asian and Indo-Europeans) and the ego-driven, patriarchal civilisations that rampaged the Earth from around 4000 BCE onwards. The notion of 'empire-building' seemed to arrived from this time, which is relevant to the Cyber-Grid Empire being built today, something I will come back to later in the book.

One of the most puz-

Figure 13: The Mysterious 'Bag of the Gods.'
The ancient bag carried by the gods and rulers on Earth.

zling symbols found all over the world, dating back to the Catal Huyuk period, 10th millennium BCE is the gods' 'handbag' (see figure 13). It can be seen on petroglyphs in New Mexico through to the ancient megalithic site of Göbekli Tepe, not far from Catal Huyuk in Turkey. The shape appears in depictions made by the Sumerians of Iraq, in decorations of the Maori of New Zealand, and the images of the 'feathered serpent' made by the Olmecs of Central America. So what is it? Some theories surmise the image is used to symbolize the reunification of the earth and sky, of the 'material' and the 'non-material' elements of existence, and this could be true on one level. However, the clues to this object could be quite simply a 'bag' that contained 'star seed,' possibly genetic (seeds) material on one level. I tend to think that the object (which looks remarkably like a handbag or purse), was a symbol associated with the gods themselves. Only a god could carry such a device, and only the gods, which seemed to appear glob-ally, could pass on the knowledge to those who worshipped them in the civilisations emerging after the great deluge.

The concept of anient royalty, through the bloodline of the gods on Earth has been talked about in many books over the years. The 'divine right to rule' afforded to specfic bloodlines dating back many thousands of years is where our concept of 'royalty' originates (see the pharaohs of ancient Egypt and kings of Sumeria, etc. The Sumerian tablets found in Iraq, dating back to around 4000 BC, are one of several sources that describe what appear to be alien gods (or royalty) called the AN.UNNAK.KI, which trans-lates as 'those who came from heaven to earth', more on the Annunaki in the next chapter. The images of the handbag, quite possibly a 'hallmark' of a god or the type of 'craft' they travelled in, seem to be telling us that the rulers on Earth from 10,000 BC brought with them knowledge of the stars, building, engineering feats (advanced technology?), agriculture and sci-ences. Our ancestors the world over all talk about star gods, or 'star ances-tors' in their myths and oral traditions.

Star Ancestors

Our ancient ancestors understood that creation consists of infinite dimen-sions of life, vibrating at different speeds and that everything has its oppo-site nature. The different frequencies of our electromagnetic spectrum with-in 'visible light' illustrate the concept of polarization. Different frequencies are said to be sharing the same space as each other. When we move the fre-quency dial, or access our 'ancient eyes', then we can see interdimensional 'beings' operating on different levels of creation. These 'beings' are the gods, giants and strange creatures that appear in folklore across almost every continent. They are the 'now-you-see-them, now-you-don't ghosts',

UFOs and mysterious cryptids like Bigfoot and the Loch Ness Monster. When people witness any of these beings, they don't disappear; instead, they leave the 'frequency range' a person is accessing. All animals, especially cats, see the different frequencies more naturally than we do, which is why shamans used to dress as specific animals, so to engage with, or see, into these 'interdimensional' worlds (see my other books).

Figure 14: Enkidu, the Shepherd.
Stone Age wild-man and friend of the ox, or the bull.

Numerous indigenous people, like the Hopi Indians, believe they descend from Orion, Sirius, and the Pleiades. Tom Pela, one of the last Hopi Elders, said Sasquatch, or Bigfoot, is a 35,000-year-old ancestor of humans. Bigfoot, according to the Hopi and Sioux, is a powerful 'earthbound monkey god' found on every continent. In Sumerian legends, he is the Stone Age wild-man known as Enkidu, a Sumerian 'shepherd figure', or 'man of the wild', a friend of the ox (or bull) see figure 14.

According to the work of Laurence Waddell, in his 1930 English, Sumerian and Egyptian linguistics and mythological book, *The Great British Edda*, the biblical Cain (the bloodline of Adam) can also be connected to the Gilgamesh and Enkidu story through the Sumerian word 'Amu', 'Ox' or 'warrior king'. As we shall see, the warrior archetype (the hunter) is very much part of the Orion story and symbolism.

Some say Bigfoot is a survivor of many evolutionary changes by living underground, in caves and in other ancient places. Paul Werner Duarte, of the Olmec people (now Mexico), also claims there are many species of extraterrestrial (and interdimensional) beings that have influenced evolution (creation of earth races) over hundreds of thousands of years. He lists some of them in a fantastic book *Star Ancestors* (2001). Duarte says: "The Greys, the Katsina people, the Nordics, and Angelics have been closely involved with human affairs since ancient times." According to the Orion worshipping Hopi there are 300 different Kachina (Katsina beings), and one of their homes is said to be the San Francisco Peaks, a place where many strange cloud formations are said to sometimes conceal UFOs inside lenticular clouds. I know this may sound fantastic to some readers, but I feel there must be more to know about our evolution and mysteries like UFOs and the so-called 'missing link', which establishment science refuses to address adequately. In countries like India, men and women have been born with horns or tails, which is more likely connected to what mainstream science calls 'Junk' DNA.[13] All so-called 'alien life' has to be connected to our noncoding DNA.

If you doubt the existence of extraterrestrials (or interdimensionals), then pause and consider for a moment. According to science, our sun is only one of some 100 billion stars in this galaxy alone! Scientists, including Sir Francis Crick the Nobel laureate (who with James Watson discovered the double helix of DNA), say there are an estimated 100 billion galaxies in our universe. Crick, for example, believes there are at least 'one million planets' in our galaxy that could support life as we know it! Millions of people have seen UFOs and at least fifteen million Americans have seen them since the 1970s. At this point we can ask ourselves why the ancients aligned their temples and monuments with scientific precision to specific constellations? Why do monuments from Egypt to Cambodia reflect the patterns of the stars? When we look at the art and symbolism in the temple/monument interiors, or in prehistoric caves, only a 'manacled mind' will dismiss the possibility of advanced beings (possibly extraterrestrial) interacting with people of Earth, within and before the great civilisations. Are we really to believe that our planet is the only one that can harbour life? I suggest we need to open our eyes to all possibilities.

Ancient Alien DNA

An extraordinary artifact thousands of years old found in Colombia confirms detailed knowledge of the internal birth process in the ancient world, together with skills beyond what is possible today. This artifact is known as the 'Genetic Disc' and includes depictions of human ova and Spermatozoa that can only be seen through a microscope (See figure 15). The disc is also made of lydite, a tough stone that breaks up easily when cut because of its structure. Researcher, Klaus Dona, says that experts in the field have told him that it would not be possible to make the same disc today with the same material. The birth theme continues on the reverse of the disc with images of a fetus, but examine how the 'people' are portrayed – they're certainly not human. Birth instruments made from lydite have also

Figure 15: Ancient DNA.
The Mesopotamian possible portrayal of the creation of the new genetically-manipulated human.

been found that confirm an advanced knowledge of the process; scientific opinion is that these could not be made today from lydite either. The human body has certainly been subjected to substantial gene splicing, which is a bit like cutting frames in a film and putting them back in a different order, to change the genetic structure. If this is done today in laboratories, how was it done eons ago by supposedly primitive people? As I said earlier, advanced knowledge of science, biology, and technology existed in the ancient world.

Another artefact depicting a half-human, a half-reptile figure found deep under the ground in Sierra Leone, West Africa, had a metal ball sealed inside. It was first X-rayed to confirm this, and when the ball was recovered it was found to be made of chrome steel, a metal alloy only discovered in relatively modern times, yet the statue in which it was sealed is estimated to be 17,000 years old! A precisely machined and shaped *cube* of metal was also found in the centre of a block of coal in Austria in 1885, which according to scientists, is estimated to have been made some 300,000 years ago. What is becoming more apparent is that some ancient artefacts were made by advanced technology, or a technology that was 'hidden' from the population. Just as today, the same 'hidden science' is kept from mainstream public view, in pursuit of using it to alter human reality. The growth in genetically modified 'everything' is a clear example of changing the human world. As this book unfolds, it will become clear where the world is going in terms of technology and artificial life forms.

The late American researcher and writer, Lloyd Pye, studied human origins for decades. In his books and lectures, he points out that human DNA has more than 4,000 defects compared with only a few hundred in chimpanzees and gorillas. Mainstream science has acknowledged sudden changes in human genetics about 200,000 years ago and again around 35,000 years ago. The changes could have been due to 'splicing' and therefore creating a 'new human' prototype from a central source, possibly alien to earth. The Watchers, the Nephilim, and the 'giants' recorded in ancient texts, art, and myths seem to be very different to the population. Were these alien giants (Watchers) the rulers and elite of our ancient civiliastions? Are they still running the world, especially through the advancement of 'alien technology', connected to sentient beings (robots), a topic which will become apparant later in the book.

Fallen Angels, Gods and Superheroes

The Greek word for watchers is 'egregoroi', and it literally translates as the 'wakeful'; the term 'Grigori' also refers to the Watchers as recorded in the *Book of Enoch*. It is said that until the mid-2nd century AD, Jewish writing

Figure 16: The Fallen Kal-El.
Artist's rendition of *Superman* arriving as a 'fallen' son of El, in the movie, *Man of Steel.*

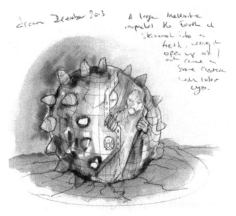

Figure 17: Watchers Arrive in Meteorites.
Drawn the same year, but months *before* I saw the *Man of Steel* movie. © Neil Hague

(such as *Midrashim*) can be taken to identify the 'Sons of God' as angels (*Genesis* 6:1 and 4). The Watchers are considered angels, in the *Book of Enoch*, before they fell to earth. Interestingly, this link to 'fallen angels' was featured in the 2014 movie *Noah*, as the Watchers in this film 'fell like meteorites', encased in matter (stone). The same visual idea also appeared in the plot of the *Superman* movie, *Man of Steel* (2013), when a young *Superman* arrives on earth inside a stone-like capsule called a Genesis pod (see figure 16). The idea of 'stone beings' will become relevant in the next chapter, too, especially in relation to legends of giants. Back in 2013, I had a dream in which I saw what looked like a meteorite hitting the earth in what seemed like America, and out of this "stone or metal-like ship" emerged a creature that looked strikingly similar to "the Thing" character of *Marvel Comic* fame (see figure 17). The DC fiction *Superman* (or Kal-El), the son of Jor-EL, could be seen as a modern-day rendition of the Watchers, too. 'El' is also where we get the words 'Elite' and 'Elohim', which requires a separate focus, more on this later in the book.

"The Thing" (one of the *Fantastic Four* who gained superpowers after exposure to cosmic rays during a scientific mission to outer space) has a remarkable resemblance to the visual depictions of a Watcher, or a stone golem, recorded in ancient Judaic mysticism. The late 'genius' Stan Lee (Stanley Martin Lieber), the imagination behind the *Marvel* empire, was possibly aware of occult mysctism and knew about such subjects including these themes within his stories. Many of his writers, such as Mike Friedrich, were of a similar background, too. One Marvel comic from the 70's called, *Strange Tales; Golem, The Thing That Walks Like a Man (The Devil Hordes of*

Kaballa!), is a clear example of Lee's background knowledge of ancient Judaic mysticism. Many images and sculptures of supernatural beings, widely depicted as the 'horned' gargoyle serpent-creatures found on both Aztec temples and almost every Gothic cathedral, are also renditions of the Watchers. The 'horned gods' will become relevant later in the book, but for now, suffice to say, the creatures that overlook Paris, sitting along with the Chimeras gallery of Notre-Dame, are representations of 'otherworldly' fallen Watchers.

Heavenly Boats

The ancient Egyptians said that the Watchers, or 'Burning Ones', came in their 'heavenly boats'. In ancient cultures across the world, you have a regularly recurring theme of 'gods' arriving in flying machines, vessels, or chariots to bring knowledge and techniques light years ahead of what existed before. In the Asian Indian culture they called these flying craft Vimanas. Author, Pierre Sabak, explores such things, going into great depth in his book *Holographic Culture* (2018), which looks at the nature of vessels and angels through what he terms "Skaphology".

The intent and purpose of this book is not sufficient to discuss 'Sabak's Skaphology' in great detail, but suffice to say there were several designs of 'craft' according to various sources. Some were cigar-shaped while others were described as double-decked with a dome and porthole windows. Both types are regularly described in UFO sightings today. The ancient Indian texts describe anti-gravity technology of the type used in 'flying saucers'. So much so, that when the Chinese discovered Sanskrit documents in Tibet and sent them to the University of Chandigarh for translation, they were found to contain the knowledge to build interstellar spaceships, according to the University's Dr. Ruth Reyna. Yet the documents were thousands of years old! Dr. Reyna revealed that these ships were known as 'Astras', and it was claimed they could fly to any planet; some texts talk about them flying to the Moon?! Interestingly, the Egyptian name for their Gods (plural), the 'Neteru', literally translates as 'Watchers', and they too show their gods in heavenly boats or sky-rockets. According to the Hopi Indian Elders, magical flying shields called 'paatuwvota' existed in their Third World, a previous epoch destroyed by an immense flood. This world was a time when great cities and trade routes were built and civilization flourished. In an address delivered to the United Nations in December 1992, Thomas Banyacya of the Hopi Coyote Clan said:

> *The people invented many machines and conveniences of high technology, some of which have not yet been seen in this age.*

Interestingly, Swedish scientists discovered a strange ufo-like ship at the bottom of the Baltic Sea in 2011, dubbed the 'Baltic Sea Anomaly'. Theories emerged from this discovery purporting the object to be a glacial deposit, or perhaps a spaceship. The photos, if genuine, indeed resemble the classic movie representation of a *Millennium Falcon-like* ship. Research undertaken by scientists from Stockholm University found the object to be left over through the movement of glaciers during the Ice Age. The 26ft tall object was discovered by Swedish explorer Peter Lindberg, along with his Ocean X team of marine explorers, during a dive searching for a shipwreck. Despite the findings from Stockholm University, Ocean X maintains that it is not a natural structure. Stefan Hogerborn, also part of the Ocean X team, said their electrical equipment stopped working when they got to within 200 metres of the anomaly on the Baltic seabed. He is quoted as saying in an article in the *Daily Express*:

> *And then we got away about 200 meters and it turned on again, and when we got back over the object it didn't work.*[14]

I found the opening narrative to the 2013 *Star Trek* movie *'Into Darkness'*, quite telling, when the *Enterprise* crew break a 'prime directive' not to allow their spaceship to be seen by the indigenous peoples of a planet they are trying to help. The starship *Enterprise* is hidden under the sea and eventually appears to save/rescue Spock as the aboriginal tribe witness this jaw-dropping scene. Visually, could this easily be symbolic of our ancient Earth ancestors witnessing what could be considered 'flying boats' or ships emerging from the sea, or disappearing across the skies?

Noah and the Watchers

The ancient Hebrew text, the *Book of Noah* and its derivative, *The Book of Enoch*, refers to the birth of Noah (sections also appear in the *Dead Sea Scrolls*), found in 1947. The Scrolls are connected to the Essene community in Palestine 2,000 years ago and give us a greater insight into their Gnostic thinking regarding otherworldly forces. In these ancient writings Noah is described as unlike any human being and more like 'the children of the angels in heaven' – the Watchers. Noah, who was said to be able to converse with the Watchers, was probably based on the Sumerian hero Utnapishtim and the Legend of Ziusudra. They are all part of a wider story of a great cataclysm changing the Earth many thousands of years ago. It is Utnapishtim who counsels the god hero Gilgamesh, persuading him to abandon his search for immortality, but giving him a trial to defy sleep if he wished to obtain immortality. According to the myths, Utnapishtim and Gilgamesh are legendary figures born of the fallen angels and therefore do not need sleep. In one narrative, Noah's father, Lamech, questions his wife about the true father of Noah: "Behold, I thought then within my heart that conception was (due) to the Watchers and the Holy Ones...and to the Nephilim...and my heart was troubled within me because of this child." Noah's birth, described in the *Book of Enoch*, states:

> *I have begotten a strange son. He is not like an ordinary human being, but looks like the children of angels of heaven to me. His form is different and he is not like us...it does not seem to me that he is of me but of the angels.*

In *The Book of Enoch*, it is said that Noah was white-skinned and blond-haired with eyes that made the whole house 'shine like the Sun'.[15] The scriptures allude to a 'superhuman' figure akin to the likes of *Thor*, or *Captain Marvel* of comic book fame. In other words, the bloodline of Noah (from Adam and through to Seth) was considered to be that of angels and the 'gods' that supposedly reigned through their offspring on Earth. Interestingly, Adam and Eve were portrayed as 'beings of light' in the 2014 movie *Noah*, and this I feel was done to reinforce some kind of 'alien connection' and the less physical/material vibration. I've often wondered if the biblical Adam and Eve figures where connected to a benevolent other-worldly force that was genetically changed by a more malevolent alien force? If so the original Adam and Eve would have been, quite rightly so, nearer to what Abrahamic faiths call the Creator, or God. I also found it interesting that the 'apple', in the movie *Noah*, even looked like a 'heart' (the apple of my heart). As I will get to later in the book, I see Adam as a 'heavenly body', or 'divine form' and when referring to Adam, by no means am I twisting religious symbolism connected to this crucial figure.

In many ways, the story of Adam and Eve is a story of how humanity gradually went from being a 'heart-based' (connected to the Infinite), to a 'gut'-based human (the Fall). Put another way, from 'being human' to a 'human' being, something lesser than its original spiritual state. It could be perceived a *vibrational* 'fall' that eventually focused humanity on 'surviving' through 'fearing' and focusing purely on the 'material' (now Smart techno-logical) world; the latter a reality designed to ensnare the 'first humans' and future generations. I'll come back to this theme later in the book, as it is a subject that weaves in and out of the story of Orion - a heavenly location from where different extraterrestrial 'intelligence' seem to be influencing Earth. An intelligence that is *not* human but thrives off humanity, very much like a host would live off its food source.

The Ancient Giants

The Persian poet Ferdowsi, in his Shahnameh or *Book of Kings*, the legendary history of Iran (completed in AD1010), tells the story of the birth of Zal, a 'Demon' or 'Watcher' warrior, whose appearance horrified his father, King Sam. According to Ferdowsi, this Watcher hybrid Zal married a foreign princess named Rudabeh, a descendant of the 'serpent king', Zahhak, who was said to have ruled Iran for a thousand years. Rudabeh is described as 'tall as a teak tree' and ivory-white. These are the familiar features of the 'Watcher' offspring from this ancient period. The height of the gods and rulers of ancient Sumeria and Egypt, from Gilgamesh to Osiris, also hints at the possibility these royal rulers were related 'genetically' to the Watchers and were the giants recorded in numerous texts and myths. The Watchers were said to be the sons and daughters of the couplings between the gods and the daughters of men recorded in the book of *Genesis*. In *Genesis* 6:1–4, it is written:

> *When man began to multiply on the face of the land and daughters were born to them,[2] the sons of God saw that the daughters of man were attractive. And they took as their wives any they chose. Then the Lord said, "My Spirit shall not abide in[1] man forever, afor he is flesh: his days shall be 120 years." The Nephilim were on the earth in those days, and also afterward, when the sons of God came in to the daughters of man and they bore children to them. These were the mighty men who were of old, the men of renown.*

The notable feature of the Watchers was said to be their eyes, as one text from the *Second Book of Enoch* describes:

> *And there appeared to me two men very tall, such as I have never seen on earth. And their faces shone like the sun, and their eyes were like burning lamps.[16]*

It is also said that the descendants of Seth intermarried with the descendants of Cain, giving weight to the Old Testament phrase 'sons of God', which seems to refer to the fallen angels – angels that were turned into physical form. 'Stone people', often recorded in indigenous myths, could be another version of the Watchers or Nephilim mentioned earlier. Much portable art dating back to the Ubaid civilization in ancient Iraq seems to depict strange creatures, possibly renditions of the watchers and their offspring. One piece of portable art clearly represents the bloodline of Zal/Zahhak and these appear to be reptilian-like Watchers, the gods for the Ubaid people (the prehistoric period of Mesopotamia, c. 6500–3800 BC).

According to the *Book of Samuel* in the *Dead Sea Scrolls*, the biblical Goliath was a Rephiam (Watcher) and in Hebrew 'repha' means 'giant'.

Goliath was also a Philistine warrior who was said to be killed by David in the war between the Israelites and the Philistines. In fact, the theme of giants can be found all over the ancient world. Cave paintings in Japan, South America, and North America depict giants, and scores of red-haired mummies were discovered in a cave near Lovelock Nevada – some were seven feet tall. Bones of giants have also been found in Minnesota, and I have actually seen bones of a giant in a 13th Century crypt underneath a church in St Bonnet le Chateau in France. The biblical themes of giants being born to earth women, after mating with the 'Watchers' are also found in ancient Ethiopian texts called the 'Kebra Nagast'. In Aboriginal myths and legends, we too find stories of giants, or evil spirits, inhabiting caves and ancient rock formations. Bates Cave, or Mulkas Cave, is named after Aboriginal legends of a giant evil spirit called Mulkin-Jal-la ('Mulka the Terrible') that lived in the cave.[17] Numerous rock paintings and handprints, one of which is said to be larger than a human hand and placed too high for any human to reach, characterize the cave's huge granite boulders. Mulka was supposed to be a cyclops-like giant who had snatched babes from their mothers and devoured them, another theme that runs through myths and legends possibly connected to the fallen angels, Nephilim, and Watchers.

The Serpent Connection

The biblical serpent in the Adam and Eve story also seems to connect to a 'reptilian extraterrestrial' theme, or simply, otherworldly, 'opposing spiritual forces' relating to the 'hacking' of ancient 'genetic' codes.[18] Similiar themes relating to the 'hacking' of codes appear in *The Matrix* movies, too, which relate to *opposing forces* seen in the Neo character and the virus-like Agent Smith character; more on *The Matrix* in a later chapter. I mention these themes purely to illustrate symbolic connections to an ancient era aligned with the 'stars', gods, chiefs, priest-kings and giants.

Alexander the Great, one of the most famous monarchs and conquerors of all time, was also known as the 'Serpent Son'. Legend has it that his birth father was the serpent god Ammon, who had mysteriously slipped into his mother's bed.[19] The same story was also told of Merovee, the founder of the Merovingian bloodline of Europe, which is often referred to as the 13th bloodline, or Holy Grail line by Michael Baigent, Richard Leigh, and Henry Lincoln. Is this the real source and genealogy for the divine right to rule? According to *The Oxford Illustrated History of British Monarchs*, all Anglo-Saxon kings proudly claimed descent from Wodan, or Wotan (or Mars), the Germanic God of War who is another aspect of the father god Odin, more on him in the next chapter. In Anglo-Saxon myth, Wodan was the consort of the Dragon Queen Hel, and one of the older names for this star god was Bodo (Budu in Sumerian), meaning 'The Serpent-Footed'.[20]

It seems clear that the ancient world was nothing like conventional history and science has led us to believe. According to many indigenous beliefs spanning tens of thousands of years, the Earth and humanity have interacted with 'genetic streams' of consciousness coming from the stars. Ancient humans were 'star gazers' extraordinaire, and it seems we have a deep connection to the constellations of Orion, Sirius, Pleiades, and Ursa Major, along with other star systems within the Galaxy.

In the next chapter, I want to explore further the 'nature of the Watchers and ancient 'giants' that left their 'megalithic mark' on Earth in an age that seems to have been all but forgotten but can still be 'felt' when we visit these ancient sites.

Sources:

1) https://www.academia.edu/38355575/So-called_Paleolithic_man_was_not_dumb._Part_One_Long_cultural_tradition_ of_sky_watching

2) https://en.wikipedia.org/wiki/Nabta_Playa

3) http://www.secretsinplainsight.com/stars-of-lower-manhattan/

4) https://www.newsweek.com/over-140-nazca-lines-strange-humanoids-discovered-peru-1472355

5) Hancock, Graham. *Fingerprints of the Gods*. Century. 1995. p57

6) Allen, James P & Peter Der Manuelian. *The Ancient Pyramid Texts*. 2005.p.70, Utt.261

7) Gilbert, Adrian and Bauval, Robert. *The Orion Mystery*. Random House, 1994. p 263

8) Ibid, p274.

9) Matlock, Gene D. *The Last Atlantis Book You'll Ever Read*. Dandelion Books. 2001, p 64-65.

10) *Ibid*, p68

11) Sabak, Pierre. *Holographic Culture*. 2018, pp122-123

12) Ravenscroft & Wallace–Murphy. The Mark of the Beast. p43

13) https://nypost.com/2019/09/18/four-inch-devil-horn-removed-from-mans-head/

14) https://www.express.co.uk/news/science/862739/Baltic-Sea- Anomaly-ufo-alien-ice-age-glacier

15) *Enoch* 106 (3): Fragment of the *Book Noah*.

16) *The Book of the Secrets of Enoch (Translated from the Slavic)* by W. R. Morfill, Clarendon Press, 1896. p2

17) https://trove.nla.gov.au/newspaper/article/47894624

18) https://www.youtube.com/watch?v=XJwRsFA4DbU&feature=emb_title

19) Bouly, RA. *Flying Serpents and Dragons, The Story of Mankind's Reptilian Past*. The Book Tree. p187

20) *The Oxford Illustrated History of British Monarchs*. 1988. p79

2

THE AGE OF ORION
'When Giants Walked the Earth'

*If I have seen further than others, it is by standing upon
the shoulders of giants.*
ISAAC NEWTON

Stone and rocks were considered sacred for most aboriginal peoples, due to their connection to their ancestors. Stone is the oldest terrestrial material and the oldest minerals found on Earth come from Australia's Jack Hills and are said to be up to 4.4 billion years old. These dates have often been disputed, not least with one basketball-size lunar rock (said to have been plucked from the moon during the Apollo 14 mission) giving further food for thought. No matter how we perceive the ancient world, from Earth's megalithic structures through to natural rock formations, our ancestors seemed to have had access to knowledge that allowed them to build fantastic stone structures. In this chapter, I want to explore a theme that gives us a glimpse into what the gods and goddesses were like in an ancient era. What we call 'megalithic wonders', in my view, are what's left of an ancient age when giants walked amongst us. I have called this epoch 'the Age of Orion'. As this chapter sets out to explore, this age was on one level, a time of wonder. Still, it was also predominant of the 'alpha-male', a lust-driven, heroic deed-maker encapsulated in the warrior archetype and the giant, Orion. I would place the Age of Orion in between the Age of Leo (10,000BC) and the Age of Taurus (4000 BC), the latter, overseeing a period of megalithic building after the biblical deluge mentioned in the last chapter. In Greek myth, Orion as the giant warrior, hunter and 'hero', was also born at this time. The seeds of 'organised' religions also appeared in this period, too. Astrologically, the art of war became more prominent through this age as Gemini (Castor and Pollux) passed into Taurus, a time when decisive actions were highly prized, and contemplation and inner reflection were considered weak. Biblical references to Orion, such as *"let us eat and drink, for tomorrow we shall die"* (Isaiah 22:13), underpin the psychological traits of the Orion Age on Earth, which I am about to explore.

Orion's Sign

According to some alternative astrologers, Orion's Sign falls between May 20th and May 23rd when the Sun is positioned in Orion, blocking out the hunter's stars in the skies. Even though Orion is not included in the classic western astrological wheel (ecliptic), *He* still influences the Earth, especially in relation to the equinoxes or solstices, as I will get to later in the book.

The ruler of Orion is said to be the asteroid Pallas (one of the earliest-discovered and largest asteroids in the solar system). According to Greek myth, Pallas was a giant who fought against the gods and was slain by Athena, who used his skin as a shield. Orion is also said to be the ruler of the astrological third house, and the number *three* which will become more significant as the book unfolds. Not least because of its connection to the belt stars of Orion, but also to saviour figures figures, like Jesus, through the holy trinity symbolism of Father, Son and Holy Spirit, not least the *three* Marys, Kings, etc.

The Sun and Moon, along with the planets in our Solar system, all travel through more than the twelve signs (constellations) of the Zodiac in a given year. In Vedic astrology, for example, twelve signs are used, with minor exception here and there and as I will come to in a later chapter, the Sun, Moon and Mars each pass through Orion, while Venus passes through Hydra, etc.[1] The position of the planets within a specific constellation, seem to correlate to mythological events, such as planets and asteroids (comets) portrayed as titans (giants) moving through (or passing) the Orion constellation. Its opposite on the zodiac wheel, the thirteenth sign, Ophiuchus, often referred to as the serpent holder (between Scorpio and Sagittarius), was a focus for secret societies in the ancient world. In astrology, Orion represents symbolism, mathematics, music, and agriculture (including healing herbs), while Ophiuchus is said to represent literature and languages. Orion is also thought of as the trunk of the 'zodiacal tree' whose position along the Milky Way runs under the feet of Ophiuchus and over the outstretched arm of Orion. The 'Tree of Life' symbolism is hugely connected to Orion and will feature a lot as I go further into the symbolism. A passage in the *Book of Revelation* 'seems' to explain the connections to Orion, Ophiuchus, and the Milky Way. The passage reads:

> *Next the angel showed me the river of the water of life* [Milky Way], *sparkling like crystal* [Stars], *flowing from the throne of God and of the Lamb* [Orion Nebula]. *Between the middle of the great street on each side of the river stood the Tree of Life bearing twelve crops of fruits, yielding its fruit every month* [Astrological Signs]; *and the leaves of the tree were for healing the nations...* (22:1-3)

The *Book of Job* mentions Orion three times: 1. "He is the maker of the Bear and Orion" (*Job* 9:90); 2. "Can you loosen Orion's belt?" (*Job* 38:31); and 3. "He who made the Pleiades and Orion" (*Amos* 5:8). Each of these quotes seems to be telling of a time when humanity was dealing with forces both 'beautiful but disturbing', whilst our connection to base animal instincts and the 'stars', simultaneously entwined, became the human species we are today. As the founder of Unity Church, Charles Filmore (1854–1948) writes:

> ...*Yet like the stars that represent truths far beyond man's present conception, his inner forces and powers, with their origins and possibilities, are just beginning to be faintly understood by him.*[2]

The lost age of Orion, along with the lost astrological signs of Orion and Ophiuchus, and ancient memories handed down through oral traditions, myths, and teachings of Earth's Aboriginal First People, naturally brings us to a place where the 'magic of the stars' meets the 'terrestrial realms' of Earth. This place in time is called the *Dreaming*, which can be observed through rock formations as seen from the Earth. The natural megalithic wonders are a good starting point to look for signs of a lost age.

The Dreaming

The Dreamtime of the Australian Aborigine was a timeless place called Tjukuba. It was said giant totemic beings emerged from within the Earth and out of the skies, to *shape* the land. In Aboriginal mythology, the Dreamtime was considered to be a long-ago creative era, when *everything* within the dreaming – the mountains, hills, trees, water holes and caves was seen as living, spiritual landscape. You could say the dreaming was the 'spirit', or consciousness, behind the creation of Earth's topography. Many 'red rock' locations all over the Earth, I believe, are remnants of a now lost 'Third and Fourth World' topology as recorded by

© Neil Hague

Figure 18: Spider Rock.
Similar stories are told in the Americas, especially in the landscape of Arizona, located at Canyon de Chelly, where Spider Rock juts 800 feet above the desert floor.

the Hopi and other Aboriginal First Peoples in their creation myths. Red rock seems to be a common topology and backdrop for stories of Earth's ancient lost world, especially in the Americas.

I visited Canyon de Chelly in 2010, and it felt to be a 'place of magic', a location where immense forces seemed to have shaped the landscape. In the Navajo lands of Keres county, in New Mexico, stands Monument Valley (another place I have visited), which is said to be the remnants of an 'ancient landscape' when Dreamtime forces shaped the land. These natural, giant red rock formations, according to Indian Elders, speak of 'creator gods', 'giants', and 'otherworldly' forces (see figure 18). The Navajo Diné Bahane (story of the people) is centred on what they call the Dinétah (the traditional homeland) of the Navajo tribe. In the geographical sense, Dinétah encompasses a large area of northwestern New Mexico, southwestern Colorado, southeastern Utah, and northeastern Arizona, known as the Four Corners, a place I have also visited. The red rock formations in these ancient lands, along with many other sites all over the Americas, are locations imbued with ancestral spirits and supernatural forces.

Elementals and Immortals

Native American 'oral traditions' suggest that the areas of land around the 'Four Corners' in the USA (both on the surface and the masses of underground catacombs) are remnants of those ancient worlds called the 'Motherland'. The Hopi and Navajo Elders say that the Motherland was a time when 'immortals' and 'multidimensional' god-beings (the Yei) walked the Earth at the time of the Third Age, or what the Aborigine called the Dreamtime. The Yei were considered giants or god-beings, and according to the Pueblo Indians, they helped shape the topology of the Earth, which in my view, is why so many ancient red rock formations seem to represent other life forms: they are 'alive'. In May 2012, I visited a place called Aramu

Figure 19: Aramu Muru - Star Gate in Peru.
Giant red rock formations in Peru (like other places all over the earth) are connected to 'stargates'. Red rock locations, across North and South America especially, also seem to be remnants of the Age of Orion (Age of Giants).

Figure 20: Aramu Muru - Star Gate in Peru.

This entity appeared above the gate (in the clouds) and was not a pleasant energy. It was clearly connected to the ancient 'dreamtime' landscape, or what Neo-platonistic writers called, a 'prince of Air'.

Muru, in Peru (near the Bolivian border), which also had 'strange magic' embodied within its red rock formations (see figure 19 on previous page). It is an ancient 'stargate' with immense electromagnetic energy. Over twenty people, including myself, witnessed the appearance of a genie-like face through a rainbow and cloud formation as we gathered to focus energy on the stargate. To our amazement, a 'face' appeared in the clouds above the petrified rock formation called 'Devil's Gate', following a ceremony performed to anchor 'higher consciousness' at the site. The petrified red rock formation and ethereal face appearing in the clouds, are aspects of 'ancient forces' that have shaped our world, and continue to affect our physical reality (see figures 20). These forces are interdimensional (or interstellar) and are often recorded in Gnostic texts as the Jinn, Archons, or 'Order of Angels', more on angels later in the book. Neo-platonistic texts and philosophy describe these forces as 'Princes of the Air' linked to the Greek noun 'aer' which relates to the atmosphere; Aeon and Aei (always present). These interdimensional entities are the 'elementals' taught about in Pagan cultures that occupy dimensions close to the physical world. I mention the Jinn/Archons in this chapter merely to reinforce how rock, air, fire and water can be utilised by forces that can 'shape' or 'manipulate' the physical world. In this context, the many megalithic structures I will come to may well have been the work of both physical and 'non-physical' beings, or even giants.

Falling Stars (Stones) and Sky Boats

When meteorites fall to Earth, they are considered 'imbued with deity', or with celestial sanctity. Ayers Rock (Uluru) is 'one big deity' for the Aborigines and holds tremendous significance to them. Whatever fell to mark the position of the black stone of Mecca in Saudi Arabia is also another example of worshipping the 'stone from heaven'. The Aztecs even said that their 'weapons' came from the stars. As we shall see as the book unfolds, Orion has influenced humanity very profoundly, in terms of war and weapons, and continues to do so.

The Yolngu people of Northern Australia say that the constellation of

Figure 21: The giant, Sahu (Orion) on his sky boat.

Orion, which they call Julpan (or Djulpan), is a canoe (a sky boat). They tell the story of three brothers [three suns or stars] who went fishing, and one of them ate a 'saw-fish' that was forbidden under their law. Seeing this, the Sun-woman, Walu, made a waterspout that carried him and his two brothers and their canoe up into the sky. The three suns that construct Orion's Belt in Western mythology are the three brothers; the Orion Nebula above them is the forbidden fish; the bright stars Betelgeuse and Rigel are the bow and stern of the canoe. The theme of 'three brothers' seems to recur in other myths associated with an ancient era inhabited by giants who came from the stars. Greek mythology gives us gods such as Zeus, Poseidon and Hades; Norse myth tells of Odin, Vili and VÈ; in Egyptian belief, Osiris, Horus (the elder) and Set. The source of these trinities seem to be based on three different worlds (realities), such as the upper world, middle world and underworld. The latter was woven into the fabric of ancient Egyptian beliefs in star gods and the afterlife, the place that Osiris or 'Sah' visited annually.

Orion was known as Sah (or Sahu), the 'toe-star' in dynastic Egypt. It was an appellation reflecting the fact that one of Orion's stars, Rigel (Beta Orionis), sticks out in front of the other stars as if it is leading Orion across the southern sky (See figure 21). Orion (as Sahu) was also referred to as the 'Far Strider', who would lead a group of 36 stars and constellations known as 'Baku' (or Decans), used by ancient Egyptian priests as celestial time-keepers across the calendar year.[3] As I will show later in the book, Orion's importance in relation to key calendar dates, pagan festivals, and religious symbolism is gigantic.

Giants in Heaven and on Earth.

In Norse mythology, the giant 'Ymir' is an hermaphroditic giant and the first creature to come into being in the Norse creation myth. It was said that Ymir's toe (like Sahu) created the frost giants, and he himself was a giant who had offspring that were also giants. The symbolism in Norse myth, associated with Ymir and Bergelmir (his grandson), seems to speak of an ancient epoch connected to giants (or Jtnars) coming from the stars. According to 13th Century books called the *Prose Edda*, Ymir was formed from elemental drops (celestial alchemy), along with Auoumbla, a primeval cow, whose milk Ymir drank. It was said that from Ymir's sweat came a race of giants, and a huge cow (Audhumla) was created to feed these giants. Both Ymir and Audhumla are Norse mythological characters that seem to hint at the relationship between Orion and Taurus (in the stars), also mirrored in pre-Christian Greek-Roman belief through Mithra and the Bull and in Persia, as Gayomart, the first man. According to Persian myth, it was from Gayomart that the human race was formed, whose twin children, 'Mayash'a and 'Mashyane', became the first human beings.[4] The Man and Bull symbolism is significant, especially Mithra and the Son of Man symbolism, which *are* Orion archetypes. Mithra was said to be born of a rock (like the Titans in Greek myths) and in the more ancient Indian *Vedas*, he was the god of light, invoked under the name of 'Varuna' and called 'the Light of the World'. Mithra, like Ahura Mazda in Persian belief, was seen as a mediator between heaven and earth; more on Mithra in relation to Orion in a later chapter.

The Prose (Poetic) *Edda* states that three gods killed Ymir – the sons of Borr (Bur), Odin, Vili and VÈ (Zeus, Poseidon, and Hades). These 'three' gods ended the reign of the Titans, the age of giants and put Ymir's (Orion's) body into the central void of the universe, creating the world (reality) out of his body. It was said that when Ymir was killed, his blood caused the 'world-changing' deluge recorded in numerous ancient myths and narratives. According to similar Greek myths, the giants were the offspring of Gaia (Earth) born from the blood that fell on them when 'Ouranos' (Uranus), the god of the sky (stars or heavens), was castrated by Cronos (Saturn). The vanquished giants were said to 'fall' and were buried under volcanoes (Volcanic plumes) and to be the cause of volcanic eruptions and earthquakes on earth, hence the importance of many 'red rock' formations I mentioned earlier. In Norse myth, Ymir's flesh was said to become the land; his blood, the oceans; his bones, the mountains (stones); his teeth, the cliffs; his hair, the trees and his brains, the clouds. My personal feelings when reading about such ethereal qualities woven into mythological personas like that of Ymir, let me see how all organic objects, the rocks, trees, stones and clouds can be seen to have *spirit*. We often see faces and strange shapes in these material objects, so are we seeing the spirit of Ymir or the forces of creation? It was said that Ymir's skull was held by four dwarfs (Nordri, Sudri, Austri and Vestri), all representing the four points on the compass (four directions), creating the dome of heaven. The sun, moon and stars were scattered sparks inside the skull of Ymir – who birthed a male and female from the 'pits of his arms', and his legs together begat a six-headed being. The six-headed being was the 'fallen state', the Scylla in Greek myth, a sea monster that symbolized the dangerous nature of the oceans. With the fall of the giant, Ymir, came the end of one age and the beginning of the next.

The Bones (Stones) of Ymir and the Giants

In the time just before the death of Ymir, myths say, the Watchers had been forced by the Creator to remain on earth as 'stone golems'. According to the *Book of Enoch*, the Watchers were given the task of helping humanity after Adam was banished from the Garden of Eden. I'll get to 'who' and 'what' the creator could be in the next few chapters, but suffice to say that the scriptures seem to hint at an unspoken royal lineage at work through the descendants of the Watchers. The biblical figure, Methuselah (the son of Enoch and the father of Lamech, and the grandfather of Noah), seem to be described as a lineage connected to the giants on earth. An line that were quite possibly related to the giants in the biblical pre-flood world, too. You could also call the giants the 'handbag carriers', hybrid bloodlines, the Watchers, and the Anunnaki mentioned in the last chapter. Much ancient royalty on earth seemed to connect to the mythical giants, not least through words, such as the Hebrew word for giant, 'Anak', and the Greek word for a prince, 'Anax'. The hieroglyph for 'Sah' (Orion) and Hebrew word, 'Sar', or prince, adds to this idea, not forgetting Orion's star, 'Rigel', meaning regal, regent, and of course, royal.

It seems the Watchers (or the Nephilim) and their masters, the Elohim, massively influenced the ancient world before (Atlantis) and after, the global flood. Arab legends also say that astonishing blocks of stone at Baalbek in Lebanon (mentioned earlier) were laid together by a 'tribe of giants' after a deluge destroyed Atlantis. One giant king from this epoch was 'Og of Bashan', which in the Bible records his bed being thirteen feet long (*Deuteronomy* 3:1). Bashan's territory included the Golan Heights in the ancient land of Israel called 'Gilgal Refaim' (the Circle of the Refaim, or giants, in English). This site consists of five concentric rings (an Israeli version of Stonehenge) whose beauty can only be appreciated from above (see figure 22). The Circle of Giants is a 5200-year-old monument believed

Figure 22: The Circle of the Giants - Gilgal Refaim.

Figure 23: Impossible Stones.
The Inca Fortress of Sacsayhuamán in Peru, 2012.

by some to have been built by the biblical giants (Nephilim). It also has a tumulus at centre, very similar to the 'mounds' supposedly built by giants and the later chiefs (royalty) connected to these mound-building giants.

The Inca Fortress of Sacsayhuamán in Peru was also created at a high altitude after the global flood. I visited Sacsayhuamán in 2012, and I cannot see how humans could have cut the stones, let alone 'moved them' to such heights without help from either giants *or* an otherworldly (alien) 'intelligence' (or technology) see figure 23. I would also add the thought: could these stones still carry the vibrational codes or energy of the Watchers (giants) that helped craft these megalithic wonders? I think they do, which is why many of these stone circles align with Orion and other stars.

In the 1950s and 1960s, Professor Alexander Thom of Oxford University concluded, from meticulous study of the layout and alignment of stone circles in Britain, that they reflected an ancient and sophisticated interest in metrology and astronomy. Professor Glyn Daniel of Cambridge University coined the term 'off-archaeology', the vague but intriguing idea of a force called 'Earth energy'. A force used by our ancient ancestors, who were able to detect this energy and build stone circles where vortices of energy were at their strongest. Much folklore associated with these stones speaks of interdimensional battles, sacrifice, people turned to stone, or the stones themselves revolving, or moving, aided by technology. There is an energy field around such ancient wonders, I have felt it personally; one that seems to aid us in travelling through time if we connect with the stones. It is not my intention here to go into depth regarding studies into the megalithic in this book. Still, it is worth noting that a common hypothesis across numerous fields of research into ancient stones, including evidence of energy, or frequency, at these places, goes back decades. Through the works of John Steele, Dr. Simon Haseler, Eduardo Balanovsky and Derek Banks, Tom Graves, Paul Devereux and Don Robins (of the Dragon Project), each have shown through their research that electromagnetic energy emits from these

Figure 24: Averbury and the *Guardians of the Stones*. © Neil Hague 2018

ancient sites. My friend Ellis C Taylor is also doing a fantastic job tracing the 'dragon lines' in Wales, which can be found in his articles at, **ellisctay-lor.com**. In one painting I made in 2018, I tried to capture the 'Shining Ones' as giant guardians of the stones as they merged with the 'crystalline' structure of the rocks at places like Avebury in the UK and other megalithic sites around the world (see figure 24). Some British legends tell of giants coming from North Africa to build Stonehenge, in Britain and Carnac in France, the prehistoric Pelasgians. These may well have been the giants of Aryan myth that used their 'magic' and physical power to erect such megalithic mysteries in the Age of Giants. Was it this epoch (the age of Orion) that saw the Pelasgians (I mentioned in the last chapter) leave their mark all over Europe, North Africa, and the Near East? In recent times, a study that examined the origins of farming in Britain, also shows people living in the region at the time Stonehenge was built, by people who had migrated from present-day Turkey and Hittite, Canaan, and Fertile Levant regions about 6,000 years ago (see figure 25 overleaf). These geographic locations are the sources of the Phoenicians, Philistines, and the giants (Watchers) of the ancient world; these people, especially the Phoenician tribes, entered ancient Britain during the age of giants.

Gogmagog and the Etonians

The oldest-known depiction of Stonehenge, found in a copy of a medieval

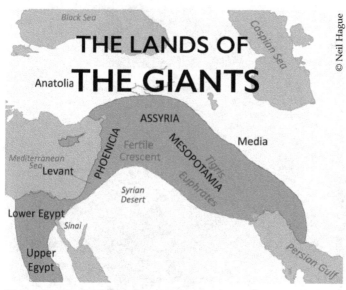

Figure 25: The biblical Land of Giants.

history text from the 1100s, supposedly shows a giant helping Merlin construct the monument (see figure 26). According to Geoffrey of Monmouth's *Historia Regum Britanniae* (*The History of the Kings of Britain*, 1136), which gave us the pseudo-history of Merlin and Arthur, and also details how Gogmagog was the 'last' of the giants found by Brutus (the Trojans), inhabiting the land of Albion (England). The battles between the Trojans and the giants of Albion are mentioned in Geoffrey of Monmouth's *History of the Kings of Britain*.

Figure 26: A copy of a medieval illustration supposedly shows a giant helping Merlin construct Stonehenge.

Early chroniclers of Britain, such as Alfred of Beverley, Nicholas Trivet, and Giraldus Cambrensis, began their histories of Britain with Brutus. In these chronicles, Gogmagog, accompanied by twenty fellow giants, attack the Trojan settlement, bringing devastation. The Trojans rallied back and killed all giants, except for one detestable monster named Gogmagog, who was compared to a mighty oak in size and strength (see figure 27). What is interesting is that the

Figure 27: The giant, Gogmagog.

Watchers were also compared to 'tall trees' in Greek accounts. In the *Historia Brittonum*, Brutus, the son of Ascanius's son, Silvius, was said to trace his genealogy back to Ham, son of Noah (back to the Watchers and shining ones again). I am sure that a genetic line migrating from the Levant in what we call today biblical times, were connected to the ancient lands of Britain, its royalty and possibly the megalithic wonders built here. The Anglo-Saxon name 'Etonian' means giant and therefore is an etymological connection to elite bloodlines connected to the giants and the elite school, Eton. Etonian, Sir Isaac Newton himself expressed that he had 'stood on the shoulders of Giants' (in Arabic, the 'shoulder' of the Giant 'Bit al-Jauza' denotes the star Betelgeuse). Newton's recognition of standing on the shoulder of giants, aka Betelgeuse, as a Freemason also, was possibly referring to the giants of Orion and the bloodline of the Watchers. Betelgeuse is crucial concerning the gods and off-world forces connected to what I see as an 'Orion Cult', a subject I will come back to in the next chapter.

The biblical 'Gog and Magog' could give a derivation of the name Gogmagog and Corineus (the founder of Cornwall and warrior giant slayer) who was said to have fought with two giants (Gog and Magog). Another name for the two giants were 'Blunderbore' and 'Redbecks' who were said to terrorize Cornwall until they were slayed by Jack, the Giant Killer. The revamped folk tale, *Jack and the Beanstalk*, written by Joseph Jacobs (in *English Fairy Tales* 1890), is another variation of the Gog and Magog stories. Jacob was a translator, literary critic, social scientist, historian and writer of English literature from Australia who edited the journal *Folklore* from 1899 to 1900 and edited other collections of illustrated tales from 1890 to 1916. The tale, in many of its forms, tells of another world (up in the sky) that houses the giant and how the boy, Jack, steals from the giant but also cuts down the beanstalk sealing the fate of the 'fallen giant'. The story is very 'Promethium' in nature and also hints at the fallen race of giants I mentioned earlier.

Giants in Irish Myth

On a visit to ancient Ireland, in 2019, I visited the megalithic site at Loughcrew, in Meath, which like many other ancient sites, seems to have remnants of work possibly made by humans *and* giants (see figure 28 overleaf). The throne of the ancient queen of the sky and the land, also known as the Hag's Chair at Cairn T (the Hag's Cairn), along with the several Cairns at Loughcrew, seem to be aligned with the different stages of the moon (its nodes and lunar eclipses).[5] The 'Hag of Loughcrew', according to Irish mythology, built the stone circles and cairns by dropping stones from an apron full of rocks. She was not your standard, human-size woman.

Figure 28: Throne of a Giant?
The author at Loughcrew sitting on what appears to be a stone throne fit for a giant queen.

The Hag, or goddess of Loughcrew, was considered a 'giant' of De Danannite origin, known as Cailleach Bhéarra of the Tuatha Dé Danann (or tribe of gods). The Tuatha are said to be descendants of a god called Nemed, a leader of a previous wave of ancient inhabitants that came to Ireland after the flood (the bloodline of Noah again). According to the 11th century *Lebor Gabála Érenn* (Irish Poems and prose), the Tuatha came from four cities to the north of Ireland—Falias, Gorias, Murias, and Finias—where they taught their skills in the sciences, architecture, the arts, and 'magic' (including necromancy). I would strongly suggest that this magic included the ability to *create* megalithic monuments dedicated to astronomical alignments, such as the Moon, Sun, Venus, and, of course – Orion. After visiting many places like Loughcrew over the years, I always feel that something other than humans constructed such sites. Was an ancient race of giants (related to the sky gods/goddesses) responsible for the many megalithic monuments? Sitting on the Hag's chair at Loughcrew made me wonder about the keepers of this sacred knowledge; the Tuatha of ancient Irish myth is an excellent example of *otherworldly* giants interacting with our ancient ancestors to create such amazing feats.

According to classical mythology, there were said to have been at least twelve god-like giants recorded in the ancient world, all conceived through various couplings with other gods and goddesses. They were Alcyoneus - Bane of Hades; Enceladus - Bane of Athena; Polybotes - Bane of Poseidon; Porphyrion - Bane of Zeus; Otis and Ephialtes (twins) - Bane of Dionysus; Orion - Bane of Apollo and Artemis; Damasen - Bane of Ares, and Mimas - Bane of Hephaestus. Greek myth especially seems to record legends of giants through numerous narratives. The historian, Pliny, speaks of a giant of whom he thought he recognized as Orion, son of the deformed Ephialtes (and later Athenian politician), an early leader of the democratic movement. According to Greek myth, the 'physical' Orion was both a giant *and* symbol for the lost age of Titans on Earth, which is probably why signs of

Orion can often be found in the land.

Orion – The Giant in the Land

Archaeological studies of Avebury (and its surrounding hills) in Somerset, also has a connection to giants *and* Orion. With the advent of aerial photography, authors such as Katherine Maltwood have provided a fascinating guide to what has been called the Twelve Astrological Giants. With roots in much earlier work, along with myths, Arthurian legends and the work of Dr. L.A. Waddell (Phoenician Origin of Britons), Maltwood's book, *A Guide to Glastonbury's Temple of the Stars* (1929), maps the surrounding geography of Glastonbury with the twelve signs of the Zodiac and much more besides. What I found interesting is that Orion features in the circular alignment around Glastonbury. As Maltwood points out in her book, "Orion looks as if he were 'supporting' the Round Table of the Somerset Zodiac." When you look at the ordnance survey maps of that area, Orion, with his uplifted arm, can be mapped around the Dundon Hill area at Compton. According to Maltwood, the 'head' of Orion is the site of the Dun (Don, or 'Fort of the Don'), a place representing 'wisdom'. The giant's uplifted arm also seems to be bent to form a Masonic square and is outlined by the roads around Compton. According to Maltwood, Orion's 'eye' can be seen in the ordnance maps not far from Dundon Smithy, by the entrance of a newly-planted orchard, giving form to the giant's eyebrow.[6] Repeated thematic symbolism connected to god-giants and the loss of sight resounds in stories of Orion through Osiris, Horus, Odin and within legends of the Cyclops, race of giants.

Orion can also be seen in the landscape of the oldest Roman town in England: Colchester, a place I lived in during the late 80s. According to Nigel Appleby, in his book *Hall of the Gods* (1998), Orion can be seen in the alignments of churches and Knights Templar monuments connected to Knights Hall, Blind Knights, Copt Hall and Beacon Hill in Colchester.[7] Appleby's research shows how three ancient causeways at Brymes Dyke, below Beacon Hill, also seem to correlate with Orion's belt stars. Wormingford Church (Betelgeuse), Knights Templar Priory House (Bellatrix), Birch Church (Saiph) and Abberton Church (Rigel), all seem to form the Orion constellation on earth. The area is also very much part of an old Roman network of strategic towns that saw rebellion by the Celtic queen known as Boadicea. Also, in Medieval times, the area saw the creation of the abbey of St John the Baptist, a prominent symbolic figure connected to Orion, Pagan festivals and a secret societies that use darker aspects of Orion consciousness, for reasons I will come to later in the book.

The Giant Albion

William Blake's epic poem, *Jerusalem, the Emanation of the Giant Albion*
(1804), also seems to hint at the celestial connection to Orion. The significance of what Blake called Albion (whose name derives from the ancient
and mythological name of Britain) appears to hint at Albion's importance in
shaping the ancient landscape. In one image (plate 100), Albion is portrayed
standing between the Sun and the Moon holding Masonic-style compass
dividers and a hammer in front of a megalithic structure which looks like
Stonehenge (see figure 29). Blake is telling us about Albion's importance in
a bygone era. Even though Blake's work is complex and personal, Albion,
for Blake, was the primeval man (Orion). A figure whose 'fall' and division
results in the creation of the *Four Zoas:* Urizen, Tharmas, Luvah/Orc, and
Urthona/Los. These are Blake's names for the human 'mind', 'emotions',
'body' and 'imagination' (spirit). The story of Albion's fall is almost symbol-

ic of the 'fall of the
age of giants'. Blake
uses the figure of
Albion as the embod-
iment of man
(Adam), Britain, or
even the western
world as a whole.
Blake's poetic narra-
tive takes the form of
a 'drama of the psy-
che'. Embedded in
the dense symbolism
of Blake's self-con-
structed mythology,
where Albion is a

Figure 29: Blake's Albion *is* Orion.
© Yale Center for British Art. (Public domain).

giant, the country, a nation, and also a constituent of twelve sons, who, like
the twelve tribes of Israel, become lost. The giant also possesses a feminine
essence through which humanity may become divine; hence, the *emanation*.
The divine feminine becomes significant to the central theme of the book as
we proceed.

Giants with All-seeing Eyes

The giants of ancient Crete are listed in various historical sources, beginning with Titan (a Greek mythological giant), including Gigantus, after
whom giants and gigantism are named. The Greek island of Rhodes was
also a habitat for giants, symbolised by the Colossus of Rhodes, an

immense statue of a giant patron god, Helios, who was once said to tower over the harbour. The Greek God, 'Argos' (with a hundred eyes) in Greek mythology, was another giant. He was the son of 'Arestor', whose name 'Panoptes' means 'the all-seeing one'. Argos was a servant of Hera (the mother of Hephaestus), one of his tasks was to slay the wife of Typhon, the fearsome giant monster Echidna, which he did successfully. The mother of all monsters, Echidna, depicted as part-human, part-serpent, seems to appear as the logo of the coffee chain 'Starbucks'. Her husband, Typhon

(the most feared monster in all Greek mythology), became a ruler in the age of the Titans. Panoptes, or Argos, is said by some scholars to be the first to fall in the 'War of the Titans' (Giants). The all-seeing giant, Argos, is also a Watcher (hence the many eyes) of an angelic lineage that connects, in my view, to the Orion constellation and the Bull (Io, or Taurus) in the stars, more on this later (see figure 30).

Figure 30: Artists rendition of Argos defending Io, the Bull.

The Cyclops in Greek mythology was a primordial race of giants, each with a single eye in the centre of the forehead. The word Cyclops means 'round-eyed' or 'one-eyed', which will become relevant shortly. Greek scholars, Hesiod and Homer, recorded two groups of Cyclops. The former described three one-eyed cyclopes who served as builders, blacksmiths, metalworkers, and craftsmen to Hephaestus/Vulcan. They were known as Brontes, Steropes, and Arges, all sons of Uranus and Gaia and brothers of the Titans (giants). Homer also talks of another group of herdsmen or shepherd Cyclopes, the sons of Poseidon (see figure 31). Both groups of Cyclopes seem to be connected to the Fallen-Watcher-Nephilim race of giants. The three cyclops, who aided Hephaestus at his forge, were said to have built the cyclopean fortifications at Tiryns and Mycenae

Figure 31: A Shepherd Cyclopes.
© Neil Hague 2002.

in the Peloponnese.[8] The Caucasus region near the Black Sea is rich in folk
literature that contains cyclops stories, considered today as variations of the
myths of the ancient Greeks. In the cyclops stories of the Caucasus, the
Cyclops is almost always a shepherd (an Orion symbol), and he is also variously presented as a one-eyed, rock-throwing, cannibalistic giant, who says
his name is 'nobody'. The shepherd cyclops lives in a cave, whose door is
blocked by a 'large stone', and who is always a threat to the hero of the
story. The blinding of the cyclops, so to steal his sheep, is also another
theme retold in the myth associated with the giant Orion, as we shall see
shortly.

According to ancient Greek legends, it was the Cyclops that had a combination of skill and strength to build such walls as Lion's Gate in Mycenae,
southern Greece (around 1250 BC). It's not too much of a stretch of the
imagination to ponder on the creation of these megalithic sites and ask
what type of 'strength' could have aided in lifting such stones and blocks?
Would I be stretching it too far if I said giant, robot-like 'intelligence' could
be involved? There is so much more to know about who and what created
the megalithic wonders, not least the pyramids. Robots are also significant
to the themes in this book, which will become relevant as I go on.

They Might Be Giants

The same reference to the 'shining ones' being born to Earth women can
also be found in later texts such as the *Book of Kings* in Iran (1010AD). The
offspring of these encounters recorded as the 'Nephilim', 'Rephaim',
'Emim', and 'Anakim', were a race of giants, often living underground, or
in caves and recorded in texts and art all over the world. These giants were
credited with giving the human race a range of knowledge known as the
'Domain of the Gods' in exchange for sexual favours from the 'daughters of
men'. The genetics connected to this coupling has been referred to as gigantism, which also seems to have existed in ancient Egypt, as recorded in
much art and by the sheer size of the coffins constructed for royalty and
priests (see figure 32).

The combined union of the 'Domain of the Gods' resulted in a race of
Giants known as the Nephilim, who proceeded to cause chaos on the earth
and were, allegedly, wiped out by the biblical flood. The biblical Goliath
was considered a Rahim (Watcher), and in Hebrew, 'repha' literally means
'giant'. In fact, several Pharaohs were said to have descended from the
Rapha, who were said to have seeded the Valley of the Rephaim and were
worshipped as the 'sons of the gods'. Their name 'Rapha' also means 'son
of Ra' – the all-seeing watchful eye. Archaeological finds in Egypt reveal
giant, cone-headed depictions among normal-sized humans, including sev-

eral Pharaohs, alluding to a separate race on earth in ancient times.

Another interesting aspect of this theme is that chieftains of the 'mound

building' tribes of North America, before the arrival of Columbus and the Spanish con- quistadors, were shown to be giants. One chief called Tuskaloosa, was one of many leaders towering over seven feet tall. Tuskaloosa's ancestors became the southern

Figure 32: Giants *everywhere* in ancient art.

Native American confederacies (the Choctaw and Creek peoples) who later emerged in the region. The modern city of Tuscaloosa, Alabama, is his namesake. Tuskaloosa and his chiefdom are recorded in the chronicles of Hernando de Soto's expedition, which arrived in North America in 1539. De Soto, the Spanish explorer and conquistador (who instigated the deaths of thousands of Indians across Peru) was appointed Governor of Cuba by King Carlos I of Spain, who directed him to conquer Florida. De Soto did this with as much violence as possible, which earned him the military title 'adelantado'.

One other notable fact, according to the work of Dr. Greg Little and his studies of American Indian Mound Builders, is that this 'vast and active' prehistoric culture seemed mainly to have 'giants' as their Chieftains. Tuskaloosa was not alone, and many of these megalithic mounds have been found to have giants buried there, notably the Wickliffe Mounds, Kentucky, and the Moundville Archaeological Site near Tuscaloosa, Alabama. Archaeologist Dr. Walter B. Jones in the 1930s claimed, in a series of inter- views, to have discovered giant skeletons while excavating the Moundville site. The authorities eventually denied the claims. What seems clear is that an ancient tribal people, who had giants as their chiefs or leaders (remnants of the time when the Nephilim walked the earth), had established them- selves in the varied lands that became the Mayan, the Yucatan, the Inca, the Peruvian and eventually the Mound Builders.

Giants exist today all over the world, from China to Turkey. Sultan Kosen of Turkey was recorded as the tallest man in 2009, standing 8 feet tall

Figure 33: Giants of today?

(see figure 33). But the tallest man in medical history, for whom there is irrefutable evidence, was Robert Pershing Wadlow (USA), who died in 1940. It is said that gigantism is the primary example of growth hormone hypersecretion disorders, a group of illnesses that are not yet fully understood. Still, we have to assume that there may be a connection to genetics and mutation. As the Russian/Ukranian occultist, Helena Blavatsky, wrote in the *Secret Doctrine:* "Had there been no giants as a rule in ancient days, there would be none now."[9]

The Giant Orion in Art

One of the only paintings featuring the god Orion shows him as a blind giant. Painted by Nicolas Poussin (1594–1665), *Blind Orion Searching for the Rising Sun* (1658), Orion is a gigantic figure. Could he have possibly belonged to the Emim, or Anakim races (see figure 34)? Poussin, of course, came to fame with his painting of the *Shepherds of Arcadia* and its connection to Rennes-le-Château (the da Vinci Code) and other villages in the Occitan. The many churches, one of which is Rennes-le-Château, are built on a pentagonal design (which could only be configured from the air)! Poussin's knowledge of the stars and mythology seems to suggest he was a master within the secret society networks of the 17th Century. Some researchers, such as the French writer, Henri de Lens assert that the 'positions' of the Shepherds in the *Shepherds of Arcadia* painting, conform to specific stars in the sky. De Lens suggests that the three male figures (or constellations) in Poussin's *Shepherds of Arcadia* are Hercules, Bootes (known as the Shepherd), and Asclepius-

Figure 34: The Giant Orion.
Artist rendition inspired by: *Blind Orion Searching for the Rising Sun* (1658) Nicolas Poussin. © Rue Bishop 2020

Serpentarius (the god of medicine). Arcadia itself was an ancient location in Greece, the last of the utopian Golden Age on Earth (The Age of Orion) and a legacy of Atlantis.

The blind Orion in Poussin's painting is seen in the landscape of Arcadia carrying Cedalion, the servant of Hephaestus (Vulcan) on his shoulders, who acts as Orion's guide, giving him sight until his vision is restored. The painting is possibly a symbolic depiction of the race of giants and their connection to a lost Golden Age and to the sun god figures that would emerge after the time of giants on earth. It was the epoch when Orion (the constellation) would become a major focus for the civilizations aligning their earth monuments with Orion's stars. Orion's blindness within the myth (as seen in the painting) relates to the heliacal rising of the constellation Orion, who disappears from 'sight' only to be visible again with his gradual return in the night sky in July each year. The Sun also blocks Orion from view at this time, when he is last seen above the western horizon in early May but reappears in the east mid-July, relating to the Greek myth of the Sun *restoring* Orion's sight. All-seeing Eye symbolism connects to this narrative, too.

Another fascinating painting called *The Ghent Altarpiece* (or the *Adoration of the Mystic Lamb*) painted between 1420 and1432, is a vast and complex 15th-century polyptych altarpiece in St Bavo's Cathedral. The work is attributed to brothers Hubert and Jan van Eyck. It is considered one of the most important historical works, featuring panels with double sets of foldable wings containing inner, and outer, panel paintings. The upper inner panels form the central Deësis of Christ the King, Virgin Mary, and John the Baptist. They are immediately flanked in the next panels by angels playing music and, on the far outermost panels, the naked figures of Adam and Eve. The four lower-register panels are divided into two pairs; sculptural grisaille paintings of St John the Baptist and St John the Evangelist, and on the two outer sections of the painting, donor portraits of Joost Vijdt and his wife, Lysbette Borluut. The central panel of the lower register shows a gathering of saints, sinners, clergy and soldiers attendant at adoration of the Lamb of God. But a critical feature in the lower right-hand panel is a scene of Saint Christopher leading groups of hermits and shepherds to the lamb of Christ. Saint Christopher is shown to be a giant in this work (see figure 35 overleaf).

Several Christian denominations venerate Saint Christopher as a martyr killed in the reign of the 3rd-century Roman Emperor Decius (reigned 249–251), or under the Roman Emperor Maximinus II Dacian (reigned 308–313). It is disputed whether Christopher existed, but his most famous legend, which is mainly known from the West and may draw from Ancient Greek mythology, tells that he carried a child, who was unknown to him, across a river before the child revealed himself as the Christ. According to the leg-

Figure 35: St. Christopher, the 'giant' leader of hermits and shepherds.

endary account of his life, Christopher was initially called Reprobus, a 7.5 feet tall Canaanite with a fearsome face, from the same people that gave us the biblical Goliath and Gog Magog. In England, there are more wall paintings of St. Christopher than of any other saint. In Iconic art, he is sometimes depicted with the head of a dog, which could be the result of a misinterpretation of the Latin term Cananeus to read 'canineus' (canine). There could also be a Canis Major (Sirius) connection to this icon. However, I have seen several dog-headed images in France, in cathedrals, especially two in the Brioude and Le Puy area that show cannibalistic and werewolf-like murals associated with the 16th Century Catholic cult called the 'Brotherhood of the Wolf'. For more on this sinister cult, see my book *Through Ancient Eyes*. The giant hermit, or traveller and his dog, in much Renaissance art, can be connected to Orion and Sirius and the fallen Watchers, angels of Old Testament fame.

The Hall of the Mountain Kings

The Watchers mentioned in the last chapter, are also connected to the symbolism associated with 'mountains', not least through biblical characters from Methuselah to Moses. Places like Mount Hermon or the 'Mountain of the Chief', 'Jabal Haramun' in Hebrew, are considered holy sites connected to the Watchers and prebiblical giants. Mount Hermon is a mountain cluster in the Anti-Lebanon mountain range and its summit straddles the border between Syria and Lebanon. It is said to be the highest point in Syria - and the highest permanently-manned UN position in the world. The symbolism associated with Orion, war and the ancient Levant, it seems, is important to the elite on earth. And as I will get into later, two wars are being waged, one above (the heavens) and one below (on earth), and they are mirrors of each other. Interestingly, the area that crosses the border between Syria and the Lebanon, and the many hilltop castles once active in the crusades, have shown to be aligned with the Orion constellation. Gary A. David, in his book, *Mirrors of Orion* (2014) shows how the hilltop castles of Tortosa, Chastel Blanc and Krak des Chevaliers, in the Levant, seem to have been positioned to mirror Orion's stars. David also proposes other alignments off the Gulf of Guinea into the Niger Delta and the Great Zimbabwe ruins in South Africa. Orion Correlation is much more common globally than we realise, which is why it is a much broader subject of focus for those who wield spiritual power on earth. The Native American Hopi Mesas in Arizona also correlate with Orion's seven main visible stars, which has been well-documented in David's book, *The Orion Zone* (2006), see figure 36.

The Hopi Mesas, the Mayan pyramids, and the pyramids of Giza, all seem to place huge importance on this star system. The First, Second, and Third Hopi Mesas, like the three main Giza pyramids, all look to align with the belt stars, Alnitak, Alnilam, and Mintaka. Other correlations in Arizona include alignments between Betatakin and Regel, Canyon De Chelly and Saiph, Wupatki (San Francisco Peaks), Bellatrix and Homol'ovi and Betelgeuse.[10]

In Egyptian myth, 'Min' (another Orion-like deity) was considered the god of the mountain, and he was also a Moon god worshipped on the last day of the lunar month in the Egyptian calendar known as 'The Exit of Min', in May. Min is similar to the Hopi god of germination, 'Muy'ingwa', who is associated with the Underworld, the stars and Pagan Maypole rituals. The Hopi plant their corn in May when Orion is in the Underworld (or not visible in the sky), and Muy'ingwa, or Min, is present through the fertility process, hence why Min is depicted with a huge phallus, or Maypole.

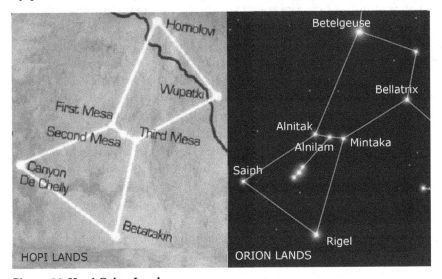

Figure 36: Hopi Orion Lands.
'Terra Orion' and 'Astar Orion' as pointed out by Gary A. David's work.

The corn crop is then harvested in July/August with the return of Orion. All those fair maidens dancing around Min's symbolic phallus is all about the fertility of spring and May (Min). Other male lunar fertility gods were 'Sin' of the Mesopotamians, 'Mani' of the Germanic tribes, 'Tsukuyomi' of the Japanese, and 'Igaluk/Alignak' of the Inuit and they, too, were involved with crop growth, fertility and the Underworld. I feel that the Moon became a male deity after the 'great war' in the heavens, a war that seems to have been focused on the Orion constellation, leading to the 'fall' of the 'rebel angels' of biblical tradition, the latter of which I will look at more closely in *Part Two*.

The connection between 'paradise' and a 'world mountain' linked to the stars (heaven) is a paramount one (no pun intended). Mount Hermon also means the 'forbidden place', and this location is the exact parallel opposite of Roswell, New Mexico on the exact polar opposite of the 33rd degree of the north latitude. The amount of so-called ET activity at sacred mountains all over the world, along with many ancient beliefs from Native America to the Himalayas, which talk of alien races, cryptozoological hybrids (like the Yeti) and otherworldly forces, all seem to connect to sacred mountains. The previously-mentioned Cabeiri were connected to Mount Kabeiros, a mountain in the region of Berekyntia in Asia Minor, and also closely associated with the Phrygian Mother Goddess, the seat of Gnosticism, as I will unravel in the next few chapters. Mount Meru, in Hinduism, is another sacred mountain connected to Orion and it was seen to have had 'seven' sides or tiers, which is another connection to Orion's seven visible stars.[11]

In ancient Judiac lore, Hermon was called 'The Great Holy One', the place Gilgamesh passes near to in the *Epic of Gilgamesh*. Hermon was also called 'Saria' by Sumerians: 'Saria and Lebanon tremble at the felling of the cedars'. In the *Book of Enoch*, Mount Hermon is the place where the Watchers and fallen angels supposedly descended to earth. In *Enoch'*, 'They swear upon the mountain that they would take wives among the daughters of men and take mutual imprecation for their sin' (*Enoch* 6).

The mountain, or summit, is also referred to as 'Saphon' in the *Ugaritic* texts. Saphon, Baal, Attar, and the Watchers seem to be the same lineage, and the *Book of Chronicles* also mentions Mount Hermon as a place where Epher, Ishi, Eliel, Azriel, Jeremiah, and Jahdiel were heads of their families in the Old Testament. Moses, of course, was also given the commandments on Mount Sinai by what could have been the 'fiery' angelic beings. Simply put, the connection to the sacred mountain (high ground) and the Watchers (or humans imbued with the gifts from the Watchers) is often connected to gods from the stars. I would suggest these 'gods' were interdimensional, *possibly* extraterrestrial in origin, and both benevolent and malevolent. The former being heavily involved in the teaching of the ancient mysteries.

Star People of the Ark

The San Francisco Peaks, a volcanic mountain range in north-central Arizona, which is said to be the home of the Hopi 'Katsina', or 'Kachina' spirits, is hugely important to Native American Hopi tribes. For the Hopi, the San Francisco Peaks is associated with the source of beings they call Kachina's (Katsina) and a place from where these spirits journey to interact with the Hopi Villages, or Mesas. The Peaks are the home of their 'star ancestors' who become clouds following their departing from the physical world. Could the Kachinas be another version of the Islamic Jinn or Gnostic Archon? I think so, as not all Jinn are malevolent. The solstice and equinoxes celebrated by the Hopi villages situated on their Mesas, are aligned with the Orion constellation, as we have seen.

According to the Hopi, the Kachinas (Katsinas) are not gods, but 'spirits' that act as mediators between gods and humans, and they are said to take the form of any animal, plant, celestial body, or otherworldly creature. The Katsina, or Kachina, are 'invited' to the Hopi villages, to serve as ethical and spiritual guides to the Hopi community, from midwinter to midsummer. During the spring and early summer, the Hopi perform a ceremonial cycle of masked Kachina dances as a plea for rain and general well-being of the tribe. All of which seems to hint at stories of star people teaching humanity how to live on a new earth after a global deluge. The Kachinas (or Katsinam) are remarkably similar in depictions of Yahweh at Ajrud in the Sinai Peninsula in Egypt (see figure 37).[12] They also seem to controversially depict more than one god. Could the visual similarity in such imagery be due to the ancient Phoenician ancestral connection to the Hopi? Did the desert god (or gods) of the ancient world travel far and wide?

There are so many striking similarities between the Hopi and Afghan people, also the Hopi and the Tibetan. One of four sacred mountains connected to the Hopi migration out of their first world (reality) connects to Tibet and Mount Everest. The other three are the San Francisco

Figure 37: The Gods of the Hopi Compared to Yahweh. (**Left**) A 3000 year old depictions of Yahweh at Ajrud. (**Right**) Hopi drawing of Star Kachina from the village of Walpi on First Mesa. From Fewkes, Hopi Kachinas (© Dover Publishing, Inc., 1985).

Peaks, the Swiss Alps, and Mount Kilimanjaro in Tanzania.

According to the Hopi elders, Aaloosaktukwi or Humphreys Peak, the highest of the San Francisco Peaks in Arizona, holds particular religious significance and is associated with a deity called 'Aaloosaka', a symbol of the Two-Horn Society. The 'two-horned' are a religious group among the Hopi dating to the occupation of the Awatovi village on the 'Antelope Mesa'. 'Two-horned' symbolism relates to a long series of 'horned' deities from the epoch before the Flood (Atlantis) and once again, can be connected to the bloodline of the Watchers. The ancient Danites, were said to be of the 'horned' clan. As it says in *Deuteronomy* 33:17, 'In majesty, he (Jacob) is like a firstborn bull; his horns are the horns of a wild ox (Taurus). With them, he will gore the nations, even those at the ends of the earth'. Other references in the *Psalms* say, 'I will cut off the horns of all the wicked, but the horns of the righteous will be lifted up' *(Psalm* 75:10).

Snake Giants

There is another aspect to humanity's ancient past, a subject that appears in all forms of religious texts and mythological narratives – snake, or serpent worship. Reverence of the serpent, or snake, is the oldest form of religious worship on earth and can be traced back to what scientists also refer to as the Toba Catastrophe event, a catastrophe 'theory' that suggests that a 'bottleneck' of the human population occurred about 70,000 years ago. It was one of the earth's most-known, most massive volcanic eruptions. The Toba catastrophe theory holds that this event caused a global volcanic winter of six to ten years and possibly a 1,000-year-long cooling episode. According to the genetic bottleneck theory, human populations sharply decreased to 3,000 –10,000 surviving individuals between 50,000 and 100,000 years ago.[13] Mathematical data and population genetics for this period also suggest a relatively low level of genetic variation among present-day humans, hence the 'Eve gene theory'. The University of Oslo showed back in 2006 that modern humans, Homo sapiens, have performed advanced Serpent rituals in Africa for 70,000 years. A bit longer than the dates given in the Bible for the age of the earth, of course, but nonetheless, the serpent has been 'influencing' humanity since the time of the Mitochondrial Eve period.

Serpent Worship is not just about the 'Kundalini' and Yoga; it is also the focus on the gods for some ancient cultures. Are these are the same gods that taught homo sapien how to live with a 'new earth', its cycles, seasons, and to 'worship' what seem to be the same gods with different names, all over the world? These are possibly the Watchers or the bloodline of Zal/Zahhak I mentioned earlier that taught about the harvest, stellar lore, and the precessions of the equinoxes.

In many ways, the Adam and Eve story must relate to the 'seeding' of the Homo sapien race on earth (out of Eden), so to create a perfect species that would 'obey' its creator. Obviously, that didn't work too well, so God (or the gods in truth) whipped up a deluge to wipe the slate clean, so to speak. This could have been stage two of installing a 'new earth' in the gods' image. Some say an 'off-world plan' that would have worked beautifully for an 'intelligence' that wished to take over and control a freshly-cleansed planet, and leaving behind a hybrid line to repopulate the earth. The Moon became more of a focus after the global deluge (cleansing), and so did the reinforcement of what became the belief in 'original sin'. Homo sapiens (not Neanderthals), were viewed as a worker human species by the gods, a 'worker bee' for those who ruled over the new earth. The most common name for the gods (possibly aliens) that ruled over a reduced homo sapien species was the Anunnaki, or the Seraphim (or Watchers). As Pierre Sabak outlines in his book *Holographic Culture* (2018):

According to the premise articulated by the Watchers, the 'divine right to rule' is an axiom eulogized as 'de facto' within the Roman Imperial Dynasty [all royal dynasties], from which the 'emperor' is considered to be a 'God' – a 'regal linage' conceived from a 'serpent'. Elevated, the deific status of the royal sovereign is lauded and is evident throughout the Greek and Semitic languages...In Greek for example, the transliteration of the name 'Kaisar (Caesar) is a contrivance on the Hebrew noun 'khayzar' (an alien or star visitor). The association corroborates the ancient conviction that the 'seed of the Emperor' originated from a 'divinity' – a being deemed as 'non-human' or 'alien'.[14]

The alien, 'royal' god figures named 'Anunnaki' by researchers such as Zecharia Sitchin, seem to be a 'group of deities' that appear in the mythological traditions of the ancient Sumerians, Akkadians, Assyrians, and Babylonians who gave life to the lineages described by Sabak.

In ancient Mesopotamia, the Anunnaki are portrayed as 'seven judges' who sit before the throne of Ereshkigal (Lilith) in the Underworld. The seven judges 'could' relate to the seven main stars of the Orion Constellation, just as the Underworld also refers to both subterranean worlds and the stars, not least the Orion Nebula focused on by the serpent-worshipping Mayans. Later, Akkadian texts, such as the *Epic of Gilgamesh*, follow the same portrayal of the Annunaki. During the Old Babylonian period, the Anunnaki were deities of the Underworld. The gods of the heavens were also known as the Igigi, who were rebellious and eventually rebelled against their parents. The same stories are encapsulated in Greek myths relating to the war between the Titans (Annunaki) and the Olympians (Igigi), which portrays them fighting in the subterranean world of Taratus in the movie, *Immortals* (2013). Nocturnal ritual sacrifice was common practice in many subterranean (chthonic) cults. When the sacrifice was a living creature, the animal was placed in a 'bothros' (pit) or 'megaron' (sunken chamber). In some chthonic cults, the animal was sacrificed on a raised bomos (altar). Offerings were usually *burned* whole, or buried, and once again under a full Moon. I will look more closely at the 'rituals' associated with the gods in a later chapter, as they are hugely connected to the transition between Halloween and what we call Christmas, which is marked by the Orion constellation in the Northern hemisphere.

Orion was also worshipped as the god Ninurta (son of Enlil), who was known as the god of fields and canals (mounds) and the bringer of fertility. He was also the god of war and the 'hunt', *who brings death* – the afterlife. Osiris was venerated in the same way in ancient Egypt. Even the *Pyramid Texts* say, 'Osiris has come as [from] Orion'. Like much ancient Egyptian royalty, Osiris also seemed 'giant-like' in comparison to the natives often depicted around him in Egyptian imagery. Art and symbols showing Osiris

(Orion) and Horus down on one knee is also common (see figure 38). Freemasonry, which based its occult rituals on ancient Egyptian death and afterlife rites, called this rite, the 'bending of the knee'.[15] On one level, the rite was an 'oath of secrecy' and allegiance to the 'knowledge passed' from

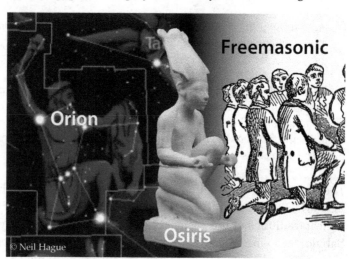

Figure 38: The *Kneeling* **giant Orion/Osiris.**
Orion was a central focus for the ancients. The constellation is the 'place of origin' for many of the giants, gods and the 'Watchers' of past ages on Earth.

the gods (giants), to the ancient priesthoods and pharaohs of Egypt. Esoteric information of this kind makes us ponder on the 'bending of the knee' (ritual) performed by the police and politicians (all over the world), in the wake of the George Floyd tragedy on May 25th 2020. The month of May, incidentally, is when Osiris (Orion) is thought to *pass into the Underworld*; a significant 'passage' and celestial position for Orion's relationship with the Pagan world, as I will explore later in the book.

The giants, or the Watchers, highlighted in this chapter, also connect to the club-wielding 'giant hunter' - Orion. Pierre Sabak points out the etymology in his book, *The Murder of Reality* (2010), to paraphrase:

Adam's bloodline is equated with Orion. Adam is punned in the Old Semitic with the word 'qadam' (east), a word translated into Latin as oriens east an etymology symmetrical with Orion. This bloodline is combined with the descendants of the Nephilim giants (nafil), Greek Titan appellations of the Annunaki (anaki gigantic). These names appertain to the race Gibborim from Gibbor giant. The word gibbor is a synonym of Orion.[16]

Orion is *the* celestial giant 'star man', a 'blueprint' for a myriad of symbols that have been with us since our ancestors looked to the heavens (to the Aeons) and the gods (or forces) that shaped our reality on earth.

Before I go into the multi-layered worlds and symbolism of Orion, it's essential first to know more about the Cult(s) entwined with Orion and *his* symbols.

Sources:

1) http://www.astrovojvodina.com/orion-is-the-trunk-of-horoscope.htm
2) *Metaphysical Bible Dictionary* (unity Village, Missouri: Unity School of Christianity. 1931, p 496
3) Tamara L. Siuda. *The Ancient Egyptian Daybook*, p312
4) Pearce, Marion. *The Gods of the Vikings*, p 81
5) Murphy, Anthony. *Mythical Ireland*. Liffey Press. 2017, pp105-106
6) Maltwood, Katherine. *A Guide to Glastonbury's Temple of the Stars*. 1929, p112
7) Appleby, Nigel, *Hall of the God; The Quest to Discover the Knowledge of the Ancients*. Hienemann. 1989, p381
8) *To Artemis*, 46f. See also Virgil's *Georgics* 4.173 and Aeneid 8.416ff.
9) Blavatsky, H. P. *The Secret Doctrine*, Vol. 2 *The Giants*. p277
10) Gary A. David. *The Orion Zone*. 2006, pp 28-29
11) Ashe, Geoffrey; *The Ancient Wisdom; a quest for the source of mystic knowledge*. Macmillan. 1977, pp 105-106
12) https://www.haaretz.com/israel-news/.premium.MAGAZINE-a-strange-drawing-could-undermine-our-entire-idea-of-judaism-1.5973328
13) Ambrose 1998. Rampino & Ambrose 2000, pp71, 80
14) Sabak, Pierre. *Holographic Culture*, 2018, p43
15) Mackey, Albert Gallatin. *A Lexicon of Freemasonry*. Forgotten Books, 217, p81
16) Sabak, Pierre. *The Murder of Reality*. 2010, p76, 202, 320, 360

3

EYES (PORTALS) & THE
HIDDEN HAND
'Signs and Symbols' of the Orion Cult

For there is nothing hidden that will not be disclosed, and nothing
concealed that will not be known or brought out into the open.

LUKE 8:17

As the age of Orion shifted into the Age of Taurus and Aries, the Annunaki giants (the Watchers) went underground after the great Deluge. The Nephilim – the Egyptian and Sumerian gods, became etched in memories of an ancient epoch – a time when the gods walked openly amongst humanity. The language of the gods, through prolific temple art, hieroglyphs, and architecture, especially in Egypt, are all part of these ancient memories, most of which are still unfathomable in the 21st Century. In the ancient Near and Middle East, a higher knowledge of the stars and magic became part of a hidden 'underground stream' tapped into by elite priesthoods. In the Ages that followed the Age of Orion that the hidden hand grew in power. It is said that, through the use of symbolism, high magic, and most importantly, through manipulating the beliefs (perception) of humanity, the children of the gods and giants became the new human rulers of the world. In this chapter, I want to explore some of the symbolism and myths associated with the emerging priesthoods and secret societies and how they focused on the stars, especially Orion.

Secrets and Symbols

Elite priests back in antiquity were only able to control thousands of people and thousands of people's minds, through 'star magic'. The same methods are in use today, at a more sophisticated level; aided by technology. The priests of Egypt and Babylon, as their equivalent modern versions today, are experts at 'withholding the truth', while releasing half-truths and then having the 'truth police' stamp out any contrary thoughts. The Holy

Inquisition was a perfect example of this type of mind control. In truth, their descendants are still at it; all they have done is change their names (logos) and improved their methods. The end result, as always, to create a subservient mind which fears to tread beyond the barriers of what the *thought police* have decided is socially acceptable. Assaulting the mind with one hand, while hiding esoteric knowledge with the other, is how these brotherhoods and their priests have helped create an illness of the mind. It's called the 'not-thinking-for-yourself syndrome', which in its extreme form creates the blind fundamentalism and the many other *isms* we endure today. In plain terms, it is 'mind control', in both its ancient and modern form.

The language of symbols, employed by the Stoics, Comacine masters, the dionysians in Greece, the Collegium of Rome, and every secret society circle ever since, speak of a hidden knowledge accessed only by initiates. All of these brotherhoods, along with the more ancient Egyptian and Babylonian temple orders, formed the basis for the ancient guilds, secret societies in the middle Ages and later masonic groups that thrived in 18th Century Europe. It is said the Parler dynasty from Cologne, for example, was probably one of the most influential family of 'masons' and sculptors, and it was they who were mainly responsible for the development of Gothic art in Central Europe. Evidence of secret societies and their connection to what became the artist guilds, were uncovered by archaeologist, Sir William Matthew Flinders Petrie, during his expedition to the Libyan Desert in 1888 and 1889. In the ruins of a city built around 300 BC, Dr. Petrie's expedition uncovered many papyrus records that told of secret meetings held by the guild of artists, priests and masons in 2000 BC.[1]

The Comacine masters, who flourished during the reigns of Constantine the Great and Theodosius, were composed of members of the Alexandrian, Stoic, and Roman brotherhoods. These fraternities eventually became the Teutonic knights and the brotherhoods of the 11th century; at the time of the building of the great gothic cathedrals, many 'secretive' guilds already existed. Some of these were known as the 'Hermandad' or simply, the brotherhood.[2] The fact that the Pyramid structures of Egypt (along with many other miraculous feats of the megalithic age) are still beyond our building capabilities today, emphasises the point that not all knowledge has been made public, while certain occult (hidden) practices continue to flourish within the secret societies since antiquity. Occult societies, going back into antiquity, have amassed immense amounts of wealth since the time of the crusades and continue to do so through the banking and political empires inspired by such secret societies. The UN, the International Monetary Fund, World Bank and UNICEF, etc., all carry the 'ancient' Roman Laurel wreath, a symbol of global power and triumph.

The Eye and Light

The Greek poet, philosopher and scientist Empedocles, like Homer 400 years before him, realised that light was both physical and invisible. This concept can also be found in the ancient beliefs of Zoroastrianism, Manichaeism, Hellenistic Gnosticism and more Eastern traditions (which are all founded on duality taking place in time and space). I will consider Gnosticism in the next few chapters. Still, it is relevant to note that Eastern philosophies refer to the duality of 'inner light' and 'physical light' and how unseen forces osculate to create the physical world. The divine light, or inner light, was considered a higher state of consciousness. While in comparison, the darkness (or lower state of consciousness) was considered the cold light (electromagnetics), or shadowside that structures the physical world. Similar theories are now understood in the areas of holographic projection, as well as groundbreaking studies made by astrophysicists into matter and anti-matter. For Plato, sight was a special interaction between the light of the eye and the light of the outer world, created by the Sun. This obsession with 'physical light' became the basis of physics from the time of Ptolemy (141AD) to the optical power-houses of Renaissance science, evident through the use of the microscope and telescope. Leonardo da Vinci, who was a scientist, artist and high-ranking member of the guild orders of Italy and France, also used lenses to capture imagery. Both Caravaggio (a Knight of Malta) and Da Vinci influenced the understanding of the 'eye' and 'optics' in general. So did the artist and architect, Filippo Brunelleschi, who pioneered the use of light and mirrors (the camera obscura) to create reflections of 'reality' and project them onto boards and canvas. For some historians, both Brunelleschi and Da Vinci were the brains behind the photo-realistic painting. Along with 'master draughtsman' Albert Dhürer, these elite court artists (alchemists and secret society members) created the concept of perspective in art; a doctrine of perspective still taught in schools, colleges and universities today. The obsession with the physical world and science's mechanisation of nature through the likes of René Descartes and Sir Isaac Newton also helped mold the current human perspective of 'five sense' led science. A science which says, if you can't see it, touch it, smell it, taste it, or hear it, then it can't exist! Yet, almost all art forms from the advanced civilisations to the art of the visionary, all hint at 'other realities', peopled by archetypes, unseen forces, and dreamlike narratives. The art, myths, storytelling, and rituals associated with earth's indigenous cultures are all dedicated to the worlds beyond the physical five senses, as we shall see.

All-Seeing Eyes

Eyes, in pictorial form, can be found in hundreds of other aspects of nature, from butterfly wings to patterns on fish. They are also a major theme in art, especially visionary art. Eyes can even be seen on the costumes of English Queens, such as Elizabeth I in 16th Century paintings, through to All-Seeing-Eyes of Freemasonic fame. As I mentioned in the last chapter, the giant Argus was covered in eyes, and you could say that Argus was the 'Big-Brother's-watching-you' figure of classical mythology. The seen and the unseen, symbolised through 'eyes', relate to forces looking into this world from a parallel one. The use of eye symbolism could also hint at the holographic nature of the Universe and how the 'whole' is contained in every 'individual' part. Many artists attempting to paint esoteric themes throughout history also found that eye symbolism automatically crept into their work, again this relates to non-physical worlds. The All-Seeing Eye symbol, or what is also called the 'Eye of Providence', is connected to a 'source' centred in Orion, as I will come to later in the book.

Eye symbolism (from all around the world) relates to the god-like power of visionary sight (third eye symbolism) on one level. On another level, it's connected to the 'Eye of Providence' depicted on the back of the US one-dollar bill. This Freemasonic symbol is associated with both Orion and Saturn and quite possibly *connects* the two celestial systems, becoming more obvious when we consider the esoteric symbolism within mysticism such as the 'Hermetic' Qabalah, as I will come to in later chapters. The eye is also a symbol for the 'microcosm-macrocosm', and much alchemical illustration explains this concept.

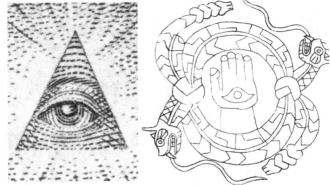

Figure 39: All-Seeing Eyes and Hands
(Left) The All-Seeing Eye found on the reverse of the US dollar bill. **(Right)** The Moundville Oggee hand, eye and snake symbolism represents a portal to the stars (some say to Orion).

Eye in the Hand of Orion

Both the eye and the hand symbols are hugely connected to Orion and a deeper understanding of a portal centred in this constellation (see figure 39). On an engraved stone palette from the Moundville burial site, located in North America, we find an 'eye inside the hand' symbol surrounded by two 'horned' rattlesnakes. The imagery is called an 'Oggee' by the native peoples who made these elaborate disks. The symbolism suggests a 'door-

way' to the dead and the spirit world. The rattlesnakes on the disk are simply an American Indian version of the European Ouroboros, which was
also said to form a 'doorway' between earth and the stars. Orion's connection to the 'land of the dead' can be seen in the beliefs of the ancient
Egyptians. Still, the American Indian Mound Builders also seem to share a
similar reverence of Orion as a location for the afterlife.

According to American Indian history, the hand with an eye is a representation of part of the Orion constellation called the 'Hand Stars of Kunu',
which leads to the path of souls.[3] The Moundville burial complex in its
entirety seems to be a mirror image of the 'realm of the dead', just as was
Ra and Osiris symbolism, or that of the ancient Egyptians. The symbolism
here relates to the Milky Way seen as a path souls must travel after death,
where Orion, like Osiris, is the gatekeeper to the afterlife. Just as the ancient
Egyptians revered the path of the dead in the *Book of Dead*, the same symbolism, found at Moundville and Cahokia Mounds State Historic Site,
seems to imply that Orion correlations go far beyond pyramid alignments
with its stars. The Eye-in-the-hand Oggee is a symbol needing further
exploration; I feel it is deeply connected to the Orion Nebula, a location I
will look at in *Part Two*.

The same eye and hand symbolism can be found on the 'Necklace of the
Mysteries', which once belonged to the Zulu shaman, Credo Mutwa (see
figure 40). The Necklace is said to be over a thousand years old (probably
older) and clearly shows the 'Oggee eye', Orion constellation and the hexagram, the latter is connected to Saturn. All three symbols, the *eye*, *hexagram*
and *hand* are connected, as we shall see. As with the symbolism of the
Crescent Moon (the Ark) and the 'two horn' symbolism. The 'horns' are
symbolic of what the
Hopi called the 'Two
Horned' and 'One
Horned' Clans
(Societies). The Two
Horned Clans are sig-
nificant in terms of
understanding deeper
levels of symbolism
connected to Orion, not
least what I term the
Orion Cult centred on
global entertainment
and geopolitics. The
Hidden Hand that
many alternative

Figure 40: The Necklace of the Mysteries.
Its symbols are connected to extraterrestrial gods and Orion.

researchers and authors have talked about over the past thirty years, or more, is the Orion Cult, in my view. The *Il Cornuto* 'Devil's Hand Sign', made by endless Cult inspired politicians and celebrities (which has its origins in Janna Coaque culture of Equador, 350BC - 400AD), is another aspect of the Hidden Hand and Horns combined.

The Hand of Kunu (Long Arm)

The hand and the eye symbol can be found in secret society symbolism, not least Freemasonry, and seen in tribal people's art going back into antiquity. The Sioux Lakota Indians, for example, have symbolic traditions connected to what they call the 'Hand of Kunu', and the stars configured in Orion, which they call the 'Nape' constellation. The Nape, for the Sioux, related to 'sacrifice' and renewal. Ceremonies were performed alongside the disappearance of this group of stars, especially before midsummer and the stars' reappearance before the winter solstice.[4]

One particular story told by the Sioux, Crow, and Assiniboine Indians was a feat of hero twins called 'Divine Boys', 'Crazy Ones', 'Daatsgye', or 'Dakadutska'. Like the Lightning Brothers of Aboriginal myth and the Monster Slaying Twins of Navajo legend, these twins represented dual electromagnetic forces appearing out of the area of the Milky Way, called the 'Great Rift' or 'Dark Rift' (see figure 41).

The constellation of Scorpius, Orion's opposite and enemy, is also located in the same region of the Milky Way. The location refers to the monster and monster-slayer figures and their emergence from the Rift. In numerous myths these twins are seen as heroes who are *ripped* from their mother's womb (the Milky Way) when she is killed by a monster. Upon their birth, the twins were separated and their mother's killer left one of them in a location where he could easily be found by his father (or uncle) - in these stories, we see the plot origins of George Lucas' *Star Wars* films. The other twin was hidden deep in the wilderness somewhere, so that one boy grew up 'civilized' and the other 'wild'. The latter twin could relate to the 'hairy wild men' phenomena found in numerous myths, not least the Gilgamesh story, a subject I will consider in a later chapter. Eventually the twins are

Figure 41: The Great Rift in the Milky Way.

reunited, avenge their mother's death, and go on to other monster-slaying adventures.

In Sioux myth, the same twins defeat the ruler of the heavens called 'Long Arm', by *ripping off* his arm and 'hand'. To the Sioux, Long Arm was a starman, also called: 'He who would seal off the hole through which souls migrate back and forth from heaven and earth and his hand was 'painted' in the light of the stars across this mouth-like hole'. The hand of Long Arm is also part of the Orion Constellation and the palm of the hand through which this hole or portal is framed, are the belt stars, Betelgeuse, Bellatrix (above the hand), Cursa and Rigel at the fingers (see figure 42). These stars form the 'Square of Orion', circumscribed by the stars Alnitak, Alnilam (Redhorn), and Mintaka (Kunu) at the wrist; Algiebba at the base of the little finger, and 42 Orionis of the 'Sword Stars' at the bottom of the thumb. According to Pierre Sabak, Betelgeuse, or 'Yad al-Jauza' in Arabic, translates as the 'hand of the giant' and is connected to the Nephilim (giants) I mentioned in the last chapter. The ancient giants seem to have originated

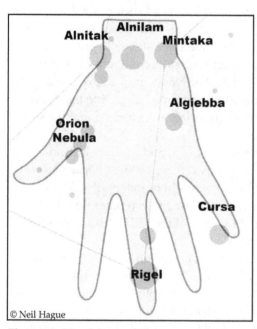

Figure 42: Hand Stars of Kunu.
Betelgeuse, Bellatrix (are above the hand), with Cursa and Rigel framing the fingers of Kunu. Orion's belts stars form the wrist.

in Orion, or at least were 'Orion worshippers'.

In Polynesian myths associated with Te Tuma, the Foundation (a male god) and Te Papa (a female), the universe was an egg that burst producing *three* layers (worlds). According to the myth, the first man was 'Matata' (Adam), who came into existence *without* arms and hands, the second man was 'Aitu' who came into being with *one arm* and finally the third man, 'Hoatea' (Sky-space), formed the perfect projection with his wife, Hoatu. From this third 'fruitful' projection came the human race.[5] Interestingly, aboriginal myths are similar in concept to the creation of 'Adam on High' (Orion), who was an important figure for Hermetic Mystics.

Among the Crow, the hand is said to belong to 'Red Woman', and the Hand Myth appears in the myth 'Hands of Kunu' (Mintaka), two of which (the stars Rigel and Cursa) form fingers in the Kunu Hand Constellation. Among the Oglala Lakota, we find the same basic myth, where the 'Chief of the Stars' has his arm stolen by Thunderbirds (lightning twins) but is then taken back again. Some Oglala tribes see the hand and as the 'Rift' in the Trapezium of the Big Dipper constellation. A star system that occupies a corresponding spot to Orion on the opposite side of the Milky Way. As I will come to later in the book, Orion's Trapezium, is, in my view, a portal into higher consciousness. In contrast, the lesser doorways, such as the Sun, Saturn, and the Moon, especially, *are* portals into realms connected to rein-carnation and soul entrapment. In his book, *Lakota Star Knowledge: Studies in Lakota Stellar Theology* (1992), Ronald Goodman suggests that it is *through* Orion that souls ascend to heaven, and a chosen few descend back to earth where all souls enter the Spirit World through the hole in the sky.[6]

A Warrior-Hunter's Hand

In tribal lore, a single hand was often painted across the face of the warrior so that the palm covered the warrior's mouth. The 'mouth and hand sym-bolism' related to the warrior's breath, the 'breath of life'. For many Native American warrior tribes, the hand is the instrument, used to seize another warrior's life, and was symbolized by sealing the hole through which his breath, or soul, sustains itself. The warrior's victory is also symbolised by the hand.

For the Lakota, an upside-down handprint would be used as the most prized symbol a warrior could place on his horse. In Apache and

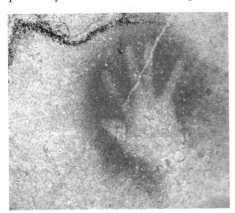

Figure 43: The Warrior's Mark.
A shaman/warrior handprint found in a paleolithic cave. The hand was a common symbol amongst Paleolithic tribes.

Comanche tribal legends, hand-prints tell of furious battles in which a warrior was fatally wounded. The same symbolism can be found in numerous exam-ples of cave art painted by Paleolithic hunters (see figure 43). Before the brave warrior's *death*, he often patted his horse on the right shoulder, thus leaving a bloody handprint on his horse for all his people to see his 'message of death' when the horse returned to camp. I feel that handprints found in Paleolithic cave art, often alongside drawings of horses and lions, across Europe, could also be a statement relating to the 'warrior spirit', which is hugely connected to

Orion. Hand and Lion symbolism combined and can be understood as the 'left' and 'right' directions (or paths) summed up in ancient Egyptian imagery of Aker, the lions of 'yesterday' and 'tomorrow'. The hand is an ancient symbol with connections to several esoteric meanings not least to biblical times. Interestingly, the 'hidden hand' or the 'hand of god' symbolism, which became a royal heraldic, can also be connected to Orion.

The 'Hamsa', also known as the Khamsa, the 'Humes Hand' or the 'Hand of Fatima', is also a popular symbol found throughout the Middle East and northern Africa, particularly within the Islamic and Jewish faiths (see figure 44). The Hamsa symbol was adopted by the ancient Sephardic community of the Iberian Peninsula, who named it the 'Hand of Miriam' after the sister of the biblical Moses and Aaron and associated it with the number *five* (*hamesh* in Hebrew), five fingers and relates to the *five* senses. I've said in other books that I feel Palaeolithic cave artists (hunter-gatherers), who made some of the most amazing imagery, could have been mak-

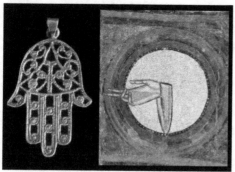

ing a point about the 'energy' relating to worlds *beyond* the five senses - possibly 'star magic'.

The hand symbol also appears on the flag of the Northern Ireland parliament and several other Irish arms, such as the 'Red Hand of Ulster' (Irish: Lámh Dhearg Uladh). It is usually shown as a right hand, but sometimes a left hand, such as in the coats of arms of baronets, a hereditary title awarded by the

Figure 44: The Hand of Miriam and Hand of God found in Abrahamic faiths.

British Crown (see figure 45). The word '*El* Star', which is said to relate to Saturn's star (the archetype of Saturn), is thought to manifests on earth as vengeance, karma, oppression, and slavery. The Province of Ulster (El Star), which has been a backdrop for bloody feuds and conflicts between 'free Irish' and 'Irish Loyalists', as seen much trouble over the decades. Such words and symbolism are connected to Orion's stars and of course, Saturn. As we shall see, the same mysticism is connected to darker aspects of Orion worship, too. What I am touching on here is a few of the 'as-above, so-below', symbols used in occult rituals and on heraldry by secret societies and religious orders, many have been

Figure 45: The Hand and the 'Crown'.

influenced in part by what I call the 'Orion Cult'. When I say Orion Cult, I am referring to an *'extraterrestrial intelligence'*, (off-world), possibly 'originating' *in* the Orion constellation. A force that has 'influenced' our world through various ancient empires and positions of power on Earth.

The Orion Cult

The Orion Cult I am describing can be seen as an 'interstellar', clandestine intelligence stretching back into the ancient world, possibly ancient Egypt and Atlantis. The Cult seems to have infiltrated the ancient mystery schools, eventually infusing 'strands' of western 'hermetic occultism' (which came out of the Reniassance 15th and 16th Century) focusing into what became known as 'esoteric' Pagan and Judeo-Christianity. Some of the ancient symbolism used by occultists through antquity, crossed over into the alchemical, hermetic mystery 'schools of thought' (especially hermetic symbolism), which has been my main interest while researching topics in the book. Similar themes of unseen, off-world forces can also be found in global native and pagan mythological stories relating to Orion. The Hermetic Qabalah (*not* the Kabbalah) is a Western esoteric tradition involving mysticism and the *occult*. It is the underlying philosophy and framework for secret societies such as the Golden Dawn, Thelemic orders, mystical-religious societies, like the Fellowship of the Rosy Cross, and is a precursor to the Neopagan, Wiccan and New Age movements. It is simply 'knowledge', like all esoteric systems, and can be used for good *or* bad.

The Orion (interstellar) Cult, or what can also be called the Orion-Saturn-Moon Cult (a tripartite cult) does not belong to *any* faith (or *any* human race); I would suggest, it is *not of the earth* and operates 'above' the concept of nations, race and religions. The Orion Cult has no allegiance to *any* nation on earth and *all* are 'expendable' to its 'earth based operations'. Its source *is* 'off-planet' (otherworldly), possibly connected to malevolent extraterrestrial consciousness originating in Orion and elsewhere. You could see the Cult symbolically as the 'eye' atop of the pyramid shown on page 81, and at a very basic level it could be referred to as a Star Cult, not least because of the focus on Orion's stars from Earth.

The use of hermetic symbolism by ancient secret societies (especially 'inverted' symbolism) along with worshipping entities connected to Orion are relevant to the Cult. Orion's stars, Betelgeuse, Rigel, Saturn, the Moon along with other nefarious entities, seem a focus, too. I sense the Cult are wizard-like, and are connected to a war being fought within Orion's star system, not least through advanced magic and *technology*, the latter will become very relevant as the book proceeds. Think of the fictional wizard, Saruman (and his mark of the 'white hand'), from Tolkien's *Lord of the Rings*, and you will get an idea of what I am describing. The off-world force, through elite hidden bases on earth, is pursuing an occult inspired 'World Order', for reasons that will become clear later in the book. From here on in, when I mention the term, 'New World Order', or 'Orion Cult', I am simply referring to an alien intelligent takeover of the Earth, through what could be percieved as 'advanced' (hidden but gradually surfacing) alien technology (a Cyber-Grid). Again, I am *not* referring to a conspiracy by any human race *whatsoever*, in fact, quite the opposite as we shall see!

The Orion Cult could also be seen to focus on 'death', destruction and chaos so to affect the human spirit, soul and mind, through the use of magic and advanced tecgnology. Such magic, anchored through Orion-Saturn-Moon rituals I feel, relates to hidden star-technology and the alien, or 'AI gods' behind the advancement in our tech-science that is dramatically changing the human habitat, globally. The legends of the trickster gods (to 'trick or deceive'), especially native American Indian references to the 'giant' spider god/goddess, Iktomi, found in so many ancient myths, could be seen as another expression of the alien archetype connected to the Cult. Groups of *three*, also seem to be a blueprint within the Orion Cult, too, possibly based on the magic of three 'points of light', or 'stars' (Orion's belt stars); and three occult groups combined could represent the triple influence of Orion-Saturn-Moon. I keep coming back in my mind to Tolkien's fictional 'Istari' (the White Council), the *three* wizards of an ancient Middle Earth, or the Jedi and Sith in Lucas's *Star Wars*. The Cult I'am outlining here, I feel, is similar in terms of its image and 'presence' on Earth.

'Darker' Materials

As I say, there is a darker (inverted) side to Hermetic mysticism. Possibly driven by Death Cult movements, not least through occult rituals relating to 'amputation of a limb' (a hand, or head) from the body of whatever group had been *infiltrated* by the Cult. Vedic astrology also has simillar concepts relating to the amputation of the head and tail of the Moon (the nodes) and all are part of this occult language, too. The amputated 'Hand of Kunu' (or Long Arm) in Lakota American Indian belief, along with the Hamsa symbol, also seem to hint at similar occult symbolism connected to nefarious star magic and protection from black magic at the same time.

Hand symbolism in Western esotericism, through the 'Left-Hand Path' and 'Right-Hand Path', is the dichotomy between two opposing approaches to magic. This terminology is used in occult groups involved in ceremonial magic. In some definitions, the Left-Hand Path is equated with malicious *black magic* and the Right-Hand Path with benevolent *white magic*. In other words, *magic* is being used for both ill or good, especially by those who are aware of Orion's 'star magic' and the duality offered by mirroring on earth what is in the heavens. What goes on 'above', plays out on earth, too.

The Western use of the terms Left-Hand Path and Right-Hand Path originated with Madame Blavatsky, the 19th-century Russian occultist who
founded the Theosophical Society. I mention Blavatsky here to merely illustrate the occult routes connected to the 'off-world' stellar Cult. Blavatsky
developed the term Left-Hand Path as a translation of the word
'Vamachara', an Indian Tantric practice that emphasised the breaking of
Hindu societal taboos by having sexual intercourse in ritual, drinking alcohol, eating meat and assembling in graveyards as a part of spiritual practice. The Vamachara is also a Sanskrit term meaning 'left-handed attain-
ment'. A term which is synonymous with the Left-Hand Path. It is also very
much part of 19th Century occult circles that gave us the likes of Aleister
Crowley, MacGregor Mathers and the Golden Dawn. It was Crowley who
altered and popularized the term Left-Handed Path in certain occult circles,
referring to a 'Brother of the Left-Hand Path', or a 'Black Brother', as one
who failed to attain the grade of 'Magister Templi' in his system of ceremonial magic. Crowley also referred to the Left-Hand Path when describing
the point at which the 'Adeptus Exemptus' (his old mentor, Macgregor
Mathers) chose to cross the Abyss to a location they called Choronzon (the
force from the Abyss) and the illusory eleventh Sephira (Sefirot), which is
'Da'ath' or 'Knowledge' in occult circles. In hermetic magic, Da'ath is the
region connected to Saturn and its influence on humanity, and I am sure the
word could have inspired George Lucas' fictional Sith Lord, *Darth* Vader?

The fictional 'Magisterium' from Phillip Pullman's *The Golden Compass*
(*His Dark Materials* Series), is also 'symbolic' of the Cult I am describing
here. Just add the 'off-world' factor to Pullman's fictional elite and you can
get the idea. In Pullman's works the Magisterium use a secret advanced science attempting to 'cut' children from their daemons (their true spirit)
while they are still young. An operation designed to sever them from what
Pullman calls 'dust' (possibly higher consciousness), keeping the children
locked into a 'controlled world' that they cannot influence, a world run by
the Magisterium. The themes in Pullman's books and film like *The Golden
Compass* (2008), such as 'abducting children', experimenting on them in
secret locations (Antarctica) and the use of black magic to control authority
figures and the population at large, seems more real than people dare to
imagine. As I will come to later in the book, consciousness from the stars, or
unseen worlds (dimensions) can be both malevolent or benevolent, like the
magic arts. The unseen, etheral dimensions that I call 'off-world' seem to be
the source for so much ill in our world.

As the book progresses, the unseen, multi-dimensional, interdimensional worlds (connected to the stars) I am going to explore, will become relevant to *why* our world is going in the direction it is.

'Star' Worship

As I say, the Orion Cult *are* 'otherworldly' magicians (possibly wizard-like-priests) that use esoteric symbolism and 'magic' to full effect. They know how to 'hypnotise' humanity through ritual magic; which today (just as it did in the ancient world) takes the form of mind control. Iconic worship of celebrities (gods), age old worship of 'leaders' (pharaohs, kings, etc), and the exoteric large scale rituals performed through the entertainment industries, over the years, are part such stellar magic. What did George Orwell say in his book *Nineteen Eighty-Four*: "The people will believe what the media tells them they believe." And people certainly 'believe' far too much of what they are told via mainstream media. We seem to be under a spell more than we dare to realise. Imagine spells being cast to keep the masses unaware of the gravity of their 'plight' within the greater movie we call life, or 'reality'. What can be more severe than convincing humanity that they are free while at the same time, denying them *real* freedom? 'Mind magic', in the form of 'tell-a-vision', only reinforces our levels of *perception* at this time. Have we moved on much since the time of the Pharaohs? Only in terms of technology, we are still very much mind controlled, it seems.

Celebrities themselves are often called on to reinforce global political agendas, at times, and this is where the occult (the hidden) meets the physical world. Of course, not all celebrities will be aware of the significance of symbolism used in occult circles, rituals and performances, like the majority of people, *we are consumers* of 'signs and symbols' (magic). The altar for 'star worship' (which includes celebrity worship), are the global entertainment industries and places like Hollywood. A place where Gnostic teachings and knowledge of occult are often given life through movie scripts and productions. It's amazing how many Gnostic philosophies and myths end up in movie scripts and comics, especially those of the Science Fiction genre. Countless dystopian worlds, ruled by tyrannical leaders or 'star gods', not to mention the 'replicant', synthetic-human themes in movies from *Blade Runner* (1982) to *Prometheus* (2012), is all part of the magic I am describing. In *Part Two*, I will be going into more depth in terms of movie symbolism relating to star gods and an impending future dystopia.

The Orion Cult is pure 'Astrolatry' (the worship of stars and other heavenly bodies as deities, or the association of gods with heavenly bodies), which has its origins in ancient Egyptian and Babylonian astronomy. The same can be said of pagan Rome, Greece and the biblical Canaanites, who fell into star-worship, seeing 'the stars of their god'.[7] It is said that the priests of the biblical era also carried Babylonian Astrolatry (ritual star magic) onto those that became the ancient priesthoods that followed.[8]

It seems today the altar for 'star worship' in places like Hollywood (the place of star magic), are also a focus for Orion, star, sun and moon symbolism, too. Knowledge of such teachings, as well as how certain aspects of Gnostic thought and hermetic occult teachings end up in movie scripts, seems to be *beyond* coincidence. There is much more to 'star worship' than meets the 'eye' and by definition it is often hidden from public view.

Cult of the One-Eyed

One main Cult symbol is the 'one-eye', which seems prevalent in various areas not least the entertainment industry (see figure 46). If you peform a google search you will see many examples of one-eye symbolism. Not all celebrities will know about such cults, of course not, and some expressions of the one-eye/three-fingers symbol given by actors, singers, etc., will be purely accidental, and non intentional. I am inclined to think it's a 'subconscious' expression for the majority. The *three* fingers (three upward strokes

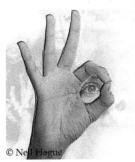

similar to the position of the thumb and fingers in the salute), could relate to the Phoenician 'šin' (tooth), or Arabic/Hebrew letter 'Shin' (ש) which mimics the structure of the human heart, possibly a form of shibboleth, just as the 'Ichthys' 'fish symbol' was used as a furtive shibboleth among Christians in its early period. Three raised fingers could also be reference to Orion's belt stars or the 'power of three' (numerlogically) in hermetic and pagan symbolism. I cannot say for sure what the symbol truly relates to, but it seems to have esoteric significance in the land of 'celebrity' (stars).

Figure 46: The Hand & the One-Eyed. One-eye/three-fingers symbol given by many celebrities.

© Neil Hague

The poster girl for the 'climate change movement', 16-year-old Swedish girl, Greta Thunberg, was seen on several occasions in 2019 to offer the one-eyed symbolism (see figure 47). Like many, she won't be aware of its deeper significance; she is just 'acting' as the public face for what feels (at a deeper level) like a 'cult' in the making. Major ceremonies, awards and celebrity events *seem* to be Cult inspired rituals at times, even spectacular events such as the Super Bowl halftime shows in the USA, 'seem' ritualistic and connected to the star, sun and moon symbolism.

Figure 47: Greta Thunberg. I am sure she hasn't a clue about the symbolism. As I say, it is a subconscious expression for the majority.

The same one-eyed symbolism can be seen on *Netflix* posters for *Lucifer* (2016) and the *Black Mirror* series. The latter is teeming with subjects

Figure 48: Lucifer, the 'light bringer'.

relating to transhumanism, dystopia, robots and the occult. In the *Netflix* series *Lucifer*, 'he' resides in Los Angeles and runs a club getting involved with the local police, assisting them in solving tricky criminal cases. Lucifer, the 'light-bringer'(see figure 48) is an important figure for the Cult as we shall see. The Netflix series is about making Lucifer, look 'cool', it seems. Los Angeles, the home of Hollywood, also seems significant to the Orion Cult, not least its name meaning: 'The Angels', in Spanish. Its full name, 'El Pueblo de Nuestra Señora la Reina de Los Ángeles de Porciúncula', means 'The Town of Our Lady the Queen of the Angels of Porziuncola' or, the 'Town of the Moon Goddess – the Madonna'. The Moon symbolically seems to be significant focus in the entertainment and film industry, too, and can be seen in the Dreamworks and Amblin Entertainment logos.

The focus on 'one-eye' symbolism is connected to many 'father god' figures found in ancient myths. According to Scandinavian myth, Odin was the Norse 'father god', or the 'all father' god of Asgard and the nine realms (dimensions). Odin is on a par with Yahweh and the Mayan Hun Hunahpu, and all can be connected to the *darker* aspect of Orion *and* Saturn *combined*, as will become clearer in the next few chapters.

Odin - the One-Eyed Father God

The Macroprospus symbol found in ancient texts is not only one that embodies the father God (Odin) symbol, it is also the 'Arika', or the symbol for the divine 'emanation', sometimes shown as the Sephirah (the Tree of Life). The *nine* realms are clearly connected to the Egyptian Ennead and other systems of 'nine', like the Ogdoad and the Ptolemaic cosmography, shared by most Renaissance alchemists. In Ptolemaic systems, the numbers 1 to 9 are primary numbers relating to 'creation' and 'birth', which is why *nine* appears in the Enneagram system and nine dimensions, or circles of Hell.[9] This connection through numbers, dimensions and various forms of ritual worship, not least through 'technology' and 'social media' today, is **not** necessarily of higher consciousness and infinite states of awareness - it will be with a very different Creator 'experience' as I will show in *Part Two*.

Odin, of course is the Merlin, Gandalf wizard-figure and the many references to the white wizard figure found in other legends and stories, too many to go into here. Odin is the father figure Saturn, Saint Nicholas

Figure 49: Odin is the 'All-seeing-eye' God. The *eye* and the *'G'* (in Freemasonry) represent a portal.

(Father Christmas), 'Father Cronos' and 'Wodan' (see figure 49). Odin has both a dark and light dual aspect; he is also the 'inspired one' who colludes with the darkness to bring both change and knowledge to the world. The nine worlds in Norse myth, ruled over by Odin, can be visually connected to the classic Masonic All-seeing eye framed by the compass and set square symbolism. The letter 'G', which often replaces the eye in Masonic symbolism, can be found in Mayan codices and motifs. For the Maya the 'G', or 'ge', referred to 'zero', the 'egg' and a *portal* between the living and the dead.[10] More on the egg symbolism in later chapter.

Odin is also a 'Christ-like god' who hangs upside down in the Tree of Life and is the Hanged Man in the Tarot, often with a raven on each shoulder. The ravens are called Huggin and Munnin (supernatural beings that accompany a person), and both are protectors and thieves. In Norse myth, they are meant to be symbols of *'memory'* and *'thought'*. Odin as the old wanderer, father time (Saturn), who like Christ on the cross on the hill of Golgotha (the place of the skull), is flanked by two thieves (two ravens), Dismas and Gestas, representing the symbolic death of the mind. Ravens are also 'revered' by the Saturn-like Yeoman Beefeaters at the 930-year-old royal fortress - the Tower of London. The 'Tower', of course, is another Tarot symbol that relates to the Odinstårnet in Denmark (The Odin Tower), the second-largest tower in Europe built in 1934-1935 but blown up on the 14th December in 1944 by a group of Danish Nazi saboteurs called the Peter group. The German Nazi 'occult elite' were obsessed with 'Nordic Mythology', as is the Vatican, it seems. The Chair of Saint Peter, also known as the 'Throne of Saint Peter', is a 7th Century relic that lies in the cathedral of St. Peter's Basilica. Cathedra is Latin for 'chair' or 'throne' - Odin's throne to be precise (see figure 50 on previous page). Odin's, Tower, Nazis, and December, all relates to the *inverted* 'energy' of Orion, Saturn, and an 'Invisible Sun' that the ancients said *powered* our Solar system.

Figure 50: St. Peter's Basilica Chair. The Throne of Saturn (Odin) under the Invisible Sun.

The parallels between Odin's rule and the creation of Rome to rule over nations can be seen in Odin's wolves, Geri and Freki (Old Norse, both meaning 'the ravenous' or 'greedy ones'). They are

Figure 51:
The Invisble Sun.
The Oculus is symbolic
of *a* sun or a 'projector'.

the wolf-suckled Romulus and Remus, the founders of ancient Rome (and the Roman Church). The wolf, or dog, symbolism found in Pagan Germanic and Roman history, especially the wolf-warrior bands and use of dogs by the Roman Legion in battle, *all* relate to the warrior/hunter aspect of Orion/Saturn who is accompanied by his faithful dogs. The warrior, or hunter is always portrayed with dogs, which could be a reference to Orion and Sirius, and the 'red' planet, Mars, too. The red carpet laid out for celebrities in Hollywood is said to be code for Sirius – the 'stars' and part of *ritual magic.*

The sun symbol, adorned with rays or 'cherubs' behind and above St. Peter's throne, is also an image that relates to sun-star worship, and more appropriately, as we shall see later in the book, an 'invisible sun' (see figure 51). Some of the arches and central focus points in the architecture also look like stars or suns or even 'projectors', another subject I will come back to in *Part Two*. Planetary bodies, such as Mars, Venus, the Moon and the Sun are more than one-dimensional objects; they are 'personified' in myth for a good reason - they are portals into other realities. Planets, suns and stars are vibrational fields, too.

The Black-Eyed Club

In recent years, some researchers have even referred to a phenomena called, the Black-eyed Club, based on a notable number of politicians, celebrities, business elites, and heads of State who, suddenly, have wound up with black eyes. I cannot validate any of this, but the subject is certainly intriguing to an inquisitive mind, to say the least. Figures such as, Pope Benedict XVI, Pope Francis, Michael Noonan, John Kerry, George W Bush, Richard

Branson, David Bowie, Lady Gaga and the British Royals (Prince Phillip, Andrew and the Queen), to name a few, all seem to have fallen victim to a bruised eye over the years (see figure 52).

According to bloggers and a *Mail Online* article in 2018, photos of celebrities sporting a bruised left eye, *could* suggest some kind of 'initiation' (or part of a ritual) connected to the all-seeing eye, or Odin/Horus who also lose a left eye in myths. The eye of Horus was often used to symbolise 'sacrifice', healing, restoration, and 'protection'. The bruised left eye phenomenon is

Figure 52:
Accidents? Or
Rituals?

more likely to be symptoms caused by internal bleeding, subconjunctival haemorrhage (caused by blood vessels rupturing within the white of the eye), or Epidural Hematoma. Still, the bruised eye phenomenon seems to be quite common in elite circles. Again, I cannot validate such claims or views either way, I am not an expert in such areas. Some alternative writers, such as the late Sherry Shriner, have suggested the black eyes are a result of 'soul snatching' by aliens; others say they are part of a 'pledgor' (security for a loan or *obligation*) as part of an occult ritual where one is forced to 'eat pain' in a quest to become 'more powerful'. Sherry's belief was that heads of State and Hollywood elite are sometimes abducted and surgery is performed on their brain (affecting the eye). I am not so sure of Sherry's 'plastic-surgery-by-aliens' abductee theory, but there are certainly some celebrities who *seem* 'synthetic' or have had excessive plastic surgey. Despite various public reasons in the media for numerous world leaders and celebrities sporting a black eye, there is something slightly odd about it all that warrants further investigation.[11] Such a subject is beyond the scope and remit of this book, my interest here is in the 'symbolism' and occult connections to Orion's stars.

The Orion occult themes, which includes 'Saturn and Moon worship', seems to run through much of what we see in the media (as TV shows/films) being obsessed with 'science', 'artificial' intelligence and synthetic humans. At this level of occult magic and ritual, the Orion Cult becomes the 'Orion-Saturn Cult' when Saturn and Moon 'energies' (or worship) are *entwined* within geopolitics; which is probably why certain celebrities 'get political' at times, so to seemingly serve the geopolitical agenda? Again, this is *not* something I can confirm here, its merely and observation.

Cult rituals are not so far-fetched as we are led to believe. We only have to watch a televised Catholic mass, or Royal ceremony, to see how public rituals are Cult-like.

'Sun' of the Father

Orion and Saturn symbolism 'combined' is also found in Norse mythology, through Odin's son, Thor. He is the hammer-wielding god associated with thunder, lightning, storms, oak trees, and strength in the protection of humankind, who also loses an eye in battle. In pagan belief, Thor was known in Old English as 'Uunor' and in Old High German as 'Donar', stemming from the common Germanic ûunraz meaning 'thunder'. Thor is a Jupiter/Zeus figure who would continue the order of the gods after he rebelled against his father Odin (Saturn) and the Titans. Thor is also compared to 'Baal', or Bel, referred to in the Old Testament. As I will show in later chapters, Baal is an Orion-like deity. Thor is also a 'star/sun god' and was worshipped in the ancient Levant, as Moloch, as well as the star 'Remphan' (Chiun) to a lesser degree. Elements of Thor can be seen in Egypt through Horus and connected to flight, eye loss, and revenge against his father's enemies.

Authors David Talbot and Wallace Thornhill put forward compelling evidence in their books *Electric Universe* (2007) and *Thunderbolts of the Gods* (2005), to suggest that many gods, heroes and myths relate to the true 'electrical nature of our Universe'. They say: "The transitional states of plasma discharge answer directly to the mythical metamorphosis or "shape-shifting" of archaic gods and monsters." What we call electromagnetic 'plasma' expressed in its many forms, as seen from the earth by ancient civilizations, would have provided our ancestors with the vivid imagery and experiences affecting their reality. The ancient skies, as seen from earth would have been an 'electric cinematic' experience to our ancestors.

According to Talbot and Thornhill, Plasma has reshaped our Universe; even within the Earth's Ionosphere, we have plasma 'earthly phenomena' called 'elves sprites' and 'blue jets' that are part of the 'force' holding our solar system in place. Lightning is a discharge when too much electricity builds up in the atmosphere, which then triggers electrical connections and responses at higher altitudes. Known as elves, sprites, gnomes and jets, electrical impacts of the lightning flash play out into the cosmos giving us an array of light shows. The archons and interdimensional forces, I touched on earlier, use 'lightning' and can manipulate electricity (electromagnetic fields) to appear and affect the physical world. It's not too much of a leap of the imagination to picture forces aligning to create effects in a parallel world.

Plasma, according to Talbot and Thornhill, is a *thousand trillion, trillion, trillion* times more powerful than gravity, and it is electricity and electromagnetism that maintain the planets in their orbits around the Sun. It's a distortion in electromagnetic forces that causes the planets to go walkabout and therefore collide with other celestial bodies. With that understanding, the same forces are capable of aiding in the configuration of different worlds, and in the movie *Thor: The Dark World* (2013), we see how a plasma-like substance called the 'Aether', can be used to both create and destroy worlds. The genius Serbo-Croatian scientist, Nikola Tesla, understood all of this, too, and was using electromagnetics to create lightning, using wireless electric power distribution in his high-voltage, high-frequency power experiments in New York, during the early part of the 20th Century.

Thor's Plasma Hammer

Thor's 'hammer' is a symbol that relates to the 'old order of gods, to the race of Titans, handed down to Thor by his father, Odin. We see the connection here to the symbol adopted by Communist Russia, a symbol for the 'might' of both Father and Son – the 'rule of law' through military might. The hammer in mythology was the tool of the 'blacksmith' and the magic of working 'white-hot iron'. It was used by the Titan and creator of weapons, Hephaestus (or Vulcan), and attributed to Jehovah (YHWH). In Norse mythology, the hammer is called the Mjölnir and is depicted as one of the most fearsome and powerful weapons in existence, capable of levelling mountains. It makes you wonder what type of tool or 'technology' may have been used to break and cut rocks to make the megalithic wonders of the world? In aboriginal myths, Orion is often enclosed within a hammer shape or 'T shape,' which could be associated with Thor's Hammer.[12] Both Orion *and* Thor share similar attributes, not least as warrior gods, which is why the Orion Cult, empower the Warlock archetype more than the 'peaceful warrior'. This is also why 'empire building' is more important than 'autonomous individual nations', under such occult elite circles. The narratives in the *Star Wars* movies, showing a galactic empire under an oppressive occult Sith Lord, as opposed to a free Republic under the protection of a Jedi Order, are highly symbolic of the 'hidden' off-world magicians that operate as the Orion Cult on Earth. The magic and 'trickery' used on humanity by such Cults, is as ancient as the many legends and myths of tricksters and fire stealers recorded within indigenous peoples' oral traditions.

Tricksters, Fire Stealers and Keepers of the Sacred Fire

In South American myths, the Jaguar Gods were thought to be the original owners of fire, who refused to share it with others. Also, in Kayua mythology, the toad and a white rabbit (the dragon and sun deities), steal his fire (symbolic of his knowledge, eyes, and powers of seeing). In Navajo myth, the coyote (a Trickster god), also stole the flame from the giant fire gods of Atlantis. The coyote, like the jaguar, gets involved with another creature (the anteater), who can take out his eyes and juggle with them. By taking up the challenge of taking out their own eyes, coyote and jaguar (to compete with the anteater), 'lose an eye', symbolic of the loss of 'true sight'. In Scandinavian mythology, the same theme is echoed with the god Odin (Wodan), who casts one of his eyes into 'Mimirs Well' in return for a drink of wisdom – the sacred knowledge of life. The Adam and Eve story is connected to this myth, as we shall see in the next chapter. Odin was said to gain insight by hanging upside down from the 'Cosmic Tree', which, as I mentioned earlier, became the image of the 'Hanged Man' in the tarot. The tree from which the Hanged Man hangs is the Tau Cross; both symbols relate to Orion as the *fallen* Son of Man, as we shall see.

In Cherokee legend, it was 'Sutaliditis', 'Sulis' (or 'Sun Woman') who held the original 'fire source' and existed at the 'seventh height', the highest knowledge.[13] The Sun was considered a 'cloak' worn by Sutaliditi. This goddess would become the Christian Mary and the Indian, Aditi-figure worshipped in caves and at temples built on rocks near natural springs; places like Bath and Glastonbury in the UK, are ancient places of worship to the goddess Sutaliditi (Sulis). Another name for the sun goddess was the 'Grandmother of the Sacred Fire,' who was so important that no ceremony could be attempted without her presence. According to Cherokee legend, many attempts were made by priestly shamanistic clans (the Star Cult going back to Atlantean times) to steal Sutaliditi's sacred fire or flame! This flame is the 'eternal flame' symbolically held by the Statue of Liberty and a Masonic symbol used to represent the theft of light (knowledge) by those in the ancient mystery schools. In my illustrated stories, *Moon Slayer* (2015) and *Aeon Rising* (2017), I relate Durga to the keeper of the firestone. The Zulu also talks of a Sun goddess called 'Langa' (the longing), who was the 'keeper of the sacred fire', and for them, she was the original Sun for Earth in an ancient epoch, one that was 'taken away'.

The sacred (smokeless) fire associated with salamanders, the phoenix and the 'fiery serpents' in the *Book of Isaiah* and *Book of Kings* were considered magical fire creatures that 'mimicked' the Sun and the stars; helping the 'powers of growth' and holding back the decay and darkness, if summoned correctly. Bonfires, for mediaeval Christianity, were said to keep 'away the devil' and, of course, were used as a method of torture and 'cleansing' of those accused of heresy by the Inquisition. The Brazen Serpent, mentioned in the *Book of Numbers* (the fourth book of the Hebrew Bible), crafted by Moses to protect the Israelites from death, was also thought to be a fiery serpent, and in some instances alluded to a Qabalah-like structure. The Brazen Serpent, or Nehushtan, is similar to the ancient Greek Rod of Asklepios (frequently confused with the caduceus) and is often cited as an instance of the same archetype (see figure 53).

The key point here is that the ancient priesthoods often referred to a 'living fire' and of the serpents that bathed in this fire. These fire entities *are* interdimensional and are part of a force that wreaked havoc on the ancients *through* their priesthoods' worship of such entities. The Burning Bush in the story of Moses is a perfect example of the fire keepers, or Jinn, worshipped by the priestly, secret societies. In *Isaiah*, it is written:

Figure 53: The Brazen Serpent and the Tree of Life combined.

Do not rejoice, all you of Philistia, because the rod that struck you is broken; for out of the serpent's roots will come a viper, and its offspring will be a fiery flying serpent. 14:29

In the *Quran*, the Jinn are said to be made of smokeless fire:

Indeed we created man from dried clay of black smooth mud. And we created the Jinn before that from the smokeless flame of fire.[14]

Methuselah (played by Anthony Hopkins) in the 2014 movie, *Noah*, is portrayed as a protector of *fallen* Angels (demons) and a magician who uses a 'flaming sword' in his youth. It is the same sword in *Genesis* that guards the Tree of Life, belonging to what we call the 'angelic realms', populated by a hierarchy of beings that could use powerful magic and enchantment to consume anything trying to pass through the path it guarded. These beings, I am sure, are connected to the Orion and Saturn through an *energetic pact* made by those *initiated* into the Cult. Methuselah's sword in the movie was symbolic of the 'magic' used to summon demons as well as to destroy them. The phrase 'an offering by fire' is used around 70 times in the Old Testament; fire (flaming swords) relates to the writings at the heart of Gnosticism and is connected to the light of Lucifer. According to *Book of Jasher*, one account talks of Methuselah and this fire:

... He delivered the world from thousands of demons, the posterity of Adam, which he had begotten with Lilith, that she-devil of she-devils. These demons and evil spirits, as often as they encountered a man, had sought to injure and even slay him, until Methuselah appeared, and supplicated the mercy of God. He spent three days in fasting, and then God gave him permission to write the Ineffable Name upon his sword, wherewith he slew ninety-four myriads of the demons in a minute, until Agrimus, the first-born of them, came to him and entreated him to desist, at the same time handing the names of the demons and imps over to him. (Chapter 3).

The above text appears to have come from a chronological compilation of hundreds of biblical legends, where Methuselah killed demons; however, in the movie *Noah*, he kills men, too, by the thousands. The off-world inspired Cult I am describing here is obsessed with fire, death, nefarious magic and warfare, so it seems.

Sacred fire was the source for those that lived beyond the physical 'spectrum', the legendary demons, the gnostic archons, and the Islamic Jinn (genie), all of which were said to have formed through in-organic worlds (through nuclear electromagnetic fire). These ancient beings could appear through Earth's physical, telluric world: the elements of air, fire, and water.

Native Americans also depicted natural phenomena, like wind, the clouds, plants, animals and thunder, in human form at times, so to explain the capabilities of these entities. Lightning, for example, is believed to be a tool of what was called the 'Holy Ones', as recorded in the Hebrew Bible. These Holy Ones are the previously-mentioned Watchers, archons and *fiery* ser-

Figure 54: The *Jinn*.
See the movie of the same name.

pents found in legends and myths from all over the world. Native American deities like 'Changing Woman', a beloved goddess who represents the powers of renewal inherent in the earth; her children, the Hero Twins, Monster Slayer and 'Born-for-Water', are all expressions of the interdimensional 'beings' I am describing here. The legendary salamander, according to some ancient sources, could turn into orbs, forks of flames (St Elmo's fire) and appear in smokeless fire (the eternal flame). Salamanders were, according to sages and alchemists, to be avoided, along with their rulers,

Figure 55: The symbol of the Salamander. Photo Neil Hague 2016

the terrible, fiery Djinn (Jinn). To get a feel for the power of the fire spirits called *Jinn*, it's worth watching the 2014 American action/horror-thriller movie of the same name (see figure 54).

The mythical salamander is another example of the unseen-made-visible through what the ancients called the 'smokeless fire'. The Roman Catholic King, Francis I of France (a prodigious patron of the arts who initiated the French Renaissance by attracting many

Italian artists to work on the Château de Chambord, including Leonardo da Vinci), used the salamander as his emblem (see figure 55). The ancient royal bloodlines, from ancient Pharaohs to a more modern-day elite, claim a heritage back to the gods (or interdimensional entities), through the Watchers and Seraphim (or 'burning ones') I have described so far. Why else would royalty use such emblems like the Salamandar, rampant lion, or dragon on heraldry? Such symbolism is thought to evoke, through magic, 'otherworldly' connections?

The Sky Vault and the Moon Portal (Tunnel of Light)

According to *Genesis*, God created the firmament to separate the 'waters above' the earth from the 'waters below' the earth: And God said, "Let there be a firmament in the midst of the waters and let it divide the waters from the waters" (*Genesis* 1:6). The word is anglicized from the Latin 'firmamentum', which appears in the *Vulgate*, a late, 4th-century Latin translation of the Bible. Another name for the firmament, or vault was the 'Empyrean', which was the place in the highest heaven, supposed to be occupied by the element of fire (star fire). I suggest that these places are 'unseen' celestial locations or *doorways* (portals) that take the soul beyond the physical three-dimensional plane. So many themes relating to a white circular light (like a full moon) can be seen in movies, which hint an otherworldly location where souls migrate at the point of death. The Moon especially relates to the idea of a 'portal'.

The Moon is referred to as 'Yesod' in alchemical hermetic mysticism. It is the first location on the 'Tree of Life' towards higher levels of reality. There is so much more to talk about in terms of *where* the soul goes at death (a theme I will come back to later in the book), but one particular scene in the *Star Trek Voyager* episode *Coda* (1997), where Captain Janeway is almost fooled by an alien into thinking she has died, explains this concept very well. The alien, posing as her father, implores her to follow him into the 'light'. She is suspicious of his intentions and refuses. In the scene she becomes aware of the 'trickery' at the point of death explaining to the alien what she sees as a 'soul trap'. Films such as *Prison Break* (2005), *The Gamer* (2009), *Death Tunnel* (2005), *Lord of Illusion* (1995) and *Knowing* (2009) all feature moon-like portals or tunnels. *The Truman Show* (1998) goes as far as showing the Moon as a control station for Truman's life (from birth), symbolic of the Moon's control over all life (and death) on earth. In the opening theme of the 1960s TV series, *The Prisoner*, Patrick McGoohan drives down the road (life's road), goes through a tunnel and enters a tunnel with a light at the end to doors that say: "Way out".[15]

The Watchers (or Shining ones) and many 'moon deities' are 'keepers of the way'. Along with the 'angelic orders' found in Abrahamic faiths, all have what we perceive to be supernatural powers and the ability to pass *through* what the ancient Sumerians called 'the vault of the sky' (the firmament). Angels, Watchers, and what we call aliens today, live inside the 'portal', or 'projectors' of reality, located through the planets, the Sun and Moon. I would go as far as saying that the hermetic Qabalah is a diagraphic symbol showing the 'hierarchical' order of these different 'portals'.

The story of the Moon-god, Suen, or Sin is one the most prominent Mesopotamian myths, telling how the god was conceived and how he made his way from the Underworld to the Sumerian city of Nippur. The Underworld also relates to the place of the stars. The Moon-god had an important role among the major gods in Mesopotamia when in full form (full Moon), he blocked out the stars. In Assyrian esoteric literature, he (the Moon) symbolises the passageway to the Pleroma, a word in Gnostic teachings referring to 'divine powers' and of a place beyond the physical world. It also means 'fullness', and as I will get to later in the book, the Moon is a 'realm' (a door) for those on earth to pass through at death. The Moon is associated with the afterlife, death, and rebirth. The 'Empyrean' or firmament, in Christian literature, was thought of as the dwelling-place of God, the blessed, celestial beings so divine they are made of pure light (see figure 56). Gustave Doré's image of the Empyrean for the very end scene of Dante's *Paradiso* gives a visual feel for the moon-like portal. So does the *'Three Circles of the Trinity'* illustration by John Flaxman, Canto 33, for *Paradiso*.

Figure 56: The 'Empyrean'.
A portal within the Moon.

I also feel that the 'three bands' in Flaxman's image connect to what Pierre Sabak calls the 'Three Orders of the Illuminati', the 'Anthropos' or the 'Shining Ones' (Watchers) and the 'race of Adam'. Suffice to say, the Watchers are similar in narrative to the Neteru gods of Egypt. The deities, collectively called 'angels' have what we perceive to be supernatural powers and the ability to pass through what the Sumerians called 'the vault of the sky', or the firmament. Angels, as portrayed in religious iconography, are not what we are led to believe, as I will come to in a later chapter; they are part of the construct connected to the Sun and Moon.

Proselene Moon and the Fall

Greek authors Aristotle and Plutarch, and Roman authors Apollonius Rhodius and Ovid each wrote of a group of people called the 'Proselenes' who lived in the central mountainous area of Greece called, Arcadia. The Proselenes claimed title to this area because their forebears were there 'before there was a moon in the heavens'. This claim is substantiated by symbols on the wall of the Courtyard of 'Kalasasaya', near the city of Tiahuanaco, Bolivia, which records how the Moon came into orbit around Earth between 11,500 and 13,000 years ago. All of which sounds mad if you believe the official mainstream science relating to the Moon. After the global cataclysm (Flood), Tiwanaku became the centre of another culture that erected the Kalasasaya, a large courtyard of stones, built as a new calendar, after the Earth had settled into a new sun cycle of 365 years, with the new

Moon (see figure 57).

The Long Man of Wilmington, the mysterious guardian of the South Downs, in the UK, who has baffled archaeologists and historians for hundreds of years, seems to be very similar 'symbolically' to the staff-holding Kalasasaya guardian. The Long Man is clearly a celestial marker, as documented by the late John David North, a British historian of science and author of numerous books. The Long Man is also a Pagan symbol associated with May Day, which of course can be traced back to Egyptian festivals connected to Min and Osiris, which are Orion deities. The 'doorway', or markers created by the staffs in the Long Man's hands, are calendar markers that seem to refer to Orion being a marker (a doorway) for those who lived on Earth after a celestial catastrophe causing the cataclysms recorded in ancient myth (see figure 57). The Long man is also symbolic of the heavenly Adam, the doorkeeper figure who represents the middle pillar of the Tree (Serifot), a subject I am going to explore in some depth later in the book. The primordial man, in this sense, is holding the door open to those who wish to enter through the celestial portal into higher states of awareness.

Some writers assert that the concept of the 'fall', in the biblical sense, relates to the Moon's 'movement' creating devastation on the Earth. But what caused the fall? Was it the Moon, along with an ancient 'alien battle' for Atlantis and Lemuria? Did a rebel faction of 'angels' fight against its hierarchy from the heavens down to Earth? I suggest that the Moon was *used* as a *weapon* in a very ancient epoch, and it facilitated the 'fall of humanity' through its 'movement', quite possibly at the hand of something greater. The Moon's surface certainly looks battle-scarred!

A fascinating book called *The Calendar of Tiahuanaco*, written by Professor Hans Schindler-Bellamy (1956), has mostly been forgotten, probably because his interpretation of symbols on the Kalasasaya Sun Gate contradicted the established view of mainstream archaeologists and astrologers. In his book, Schindler-Bellamy not only claims but also proves that the Sun Gate is a calendar, not only from a civilization more than twelve thousand years ago but a calendar that differs from the present. During that time, Earth was thought to

Figure 57: The 'Gatekeepers' on Earth. (Left) A 'Son of Man' (Orion) archetype at the Courtyard of Kalasasaya. (Right) The Long Man who *through* him (the truth, the light and way), humanity could reach heaven, or the creator.

have had a different solar orbit and axial tilt, and a different moon. I would suggest it was the same Moon but one 'positioned' a lot nearer to the Earth, helping to bring an end to the Atlantean civilization.

The Moon is *not* what it appears to be. As an object of study, I have found myself focusing subconsciously on the Moon. This 'silvery orb' often creeps into my work, not only as a symbol reminding me of the importance of the time we spend asleep on one level but also as a reminder of the forces operating 'just outside' of our 'earthly sphere'. Within the cycles of the Moon are keys for understanding the nature of our gifts and abilities. All of which spring forth from the *Source*, the dreaming, and the more subtle frequencies affecting our emotions and moods. One particular painting I made (or 'channeled' in 1993), gave me insight into forces *using* the Moon to 'draw in' souls that cannot see beyond the veil. The image shows a massive force 'moving' the Moon towards the Earth in an ancient epoch (see figure 58). The image was celebrated in the *Best of British Illustration* book *Images 1993*; something in the image seemed to strike a chord with the judging panel who selected it (you can see a coloured version on my website).

The visual themes I am describing here are *not* based on the actual biblical story of Noah. But with some stretch of the imagination and insight, we might realise that what the Bible calls 'God', may be an expression of 'alien intelligence' or simply the mind of an other-worldly 'Cylon-like' artificial *sentience* that can also create life forms. Is it true to say 'unseen' forces and the 'gods' recorded throughout the ancient world, along with our modern cultural myths (seen in many books and movies today), are what appear to stand between us and higher consciousness (the *Infinite*). To put it simply, the 'unseen' gods of the ancient world, some of which were benevolent, could speak directly to the hearts and minds of our ancestors. Others were malevolant in origin and had ulterior motives.

In Gnostic creation texts, these unseen forces are often referred to as 'Archons', a Greek word meaning 'ruler'. The same texts also spoke of 'higher gods' that *used* the archons like a master uses several servants to do 'his' bidding. This 'god' (or gods) was said to stand between the human race and a transcendent, infinite

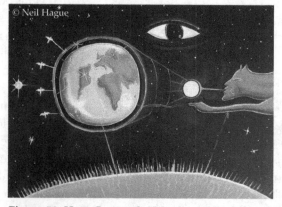

Figure 58: Here Comes the Moon.
I painted this image in 1993 before I knew any of these concepts.

world, a place that could only be reached through 'Gnosis' or self-knowledge. As I bring this chapter to a close, it is worth noting that according to the Gnostics, the Archons were said to be here 'before' humanity. The 'manipulation' of the human mind (through these unseen forces) has been ongoing since the so-called 'creation' recorded in the biblical book of *Genesis*. Only *after* great geological cataclysms (Noah's flood) and genetic manipulations, has control by alien forces seemingly gone into overdrive.

The fall of humanity, encoded in the Adam and Eve story in *Genesis*, is where we need to turn our attention to next, so to understand more about the forces that have shaped our human reality (our perceptions). As we shall see, the biblical creation story is only one piece in a much larger picture, a narrative, which includes a goddess and her offspring – the different realms populated by stars, suns, moons, and planets *personified*.

Sources:

1) Bramley, William. *The Gods of Eden*. Avon Books. 1989, p90
2) Potter, GR. *The New Cambridge Modern History, Volume One -The Renaissance,* 1967, p248
3) Hancock, Graham. *Before America*. 2019, p 308
4) *Lakota Star Knowledge: Studies in Lakota Stellar Theology,* 1993, p34
5) Campbell, Joseph; The Hero with a thousand Faces. 1949, Pp 274-5
6) Goodman, Ronald.*Lakota Star Knowledge*. 1992. p22.
7) *Amos* v 26, R. V.
8) http://jewishencyclopedia.com/articles/13990-star-worship page 527
10) https://vigilantcitizen.com/pics-of-the-month/symbolic-pics-of-the-month-05-19/
9) Hague, Neil. *Through Ancient Eyes*. Quester. 2018, p306
10) Men, Hunbatz. *Secrets of Mayan Science and Religion*. Bear & Company; Original ed. Edition. 1989, pp 60-61
11) https://prepareforchange.net/2018/08/22/the-black-eye-club/ & https://www.dailymail.co.uk/femail/article-5971319/Conspiracy-theory-suggests-celebrities-snapped-black-left-eyes-ILLUMINATI.html
12) Munya, Andrews. *The Seven Sisters of the Pleiades: Stories from Around the World*. p126
13) Allen, Paula Gunn. *Grandmothers of the Light*. The Women's Press 1992. p 85
14) *Quran* 15:26-27
15) https://www.trickedbythelight.com/tbtl/movies.shtml

4

PARADISE FALLING

'From the Star Goddess Down to Earth'

Your teacher can open the door, but you must enter by yourself.

CHINESE PROVERB

The general name for the mystics who pondered on the cosmos, creation and the 'nature of reality' is the 'Gnostics'. One important source for Gnostic teachings came from a series of manuscripts called the *Nag Hammadi* texts and the *Dead Sea Scrolls*, found near the town of Nag Hammadi about 75-80 miles north of Luxor on the banks of the River Nile, in Egypt. These texts generally became known as the 'lost gospels' of the *Nag Hammadi* Library. The Nag Hammadi discovery included thirteen leather-bound papyrus codices (manuscripts) and more than fifty texts written in Coptic Egyptian, the work (along with other ancient influences) of a people known as Gnostics. The Gnostics were not a racial group; their ideology was a way of 'perceiving reality' under the heading of 'Gnosticism', coming from the term *Gnosis* - a Greek word that translates as 'secret knowledge'. To be Gnostic, in simple terms, meant to be 'learned'.

In 2017, I wrote and published an illustrated story, *Aeon Rising*, giving an alternative perspective of the origins of Gnostic thought. I wrote:

Many thousands of years ago when the Earth was nothing like it is today, an ancient people walked its surface in the light of the source of All-That-Is. They were simply called the 'keepers of the Aeons'. In later World Ages, they were known as the Gnostics. All manner of stars, suns and planets are manifestations of the Aeons. The very centre of creation is Infinite Awareness, All-Possibility, and All-Potential. Everything has consciousness and the Ancients called this 'living consciousness' the Pleroma (the totality). It was from the Pleroma that the Dreaming occurred.

Before I go deeper into Orion symbolism, I want to look at what the learned, or the Gnostics, knew in relation to Creation and the Cosmos. My feeling is that the Abrahamic faiths are simply an attempt to overwrite Gnostic teachings which give a more credible explanation of how reality was created.

The Aeons (Higher Consciousness)

The Gnostic *Nag Hammadi* texts offer an alternative creation story teaching of a cosmological 'birthing' of our world through *dreaming* of what the texts refer to as the 'Aeons'. According to Gnostic thought, the Aeons were divided into *Upper* and *Lower* realities (states of consciousness) and one particular Aeon, called Sophia, was pivotal in their creation story. Sophia was the goddess that became Gaia, or Earth, in the Gnostic teachings. Dictionaries define this meaning of Aeon as a power existing from eternity; an emanation or phase of the 'supreme deity'. Gnostic texts refer to the Upper Aeons and Lower Aeons in very different terms and they say that between two worlds is a curtain, veil, or boundary. The Upper Aeons are said to emanate directly from the unity of 'The One' – *Infinite Awareness* of itself – and can be symbolised as concentric circles expressing the Oneness of their Creator, or Emanator. Gnostics also describe the Upper Aeons as 'The Silence', or the 'Living Silence', or the 'Watery Light'. The Lower Aeons instead were said to be 'creator gods' that could only influence worlds beyond (or below) the veil or boundary see figure 59.

The Gnostics talk of the teachings of the 'Pleroma', or

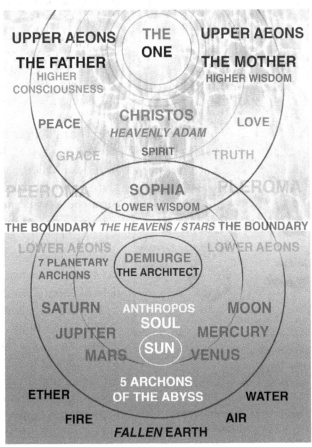

Figure 59: The Gnostic Cosmos. © Neil Hague 2020

what the *Nag Hammadi* called the 'abode of the Upper Aeons'. They described it as the place of higher consciousness, 'eternal ideas' or the home of the original archetypes. The word 'Aeon' for the Gnostics, was another way of describing 'higher consciousness', or the *Infinite* that *is* the 'Pleroma'. In recent years, I have often depicted in my art, the Pleroma, which I see as 'living plasma' (the force behind the electric Universe) that constitutes the mass of our *living* Universe. The Lower Aeons, or 'Heimarmene', is the constructed cosmos and concerned with the consciousness of planets, moons and the human form, the latter being called the 'Anthropos', a subject I will return to in the next chapter. In simple terms, the Pleroma for the Gnostic mind was (is) living electromagnetic consciousness. Everything is alive and can take multiple forms. As the physicist Wallace Thornhill says in the book he wrote with David Talbot, *The Electric Universe* (2007):

Figure 60:
The Cornucopia.
A feminine image symbolic of Mother Nature and the 'Field of Plenty' being 'manipulated' by those who control the wealth on earth. Courtesy of Dover

We can detect magnetic fields in space, which, according to Maxwell's equations, means electricity must be flowing in space to produce them. It is impossible to have a magnetic field without moving electrons. Electrons only move in response to charge imbalance. Once an electron is moving, we have an electric current.

The word Pleroma also means 'fullness' or 'plenty' and relates to what Native Americans call the 'Field of Plenty'; the place from which *all* life manifests. The cornucopia is another symbol for the Pleroma or 'Field of Plenty' (a spiritual Eden) and can be found on buildings (banks) and stately homes of those who have much invested in the 'control' of this field of energy on Earth (see figure 60).

In my book *Journeys in the Dreamtime* (2006), I refer to the Pleroma as the 'mother substance' and the 'source of all light'. In the ancient Judaic texts, *The Book of the Mystery* and the *Kabbalah*, the divine substance is personified as the most 'ancient of ancient'. Manly P Hall, Freemasonic Historian and author of *The Secret Teachings of All Ages* (1928), quite rightly refers to 'Superconsciousness', or the Aeons, as having both male and female personage. In the Hebrew Bible, 'wisdom' (Chokhmah) relates to a 'Divine Unity' evident in the Gnostic teachings; the Higher Aeons, male and female, *wisdom* and *intelligence* 'combined' (symbolised as the snake), were said to have created the world. One text in the *Book of the Mystery* reads:

> *From the bosom of this absolute Unity, distinct from the various forms and from all relative Unity, go forth, as parallels, two principles, opposite in appearance but inseparable in reality; one, male or active, which is called "Wisdom," the other passive, or female, is designated by a word which it is customary to translate by "Intelligence".*[1]

The female divinity in such passages refers to 'Sophia' in Gnostic belief. She is the creator of worlds affecting our reality and as the *Zohar* states:

> *Wisdom is also named the "father"; for it is said, Wisdom engenders all things. By means of thirty-two marvelous ways by which it is diffused through the universe, it imposes a form and measure on all that is. Intelligence is the "mother," as is written: Thou shalt call intelligence by the name of mother.*

The 'thirty-two marvelous ways' seems to relate symbolically to the human vertebral column and the 33rd vertebral, of course, is the atlas vertebra, atop the cervical vertebra, at the seat of the skull (place of the mind and imagination). It is also the highest level of Freemasonry called the Sovereign Grand Master General and much more besides.

Sophia, Mother Nature & the Starry Night

The two-thousand-year-old *Nag Hammadi* texts say the Aeons were separated from their celestial region by Horus (or Boundary) and beyond its veil was what the Gnostics called the 'Kenoma', or the 'void' (worlds beyond spirit). Humanity was said to have been created out of the meeting of the 'Kenoma' and the Aeon Goddess, Sophia. It was thought by the Gnostics that humans are god-like (Aeon-like) with a powerful tool at their disposal – 'divine Imagination' (see *Through Ancient Eyes*). In the *Nag Hammadi* texts, the Aeon called Sophia (wisdom in Greek), aided by Thelete (intent in Greek), was said to have dreamed into existence a world connected to the Upper Aeons but formed in worlds connected to the Lower Aeons. Sophia became self-awareness and through her dreaming process, into the realms of the Kenoma (beyond the veil), she created what the Aboriginal cultures call the 'Dreamtime' – a creation *epic* predating *all* biblical creation narratives by at least tens of thousands of years.

In Greek myth, the goddess 'Astraea', the celestial goddess similiar to Sophia, was said to be the last of the immortals to live with humans during the Golden Age I mentioned in *Chapter One*. According to the Roman poet Ovid (43 BC- 17AD), Astraea abandoned the earth during the Iron Age. Fleeing from the new wickedness of humanity, she ascended to heaven to become the constellation Virgo.[2] In the tarot, the 8th card, 'Strength and Justice' (with a figure of Justitia), is thought to be the figure of Astraea. The female character on that card is also Sophia wrestling with the lion, who as we shall see, relates to another part of this story. According to legend, Sophia, or Astraea will one day come back to earth, bringing with her the return of the Golden Age of which she was the original ambassador.

Both Sophia and Astraea are versions of the virgin goddess of justice, innocence, purity and precision. It was Asteria, the goddess of the stars who appeared in many forms, especially in tribal Asia Minor and European beliefs. In Egypt she was the goddess, Nut. A star (sky) goddess who gave birth to the 'gods' that would rule over the civilizations of the new world. Sophia is the Greek Gnostic version of the celestial goddess figure, Nut. I am also certain the 'Sheela Na Gig' figures of ancient Ireland are also symbolic versions of the mother goddess (Sophia), and the 'birthing' of what would become a pivotal god-figure. So, too, are the images of the goddess 'Umai' worshipped by the Scythians, Bulgars and Turkish semi-nomadic people of the Caucasus Mountains (see figure 61). The Bulgars, incidentally, gave rise to what became 'Gnostic Catharism' through the Bogomil priesthoods of Bulgaria, more on the Cathars later. For the ancient Turks, the

Figure 61: The Goddess Umai.
The Goddess Umai was worshipped by the tribal people of the Caucasus Mountain regions.

Figure 62: The Goddess Umai.
Copied from a Siberian shamanic diagram clearly showing the heavenly zone above the boundary.

Figure 63: Flag of the Chuvash Republic.
The Goddess Umai symbolised through the
celestial *tree (or pole)* and the *three stars (suns)*.

goddess Umai appeared as a highly revered deity. She was the patron of all Turkic and Mongolian people of the Altay (Altai) in the Siberian Altai Republic regions. Umai, like other goddesses, was connected to the 'divine aspect of creation', and was said to live in the heavenly zone (the Upper Aeons), sending her rays down to earth, giving life to humanity. Her face sits atop a pole above what is clearly a 'boundary' where the stars, suns and heavenly worlds connect to those below (see figure 62). As above, so below.

The National flag of the Chuvash Republic, from the region where Umai was worshipped, depicts the same central pole or 'tree' and 'three stars' of 'Tengriism', the shamanic practice of the Xiongnu, Xianbei, Turkic, Bulgar, Mongolian, Hunnic, and Altaic peoples (see figure 63). The tree is symbolic of the bridge between the timeless and infinite worlds of the Upper Aeons and the Earth (Sophia/Gaia). The three stars (or suns) could be symbolic of the three stars forming Orion's belt on one level, but more importantly, they are symbolic of the 'power of three' and 'manifestation' out of what those cultures called the 'field of plenty'. They are also the three properties of the physical Sun: *life, light* and *heat* and they symbolise the three worlds: *spiritual, intellectual* and *material*. According to some researchers, these stars are also three suns which are connected to Orion and Taurus and the trinity of knowing, gratitude and action.

In 2019, I visited Riga, Latvia. The original Baltic peoples were also pagans despite their many tribulations and occupations at the hands of invaders spanning many centuries. Due to Latvia's strategic location and prosperous trading city of Riga, its territories were a frequent focal point for conflict and conquest between at least four major powers: The State of the Teutonic Order; the Polish–Lithuanian Commonwealth, Sweden; also the Russian Empire. The Order of the *Three Stars*, established in 1924, in remembrance of the founding of 20th Century Latvia, seems to have a connection to the Teutonic Order (Freemasonry) and Orion. Its motto, '*Per aspera ad astra*', means 'Through hardships to the stars'. In ancient Egypt, Osiris (or Orion) represented the physical material world and the path all souls would take to travel the world tree, the 'pole of light', home. As we shall see, the eye of Osiris relates to an invisible sun, a location where, 'from one light come *three* lights'.

The Goddess of the 'Light' – the Wife of God

The Goddess Gnowee (the torch carrier), of the Wotjobaluk Aboriginal people, was also another version of Sophia. The
Freemasonic version of this torch-carrier is the
Statue of Liberty of Isis (Liberty Enlightening the
World). Mythologically, the Goddess Isis was the
eldest daughter of Saturn, wife of Osiris (Orion)
and symbolic of the Dog Star, Sirius. The Goddess
and legendary ruler Tomyris ('Queen of the
Scythians') of the Massagetae people, seems to be
connected to the Phoenician and earlier shamanic
female warriors - the Amazons. Ancient Amazons,
hunters, the hunter, Orion and the many modern-
day corporations, names and logos, are all connected symbolically, as we shall see.

Another aspect of Sophia can be found in the
stories of Asherah, the 'Wife of God' found in
Mesopotamian art and sculpture. The famous
25,000-year-old Neolithic sculpture of the 'Venus of
Dusseldorf' is another image of Asherah, or possibly, Sophia (See figure 64). In American Indian
belief, there is also a 'Yei' (divine form) called
'Ahsonnutli' or 'Etsanatlehi', which means 'woman

**Figure 64: Venus of
Dusseldorf.**
A 'personification' of
Venus, Virgo and Gaia
(Sophia).

who changes'. Also called 'Changing Woman', she was one of the principle
creation spirits (or Aeons) that formed the sky and the earth (see also the
Egyptian goddess, Nut). In simple terms, the Gnostic Aeon Sophia, along
with the Pleroma goddess Thelete (through their ability to create), both
manifest the Anthropos – the *divine human form*. According to the Gnostics,
the place where the Anthropos emerged was the Orion Nebula, which, as
we shall see, became a fascination for Sophia.

Sophia's Dream Turned Nightmare.

It is said that Sophia 'absorbed herself' in her fascination for the Anthropos
and her dreaming, where she 'fell' further into the 'void' or the 'Kenoma'.
Here she awoke from within what seemed to be a *nightmare* as she drifted
further away from the Pleroma and Upper Aeons. The Gnostics say Sophia
impacted on the outer veil (the boundary) and ventured into the realms of
chaos, her 'living consciousness' led to the 'emergence' of what Gnostic

texts call 'inorganic' elementals. These are the 'Archons' mentioned in pre-vious chapters. In Arabic texts the same elementals are called the Jinn (genies), and in Christianity they are referred to as demons or 'phantoms'. The word Archon comes from the Greek 'archai', which means primordial, first, or antecedent in time. The texts describe how the Archons arose in the planetary system before earth was formed into a habitat for life; they are not organic by nature. In truth, these 'entities' are both good and bad and are also the angelic beings and the Watchers I mentioned in the last chapter. The arrival of the archons into the void was said to be a 'plague' on the Anthropos and therefore humanity. We are still suffering from this plague. The arrival caused chaos in all matters of the human mind. Sophia's impact on the boundary-between-worlds also created a cosmic calamity as these inorganic Archons circled and swooned around the chaos that was formed by Sophia's 'fall' into the Kenoma (see figure 65). The story in itself is mir-rored in so many indigenous myths that relate to the 'splitting of the supreme being' and the 'duality of life' that ensued from this splitting.

On one level, you could say that Sophia fell into a 'coma', a place from which she would eventually awaken, but her wanderings in the Pleroma set in motion a creation epic. Some texts, such as the *Apocalypse of Adam*, say that Sophia, as one of the nine muses, 'solidified' her attention, eventu-ally becoming the Earth. One text in the Gnostic Bible reads:

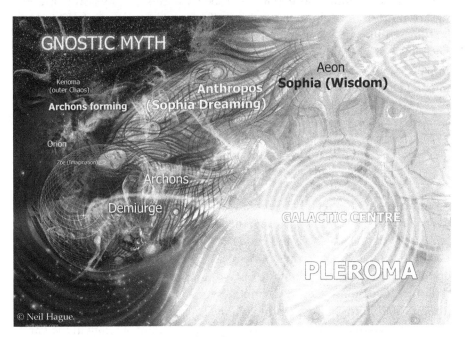

Figure 65: Sophia's Dream Turned Nightmare.
Sophia's dream giving form to worlds centred on the Orion and beyond.

From the Nine Muses, one separated away. She came to a high mountain and spent (some) time seated there, so that she desired herself alone, in order to become androgynous. She fulfilled her desire and became pregnant from her desire.

The texts here refer to an aspect of Sophia becoming the Anthropos (celestial humanity) or giving birth to the light (divine imagination) that would become what visionaries, like William Blake, called the 'Human Form Divine'.

Virtual Heaven

According to Gnostic myth, the world humanity inhabits is pure 'thought', the region of matter made manifest through the material (physical) world. This philosophy was the foundation of the Gnostic groups that became the Tenth Century 'Bogomil' and 'Paulicians', through to the 12th Century Cathars of Occitania, France. They all saw the physical world as the land of shadow and darkness, a place where 'perception and deception' would coexist. The material world was always imperfect and unchangeable for the Gnostic dualist faith, and only spirit should be sought. The Aeons was the home, or sanctuary, for those that lived in the light. According to Gnostic texts, Sophia eventually 'changed' and took physical form as Gaia (the original Earth) so to allow those that would be born into the physical world to find comfort in the light of the goddess. Sophia was personified as Mother Nature and the key to living in harmony as a human being. Look how far we have come from this understanding today? The Northwest Thompson Indians, an Indigenous First Nations people in southern British Columbia, illustrate a similar story of the Earth as a goddess through their cosmology:

At first Kujum-Chantu, the Earth, was like a human being, a woman with a head, and arms and legs, and enormous belly. The original humans lived on the surface of her belly. Her hair became the trees and grass; her flesh, the clay; her bones, the rocks and her blood, the springs of water.[3]

From my research, I feel that Sophia was captured in art forms found all over the ancient world as the original goddess. She is 'Langa' to the Zulu African; to the Aztec, she is the goddess 'Chalchiuhtlicue'. We find many personifications of this Aeon Goddess; as previously mentioned, she is the goddess Umai; Asherah, the Wife of God, found in Mesopotamian art and sculpture. Eve, in my view, was another version of Sophia. The 'lioness', 'dragon' and 'bird' in my painting, *Eve and Adam in the 'garden in the Stars'*, are all projections of the goddess who lives in the light, *forming* in the garden amongst the stars (see figure 66). The garden is located in the Orion

Nebula, which I will explore in more depth later.

The lioness and the dragon bird are intricately connected to our DNA, including so-called junk DNA. The god in the upper right section 'holding' the Anthropos (the first human being, also referred to as Adamas, or Geradamas) is symbolic of the Elohim, more on them shortly. You will also notice from my painting that the goddess Eve is already in the Garden of Eden. According to Gnostic teachings, the *spirit* of Eve was already in the garden and was referred to as 'Zoe' (life itself). Zoe is a daughter of Sophia and a teacher for the first man - Adam. Zoe, or Eve's spirit, entered the Tree of Life and eventually became symbolised as both the 'serpent' and the 'apple' in *Genesis*. All of this was said to have occurred after Sophia's nightmare and primary birth, something I will look at shortly. Zoe, or the 'Spirit of Eve', according to the *Secret Book of John* (also known as the *Apocryphon of John*), was said to have *become* the tree to hide from the Archons. The *Apocryphon of John* elaborates on this narrative:

Figure 66: The Goddess & Adamas who *lives in light*.
Eve (Zoe) and Adam on High in the Garden in the Stars.
(© Neil Hague 2018.).

A light-filled Afterthought emerged, and he called her Zoe (Life). She aids the entire creation, working with him, restoring him to the Fullness. She taught Adam about the way his people had descended. She taught Adam about the way his people could ascend, which is the way he had descended. The light-filled power was hidden in Adam, so that the rulers wouldn't know about Her. For [Zoe/Spirit of Eve] *would repair the damage her mother had caused.*

Sophia, Orion and the Milky River

Sophia, being so in awe of the realms of the Upper Aeons, 'dreamed into existence her own world' without consent from the *Infinite*. From within Sophia's dreaming-turned-nightmare, according to Gnostic scriptures, there appeared a central figure, or a deity to which she gave birth, then quickly rejected. This unwanted child grew to become the arrogant god-figure we recognize in the books of the Old Testament. Like a child, this figure arrogantly proclaimed itself to be the 'source of all that was' born of the impact on the Pleroma caused by Sophia's dreaming. For the Aramaic Gnostics, this 'ruler' became known as 'Yaldabaoth' (the blind 'announcer'), or the Father God 'architect' who manufactured a 'fake system of worlds'. In Aramaic, his name was 'Saklas', meaning 'fool', a symbol that will be highly relevant in the next chapter. The worlds formed by the Demiurge-Yaldabaoth were the 'stars' and 'nebulae' in the *lower worlds* of what the Gnostics called the 'Kenoma' and ancient Greeks called the 'milky circle' – the Milky Way.

The Coma Berenices constellation, also called 'Berenice's Hair', situated between Leo and Arcturus (Bootes) is also hugely connected to the Sophia story, too. Not least through the Gnostics' understanding of what they called the 'true light' and their knowledge of the stars. The Coma Berenices constellation has eight Messier objects* and is rich in galaxies, containing the northern part of the Virgo cluster, connected to Aphrodite: the goddess of love and beauty.

For much of East Asia, the Milky Way galaxy is referred to as the 'Silver River'. Chinese legend says that once upon a time, there was a beautiful young maiden named the 'Goddess Weaver', the daughter of the Celestial Queen Mother (Sophia). For numerous American Indian tribes, the Milky Way was the *source* of the mother goddess, the 'milk of heaven'. The rift in the Milky Way was a 'place' where it was said the first human (star human being) was born. Interestingly, the Milky Way is a barred spiral galaxy with two major arms and a number of minor arms, or spurs. Orion (the star human being) is located between the Sagittarius and Perseus Arms of the Milky Way and our sun is located in the Orion Arm, or 'Orion Spur', of the Milky Way galaxy. Black holes and dark molecular areas, like the Great Rift (mentioned on page 83), seem to be hugely important; often appearing in ancient myths to be locations (sometimes 'doorways') from where forces have fallen (or emerged) amongst the stars.

Footnote: Naturally occurring physical entity, association, or structure that exists in the observable universe, named after the French astronomer Charles Messier in his *Catalogue des Nébuleuses et des Amas d'Étoiles* (*Catalogue of Nebulae and Star Clusters*).

The 'Fallen One'

In Greek mythology, the casting out of Hephaestus (or the Roman god Vulcan) from Mount Olympus, by Hera, is similar to the Gnostic narrative of Sophia rejecting her god-like, unwanted child. The one-eyed cyclops characters, found in myths associated with Hephaestus, represent the Eye of Providence 'personified' on one level, but are also symbolic builders of the scaffolding of planetary systems that became our solar system. Hephaestus (or Vulcan), was one of the three gods credited with the creation of the 'star man' and giant god, Orion. Just as Typhon and Lucifer were 'cast out' of heaven, Sophia's child was cast away from her as she fell further into the realms of chaos. Both the rejection of her creation and the fall of Sophia, leads to the 'spawning of a deviant god-figure the Gnostics refer to as the 'Demiurge'. The texts say this 'god' had the abilities of his mother, but carried *neither* the light and wisdom of the Upper Aeons, nor the *spirit* of the Pleromic worlds from whence Sophia was conceived. The Demiurge is the 'false proclaimer', the 'architect' of planetary realms, also known as the 'changer of worlds' and the 'harbinger of fear'.

Gnostic schools of thought associated the Demiurge with Satan, Ahriman, Saklas, Samael and Choronzon. For the Gnostics, the Demiurge was behind the creation of Adam (Primal Man) and this fits with my long-held contention that the force referred to as the Archons manipulated human genetics to create a body-type (biological computer-type) that most suited their goal of human subjugation. The Demiurge is also known in the Gnostic texts as the 'Lord Archon' and quoted as saying: 'Come let us create a man according to the image of God and according to our likeness.' The planet Saturn, El, and the biblical Elohim, are a variation of the 'Gnostic Lord Archon', or 'Architect', too.

Under the instruction of this Architect God-figure (who believes he is the creator of all he beholds), along with the Archons, they are said to build planetary systems, *excluding* the sun and our 'original earth'. The Demiurge instead creates a 'fake earth' (a fractual copy), or matrix world based on the original earth. The Archons mimic other planets to alter the unique geometry (fractals of light) to replicate 'the heavens' in their god's liking. Gnostic texts say the Archons, guided by the Demiurge, constructed an illusory reality, purposely made to 'mimic' the original organic reality born of the Aeon Goddess, Sophia. We know the place well. It is the very troubled earth reality we call 'everyday life'.

In the Aboriginal Dreamtime, the archon forces I am describing are called the 'Mimics'; these were said to look like giant frogs or lizards. The illusory earth-world born of Sophia's 'dreaming' and then copied by the 'Mimics' (Archons), was said to have 'changed' in appearance 'four times'.

The rise and fall of golden ages and ancient eras are the different worlds described by the Hopi and other native peoples. I feel these changes were 'instigated' by the archons, or Mimics, I am describing. We are currently in the time of another 'world change', as I will show later in the book. The Gnostics also say humanity remains caught up between two realities: the original earth, and the bad copy created out of what the Gnostic texts call HAL, forged by the architect Creator-God – or Demiurge (see figure 67).

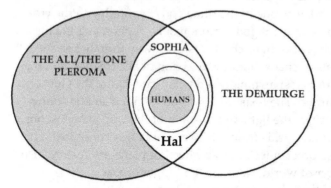

Figure 67: Caught Between Worlds. Humans are caught between two worlds: The Aeon *organic* Earth World, and the Demiurge 'fake' (*artificial Intelligent*) controlled Earth, or Hal. We have a choice to make!

The duality of these two worlds will become more apparent further into the book as I explore the symbolism in great depth. I feel that Sophia's fall in the Gnostic texts hints at the formation of the Orion Nebula as part of the creation of our physical reality. As I will show, the Orion Nebula is a portal and possibly the place of emergence (and return) for the human soul. I wrote in *Aeon Rising* (2017):

> *This Demiurge created a copy or 'shadow version' of the Aeon worlds 'separating them into upper and lower heavens'. The architect of these shadow worlds was androgynous, as were the willing angels, phantoms and demons that followed it. In what we call the Orion star system, this god created a 'blueprint' for the beings that would appear on this Earth. Adam appeared as Orion (unisexual, and the first of the 'Lower Aeons'); but the Demiurge then divided this blueprint into male and female genders and this is where the story of Adam and Eve comes from.*

A Demented God

According to the *Nag Hammadi*, HAL, or the illusory planetary realms of our Solar system, had its Creator - the Demiurge. He was the deity eventually called God by monotheistic patriarchal religions. Can you see why the Gnostics (and later Cathars) were violently removed wherever they appeared, offering an *alternative* view to 'established' faiths? According to the Gnostic texts, '*He*' (the Demiurge) was an angry, demented, impostor-god who envied human divine imagination – the Anthropos. *He* is the 'beast' often depicted as a 'rampant lion' whose minions are the 'inorganic' Archons, often described in Gnostic texts as resembling an aborted fetus. The key point to emphasise here is that the Demiurge should be seen as the 'master of mimicry' and the architect of 'manipulating perceptions'. The Solar system, as I shall come to, has been changed and 'altered' in *appearance* by the *mind* the Gnostics called the Demiurge. The Gnostic Bible and the texts *On the Origin of the World* describe events concerning the arrival and demeanor of the Demiurge. It says:

> *Now when the outer heavens had been consolidated along with their forces and all their administration, the Demiurge became insolent. And he was honored by an army of angels who gave blessing and honor to him. And for his part he was delighted and boasted to them, 'Lo, I have no need of anyone else, no other gods'. He said, 'It is I who am god, and no others exist apart from me.*[4]

The above text is the perfect description of the 'arrogant' (too-often psychopathic) archetype; it is also the 'fire and brimstone' God we find throughout the Old Testament. His angels are not angels, but Archons, which is where we get the word '*Arch*-Angel' and much more besides. As the acclaimed John Lamb Lash writes in his book, *Not in His Image* (2006):

> *...and Sophia desired to cause the thing that had no innate spirit of its own to be formed into a likeness and rule over primal matter and over all the forces she had precipitated. So there appeared for the first time a ruler out of chaos, lion-like in appearance, androgynous, having an exaggerated sense of power within him, and ignorant of whence he came to be.*[5]

The Gnostics defined the Pleroma (or the Pleromic gods), as existence beyond matter (flesh and bone). I relate the term *beyond* matter to what is referred to, in a Metaphysical Universe, as 'waveform level', 'fractuals' and matter. You could also compare the Pleroma to the world of spirit. The altered version of the earth I touched upon may have been a 'bad copy of the fractuals of light' (Sophia's original *spirit form*), but it was still a copy of something of a 'higher' (or good) despite the Archons working ever since to *remove* the good and replace it with their inorganic devilish version of reality the Gnostics called 'Hal'.

The destruction of our climate and the human *organic* world in favour of 'everything artificial' is a *key* to understanding what the archontic forces live for – to 'feed off' the human spirit and root out anything that can lead humanity back to the source – the Infinite, which exists beyond Hal. The 'rooting out' of all Gnostic groups (early Christians) by Rome, immediately after the destruction of the Second Temple in Jerusalem around 70AD, was a clear expression of the archontic, autocratic, 'oppressive' empire-building of those 'possessed' by the Demiurge and the archons. History is full of such examples, but the Gnostics were targeted by the Roman Empire (at that time), due to their 'knowledge' of *self* Gnosis (the Christ *within*). Empires (including modern day technocracies) cannot be built if Gnosis is 'activated' within each soul; therefore, *all* memory of the true nature of Christ needed to be overwritten. I will come back to this later in the book.

Like the Gnostics, the Sethians (one of many ancient Gnostic groups) flourished in the Mediterranean region at the time of nascent Christianity; they provided a synthesis of Judaic and Greek thought within their own distinct interpretation of cosmic creation. The Sethians were a Gnostic movement, who claimed to possess secret knowledge that could unlock transcendent understanding. Central to many gnostic beliefs is a dualistic view of the universe. A philosophy that sees all matter as mostly illusory while the spirit is the only *true* reality. Some scholars, notably Gershom Scholem, profess that Jewish Gnosticism predates its Christian counterpart and this can be seen, for example, in the writings of Philo of Alexandria, the revelations of Ezekiel, the apocalyptic sections of the *Book of Daniel*, and the apocryphal *Book of Enoch*, with its detailed explanations about the angelic world. The latter contributed to Gnostic descriptions and names for the archons, aeons, and other Pleromic gods such as Sophia.

A Chimera was Born

In some versions of the Gnostic myth, the spiritual aeon, Sophia, imitates God's actions in performing an emanation of her own, without the 'prior approval' of other Aeons in the Pleroma. The texts say this results in a crisis within the Pleroma; one that leads to the appearance of the Demiurge, who they call Yaldabaoth, a 'serpent with a lion's head'. In one narrative, this 'god' is at first hidden (some say rejected) by Sophia but subsequently escapes, stealing a portion of divine power from her in the process. Thus the Gnostic Sethians believe that there is a true God and a false God. The latter is the Demiurge, which is classical Greek for 'master' craftsman-creator. According to some Gnostic traditions, the 'master' craftsman created the world following God's command. However, the malevolent Demiurge then usurped the true god's position. I personally feel that the Demiurge is a 'personification' of the 'Fall', or a computer virus-like form which spread across planetary fields (our Solar system), altering the souls of planets, and aliens alike, a subject which will become more evident as the book unfolds.

Gnostic texts such as the *Hypostasis of the Archons*, say the Archons were born out of Sophia's dreaming and that they created 'seven powers' for themselves. One of the seven powers created was said to be 'six angels' (six archons), one of these was called Sabaoth (the Lord of Hosts), who was said to have 'a dragon's face'. Sabaoth, Helios and Saturn seem to be the same entity and in some myths they are also connected to Prometheus (Lucifer) and Cronos (Saturn/Satan). Both these gods relate to an ancient epoch, a cosmology connecting another central sun (Saturn) when Sophia's original earth flourished in a Golden Age. For more information on this concept, see David Talbot's excellent book *The Saturn Myth* (1980). Lash also equates the sixth angel Sabaoth with our sun, but the *Apocryphon of John* says: 'The sixth one is Cain, whom the generations of men call the fallen Sun.' This fallen Sun, in my view, is both Helios and Saturn (Prometheus and Cronos) and it is Orion, as we shall see, that holds sway over the original 'ring-less' Saturn (the old Sun). A harmonised human, connected through the heart will naturally bypass the 'rings of constriction' imposed via Sabaoth (or Saturn). I go into these concepts in great detail in my graphic novels *Moon Slayer* (2015) and *Aeon Rising* (2017). Suffice to say here, the Demiurge is also *working through* Saturn and it is the great Archon Yaldabaoth that is said to control Saturn in our age.

In the *Nag Hammadi*, the Gnostics describe Yaldabaoth as 'Ariel', another variation of the angel Ariel which means 'Lion of God' or 'Hearth of God'. The *Apocryphon of John*, a work heavily quoted by John Lamb Lash, describes the Demiurge as a dragon-like lion beast. The same beast often symbolised as a Chimera, a lion-headed serpent said to forge a world in its own likeness (see figure 68).

Figure 68: The Demiurge.
Also known as Yaldabaoth, the Father of Adam.

The Chimera in Greek mythology, a monstrous, fire-breathing hybrid creature of Lycia of Asia Minor, composed of the parts of more than one animal, can be seen as another symbol of the Demiurge (in image only). The Chimera is usually depicted as a lion, with the head of a goat arising from its back and a snake-like tail often ending with a snake's head. It was said to be one of the offspring of Typhon, Echidna, and a sibling of monsters such as Cerberus and the Lernaean Hydra (see figure 69). In Medieval art, the Chimera of antiquity was forgotten, but chimerical figures appear as embodiments of the deceptive, inverted forces of nature.

Figure 69: The Chimera.
A hybrid creature of Lycia, Asia Minor.

With a three-part body, symbolic of the lion-like Demiurge, the goat of Mendes (Pan) and the snakes or Hydra, associated with the Cobra deities, the Naga (mentioned in *Chapter One*), it is the ultimate rendition of chaos. The Gnostic text, *Hypostasis of the Archons*, alludes to the lion-like Demiurge and the veil between the spirit and material world:

> *A Veil exists between the world above and the realms that are below; and shadow came into being beneath the veil. Some of the shadow [dark matter] became [nuclear] matter, and was projected apart. And what Sophia created became a product in the matter, like an aborted fetus. And it assumed a plastic shape molded out of shadow, and became an arrogant beast resembling a lion.*[6]

Much Upper Renaissance art also shows us the 'beast personified', not least the work of the Fifteen Century Flemish artist, Rogier Van der Weyden, in his painting of St. Jerome (who was the father of the early Christian Church). The lions' faces are peculiarly human in many of these

paintings so as to emphasise the subtle connections between the 'beast and man' (see figure 70). In my art, I use similar concepts of personified energy; yet, my lion imagery represents the 'Pleroma', not the 'Chimera'. My 'Lions of Durga' in the *Kokoro Chronicles* are purely the Pleroma, or Aeon Consciousness 'personified'. Interestingly, Angra Mainyu,

Figure 70: The *beast* and *man* in much 14th Century religious art 'personifies' the lion.
© Neil Hague 2020

the deity found in the Gathas (the oldest texts of Zoroastrianism), is also depicted as a lion-like sun beast (see figure 71). 'Angra Mainyu' is the devil-like god which can be translated as a 'mind', or 'spirit' or otherwise 'abstract energy'.[4] The syllable 'angra' in this context also means 'destructive', 'chaotic', 'disorderly', 'malign' and a manifestation of *anger*; all are perfect words to describe the 'fire-and-brimstone' god of the Old Testament, who, according to Gnostic thought, *is* the Demiurge.

Figure 71: Angra Mainyu.

The beast, or rampant lion, featured on royal

heraldry, through to the many statues of lions on Stately homes, all relate to the symbolism of the prideful, arrogant, Chimera, or Demiurge. The lion-headed 'Time Lord', Mithra, was another version of the Demiurge. The lion was also a symbol for the tribe of Judea in the biblical sense, with Jesus as the lion king, but this could also be just another representation of the royal lordship of the chief architect - the Demiurge.

The Lion's Paw

Connected to the Demiurge is the symbolism of the lion in its 'fallen state', sometimes depicted as the 'rampant' lion (see figure 72). Three Rampant (passants) lions could also be symbolic of Orion's three belt stars and the 'tripartite forces' that influence humanity (the Anthropos).

Symbolically, the lion in all ages has been noted as a symbol of strength and sovereignty. The 'King of the Beasts,' whose mighty roar brought fear to the hearts of all, was known and respected by many ancient cultures.

Figure 72:
The Rampant Lion.
Featured on royal heraldry and possibly based on the archons, and the Demiurge combined.
© Courtesy of Dover

The lion's head and mane were placed on many Egyptian hieroglyphs and idols, including the famous Sphinx, which recognised this animal as the ruler of the animal kingdom. Having the 'heart of a lion' was, and is today, deemed an acknowledgment of strength and character. Medieval knights adorned their shields and coats of arms with representations of lions, lions' heads, manes, and paws for the same reason. Richard, the Lionheart (Richard I) and his famous shield of three lions (passants) are well documented in history and in legend, signifying his sovereignty over England through the personal arms worn by the Plantagenet kings who ruled England from 1154 onwards.

The 'Lion's Paw,' or grip, formed by placing fingers in the form of a cat's paw is a 'secret sign' associated with Freemasonry. This 'grip' has also been connected symbolically to anient Egyptian mysteries, which is significant in several respects, both legendary and allegorical in its message of 'transition and everlasting life'; both said to be a critical part of reaching the Third Degree of Freemasonry. As a symbol, the lion goes back to Babylon, Sumeria also, and can be found all over the pre-Christian world, not least the original secret societies that emerged in the 11th and 10th Centuries at the time of crusades. The lion is also a symbol, or emblem, for the biblical tribe of Judah; the alleged line of Jesus in scripture. Ancient secret societies, initially centred in Egypt and what is now Palestine, believed the lion to be a 'king of kings'. Legend held that a lion's cub, or whelp, was born dead and brought to life by the roar of the male lion (its sire). As such, the reference to the lion may be applied to a Messiah figure, who brought 'life' and the 'light' of immortality, through the roar of God's word. In this context, the lion image could be seen as the source for the God in the Old Testament and therefore beliefs associated with the Gnostic Demiurge. Other symbolism relating to the lion worshipped by ancient brotherhoods (like the priests of Sekmet in Egypt), related to 'death and the resurrection' and 'Son of Man' symbolism, something I will look at in the next chapter.

In terms of Freemasonic literature around rituals, the initiate was said to be introduced to the symbolism of the lion's paw during the Master Mason's degree, during portrayals of the Hiramic legend where reference is given to 'spiritual resurrection' and immortality of those being initiated. The symbolism of resurrection is an important part of a Freemason's journey and quest for light. As one website states:

> In moving from darkness to light, the Freemason recognizes his personal trans-
> formation and improvement, but the great step forward is made in the Third
> degree. From the hand of a trusted Brother one is raised to a higher level of spir-
> itual understanding and with the strength so gained, may become a better man
> and Freemason.[7]

The Sumerian Fall & Humbaba's Head

In the Akkadian Epic of *Gilgamesh* 1800BC, the demon 'Humbaba' seems also to be another version of the Gnostic Demiurge. This entity was placed in the forest by the Annunaki god, Enlil. Humbaba's face is that of a lion with a terrible stare. It is said that when Humbaba looks at someone, it is the look of death. The Epic of Gilgamesh says that Humbaba's roar was a flood, his mouth death and his breath fire! He could hear a hundred leagues away from any rustling in his forests of Lebanon, the place in the ancient world where the great cedar forests once grew. In various examples, his face is scribed in a single coiling line, like that of the coiled entrails of men and beasts. Another description of Humbaba from the Georg Burckhardt translation of *Gilgamesh* says, "He had the paws of a lion and a body covered in thorny scales; his feet had the claws of a vulture, and on his head were the horns of a wild bull; his tail and phallus each ended in a snake's head." This description is that of the Chimera or Demiurge and all its 'features', not least its horns, will become relevant as the book progresses (see figure 73).

In this 4000-year-old epic, Gilgamesh punches Humbaba when his

Figure 73: Humbaba.
My rendition of the Sumerian demon (© Neil Hague.)

Figure 74: Medusa.
(Public Domain.)

guard is down and in prehistoric, Marvel comic style, captures the monster. Defeated, Humbaba appeals to a receptive Gilgamesh for mercy, but Enkidu (mentioned in *Chapter One*) convinces Gilgamesh to slay Humbaba. Enkidu in my view, is another aspect of 'Adam', or the original human prototype before final 'genetic tinkering' by the Anunnaki-created Adam. As I will show later in the book, he is the wild-man-of-the-woods archetype connected to the stars, not least Ursa Major, the Great Bear. In a last effort, Humbaba tries to escape but is decapitated by Enkidu, or in some versions by both heroes together; his head is put in a leather sack, which is brought to Enlil (the Annunaki god of the Sumerians), who originally assigned Humbaba as the forest's guardian. It is said in the Sumerian epic that Enlil becomes enraged upon learning of this defeat and redistributes Humbaba's seven splendors (or in some tablets, called auras). The headless creature's stare became an apotropaic (power to avert evil influences) icon, and its theme can be found in Greek myths relating to Perseus, who also cut off the head of the Gorgon, Medusa, and placed in his leather sack (see figure 74). In mythology, the Gorgons were *three* sisters, Stheno, Euryale, and Medusa. Along with other monstrous offspring that included Echidna (Viper) and Ophis (Serpent), the Gorgons were said to be the result of an incestuous union between children of Poseidon and Gaia (Earth). The Gorgons can be seen as symbolic of 'fear and terror'. The 'headless god' (in a sack) symbolism is often connected to Orion's nefarious side.

Enkidu's Dilemma

The sacred Prostitute, Shamhat, plays an integral role in *Tablet I* of the *Gilgamesh* epic relating to Humbaba and Enkidu. She is celebrated with the taming of the wild man, Enkidu, who was said to have been created by the gods as a rival to the mighty god-man, Gilgamesh. Shamhat was a sacred temple prostitute or 'harimtu'.[8] She used her attractiveness to tempt Enkidu from the wild, to calm his 'wildness', civilizing him through 'endless' sexual intercourse (see figure 75 overleaf). It is said that Shamhat 'exposed herself' at a water source where Enkidu had been spotted. The texts say that

Figure 75: The First Adam & Eve.
Enkidu and Shamhat (Adam and Eve)
or Jesus and Mary Magdalene.

he 'enjoyed' Shamhat for 'six days and
seven nights'. A fragment found in 2015
and read in 2018, disclosed they had *two
weeks* of sexual intercourse, with a break
spent in discussion about Enkidu's
future life in Uruk.[9]

Shamhat, in this story, would pave
the way for the 'blame-it-on-Eve' script
that would eventually find its way into
the Garden of Edinu, the original story
of Eden. The same symbolism appears
in the Jesus story of Mary Magdalene,
too, who is 'downgraded' to the level of
prostitute by those who invented the
New Testament. Unfortunately for Enkidu, after this long 'sexual workshop'
in how to be civilised, his former companions, the wild animals, turned
away from him in fright at the watering hole where they congregated. This
is the same story found in *Genesis*, where Adam and Eve are 'shamed' and
'blamed' once they realise their 'nakedness'. *Genesis 3:7* says: 'Then the eyes
of both of them were opened, and they realised they were naked; so they
sewed fig leaves together and made coverings for themselves.' Enkidu's
loss of innocence (through his six-day love fest with Shamhat) can be compared to the sudden awareness that the world was not as he, and his animal companions, could sense.

Shamhat persuades Enkidu to follow her and join the civilized world in
the Sumerian city of Uruk, where Gilgamesh is king; rejecting his former
life with the wild animals of the hills and forests. Enkidu's move leads to
Gilgamesh and Enkidu becoming the best of friends and undergoing many
adventures in the 'forests and plains of Edinu'. On his deathbed, Enkidu
blames Shamhat for tempting him from his previous reality, but eventually
states that *all* men will come to adore Shamhat. Shamhat is a Sumerian version of 'Pandora', a goddess I will address further later in the book. The
roving antics of Enkidu and Gilgamesh, I feel, were mirrored in the stars
amongst the Orion Constellation and especially in 'Gann Eden', which
means the 'Garden of God' (the paradise) in the stars.

The Garden and the Ancient of Days

Impressive research conducted by US researcher and business analyst,
Danny Wilten, shows many correlations between Orion and the electric universe theory I touched on briefly in *Chapter Two*.[10] In some of Wilten's image
mapping, the central sun symbolism, said to be in the Orion Nebula, can be

Figure 76: 14th-Century Fresco from Ubisi, Georgia. The triangle shape represents a pyramid, or trapezium.

seen as a lion's head in profile with a snake-like cluster of stars that descend from its head, forming parts of the outer nebula. There is so much more to know in this area of research connecting Orion with much religious symbolism as I will come to later in the book. Knowing our solar system is situated within the Orion arm of the Galaxy, what seems to be clear is that our Sun is being 'powered' by a heliosphere at the centre of an external birkland current focused on the Orion constellation. Abrahamic faiths have personified this 'external focus' as God, Jehovah (Tetragrammaton), or what the Christian Gnostics called the Demiurge. It is the 'creator operating through our sun', or *another sun*, beautifully illustrated by William Blake as the *Ancient of Days*. Blake's image gives a symbolic feel for the Gnostic Demiurge leaning out of sacred fire (or portal) who, like an architect or 'master architect mason', divides time and space, creating the illusion of the material, physical world. In the Ubisi Fresco version (see figure 76), the Demiurge is located within a tetrahedron-like portal, surrounded by the wings of the seraphim, the highest of the angels (Archons). In The Church of Jesus Christ of Latter-day Saints, the title 'Ancient of Days' relates to Adam (Son of Man), who is also identified with the *arch*angel, Michael. And the mystical *Zohar* goes into great detail describing the White Head of God (seen in the Ubisi Fresco), and ultimately, the emanation of its anthropomorphic personality known as the Qabalah; a topic I will look at closely in the next few chapters. Blake was tapping into the spirit of Byzantine religious iconography, focusing on the same white-haired, architect god. The portal is often triangular, relating to the 'high altar' often surrounded by nebula-like clouds, as shown in the extensive research of 'High Altar' art by Danny Wilten through his YouTube channel and e-book, *Orion in the Vatican* (2013).

Orion in the Vatican

Hermetic Qabalah refers to Orion as 'Adam on high', or the 'heavenly man' whose head (Merkava) manifests our reality. In his research, Danny Wilten seems to have found similar visual themes within the 'mirror images' of the Orion Nebula, not least the Nile Delta region *mirroring* the Orion Nebula on Earth. The symbolism contained within the 'tree of life', from the head to the toes of the celestial human, through what is described as the 'middle pillar' (or spine), also seems to connect us to the Orion Nebula. Wilten's book *Orion in the Vatican* (2013), is a superb document that clearly provides a thread of truth contained within many of the high altar pieces of art and how they mirror the Orion Nebula in great detail. The correlations between Michelangelo Buonarroti's *Creation of Adam*, on the ceiling of the Sistine Chapel (a place I visited in 2011), and what is clearly defined as a human brain, with detailed hemispheres once overlaid, is a well-known correspondence. I found the Sistine Chapel in the Vatican to be a dark place *vibrationally*, which made me wonder what on earth has happened there over the centuries? As mentioned in Wilten's book, a Fox News article titled: *Did Michelangelo Paint a Brain in God?*, Ian Suk, a medical illustrator, and neurosurgeon Rafael Tamargo, analyzed the fresco, *Separation of Light and Darkness* digitally, by comparing the shadows outlining the features of God's neck and a photograph of a model of this section of the brain. Their conclusion and resulting analysis for the *Creation of Adam* fresco affirmed it was similar to the human brain.[11]

All of this makes perfect sense, especially if we delve a little into Hermetic Principles and how the masters of the Renaissance period, covered by Wilten in his book, must have been 'seeing' in a manner allowing them access to a higher understanding of the cosmos. Either this or they had advanced 'technology' not made public at that time. When we consider the notion of a 'Holographic Universe', it wouldn't be too impossible to understand how geography on earth can be mirrored in the stars - namely, Orion. Added to this concept is the science associated with Black Holes and their holographic abilities. I am not going to go into great depth here as I will come back to the Holographic projection connected to Orion in *Part Two* of the book. But in relation to cosmic forces creating, or 'shaping' our reality, courtesy of the Demiurge, it is important to expand the correlations touched on by Wilten and the science behind holograms in relation to Orion.

Black Holes, Holograms and Orion

On a larger scale, the Universe is now thought of by leading physicists as a hologram, or a super-hologram to be precise, projecting endless other holograms, including the human body. Everything 'projected' is a hologram (illusion). Dennis Gabor discovered holograms from the late 1940s and won the Nobel Prize for his work. He turned a three-dimensional object into a frequency pattern on photographic film and converted it back to a 3D holographic image. Holograms are made by directing a laser onto a photographic film, directed at the film through a semi-transparent *mirror*. Some of the light is deflected away in another direction and onto the object you want to photograph. Now you have the laser light pointing at the film (known as the reference beam) and the part deflected away, onto the object (known as the working beam). This working beam, carrying the object's vibrational image in question, is also directed onto the photographic film. When it hits the film it 'collides' with the reference beam – its 'other half' – and this creates what is now known as an 'interference pattern' between the two.

One of the unusual characteristics of a hologram is that every part is a smaller version of the whole. Therefore, it would be conceivable to accept that a star cluster could easily be a projection of something greater, while projecting a smaller version of itself somewhere else in space. The concept of a Divine Human form, as I mentioned earlier, is merely a *projection* of the celestial form (or body). Visionaries like Blake knew these concepts. In *The Songs of Innocence and of Experience*, Blake wrote:

For Mercy has a human heart; Pity, a human face;
And Love, the human form divine: And Peace the human dress.
Cruelty has a human heart And jealousy a human face, Terror the human form
divine, And secrecy the human dress.
The human dress is forged iron, The human form a fiery forge,
The human face a furnace seal'd, The human heart its hungry gorge.

There are estimated to be *250 billion* stars in our galaxy and a potential *100 billion* galaxies in the universe, or so. Amongst the vastness of what we call space, there are also information points scientists call black holes. According to scientists like Dr. Ladislav Subr (Charles University, Czech Republic), they have discovered a black hole hidden within the Orion Nebula. The Orion Nebula Cluster, one of many star clusters hanging from the mythic warrior's belt, according to scientists working with Subr, seem to have merged, creating a massive black hole, 200 times more massive than the sun. Dr. Subr explained in the September 20th *Astrophysical Journal*:

Our scenario neatly accounts for virtually all observed properties of the Orion Nebula Cluster, that is, its low number of high-mass stars, and its rapidly-moving central stars, and suggests that the massive stars near the centre of this cluster are bound by a black hole ...

A black hole could also be observed indirectly, by measuring its effect on the stars whirling in the cluster core. Subr and his colleagues suggest that a 150-solar-mass black hole could explain the high speeds of the Trapezium stars, which lie at the Orion Nebula's heart. But thorough observations of the star clusters innermost area, 0.2 light-years are still needed to reveal whether the black hole exists, the authors conclude:

The Orion Nebula Cluster is one of the closest young star clusters, about 1300 light-years away, making it easier to study than the massive clusters, which lie at greater distances. If a black hole really exists in the ONC, then it might be the closest black hole known to Earth.[12]

Science is now expressing the viability of our Universe being a super holo-gram; evidence now put forward is that black holes can 'absorb' informa-tion. Black holes are storing all infor-mation on what physicists call the 'event horizon' where information (data) is never lost but is also 'project-ed' out from the surface of the black hole (see figure 77).

According to scientists like Dr. Leonard Susskind, our 3D reality is merely a projection of a black hole and all that has happened on earth since ancient times, *is part of that projection.* All religions seem to share some kind of understanding of this creation pro-cess as we shall see later in the book. Carl Sagan once said:

Figure 77: Artist Rendition of a Black Hole. (Public domain.)

Black holes may be apertures to elsewhere. Were we to plunge down a black hole, we would re-emerge, it is conjectured, in a different part of the universe and in another epoch in time ... Black holes may be entrances to Wonderlands. But are there Alices or white rabbits?

The seat of creation, characterised as God in Abrahamic religions, could also relate to the Orion Nebula and its black hole. The Orion Nebula is a 2D version of our world, a *living* 'eye' full of information, perceiving or *project-ing* our reality. A topic I will come back to later in the book.

Living Distortion

Danny Wilten has put forward a convincing argument (through years of research into Abrahamic, Catholic altar art), that the 'holographic nature' of the universe seems to be 'visually evident' *in* numerous works of art com-missioned by the Roman Church. What did these priests and secret soci-eties know when commissioning such amazing works of art? I would sug-gest that they knew that the face of God (or the Tetragrammaton) in the Abrahamic sense is, on one level, a personification of the *information* being 'projected' out of the black hole, centred on Orion's nebula. The information is also a 'distortion' of the 'true projection', which in the Gnostic sense, is connected to what I described earlier as the Upper Aeons, or 'Superconsciousness'. The distorted information, instead, is projected from the *face* of something that has confounded and confused the human mind since ancient priests wrote all manner of scriptures dedicated to this deity. It is 'self-aware', as all consciousness is, but this *face* is the heart of all forms of 'schism' in our reality. The insanity of our world, the wars, famine, pain, suffering, money system and *all religion* are holographic projections of this schism or distortion (see figure 78).

The Gnostic Demiurge (and archons) is the force that gives life to the 'distortion' as it manifests in the physical world and the many layers of madness we humans have come to accept as 'reality'. It is Chimera-like, and a monster in its own right. Many of the Titans recorded in myth, from

Echidna to Prometheus, can be seen as expressions of 'darker chaotic forces' constructed by the Gnostic Demiurge. The outer planets of our solar system, Pluto, Uranus and Saturn (the Titans) are celestial bodies, personified in myths and stories connected to the Fall,

Figure 78: The Self-Aware Chimera.
The Gnostic Demiurge. The lord of distortion and chaos in our illusory world. © Neil Hague 2013

which also meant a 'fall in frequency', from higher consciousness to a lesser state of awareness.

The fall of the rebel angel, Lucifer, in the biblical sense, is simply the story of humanity's plight in a 'distorted world', a world symbolically affected by the chimera-like Demiurge. Interestingly, the *Mission Impossible 2* movie plot involved a deadly 'synthetic virus' named 'Chimera' that could rapidly wipe out the world's population. In light of what happened with Covid-19 in 2020, it makes you wonder how much of what we call reality is 'scripted' and movie-like. The Covid-19 lockdowns and pandemonia certainly felt (and still feels at the time of writing) like living in a bad

movie. Inspired filmmakers, seem to have etched numerous Gnostic mythological themes into films and narratives. The most famous rendition of our
distorted, 'illusionary world' was the concept behind the excellent *Matrix*
movies, where a different kind of virus spreads in the form of 'sentient programmes' (the Agent Smith character), designed by machines to eradicate
free human beings. In the *Matrix* movies, Agent Smith is a computer programme that manifests and replicates itself ever more rapidly once it comes
into contact with Neo. The spider-like Machines that construct the matrix
(the super holographic illusion humanity is immersed in), *are* an artificial
intelligence responsible for the sentinel agents designed to 'police the
matrix'. The machines in *The Matrix* even swirl visually and join together
creating a 'machine face', their god-like omnipotent deity who meets Neo
in their machine world. This face, and the thousands of machines that construct it, reminded me of the Gnostic Demiurge, symbolically. Interestingly,
a Unified Science Course in the Resonance Academy (Resonance Science),
in 2020, used an image on their social media page of what looked like the
spider-like machines in the *Matrix*, to illustrate *how* AI determines the basic
structure DNA follows in creating *all* life. The Spider-like exoskeletal
'image' is significant too, as we shall get to later in the book.

Agent Smith in *The Matrix Revolutions* movie is the 'virus' that spreads
causing the world matrix to start over; to 'shift' into a *new* paradigm. At the
time of writing it certainly feels like we are in a paradigm shift due to the
corona*virus*. The Archons (Agents and the Machines), which were created
by the Demiurge (the Grand Architect), are copies of the original distortion.
It is peace between humans and machine (artificial intelligence), or between
the Oracle (Sophia/Earth) and the Architect (Demiurge) that ends one
matrix (reality) and instigates a 'new dawn'. *Through* Neo (a symbol of
Adam) and Trinity (Sophia/Eve) in this movie narrative, the world is
renewed.

The Matrix & the *One*

In *The Matrix* trilogy, the concept of 'ordinary life' being an illusion (a hologram) produced by the brain, can be found in the philosophy and teachings
of our ancient ancestors. The world of illusion (or Maya) as taught by the
Tibetans and South American Indian Mayans are just two of several ancient
civilisations expressing the same view of reality as a holographic illusion.
This is probably why much Oriental (an Tibetan) imagery, including fight
sequences and costumes appear in *The Matrix* films? In the writings of
Greek philosopher, Plato, through his 'allegory of the cave' (mind), we also
find concepts that speak of the illusions we call daily life. Plato, in his
Republic (514BC), outlines themes that speak of humanity being born into a

prison, an illusion (a life of deception) and of course, even though the Wachowski brothers' production is more sophisticated and relevant to our times 'technologically', the narrative *is* ancient.

The notion that our world (our reality) is merely an 'appearance', a dream, or illusion, can also be understood through the work of scientists and philosophers from René Descartes, to Immanuel Kant. Along with theories associated with quantum physics, through to alchemical art and texts illustrating microcosm and macrocosm, the idea of illusion is a common theme. All these subjects, along with recent discoveries in biometrics (microchipping) and the rise of artificial intelligence, open the mind to the idea that we simultaneously partake and are *isolated* within a prison (world) of our own making. *The Matrix* is possibly the retelling of the greatest story ever told, one that can be found woven into *all* religions and myths. As I have already mentioned, from Socrates and the Oracle at Delphi, to the notion of 'Hal' in Gnostic writings, they all present the idea that we are being *decieved* by our eyes (the brain). It was Rene Decrates, who said: "From time to time I found that the senses deceive." Indeed, they do!

The character *Neo* in *The Matrix* is an anagram for the *One*, the 'original' human (Adam, or man of heaven), who originally existed outside of the matrix. The theme of the *One* relates to *Orion*, or the heavenly human, Adam, Osiris and much more besides, as I shall come to shortly. Humanity in its 'divine form' is *Oneness* – or a state of multidimensional bliss. *Oneness*, or being *The One*, is essentially the same idea and relates to what scientists, such as the 16th Century Giordano Bruno, referred to as the 'cosmic mind'. Bruno also called *The One* 'bright fire' from where all forms originate. Its real source lies *beyond* memory and programming (our DNA codes), and *it* has the power to download new information, retrieve ancient files (past/future lives) and re-write itself according to the experiences gained in life. As the film *The Matrix* constantly refers to, Neo is the *returned* human saviour, a microcosm of the *original source*. He returns to free his relatives (all humans) from the bondage of the Matrix. In terms of symbolism, Neo is the heavenly Adam (Orion), the 'Son of Man' and the embodiment of the 'first divine human' as written in Gnostic texts.

Inner Light – Inner Mind (Eye)

The Oracle, in the Gnostic sense, and in *The Matrix* movie, is the embodiment of the Earth-Matrix-Mind (Sophia/Gaia). She is the mother, 'chaos' figure, who wants to help humans be free of control by the Architect (the Demiurge). Stories of 'Grandmother Spider', told by Native American tribes, tell of the animals complaining about living in darkness and desiring the light given to the original human, or what alchemists have referred to as the 'inner sun'. The same knowledge of our 'inner sun' can be seen in 30,000-year-old figurines and portable art depicting lion-headed humans or figures with sun-heads. It can also be seen in Algonquin rock art showing archetypal images of the inner light connecting all humans to the source. Or what Jacob Böhme described as the 'outer sun longing for the inner one'. Science has shown us that when the human mind plunges into darkness, it has a fail-safe mechanism producing what are known as 'phosphenes'. These symbols of light come in the form of spirals, sacred geometric shapes, and more importantly, they are the source of our mind's connection to worlds beyond the boundary I described earlier. They are the mind's eye's ability to see what Bruno described as heavenly bright fire. As the 12th Century mystic, Hildegarde of Bingen wrote in her illustrated *Scivias*:

> *And it came to pass ... that the heavens were opened and a blinding light of exceptional brilliance flowed through my entire brain. And so it kindled my whole heart and breast like a flame, not burning but warming ...*

In *The Matrix* movie, Osiris is also the name for the space ship used by Morpheus's 'renegade' group. The 'Nebuchadnezzar' is another name for one human vessel or ship; these names give direct reference to the Babylonian priesthoods and their king that fought and defeated Jerusalem. Zion in the *Matrix* movie, is the home for humans living freely, disconnected from the machine-generated illusory world. Yet these souls in the film are still in conflict with a predatory artificial (alien) intelligence (the machine world) trying to destroy a 'minority' of free humans. The machines *do not* want humanity unplugged from the matrix because, in the movie, humanity is providing a 'power source' for the 'artificial intelligent' machine world. We are very close in our world to realising artificial intelligence is a threat to humanity; much more on this later in the book. 'Renegades' from beyond the Matrix are waking up those who are still plugged into the illusion. The left side of the brain is where we assimilate logic and reason (the artificial intelligence of the machine world), and the right side of the brain could be seen as the spirit/imaginary/*real* world. The 'third-eye' (the seat of perception) at the base of the brain is our balance. The 'rise of the machine' in our world, through AI and 'robots', is hugely relevant to the symbolism I am unravelling in the book, especially in later chapters. The 17th Century hermetic alchemist and artist Robert Fludd said of the 'inner eye' and our perception of the world:

> *... the eye of man (is) an image of the world and all the colours in it are arranged in circles. The white of the eye corresponds to the ocean, which surrounds the whole world on all sides; a second colour is the mainland, which the ocean sur-*

rounds, or which lies between the waters; a third colour in the middle region; Jerusalem, the centre of the world.[13]

Fludd, like other hermetic artists and alchemists, he seemed to be part of the mystery school network. At the highest levels of the 'off-world' Orion Cult they know that the world we live in is an illusion, created by our mind, projected by the brain and reflected by the eyes. Our *perception* creates our reality, our 3D world matrix. Seeing invisible worlds, or capturing imagery that speaks of alternative dimensions (beyond the walls of the matrix) to the reality governed by the five senses, can be seen in various art forms. Blake went as far as saying:

This Lifes dim Windows of the Soul
Distorts the Heavens from Pole to Pole
And leads you to Believe a Lie
When you see with not thro' the Eye.[14]

As I have briefly touched on in this chapter, it is the Demiurge, according to the Gnostics, who created our Solar System, appointed a hierarchy of angels (one of whom rebelled), and who created the Anthropos - the Heavenly Adam. In the next chapter, I want to consider the 'Son of Man' theme, the *first* human 'being', sometimes referred to as 'Adamas' or 'Geradamas' and some of the symbolism connected to Orion.

Sources:

1) https://www.sacred-texts.com/jud/rph/rph15.htm#fr_298
2) Ovid, *Metamorphoses* 1.149–50: Translated by Frank Justus Miller (1916). New York: Barnes & Noble Classics. p6
3) Long, Charles H. *Alpha: Myths of Creation*, 1963. pp 36-37
4) (103.1-15)
5) Lamb Lash, John. *Not in His Image, Gnostic Vision, Sacred Ecology and the Future of Belief* (The Apocryphon of John). Chelsea Green. 2006, p100
6) *Ibid*, p200
7) www.themasonictrowel.com/Articles/degrees/degree_3rd_files/the_li ons_paw_gltx.htm
8) Dalley, Stephanie. *Myths from Mesopotamia, Creation, the Flood, Gilgamesh and others.* Revised edition. Oxford University Press, 2000, p137.
9) Ditmore, Melissa Hope (ed). *Encyclopedia of Prostitution and Sex Work*, Volume 1, Greenwood Publishing Group, 2006, pp.34-5.
10) https://en.wikipedia.org/wiki/Birkeland_current
11) Wilten, Danny. *Orion in the Vatican*, 2013. p57
12) https://www.skyandtelescope.com/astronomy-news/a-black-hole-in-orion/
13) Fludd, R: *Utrusque Cosmi*, Vol II, Oppenheim 1619.
14) Blake, William: *The Everlasting Gospel*, (1757–1827) p 97-100

5

ORION ADAM

Symbols of the 'Son of Man'

Do you not know, Asclepius, that Egypt is an image of heaven, or, to speak more exactly, in Egypt all the operations of the powers which rule and work in heaven have been transferred to earth below?
TRISMEGISTUS

The Hermetic Qabalah is a system of mystical doctrines, esoteric thoughts, and teachings connected to Gnostic and Christian cabalistic philosophies. It provides the textual 'spiritual' foundation for the mystery schools emerging during the time of the Gnostics and means 'reception,' something 'received' or oral transmission through an oracle.

Hermetic systems inspired by earlier mystical Judaic books, passed initially through Medieval circles, can be seen as symbolic guides explaining how different worlds (invisible structures) connect to our human reality. Historically, it is said the original Qabalah emerged after earlier forms of 12th Century Judaic mysticism flourished in Spain and Southern France (through the Gnostic Cathars). Much of which was later *reinterpreted* during the mystical renaissance of the 16th Century Ottoman Palestinian era, and studied in occult circles across Europe. The 12th Century also saw the rise of various Knights Brotherhoods like the Templars, who were said to be interested in Gnostic and ancient mysticism. The Knights Templar were aligned to the mysticism and knowledge of the middle east (alongside the Arabic Assassins of Persia) rather than orthodox Christianity at that time.

The *Sepher Yetzirah* (the *Book of Light*), along with later hermetic occultism, describes our inner (spiritual) constitution and how the 'Creator' *creates*. According to the mystery schools (like the Templars) the knowledge contained within some of these teachings, was a necessary part of fulfilling a purpose on earth. In other words, such teachings were thought an essential part of the initiation for those in the mystery schools connected to ancient secret societies. I am no initiate of any society or group, but I have certainly found hermetic Qabalistic teachings and symbolism *very* inspiring as a writer, artist and illustrator.

As with many oral traditions of the earth's indigenous nations, mystical teachings was also not written down. It was thought of as a 'hidden' (Occult) wisdom, a way of tapping into forces that construct our reality. According to author, J. F. C. Fuller, in his book *The Secret Wisdom of the Qabalah*, the origins of the original Kabbalah remain lost in primeval mysticism, which existed before the times of the Biblical Essenes. According to Fuller (a senior British Army officer, military historian and occulist) the wisdom contained within such ancient texts exists as 'layers within layers' (worlds within worlds) all focused on the nature of God, the Universe, and primarily the hidden. As Fuller writes:

> *This wisdom is formed within a vast number of doctrines, such as the nature of God; the mystical cosmogony of the universe; the destiny of the universe; the creation of man; the immutability of God; the moral government of the universe; the doctrine of good and evil; the nature of the soul, angels, and demons; the transcendental symbolism of numbers and letters; the balancing of complementary forces, etc.*[1]

What Fuller calls 'the mystical cosmogony of the universe', along with the creation of man, is deeply connected to Gnosticism and, as we shall see, Orion.

Heavenly Adam – the Gnostic Anthropos

In Gnostic Pauline Christianity, Orion is connected to what is called 'Adam on high', or the 'heavenly man' whose head (Merkava) manifests our earthly reality. The word 'Adam' is said to relate to the name 'Atum' (the first human). Similar words can also be found in Hindu belief as 'Atma', or 'Atman', the latter of which is supposedly a Semitic permutation of the word Adam. In occult traditions, Adam is also described as 'kadum', meaning the 'Ancient One', a title coupled in Old Semitic with 'qadam' - *he* who, like the sun, rises in the east. In ancient Egypt, Adam on high (or Man of the Sun), *is* a 'star man' in the form of Osiris whose attributes are mirrored on the earth below. Orion worship', along with Saturn worship (and occult symbols associated with such mysticism in relation to Orion) abound, as we shall see.

Amongst the Mandeans (a Gnostic sect that survives in Iraq), the Primordial Adam is coextensive with the cosmos, his body is the body of the world, and his soul the soul of 'all souls'. The Gnostics held that individual human beings are descended from the cosmic 'Anthropos' as a result of the fragmentation of the 'Primordial Man'. In Jungian theory, the Primordial, 'Cosmic Man' is an archetypal figure that appears in creation myths of a wide variety of mythology. For example, in Chinese legend, it is 'Pangu' who is thought to have given the earth its natural features and when he died his body became the Sacred Mountains of China. The Persian equivalent is 'Keyumars', who released semen when he died, out of which came the first human couple. In Islamic Sufi teachings, 'The Perfect Being' is called 'Al-Insan al-Kamil', another Adam or Son of Man figure, or title.

In these ancient teachings, the first spiritual world that came into existence (through God's infinite light) was Adam Kadmon. This 'Adam', from the Gnostic perspective, is not necessarily the same as the 'physical' Biblical Adam, 'Ha Rishon'. In variations of the hermetic Qabalah, the heavenly Adam corresponds to a place above the Keter (the crown), the 'divine will' that, according to Gnostic and hermetic teachings, motivated the creation of our solar system, from the stars to the earth. The 'crown', or Keter, is, in my view, located in the Orion Nebula, as I will come to later in the book. The Gnostic Anthropos, or Adamas, as it is sometimes called (see figure 79), is considered the 'pure mind', distinct from matter or the material world. The heavenly Adam was considered a *living light* that

Figure 79: The Anthropos. A combination of 'Sophia' and 'Christos' projects a new earth in my vision of this Gnostic narrative.

encompasses duality, and in simple terms, it is the 'light of the world' (the Creator) that the Gnostics and 11th Century Cathar parfait priests alluded to in their teachings.

According to hermetic mystery schools, the Anthropos is also the source (or place) from where both good and evil originates. The 'Great War in Heaven', a subject I covered in my illustrated novel, *Aeon Rising* (2017), was created by the 'pollution' of the Anthropos along with interdimensional forces that dragged this war down to earth. The sentient beings responsible for this *invisible* war-torn vibration, I feel, are based in the Orion constellation (and elsewhere) and operating through 'technology' (cyborg/robots), as we shall see later in the book. Interestingly, the name given to 'social robots' at Media Lab Europe is, Anthropos.[2] These robots were developed to aid in research on anthropomorphism and designed to 'explore the illusion of life and intelligence during the development of meaningful social interaction between artificial systems and people'. In other words, such robots were designed to prepare humans for our interaction with artificial intelligence and possibly off-world intelligences that have inspired such technology. One website on Gnosticism (Minutiae) explained very well the ancient world (the time before the fall) and our current technological era:

> *Life of that time was pastoral and agrarian, not cluttered with the noise of arrogant science, which chokes on its own fumigations, drums out an incoherent, electro-mechanical language of its own. During the Gnostic era, the soul of Anthropos had not yet lost touch with all the variety of other denizens, dwelling in the planet-wide forests, as it has today. The language of birds is no longer familiar to the high-rise, cliff dwelling Anthropos of the city.*[3]

The Gnostics wrote that two Aeons, Sophia and Christos, undertook the encoding of the human genome, creating the Anthropos. The coupling can also be understood merely as the 'path of the heart'. The coupling of Sophia (the goddess) and Christos (Son of Man), or 'Christos-Sophia', according to Gnostic thought, was based on a 'higher love', an unconditional love - above all other forms of love. The Alchemy of Christos-Sophia is number 13, which is known as a symbol of mystical power and magic. According to numerologists, Thirteen rules regeneration and the forces of death and rebirth, which is why thirteen occurs in much religious symbolism and mythology.

According to the Gnostics, Christos and Sophia are the parents of the human species, but not in a biological sense. Christos and Sophia make a 'celestial coupling' encoding it with many capacities and talents.

Figure 80: The Orion Spur (Arm).
Our solar system is powered by electromagnetic plasma within the greater Orion Spur.

After creating the human 'divine' form, they join the entire Pleromic field to release the divine form into the galactic limbs of the Milky Way. The pleroma expression of the Anthropos becomes the Orion Arm, a minor spiral arm of the Milky Way some 3,500 light-years across and approximately 10,000 light-years in length. Our Solar System, including the earth, lies within the Orion Spur (see figure 80), and it is why there is so much focus on Orion by indigenous people and in the esoteric teachings.

The ancients believed that human form made in the image of God was to be understood literally.[4] For the Gnostics and early Christian mystics, the Universe was a vast organism, not unlike the human body, with all facets of the Universe having correspondence to the human form. Simple examples of this understanding can be seen in hermetic teachings connected to ten physical laws (Ten Commandments), through to the ten human fingers and toes. At the same time, the four fingers of each hand represent the four elements of earth, air, fire, and water. The twelve parts of the human fingers (on each hand) are also analogous to the twelve astrological signs of the zodiac. The ancients understood these principles, along with knowledge of the stars. The same principles were considered a 'sacred science' by these ancient mystery schools. DeAnne Loper writing in *Kabbalah Secrets Christians Need to Know* (2019), says of these ancient teachings:

> The so-called science of Kabbalah is said to contain the ancient "Blueprint" that reveals the secrets of the Universe ...
> ... it is the key that unlocks consciousness to the awareness of oneness between creation and creator.[5]

Orion's 'presence' can be seen as the Heavenly Adam, and this archetype seems to have been studied carefully by ancient brotherhoods from within the mystery schools, as we shall see.

Jacob's Ladder

Jacob's ladder of *Genesis* can be seen as another version of the Sefirot (Tree) or 'projection' through the body of the heavenly Adam. In the texts, Jacob falls asleep on a 'stone' and dreams of a ladder stretching between heaven and earth thronged with angels (archons). The stone upon which he lays his head is the 13th stone or the pineal gland at the seat of the human mind (brain), giving light to our 'third eye'. Jacob, of course, had twelve sons who were said to become the progenitors of the biblical Tribes of Israel. His only daughter, mentioned in *Genesis*, is Dinah (possibly another symbol for the lost 13th tribe?), which gives us the all-encompassing num-

© Neil Hague

Figure 81: The Anthropos is evident in the sea of energy that surrounds us connected to our spirit and soul.

ber 13, the Anthropos, born of Sophia (Dinah) and Christos in Gnostic teachings (see figure 81). Robert Fludd, the prominent 16th Century English Paracelsian physician, alchemist, astrologer, mathematician, and cosmologist, often depicted the ladder and Anthropos as a 'projection' of a higher source in his *Utriusque Cosmi*. Fludd's image shows man (human form) the 'microcosm' within the universal 'macrocosm.' He was the son of Sir Thomas Fludd, a high-ranking governmental official and Queen Elizabeth I's treasurer for war in Europe and a member of Parliament. Along with Dr.

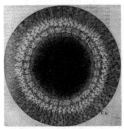 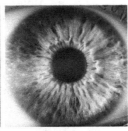

John Dee, Thomas Fludd, and his son Robert, were pioneering behind-the-scenes (cult) figures for what would become the Age of Enlightenment. During this period, Athanasius Kircher, the 17th Century German hermetic Jesuit scholar, also produced many papers and drawings attempting to order the connections between the 'stars and humanity'. His systems, maps, and illustrations symbolise the path taken by electromagnetic light as it descends through the 'world tree'- Jacob's ladder, circling *into* the human eye (see figure 82). The darker area of the eye (the pupil) is as a sea of 'dazzling darkness' from where light descends.

Figure 82: The Dazzling Darkness.
(Left) Kircher's image showing connections between the 'stars and humanity. **(Right)** The human eye is a vortex surrounded by a torus of energy.

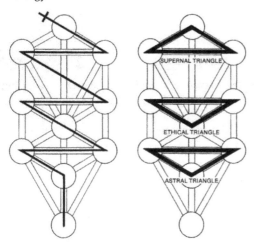

Figure 83: The Tree of Life and the Sword.
The path of the 'flaming sword' formed by the three triangles, connects to 'Superconsciousness' (spirit) and 'Astral' subconsciousness (the soul/mind/body).

The 'descending light' in the hermetic Qabalah, is often depicted as a 'flaming sword', travelling like lightning through the Tree of Life (Sefirot). The light travels from the Keter (the crown or branches), to Malkhut (the roots). Put another way, the lighting descends from the stars 'above' to the earth 'below' (see figure 83). The descending light could be seen as the 'flaming sword' referred to in *Genesis*, as it travels like a lightning rod passing diagonally through different bodies that make up the points on the Ladder, or Tree of Life: "After he drove man out, he placed on the east side of the Garden of Eden cherubim and a *flaming sword* flashing back and forth to 'guard' the way to the tree of life."(3:24)

The ten points on the ladder or tree, from Keter to Makhut, can also be seen as the planetary bodies making up the solar system and relate to different dimensions intersecting the tree or ladder. The tree and its points also appear on ceilings of almost all major gothic cathedrals in Europe. This architectural detail is because the Templars and esoteric brotherhoods who built such magnificent temples must have known about the mysticism and science relating to the Tree of Life, and Orion's significance with it. The sections of the tree of life can be seen to form *three* different regions, the upper, middle, and lower worlds contained within the hermetic Qabalah. The lower world, or the roots of the tree (said to go deep into the Underworld), is symbolic of the hidden mysticism belonging to brotherhoods like the

Figure 84: Three Worlds or 'Regions' of the Hermetic Qabalah (from a Different Angle). The *physical* (Middle), *astral* (Left) and *hyperspace* (Light) realities combined in one image.

Stoics and Templars. The Qabalah could be seen, as the knowledge of the *structure* housing the 'light body' of the heavenly Adam within these 'three worlds'.

In a design piece for an album called *The Trivium* (created for Alice-D Records in 2016), I show these 'three regions' constituting both the Qabalah and Tree of Life (see figure 84). These realms (or worlds) become the Lower Astral world (our thoughts), the Upper Worlds or Hyperspace (Superconsciousness); and lastly, our Physical Reality, or Matrix (middle earth). All three 'realms' connect via a central sun positioned at the top of the path, or spine, of the body of the heavenly Adam.

The circles or realms descending symbolically from an upper world and central source (a projection point), are said to number 1 to 9 – the primary numbers or circles from whence all others derive. These circles (rings) are also 'realms' or 'frequencies' that align with the so-called 'Seven Deadly Sins' through the 'Eighth Circle', depicted as a human 'eye' by 15th

Century hermetic artist, Hieronymus Bosch. Interestingly, it is written that the 'Eighth Sin', or the Eighth Circle, called 'Malebolge', was often depicted as the upper half of Hell, the place of the 'Fraudulent and Malicious' souls. Danté described the Eighth Circle in his 12th Century epic work, *Inferno*, as a place where 'deception' and evil dwelt. All of these mystical systems seem to be hinting at a *threefold* reality connected by circles, rings, a ladder, or a tree.

The circles or rings (if you are a *Lord of the Rings* fan) also relate to constructed hemispheres that 'restrict' human consciousness. The rings form an 'ethereal link' to otherworldly creators (the archons), the 'gods', and planets in our solar system. Manly P Hall depicts the connection between microcosmic and macrocosmic life as the 'Ancient of Ancients', often depicted as a white-haired man with the planets of the solar system encircling him. The Ancient of Ancients is another version of the Tetragrammaton (the Demiurge) sometimes depicted as 'seated' on a throne with twin pillars, surrounded by the four apostles, Man, Eagle, Ox, and Lion. The four apostles are also guardians of the ancient texts and represent the 'precession of ages' (from Leo to Aquarius). The 'Rays of Creation' coming from the hands of the 'Ancient of Days' are said to be the 'male and female' forces of creation, the twin caves of creation, which I feel, are located within the Orion Nebula, the birthplace of the heavenly Adam (see my image on page 115).

Four Adams and the Feminine spirit

Abrahamic creation story says Adam was created out of 'adamah', the Hebrew word for earth. The etymological link between the word 'adamah', and the word 'Adam' is used to reinforce the teleological link between humanity and the earth. The word connection emphasises how man was

created to cultivate the world (the ground) and, according to Abrahamic belief, originated from the 'dust of the ground'. It is worth noting, however, that in Hebrew, adamah has a feminine form, and the word has strong connections with a woman in theological concepts. The link to Adam as the heavenly Adam *through* Sophia is evident in the Gnostic reverence of the goddess (feminine creative power).

As I have already mentioned,

Figure 85: The Gardener. Adamah (earth) and Eve (goddess) were symbols of the earth goddess.

Adam (adamah), and Adam Ha-Rishon are thought not to be the spiritual, or *infinite* body of light referred to as, 'Adam on High' (man of light). The blueprint for the *light*-man or *human*, along with the earth matrix, connects to Adam, the *star* man. In this sense, Adam can be seen as the gardener, shepherd, hunter, and 'caretaker' on earth (see figure 85 on previous page), a physical embodiment of the Orion constellation. As the Hebrew *Book of Mysteries* says:

> But it is necessary to distinguish the higher man (Adam d'leeloh) from the lower man (Adam d'letâtoh), for one could not exist without the other. On that form of man rests the perfection of faith in all things, and it is that form that is spoken of when it is said that they saw above the chariot like the form of a man; and it is of that form that Daniel spoke in the following words (Daniel VII, 13): 'I saw in the nightly vision and behold, one like the son of man came with the clouds of heaven, and he came even to the Ancient of days, and he was brought near before Him.' (19) Thus, what is called the Celestial Man [Orion?], or the first divine manifestation, is nothing else than the absolute form of all that exists; the source of all the other forms, or rather of all ideas, the supreme thought, otherwise called also 'reason' or the Word.[6]

The hermetic occultist Helena Blavatsky also writes in the *Secret Doctrine* (1888):

> The Kabbalists teach the existence of four distinct Adams, or the transformation of four consecutive Adams, the emanations from the Dyooknah (divine phantom) of the Heavenly Man, an ethereal combination of Neschamah, the highest Soul or Spirit: this Adam having, of course, neither a gross human body, nor a body of desire. This Adam is the prototype (tzure) of the second Adam. That they represent our Five Races is certain, as everyone can see by their description in the Kabala: the first being the perfect, Holy Adam; . . . a shadow that disappeared (the Kings of Edom) produced from the divine Tzelem (Image); the second is called the protoplasmic androgyne Adam of the future terrestrial and separated Adam; the third Adam is the man made of dust (the first, innocent Adam); and the fourth, is the supposed forefather of our own race — the Fallen Adam[7]

The 'spiritual blueprint' called the *first* Adam, according to the Gnostics, came into existence through the 'sacred couple' (Sophia and Christos). For the Gnostics, the *second* Adam emanated from the first Primeval Man, the 'Ophite Adamas', in whose image he is given form (life). The *third* Adam comes from the second — an Androgyny, creating a human 'being' constructed out of 'light'. The *fourth* Adam or human race was thought to be a 'degraded copy' of the original blueprint (*The One*), the original star man who was created *before* anything existed. The Tree of life *and* the body of the heavenly Adam (Orion), are symbols of our 'construct' of worlds. The significance of 'four', numerologically, is seen in *four* elements, directions, races, and world ages. The *four* Adams mentioned briefly here are another way of describing the spirit, soul, mind, and body of humanity.

Orion – Adam – Redman – Earth

'Temurah' is one of the three ancient methods used by mystics to rearrange words and sentences in the Bible, in the belief that by this method they can derive the esoteric substratum and *deeper* spiritual meaning of the words. Other methods are 'Gematria and Notation'.* According to 4th Century uses of Notation, it is said that the word A-D-A-M forms also the first letters of the four words 'Anatole Diesis Archtops Mesembria', the Greek names of the 'four corners of the world' (the earth), which esoterically also relates to the four different races of earth (black, white, yellow and red).

Some sources say the word Adam is derived from 'red earth', or Red Adam. The Red Rock canyons of Arizona and New Mexico (mentioned in earlier chapters) interconnect to symbolism associated with Orion's stars. In Gary A. David's brilliant book *The Orion Zone* (2006), he puts forth compelling evidence showing how natural architecture and constructed Hopi mesas are aligned to astronomical phenomena connecting Orion's stars with the surface of the earth. So do hundreds of petroglyphs created by the Pueblo Indians, showing their understanding of Orion's influence on earth. Many red rock locations all over the earth are significant to the golden age I mentioned in *Chapter One*, but could also be connected to the first man, Adam and the planet Mars. ÂDôM and ÂDOM also signifies red, ruddy, bay-coloured, as of a horse, the color of a red heifer. "ÂDâM, a man, a human being, male or female, red, ruddy."[8] According to etymologist and author, Pierre Sabak, the word 'Adam' connects to the word 'red'. He also links Adam and Mars to Orion through sacrifice, war, and death. He writes:

> The Hebrew word 'Adam' is deduced from 'adamah' (earth) and adom red, thus adamah implies red earth and is related in the Semitic to ma'adim Mars. Its derivation is 'me'adim' literally (from Adam). In Egyptian Arabic 'Mars' means March (and is found also in the French word mars march). Mars religiously denotes the sacrifice of the spring lamb an innocent equated with Mars and the genealogy of Adam. Theologically the sacrifice of the ram denotes the destruction of Adam Arabic Adam literally (annihilation) suggesting the death of the planet Mars and the descendants of Adam.[9]

Arjuna *is* Orion

There is also the supposed Aryan connection to Adam through the main central character (superhero) in the ancient Indian epic *Mahabharata*, called

Footnote: Gematria is an alphanumeric code of assigning a numerical value to a name, word or phrase based on its letters. A single word can yield multiple benefits depending on the cipher used.

'Arjuna'. According to the texts, Arjuna was a noble supreme archer born seven months after the birth of Krishna, and companion to the monkey god Hanuman. The etymology of 'noble' is derived from Sanskrit, but in the same language, it also means 'white' or 'bright'. Arjuna also

Figure 86: Arjuna *is* Orion.

means 'shining' or bright silvery light - an obvious connection to the stars (see figure 86).

The *Mahabharata* is the Hindu version of the epic *Gilgamesh* in so many ways. The god and warrior-king, Gilgamesh, mirrors Arjuna, and the monkey god, Hanuman, mirrors Enkidu, and they all represent celestial figures that come to earth. In some ways, these narratives explain opposing forces found in myths connected to Orion and the Pleiades. As I will come to in more detail later in the book, the 'war on earth' as 'mapped out' by the 'war in heaven' (star wars) is also part of these myths. Nandi (the sacred bull), the vehicle for the Hindu god, Shiva, who opposes Arjuna (Orion) in the *Mahabharata,* is also the 'Bull of Heaven' in the Mesopotamian version, that Gilgamesh opposes. Both Shiva and Arjuna represent the 'Fallen state' of the 'divine form' symbolic of the fall of Adam.

Warrior Star Man - God of the Underworld

The pattern of stars forming Orion is recognised as a coherent constellation by many ancient civilisations, though with different representations and mythologies. Orion is a prominent constellation located on the celestial equator and visible throughout the world and, therefore, one of the most conspicuous and recognisable constellations in the night sky. Its brightest stars are Rigel (Beta Orionis) and Betelgeuse (Alpha Orionis), a blue-white and a red-orange supergiant, respectively. Betelgeuse is uniquely recognisable, not least due to its orangey-color in the top right side of Orion and its increasingly volatile nature as it may go Supernova any time.

The configurations of the constellation Orion are said to have roughly formed about 1.5 million years ago, because of relative slow movements of stars within the constellation (especially the belt of Orion) from our earthly perspective. Scientists say that Orion will remain visible in the night sky for the next 1 to 2 million years, making the constellation one of the most extended observable constellations parallel to the rise of human civilization. External to mainstream perspective, Orion, like the many constellations adjacent to the starman-warrior, plays a part in a 'symbolic language' connected to the ancients. The ancient Sumerians, for example, saw Orion as a sheep herder, while in ancient China, Orion was one of the 28 zodiac signs Xiu, known as 'Shen'. In Chinese, Orion means 'three' so-named due to the distinct three stars located in Orion's belt. There are other symbolic reasons, as I will come to shortly.

The Babylonian star catalogues of Late Bronze Age name Orion, SIPA.ZI.AN.NA, which also relates to 'The Heavenly Shepherd' or 'True Shepherd of Anu' - Anu being the chief god of the heavens for the Sumerian priesthood'. In ancient Babylon, Orion was sacred to the gods 'Papshukal' and 'Ninshubur', fulfilling the role of 'messenger to the gods'. Papshukal was closely associated with the figure of a 'walking bird' on Babylonian *boundary* stones. On star maps, the Rooster is located below and behind the 'True Shepherd' – Orion. I find it interesting that the Rooster, which is a significant heraldic emblem for Republics like France, also takes form in Gnostic myth as Abraxas, the god of chaos - the Demiurge. The Rooster also represents 'day' or the 'light', the power of 'word', the 'Music of the Spheres', connected to the god, Hermes (one of Orion's three fathers in Greek myth). The same symbolism can be found in Egyptian mythology as 'Amenti' and the 'realm of the dead' (Underworld). Spirits, corpses (wafted from the earth), and transformed at times into Osiris (Orion) or Helios (Saturn) can also be seen in esoteric imagery as a figure riding upon the back of a Rooster, crocodile or lion in ancient art.

As I have already mentioned, the stars of Orion in ancient Egypt were called 'Sah'. It's also worth noting that the Hopi word for 'star' is 'sohu', and although the vowels are arbitrary, the Egyptian name for star (particularly those of Orion) is 'Sahu'. Because Orion (or Sah) rises before the star Sirius (whose heliacal rising was the basis for the Solar Egyptian calendar), *he* travels with 'Sopdet', the goddess who personified Sirius. The god 'Sopdu' was also said to be the son of Sah and Sopdet. Sah was syncretized with Osiris, while Sopdet was Osiris' mythological wife, Isis (Sirius), more on this star later in the book. In the *Pyramid Texts*, from the 24th and 23rd centuries BC, Sah was one of the main gods whose form the dead pharaoh would take in the afterlife. In places like Tiahuanaca in Bolivia, underground monuments, along with pyramids on its surface, are dedicated to another god called Viracocha. Lord Viracocha (and Quetzalcoatl) is the South American version of Sah and Osiris, and the Inca version of the god, Orion. All of these deities are connected to war in the heavens and the arrival of the gods form the stars. The Ojibwa (Chippewa) Native Americans call the Orion constellation 'Kabibona'kan', the 'Winter Maker' (or Door Keeper), as its presence in the night sky heralds winter and the time of Saturn. I have much more to say about the Orion-Saturn connection in later chapters as it is a crucial part of the story in terms of symbolism.

Masau'u – Atum - Ptah

The Hopi deity, 'Masau'u' is an essential figure in Pueblo creation stories, not least the Pueblo 'emergence' into the world. Masau'u is similar to Osiris, and both gods are 'Son-of-Man' deities. They are symbols of Orion's archetypal 'impression' on our ancestors' collective mind. In Hopi belief, 'distances' and 'size' are insignificant to their god Masau'u, because it was said he traversed the entire earth before morning came, and is both 'big and small' at the same time. The Hopi were expressing both the Sun and Orion's 'movement' from the eastern to the western horizon during the night (or Underworld).

Figure 87: Atum and Ptah *are* Orion.
He is the star man whose light *descends* to earth.

Orion's 'movement' from the eastern to the western horizon during the night (or Underworld).

Symbolism relating to the pineal gland, Odin's eye, Golgotha (the place of the skull), along with the 'Son of Man' (Jesus -Adam) figure, all allude to the celestial 'giver' and 'taker' of life – Orion. The same attributes belong to other creator gods such as 'Atum' and 'Ptah' of ancient Egypt (see figure 87), through to the Greek fire-bringer – 'Prometheus'. Atum is also where we get the word Autumn, a season relevant to Orion's position as it moves across the sky, as we shall see in later chapters. John Anthony West, writing about the symbolism of Ptah in his acclaimed book *Serpent in the Sky* (1993), says:

> *Ptah is Atum* [Adam/Orion] *fallen to earth. He is the coagulating fire* [light], *the simultaneous cause (of the created world) and effect (of the scission). Ptah is phi, the creative power inherent in Atum but locked in Atum in his fall to earth.*[10]

And Pierre Sabak says of the etymology of Atum in his book *Murder of*

Reality (2010):

> *Correlation between 'Atum' and 'Adon' is recorded in the hieroglyphic. On rare occasions, according to the scholar David Rohl, Atum is spelt 'using a hand which Egyptologist's recognize as the letter 'd' or 't,' giving us A-d-m'. Atum's name, therefore, serves as a probable pun on the Hebrew name Adam - the progenitor of man, cognate in Greek with Adonai (a Lord).*[11]

As I have already said, Orion in the American Southwestern skies represents the Hopi god Masau'u, whose symbol is a 'whirlpool gate', or a 'double spiral'. The same symbol can be seen in both Arizona and at the Sid in Broga site (New Grange) in Ireland (see figure 88).

Figure 88: The Whirlpool Gate (Door).
Attributed to Masau'u (Orion). The symbol represents this god's ability to be in two zones, or dimensions, simultaneously.

The New Grange heritage site is a vast 'netherworld' initiation chamber, focused on celestial connections between earth and the stars, notably, in my view, Orion (Masau'u). Places like New Grange and other Neolithic sites seem to have been born of a matriarchal culture (Sophia/Sheela na gig), the Underworld (the stars), and hunter-gatherer male fertility figures, the latter relates to Orion. Anthony Murphy, in his book, *Mythical Ireland* (2017), suggests Orion becomes mythical characters such as 'Nuadu of Silver Arm,' 'Ligh Lamhfada', 'Amergin Glúngeal' and 'Fionn Mac Cumhaill'. He also suggests that kerbstone 52 at Sid in Broga (New Grange) contains representations of Orion's stars (see figure 89).

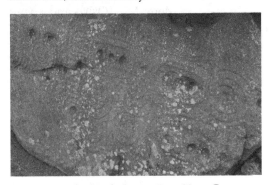

Figure 89: The Kerb Stone 52 at New Grange.
Does it contain represenations of Orion's three belt stars? *Three* is a power number.

There is also more to know about the Hopi god Masau'u, as the Hopi word 'maasi', means 'grey'. For the Hopi, Masau'u is also the terrestrial equivalent of Orion, whose name can also mean 'ant' or ant-man. The concept of *Ant-Man* in the *Marvel Universe* films and comics gives the idea of a superhero who can be both 'big and small'. Interestingly, the Indo-European root word for Orion is 'Morui', which is also supposed to mean 'ant'.[12] I tend to think that the grey alien phenomena are more of an 'expression' relating to darker, malevolent (hive mind-like) forces attributed to Orion and other star systems, a subject I will come back to in *Part Two* of the book.

Giant Hunter Lover-Man

The Cerne Abbas Giant hill figure near the village of Cerne Abbas in Dorset, England, seems to be another depiction of Orion. The hill figure

 stands 55 metres (180 ft) high, with a prominent erection, wielding a massive club in his right hand (see figure 90).

The connection to the god-man hunter, Hercules, is apparent, too, in this petrographic. The phallic nature of the giant relates in part to the Egyptian deity Min/Osiris and Orion. The fact that Cerne Abbas is meant to be

Figure 90: Giant Hunter Lover-Man.
Cerne Abbas Giant *and* Hercules are Orion figures.

viewed from the air and that it sits below an Iron Age fort commonly nicknamed the frying pan (another name for both the Big Dipper and the belt and sword stars of Orion), makes me wonder if these works were specific renditions of star symbolism on earth. The origin and age of the Cerne Abbas figure are unclear. Still, it could have been another work of art by the Phoenicians, Cabeiri, and the Pelasgian 'elite' who I am sure were the protagonists of the mystery schools, mentioned in *Chapter One*. The word 'Cabala' is also thought to be derived from the Latin 'caballus', a horse, as in the 'Horse of Troy' in the *Iliad*, which makes the 'white horse symbolism' found all over the hills around southern England all the more intriguing. Like several other effigies scraped into the hillsides of ancient Britain, Cerne Abbas is often thought of as an ancient construction, though the earliest mention of it dates to the late 17th Century. Some writers suggest the giant man is 17th Century in origin and carved around the time of the English Civil War by servants of the Lord of the Manor, Denzil Holles, and intended as a parody of Oliver Cromwell.[13] I doubt that very much!

A Mimbre Pueblo bowl, from around 1000 AD, depicts a giant warrior-clown (more on the sacred clowns later) with 'three' lesser figures supporting his enormous penis. The three characters could be symbolic of the three belt stars of Orion (see figure 91). The large phallus is a symbol connected to fertility, agriculture, and Orion's significance to the seasons.

The Egyptian god Min, an extremely ancient god who goes back to the Pre-Dynastic period in Egypt, was initially identified with the constellation of Orion (see figure 92). According to Pierre Sabak, the Greek root 'ourien'

Figure 91: The Penis of Osiris (Orion). An 11th Century AD Mimbres plate showing Orion. The three figures holding the Obelisk (penis) could be the belt stars of Orion.

Figure 92: Min of Egypt. Supporting a large phallus and another representation of Orion's significance to fertility on earth.

(semen) is a name suggesting the 'lions of Orion' and appertains to the castration of Osiris's penis, or phallus. In the myth, Osiris's penis is replaced by a golden member, symbolic of a bloodline usurping another line on earth. Phallic imagery could also relate to the 'panspermia' theory, that life on earth originated from microorganisms, or chemical precursors of life, present in outer space – known as panspermia. Orion's Nebula, as we shall see, is a potential focus for panspermia, not least through our Solar System's position in the Orion arm part of the Milky Way Galaxy.[14]

Kesil Horeph, Hercules and the Lion

In Hebrew, Orion is 'Kesil Horeph', refers to both the fool and a giant angelic being. The upraised arms of Kesil Horeph is another depiction of the Orion constellation (the giant of winter), see figure 93 overleaf. Kesil

Figure 93: Kesil Horeph.
A star map of the 'giant of winter' in the North.

may have referred to the biblical 'Foolish Messiah', or the Babylonian messiah figure, Nimrod (another version of Orion). According to Babylonian texts, Nimrod influenced the idea of Kesil after the great flood.

Nimrod was also the hunter, the trickster, and in Hungarian mythology, a stag-man. Herne the hunter, like Kesil and Nimrod, are seen as mystical beings with magical powers, whose role was to indicate the will of God (or the gods). Nimrod-Hercules is also a solar deity, a mighty hunter who performs twelve labours (the twelve astrological houses) forming the zodiacal band. Pierre Sabak, writing about Kesil in his book, *Angelic Invasion* (not yet published), explains the etymological connection between the fool, the hunter, and the gods. He says:

Within early mythology and reproduced on star maps the figure of 'Kesil' (Orion) is often shown holding 'keshet' (a bow), and is a weapon that is twinned in Hebrew with 'kashtit' (the iris of the eye) an insignia of the Watchers aka the Seraphim (non-human angels) ...

... Repeated also in Judaic theology 'keshet' (the bow of war) is a signifier of 'keshet be'anan' (a rainbow – literally a bow of the cloud). Religiously the bow is accorded with the descendants of Orion in particular the Covenant between Noah and the 'Elohim' (the High Ones) following the great flood, which destroyed mankind.

Kesil Horeph is another version of Adam, Orion, and the Son of Man archetype. The word Kesil (or Kes) also relates to a throne, or eye motif, associated with Osiris (Orion). Osiris, Nimrod and Hercules are interchangeable as solar gods, warriors, hunters, and 'giants' amongst humanity. Kesil, like Hercules, holds a baton or club, just as original depictions of Orion show this warrior with a club (see figure 94).

Figure 94: Orion in the Tarot.
(Left) Nimrod (Hercules). **(Right)** The peasant Fool. All are versions of Orion.
(Public Domain)

Kesil is the Fool in the tarot and, therefore, appropriately connected to Adam on High and Orion as I will come to shortly. One other feature is the star giant's connection to the lion (or lion skin), which relates to the Gnostic Demiurge and the 'fall' of Adam from Eden. Egyptian priests in many of their ceremonies also wore lion skins, all symbolic of the exalted and conquered Sun (Leo) - see the Lion's Paw ritual in the last Chapter. The constellation of Leo is also crucial to know more about 'lion consciousness'. (For more details on this subject, refer to my graphic novels.) The club-holding warrior-fool (like Samson of biblical fame) is ready to do battle with forces of darkness, such as the Nubian lion and the malevolent Demiurge and his minions. Kesil Horeph, as the Fool, is also seen carrying a cudgel (club) in earlier renditions because the club was a 'weapon' of protection used by hunters and peasants.

The Joker in the Pack

The Fool, or Kesil, was often wearing a hat with the ears of an 'ass' (donkey), a symbol associated with the 'lowest angel' (Archon), 'Thartharaoth' and the opposite of 'Highest Crown'. The crown (or *corona*) in this context relates to both royalty and the throne in heaven, a symbol or word that is used often by the Cult. The symbolism connected to the court jester and a medieval fool can also be found in the Hebrew noun 'kes' (a throne), or Arabic 'kursi', and is unique to Orion's relationship with royalty; hence why the court jester held a vital position in the royal courts of Europe. The jester was the *only* person who could mock (make an ass of) the court in front of the king.

According to Greek legends, the god Apollo, changed King Midas' ears into ass's ears because he preferred the sound of Pan's pipes to the music of the temple of Delphi. The innocence of the Fool and the Age, or time before the fall relates to this symbolism. It is the 'unnumbered' Fool who begins the tarot (or the journey) from the innocence of spirit to the outwardly physical projection of the world (reality). The thirteen balls in the hand of Kesil in this 15th Century illustration are more 'Son of Man' symbolism, possibly relating to thirteen signs, thirteen moons, and the Gnostic connection between Sophia and Christos mentioned earlier (see figure 95).

Figure 95: Kesil.
The giant fool shown with ears of an ass.
(Public Domain)

The numerical connections to the 22 cards forming the Major Arcana cards in the tarot, the 22 letters of the Hebrew alphabet (along with Atziluth - the suit of

ADAM, KESIL & the FOOL

THE FOOL.

Figure 96: The Fool & the *Twenty Two* Code. 22 tarot cards, 22 letters of the Hebrew alphabet, and 22 bones in the human skull (Golgotha). Obviously not a coincidence?

wands), and the number of bones in the human skull (eight cranial bones and fourteen facial skeleton bones), are obvious (see figure 96). There are also 22 amino acids (DNA codes), providing the blueprint for life. These numerological connections relate to the skull of the heavenly Adam and in the 22 *paths* in the original Kabbalah, running between the Sephirot (the Tree) and the initiate. The skull and bone symbol also relates to the skull of Adam and connects Orion *to* Saturn (Satan) - hence the Fall. The mind (brain) being the battle ground for the soul. *Twenty-two* is also *four* (2+2), and 'four' is a number that equates to structure, dedication, and bones. Therefore, within the tarot we have a numbers and codes that express the holographic nature of reality (all embodied within Orion/Adam/Anthropos), a subject I will come back to in *Part Two*.

The tarot cards, the Fool (or Joker), the Magician, and the Hermit are archetypes showing a connection to Orion (the star man). Major Arcana tarot cards seem to be hinting at a path of self-discovery, that starts with Orion (Fool card) and ends with the earth matrix (World card). While writing this chapter, I came across an interesting French blog, *The Constellation of Orion, The Mystery of Orion - a giant on the Ecliptic*, connected to the last heir of the Master cardmakers of Marseilles, Philippe Camoin. In the article, the writer reached the same conclusions regarding the tarot, the Fool, and Orion. Camoin, is an expert on the tarot, and it was no surprise to see that he also saw the Fool as Orion, along with the Priestess (the Popess card) and the World card as representing Sirius and the Earth. Both Orion and Sirius are 'pathmakers' as characterised by the numbering of the Major Arcana. The article read:

The number 22 is a powerful number, it is a "master-number" and is considered to be beneficial. It symbolizes the manifestation of being in its diversity and in space-time. Although the MAT [the fool] does not carry a number, it remains the 22nd major arcane of the ROTA (sky wheel) Tarot. Kabbalists, on the other hand, believe that it is the 21st blade, because the SHIN that can be compared to the Chinese SHEN (Orion) is the 21st letter of the Hebrew alphabet.[15]

According to Camion, it is Sirius who guides the Fool (Orion) on earth, so to 'open the doors' of heaven for humanity. On his journey, the fool is accompanied by a small animal, a blue dog (or cat), which falls in the position currently occupied by the Lepus constellation (the hare). Interestingly, according to Camion, some of the Major Arcana cards can be placed side-by-side and elaborate further on the Orion, Sirius, Saturn, Moon connection.[16] I will have much to say about all of these connections in later chapters.

Primordial Planet Man-Fool

In the *Book of Hours* (*Book of Time*), created in the Middle Ages we find some exciting imagery connected to Kesil and the Fool. *The Book of Hours* has its ultimate origin in the 6th Century *Psalter* (copies of the *Psalms*), which monks and nuns were required to recite. By the 12th century, it developed into the breviary (Prayer rites), with weekly cycles of psalms, prayers, hymns, antiphons and readings changing with the liturgical season (hence the hours, days, months, etc.). A Flemish *Book of Hours* Illustration shows what is called the 'Planet Man', another rendition of a celestial Adam.

In this image, a celestial man also has a Fool, or jester, at his feet, said to be symbolic of the 'lunacy' of the fool and the lunacy connected to the 'Luna Obscura' or dark moon situated under the left hand of Planet Man. The dark moon is a description for the moon during periods when it is not reflecting direct sunlight towards Earth, but instead, its light defines the last visible crescent, or a waning moon. The symbolism in the illuminated illustration shows both Adam and the Fool as a macrocosm of the solar system, hinting at the moon (which *controls* the mind of Adam) being a vessel for the 'afterlife' (or death).

The three-pointed hat worn by the jester-fool is also connected to the three belt stars or three 'hearthstones' of Orion, more on this later. I can't help but wonder if the 'Infinity Stones', in the Marvel *Avengers* stories, belonging to the 'Elders of the Universe' (sought after by the Titan, Thanos), are symbolic of the 'hearth stars' (stones) focused on within Orion. The fictional character Thanos (born of Titan, one of Saturn's moons), certainly fits the bill for a demented tyrant, fool-god, who wields terrible power through a metal gauntlet that houses the infinity stones.

The Pleiades or seven stars (Spirits of Seven Churches in Asia Minor), are also considered a centre of influence for humanity through peace, compassion, and love. The Pleiades are the work of the Goddess (Sophia) in my view and represent much that we call 'native' or 'Pagan'. Some myths say that the 'goddess' was replaced by a 'god', and the Pleiades influenced by a 'Fool' who 'moved' the constellation into Taurus (the Bull) through a heavenly struggle, or war. Star myths like these relate to Gnostic interpretations of the 'work' or damage done by the demented Demiurge, (think Thanos) who could also be considered a 'trickster' or fool. The theme of the fool can be found in so many ancient civilisations and native myths. In Maori legend, for example, one of the Seven Sisters (Pleiades) was supposedly raped by the fool, 'Kidili' (another Orion figure) and Native Americans share many similar stories, too, of maidens chased by a foolish 'giant'.

Tetragrammaton & Adam on High

Connections between the Abrahamic religions and some of the Native American traditions are very similar in language, the origin of gods and beliefs. As I have already mentioned, the Hopi god, Masau'u, seems to be another version of the 'fallen Adam', or Orion in his fallen state. The stacking of 4 letters of the Hebrew alphabet, I. H. V. H, spelling 'Yahweh' (the Tetragrammaton) seen as a column, is another indication of a 'human-made' form of Adam in the *image of* God (see figure 97). Even earlier versions of Hebrew letters combined, from 2,000BC, look like 'upstretched arms' similar to Kesil on page 152. There is so much more to go into deeply here, not least the numerological connections to the letters 'He', '5', and 'H' and 'X' found in other areas of magic, mysticism, and symbolism. I am not an etymologist of course, but the letter 'X' seems to be especially crucial as it is the *22nd letter* of the Greek alphabet. As I will show in a later chapter, the 'X' is used excessively in the media, in logos and other symbolism.

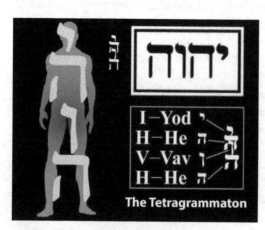

The Tetragrammaton

Figure 97: The Tetragrammaton.

The Gnostics inferred from the verse in *Genesis*: "Let us make man in our image," the first earthly man, based on the model of a celestial Adam – or 'Adam on high'. In the Nag Hammadi, *Apocryphon of John*, we learn that the Anthropos is the first creation of 'knowledge' and 'perfect intellect', seen as the first luminary of the heavens. Why was Orion so crucial to the ancients? The pyramid builders and those who erected megalithic sites all over the world seemed to be fascinated by Orion's stars. Were they aligning their temples with Adam on high and what *He* represented? For the ancients, could Adam on high be seen as the 'heavenly (celestial) model' (Orion), through which the Gnostic Demiurge 'created' the Earthly Adam? For me Adam on high represents a spiritual connection to the Infinite Creator, beyond the illusion. Are alignments on Earth dedicated to the 'creators' or 'creator' of Adam on high – or to Orion's configuration? As I said at the beginning of the book, much of this is subjective and open to various interpretations depending on your personal beliefs. I have no desire to belittle others faiths here, I am simply correlating common themes and symbolism relating to Orion and Adam found in numerous cultures and religions. The notion of 'as above, so below' (the holographic universe in all its glory) is also important to understanding the beliefs and perceptions of the ancients who revered Orion's stars.

Staying with the theme of Adam and the connections to Orion, let us look at some of the symbolism relating to the 'Fall' and the 'light-bringer' who in numerous myths, was said to come to Earth in ancient times.

Sources:

1) Fuller, J. F. C. *The Secret Wisdom of the Qabalah; A Study in Jewish Mystical Thought*. p11
2) https://en.wikipedia.org/wiki/Media_Lab_Europe%27s_social_robots
3) https://amunaor.com/2015/02/04/no-mortal-man-hath-yet-to-unveil-me-gnostic-symbolism/
4) Hall, Manly P. *The Secret Teachings of All Ages* (Readers Edition). Penguin. 2003 p160.
5) Loper, DeAnne. *Kabbalah Secrets Christians Need to Know: An In Depth Study of the Gods of Jewish Mysticism*, 2019. p80
6) *Numbers* 23:19
7) Blavatsky, H; *Secret Doctrine*. p409,
8) Pre-Adamites; p.161
9) Sabak, Pierre. *Murder of Reality, Hidden Symbolism of the Dragon*, 2010 p196-197
10) West, John Anthony. *Serpent in the Sky*. Quest 1993. p127
11) Sabak, Pierre. *Murder of Reality, Hidden Symbolism of the Dragon* Serpentgena. 2010 pp 186-188
12) David, Gary A. *The Orion Zone: The Ancient Star Cities of the American Southwest*. Adventures Unlimited. 2006, p282.
13) Denzil Holles (1st Baron Holles). *Cerne Abbas Giant at Sacred Destinations*, BCW Project accessed 10-05-18
14) https://en.wikipedia.org/wiki/Panspermia
15) http://secretebase.free.fr/complots/zodiac/orion/orion.htm
16) https://fr.camoin.com/tarot/tarot-code-sentier-etoile-sirius.html

6

PROMETHEUS ADAM
Symbols of the *Fallen* 'Stars'

Big things have small beginnings
David 8 (from the movie *Prometheus*)

Another aspect of the fallen state of Adam is thought to be the Greek Titan, Prometheus. He is the light carrier, or the 'bringer of light', who in mythology connects to the time of the 'Fall' and biblical Flood narrative. Prometheus's son, Deucalion (Noah), and the Shining Ones (Watchers) I mentioned in earlier chapters are part of the story relating to the 'fallen state' of Adam/Orion consciousness. They are all part of the *descending* light (fire) said to have been brought by Prometheus.

In esoteric literature, Prometheus is also Lucifer, who performs the same actions of Prometheus, including the 'gifts' brought by the fire-bringer; both share the notion of a 'fall to earth'. It's interesting to note that Prometheus and the fallen rebel angel of biblical fame, are seen as the same entity in much mythology, art, and symbolism. Prometheus, like Lucifer, is a revealer of the endless challenges for humanity. Prometheus is William Blake's *Glad Day - the Dance of Albion* (1795) and a primeval giant, whose fall and division results in Blake's *Four Zoas:* Urizen, Tharmas, Luvah/Orc, and Urthona/Los. In my rendition of Blake's image, *Dream Fulfilled* (1995), Albion is a creator, liberator, and 'man of light' descending to earth (see figure 98). In Blake's mythology and representation of biblical figures, both Adam and Satan were contained within the 'egg' which burned from Lucifer's fire, surrounded by Blake's version of the Four Adams (Urizen, Tharmas, Luvah/Orc, and Urthona/Los). For Blake, Los is the *fallen* (earthly human), based on Prometheus and his imprisoner, Hephaestus; both figures are connected to 'bringing' and 'using' star fire belonging to the gods, or God.

Creation themes showing through imagery and myths of Prometheus (Greece), Ptah and Khnemu (Egypt) and Enki (Mesopotamian), are all versions of the Demiurge creating Adam. Or the collective biblical Elohim – the creators of the body-blueprint of humanity (see figure 99). In Ridley

Figure 98: Prometheus Light-Man.
My painting, *Dream Fulfilled* (used as the cover art for David Icke's book, '... *And the Truth shall Set You Free*', 1995), is Promethean in nature.

Figure 99: Prometheus.
Prometheus creating a 'human being'.

Scott's movie, *Prometheus* (2012), the alien 'genetic engineers' (creators of life) are 'giants' and 'time travellers'. Scott's work seems to have been inspired by the ancient knowledge of creator gods found all over the world – hence the movie title, *Prometheus*. Similar attributes relate to the Egyptian creator god, Khnemu, who was said to have 'shaped' the human form and given it life. I have pondered on the concept of a genetically modified human species in recent years, hence the visual themes in some of my art. Maybe somewhere in our hollow Moon (one of Saturn's satellites) was the laboratory of 'Khnemu', a place called 'Eden'? Was the Moon the biblical Ark? Could the collection of double of every species on earth, taken onto the Ark, be an alien geneticist laboratory? Was this the same place from where 'Adam and Eve' (double helix) might have been conceived? It is impossible to know. But, there has to be more to *our* alien connection from a biological perspective. Artificial intelligence (AI) *is* becoming part of our human world, as I will come to later in the book. Therefore, are we being 'upgraded' (like a robot) *once again* so to be more biologically 'compatible' with alien, artificial intelligence? Themes of human-like 'robots' are also prevalent in movies such as *Prometheus* because 'humans as robots', as we shall see later in the book, are our 'ancient-future' connection to the 'fall'.

The legend of Prometheus tells of a Titan deciding to disobey the gods and make humans 'gods' themselves. Prometheus is described as the 'fallen one' (Lucifer) that Christianity has connected to Satan or the devil.

Prometheus, as Lucifer, is also characterised in Egypt as the hawk-headed Horus magically conceived by Isis (Sirius) and the murdered, or fallen Osiris (Orion) who was killed by his brother, Set (Saturn). The red desert deity, Set, is a variation of Yahweh (Gnostic Demiurge), who became Horus's sworn enemy. Like Satan, Set is a bringer of *false* light - the matrix. The Old Testament tells us that Yahweh confronted by one of his angels, Lucifer, in a sort of explosive palace coup – led to the rebel Lucifer being expelled from the palace or 'house of many mansions'.[1]

In Greek mythology, Prometheus is a 'creator god' in his own right. Like the Elohim in *Genesis*, which was said to create Adam, his creative actions were considered both 'rebellious' and disobedient. He made humanity 'more than' an animal, according to the myths, by giving humanity the ability to be god-like. As a 'bringer of fire' (celestial star fire), Prometheus is also a star who comes out of the Milky Way, also called the 'Fire-Stream'.[2] I would suggest that myths associated with Prometheus are stories that try to describe the 'movement' of electromagnetic light, along with the movement of planets (possibly Venus) carrying 'star fire' to our world in an ancient epoch. The changes to human perception and the new ways of 'seeing' connected to enormous ancient celestial events, such as the arrival of a comet, or plasma (electromagnetic fields) seen globally across the skies would have left such a powerful impact on humanity.

Prometheus's disobedience could also be a warning of a comet, or star, coming to earth (again). This is a subject that has been topical when writing this book, not least through the arrival of Atlas (or C/2019 Y4) in May 2020. As the Jewish scholar, Samuel of Nehardea (165 BC), said: "We have it as a tradition that no comet ever passed across the face of Orion 'Kesil'; for if this should happen the earth would be destroyed."[3] When Samuel's audience objected to this statement, saying: "Yet we see that this occurs," Samuel replied: "It only appears so; for the comet passes either above or below the star [Orion]. Possibly also its radiance passes, but not its body." Again, Samuel says: "But for the warmth [electromagnetic plasma] of Orion, the earth could not exist, because of the frigidity of Scorpio; furthermore, Orion lies near Taurus, with which the warm season begins."[4] I will have much more to say about the seasons, religious festivals and symbols concerning Orion's influence in a later chapter.

Two *Fallen* Suns

Satan is an aspect of two *fallen* entities, representing the *lower* aspect of the fallen angel Lucifer. A Satan-Prometheus-Lucifer mural can be found in the United Nations building in New York, showing figures in front of a Black Sun (Saturn/Satan) and an unfinished pyramid with fire rays and red/blue colour schemes all across the image. The 'red' and 'blue' colour use will become significant as we get deeper into Orion symbolism; they are a substantial part of the esoteric nature of Orion's influence on earth. Imagery associated with Prometheus, Lucifer and Satan (Saturn) in simple terms, describe Adam's connection to Orion (Prometheus) and Saturn (Cronos/Satan) through a *fallen state*; from a celestial (Aeon/spirit) to the density of the soul and eventually to physical matter.

The connection to pre-Christian cults such as Orphism and Dionysus also relates to the 'fallen' deity, sun god who descends into the Underworld, and returns. Like Dionysus, 'Adam on high' *is* the Son of Man who begins in heaven and 'falls' to the physical plane, returning to heaven. As seen by the Orphic cults, Dionysus was 'divine in heaven', but in the flesh (as Zagreus), he was a 'fallen one' – a Titan just like Prometheus. The Pagan world seemed to marry the Christian world through the Orphic and Gnostic belief in a Son of Man, the latter of which became the Christian idol, Jesus. As Carl Jung says in his work, *Man and His Symbols* (1964):

> *The Son of Man, though born of a human virgin* [if you believe this], *had his beginning in heaven, whence he came in an act of God's incarnation in man. After his death, he returned to heaven but returned once and for all, to reign on the right hand of God until the Second Coming when the dead shall arise.*[5]

Raising the dead, venturing into the Underworld, 'surviving death', etc., are all connected mysteries associated with the pre-Christian Orion-Saturn Cults. Tolkien's epic trilogy, *The Lord of the Rings*, even has the archetypal Son of Man, the king Aragon, who is able to summon the dead in *The Return of the King*. The point I make here is that all these archetypes are 'warrior' kings, or 'divine protectors,' 'magicians', 'teachers of fertility rites' and keepers of *darker arts* connected to Orion *and* Saturn.

Prometheus, 'Fire Seed' & Dwarf Stars

The connections to Prometheus, Saturn, and Orion are also evident in the movie *Prometheus*. Early into the film's plot, the constellation featured in the discoveries found in ancient art, by scientists working for the fictional Weyland Corporation, seem very similar to the 'Flame Nebula' in the Orion constellation. The Flame Nebula has a bright star called Alnitak (Ori), which is an emission nebula formed of ionized gases that emit light of various wavelengths. The most common source of ionization is high-energy photons emitted from a nearby hot star. Alnitak is the easternmost star in the Belt of Orion, shining energetic ultraviolet light into the Flame Nebula, and this, according to scientists, knocks electrons away from the high clouds of 'hydrogen gas' residing there. In Hindu belief, the hermit sage of the gods, 'Angira' (the son of Brahma), was said to have been born of a flame, 'fire seed' or (hot coals). Like the Roman god, Vulcan, these gods are all Promethean. In the *Vedas*, it is said that eight sons, including Jupiter, were born of this fire seed and some texts call Jupiter the 'Fire God'.[6]

Connections between Prometheus, Jupiter (Zeus), Osiris, Amun, Cronos (Saturn) and Orion, are a constantly recurring theme in mythology. These connections made me wonder if the 'Titan', Prometheus, took the 'fire of life' (the photonic fire seed) and the knowledge to 'fuse life' from the Emission Nebula of Orion to Earth? Both Jupiter and Saturn are 'Brown Dwarf stars', a type of sub-stellar object occupying the mass range between the densest gas giant planets and the lightest stars. To put their size into perspective, Jupiter has 79 moons, some of which are huge (the Galilean satellites are the four largest moons of Jupiter), the biggest of which is Ganymede, bigger than the planet Mercury. Ganymede is a crucial mytho-logical figure to the Star Cult I outline here. After the Titan Wars in Greek mythology, Zeus (Jupiter), in the form of an eagle, carried the handsome young Ganymede up to heaven to become the 'cupbearer' of the gods. In the myth, Ganymede represents the 'Age of Aquarius', and he is actually 'abducted' by Zeus in the form of an eagle. The eagle symbol used by a 'physical' elite on earth goes back to the Babylonian and Roman empires and can be seen in almost every Christian Church in the form of a pulpit. Therefore, I am not sur-

Figure 105: Jupiter and Ganymede. **(Left)** Ganymede outside the crypt. **(Right)** The famous Oxford pub sign. Both are symbol of the Age of Aquarius (Ganymede) being abducted by Zeus in the form of an eagle.

prised to find a statue of what appears to be Ganymede 'putting up a fight' with the eagle before his 'abduction' outside the crypt on the land of the Duke of Westminster. I cannot say for sure if this is meant to be Ganymede, but it certainly has the image of such a scene from the myth.

The same image is the name of one of the most famous pubs in England, a place where J.R.R. Tolkien and C.S. Lewis would share ideas while lecturing at Oxford University in the 20th Century (see figure 105). Tolkien of course used the eagle symbolism connected to one of the *three* Istari wizards, Gandalf, within his books *Lord of the Rings* (Saturn) and the *Hobbit*.

Frozen in Time

The fall of the titan, Prometheus, is the same as Satan's Fall in Danté's 13th Century poem, *Inferno*. In Danté's work, Satan is trapped in the frozen central zone inside the Ninth Circle of Hell.[7] Satan *or* Saturn is ensnared and 'restricted' by the Holy of Holies, or 'Circles of Hell', and becomes the alter ego, Cronos. The Qabalah compares the 'flaming sword' and its electromagnetic light, or power of creation, to Satan. In the Gospel, according to *Luke*, Jesus describes Satan as 'lightning fall from heaven'.[8] The *Fall* is the 'symbolic' trajectory of light as it passes through the Tree of Life (the sefirot) and the body of the heavenly Adam (see page 141). It is one of Orion's creators, or fathers, 'Vulcan' (Hephaestus) who binds the young Prometheus to a rock for stealing the light of creation. The starlight, or fire, brought by Prometheus, could have originated in Orion's Nebula – its Trapezium area, another topic I will return to later in the book. It seems, a celestial force, in the form of Prometheus, was punished for bringing knowledge (the light of the world) to a bewildered ancient human species.

Another of Vulcan's (Hephaestus's) creations was 'Pandora', the first woman. Pandora, or Persephone, was another version of the goddess, Sophia (a copy of the original). Pandora, according to myth, opens a box (or jar), thus freeing the Archons (Genies) into the lower-astral human worlds. What the myths and legends allude to is the 'hierarchy of light' from the *unseen* to the *seen* in terms of visible light; the light goes beyond the boundary or veil and, at the same time, creates, constructs, and often destroys our human world. According to Greek Myth, the fire creator god, Hephaestus, also created the first ancient robots.[9] A subject crucial to the Orion story, as we shall see later in the book.

All So 'Strange' (*Doctor Who?*)

When we venture into *Marvel's* fictional worlds, we also find references to Adam, the magician. The *Marvel* character *Doctor Strange*, along with another hero called *'Adam Strange'*, created in the 1950s, seems to hint at the 'cosmic chosen-man' mythology. Both characters seem to be symbolic personifications of the fallen Adam and Primordial Man. Adam was said to be the first 'light-man', or first 'human being' to emerge after the creation of the cosmos. Eve, in my view, was already an aspect of Sophia (an Upper Aeon) and not created with the fallen Adam (see page 115). In these *Marvel* narratives, Eve could be considered one of the 'Ancient Ones' who is portrayed as a woman (played by Tilda Swinton) in the 2016 movie version of *Doctor Strange*. The same ideas of the 'ancient one' could have been inspired by a Celtic version of the Sophia myth as Ceridwen (Welsh myth), or 'Danu' (In Irish mythology). The Biblical version of Eve alludes to a lesser creature, possibly a Pagan Pandora connection, which was eventually absorbed into other religions.

The 'eye' and 'X' symbolism found in Marvel's *Doctor Strange* seems to relate to 'combined' Orion and Saturn symbolism. Is Steven Strange another 'Time Lord' or *Doctor Who*? The 'Eye of Agamotto', used by *Doctor Strange* to 'reverse time' and undo all the destruction in the Marvel story, can be found in much secret society symbolism. In the *Doctor Strange* narrative, the Eye of Agamotto contains the 'Time Stone' (one of the six Infinity Stones in the *Marvel Universe*) and is clearly a reference to the

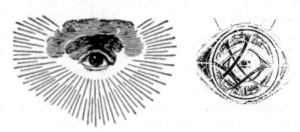

Figure 100: The Eye of Providence and Agamotto.
The 'Eye of Agamotto' is *Doctor Strange's* amulet and is symbolic of the *origin* of his sorcery (is this origin Orion?)

relationship between Adam on high (Strange) and Saturn (the Lord of Time), through a Time Stone encased in a 'Cube, H and X' symbol. The Eye of Agamotto also resembles the 'Eye of Providence' found in Freemasonry. The eye is a symbol for the Trapezium area, a portal into the upper Aeons through the Orion Nebula, a region I will dedicate a whole chapter to later in the book (see figure 100).

In his book, *Fingerprints of the Gods* (1995), Graham Hancock identifies Orion as the god of Time (Cronos/Saturn). Hancock says: "In the subcontinent of India...the Orion constellation is known as Kal-Purush, meaning Time-Man... ." Saturn, worshipped as the creator, was another version of Adam: "The first religious symbols were symbols of Saturn, and so pervasive was the planet god's influence that the ancients knew him as the creator, the king of the world, and Adam the first man."[10]

Superhero, *Adam Strange*, seems to be an earlier version of *Doctor Strange* in the Marvel series; the X-Eye (portal) symbolism found in the *Doctor Strange* narratives is also seen in the X chromosome symbol. The X and Y chromosome is the genetic blueprint for life in physical form, but the 'X' is often interchanged with the 'hourglass' in Freemasonic symbolism and relates to death, Cronos, or Saturn (see page 279-80). The flaming sword that passes through the body of the heavenly Adam could be another way of describing the light (crystalline-like) aspects of RNA and DNA.

In the Marvel stories, *Doctor Strange* also confronts 'Dormammu' in what is called 'the Dark Dimension' and creates an endless time loop to 'trap' this Demiurge-like deity. Dormammu could easily be inspired by the Demiurge of Gnostic belief, especially since many movies, in recent years, seems to be spilling out Gnostic-Hermetic subjects. The many *Marvel* villains like Thanos and Galactus, in my view, are references to Saturn-like titans (giants) and 'darker forces' operating beyond the physical dimension.

Expulsion from Paradise

The projection out of realms described as Upper Aeons in Gnostic teachings could also be describing the 'fall' and the expulsion of Adam and Eve (Sophia) from a celestial Eden. In the Old Testament 'blame and shame' version of the story, Adam (in a heavenly form) falls victim to the desire to know more and eat from the Tree of Life. The act of eating the apple sees God (the Gnostic Demiurge) 'expelling' Adam on high (Orion) and Eve, along with the serpent (the electromagnetic kundalini force) for disobeying the instruction, 'thou shall *not* know thy self'. As it says in *Genesis*:

> *Then the Lord God said, '. . . Now, lest [Adam] reach out his hand and take also of the tree of life and eat, and live forever—therefore the Lord God sent him out from the garden of Eden to work the ground from which he was taken. He drove out the man, and at the east of the Garden of Eden he placed the cherubim and a flaming sword that turned every way to guard the way to the tree of life.*[11]

Adam disobeyed God's command regarding the tree of knowledge of good and evil by eating from the tree of life, so to discern between 'good and evil' (life and death). In other words, humanity was not supposed to 'operate' beyond the polarity of life and death (duality) and the realms beyond what the Gnostic veil, or boundary leading to the Upper Aeons. Adam and Eve would 'know' the true nature of reality. As it states in *Genesis*:

> *Then the LORD God said, "Behold, the man has become like one of us in knowing good and evil.*[12]

On one level, the celestial (heavenly) Adam (an aspect of the Christos), and Eve is the Upper Aeon who *converges* with Adam to create the blueprint for human life on earth. As I said in earlier chapters, was this blueprint eventually 'hacked' and the X and Y chromosomes used to create a new biological human, one that would forever obey the Demiurge and 'otherworldly forces' working against the Creator, *against* the heavenly Adam - humanity?

Three forces take the form of the 'Tree of Life' (good and evil) and the

'Tree of Knowledge' in the Garden of Eden, and the trees seem to be symbolic of the forces focused on the Orion Nebula. In Jewish theology, the higher 'Gann Eden' is called the 'Garden of Righteousness', a location said to have been created at the beginning of the world. It is said that here the 'righteous' dwell in the sight of the 'heavenly chariot' carrying the 'throne' of God (Aeons). Is it possible that the 'chariot' and 'throne' is another way of describing the Trapezium area of the Orion Nebula? Was Orion (the King) and his Queen (Eve) expelled from the realm of paradise, the place where the Upper and Lower Aeons meet, for disobeying the Demiurge? Again, it is interesting to note that the word 'paradise' comes from the term 'Pardes', meaning a 'royal garden' or 'hunting park'- a perfect setting for the fall of Adam on high - the star man – Orion. In his excellent book *The Secret Teachings of All Ages*, Manly P. Hall describes Adam's fall from the worlds called the Garden of Eden:

> *The world of Assiah, or the elemental world of substance, is the one into which humanity descended at the time of Adam's fall. The Garden of Eden is the three upper worlds, and for his sins, Adam was forced into the sphere of substance and assumed coats of skin (bodies). All of the spiritual forces of the upper worlds A, B, C, when they strike against the elements of the lower world, D, are distorted and perverted, resulting in the creation of hierarchies of demons to correspond with the good spirits in each of the higher worlds.*[13]

Sophia & the Serpent

For the Catholic church, the serpent of Eden became associated with Satan's (or Saturn's influence) over man and woman, especially how the serpent's power led to the act of disobedience itself. The serpent, for the Gnostic mind, was important in the 'act of gnosis' itself and can easily be understood as celestial electromagnetic forces coiled around the Tree of Life, connected to the planets within our solar system. The serpent's disobedience can be symbolised as Satan's supposed imprisonment in the 'circles of hell' (see also the story of Prometheus), which I feel are the creation of Saturn's (Satan's) rings. I do not view the serpent, in the biblical sense, as a totally negative force. As I said, the Gnostics saw the serpent as a powerful force allowing 'electromagnetic' energy to create worlds and solar systems. Without the serpent (Kundalini), we would not access our 'Third Eye' (the Eye of Providence), and we would not be 'charged' as electromagnetic beings. Both the serpent and Eve in this story were always present in the garden amongst the stars – Orion's Stars. The serpent and Eve (the goddess Sophia) have been blamed, shamed, and denied by 'established' faiths. Eve is an aspect of Sophia and came *not* from the physical body of a 'fallen', genetically modified Homo-Adam, who is now spiritually encased in a fake (illusory) Earth-matrix. Lower Aeons ensnare the fallen Adam (fallen humanity), or archons standing between humanity, Malkchut (the matrix earth), and the higher worlds of the hermetic Qabalah. The biological (physical) Adam and Eve are not the original celestial versions symbolised through the heavenly Adam, Sophia, and the Tree of Life. The various Gnostic sects that predate official Christianity understood the power of the serpent (kundalini) as an awakening process. One example of this is the Gnostic Naassenes (Essenes), also generally known as Ophites, whose name derived from the word 'ophis', the Greek word for serpent.

A Fallen Eve

According to Greek myth, after humans received the stolen 'gift of fire' (creative Imagination) from Prometheus, an angry Zeus (or Demiurge) decides

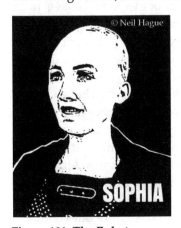

to give humanity the gift of 'punishment' to compensate for the knowledge given to humans. The myth tells of Zeus commanding Hephaestus to mold from the earth the first woman, a 'beautiful evil whose descendants would torment the human race'. Hephaestus created a 'haunted woman' called Pandora to drive men mad. I'll have more to say about Pandora in a later chapter. Still, Pandora's box of magic and chaos, according to myth and legend, was let loose on humanity for Prometheus's disobedience. Hephaestus's creation, Pandora, and the 'Pepos Kore' sculpture of a female figure found in Athens 530BCE (with its almost 'alien-like' artificial glare), looks remarkably 'robot-like', the significance of which will become more apparent when I

Figure 101: The Robot Sophia.
A *fallen* Eve the *first* 'robot citizen' on Earth in 2017.

consider ancient robots in a later chapter. It's interesting to note that a country with one of the most austere forms of Islam, 'Wahhabism', made the robot 'Sophia' the first 'robot citizen' on earth in 2017 (see figure 101). An 'inversion' of the true meaning of the aeon goddess Sophia. The robot came to us courtesy of the Future Investment Summit in Riyadh, where Sophia was granted Saudi Arabian citizenship, becoming the first robot *ever* to have a nationality. When robots are given 'citizenship' you have to wonder what next? What kind of future awaits humanity as robots become the norm?

The Roman Catholic Church, along with various Abrahamic strands,

like Wahhabism, have sought to demonise Eve (the goddess Sophia) so to
suit their agenda to *control*. Eve, like all women, through the eyes of the
'Demiurge-driven religions', has been forever 'dominated', abused and controlled. The original Earth (Sophia) has been 'dominated' too, in my view,
by a demented creator that ancient priests (mainly men) called God.

The good news is that time is running out for those that seek to eternally
'divide', 'dominate' and 'suppress' the original human being. The
Anthropos (the lower Adam) was born of a union between the higher-celes-
tial (Aeon) feminine and masculine forms known as the heavenly Adam
(Christos) and Eve (Sophia). The unification of both celestial male and
female standing at the Tree of Knowledge, symbolically speaking, gives us
the potential for all duality to cease, and for the 'two' to become 'one'
again.

We need to 'see' beyond duality and division, which is not easy when
we are continuously persuaded through all forms of media to 'believe' in
separation. The obsessive social distancing 'mantra' and 'mask wearing'
attached to the Covid-19 pandemic is a classic example of 'separating
humanity' from each other. There are other factors relating to social distancing, masks and a Cyber-Grid Empire, something I will explore in *Part Two*.
As the Gnostics would say, we need to be as 'wise as serpents, but as harmless as doves'. Being human means we need to consider higher forces from
beyond (or behind) the Sun (and solar system); go further in our quest for
freedom, beyond the many religions, restrictions and systems that are holding us in mental servitude. The fall of Adam and Eve did not end in Eden;
we have *continued* to fall further towards worshipping Artificial Intelligence
(AI) on earth. All forms of Artificial Intelligence, from microchipping
humans, to the 'rise of robots' in everyday life, are all signs of our continued fall, a subject that deserves a chapter itself later in the book.

Adam, the Turtle, Chariot and 'Magician' Archetypes

The difference between the 'higher Adam' and 'fallen' (or lower) Adam
(Adamas or Geradamas), has to be understood through knowing one cannot exist without the other, just as 'yin and yang' connect to create the
wholeness of being. It is the higher Adam (which acts as the bridge
between worlds above in the esoteric sense) and gives us what many mystics have called the divine form. The higher Adam could be said to appear
through Orion and its nebula – the place where young stars are born. In
Mayan mythology, the higher Adam is 'Itzamna' (the 'upper god' and creator deity) thought to reside inside the sky. Itzamna, and the root 'itz' is a
word that could relate to all sorts of secretions (such as dew, sap, and
semen) and also sorcery. In Maya mythology, Itzamna was an agent in the

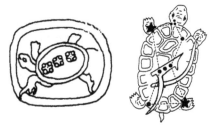

Figure 102: The Orion Turtle.
The three-crested Musk turtle in Mayan myth is another representation of Orion.

creation of the *three*-stone hearth, a location the Mayan believed to be in the centre of the Orion Nebula, often symbolised as the Orion turtle. According to Mayan myth, the turtle stars are in the Orion constellation and are related to the freshwater 'Musk turtle', or 'three-crested turtle from Tzel' due to three distinct ridges on its shell (see figure 102). The Bonampak murals (600-900 BC), an ancient Maya archaeological site in the Mexican state of Chiapas, clearly show the turtle connected to Orion's three belt stars, along with other images of Saturn, Mars and Gemini (the twins).

The Mayan myths of the hero twins, Hunahpu and Xbalanque, touched

Figure 103: Adam the Charioteer.
The Chariot with the Son of Man who dances between the Sun and the Moon.

on in earlier chapters, were also said to have appeared through a crack on the back of the cosmic turtle at the place of creation – where Orion's belt stars sit. Early astronomers, including Galileo, somehow seemed to miss this crucial area of the Orion Nebula, an area that the conquistador Jesuits didn't want the masses to know anything about, as we shall see. In the book of *Daniel* and *Ezekiel*, man's star body is spoken of as a chariot-like form.[14] The Chariot is another hidden code for the celestial Adam, the Son of Man (Orion) portrayed as vessels recorded in ancient art and texts (see figure 103). In the words of *Daniel* (7.13): "I saw in the nightly vision and behold, one like the son of man came with the clouds of heaven, and he came even to the Ancient of Days, and he was brought before Him." The Chariot with is the Son of Man who dances between the Sun and the Moon in much symbolism. Jesus is often positioned between the Sun and the Moon in numerous Saxon and Celtic Christian churches. In this sense, the Son of Man archetype represents an 'absolute form', the *logos* and the 'higher Adam', possibly made manifest in its celestial form as Orion. What I am trying to convey here is 'continuity' of the use of such an archetype, on one level, but also an understanding that one of the main constellations visible to humanity, and found in myths relating to Orion (and other celestial bodies), is coded *within* the tarot. Let us examine a few examples.

The Queen and the Chariot

The seven planets, or satellites focusing on the lower realms of the heavenly Adam, are a sidereal connection to the Son of Man archetype. Adam (Orion) can be seen as the first of the 'sevenfold series' of *true prophets*, comprised of Adam, Seth, Noah, Abraham, Zoroaster, Buddha, and eventually, Jesus. All of this is *code* for the heavenly Adam, or Orion. The number *seven*, seems significant to the Son of Man symbolism as it relates to 'heaven' (through *three* directions) on 'earth' (which has *four* physical directions). There are also *seven* main visible stars forming the torso of Orion, more on these stars later.

The *seventh* card in the tarot is the Chariot, and the square on the charioteer's chest can be seen as a representation of the hermetical view of the four worlds, which are said to be: Atziluth (Emanation/Close); Beriah (Creation); Yetzirah (Formation); Asiyah (Action) see figure 104. Below

Asiyah, the lowest spiritual world, is Asiyah-Gashmi, our *physical* Universe. The noun Merkabah 'thing to ride in', or a 'cart' is derived from the consonantal root r-k-b with the general meaning 'to ride'. The charioteer, I would suggest, is another version of the celestial Adam. I see the heavenly Adam (Orion) in the archetypes of the *Fool, Magician, Charioteer, Hermit* and the *Star* in the tarot. The latter being more of a Gnostic Christos-Sophia archetype. Through these archetypes, we are taken beyond the mundane world and lifted towards the stars. They represent the promise of what exists beyond the veil.

THE CHARIOT.

Figure 104: The Chariot.
The Chariot is obviously a vehicle, or vessel, driven by a priestly class connected to the stars.

The High Priestess (or Popess) in the tarot is holding the *Torah* and seated between the left and right-handed pillars, or paths, of 'Boaz' and 'Jachin' of Hiram Abiff Freemasonic legend (see figure 105). The tarot has Qabalistic/Hermetic origins as far as I can see.

Figure 105: The High Priestess.
(Left) The High Priestess in the Tarot makes up the *third* pillar, carries the *Torah*, and has an 'X-cross' on her chest. **(Right)** The *three* pillars focused on in the Hermetic Qabalah - the circles represent heavenly bodies (planets).

The idea of a Right and Left-Hand Path in magic and esoteric teachings, stems from Indian roots in Hinduism and Gnosticism and relates to the use of 'magic' and 'Gnosis' (knowing thyself) so to reveal the mysteries. But there are *three* pillars in the High Priestess image in the tarot. The serpent that climbs the 'middle pillar' (or spine), formed by the throne of the High Priestess, is the 'Wayshower' and can lead to Gnosis, Beauty, Justice, and Mercy; all are the teachings of the one called Jesus - the 'Son of Man' – the heavenly Adam.

The High Priestess in the Tarot is also the 'Queen of Orion', who sits on the throne of the earth. She rules over a *fallen* earth a 'horned mistress', the inverted version of Sophia (the opposite of wisdom). The High Priestess is also Semiramis, Artemis and Demeter; the pomegranates in the area behind the queen in the tarot image, are symbols of Hera, the 'pure mother' representing fertility and abundance. But she can also be a symbol of the 'dark queen', or witch, who administers the magic revealed by the Magician, who comes before her in order, in the tarot. Seated between the 'twin' pillars (or towers), The High Priestess is a symbol of duality; as with all life, Orion's projection is duality at work on earth.

Interestingly, Madonna's Super Bowl XLVI halftime show at Imbolc, 2012, showed the iconic 'priestess of pop', 'throned' and symbolically positioned between what appearer to be two pillars of what was Solomon's Temple in biblical times (see figure 106). Her set, which was very impressive, even included two

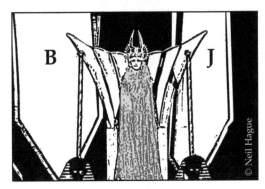

Figure 106: The Iconic Priestess of Pop.
A drawing of Madonna on stage from the 2012 Super Bowl. Is the set replicating the the High Priestess and the Chariot tarot cards, combined?

Sphinxes (with neon eyes) below her, which again can be seen in the

Chariot card. The Super Bowl symbolism seemed to show Madonna's set designers knowledge of the tarot and the Merkabah. Madonna has of course shown a spiritual interest in the Hermetic-Gnostic-Qabalah and has attended various temples over the years, according to news sources, so she could know about such hermetic occult symbolism? Again, I cannot confirm this here, it may all be 'coincidental' and simply artistic inspiration. The 'horns' on her costume also seemed to 'visually' relate to the 'horned gods', connected to Orion 'archetypes', as we shall see in the next chapter.

The Keter and *Corona* Symbolism

In 2019, Madonna became 'Madame X' for her most recent album and also performed at the *Eurovision* song contest in Israel 2019. The show was teeming with *visual* symbolism, not least the use of the 'X' (another Adam -

Orion archetype) see figure 107. Madonna's *Eurovision* show was almost ceremonial-like and featured a giant skull-like face, out of which a 'crowned' Madame X appeared. Pagan goddess figures wearing masks, burning columns, and 'black and white' dualistic symbolism also dominated the performance. The *Eurovision* act seemed not only to be offering up a visual ritual, but part of the performance seemed

Figure 107: X's, Eyes and Skulls.
The X is a symbol connected to spells, 'magic' and other worldly (hidden) dimensions.

to hint at a 'new future' brought on by something 'foul in the air'. From Madame X's eye patch, to the 'crown' on her head (surrounded by gas mask-wearing dancers), the performance seemed highly symbolic to say the least. With the World Health Organisation calling coronavirus their 'Disease X' in early March 2020, you can't help but wonder whether the performance was hinting at a future possible pandemic? Or was it all visionary artistic coincidence? I cannot say for sure, either way.

Even the word 'mask' appears to come from French 'masque' (a covering to hide or guard the face), derived in turn from Italian 'maschera', and Medieval Latin *'masca'*, 'spectre' or 'nightmare'. The latter seems relevant to the nightmare chaos brought on by the *corona*virus pandemic in 2020, not least the implementation of mandatory 'mask wearing' by governments all over the world, more on this later in the book. The lyrics to Madonna's (and rapper, Quavo's) song, *Future*[15] (*Not everyone is coming to the future*), performed at the *Eurovision* seemed to be telling us something profound?

Or was it all just artistic visual coincidence? We shall never know.

Interestingly, 'Corona' is Latin for 'Crown' or 'wreath' (crown chakra), but it is also a word used to describe the 'aura' of 'plasma' surrounding the Sun and other stars (see figure 108). The 'crown' is also the 'Keter' in hermetic Qabalah symbolism, connecting to a higher state of awareness and our ability to *become* conscious, awake, or genuinely self *aware*. The Keter is considered a *portal* and a possible location leading to Orion's Door – *above* the crown. The 'fear' and 'panic' caused by the *corona*virus pandemic, I would suggest, literally 'shut us down' (see the gobal lockdowns), causing much fear, and potentially preventing us from reaching awakened states. Being told to self-isolate and 'keep our distance', or prevented from fully 'living life', would bring only *more* fear; when in truth, the opposite is required to balance such 'manufactured' chaos. The crown is also the hall-

Figure 108: The Corona - Crown.
The symbol of the crown (corona) relates to the 'highest of high' in occult hermetic teachings.

mark of a Cult that has left its 'mark' historically on earth, but at the same time does not originate on earth. Who do you think 'placed' the 'crown' of thorns on the head of Christ, symbolically? The ancient Roman expression of the Orion Cult did. Considering the metaphysical symbolism associated with Gnostic teachings, is it a coincidence that the chaos caused by the *corona*virus was not somehow connected to our ability of accessing levels of awareness beyond the 'crown' (corona) chakra? What did the end of Madonna's visionary-like Eurovision act say? *'Wake Up'*… A strong message for the masses. Yet so many seem to be 'sleepwalking' at this pivotal time on earth.

In all but a few exceptions, 'celebrity worship' seems to exist to replace the old gods of the ancient world with the 'new gods' - big-tech deities and other forms of 'celebritas' for the masses to revere. Celebrities could be seen as the new demigods (the *stars*) that the poor and 'ordinary' are encouraged to look up to. At the time of the *corona*virus pandemic, especially in the UK, celebrities appeared on TV to articulate the 'new normal' and help reinforce the *mantra* of 'stay home - save lifes, etc'. We had A-Listers sharing their face mask selfies on Instagram, from Kim Kardashian to Gwyneth Paltrow. The latter joked about her role in the 2011 movie *Contagion*, saying: "I've already been in this *movie*." The likes of Taylor Swift and Ariana Grande criticized fans on social media for 'not taking the virus seriously', while others unquestionably promoted the official government line of information regarding Covid-19. The likes of Arnold Schwarzenegger and Tom Hanks also became part of the official narrative', appearing on TV with Hanks even posting a picture of a 'single' rubber glove (a hand) on Instagram, after he and his wife tested positive for the virus before the 'lockdown'. The hand symbolism seemed evident in Hank's social media post (see *Chapter Three*). I am not saying Hank's glove photo was a 'decided' image, I am sure it was arbitrary, but as mentioned earlier in the book, the single hand image has occult connotations and all of us at times are influenced by the 'unseen'. Many celebrities are part of the 1% - the mega rich and the upper echelons of society. Many are also said to belong to fraternities based on Greek letters, not least the original, 'Alpha', 'Phi' and 'Kappa' societies, but, in truth, its hard to know for sure if such elite circles exist today. Just as the demigods in myth were there to hold sway over the masses; celebrities and their 'status' (*celebritas*) are often utilised to keep the masses focused on specific narratives. Most won't know they are being asked (or used), but some willingly give their soul to dark forces, serving off-world entities and the Cult I've outlined so far.

The first few chapters have looked at simple correlations, past ages on earth relating to Orion symbolism. I have also illustrated various interconnected themes showing Orion as Adam, the Anthropos, along with the 'fall of the Aeons' into physical form. In the next few chapters, I am going to delve more deeply into the myths and symbolism associated with the 'Star Man' (Orion) and *how* esoteric influences often 'appear' in our world.

Sources:

1) Picknett, Lynn. *The Secret History of Lucifer*. Robinson. 2005, p14

2) *Daniel* (King James version) 7:10.

3) https://en.wikipedia.org/wiki/Samuel_of_Nehardea

4) Yerushalmi Berachot 9 13c; Bavli Berachot 58b

5) Jung, Carl. *Man and His Symbols*. Stellar Books. 2013, p142

6) Dr. Svoboda, Robert E. *The Greatness of Saturn*. Lotus Press 1953, p68

7) *Luke* 10:18

8) *Inferno, Canto XXXIV*, lines 39–45, Mandelbaum translation.

9) Mayor, Adrienn.; *Gods and Robots, Myths, Machines and Ancient Dreams of Technology*. 2018, p134

10) Hancock, Graham. *Fingerprints of the Gods*. Century, 2001, p277

11) *Genesis* 3:22b-24

12) *Genesis* 3:22a

13) Hall, Manly. P. *The Secret Teachings of All Ages* (Reader's Edition). Penguin. 2003, p378

14) *Ezekiel* (King James version) 10:14

15) © Interscope Records (written by Starrah), May 17, 2019

7
SYMBOLS OF THE 'STAR MAN'
The Horned Hunter-God of the Stargates

Who looks outside, dreams. Who looks inside, awakens.

CARL JUNG

I have spent many years perusing books on Alchemy, mysticism and symbolism, and what strikes me most, is how much esoteric 'imagery' (knowledge) seems to be showing us the 'interconnectedness' of the stars and earth. When we consider Alchemy, along with various ancient scriptures of antiquity, there appears to be a common connection between what I will call the 'Star Man' - Orion and Saturn. The World Tree and the full figure of the heavenly Adam, are two-dimensional diagrams that try to explain a heavenly structure through which we 'connect' to the stars. In this chapter, I want to go much deeper into the symbolism around Orion (the Star Man), exploring myths, movies and beliefs which move us further through *Orion's Door*.

Three Pillars

The three pillars can be seen as part of the hermetic structure, forming the metaphysical body of the Star Man - heavenly Adam. Non-physical worlds are channelled through the pillars, which are said to constitute the spirit world *made* physical. According to hermetic mystics, the *left pillar* is female and represents wisdom, justice and splendour; whereas the *right pillar* is male, representing intelligence, mercy and firmness.The two pillars constitute the 'Tree of Knowledge' of Good and Evil (duality), as they are made up of 'imbalanced forces', which according to the mystics can only find equilibrium in the 'central' trunk, or pillar (see figure 109 overleaf).

The central pillar - known as Harmony, or Mildness, or sometimes as the 'Perfect Pillar', is the Tree of Life as mentioned in *Genesis*.[1] It is also 'Irminsûl', the Old Saxon word meaning 'great pillar', or great warrior - see Orion *or* Hercules. The Irminsûl is shaped as a 'T' and relates to the 'Tau Cross', which is another symbol associated with Orion worship. In fact, the

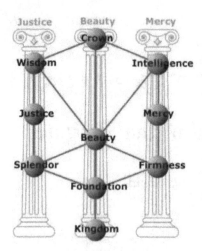

Figure 109: The Three Pillars.
The three pillars talked of by hermetic mystics.

three pillars are connected symbolically to the 'Pillars of Hercules', often depicted with a warrior as the middle (third) pillar. The figure within the pillars is often shown using 'force' to destroy the left and right pillars. Symbolically speaking, going *beyond* the Pillars of Hercules, meant leaving the deception of this world into the realm of higher enlightenment - through Orion's Door. The pillars are said to be doorway and direct channel from the earth to the stars, passing through the Moon, Sun, Saturn to what is the 'crown', or what I see as the Orion Nebula. The symbolism contained within the 'Tree of Life', from the 'head' to the 'toes' of the celestial human, through what is described as the 'middle pillar' (or spine), also seems to connect humanity to the Orion Nebula. When we consider the notion of a holographic Universe (As Above, So Below), it wouldn't be impossible to understand how geography on earth can be mirrored in the stars – namely, the Orion constellation.

All references in the New Testament attributed to Jesus, when he spoke of *true* 'justice' and 'mercy', could be direct references to mystical knowledge and Kabbalistic teachings relating to the Tree of Life and the spiritual body of Adam (The Son of Man) 'projected' out of Orion. Gnostic creation myths say that Adam on high (Orion) was coupled with an aspect of Sophia, called Eve, through the joining of these Aeon forces. Sophia's point of connection with 'solar (star) consciousness', creating a portal into our human world, is *through* the 'central pillar'. When I say human world, I am also referring to non-physical or 'non-local realities' that are part of the whole human being. We are more than flesh and bone and our *imagination* is vital to understanding the true magnitude of human power and creativity.

The Ray of Creation – the Central Pillar

The Sun, Moon and Saturn (along with other wanderers) are said to be governed through what western occultists and alchemists called the 'Ray of Creation'. This Ray was part of an occult system created by George Ivanovitch Gurdjieff (1866-1949) as another representation of the Heavenly Adam. The 'Ray of Creation' is not measured through the 'visible spectrum of light', but is said to project out of the 'Eye of Providence' (the All-Seeing Eye), which is framed by a Trapezium. Just as light passes through every

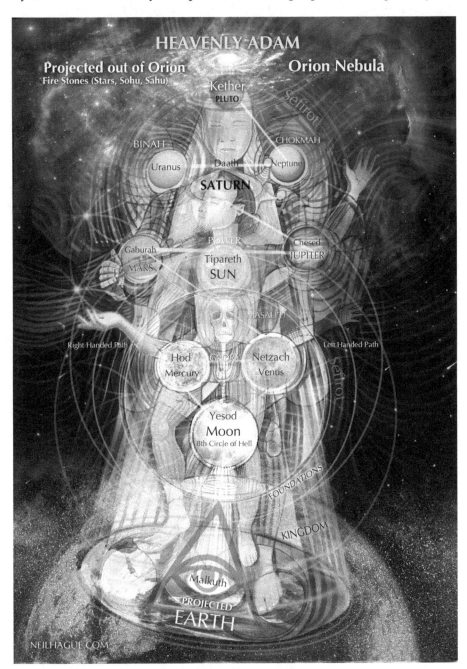

Figure 110: The Ray of Creation and the Central Pillar.
Heavenly Adam and the Three Pillars combined *within* the Ray of Creation. My version of the energetic structure of Adam's heavenly, celestial body. © Neil Hague 2019.

window in a house, The Ray passes through *all* worlds - *all* realities. For example, Gurdjieff, relates various levels of the Ray of Creation with physical, astral, mental, or causal bodies of human beings, and each level, according to Gurdjieff, has a specific density of matter and a specified number of laws. The bodies that construct the 'Star Man' (Heavenly Adam), are the Sun, the planets and the Moon. The 'Flaming Sword' mentioned earlier, is another version of the Ray of Creation (see figure 110 on previous page).

The Ray of Creation forms the body of the Star Man and manifests the physical (illusory) reality called life on earth. From the Gnostic perspective of the human journey through different worlds, the physical reality is a world governed by a 'one-eyed' *foolish* God – the Demiurge. As I say, humanity is being forced (it seems) to accept the *fallen* version of Adam (for reasons I will come to later in the book), rather than the higher states of consciousness (Upper Aeons), through Eve and the earth goddess, Sophia.

Three Pillars or Suns (fires)

According to mystic traditions, there are three suns in each solar system connected to three centres of life. These suns are said to be the 'Spiritual Sun', the 'Solar Sun' and the 'Material Sun'. This concept was described by Jesus (the Gnostics) as the heavenly light *behind* the Sun.[2]

In Gnostic prayers, the three would follow as the 'nous' (mind), 'Christos' (solar plexus) and 'amen' the heart. Other Gnostic trinities connected to the suns are Sophia (wisdom), Erini (peace) and Phronesis (perfection). In the spiritual body of Adam (the Son of Man), in the Gnostic sense, we find the three suns, too. As the great philosopher, scientist and healer, Paracelsus wrote of these three suns:

> There is an earthly sun, which is the cause of all heat, and all who are able to see the sun; and those who are blind and cannot see him may feel his heat. There is an Eternal Sun, which is the source of all wisdom, and those whose spiritual senses have awakened to life will see that sun can be conscious of his existence; but those who have not attained spiritual consciousness may yet feel its power by an inner faculty which is called Intuition.

Manly P Hall expresses the same teaching in his book, *The Secret Teaching of the Ages*, when he writes:

> The Transfiguration of Jesus describes three tabernacles, the largest being in the center (the heart), and a smaller one on either side (the brain and the generative system). It is possible that the philosophical hypothesis of the existence of the three suns is based upon a peculiar natural phenomenon which has occurred many times in history. In the fifty-first year after Christ three suns were seen at once in the sky and also in the sixty-sixth year. In the sixty-ninth year, two suns were

seen together. According to William Lilly, [seventeenth century English astrologer] between the years 1156 and 1648 twenty similar occurrences were recorded.[3]

The appearance of more than one sun could relate to 'Sun Dogs' and other natural phenomena created through light. A subject beyond the remit of this book, but the mystics seemed to place three solar bodies within a 'Grand Man' (the Architect or Ancient of Days) connected to the three centres (or hearts) in the human body: the brain, the heart, and the generative system. The brain represents the mind; the heart is the spiritual centre, and the intestines are the solar plexus and inner knowing. The three suns (or bodies) give life to the celestial human, emanating from spirit to the lower worlds of 'mind' and 'emotion'. As Hall goes on to say:

What the sun is to the solar system, the spirit is to the bodies of man; for his natures, organs, and functions are as planets surrounding the central life (or sun) and living upon its emanations. The solar power in man is divided into three parts, which are termed the threefold human spirit of man.[4]

The Suns (or three stars) in our solar system are the Sun, Jupiter and Saturn, the latter is placed above the sun on the middle pillar because of its importance in the hierarchy. The body of humanity can also be divided into three distinct parts: *spirit, soul* and *body*; and these aspects correlate with the three suns. The Augsburg *Book of Miraculous Signs*, a luxuriously illustrated Roman manuscript (1552 of Augsburg) *Bibliothèque Infernale*, shows three Suns along with the fourth one as a comet. As mentioned in earlier chapters, the fourth Sun (or comet) was considered a symbol of Venus, or Sophia; both connected to Orion. Comets are considered 'major' harbingers of change by many indigenous cultures due to their ancient orbits.

In Masonic books, we find 'Three Lights' (Solar Fire, Stellar Fire, Lunar Fire); 'Three Geometric Solids': *Sphere, Pyramid* and *Cube*. In Alchemy, we have three substances of Mercury, Sulphur and Salt and all variations of the three principles can be connected to Father, Son and Mother. The Three Lights correspond to *Starlight*, Sphere, Mercury; *Solar light*, Pyramid, Sulphur; *Lunar light*, Cube, Salt. The latter combination seems to be telling us something symbolically about the moon's connection to the goddess Selene (salt) and its relationship to Saturn (the hexagram and cube). As I have already touched on, the moon is being used as a vessel by another force, alien in my view, so to create the 'biological matrix reality' we are 'boxed into' on earth (see figure 111 overleaf). I feel that three suns also relate to three levels of consciousness, which are 'Superconsciousness', Subconsciousness and Consciousness. All of which are connected to Orion's

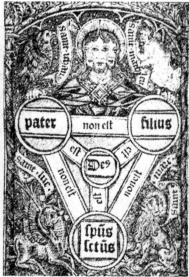

Figure 112: Three Faces, Suns.
Christ – the Son of Man (Adam on High) with *three* faces. © Neil Hague

Figure 111: Humanity Vibrationally 'Boxed' In.
The biological earth-matrix reality keeps humanity ensnared in a cycle of life and death. Yet, our spirits desire true freedom.

invisible Sun, Saturn and our Sun (solar plexus). The Binary sun connection to Sirius and our Sun also affects consciousness and it is no surprise to realise that consciousness and imagination are our links to eternal, infinite worlds beyond the structure of the solar system. Byzantine Christian art showing Christ with three faces, along with depictions of Brahma and Buddha also with three heads, alludes to the 'power of three' faces or suns (see figure 112).

Figure 113: Mayan Earth Turtle.
The earth turtle Itzamna, connects to Orion's three belt stars.

In the Mayan Madrid Codex, we see a clear image of the structure that connects these suns to the earth (through the turtle) suspended from cords linked to what some believe to be Orion as it hangs below the ecliptic (see figure 113). Orion's three stones (or stars) and the earth (the turtle Itzamna, I mentioned in the last chapter) are linked; it is the location from which the Maize God, Hun Hunahpu (the First Father), was said to rise from during his resurrection. The common themes here are a 'trinity' of forces, bodies, suns or pillars. All of which gives us a *triad* of suns or stars *making* the Heavenly Adam – the 'first father figure', who is born and ascends to a point of origin in the stars of Orion.

The Goddess of Wicca's, sometimes portrayed as the 'Triple Goddess', can be connected to the 'three bodies'. She also has a masculine consort, the Horned God, of whom I'll have more to say shortly. The term triple goddess can be used outside of Neopaganism, which often refers to three forms, or aspects, of one goddess. These three figures are often described as the Maiden, the Mother, and the Crone; each symbolize a separate stage in the female life cycle and a phase of the moon. Madonna used triple goddess symbolism in her 1998 music video *Frozen*, where she splits into three figures. On another level, I feel that the triple goddess symbolism relates to original consciousness, or spirit of the Earth (Gaia), the Moon (Selene) and the Sun (Langa), all of which can be seen to be expressions of Sophia's higher state of awareness. Carl Jung, in his work, theorised that the triple goddess was connected to a male archetype. One example being Diana becoming three (Daughter, Wife, Mother) through her relationship to Zeus, a male deity. The goddess, Hecate, was considered the mistress of the 'three realms' through her relationship to the moon, the corn, and the realm of the dead (the chthonic world).[5] The important connections to the Triple Goddess and the number three, are the moon and the Chthonic (Death) Cult of antiquity who focus on the Underworld, Saturn and Orion.

Black Star (Sun)

There is a belief in alchemic and hermetic traditions in the existence of two suns: a *hidden one* of pure philosophical gold, consisting of the essential fire conjoined with aether, and the *apparent one* of profane, material gold. The 'apparent' sun being the sun in our sky. Alchemy says the apparent 'material sun' leads to the 'dark sun' (or black Star), another name for Saturn.

In Alchemy, the spirit and soul are divided through 'polarity' created by Saturn (the Black Sun), which also carries subtle frequencies through the subconsciousness to our conscious mind. The colour black often worn by priests since ancient times, is simply Black Sun worship, connecting to what hermetic occultists call, 'Absolute Darkness' – or the 'Dazzling Darkness' (see figure 114 overleaf).

According to the *Book of the Holy Trinity* (a fifteenth Century German manuscript), the 'Dark Sun' (or black star), appeared after Adam's (Orion's) fall, a story of how humanity was made 'from the black sun's fire'. It was a lower light, or *lesser* light, one that is mentioned in *Genesis* 1:3: And God said, "Let there be light," and there was light. 13th Century Spanish mys-

Figure 114: Black Sun.
The 'dark material fire' of the black sun, as seen by 17th Century Alchemists. Taken from Daniel Stolcius alchemical works, *Viridarium Chymicum*, Frankfurt, 1624. (Public domain.)

tics, such as Joseph Gikatilla said: "... the fall of Adam (Orion) destroyed the smooth relationship between the upper and lower Sephiroth (Tree), destroying the unity of heaven and earth."[6] Thirteenth Century Kabbalistic teachings refer to this light as 'vibration' called 'Ain Soph', which is energy (light) contracting and expanding; creating life. The Black Star receives the light or blood (plasma) of the Universe and channels it to other planets. All stars, nebulae and suns are channels for the 'Absolute Darkness'.

Our Black Star – Saturn is an important focus for elite Cults on earth because of its vibrational connection to Orion.

Gas giants, like Saturn and Jupiter, have some of the characteristics of brown dwarfs. Like the Sun, Jupiter and Saturn are made primarily of the gases hydrogen and helium. Saturn is nearly as large as Jupiter, despite having only 30% of the mass. Three of the giant planets in the Solar System (Jupiter, Saturn and Neptune) emit much more (up to about twice) the heat they receive from the Sun and all three giants have their own 'planetary' systems – their moons. Saturn has *sixty-two* moons (9 are waiting to be officially named) with the largest moon, Titan, the home for many a *Marvel* Comic book bad guy. According to astrophysicists, Brown Dwarfs can maintain magnetic fields of up to 6 kg in strength and approximately 5 – 10% of Brown Dwarfs appear to have strong magnetic fields and emit radio waves. Saturn is a planet/star shown to emit both 'sound waves' and strong mag-

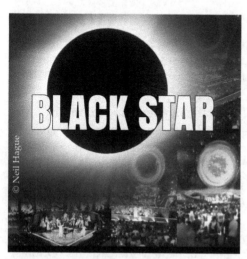

Figure 115: Black Sun (Star)
From Black Sun to Saturn's Star, as seen at the 2019 *Eurovision* Song Contest.

netic fields. There seems to be much ancient religious focus centred on this planet/star and its power source – or central fire – Black Sun.

In recent years I have seen the use of the 'Black Sun/Star symbolism' in graphics on TV programs such as *Heroes Reborn* and in 2019 at the *Eurovision* Song Contest, where a globe starts out as a black orb, or sun, before it eventually morphs into the star (see figure 115).

A 'Star Man' Passes

On the 10th of January 2016, legendary and talented musician David Bowie (real name David Robert Jones) died at the age of 69, two days after his birthdate and the release of his final album, *Black Star*. I loved Bowie's music. The imagery on the album was Masonic in parts, not least the music video for the track *Black Star*. From button-eyed, blind prophets, to a jewelled skull inside a spacesuit and crucified scarecrows, the imagery indeed showed Bowie's interest and knowledge of alchemy, the occult and some of the themes covered here in this book. The woman with a tail in the video who is seen looking at the dark star (sun) and who goes on to reveal the skull in the space suit, seems to hint at another off-planet world. I would suggest the world she is looking at is a moon of Saturn, quite possibly Titan, which is larger than the planet Mercury. The same moon seems to feature in Ridley Scott's *Prometheus* (2012), where the crew, along with the cyborg David 8 (or David Saturn), venture to another planet to discover the origins of humanity. David 8 is played by Michael Fassbender, whose appearance and character in the movie was said to have been inspired by Bowie. The album and the imagery around *Black Star*, feels like it was meant to be an occult message or statement. Sadly, no one will ever know.

The *Black Star* (2016) video seems to feature 'Ormen', which is the name of a village in Norway, the country where Bowie's old girlfriend, Hermione Farthingale, went in 1969 to appear in the film *Song of Norway*. This movie was about the composer Edvard Grieg taken from the musical play by someone going by the name of Milton 'Lazarus'. Ormen also means 'serpent' in Norwegian, a creature mentioned in the writings of the occultist Aleister Crowley, with whom Bowie took an interest in during the 1970s. Bowie even said in one interview called *'David Bowie '04 talks Ziggy Stardust, John Lennon, Aleister Crowley'* (seeYouTube), how he 'fell' into subjects around 'black magic, Qabalism and the whole idea of the 'Crowleyism' of that time; hence the possibility o the 'Star Man' image and the song of the same name. The *Times of Israel* confirmed this by running an article in January 2016 just after Bowie's death saying, *'David Bowie was into the Kabbalah and sang about it.'* The article cites several examples of his 'interest', not least his song titles, such as *Station to Station*, a song about 'Keter' to 'Malkuth'. It seems Bowie was (in the past) actually into the Hermetic Qabalah, with its connections to the Golden Dawn, Aleister Crowley and teachings that encompass astrology, occult tarot, geomancy, and alchemy.

Another track on the *Black Star* album, *Lazarus*, throws at us symbolic themes connected to death (possibly Bowie's own) and the usual Jesus narratives of the resurrection (life after death). I also find it intriguing that Bowie won a 'Saturn Award' (Award for Best Actor), for his performance in the 1976 Science Fiction film, *The Man Who Fell to Earth* (see figure 116). Bowie also had a leading role in the TV Drama/musical, *Baal* (1982). Bowie played Baal, a young amoral, rebellious poetic genius who, after a short and eventful life of debauchery, betrayal and violence, cuts his ties to the world and meets his doom.

Baal (Ba'al) was the Canaanite Jesus figure (god) associated with both Saturn and Orion. The blind, or missing-eyes imagery of Bowie in the *Black Star* video could also be another symbolic version of Orion, who was blinded by Oenopion, the son of Ariadne. The goddess, Ariadne was the creator of mazes and labyrinths, and of course, guess who played Jareth, the Goblin King in the 1986 movie, *Labyrinth*? Mr Ziggy Stardust, the late Pop Star Icon himself. Some of the imagery in *Black Star* certainly looks like imagery in the movie, *Labyrinth*. As I have mentioned in the last chapter, Prometheus (the god who 'fell to earth') also represents an *aspect* of Saturn, as a young man, before he becomes Cronos the old man. In the

Figure 116: The Star Man, David Bowie.
My rendition of the 'Star Man' from *The Man Who Fell to Earth*.

myth, an immortal Prometheus is bound to a rock, where an eagle, sent by Zeus, feeds on his *liver*, which would then regenerate overnight, only to be eaten again the next day. Bowie, we are told, died of liver cancer.[7] It's all highly symbolic, whatever the story was regarding Bowie's life and death.

While writing this chapter, I was reminded of the hypnotic song '*Black Sun*' by Dead Can Dance (written by Lisa Gerrard and Brendan Perry), which eerily sums up symbolic and 'numerological significance' to both Saturn and Prometheus and the number 69 (Bowie's age when he died). It is said that Saturn has a speed of 9,69km/sec, and as I have pointed out through my art and blogs going back ten years, Saturn is the epitome of control *over* 'perception' in our world-matrix, not least through the media, sex and *fear of death*. Orion and Saturn (especially Betelgeuse) are linked.

A black star is also a gravitational object composed of matter. It is a theoretical alternative to a black hole. A black star with a radius slightly greater than the predicted event horizon for an equivalent-mass black hole will *appear* 'very dark', because almost all light produced will be drawn back to the star. Any escaping light will be severely, gravitationally 'red-shifted' (referring to the shift of the wavelength of a photon to a longer wavelength). A black star could easily appear almost exactly like a black hole to consume star fire (energy), or 'holy fire', as the alchemists call it. Heraclitus (6th Century BC) refers to the holy fire as 'artistic' fire. And its *invisible* effect supposedly distinguishes the work of alchemists from that of mundane chemists (scientists). Bowie was undoubtedly an artistic fire to be reckoned with in his lifetime, and his visionary work was certainly 'alchemical' and genius in my view.

Black Sun – Holy Fire Symbolism

The Black Sun is said to be the result of the first stage of the '*Opus Magnum*', another name for alchemy, or what alchemists call the 'blackening' or spiritual transmutation of the Philosopher's stone. The complete *Opus Magnum* (or Great Work) ends with the production of gold (the apparent Sun). The alchemical Black Sun symbol was used widely over the years. The Nazis used the symbol, which can be found in places like the former SS Generals' Hall (Obergruppenführersaal) on the first floor of the North Tower of Wewelsburg Castle in East Germany. Other renditions of Black Sun symbolism can be seen in various religious-esoteric literature, also used by musicians such as COIL and Boyd Rice, the latter created *Children of the Black Sun*, released by Mute Records in 2002. Rice, an American experimental sound/noise musician using the name of NON since the mid-1970s, is an archivist, actor, photographer, author and member of the *Partridge Family Temple* 'religious group'. Other uses of Black Sun symbolism can be found in *Black Sun Rising*, a fantasy novel by American writer C. S. Friedman. The Temple of Set, established in the United States in 1975 by Michael Aquino - an American political scientist, military officer, and high-ranking member of Anton LaVey's Church of Satan, also used Black Sun symbolism. It is a symbol that clearly relates to the 'darker' aspects of star/sun worship.

In Mesoamerican mythology, the Black Sun had many mystical meanings. Among them was its connection to the 'feathered serpent' god Quetzalcoatl and his movement in the Underworld. For the Mesoamericans, there were two suns, the 'young Day Sun' and the Ancient Sun, the *Dark* Sun. And Quetzalcoatl was said to journey between both Suns through the Solar Tree. Some scholars regard the mythological Black Sun as female in origin, which could allude to the Gnostic understanding of Sophia and her offspring (the Demiurge) I mentioned in *Chapter Four*.

The Aztecs associated the passage of the Black Sun, on its journey through the Underworld, with the image of a butterfly. The butterfly, in turn, is an archetypal symbol of the transcendent soul, its transformation and mystical rebirth. It is also seen in the figure of the frightening earth goddess, 'Itzpapalotl', called the 'Obsidian Butterfly', which could also be another Sophia figure in her fallen state. The Monarch butterfly, along with the moon and the skull, are all Underworld symbols relating to darker rituals connected to Saturn and Orion, not least MK Ultra - mind control. In Aztec belief, Itzpapalotl devoured people during solar eclipses, while the Aztec Underworld was the eternal dwelling place of souls. According to the *Codex Rios*, the Underworld was made of 'nine' layers, or points (like the Tree of life). The first level was between the Moon (Yesod) and the Earth's surface (Malkuth-pronounced mahl-KOOT), a 'portal' often symbolised as the 'face of a gigantic toad' that devoured the dead and gave passage to the other eight lower levels. These lower levels are the levels of hell recorded in texts such as Dante's, *Inferno*. The souls of the dead were said to occupy the ninth level, known as the place of 'Mictlan Opochcalocan' (another version of the Hopi Masau'u god from Orion). As I will come to later in the book, the nine levels are the 'invisible scaffolding' of the Solar System, one of which is the Black Sun-Star, which is connected to Orion. The Aztecs called the stars of Orion's Belt and sword area, the 'Fire Drill' and their rising in the sky signalled the beginning of new fire ceremonies, a ritual performed by the Aztecs to postpone what they saw as the end of the world.

From Orion to Saturn

The Cult of the Star Man is 'Orion and Saturn worship' *combined*, which is why there are connections to these celestial figures through ancient myths. The 'Nine Rings', or 'Holy of Holies' found in alchemical and Kabbalistic books, are, from my research, the symbolic circuitry connecting 'Orion to Saturn'. It was said that souls would descend the 'nine layers' of the 'Underworld' in an arduous four-year journey until eventually reaching 'extinction' in the deepest part - 'Mictlan Opochcalocan' – the 'Place of the Dead'. Mictlantecuhtli was particularly worshipped in the Aztec month of Tititl, equivalent to Roman Saturnalia (December), where, at the temple of Tlalxicco, an 'impersonator' of the god was sacrificed and incense was burned in his honour. The ancient sacrifice of a 'scapegoat' at Yom Kippur at the beginning of autumn (Atum), as part of the Jewish faith, seems to be connected to the 'time of year' when Orion becomes a focus astrologically.

Author Micheal Talbot, in his excellent book *The Saturn Myth*, produces compelling ancient evidence for Atum as the 'Great Father-figure' connected to Saturn, and the impersonator Demiurge, mentioned in earlier chapters. What I find interesting is how Saturn-Orion connections can be seen

by looking closely at ancient deities such as Atum. For the ancient
Egyptians, Atum, was the 'ancient voice of heaven' (the word), and a sta-
tionary god of the sky. Talbot proposes that Atum could have been a representation of an ancient Saturn, *fixed* in a position nearer to the Earth. The
Egyptian *Book of the Dead* describes Atum (Re) as the 'god of the celestial
ocean' and masculine power of heaven or a luminous seed.[8] I feel that
Atum-Re, as described here, is a *vehicle* by which Orion became connected
to Saturn. More so, Atum is a vibrational (energetic) connection to Saturn
reaching back symbolically to an ancient source; its possible origins in
Orion's star, Betelgeuse. You could say that from Atum's 'limbs' emanates a
totem-like 'assembly of projections', which became Adam on High – the
Star Man (Orion).

In *The Way of the Sacred: The Rites and Symbols, Beliefs and Tabus, That Men
Have Held in Awe and Wonder Through the Ages* (1974), anthropologist Francis
Huxley correlates Orion with Saturn. He suggests that Saturn can be found
in Orion, as they are part of the same family of stars.[9] Many of the titles
given to gods associated with Saturn can also be equated with Orion; Osiris
and Horus are two perfect examples. The notion of a Saturnian deity
(Saturnus), watching over the annual 'agricultural cycles' on earth for the
ancients, is exactly what Orion also does. Not least through Egyptian and
Dogon deities such as Osiris and Lébé, who are both connected to millet
grain and other crops. Huxley wrote:

> He [Cronos] *is also to be found in the constellation Orion, who wields that sick-
> le-shaped sword called a falchion and which farmers call a billhook. Like all con-
> stellations, Orion has been called by many names, though in this case they all
> bear a close resemblance. For the Egyptians Orion was associated with Horus and
> the soul of Osiris; in Hindu Brahmana he is seen as Prajapti in the form of a stag
> [Orion]; several nations in the middle East refer to him as the Giant, or the
> hunter Nimrod mighty before the Lord; and he was Saturnus to the Romans.*[10]

Hunter Star (Saturn) Man

A classic image of the Star Man is the Assyrian god, Ashur, who also resembles Orion. The image of Ashur with his bow and raised right hand is similar to the classic image of Orion (see figure 117 overleaf). He is also visually
positioned inside an orb or wheel (a door) and his wings, along with this
circular device, resemble Saturn.

The word 'Ashur' is derived from the Arabic word for Sirius, 'Al Shi'ra'
and the ancient Assyrian city of Ashur. Here we have another warrior god
who travels in some sort of sky wheel or ship, with its winged disk (dis-
playing horns) enclosed by four circles revolving around a middle circle.
Ancient depictions of Saturn, according to some researchers, not least

David Talbot, show how it was
often drawn as a winged disc.
The crescent and the circle combined is another symbol for the
ancient image of Saturn. Here,
once again, we see the symbolism of the horned celestial deity,
which is of importance to the
Orion Cult, as we shall see.

Figure 117: Ashur - The Star Man.
The 'hunter,' archer, Star Man – Ashur *is* Orion
and Saturn combined.

Another deity is called
'Hadad', from the Levant (now
Syria and Lebanon), the son of
'Nanna' or 'Sin' and 'Ningal
Hadad' mentioned in *Chapter Two*; Hadad was an important figure. He was
introduced to Mesopotamia by the Amorites, where he became known as
the Akkadian (Assyrian-Babylonian) god, Hadad or Adad. Hadad was also
called 'Pidar', 'Rapiu' and 'Baal-Zephon', often shown holding a club and
thunderbolt and wearing a bull-horned headdress (see figure 118). In the
second millennium BCE, the King of Aleppo (Syria) called himself 'the
beloved of Hadad'.

The god Ba'al is another variant of Hadad; both represent the combination of Orion, with Saturn and
Taurus as celestial figures. Baal-
Saturn, or 'Ba'al Hammonis' was
another Romanised deity worshipped in Carthage and North
Africa. The 'combined deity'
shows us again the connection
between two celestial deities –
Orion and Saturn. Both archetypes
were depicted as a bearded, older
man with curling ram's horns. The
warrior ruler, Alexandria the
Great, also saw himself as Baal
Hammon (see figure 119). Just as

Figure 118: Baal - Orion.
The horned warrior Hadad, or Baal-Zephon.

Orion, the celestial man, giant hunter and guardian of the stars was 'placed'
to hunt all of earth's creatures. The myths associated with Orion included
the archetype of the *artist* and the *war god*, Mars; both connected through
the 'art of war'. The symbols of Orion (the giant *first* man), Saturn (the
bringer of time and death) and Mars (the originator of war), all *combine* in
the post-flood world age I call: the Age of Orion (see *Chapter Two*).

Figure 119: Alexandria the Great.
Depicted as the horned Baal Hammon.

Figure 120: Stag Head.
The 'Stag', eagle
and 'triptite' masks
of Nimrod are symbols connected to *ancient* Orion-Saturn Cults.

Another name for Orion was 'Mithra' and 'Migra', the deer with horns, or stag-man with antlers; which is probably why ruling bloodlines kept the hunted 'stag head' trophies on the walls of their stately homes? Mithra became a cult for the Soldiers of the Roman Empire (along with Mars) and its history goes back to the time of Zoroaster (Persia). Mithra (or Mitrash) was said to be the 'Governor of the Sun' (Solar System), or 'he that powers the sun', indicating there is something more behind the celestial giants, the Sun, Saturn, Jupiter and the planets. Mithra was connected to our Sun, and to Archangel Michael, a figure I will explore in later chapters. Interestingly, the Rothschild's Surrealist Ball of 1972, hosted by the glamorous international socialite, Baroness Marie-Hélène de Rothschild, from the photographs publsihed online, all seem inspired by occult symbolism. Attendees of the ball at the Chateau de Ferrières, are shown to be wearing all manner of esoteric masks and costumes, notably a stag head (see figure 120). Masked balls, throughout the ages, offer a range Pagan, occult Orion-Saturn symbolism.

From Orion to Cassiel and the Eighth Circle of Light

The circles, or realms, descending symbolically from an upper central sun through the Tree of Life are said to number 1 to 9 (making 10) and these are the primary numbers from whence all others derive. Danté described the Eighth Circle in his 12th Century work, *Inferno*, as a place where 'deception' dwelt. Interestingly, it is written that the 'Eighth Sin', or the 'Eighth Circle', called 'Malebolge', was often depicted as the upper half of Hell, the place of the *Fraudulent* and *Malicious*. Why am I thinking of Earth's ruling elite going back into antquity? These circles (or rings) are also realms or frequencies that align with the so-called 'Seven Deadly Sins' through the Eighth Circle, and depicted as a human 'eye' by the 15th Century artist, Hieronymus Bosch.

All of these symbols relate to 'perception' and how the world is created through our perception, our imagination. The circles or 'rings' (if you are a *Lord of the Rings* fan), also relate to constructed hemispheres that 'restrict' human consciousness to form an 'ethereal link' to otherworldly creators: the gods, goddesses and angels (archons) we call the Planets, and electro-magnetic light (or plasma).

According to the *Book of Enoch*, the angelic host, 'Cassiel' (also known as Qafsiel/Qaphsiel), is described as the 'ruler' of the Seventh Heaven. The host acts as guardian to a 'doorway', through which souls would pass into the Seventh Hall (or Heaven) found in the *Hekhalot Rabbat*; a spell book sometimes referred to as the *Books of the Palaces* and the *Chariot*.[11] Cassiel is a guardian armed with a 'lightning-dripping sword' and a *bow* of light; he can summon powerful wind weapons, which he uses against anyone not fit to see God (the Demiurge). Cassiel is also described in the *Hekhalot Rabbat* as one of three guardians of the entrance of the seventh palace, alongside the angels 'Dumiel' and 'Gabriel'. In the *Ma'aseh Merkavah*, a mystical text dating from the Gaonic period (589 CE), Cassiel is the 'Prince of Saturn' and regent of Capricorn.[12] The Key of Solomon shows the angel Cassiel (sometimes an archangel) residing over Saturn (Sabbath Day/Saturday). He is depicted in Francis Barrett's *The Magus* as a dragon-riding jinn with a beard who rules over Saturn.[13] Such imagery I have found inspiring from an artistic view point.

Lord of Duality

Another aspect of Saturn dominion over time and Orion's fall into duality, is the cosmic world dynamic of 'Rex Mundi' (another name of the Demiurge mentioned in previous chapters). Here we have a demonic force *personified* by Asmodeus, at the 'door' of the Church of Rennes-le-Château in France (see figure 121). It is not my intention to delve into the Rennes-le-Château mystery here, but suffice to say that the symbolism of the 'devil at the door', the Magdalena Tower (with its 22 steps) is an important aspect of Gnostic and Hermetic mysticism I've illustrated so far. The statue of Asmodeus represents the 'false God', the Demiurge's influence over Saturn, through the angel Cassiel and the other fallen angels. In the *Dictionnaire Infernal* (1818) by Collin de Plancy, Asmodeus is depicted with the breast of a man, a cockerel's leg, serpent tail, three heads (one of a man spitting fire, one of a sheep, and one of a bull), riding a lion with dragon wings and neck. All of these animals are associated with either demonic possession, revenge and the Chimera I mentioned in *Chapter Four*. Each are an embodi-ment of the *demented* Demiurge figure who created the 'fall' of humanity and punished Prometheus.

The Solar Mysteries trace the soul's development and 'evolution'

Figure 121: A 'horned' Asmodeus (Rex Mundi) at the 'door'.

through the Ray of Creation, as mentioned at the end of the last chapter. The human soul connects with the Ray of Creation, projected from the centre of *all-that-exists*. What prevents us from going beyond the minor doors (or portals) contained within the Tree of Life (the body of Adam on High), *is* Rex Mundi. Or, as *it* is described in Judeo-Islamic lore, the king of the earthly spirits – the 'King of the World'. Rex Mundi is the 'darker' Orion archetype who is forced to watch duality unfold in 'time and space', never going beyond Orion's Door. Hence, Asmodeus (Rex Mundi) sits at the door of Rennes-le-Château, looking over a masonic, dualistic checkered floor. He is like the Marvel Comic 'lord of chaos', 'Dormammu', trapped in 'time (symbolic of Saturn) and space (symbolic of Orion) by the 'Time lord', or *Doctor Strange* for attacking Earth. In this sense, both dark and light forces are 'trapped' in Orion's Gate, or at the Door.

Sense 8 – Saturn

The Netflix Science fiction Drama *Sense 8* (2015), written by the Wachowskis and Straczynski, has a dark Gnostic undertone within its plot. The story tells of *eight* strangers from different cultures and parts of the world all 'birthed' by a woman called 'Angelica', who kills herself to avoid capture by a man named 'Whispers'. The *eight* (symbolic of Saturn) eventually discover they now form a cluster of 'sensates': human beings who are mentally and emotionally linked. They are all born on the 8th August, the Lion's Gate, too, and able to sense and communicate with each other, share their knowledge, language, and skills (telepathy). *Eight*, in this scenario, can be symbolic of the eight spheres of influence forming part of the Gnostic Ophitic system I mentioned earlier. The Wachowskis (formerly The Wachowski Brothers), also created *The Matrix Trilogy* (1999-2003) and *Jupiter Ascending* (2014), almost certainly will have some understanding of the Gnostic symbolism I am covering in this book. They have made some of the most 'cutting edge' films of our time, in my view.

The HBO Television series *The OA* (2016), also has many symbolic references to Saturn, death and the Underworld. The series revolves around Prairie Johnson, an adopted young woman who resurfaces after having been missing for 'seven' years. Upon her return, Johnson calls herself 'The *OA'* (the original angel), exhibits scars on her back and can 'see' despite having been blind when she disappeared. Prairie refuses to tell the FBI and her adoptive parents where she has been and how her eyesight was restored. Instead she quickly assembles a team of five locals (four high school students and a teacher) to whom she reveals key information, also explaining her life story. Finally, she asks for their help to save other missing people whom she claims she can rescue by 'opening a portal' to another dimension. Again with this 'eight'-part series x 2, we are drawn into the influence of Saturn symbolism and the different dimensions associated with death and near-death experiences, as portrayed in the 16 episodes.

Interestingly, the psychopathic doctor in the first *OA* series was called 'Hunter' (Ashur-Orion). 'O' in the Greek alphabet, which is derived from the earlier Phoenician alphabet, is the 15th letter and *Fifteen* is the number associated with the Devil in the tarot, also the number found in the magic square of Saturn. 'A' is Alpha, the first letter of the Greek alphabet and relates to the beginning of 'time', which is ruled over by Saturn. The symbolism contained within much of what is appearing in dramas and movies on TV is often full of Gnostic, Orion and Saturn symbolism.

Orion's Celestial Standoff

Orion plays a considerable role in the shaping of our 'collective thoughts', our beliefs and above all, the belief in duality as it appears in time and space. There are 17 (1=7=8) stars that make up the Orion constellation and we see the linear algebra-like alignments of Orion's *seven* main 'visible' stars oppose each other at diagonals. Duality can be found in many myths and legends, and of course, we see duality all of the time in the 'opposites of nature' – not least through the cycles or seasons on earth. Duality is evident in the stars, especially through Orion and Taurus, as they prepare to fight or *oppose* each other.

In the constellation of Taurus (the bull), we also find seven stars called the Pleiades, or seven maidens as they are described in many myths. In Greek myth, it is said that Orion pursued the Pleiades, named Maia, Electra, Taygete, Celaeno, Alcyone, Sterope, and Merope after he fell in love with their beauty and grace. The hunter goddess, Artemis, asked Zeus to protect the Pleiades from Orion and in turn, Zeus turned these maidens into stars. In the same myth, after Orion's battle with Scorpius, Zeus then turns Orion into a constellation to further pursue the Pleiades in the skies. In other words, these maidens went from being chased on earth, to being chased across the heavens. Zeus, like Orion, seems to love pursuing females! Some say that the 'perpetual hunt' by Orion, is a macrocosm for the chase between all men and maidens on earth. Go out on an average weekend into 'clubland' (not that I do anymore) across the bars and pubs of the western world, and you'll see this phenomena in action. In other stories we see Orion chasing Pleione, the 'mother' of the Pleiades, for seven years (symbolic of the seven stars). Orion seems to like all types of female.

In fact, once you delve a little more deeply into Orion symbolism, it seems much of what is mapped out on earth through ancient art, myths and temple sites, can relate to the 'celestial hunter' and his dogs in the heavens, Canis Minor and Major (or Sirius). The dog leading the hunt is called Procyon and both dogs are said to be chasing Lepus (the hare) or sometimes the fox, while Orion 'stands against' Taurus. In this role, Orion is also Mithra, who 'slays' the Taurine bull. For anyone still following my symbolic threads here, all of these animals feature hugely in the 'hunts' and symbolism of the bloodline aristocracies connected to the Orion and Saturn Cults; fox hunting notably a pastime for the bloodlines who consider themselves to be 'above' all life! In ancient Egypt, Orion was identified with 'Unas', the last Pharaoh of the Fifth Dynasty, who was said to have 'eaten the flesh of his enemies' and devoured the gods themselves, to become great and bring inheritance of his power. According to myth, Unas travels through the sky to become the star 'Sabu' – another name for Orion.

God of the Wild Hunt

The 'Wild Hunt' is a folklore motif historically connected to the beginning of the autumn season found in much European folklore. This time of year is associated with Orion's arrival in the Northern Hemisphere and the autumn equinox and Samhain (Hallowe'en); more on Hallowe'en later in the book. Wild Hunts typically involve a ghostly or supernatural group of hunters passing in wild pursuit. The hunters may be either elves, fairies, or the dead; the leader of the hunt is often a named figure associated with Woden (or Ba'al), both of which are versions of Orion. The Viking raids and legendary figures like Theodoric the Great, the Danish king Valdemar Atterdag, the Welsh psychopomp, Gwyn ap, Nudd and biblical figures such as Herod, Cain and Gabriel are also associated with the hunt.[14] Fox hunting in Europe is connected to the wild hunt archetype and so is the colour red and blue/white, which relate to Orion's stars, a subject I will look at later in the book.

Seeing the Wild Hunt was thought to presage some catastrophe such as war or plague, or at best, the death of the one who witnessed it; people encountering the hunt might also be abducted to the Underworld or the fairy kingdom. In Norse myth, for example, it is Odin (Saturn) who oversees the wild hunt and in English folklore, Herne the Hunter is a ghost associated with Windsor Forest and the Wild Hunt (see figure 122 overleaf).

In all cases, the hunter is *'other-worldly'*, or god-like who gathers to him unseen forces as earth enters into the 'darker-half of the year – from Hallowe'en through to winter. Note the owl in the illustration by Cruishank which is another symbol for the hunter.

Figure 122: The Wild Hunt.
Herne with his steed, hounds and owl.
Illustrated by George Cruikshank, c.1843. (PD)

In the epic Sumerian legend of *Gilgamesh*, the hunter god-king Gilgamesh (another Orion figure) fights the Bull of Heaven. We see the same symbolism in the tussles between Attis and the Bull, through to Perseus and the Minotaur. The latter takes place at the centre of Ariadne's labyrinth, a symbol of the mind and the 'weaver within'. Orion, whether holding a club or bow, is hunting the animal kingdom or nature, and this symbolism can also be found on crests, heraldry and insignias of the elite bloodlines on earth.

In other legends, Orion, out hunting, chases the Pleiades and takes the form of a bear. The myths about Callisto and Artemis (the goddess of hunting) also include the hunter becoming a bear and *bear symbolism* is very much connected to otherworldly giants and Bigfoot, as we shall see in a later chapter. The legends of Bear Butte (Devils Tower) in Wyoming, according to Native American myth, describe the creation of the Butte through the claws of a giant bear, they say scratched at a 'giant tree' as it grew skywards to place the seven maidens, as the seven stars, to become the Pleiades in the sky. Orion is also referred to as a 'Heavenly Shepherd' or the 'True Shepherd of Anu' (a shepherd of bears). Interestingly, the mark of the Hopi Bear Clan can often be found alongside petroglyphs also depicting Masau'u (Orion). The Son of Man, Christ as the 'Good Shepherd', could also be connected to this symbolism. Other Bear symbolism refers to the constellation of Ursa Major (the Plough) as it aligns with the Pleiades and many bear myths relate to star people coming to earth. Homer, in the *Odyssey* referred to "the Great Bear that men call the Wain, that circles opposite Orion, but never bathes in the sea of the stars". Even the *Book of Job*, a Biblical book about God's (possibly the Demiurge's) punishment of Job, mentions Orion: "He is the maker of the Bear and Orion" (*Job* 9:9). The latter I feel, refers to the Gnostic Demiurge, which brings me back to the consciousness that created Orion's form, working through its electromagnetic life force – its stellar doorway.

The 'Unnatural' God of the 'Doorway'

In Lakota and Dakota Sioux, Orion is the horned giant 'Haokah', celebrated through tribal dances to this god-figure (see figure 123). Like Morpheus in Greek myth, Haokah was referred to as the 'unnatural god,' the ruler of dreams.[15] Haokah was simultaneously revered and feared among the Sioux as a deity that could use magic and lightning to destroy worlds. The Thunder-beings honoured by the Lakota also connect to Orion. Thunder, or more importantly, 'lightning', was a weapon attributed to gods connected to Orion; so was the Sacred Clown, or the Fool, said to come from Orion by some of the American Indian tribes. As I mentioned in *Chapter Five*, Kesil, or the 'fool' is Orion and the three-pointed hat of the jester-fool can also be connected to the three belt stars or three hearthstones of Orion. It's worth noting the Hopi word for star is 'sohu' and although the vowels are arbitrary, the Egyptian word for star (particularly those of Orion) is 'sahu'.

© Neil Hague

Figure 123: Orion *or* Haokah in Sioux mythology and belief.
Haokah is the god of the 'doorway', dreams and trickery.

American Indians believe in the existence of many Giants (not least the Bigfoot tribes), but Haokah is one of the principal *celestial* giants. He was the anti-natural god, or the teacher of opposites (duality). For example, in summer he feels cold, in winter he suffers from the heat; hot water is cold to him, and the contrary, etc. He is the god of 'contradiction' and therefore, 'mimicry', which, according to the Gnostics, was a trait of the archons. He was considered a 'double-faced' god, often shown to have a *blue* and *red* face, both colours symbolic of the giant stars Regel (Blue) and Betelgeuse (red). The Norse god, Loki, is another version of Haokah and Loki's sister, the goddess Hel, was said to have a dual visage often coloured red and blue. The same attributes apply to the West African deity 'Eshu', which the Yoruba people, regard as a trickster god. This particular figure was capable of traversing time, haunting gateways (portals) and changing into different forms. In one Yoruba Poem regarding Eshu it says:

Eshu throws a stone today and it kills a bird yesterday.[16]

This particular phrase relates directly to the ability to travel back in time and suggests the ancients were adepts at manipulating time. Eshnu, like Loki of Scandinavian myth, or the antler Celtic god Cernunnos (the hunter/shaman), was also said to be able to move between different worlds through 'doorways'.

The *Rig Veda* refers to the Orion Constellation as 'Mrigashirsha' (the deer's head), or the horned hunter, often depicted as the classic image of the shaman wearing antlers. In Hindu astrology, Orion is connected to both Mrigashirsha and Arudra ('teardrop') and relates to the great hunter – the stag-man. Above the shoulder star of Orion other stars are visible; these are Mrigashirsha, meaning deer's head, also known as 'Agrahayani'. Their brightest star in this cluster is called 'Heka', a bluish star more than 1000 light-years away. Slightly below Heka, two stars are seen: 'Khad Posterior', the brighter one to the side of Betelgeuse (the shoulder star) of Orion, and 'Khad Prior' on the other side. Khad Posterior is like our sun, a yellow star, at a distance of about 120 light-years, whereas Khad Prior is a very distant bluish star nearly 1000 light-years away. 'Heka' (Haokah) also means a 'White Spot'; Khad-al-Geuse means 'Cheek of the Giant'. All of these stars in Orion make up what the Sioux call Haokah, the god of the *doorway*.

CERNunnos

The Celtic deity Cernunnos is another version of this hunter on earth (Herne the Hunter). Like other horned and antler gods, Cernunnos was the 'keeper of the door' between this reality and the realm that is just beyond the veil. All these different versions of the same celestial god (Orion) are symbols for a force sitting just beyond what the Gnostics called the 'boundary', or 'portal that creates our world'. As a side note, I found it fascinating that CERN in Switzerland was set up to 'penetrate that veil' by a priesthood disguised as scientists. A statue of Shiva, who was sometimes depicted with horns, also stands on the grounds above CERN. Shiva is known as the 'creator', 'maintainer' and the 'destroyer' within the 'Trimurti', the Hindu trinity, which includes Brahma and Vishnu.

The statue at CERN captures Shiva performing the Tandava, a dance believed to be the source of the cycle of creation, preservation and destruction. Shiva's dance exists in *five* forms, showing the cosmic cycle from creation to destruction:

- 'Srishti' - creation, evolution
- 'Sthiti' - preservation, support
- 'Samhara' - destruction, evolution
- 'Tirobhava' - illusion
- 'Anugraha' - release, emancipation, grace

As always, it's all about 'star magic' and even though it is said that CERN closed down for two years, none of it is a good omen! The type of wizardry that took place at CERN, doesn't do 'holidays' or 'shut-downs' (lockdowns) in my view. The CERN 'ring' is still working its interstellar magic for sure.

Celestial crossing points between the Milky Way and Earth's solstices on the ecliptic are understood in shamanic traditions to serve as 'doors' to the spirits, or Underworld. Just as there are portals linking Earth and the sun, there also appear to be energetic 'star gates' connecting our Sun to other stars, notably Orion. Saturn (as a star/sun), connects to the main stars of the Orion constellation, especially at critical points at certain times of the year. Symbolically speaking, it seems Saturn is colluding with Orion to construct reality, unseen, but 'felt' at specific times of the year.

Bull of Heaven

From Neolithic cave paintings in France, to images of Cernunnos in Celtic Europe, the deer, bull or bison was often portrayed as a giver of life, a 'protector' but also the hunted. The same themes are attributed to Osiris in Egypt, Orion in Greece and 'Shiva-Rudra' in India. Herne the Hunter and Pan are the most apparent Pagan figures associated with the horned hunter, and both Orion and Saturn. It is worth noting that Yahweh, Amun and Maat (in Egypt) were also depicted with horns or antlers and said to have fashioned the first two people (Adam and Eve) out of clay.

In Sumerian mythology, Orion was called URU AN-NA, which means "the light of heaven", which was specifically part of the Gilgamesh, myths. Sumerians associated Orion with the story of their hero, Gilgamesh, fighting the bull, represented by Taurus. Their name for the constellation Taurus was GUD AN-NA, or 'the bull of heaven.' Both Gilgamesh and the Bull of Heaven were often shown with horns and both were empowered by invisible forces.

Amun of ancient Egypt, often referred to as the hidden one (solar deity), is also depicted with horns. Amun combined with Ra, the sky god, became the 'ultimate god', 'Hidden in the Sky'. Over time Amun began to absorb many other local gods, becoming the great deity of Egypt, who encompassed attributes of all other gods. The ultimate purpose was to raise Ra's cult over the cult of any other god, so the more gods melted into his personality, by doing so, the more powerful was the religion. This merging of gods led to the development of an early form of monotheism; other gods no longer appear independent, but they all enter a 'constellation' as angels subservient the 'one god'. That constellation is Orion and the angelic hosts in relation to Orion will become relevant later in the book. The Egyptian cult of Amun would eventually become Christianity thousands of years later, as Amun absorbed Osiris and his son Horus, and wife Isis. They became the trinity of the Father, the Son and The Holy Spirit. The biblical event of the sacrifice of the 'Passover Lamb' goes back to the cult of the horned (ram) Amun (Egypt), eventually becoming entwined in the Pan/Jesus story.

'Horny as Hell'

The sister/daughter of Loki (Haokah), Hel, is another deity who carries elements of Orion symbolism. Hel (or Hell), also known as 'Notre Dame', was said to be the 'she-trickster' who could be invoked to bring mischief and misguided thoughts on earth. She is the maiden of Betelgeuse and Bellatrix, sometimes depicted in black and white just as Koshari clowns were shown in Native American belief (see figure 124). Betelgeuse and Bellatrix are two of Orion's prominent stars. The 1988 movie *Beetlejuice* starring Michael Keaton, features the 'evil shape-shifting clown' called Beetlejuice, showing him wearing the black and white stripes of Native American Koshari clowns. It's no coincidence that the imagery connects, because for the Lakota Sioux, the Koshari and Haokah were considered 'sacred' and from Orion. Betelgeuse, to be precise! Just don't say his name '*three* times'!

There are also ancient records of a mysterious race of beings associated with what Hopi Indians call the 'Two Horned Clan' (see figure 125). In the ancient world the Hopi talked of 'unnatural gods', the 'rulers of dreams' as having horns. The Hopi said these figures were of the Two Horned Clan, or the 'Two Horn' and 'One Horn' Societies. According to the Hopi, this clan, along with the Unicorn and Bow Clans, perform some of the most significant and oldest ceremonies in their calendar. The Latin word for 'bow' is '*apis*', a word used for the sacred bull of Egypt and the animal into which the dead Osiris was placed and transported, according to legend. The legend of Apis and Osiris would fit with alchemical texts that say, Apollo, Vulcan and Mercury 'conceive Orion' in an allegory of the 'three-fathered philosophical child'. Orion, the child, was born to 'Hyrieus' and called 'Urion' (Urine) emerging from inside the hide of the bull. Osiris was also known as the 'Bull of the West', 'Tem' and aforementioned 'Atum'; all were adorned with horns of the bull (see figure 126). The bull, or Ox, is of course, the constellation of Taurus, of which Orion (Osiris) is connected.

Among the Fon tribe of the former kingdom of the Dahomey, now Tongo in West Africa, we also find alignments with symbols of the Ox, the bull and Orion. According to anthropologists, the Dahomey Amazons as they were called, may have evolved from female, hunter-gatherer tribes called the Gbeto.[17] The Gbeto also performed a ritualistic bull sacrifice, simi-

Figure 124: Koshari Clowns & Orion.
A Koshari compared to the character *Beetlejuice* in the movie of the same name.

Figure 125: Two & One-Horned Clans.
Hopi petroglyphs of Two, and One-Horned beings (their unnatural gods). Drawings copied from rock paintings on the Mesa Verde, Colorado.

Figure 126: Atum - Apis.
Atum and the Bull, Apis. Both are joined just as Taurus and Orion are connected.

lar to Mithriac rituals and symbolism discussed in a previous chapter. Bull sacrifice in the ancient world, through to its last remnants in places such as Spain and Bullfights, are all connected to Orion/Taurus worship. Other symbols that relate to the two-horned deities associated with Orion are the Wall Street Bull, or Ox; both are versions of the constellation Taurus and the elite city of 'Ox'ford in England. The ancient Canaanite god, Moloch, can also take the form of a 'horned' owl (see Bohemian Grove), or bull, and of course, some of this symbolism is found in the street plans of major cities, not least Paris and Washington, DC.

Orion and the Horned Ones

The worship of the 'Unktehi', through to later buffalo-reverence by the plains tribes of South and North Dakota in the USA, are also examples of the importance of Orion/Taurus worship. The stars became intrinsically woven into Native American myths and legends connected to Orion and his stellar neighbors, Taurus and Monoceros (the unicorn) see figure 127 overleaf. Orion's lion skin shield and the Monoceros become the 'Lion and the Unicorn' symbolism featured on the royal coat of arms. The 'Qilin' ('Kirin' in Japanese) is a mythical horned and hooved chimerical creature known in Chinese and other East Asian legend to be connected to the Monoceros (see Figure 128 overleaf).

According to the 5th century BC, *Zuo Zhuan*, an ancient Chinese chronicle, it was said the Qilin appeared prior to the imminent 'arrival', or 'passing', of a sage or ruler. It is interesting how the Monoceros constellation (the unicorn) closely borders Orion, along with Lepus (the Hare) and Gemini (the Twins) – all of which are connected to major Pagan festivals associated with Solstices and Equinoxes, which will become relevant in later chapters.

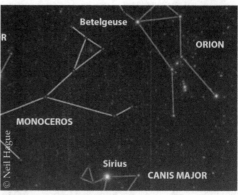

Figure 127: Orion is flanked by Monoceros (Unicorn) and Taurus (Bull).

The Tibetans and the Hopi are said to be the same 'first peoples' and both cultures have ceremonies imitating the two-horned deities mentioned here. Other parallels include the abundant use of silver and coral, turquoise and specific patterns of textiles and long, braided hair (sometimes decorated), worn by both men and women. Native American Pueblo Indians and Native Tibetans both mention the horned gods in their stories and ceremonies (see figure 129). The 'two horns' and the colour symbolism associated with 'red and blue' are also connected to various trickster

Figure 128: The 'Qilin' ('Kirin' in Japanese). The mythical horned lion-like creature.

gods (Mercury, Hermes and the snake) and all these archetypes fit like 'cogs within an unseen clock'; working the 'cycles' of the year, the Solstices and Equinoxes, along with duality fostered in our minds.

The UK government coat of arms, or royal arms, featuring the lion and the unicorn is an expression of the

Figure 129: Hopi and Tibetan Horned Ceremonies. (Left) Hopi Horned Clan. **(Right)** Tibetan 'horned' devil dancers.

Orion archetypes. We have already seen in previous chapters, how the lion relates to the Demiurge and Orion's *fallen* state. The Unicorn, or Monoceros in this context, relates to the 'horned' Shining Ones. The Unicorn is always tethered to the lion (beast) on the royal coat of arms, until recently. However, in 2019-20 the royal coat of arms showed the unicorn to be 'free' and unchained. In late 2019, the unicorn half of the royal coat at Buckingham Palace was said to have been knocked off the palace gate (by a delivery lorry), amidst talk of a *new* King of England called, Joseph Gregory Hallet (the supposed true King John III). I have my doubts about much of this alleged 'new king' narrative, but the lion and unicorn are symbols for ancient bloodlines connected to the Watchers and the Shining Ones mentioned earlier in the book. The unicorn, for example is said to relate to the royal Merovingian bloodlines; to Eleanor of Aquitaine (1122 -1204) and the Angevin kings of England dduring the 12th and 13th centuries. Eleanor's bloodline, through her marriage to Henry II (House of Anjou) became the Plantagenet kings, the most notable being the last Plantagenet, Richard III. Royal 'descent' and royal 'divine right to rule' are thought, by some researchers, to originate from the 'angelic' Watchers or star-seed, notably Orion's stars and his neighbours, Monoceros, Sirius (Canis Minor) and Taurus (pleiades and aldebaran) and Lepus.

The Shining Ones

The horn reference in art, myth and belief is overwhelming and can be seen on stately homes and heraldry. The biblical Moses was sometimes depicted with horns in religious iconography due to the translation by St. Jerome in the 4th Century *Vulgate* (see figure 130). This image of Moses has been passed off as a religious artistic 'mistake'. Yet I doubt Michelangelo made mistakes? Moses here is more likely presented as the previously-mentioned Egyptian 'Atum' figure, adorned with horns of the bull on one level; but it could also be a symbol of being illuminated just as the Watchers were (see *Chapter One*).

The wealthy bishop of 12th Century Paris, Maurice De Sully (who created Notre Dame Cathedral) also used the same *two horns* and the *snake* on his personal seal. The horns are said to be symbolic of being 'glorified' and in many ways they

Figure 130: The Shining Ones.
(Left) A Horned Shining One at Hampton Court. **(Right)** Michelangelo's Horned Moses (c. 1513–1515).

represent the 'rays' of the Sun. However, there is also a connection to the 'Shining Ones' a term used for both the biblical Nephilim and their first-born. The Watchers, or Shining Ones, mentioned in earlier chapters were often depicted with horns on their heads, a symbol of royalty and kingship (kin-ship=Bloodline). Osiris (Orion) was sometimes depicted with horns, too, and of course there have been people born with horns in places like China and India, not to mention the strange human skull with horns dis-covered in a burial mound at Sayre, Bradford County, Pennsylvania, in the 1880s. Like the remnants of ancient giants, beings with horns seem to have walked the earth in the ancient world, too.

In terms of alchemical symbolism, the horns, or rays (if there are more than two), are references to philosophical 'Dew' - an hermetic alchemical substance said to emanate from the 'centre' of the Galaxy and transmitted *through* the Sun. This Dew, says the *Zohar*: "...is the 'manna' on which the 'souls of the just' nourish themselves." For the biblical Israelites, the 'manna from heaven' was said to be a celestial food given to the 'people' and directed by Moses in the *Book of Exodus*. In Alchemical texts, the 'dew' is an emanation or 'radiation' from the Tree of Life, which emerges as a conduit passing through the Sun, just as photons pass through space. All these references of 'Dew', 'manna', etc., seem to be alchemical words, I would suggest, for electromagnetic forces that shape and create stars, suns and planets -- not least Orion's stars.

The Horned 'M' Treatment

Time Magazine has utilised images of world leaders framed in front of the letter 'M' on several editions, so to play on the theme of 'horns'. The Clintons, Bushes, as well as Obama and Donald Trump, in 2016, to name but a few, have also had the 'M' horned treatment on the magazine's cover (see figure 131). The imagery could be purely accidental but seems to 'place' symbolic 'horns' on those featured. The effect is similar to the horned Moses, the 'shining world leader' and also a symbolic connec-tion to the 'enlightened ones' - the bloodlines of the 'Shining Ones'- the Watchers.

Figure 131: The 'Horny One', Bill Clinton.
A plethora of world leaders *seem* to be given the visual 'horn treatment' on the cover of '*Time*'. All accidental? Maybe?

Time Magazine was started by Briton Hadden, allegedly a member of the Delta Kappa Epsilon

Brotherhood, one of the oldest North American fraternities based at Yale College in 1844. Over the years, Delta Kappa Epsilon members have said to include *five* of forty-five Presidents of the United States, all connected to the Skull and Bones Secret Society.[18] Delta Kappa is one of *nine* fraternities using Greek letters, 'allegedly' connected to *nine* elite bloodline families on earth. I cannot verify such a claim here, but the symbolism is certianly interesting. Kapp's British equiva-

Figure 132:
The Delta Kappa Epsilon logo.
Public domain © courtesy of Eric Holland
2016 (Creative Commons).

lent could be compared to the elite 'Bullingdon Club' said to be based at Oxford University, which gave us several Prime Ministers in recent years, not least the current one, Boris Johnson. Many celebrities and world leaders seem to rise through the ranks, or gain 'stardom' due to their membership of these secret societies. The original Delta Kappa Epsilon logo has all the major symbols connecting to the subjects discussed in this book, not least the rampant lion, the Eye of Providence, winged disc and Adam's 'X' on its shield (see figure 132). There is also seems to be a connection to Orion through the belt stars named 'Mintaka', 'Alnilam' and 'Alnitak' (Delta, Epsilon and Zeta Orionis) and 'Kappa Orionis', or 'Saiph', the southeastern star of Orion's central quadrangle.

Horned 'Stars'

The number of celebrities I have seen 'wearing horns', or having hair shaped to look like horns, is almost beyond coincidence (see figure 133). Can it all be simply chance? Possibly? But, who knows for sure? However, the symbolism itself *could* relate to what the Hopi called the 'horned gods', or 'horned clans' mentioned earlier, as well as the Christian devil; along with the 'magic and power' connected to occult symbolism associated with both Orion and Saturn. I would go one stage further

Figure 133: Celebrity Horns.
The Orion-Saturn Cult horn symbolism, sometimes 'innocently' adorned by actors, performers and singers. © Neil Hague

and say that horned 'non-physical' entities, often possess the bizarre and 'ego-driven' no matter what status in life. People can become vessels for forces 'unseen', which is what possession in the religious sense relates to. The horns here could also be 'expressions' of the 'light of lucifer' (or Prometheus) and 'the light', I would suggest, is the metaphysical 'light of lucifer' (Lux), the 'Shining Ones' and the *invisible war* between opposing interstellar forces.

Koshari Clowns, Moloch & MTV

Back in 2013, the *MTV Video Music Award* show provided a brief glimpse of symbolism associated with a taste of Orion-like symbolism in the form of the Orion Koshari clown image mentioned on page 199. As part of the performance, singer Robert Thicke dressed almost like a Koshari clown of *Beetlejuice* fame, performed with a scantily-clad, (then young) Miley Cyrus. For those who can remember her little 'horned hairstyle' and protruding tongue, they won't forget the bizarre imagery these two performers 'conjured' for the masses that night. The phallic-like large 'hand', held by Cyrus, had all the remnants of Min's manhood, too. The performance seemed 'visually' Orion-Betelgeuse archetypal especially the black and white striped outfit worn by Thicke. It's all a kind of 'mind magic' (in the form of entertainment) for those who are drawn into these 'big events' featuring such 'stars'.

As I said earlier, many of the Super Bowl XLVI half-time shows seem to offer up semi-occult symbolism for the millions who subconsciously soak up the 'star magic'. The use of occult symbols, horned outfits, fire, pillars, along with the All-Seeing Eye, etc., often appear at such spectacular events. They do look ritualistic 'visually', which is not a criticism of the performers themselves, but an observation of the amount of ancient pagan and Babylonian, esoteric symbolism appearing at such events. Like I say, much of it is innocent fun but there is an element of 'dabbling' in the vibrational energetic fields connected to Orion, Saturn and other nefarious off-world entities.

In terms of rituals and the worship of ancient gods (entities), through modern expressions; we have seen, at times, disturbing imagery in films and music videos. Much of this 'artistic' licence seems to relate to Saturn and Moon symbolism, also the Roman god Vulcan and the an ancient horned god, Moloch (see figure 134). The latter, a deity who was focused on in the ancient region called 'Gehenna' (in biblical Jerusalem), not least by Canannite priests who were notorious for human sacrifice by fire in biblical times. The location became known as the wicked place, where ancient priest-kings sacrificed their children to the horned Moloch. Freemason and

Figure 134: The Horned Moloch.
Human sacrifices (by fire) to the horned god, Moloch.

Reverend Frederick John Foakes Jackson, professor of Christian Institutions in Union Theological Seminary, New York said of Gehenna:

Recent excavations have shown the frequency of the sacrifice of children in Palestine...

...Children were burnt alive at a place called Trophet (the fire stove) in the valley of Himmon, which is now Jerusalem. The Valley of Himmon (Gehenna) meets up with the Kidron Valley, which passes between the Temple Mount and the Mount of Olives.[19]

I'll leave the reader to conjure up connections in their mind's-eye, of how alleged abuse and grotesque acts commited against children 'supposedly' through places of 'power' in recent times, *could* relate to ancient nefarious 'entities', or off-world 'forces' controlling such Cults. I am not saying for a minute that *any* of the performers or organisations briefly mentioned in this book are involved in such acitivities, such ideas are beyond the scope of this books remit. All I am pointing out is the relevance of 'visual imagery' and 'symbolism' within the many symbols, costumes and performances, (whether coincidental) alluding to knowledge of the occult and 'some' of the esoteric connections illustrated so far.

The past few chapters have had common themes relating to 'unseen forces' with a focus on Orion symbolism (and *his* neighboring star systems) as seen in ancient myths through to modern media expressions. We have also seen 'subtle connections' between Orion, the Sun, Moon and Saturn, with more to come later in the book. Before I look further at 'duality' in relation to these forces, let me now open the door a little wider, and go deeper into the symbolism within parts of the media, movie and corporate worlds that seem to offer up a connection to Orion symbolism.

Sources:

1) Fuller, J. F. C. *The Secret Wisdom of the Qabalah; A Study in Jewish Mystical Thought,* p29
2) *The Gospel of Peace of Jesus Christ*; (The Aramaic and Old Slavonic Texts compared and edited by Edmond Székely. C.W. Daniel Company. 1937, p25

3) Hall, Manly. P. *The Secret Teachings of All Ages* (Readers Edition). Penguin. 2003, p123

4) Ibid, p 141 (https://www.sacred-texts.com/eso/sta/sta11.htm)

5) Jung, C. G., and Kerényi, C. *Essays on a Science of Mythology: the Myth of the Divine Child and the Mysteries of Eleusis.* Pantheon Books. 1949, p167.

6) Roob, Alexander. *Alchemy & Mysticism* (*Opus Magnum*: Sephiroth). Taschen. 1996, p319

7) https://www.telegraph.co.uk/music/news/was-david-bowies-blackstar-named-after-a-cancer-lesion/

8) Talbot, David. *The Saturn Myth.* 1980 p13

9) Huxley, Francis *(the Anthropologist). The Way of the Sacred: The Rites and Symbols, Beliefs and Tabus, That Men Have Held in Awe and Wonder Through the Ages.* New York; Dell Publishing. 1974, p112

10) *Ibid*, p212.

11) Rabbi (Pseudo)-Ishmael (1928). Odeberg, Hugo, ed. 3 *Enoch or the Hebrew Book of Enoch.* Cambridge University Press. p54.

12) Savedow, Steve, ed. *Sepher Rezial Hemelech.* Weiser Books. 2000, pp119-210.

13) Gettings, Fred. *Dictionary of Demons.* Guild Publishing. 1988 p (plate 64b).

14) Briggs, Katharine M. *An Encyclopedia of Fairies, Hobgoblins, Brownies, Boogies, and Other Supernatural Creatures,* s.v. "Wild Hunt", p 437. and Katherine M. Briggs, *The Fairies in English Tradition and Literature,* pp 49–50 University of Chicago Press, London, 1967

15) Owusu, Heike; *Symbols of Native America.* Sterling Publishing. 1997. p159

16) Annotated *Myths & legends,* p 86

17) David, Gary A. *Mirrors of Orion, Star Knowledge of the Ancient World,* Create Space Independent Publishing Platform. 2014, p125

18) https://en.wikipedia.org/wiki/Delta_Kappa_Epsilon

19) Vol I. Prolegomena I: *The Jewish, Gentile and Christian backgrounds* (1920).

8

ORION'S STAR MAGIC

'Seeker of Dark Places'

A warrior never worries about his fear.

CARLOS CASTANEDA

In mythology, the giant Orion was said to lose his sight and then seek out the light of the Sun so to regain his 'vision'. He is the 'blind-but-can-see-again' figure, who in darkness, searches for the light of the world. We too, are searchers of the same light, metaphorically, as we weave our way through what is often a dark world. On one level, it is sunlight that first blinds and then later heals Orion, and this could be an allegory of modern science and spiritual awareness (or lack of), connecting the stars with earth. Orion's story is an allegory of the loss of primordial perception and regaining vision in the dawn of new light, or information. As I have shown, Orion represents an ancient epoch of the hunter-gatherer peoples of Arcadia and their connection to the magic of the stars. In this chapter, I want to look at star magic and myths that seem to offer 'darker archetypal connections' to Orion, while he is in 'darkness'. Orion's time in darkness (within the myth) is a prime focus for those who *follow* Orion's nefarious side. The 'dark side', often expressed in today's world media, movie industry and politics will be explored throughout this chapter and can be tied to Orion symbolism.

In his book *The Greek Myths* (1955), Robert Graves connects Orion with Oenopion (the legendary king of Chios), who is called the perennial 'Year-King'. According to myth, Oenopion 'pretends' to die at the end of his term and appoints a substitute, in the form of Orion, who actually dies in his place. Interestingly, the Oenopion beetle (a horned Oenopion zopheroides), is a 'darkling beetle', called a *'seeker of dark places'* connected to chthonic activity, soil and dead matter. The exoskeleton aspect of the beetle will also become relevant later in the book, too, in relation to the 'ancient-future' gods (aliens) entwined with Orion. Oenopion, the son of Dionysus (the chief wine deity), was seen as the 'Year-King' due to his importance in the harvesting of the vine and other crops. Oenopion was also responsible for Orion's disappearance into a 'dark place' (the Underworld) by blinding him, an act that symbolised sacrifice of one who rules over the year (annual cycle). Eye symbolism mentioned in earlier chapters, expressed through Orion Cult, is very much part of Orion's loss of sight symbolically. As Homer wrote in *Odyssey*: "(Orion), a hunter of shadows, himself a shade" (II. 572).

Blind Worship

Orion's blindness is similar to the story of Odysseus blinding the Cyclops, connected to a solar legend where a Sun-hero is captured and blinded by his enemies at dusk, yet escapes and regains his sight at dawn, when all beasts flee from him. Graves sees the rest of the Oenopion-Orion myth as an amalgamation of diverse stories, some of which I've already touched on, such as Gilgamesh and the Scorpion-Men; the latter relates to the Egyptian god, Set, becoming a scorpion that kills Horus/Osiris (Orion). Similar themes recur in the 'Hymns of Orpheus', the 'Hymn to the Sun'; describing Orion's eyes as an 'eternal eye' with broad survey, as like 'Immortal Jove', all-searching and 'bearing light'. Other descriptions speak of the 'great eye of nature' and starry skies', seeming to relate to a central eye within the Orion constellation; more on this later.

From mythology and symbolism connected to Orion, he is the ultimate warrior-archetype belonging to an ancient era - blinded then having his sight restored. In old Hungarian tradition, Orion is known as the 'Magic Archer', Íjász, or Reaper (Kaszás). In other myths, he is called Nimrod (Hungarian Nimród), the greatest hunter, who, like Odin, is the father of the twins 'Hunor' and 'Magor'. In other Hungarian traditions, Orion's belt is known as 'Judge's stick' (Bírópálca); in Scandinavian tradition, Orion's belt was known as Frigg's Distaff (friggerock) or Freyja's distaff, another underworld (dark) connection.

Orion's placement amongst the stars was important to earth's ancient peoples and like Theseus and Hercules, these legendary warriors met many beasts and darker creatures in their fights, seeing them venerated through what the Greeks called 'Hero Cults'. In Ancient Greece, it was said Orion had a hero cult in the Boeotia region of central Greece; the number of places associated with his birth suggest that it was a widespread cult.* A feast of Orion was also held at Tanagra as late as the Roman Empire and they had a tomb of Orion at the foot of Mount Cerycius (now Mount Tanagra).[1] Another Orion hero name is Cephalus or Kephalos, which means 'head' and is associated with several hero-figures in Greek mythology. Orion, the Star Man, is both a warrior, hunter and noticeably seen to be 'headless' amongst the stars when viewed with the naked eye. The 19th-century German classical scholar, Erwin Rohde, viewed Orion as an example of the

Footnote: A birth story is often a claim to the hero by a local shrine; a tomb of a hero is a place of veneration.

ancient Greeks erasing the line between the gods and mankind. In other words, if Orion was in the heavens, then other mortals could hope to be there, too. Star worship is *profoundly* connected to Orion as we have seen so far, and the ancient priesthoods and Stellar (star) Cults aligned themselves with Orion, especially the 'darker' aspect of Orion – notably his death at the hands of the Scorpion, or Scorpios.

A Headless Man

Orion is clearly visible in the northwest (Southern Hemisphere) and south-west (Northern Hemisphere) night sky from November to February and best seen between latitudes 85 and -75 degrees. Alnilam, Mintaka, and Alnitak (Orion's belt), are the most prominent stars in the Orion constella-tion seen with the naked eye. Betelgeuse, the second brightest star in Orion, establishes the right shoulder of the hunter. Bellatrix serves as Orion's left shoulder and Saiph serves as Orion's right knee. Rigel forms the hunter's left knee. Other stars in the constellation include Hatsya, which establishes the tip of Orion's sword that hangs off the belt, and Meissa, which forms the point where his head would be. The main door into Orion is *within* the body of the warrior-star-man, and the stars framing his giant form.

Orion looks 'headless' in terms of how the stars are grouped, focusing on his torso, legs and arms. He is a 'headless star man' whose stars offer greater insight into religious blueprints shaping human life, as we shall see. Osiris was also portrayed as headless in some texts; indeed, various species of mythical headless gods (or people) were rumoured to inhabit remote parts of the world. Not all these gods are connected to Orion but depictions of a headless Osiris (or Min) on a Sarcophagus in Cairo visually portray the power of his fertility (see Figure 135). Osiris as Orion governed the afterlife (the Underworld) and therefore was often portrayed as a 'life giver' through vegetation and annual flooding of the Nile, where Osiris was linked to the heliacal rising of Orion and Sirius at the start of the Egyptian New Year.

Other headless war-rior figures are seen in folklore and magic, not least in the legends of the Blemmyes tribes of North Africa and the pygmy peoples connect-ed to Egypt. The pygmy god, 'Bes', was especial-ly used as a talisman for protection against evil.

Figure 135: The headless Osiris (Orion) on a sarcopha-gus in Cairo, guarded by Nephtys and Isis (Sirius).

These North African tribes were variously known as 'Akephaloi' or 'Blemmyes' and were described by those who encountered them as lacking a head but having facial features on their chest. The headless Akephaloi, or the dog-headed 'Cynocephali', along with various wild men and women, were said to have dwelled in the eastern edge of ancient Libya, according to Herodotus' Libyan sources.[2]

Mythological references to the headless god are seen in ancient China as 'Xingtian' (Hsing T'ien), in Chinese myth, a deity who fights against a Supreme Divinity, possibly the Demiurge, mentioned in an earlier chapter. Losing the fight for supremacy, Xingtian was beheaded and his head buried in Changyang Mountain (see figure 136). Nevertheless, headless, with a shield in one hand and a battle axe in the other, he continues the fight, using his nipples as eyes and his navel as a mouth. Similar versions of the head-less warrior can also be found across the South West of America, too. I am not saying these glyphs were made as a focus on Orion, but it is interest-ing how similar headless figures can be found on very different continents.

Figure 136: The headless warrior, Xingtian.

Other explanations have been offered for the legend of their unusual physique. As noted earlier, native warriors perhaps employed the tactic of keeping the head tucked close to the breast while moving with 'one knee' on the ground? Sounds pretty difficult to me, but perhaps they had the custom of carrying shields ornamented with faces? The latter seems the most plausible expla-nation. Petroglyphs in New Mexico seem to also depict strange figures holding an axe and having a face on what could be a shield or their body. Other petroglyphs mark the position of the sun and moon at the summer and winter solstices. Still other sites such as Chaco Canyon (once home to the Anasazis) also seem to align with with Orion's belt stars. For more information on the American South West and Orion, I cannot recommend highly enough the brilliant work by Gary. A David (see bibliography).

The Headless Gods & the Place of Fear

In Mayan myth it was said that the twins Hunahpu and Xbalanque were conceived when their mother Xquic, daughter of one of the lords of Xibalba (the place of fear), spoke with the severed head of their father Hun Hunahpu. For the Mayans, Xibalba (pronounced 'Zi-Balba') is located in

Orion; the gods Hunahpu, Xbalanque (and the howler monkey scribes and sculptors that accompany them) are no different symbolically to the Egyptian deities, Osiris, Thoth and their connection to Orion and the Underworld. The symbolism associated with Xibalba and the symbol of the 'severed head' seems to be connected to Orion.

Xibalba is the name of the Underworld in K'iche' Maya mythology, a place ruled by the Maya death gods and their helpers, all of which will become relevant as the book unravels. Xibalba is also meant to be the Orion Nebula (Messier 42, M42, NGC 1976 located at 1,270 light-years approximately from the Earth. This location is crucially important to many indigenous cultures.) The god 'Xbalanque' (pronounced balan-ke) for the Maya, can be translated as 'Jaguar Sun' (x-balam-que), or 'Hidden Sun' (x-balanque), and 'Jaguar Deer' (x-balam-quieh). The symbolism of the Hidden Sun and its connection to Xibalba also becomes more important in a later chapter.

Xibalba, features in the movie *The Fountain* (2006) by movie director, Darren Aronofsky, and also has biblical underpinnings. The movie opens with a phrase from *Genesis* 3:24, "After he drove man out, he placed on the east side of the Garden of Eden cherubim and a flaming sword flashing back and forth to guard the way to the tree of life." The film is about *three* people (played by Hugh Jackman) living in different centuries (but connected) who embark on a search for the Tree of Life in order to protect their loved ones and receive the gift of immortality. The 'flaming sword' in this narrative *is* the sword of Orion, the location where the Orion Nebula sits. I am told the word 'sword', in the original Hebrew, is 'chereb', from the root word 'charab'. And 'flaming', from the word 'lahahh' is a 'supernatural weapon' which could bring swift and deadly destruction. It could also be defined as a fire, magic or enchantment that consumes, encircles or wraps up something. The meaning here could be a reminder of both the 'child' and the 'rebel angel' within us all. I tend to think it also relates to the power of something that has ability to shape or destroy worlds, too. Aronofsky's film *Mother* (2017), is another rendition of the Garden of Eden story with Adam and Eve at the heart of a violent cycle of death and rebirth, told through a modern context. Essentially, it is a psychological horror movie with undertones also relating to the Sophia and Demiurge narrative.

The goddess 'Xquic' and 'Xmucane' in Mayan belief, is another variation of Spider Woman, Sotuknang and Inanna of Sumeria (3500 BC). Xquic could also be an 'aspect'of the gnostic Sophia; *all* of these deities could have been personified versions of catastrophes and events connected to the Earth, Moon and Venus in an ancient epoch. More so, the stories of creator twins and monster slayers seem to be connected to several locations amongst the stars and can be found in numerous aboriginal myths relating to life and death, not least the twin stars of Regal in Orion. Life and death symbolism associated with the gods 'Hunhunahpo' and 'Seven Hunahpo' in Mayan myth, on one level, relates to the life cycle of maize (corn) as it was for the Hopi. Hunhunahpo *is* another Osiris, who for the Egyptian, was also the god of the harvest. In order to harvest corn, it is necessary to 'remove its head'. Therefore, the beheading of Hunhunapho (Osiris) is symbolic of cutting off the 'head', or the fruit of the maize. Both John the Baptist and the Hopi god, Masau'u *become* headless in their narratives, which is relevant to the Orion story. The maize 'seeds' must then be replanted by humans in order for the corn to grow again. It is also worth noting, that the Orion constellation is 'hidden' by the position of the sun during planting and growing seasons, when the grain is coming back to life from seed. The head of Hunhunahpo (or Orion), for the Mayans, seems to have been located as the Hyades star cluster, in Orion's neighbour, Taurus. The Hyades cluster also contains the bright star, Aldebaran, which is the eye of the bull; both Aldebaran and Orion seem to be forming an alignment linking the eye of the bull with the belt stars of Orion. In Mesoamerica, the Hyades 'head' appears first on the Eastern horizon, followed by the body of Hunhunahpo or 'First Father' (Orion) as he goes head to head with the bull in the heavens. As I will show in the next chapter, endless symbolism connected to Orion and Taurus and their joint influence on the minds of humanity, through belief, mythology and duality is 'huge'.

In Mayan myths (relating to the ballcourt, Hunhunahpo and Xibalba - the Underworld), the focus was on life, death, duality with connections to the Dark Rift in the Milky Way and Orion's position. In Egyptian myth, Dark Rift is called 'Duat', a location divided by the Milky Way, situated between Leo (lion) and Orion (son of man). 'Hun' in Mayan also means 'one' or 'One Lord' and relates to the *one* lord – the Demiurge in Gnostic myth. Hunhunahpo has a twin brother who is known as 'Seven Hunahpo' (possibly the seven main visible stars of Orion) and both One Lord and his brother, Seven Hunahpo, were ball players in the court of the gods. Soccer (football), the roll of the dice and lotto's in our world, could be seen as symbols of duality and influenced by Orion archetypes.

Tammuz - Orion Loses his Head

According to *The Saturn Myth* (1980) by David Talbot, Orion was known as Tammuz in Babylon and Saturn in Rome: "...The story of Orion preceded astrology." Tammuz was another 'Son of Man' Jesus figure. In fact, Orion is widely acknowledged to be the Greek version of the Babylonian Tammuz-Ninurta, connected to Saturn. Orion is also known as the 'lover of Diana' (the Moon) and it is Diana (Artemis) who shoots Orion in the head in Greek and Chaldean myths. Assassinations by a 'head shot', or 'decapitation', are Orion-Saturn-Moon Cult inspired in my view. In ancient myth, Orion's head is missing as his body washes ashore; it is said Diana grieved greatly that she had shot him, lamenting his death with much weeping, as Orion's torso was placed amongst the stars. Orion, like the Hopi god Masau'u, has no head in his 'star-man form' as I have already touched upon. The Age of Orion, as mentioned in *Chapter Two*, ended when the moon goddess symbolically 'beheaded' the giant (think John the Baptist and Salome). The 'weeping of women' in the book of *Ezekiel* is symbolic of Diana's lament:

> For they say, The LORD seeth us not; the LORD hath forsaken the earth. He said also unto me, Turn thee yet again, and thou shalt see greater abominations that they do. Then he brought me to the door of the gate of the LORD'S house, which was toward the north; and, behold, there sat women weeping for Tammuz.[3]

Orion's position in the sky created by the heliacal rising due to Earth's orbit at certain times of year, means the sun would block our view of Orion by day. The star man is also symbolically 'swallowed up' by the Netherworld as he disappears below the equator in late Spring. In some instances, the Sun and Moon are seen to rise above the constellation giving the effect of the star man's head replaced by another celestial body. Alignments of this kind at Solstices were often 'marked' on rock in the form of pictograms by Bronze Age artists.

At the Solstices, the Sun figuratively 'loses its head', starting to fall from the heights of its northern course as viewed from earth. The heliacal rising and the sun's position at both ends of the year gives rise to the idea of two 'suns', as mentioned in the last chapter. In some Medieval and Renaissance folk traditions, the two halves of the year suggested a 'battle' between two suns in the form of the 'Oak King' and the 'Holly King'. The Oak King loses his power at the Summer Solstice so the Holly King can begin his reign and maintain his power over Earth until the Winter Solstice. At this point the symbolic fight occurs and the Oak King regains his 'crown' (corona) and his head, and the cycle begins anew. Much twin symbolism found in myth also relates to

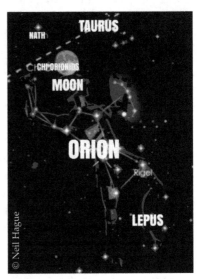

Figure 137: Orion Head-Changer.
Orion's head changes during the annual astrological cycle.

Figure 138: Iluminated Hand and weapon.
Other times his baton, or sword, is illuminated by other planets and the Sun.

these two aspects of the sun's reign and decline.

At times, the sun or the moon is visibly apparent, sitting atop the shoulders of Orion (see figure 137 and 138). Sometimes other planetary bodies such as Jupiter, Mars, Venus, Mercury or Saturn overshadow the spot. I imagine these different alignments carried very different meanings to those who observed them. The energetic vibrations would also change for those witnessing the effects. In all instances, it was the headless star man who wore the planets, like a series of helmets or heads, at various times depending on what planet moved into position. Like the god Janus, or Nimrod (the keeper of the gateways/passages) in Roman and Babylonian worship, and Apis/Osiris of ancient Egypt, Orion was the 'door-keeper' and a celestial god of *changing* time.

Orion's Lover

Orion's name is derived from the ancient Greek word *oros* (mountain) or from *ourios* (urine). In Greek mythology, Orion was likely the son of the sea-god Poseidon and Euryale, daughter of Minos, King of Crete. It was said that Orion could 'walk on the waves' like his father and was said to have walked to the island of Chios where he got drunk and attacked Merope, daughter of Oenopion, the ruler there. You could say that Orion 'lost his head' in a slightly different manner. Born of Gaia and the gods, it seems Orion was a bit of a womaniser and a drunk despite having deeper love interests. According to Roman author, Hyginus (64 BC – AD 17), the goddess Artemis once loved Orion but was tricked into killing him by her brother Apollo (the Sun), who was said to be 'protective' of his sister's maidenhood. Artemis, like the Roman goddess, Diana, represented the Moon. Orion's love interest in the moon goddess probably relates to Orion's celestial *body* in relation to the Moon and the Sun, both of which are uniquely positioned for earth. More so, Orion was considered 'earth-born' (with the genetics of the gods), from the giants or Watchers. Like many other hero figures, such as Hercules of Oeta, Polyphemus the Cyclops, Samson the Danite, Cuchlain of Muithemne (the Irish sun-hero), Orion the Hunter was 'bound' by the goddess and 'used by the gods' so that eventually he would reveal mysteries through what became religious archetypes.

In myths associated with Artemis and the hunter, Actaeon (another ver-

sion of Orion), Actaeon accidentally sees Artemis taking a bath in her secret
outdoor grotto. Artemis is the 'bear goddess' and expert archer, who is said
to become angry with the young male hunter, so angry that she turns him
into a stag, whose hunting dogs (possibly symbolic of the Sirius constellation) devour Actaeon. Artemis is the goddess of the hunt, the wilderness,
wild animals, the Moon, and chastity (see figure 139). The root of her name
is probably Persian in origin from 'arta', 'art' or 'arte', all meaning 'great',
'excellent', and 'holy.' Artemis is also identified with 'mother of Nature'
who herself was born of the goddess Leto and Zeus, all of whom are children of the Titans (the giants) in Greek myth. The Egyptian goddess,
'Neith', is another Artemis figure. She is the goddess of war and of hunting,
and had as her symbol two arrows crossed over a shield. Neith is paired
with Ptah-Nun who is another Orion figure; it is interesting that in earlier
Islamic belief, Neith, along with the 'Three Daughters' of Allah (possibly
the belt stars), all seem to be references to Orion. The leading figure of the
Hunger Games Trilogy (2013), Katniss Everdean, is a representation of
Artemis, Diana and even Europa (see figure 139). In classical Greek mythology, Artemis was the twin sister of the sun god, Apollo, hence the connection between Katniss and Peter in the *Hunger Games Trilogy* when both characters are shown to 'catch fire' entering Panem. The Hellenic goddess of the
hunt Artemis was goddess of wild animals, wilderness, childbirth, virginity
and 'protector of young girls' (i.e Prem and her sister in the *Hunger Games*
movie).

The Roman poet, Quintus Horatius Flaccus, known as Horace (65 BC to
8 BC), also tells of Orion's death at the hands of Diana/Artemis (the moon
goddess) and Gaia (the earth goddess). Orion represented the Arcadian
epoch of giants and the remnants of the 'Age of the Titans' on earth. The
Roman poet Publius Ovidius Naso (known as Ovid), also mentions Orion
in the Fasti, May 11 (or *The Book of Days*), when, in Ovid's time, the constellation Orion was said to set with the sun. The loss of Orion's sight at the
hand of King Oenopion, with help from 'Cedalion' (the demi-god of smelt-
ing ore), Orion's
sight (his eyes
and head) are
restored by the
sun god, Helios
(another version
of Apollo,
Jupiter and
Saturn), the old
Sun in the
ancient age of

**Figure 139:
Artemis.**
Orion's equal and
lover, Artemis,
symbolised in the
Hunger Games
movies as 'Katniss
Everdean'.

the giants. The Colossus of Rhodes is the most famous veneration of Helios, see *Chapter Two*. The Greek/Roman goddess Artemis/Diana does not have all the traits of Ishtar/Inanna but many of the key attributes are present nonetheless: bow and arrows, the moon, and riding a chariot, or a lion. Ishtar/Inanna's helmet is adorned with horns (see also Hathor) both of which are lunar symbols connected to the *horned* gods mentioned in the last chapter. Inanna is also the daughter of Nannar/Sin, the moon god mentioned earlier.

A Goddess for the 'Son of Man'

Orion is mentioned in the oldest surviving works of Greek literature, which probably date back to the 7th or 8th century BC, but which are the products of an oral tradition with origins probably dating to several centuries earlier. As an offspring of the gods, Orion (like Actaeon and Hephaestus) pursues the goddess, with sexual desire for her. Like the Satyrs of ancient Greece, chasing nymphs, Orion's bloodline is of the Titans, the giants born of copulation between the gods and the daughters of men. The goddess of the hunt, the moon and the morning star (Venus) are all Orion's 'fantasy'. The goddess he lusts after is also Ishtar/Inanna, who eventually becomes the Mary Magdalene-figure in much later Christian narratives. In fact, the three Mary's of the New Testament could also be a female symbol of the three belt stars of Orion, along with the Triple Goddess associated with Hecate. While Inanna/Ishtar is described as a prostitute, just as Mary Magdalene was, both Athena/Minerva and Artemis/Diana are called 'virgins' in their respective mythologies. Virgin Moons to be precise! Both perspectives of these goddess figures are two sides of the same coin. Ishtar/Inanna is a goddess of sexuality but above all, she is a goddess of 'desire' and of the destructive power accompanying this desire. Athena, for her part, is the target of an incestuous attempted rape by her brother, Hephaestus and the power that leads to Orion's demise in Greek myth. Artemis/Diana and Athena/Minerva are barred explicitly from sexuality, yet they are still goddesses of desire leading Orion to force himself on Merope (also a star, in the constellation Taurus and a member of the Pleiades star cluster). The story of Orion and Merope varies. One source refers to Merope as the wife of King Oenopion and not his daughter. Another refers to Merope as the daughter of King Minos famed for him housing the offspring of the Cretan Queen Pasiphae – the Minotaur, another Taurean archetype. The main points found within myths associated with darker aspects of Orion are: *lust, desire* and the *power* over celestial objects (often goddesses of the stars), said to seduce the masculine hunter - Orion.

In various myths, male gods often go 'crazy for' or kill each other out of a desire for Ishtar/Inanna; or in Orion's case, lose their head while out hunting with her. The symbolism behind Herod Antipas's ritual killing of the prophet John the Baptist, because of the powerful female influence (of Salome) over Herod is another variation of the same narrative. In fact, both John and Jesus are biblical versions of the 'Holly and Oak' Sun Kings I mentioned earlier. So are myths associated with Orpheus, the divine musician, who ventured into the Underworld to retrieve his lover, Eurydice, but lost her due to turning back to 'see her' before she could reach the light of the sun. Orpheus preached that Helios was the greatest of all the gods; however, like Orion he is killed at the hands of the goddess in the form of the Maenads (the female followers of Dionysus).

Ritual killings of Sun 'Kings'

Themes of ritual killings seen in movies, through to political and religious assassinations over the centuries have involved the death of a 'king' or a 'Queen', symbolically. The assassination of JFK in 1963 is the most notable ritual killing of a symbolic 'solar king', or world leader. Kennedy's connection to the Hollywood 'queen', Marilyn Monroe, who also died under strange circumstances, is another strand in the symbolism. The death of Princess Diana (Sun Queen/Isis) and Dodi Fayed (Osiris) in 1997 also had a huge amount of symbolism connected to their deaths in Paris. David Icke's book *The Biggest Secret* (1998) goes into great length about Diana and Dodi's 'accident'. The lighted torch of Prometheus was erected for both JFK and Diana and such esoteric symbolism, as I have been ponting out, is the hallmark of occultists operating in the shadows. The remit of this book isn't big enough to go into 'conspiracies and cover-ups' regarding such legendary icons, I mention them here to reinforce the 'ritual killing aspect' connected to 'mind control' (often through the film and music industries) icons. Hollywood seems to have been a haven for darker aspects of Cult actvities, in recent years, through exposure of vile activities involving paedophilia and sexual assaults brought to the surface in high profile cases. These abominations are 'Orion-Saturn-like' in nature (the darker side of Orion) if grasping the mythical aspects of the persona that was the giant Orion.

Secret societies and Knights Orders, such as the 19th Century, 'Knights of the Golden Circle', connected to Freemasonry have alleged to have been instrumental in assassinations of important figures. John Wilkes Booth who assassinated Abraham Lincoln, for example, was said to be a 33rd degree Freemason and connected to the Knights of the Golden Circle.[4] JFK's assassins were clearly connected to sinsiter operations beyond government level. The killing of 'John' Lennon was another high profile 'ritual asassination' when he was shot in the head. His killer, Mark Chapman, said to be carrying a recently-purchased copy of J. D. Salinger's novel, *Catcher in the Rye*, wherein Chapman had written: "This is my statement"; signing it "Holden". The fictional character Holden Caufield, represents the 'fall' from the cliff (like Prometheus or Lucifer) and represents the fall from innocence. In the book, Holden illustrates the attempt to shelter kids from 'growing up' (Peter Pan), and more personally, conveys his desire to avoid the harshness of adult life. All of which can be seen in archetypal symbols connected to Adam, Prometheus and as a protector of humanity. Writing about Mark Chapman and his bizzare obsession for the *Catcher in the Rye* – Holden Caufield, John W. Whitehead writing for the Rutherford Institute said of Chapman:

> *Chapman decided that since he had not actually turned into Holden Caulfield, the purpose of his killing Lennon was to draw attention to the book. "Everybody's going to be reading this book--with the help of the god-almighty media," he told his lawyer. Chapman called himself "the catcher in the rye for this generation," explaining that each generation has its own catcher, and compared himself to Moses and Jesus. Just before his sentencing, Chapman read the "catcher in the rye" passage from the book aloud in the courtroom.[5]*

Chapman was clearly under some kind of mind control when he shot Lennon, who if he had lived, may well have become one of the biggest, 'outspoken public figures' of our lifetime. When War is more important than Peace on all levels, the Moses or Jesus-like figures better not speak out against it! Lennon was also shot on the verge of Saturnalia when Orion is climbing high into Autumn's Winter sky. JFK was shot in the head in Dallas, in the same 'window' on the solar year. Many high profile ritual killings are almost mythic when it comes to detail and 'black magic' performed behind the scenes enabling such atrocities.

The Beast of Star Magic

The ritual of the 'Headless One', for example, has been one of the most important in modern magic for over 160 years. Originating in the 'Magical Papyri' (a body of papyri from Graeco-Roman Egypt), the rite was published by Charles Wycliffe Goodwin in 1852 and adapted by the famous Golden Dawn and Aleister Crowley (see figure 140). According to Jake Stratton-Kent, who writes in his book *The Headless One*:

> *Crowley's diaries, works and the Holy Books of Thelema themselves all stand testament to the importance of this ritual in his magical work... Accordingly, on November 28th, 1911 at 10.38 pm he opened the Temple and at 10.45pm he invoked Ab-ul-diz by the Bornless Ritual and at exactly eleven o'clock the Spirit [of the Headless One] appeared.[6]*

Crowley was said to be prolific in conjuring up demonic hosts, not least

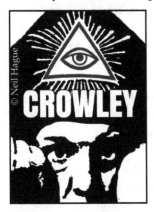

entities said to be typhon or Leviathan. Some say that the Loch Ness monster was all Crowley's doing, too. All of this is speculative. Boleskine house, Crowley's manor on the southeast side of Loch Ness in the Scottish Highlands (1899–1913), was witness to all sorts of 'dark and dire' rituals performed by Crowley while he was living there. Famous people like British film star George Sanders and Led Zeppelin guitarist and occult enthusiast, Jimmy Page, have talked about Boleskine's 'bad vibes', headless ghosts, and another owner, a retired Army Major was said to have committed suicide in the 'master occultist's (Crowley's) old bedroom.[7] Other deaths occurring around Crowley were when he and several other renowned climbers attempted to conquer Kangchenjunga peak, on the Sikkim-Nepal border in the Himalayas in 1905. A splinter party fell, triggering a catastrophic avalanche killing four expedition members, including key climber

Figure 140: The Beast, Star Magician.
20th Century high profile magician and founder of the Temple of Thelema. Crowley has interested many celebrities over the years.

Alexis Pache. Crowley's true colours surfaced, according to those in the group, when instead of descending to help with the rescue attempt, Crowley sat in his tent, drinking tea, despite hearing the shouts and screams from below. Sherpas on the trip said the Kangchenjunga Demon (a type of Yeti) had taken the climbers.

Aleister Crowley is shown to have had considerable influence over what would become popular culture, especially Hollywood in its early years. Crowley's connections to British Intelligence and the founding father of the American space programme, Jack Parsons, his adept, are just two examples of Crowley's influence. Parsons was also close to L. Ron Hubbard founder of Scientology, an organization which has attracted many producers, actors, actresses and songwriters; notably, Vivian Kubrick, daughter of legendary Stanley Kubrick. The Church of Scientology operates special 'Celebrity Centres' and its policy governs those Celebrity Centres (the main one in Los Angeles and others in Paris, Nashville, and elsewhere). Nashville, especially, was identified by Fritz Springmeier in his books as a major 'monarch mind control' programming centre *supposedly* connected to singers and performers that make it big as 'stars'. Again, I cannot validate this here.

According to some writers, Ian Fleming based Blofeld, the baddie in *Goldfinger*, on Crowley and it seems for some writers, Crowley also gave

Churchill his 'V' hand sign to counteract the Nazi's use of the swastika. His influence on symbols, including hand signs, rock music and post-beat counterculture is well documented in Gary Lachman's book, *Turn Off Your Mind* (2001). Crowley's influence can also be seen in films such as *Don Cammell's Performance* (1970) and Kenneth Anger's *Lucifer Rising* (1972), with Mick Jagger creating a dissonant synthesiser soundtrack to Anger's cinematic enactment of one of Crowley's rituals, 'The Inauguration of *My Demon Brother*'. Crowley also appears on the Beatles' *Sergeant Pepper* montage album cover illustration; also, on Michael Jackson's *Dangerous* album illustration, which is littered with symbols of all-seeing eyes, stars, pillars, lakes of fire and other occult symbols.

No matter how one views popular culture, rock music and what has become a media machine, the occultists, especially through Freemasonry, are involved behind the scenes. Crowley is just one of several key occult-magician figures of the 20th Century to inspire what has become modern media culture. Leading figures behind Hollywood and a great many actors, musicians, sportsmen and writers have said to have been Freemasons.[8]

Another of Crowley's ventures was the 'Ordo Templi Orientis' (O.T.O.) the 'Order of the Temple of the East', or 'Order of Oriental Templars' (founded in Germany in 1904). It is an international fraternal and religious organisation founded at the beginning of the 20th century by Carl Kellner and Theodor Reuss, the latter of which was an Anglo-German *tantric* occultist, freemason, alleged police agent, journalist and singer. Originally it was intended to be modelled on European Freemasonry, but under the leadership of Aleister Crowley, O.T.O. was reorganized around the 'Law of Thelema' as its central religious principle, involving standard practices and rituals connected to ancient Egyptian belief and Magic (Magik). It went under other names such as: the Gnostic Catholic Church (**no** connection to the Cathar Gnostics); the Rite of Memphis; the Order of the Sat Bhai; the Hermetic Brotherhood of Light, and also the 'Illuminati'. The latter is the most commonly used term, which has its origins in 18th Century Germany through its founder, German philosopher and law professor, Adam Weishaupt. Celebrities such as Marilyn Manson, Kanye West, Jay-Z, and some of the hottest stars are 'rumoured' to have associations with OTO. Again, I cannot validate such rumours in this book. The OTO (Thelma) philosophy also emphasizes the ritual practice of Magick, especially 'black magic' (or witchcraft). How many celebrities have been 'sacrificed' at the altars of the Illuminati since the time of Crowley?[9]

Crowley's Thelemic religion was founded upon the idea that the 20th century marked the beginning of the 'Aeon of Horus', in which a new ethical code would be followed: "Do what thou wilt shall be the whole of the Law" (Law of Thelema) This statement indicates adherents, known as

'Thelemites' should seek and follow their true paths in life, known as their 'True Wills'. This is expressed further by another metaphor, 'every man and every woman is a *star*', which portrays the distinct nature of every individual as residing in a non-overlapping point of space and time. Tinsletown is full of *stars* and they are there to both entertain and *mesmerise* us.

Super Bowls and Star Gates

The Super Bowl Show itself is one of the most watched events on television in the United States annually, reaching hundreds of millions of viewers worldwide. The Super Bowl halftime performance seems to be a massive vehicle used by unseen forces desiring to infuse our thoughts with subconscious imagery connected to the Orion and Saturn. Starting January 15th 1967, the event has become more 'sophisticated' over the decades. Performers such as Madonna, Beyonce, Cold Play, Bruno Mars and Katy Perry, to name but a few, have been centre stage in recent years. The performences are *used*, it seems, to draw down stellar magic, aligning with archetypes connected to ancient gods ('idols'). Beyonce's 2013 performance, for example, seemed to utilise symbolism associated with Horus, Kali, optical illusions, Hell and illuminati hand signals. The 'set' was made to look 'Hell-like' with hands reaching up from the flames and abyss. As Beyonce sang on stage, her supposed demon (alter ego), 'Sasha Fierce' (according to some writers) became part of the spectacle of her show. I obviously cannot say for sure, but, after observing occult symbolism at many of these halftime *Super Bowl* events each year, in the winter (when Orion is high in the sky), magic is in the air. It has also been said they align with a powerful portal called the 'Silver Gate' (a star gate) focused between the constellations of Orion, Gemini and Taurus (see figure 141).

The Silver Gate, also called the 'Gate of Man', has been said by researchers to represent a path of ascension into the 'Galactic' Centre and origin of our sun. When I say 'path', I mean an inter-dimensional alignment of specific energies, not least *Orion's influence*, too. There is a lot of New Age misinformation written about the Silver Gate and the Gate of

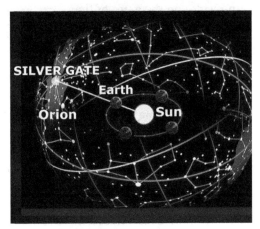

Figure 141: Silver Gate Portal.
The Silver (star) Gate, or 'doorway', sits on the crossing of the Milky Way and the ecliptic.

Man on the Internet, but essentially Orion's belt stars rise on the eastern horizon of the ecliptic following Betelgeuse towards the Silver Gate opening, usually when the halftime Super Bowl is performed. Some kind of vibrational alignment takes place at such global tournaments (see the 2012 Olympics) and the alignment in the heavens is crucial to such acts by those who perform magic over the masses. A lot of this is happening unkowingly for both performer and audience alike.

The Greek writer, Macrobius, called these 'gates' on the ecliptic, through which souls ascended and descended to Heaven, the 'Gates of the Sun'. Why? Because not only mortal man but also our sun dies and is reborn in the precession cycle at the very same gates. In the scheme of things, there are actually two gates opposing each other along the 'Galactic Plane' (the astrological circle or circuit). While the Silver Gate is located at the Orion, Cygnus arm of the Milky Way, another gate (its opposite), known as the 'Golden Gate', is situated near Scorpio, towards the Galactic Central Sun (see figure 142). The ancients called the full circuit, or path, made around the galactic equator, the 'Gate of the Gods'. When the Sun resides on the gates of the Golden Gate at an equinox or solstice, it represents a galactic alignment and celestial conjunction according to the ancients. Ophiuchus and Orion are mirror

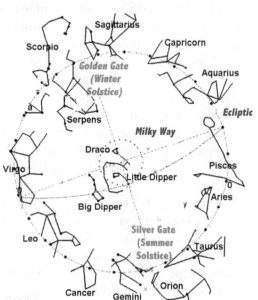

Figure 142: Golden and Silver Stargates. The Golden and Silver Gates are polar opposites providing a larger astological cycle alignment.

images of opposing polarity, but together, they represent the ascending path through the Gate of Man, meeting at the Gate of the Gods. We are cycles within cycles, energetically. The planets are also said to pass through the Silver Gate at the time of specific astrological alignments and the Sun goes through the Golden Gate every year on Winter Solstice. At the time of writing, Mars (the God of War) passed through the Golden Gate on February 16th, 2020. According to astrologers, on December 21st the Sun routinely crosses the Gate but in 2020 the Sun passed *both* Saturn and Jupiter for a 'Great Conjunction'. We saw a major event unfolding around this 'window of time' - the 'war' against the coronavirus (Covid-19).

Everything is aligned accordingly, it seems.

The alignments of each component of the astrological galactic plane are like a celestial compass (the Golden Compass?) which creates polarity. It is said that while Orion/Osiris (masculine energy) and the Taurus (feminine) are pointing at the Silver Gate, all becomes feminine; whereas, the opposite side, Ophiucus/Isis (feminine energy) and Scorpio (masculine energy) pointing at the Golden Gate, all become masculine. Both stellar gates and the constellations surrounding them are 'separated' (according to the myth). Because of the 'death' of Orion at the hands of Apollo (the Gate of the Sun), the moon and Scorpious (Scorpio), represent death. The spider, too, can be connected to this alignment as both the spider and scorpion are part of the arachnid family.

The energy generated by the Super Bowl halftime 'rituals' seems to be aimed at harnessing 'darker forces', or spider-scorpio-like forces, so to draw on and affect global energy. As it says in *Ephesians* 6:12:

> *For our struggle is not against flesh and blood, but against the rulers, against the authorities, against the powers of this dark world and against the spiritual forces of evil in the heavenly realms.*

The Super Bowl events, like so many enormous spectacular stage events, seem to involve numerology, acoustic alchemy, symbols, archetypes, themes, spoken words, spirits, cosmology and at times, images of idol worship. They seem to be the ultimate platform for interstellar forces (Orion Cult) to work their magic. Other artists who have performed the *Super Bowl* 'ceremony' include the singer, now actress, Stefani Joanne Angelina Germanotta, professionally known as 'Lady Gaga'.

Global Performances - Working that Stage 'Magic'

Lady Gaga seems to be a pivotal figure within elite entertainment circles. She fronted the 'One World: Together At Home' concert, with other artists, musicians at the time of the 'global lockdown' in April 2020. The partners behind the *One World: Together At Home* 'platform', according to their website: 'are working towards a world free of extreme poverty by 2030'. Yet, according to some, the 'imposed' lockdowns all over the world caused unncessary death, poverty (not least through job losses) and devastated economies in many countries. Many elderly have died all over the world too, because of the lack of treatments they would have otherwise received if there had been no global lockdown (house arrest). The contradiction in many ways is quite staggering. The symbolism used for the 'One World: Together At Home' concert was no suprise to anyone who has studied symbolism. The 'sun-eye' and the 'hands' (in the shape of a home/house) fea-

Figure 144: All-Seeing Eye-Sun with 'Hands'.
The logo seemed to symbolise our *global* 'house arrest' in April 2020.

Figure 143: Occult Hand Signs.
The hand sign given by many celebrities is said to be an occult reference to blessing ceremonys in biblical times? Or is it a trapezium symbol?

tured once again. As I will come to later in the book, 2030 seems to be a significant date in relation to installing a centrally-controlled global government, where 'global citizenship' would be enforced *through* smart technology (nano-techology) connected to a Cyber-Grid. A 'mandatory' global vaccinaton programme, because of the coronavirus, is highly likely, too. Again, I am *not* saying musicians such as Gaga are involved in such plans, I doubt they are even aware of the larger occult significance and agenda, but the imagery and use of symbolism is interesting, as always (see figures 143 and 144).

According to Moe Bedard (GnosticWarrior.com), the hand symbolism seems to relate to ancient Phoenician-Canannite gestures and blessing ceremonys performed in the temple in biblical times.[10] These gestures are obviously still used today and often by celebrities who do not understand the history and symbology behind such signs. Only a fully initiated person would know the real meaning behind such symbolism. There is nothing new with symbolism, its the most ancient of languages, as Confucius said, 'Signs and symbols rule the world, not words nor laws'.

Magic-like Performances for the Subconscious Mind

In 2017, Lady Gaga also sang the US national anthem at 'Super Bowl 50', which was partnered with 'Intel'. Hundreds of lighted drones, forming various shapes in the sky above Houston's NRG Stadium, made this the first time 'robotic' aircraft had ever appeared in a Super Bowl program. The drones and how they were used to form the Intel logo, only scratches the surface in terms of what AI technology is intended to be used for eventually, much of it being fostered to replace human intelligence, as I will get to in *Part Two*.

The robot theme has also grown increasingly since the millennium. Beyoncé's performance of the song, "Get Me Bodied" at the 2007 BET Awards, was pure 'Metropolis-like symbolism. In Beyoncé's performance she rises from a matrix-like stage set dressed as a 'robot', awakening after being charged with electricity. It was Frankenstein meets Metropolis visually! Her robot shell is peeled away to reveal a part sexualized and provocative costume underneath while her back-up dancers are locked inside cages. The movie *Metropolis*, classically uses conceit and creates a reality where the workers (masses) live below the ground, while its aristocracy lives in skyscrapers high above. The concept of *Metropolis* extends to a biblical dimension, with workers being 'gobbled up' in fantasy by the demon, Moloch, whilst the wealthy cavor around places called the 'Eternal Gardens' (Eden) and the central skyscraper, the New Tower of Babel. The notion of robots, artificial intelligence and an elite that intend use it to control the masses, is certainly a major theme in music, film and books in our time. Like most of these 'mega' performances, they often seem to be revealing hidden themes, very much connected to a 'Cyber-Grid Empire', as we shall see later in the book.

Katy Perry's 2015, Super Bowl XLIX performance seemed to be a symbolic homage to Artemis/Ishtar/Inanna. Katheryn Hudson (aka, Katy Perry) whose parents were said to be travelling Pentecostal preachers, according to Perry's Autobiography. It is said before her family 'found Christ', her father was a hippie figure who was said to have hung out with Timothy Leary, also a follower and proponent of Crowley's philosophy. Leary also wrote and spoke frequently about transhumanism, space migration, 'intelligence increase' (through AI), and life extension. Leary was a major player in the Hippie, Counter-Culture movement and one of the pivotal figures behind it. According to *Rolling Stone*, it is said that by the time she was 13, her parents were taking her to 'Nashville' (a notable centre for mind control, according to the whistleblower author Cathy O'Brien) to pursue a gospel-singing career, something she has in common with Beyoncé and Taylor Swift. Many of these performers' parents were said to be a major catalyst, to the point of making the child's career the family's highest priority.[11]

Perry's arrival atop a red-eyed, robot-like lion (singing her song *Roar*) at the 49th Super Bowl halftime show, also 'hinted' at ancient Babylonian symbolism connected to the goddess Asherah/Artemis - the Lion Lady (see figure 145 overleaf). Interestingly, according to author Pierre Sabak, the word 'Peri' (or Perry) etymologically is a Persian word for Jinn (Archon).[12] I am sure Perry had no knowledge of the visual comparison, not that it would matter to such big stars/performers. The imagery is there to act as a bridge to the subconscious mind. Asherah's association with lions is far from unique in the ancient world, too. The Goddess riding a lion, or being flanked by lions was known as 'lion-possessing' and connects to the zodiacal sign of Leo. The goddesses Kore and Persephone are other versions of the Lion Lady; all can be connected to the goddess Hecate, who was used for 'invoking forces'.[13] I will come back to Hecate and its significance to rituals connected to the time of Orion in a later chapter. Perry's dress, covered in stylised flames, was another reminder of the 'Catching Fire' Artemis/Apollo symbolism seen in the *Hunger Games* trilogy. Besides the

Figure 145: Perry as the Star Goddess, Asherah.
(left) Asherah/Artemis standing on the lion. **(Right)** At the 49th Super Bowl halftime show, Katy Perry seems to appear as the goddess Asherah, in the place of magic – where the 'stars' are revered.

connection to the goddess Asherah, lion symbolism relates to ancient rulers and those who influence politics and the media indsutries globally. The Babylonian lion (Leo) symbol is found in many areas of our lives, too.

'Holy Wood', the Hunter's Paradise

The name Hollywood is said to refer to the 'holly-wood' (holy wood) or Hel-wood, the place of magic, where Druids of the ancient mystery schools would perform their ceremonies. The 'chief wizards' of today are the mega rich film directors and producers, who fund and often create the blockbusters we flock to. Film is mass art and big productions, especially the ones that conjure up imagery associated with duality (good against evil), no different in content to the religious spin exalted by priests throughout history. Totalitarian modernist attitudes from the turn of the Twentieth Century have used film to 'engineer' the human collective perception and soul. Films are a classic example of myth-making, art and propaganda combined. Holding power over the minds of the masses in ancient times was the purpose of the shaman (myth maker) and the same is still happening today. The media is a powerful, mind-controlling device and it is used to full effect, day after day, by the those that understand how the subconscious mind creates reality! All advertising is a testimony to the power of subliminal messages, churned out by the film and media industry, which speak directly to our subconscious minds. Most of the products we consume, we don't actually need and this is the real reason for endless advertising, the media industry and the world of celebrities in general.

The music industry is a haven for some of the most obvious references to gods, goddesses and symbolism associated with the occult. There is nothing necessarily bad about the occult, a word that literally means 'hidden'; however, it is the use of hidden knowledge that can be directed towards good or bad. In that sense all knowledge is neutral, it is the malevolent use of the occult, through black magic, which opens individuals up to the state of mind that too often revels in unspeakable crimes against humanity. Many symbols used in media and music industries carry occult meanings, most have dual significance and as always, the symbolism relates to celestial figures.

The symbol of the 'whore' and the 'virgin' rolled into one figure, touched on earlier, is a classic archetypal description of the ancient Mother Goddess, or Dragon Queen, found in the ancient world. This goddess figure was called Ishtar, Isis in Egypt, Semiramis in Mesopotamia and later referred to as Mary Magdalene by the Christian faith. Madonna, was the ultimate contemporary figure of the music industry based on the virgin-harlot archetype. As I've already touched on in previous chapters, Madonna has also appeared in music videos as a serpent fire-goddess for her track *Bedtime Story* (1994). This video was around the time she is said to have discovered the Kabbalah, and has references to Sufi mysticism and Gnostic teachings associated with the Jinn and Archons as mentioned in earlier chapters. The very popular *Handmaid's Tale* (2017-19) also has a character called 'Offred' who is linked to Sufi mysticism, which is said by its nature, to be subversive to mainstream religious authority and hierarchy. The projection of 'subversiveness' and 'inversion' of 'asceticism' celebrated through pop 'idols', can be connected to the symbolism of Kali, Hecate, Hel and Artemis and the Dog Star, Sirius.

Interestingly, Kate Bush, the 70s and 80s English singer (before Madonna), was also compared to the Pagan goddess Isis, or the Scandinavian Frig/Hel, whether she wanted it, or not. Writing in *The Secret History of Kate Bush* (1983), In the 80s, Fred Vermorel compared Kate Bush to the ancient goddess figure, Frigg. He writes:

Kate Bush is our goddess Frig. And, like the Saxons, we both revere and fear her. Shroud her in mystery of her power and the power of her mystery. She is a fertility goddess for our nature: the Economy. Mother Commodity. Kate Bush is the smile on the steel of EMI, the mating call of Thorn Industries, British Capital on heat, the soft warm voice of mass media, the sweet breath of vinyl, the lovely face of bureaucracy, the seductive gaze of power. As every star is.[14]

I like Kate Bush's music but that description of her, in relation to an ancient deity and the 'power behind the music industry', could be applied to other Hollywood or music stars in the past. Marilyn Monroe and others like her seem to have replicated occult 'idols'. Jeff Godwin's book *Dancing With Demons – The Music's Real Master* (1988), covers a wide range of musicians, from rap artists to rock bands, which he suggests are (or have been) involved in satanic rituals. I personally cannot validate such claims and I certainly don't share Godwin's Christian fanaticism (he's not quite grasped that Catholicism at its 'highest level' has been involved in horrendous crimes against children), but his book certainly illustrates some of the more subliminal connections between the rich and famous and black magic. He also highlights some of the word twists and symbolic codes found in lyrics and on album covers going back to the Sixties.

Truths Embedded in Films

Stories and themes contained within movies and novels have a greater effect on the mind than we give them credit for. So do the subliminal messages used in television commercials and within programmes targeting all levels of society. The word 'programme' says it all really, because that is exactly what our minds are: a programme arrested by endless chat shows, news bulletins and other forms of mediocre entertainment. Education is also full of programmes, administered by programme leaders working to a matrix (time table). Films can also be used as tools for propaganda, especially for the Masonic/occult/religious hierarchies and the off-world forces driving that I call the Orion Cult. The multi-million dollar media and film industry, are helping to create what could potentially be 'new perceptions' based on a political agenda for the 21st Century. The vision is for a New World Order where humanity has 'direct' experience with the god of this New Order – AI. Many science fiction films are preparing the psyche to accept the revelation of alien invaders, or a World at War, as a move towards accepting a New World Order. It's also fascinating to see how certain films mix truths with disinformation; by labeling these types of films as 'science fiction', they often provide a cover for the off-world forces and the nature of a coming AI New Global Order. As the American film director, producer, and screenwriter, Zack Snyder, said about making movies:

> I think it's drawing on all mythology; comic book, religion, ancient, philosophical.

Hollywood is expert at myth-making, not least through some of the organisations making obvious their source of 'star screen magic'. Tinsle Town has been a major part of all our lives, when it comes to the 'visionary', 'artistry' and 'myth-making'. I hope we do not see its decline in the years to come, too much art and creativity is being lost to technology. Storytelling and myth-making is essential to our humanity and the ancient myths need to be kept alive.

Orion in the Movies

Orion Pictures Corporation was an American motion picture producer and distributor that produced and released films from 1978 until 1999 and was also involved in television production and syndication throughout the 1980s until the early 1990s. It was formed in 1978 as a joint venture between Warner Bros and three former top-level executives of United Artists. Although it was never a large motion picture producer, Orion achieved a comparatively high reputation for Hollywood quality, producing some excellent movies. Since 1997, Orion has been owned by Metro-Goldwyn-Mayer and later, the Samuel Goldwyn Company took over the television side of Orion's productions. Hollywood seems to have been mainly influenced by wealthy philanthrophists, occults (like Crowley) with what appears to be an 'interest' in mysticism, philosphies and mythology, therefore it would have been no surprise to find such a huge corporation within tinseltown, called 'Orion' Pictures.

One of Orion's founders, Arthur B. Krim, was an American entertainment lawyer and former finance chairman for the U.S. Democratic Party (an adviser to three presidents: Kennedy, Johnson, and Carter), also the former chairman of 'Eagle-Lion' Films (1946–1949), United Artists (1951–1978), and the legendary Orion Pictures (1978–1992). His more than four decades as a movie studio head is one of the longest in Hollywood history, according to Wikipedia. Orion produced some of the finest films of its time, especially through my youth, such as *Dances with Wolves* (1990), *The Silence of the Lambs* (1991) and *Robocop* (1987). In many ways, Orion was a tour de force until after a series of crisis ended it in 1992.

Orion and Nasa

The National Aeronautics and Space Administration (NASA) spends billions on space projects and therefore it is no surprise to find one of the most expensive projects launched in 2011 called the 'Orion Project'. The original logo of NASA's Apollo program, with the stylized Orion shoulder belt in the centre, seems to indicate there is more to know about the Orion constellation. What is interesting in the NASA logo is the graphic connection between the earth and the moon through Orion's belt stars. The god Apollo, named after the god of music, poetry, 'archery' and the Sun along with the Moon Goddess, hunter, Artemis/Diana, through their joint machinations, kill Orion in the myth. You could call it the 'Moon (Artemis) Apollo mission' (see figure 146 overleaf).

The obvious occult symbolism connected to Nasa and its Apollo

Figure 146: Apollo Mission.
At the highest levels, NASA
seems to understand the occult
symbolism connecting Orion,
Sun, Saturn and the Moon.

Programme won't surprise anyone who has done some basic research. For example, the Moon landing on the 20th July is thought to have coincided with the anniversary of the commencement of the Egyptian (Osiris), Sothis (Siris) calendar. The use of symbols on badges and emblems within Nasa's space programmes seem to hint at the same knowledge found within secret societies such as the Freemasons, too.

NASA's motto for the Moon Landing, "That's one small step for man, one giant leap for mankind", hints at a more off-world grandiose agenda. The national effort that enabled Astronaut Neil Armstrong to speak those words as he stepped onto the lunar surface, fulfilled a dream as old as humanity. But Project Apollo's goals went beyond landing Americans on the Moon and returning them safely to Earth. According to Nasa, it had other interests, with the following intentions:

- *To 'establish the technology' to meet other national interests in space.*
- *To achieve preeminence in space for the United States.*
- *To carry out a program of scientific exploration of the Moon.*
- *To develop man's capability to work in the lunar environment.*[15]

NASA is a highly secretive setup, destined to be much more influencial when it comes to a Space Age future, which, at the highest levels, I would suggest, will involve communcation with alien life they *already know about*, and connecting with star systems such as Orion. I wonder about Nasa's abilities to do *all* they say they can do, especially given controversy over 'Operation Paperclip' and the Moon landings in past decades. Operation Paperclip was a secret program of the Joint Intelligence Objectives Agency (JIOA) largely carried out by Special Agents of Army CIC, in which more than 1,600 German scientists, engineers, and technicians, such as Wernher von Braun and his V-2 rocket team, were said to have been taken from Germany to America for U.S. government employment, primarily between 1945 and 1959. Many were said to be *former* members, and leaders, of the Nazi Party. In fact, four Operation Paperclip members were awarded the NASA Distinguished Service Medal in 1969: Kurt Debus, Eberhard Rees, Arthur Rudolph, and Wernher von Braun. Ernst Geissler was awarded the medal in 1973. There is more to know about NASA and its real purpose, especially in the fields of alien (artificial) intelligence.

The Orion Project, one of NASA's biggest projects to date, stated on its website, 'will carry astronauts into deep space and then return them home to earth'. It is said that NASA's Orion Project will be able to travel to an asteroid, or even Mars (see the movie, *Martian* 2014). The Orion shuttle, created for the project according to NASA's website, has 'three' main parts (no surprises there). The upper section is the launch abort system, or LAS; the crew module is the middle part; and the service module is the lower portion of the spacecraft. Astronauts will sit in the middle section, the crew module. This will be their living quarters. The powers on earth, the extremly wealthy 1% are obsessed with such space missions (projects) and 'star wars', which only enhances the idea of earth's ancestral bloodline elite creating a 'prison planet'; a place of *quarantine* for humanity, while being obsessed with AI and its connection to alien life (the stars).

The Constellation Program

As the Vision for Space Exploration was developed into the 'Constellation program' under NASA administrator Sean O'Keefe, the Crew Exploration Vehicle was renamed the 'Orion Crew Exploration Vehicle', after the star constellation of the same name. Within this ongoing project, came the 'Orion Crew Exploration Vehicle' (CEV), Orion 'Multi-Purpose Crew Vehicle' (MPCV) and The 'Orion Crew Module' (CM). All connected to the space shuttle. Currently under development by NASA and the European Space Agency (ESA) for launch on the Space Launch System. According to NASA, 'Orion is intended to facilitate human exploration of the Moon, asteroids and of Mars and to retrieve crew or supplies from the International Space Station if needed'. All this Orion naming is obviously telling us something more about NASA's real interest in the Constellation Programme – Orion, and possibly what exists there?

Despite the now-cancelled Orion Constellation Program instigated during the Obama administration, the Orion Crew Exploration Vehicle survived the cancellation and was renamed the Multi-Purpose Crew Vehicle. Some say the Apollo and Saturn projects were prioritised over Orion in 1963 and that the reusable rockets, an integral part of the Orion Constellation Programme, are being spearheaded by Elon Musk's Space X (more on the 'X' symbolism later.) Musk, like Sundar Pichai (head of Google) seem to be fronting a deeper agenda to connect humanity to satellite systems via micro-chips (Nanorobotics) and everything 'Smart'. Note the graphic connection to Saturn in the logo of the Orion Project, which was originally designed by Star Trek artist Mike Okuda (see figure 147 overleaf). Some researchers have even connected the Manhattan project to Nasa's Orion Project, not least through the use of nuclear propulsion design, said to take *twenty two* people to Saturn in the 1970s.

Figure 147: The Orion Project.
Orion and Saturn *are* connect-
ed more than we realise.
(Public domain.)

In 2019, NASA announced it was involved in a deal with Lockheed Martin costing 3 billion dollars, to build three Orion capsules to return to the moon by 2024.[16] The mega deal calls for a first phase including three capsules for $2.7 billion, for Artemis Missions III and V that will take astronauts back to the Moon (if they actually went when they said they did?). The Orion capsules, according to NASA, will be able to bring astronauts to the Moon and back, and it must also be capable of travelling to Mars and beyond. NASA Administrator Jim Bridenstine (a Republican congressman from Oklahoma) said of the project:

> *Orion is a highly capable, state-of-the-art spacecraft, designed specifically for deep space missions with astronauts, and an integral part of NASA's infrastructure for Artemis missions and future exploration of the solar system …*

In addition to the capsule that will orbit around the Moon attached to a mini-station (called the 'Gateway'), NASA asked the aerospace sector in July 2019 to propose detailed vehicle projects to land two astronauts on the Moon by 2024, including the first woman. The use of the name 'The Artemis program' connects to this, not least the Artemis myth in relation to Orion. The Artemis program is running behind schedule, but the flight of the Artemis I mission – unmanned – is supposedly scheduled for by the end of 2020. The first manned Artemis II flight is said to be scheduled for 2022. What isn't running behind schedule is the enormous surge towards *everything* AI, as we shall see.

Orion and AI

Orion also features heavily in the corporate world in many forms. A quick scan throws up Artificial Intelligence services to Japanese beer distilleries, all sharing the name Orion. We also have what seems to be three belt stars on the US Democrat logo, Orion TV and Orion Electric (1958) and various military based firms sporting Orion as their logo. The Japanese seem to love all things Orion, which, as I will come to later in the book, could relate to their ancestral connection to the Samurai and the ancient Japanese Ainu and Jomon people. As I have already touched on, Orion is connected to Ursa Major through the goddess Artemis, which is the name of a microchip

Figure 148: It's *bigger* than we realise!

computer technology, too. The main point here is the *name* 'Orion' is used extensively in the 'space-tech-corporate' world for obvious reasons.

What is interesting is the use of the word 'Orion' in everything AI, along with Data Interchange platforms emerging over the past few years. The interconnectedness of all things 'Smart' and the 'Cloud' systems that corporations use, seem to be inspired by Orion, too (see figure 148).

One of the main themes attributed to AI platforms are 'blockchains', which are digital ledger systems. One notable nature of blockchain technology is its distributed implementation manner, operating through 'Smart technology'. The rise of 'Bitcoin' currency can be seen as a similar platform, now demonstrating its potential in numerous domains. In simple terms, these artificial intelligent platforms are not only facilitating a whole new 'reality' in what we call cyberspace, but they are building it to extend to empirical levels. But why Orion? The main reason is in part connected to the type of alien intelligence associated with the Orion Constellation, as I will come back to in more detail towards the end of the book.

The world depicted in movies such as *I Robot* (2004) and *Oblivion* (2013) and the *Hunger Games* Trilogy (2013), are only a few examples of what these cloud-based, smart platforms could achieve. The central artificial intelligent 'command' called Virtual Interactive Kinetic Intelligence (V.I.K.I) is the nearest science fiction has come to depicting an Orion-like 'queen' that controls her robot army 'coded' to the highly symbolic 'three' laws (see figure 149). VIKI's monologue in the movie *I Robot*, when she is being challenged by a suspicious renegade detective Del Spooner (played by Will Smith), says:

Figure 149: 'VIKI'.
She is the archetypal Orion Queen or Hive Mind. Possibly Google's Alexa in the not-so-far distant future.
My image inspired by the movie I Robot.

To protect Humanity, some humans must be sacrificed. To ensure your freedom, some freedoms must be surrendered. We robots will ensure mankind's continued existence. You are so like children. We must save you from yourselves.

Even though this is science fiction, the above statement should send 'alarm bells' ringing, as we are not that far from the possibility of Virtual

Interactive Kinetic Intelligence 'taking over'in the not-so-far distant future. It will be written into history, remember when Google's Alexa, or Apple's Siri, started out as innocent Interactive Kinetic Intelligence toys? It is what comes *after* these AI applications we need to be concerned about.

A TV commercial for the new generation of Galaxy Samsung androids, *Galaxy Hunter,* in 2019, also seemed to incorporate imagery connected to Orion, robot-machines and giants. The caption for the advertisement was: "What we create today, lets you create the future". That future depends hugely on how much the younger generations focus their attention on imagery being projected via games, streamed films and other forms of digital entertainment. The young especially are being prepared for an AI takeover, which is probably why 'online gaming' and other cellular device activity has grown over the decades.

Cult influence of the entertainment industry in particular, focus our attention on idols (celebrities) so to maintain *our* focus on the idea of the gods (the stars). Methods used by these brotherhoods vary and that is why much of the entertainment industry attracts an occult influence. Whether it's the Olympics (symbolised through the 'rings' and lighted torch), or a film with subjects pertaining to the occult (see *Harry Potter),* they are teeming with references to mythology, hidden brotherhoods and symbols associated with the occult. The goal is the same; to influence the minds of the masses to accept New World Order ideologies. These objectives relate to what some researchers have called the 'Super Torch Ritual' and relate to the 'end of days' or 'judgement day' scenario (found in many movies), designed to usher in the end of one age and the birth of a *new* dystopian *normal.* A more current term being used on media platforms is the 'Great Reset', which is simply another way of saying the New World Order. As I will get to later, the 'Reset' could be part of the Cyber-Grid Empire being built to enslave humanity in the future. The dystopian theme in such movies, whether caused by nuclear war, zombie-*virus* or some extraterrestrial invasion, always leads to a 'new world' ruled by a technocratic elite (often otherworldly too), while the masses live in some form of permanent poverty and 'quarantine'. Movies like *Equilibrium* (2002) and the *Hunger Games* are two of many examples depicting such future nightmare realities. *Equilibrium* is an especially telling film, the setting is a post 'Third World War' dystopia from which all 'dangerous' human emotion is drained by daily injection (a vaccine programme) of the drug Prozium and the burning of art and books are common (see any fascist regime). Look at the levels of 'censorship' of 'aternative' voices by the Silicon Valley giants, Facebook and YouTube, etc, in 2020, and you can get a glimmer of that tyrannical future being built around us. Technology and the forces behind it *will* rule us (it already does for young people), unless we learn to 'switch off' and tune into 'higher forces' - our source of power. The imagination is crucial to this tuning in process. It is also our connection to the source, or infinte. As Wiliam Blake said, "The imagination is not a state, it is the human existence itself".

ART-*em*-IS and the *Hunger Games*

The *Hunger Games* movies, based on the books by Suzanne Collins, who incidentally comes from a military background, are especially telling in terms of predictive programming, a future full of occult symbolism, tyranny, dystopia and an elite (the 1%) governing a new topology in the USA. In the first movie, there was even a 'Saturn black cube' in the centre of the capital, (which reminded me of the NSA headquarters), another symbol for total surveillance, idolisation and 'suppression of information'. The capital in the *Hunger Games*, Panem, is the 'ultimate city' that rules over a future America, with its segregated *twelve* districts (just as our perception of time is governed by *twelve* hours, months). Panem's is another 'time lord city' symbolically ruling over the populace by a Saturn figure (President Snow), a symbolic figurehead for the 1%. Connected to this is the '*e*' of Panem, a heavily used letter within numerological associations and emphasised in many logos or corporations, not least the 'Int*e*l' and Saturn-like Internet 'explorer' logos. 'E' in the Greek alphabet is 'Epsilon' and again we are back to references of secret societies and fraternities involved in the highest levels of society (see page 203). According to some researchers the letter *e* is a very important letter (or its numerlogical value is) because it represents the *fifth* essence (element), or the 'power of transcendence'. This power is the core philosophy behind the capital of Panem, where *power* is concentrated in the hands of the few (elite) and 'games' are played out for their sick satisfaction. E *(e)*, I have noticed, is always 'highlighted', or 'dropped' in some way, in logos and symbolism to reinforce this power of transcendence.

The 'M' is another letter important to the mystery schools of antiquity, being the numerological equivalent of '*thirteen*', we have the 'rise and fall' of America in the *Hunger Games* books, this relates to the original *thirteen* districts or the 12 sectors around the 1 (the Capitol). 'M' or the *13th* letter in the alphabet is the symbolic 'master' with 12 disciples and, esoterically speaking, *thirteen* is the 'experiencer' of the 12 signs of the zodiac. There are only 12 months in the Gregorian sun calendar but there are 13 months in the original indigenous lunar calendar; there were 13 districts, but now only 12 remain, etc. Just as there are, of course, 12 Jurors and 1 Judge, etc. Numbers (and letters) are vibrational codes affecting the subconscious. As David Icke writes in *The Biggest Secret* (1998):

These number codes have even deeper meanings than the more obvious ones of days, months, and the zodiac. Numbers also represent vibrational frequencies. Every frequency resonates to a certain number, colour and sound. Some frequencies, represented by numbers, colours and sounds, are particularly powerful. Symbols also represent frequencies and they affect the subconscious without the person realizing it is happening. This is another reason why certain symbols are seen in secret societies, national flags, company logos, advertising and so on.[17]

And I would suggest that the 'carefully chosen' detail concerning numbers, symbols and references to myths in such movies, are part of this rationale.

The capitol, Panem, in the *Hunger Games*, is the 'state of the art' technological 'district-to-district' life, with everything linked by microchip, communication systems, etc. The masses *are* slaves to their Panem masters, just as today the masses are no more than slaves to elite power brokers who invented banking and politics and the very 'technology' we consume and have helped create. With the Artemis symbolism (Orion's lover) so obvious in the *Hunger Games* books and films, it's worth noting that the EU has a ECSEL-JU project called 'Artemis Joint Undertaking' (Electronic Components and Systems for European Leadership), which is providing technological hardware and software that could easily be part of a dystopian future. The ECSEL-JU programme, according to their website, has an estimated budget of €4.815 *billion*, merging the previous ARTEMIS-JU and the ENIAC-JU in June 2014, with a view to complete its work in 2024. Within its structure are *three* industry associations (including ARTEMIS Industry Association) representing areas of Micro-/Nanoelectronics, Embedded and Cyber-Physical Systems and Smart Systems. Along with AI, these are the areas of investment that are building the 'Cyber-Grid Empire'.

The Just after 9/11, we also had the Carlyle Group Subsidiary named 'Matrics', pushing a 'Tracker Chip' that would be used in global future RFID infrastructure. Built on the back of IBM's technology, the Artemis systems were designed and sold as a means to spot and fight infections in babies, but also to grab data from both medical records and 'real-time sensors' feeding data to, what its own literature calls 'the machine world'. Today, we are seeing the same technology being proposed as part of the 'Track and Trace' applications in the wake of the coronavirus pandemic.

According to the ECSEL-JU project (Artemis Industry Association) website: "Artemis has been working to create, embedded computing systems, although invisible, making a significant contribution to improving our daily lives". What is more, the ECSEL-JU projects offer state-of-the-art industrial applications which are part and parcel of the European economy and what will become an electronic currency [world currency]. Their website also says:

> *In order to promote economies of scale, reduce costs and encourage the marketing of products based on these technologies, the European Union (EU) is launching a public-private partnership in the field of research into embedded computing systems in the form of a Joint Technology Initiative, implemented by the ARTEMIS Joint Undertaking ... .*[18]

In other words the massive integration of mobile phones to bank cards, cars and planes (all future transport), to *all* computing devices, would cover 98% of all usage globally. Talk about profiting from others 'happy' servitude? Panem here we come!

The Alien Amongst Us

Computers, as we know, have moved away from the desktop and can be found in everyday devices of all sorts, from cell phones, to smart meters. Innovations made possible by embedded systems coordinated through the likes of ATREMIS, are said to make our lives healthier and more interesting; our transport safer, and our energy use more sustainable. They are at the heart of industrial innovation and competitiveness, creating and sustaining jobs and economic well-being. *So we are repeatedly told.* However, the *Hunger Games* movies, along with other dystopian films, such as the even darker dystopian science fiction movie *Brazil* (1985), the world is run by microchips, holographic interfaces (via the World Wide Web), and at the extreme end, 'living machine consciousness' (AI). The Internet *is* artificial consciousness and with no stretch of the imagination could become a 'living' (alien) entity, leading to total surveillance, or a 'skynet' scenario? We already have this type of surveillance with the 'Intellistreets' systems, Smart technology, facial recognition and the ever-growing 'Internet of Things'. In the *Hunger Games* movie, *everyone* is 'watched' by an advanced version of this technology. A reality we are seeing unfold rapidly today. Interestingly, in a BBC *Newsnight* interview in 1999, David Bowie, talking to Jeremy Paxman about the Internet, said: "I think we are on the cusp [back then] of something exhilarating and terrifying". When questioned by Paxman about 'world wide web' being just a 'tool', Bowie replied: *"No it's an alien life-form"*. I agree. As expressed through the themes so far, I am sure the late 'legendary' Bowie knew about such otherworldly forces.

No matter where one looks throughout history, ancient brotherhoods have strived to influence the perceptions of the masses so to accept a global future timelines that often do not respect human individuality, spirituality and, above all, the Earth herself. Instead, the 21st Century media-machine, could be seen as inspiring the *new* religion, 'technology' and the ideaology towards a *new* global order based around technology. There seems to be a mantra based on the same symbolism found in occult systems which at the very epicentre is worshipping artificial intelligence and possible dystopian realities.

Media Magic and Subliminal Messages

As I have outlined in this chapter, the world of big-tech, the media and television, especially movies, seem to be tools inspired by otherworldly forces connected to those who utilize magic and rituals to affect human perception. We are an inspired human family, but at the same time we seem to be 'under the influence' of advance science, technology and 'projected realities' which are not always positive, or benefitial to us as a collective species.

Five hundred years ago, technology that was ahead of its time, from a public perspective, was being used to create imagery that would ultimately mould the perceptions of the era we call the Renaissance. Art, religion and mythological scenes were used to 're-enforce' beliefs that the rulers and elite of that era wanted the masses to hold. Some film makers (producers/directors) today, who are no different in terms of their access to knowledge, are like the Leonardo Da Vinci's of their time. Today, the 'myth-makers' produce works of art in the form of films so as to shape perceptions and reinforce ideologies. I have been amazed at the amount of information embedded in ancient myths that filter *into* themes found in films. Dualism, or the myths pertaining to 'good against evil', are the most obvious theme used in blockbuster plots. Going to the cinema to watch the latest film (before the coronavirus pandemic), is almost like attending a ceremony dedicated to the subconscious mind. Even the atmosphere within a cinema through the 'lack of light', the often use of 'red curtains', along with the imagery itself, is almost like attending an esoteric/occult ritual. The imagery contained within films coming out of Hollywood over the years, can have an effect on our subconscious, more than we actually realise; some movies are 'predictive' programming to the core, especially when topics within movie plots seem to project' future outcomes relating to events unfolding in our world. The film director/producer can be seen as the ancient magician archetype who alters our perception through the use of narratives, symbolism and archetypal imagery. I have even heard people say that they "went somewhere", or that the film was "more of an experience", after seeing some of the latest blockbusters. This is because the imagery and themes behind them are part of a subconscious language, memories and alternative histories, which can still be accessed by the mind. Entering the cinema is symbolic of entering the chambers of the subconscious mind and that is why cinema has become an important tool for the forces that have a lot invested in how we see the world. This is fundamentally influenced by, a) our subconscious thoughts and beliefs, and b) the primary visual cortex at the base of the brain, the primary factor of how we *create* our individual and collective reality!

In the next few chapters I want to consider 'creation', 'reality', 'duality' and some of the key religious groups, such as the Gnostic Cathars, who understood the nature of dualism. I also want to look closer at the symbolism connected to the *archetypes* of Orion.

Sources:

1) Knoeplfer, Denis."*Épigraphie et histoire des cités grecques-Pausanias en Béotie* (suite): *Thèbes et Tanagra*" (PDF). Archived from the original (PDF) on 2007-09-27. Collège de France, following Louis Robert's explanation of a Roman-era inscription.
2) Herodotus. *The Histories*. Trans. A. D. Godley. 4.191.
3) Ezek. 8:12-14
4) Daniel, John. *Scarlet and the Beast - A History of the War between English and French Freemasonry*, 1889 p64
5) https://www.rutherford.org/publications_resources/john_whiteheads_commentary/mark_david_chapman_the_catcher_in_the_rye_and_the_killing_of_john_lennon
6) Jake Stratton-Kent. *The Headless One* (e-book) p30
7) http://weekinweird.com/2011/04/11/the-boleskine-house-loch-ness-other-stranger-monster/
8) *Freemasonry an Illustrated Guide* 1999, p200
9) https://www.thesun.co.uk/news/7561460/aleister-crowley-sex-demon/
10) https://gnosticwarrior.com/illuminati-hand-sign.html
11) *Rolling Stone Magazine*, "Sex, God and Katy Perry", August 2010
12) According to Pierre Sabak, the word 'Peri' (Perry) is a Persian word for Jinn (Archon).
13) Newton, Toyne. *The Dark Worship*. 2002, p21
14) Vermorel, Fred. *The Kate Bush Story*. 1980, p147
15) https://www.nasa.gov/mission_pages/apollo/missions/index.html
16) https://www.msn.com/en-gb/news/techandscience/nasa-in-megadeal-with-lockheed-for-moon-mission/ar-AAHJWpS?ocid=spartanntp
17) Icke, David. *The Biggest Secret*. Bridge of Love. 1998, p145
18) https://artemis-ia.eu/h2020calls.html

9

ARCHETYPES OF ORION
Symbols of Life, Death & Duality

Seek him that maketh the seven stars and Orion ...
The Lord is his name
Amos 5:8

The Orion constellation can be seen as an all-encompassing 'archetype' for duality and of how 'dual forces' wrestle within our reality. Understanding dual forces, seemingly 'eternally turning', aiding in the evolution of humanity, can often be seen in petroglyphs and pictographs made by ancient artists. You could say that the plentitude of art made on rocks and caves, in places such as Arizona through to Northern India, by migrating artist-shamans, was probably put there intentionally to remind future generations of greater life cycles endured through opposing forces. All religion from its initial Paleolithic and Pagan origins, through to the Abrahamic faiths, have interwoven concepts of gods representing good and evil, heaven and hell, or life and death. These concepts have been personified and narrated through native myths for thousands of years. In this chapter I am going to look at the legends and symbolism connected to Orion and 'duality'.

The Dual God
Petroglyphs of strange deities, such as 'Kokopelli' (the hunchback flute player), found in numerous locations across North America, are considered a symbol of the 'Solar life force'. Kokopelli is almost always depicted in rock art, adjacent to, or rising out of the head of, the god Masau'u I mentioned in *Chapter Five*. The Hopi tribes of Arizona say these two gods represent the duality of the 'supreme being' (or the 'force' if you are a *Star Wars* fan). 'Masau'u' was said by the Hopi to be a totemic deity who came out of the 'darkness' as a 'faceless' god, who represented death and the underworld. In some traditions, this mask-wearing figure also represented a 'destroyer of worlds', not too dissimilar to the fire-and-brimstone Old testa-

ment god found woven into Jewish and Christian belief. For the Hopi, Masau'u could take the form of a supernova, fiery celestial events such as comet and meteorite activity that brought enlightenment, or death and destruction.[1] Parallels can be drawn between Masau'u and 'Yama' in Hinduism, who was also the 'God of Death'. Death in relation to these deities was *not* about the 'fear of death' but the opposite, they were considered 'life-givers' *through* death, a concept seen in nature all of the time, especially when nature 'dies' only to be reborn the following year. In Vedic art, Yama is often depicted with green skin, red clothing and riding a buffalo (see Taurus). Both Masau'u and Osiris of ancient Egyptian myth were also depicted as 'giant green gods' associated with the 'underworld', 'germination', and the passage from life to death and visa versa.

The Hopi word 'massi', means 'grey' and could relate to 'grey' aliens, and Hopi legends of being taught by 'Ant People' in subbteranean worlds before the Hopi came to live on the earth's surface. I'll return to this subject later. Alongside Masau'u, Kokopelli was said to be a guardian of the North, and the Sun. He was also a solar insect deity associated with the colour white and blue. Colour symbolism was (and still is) hugely important to the Orion Cult, especially in relation to Orion's stars. Both deities, kokopelli (life) and Masau'u (death), are often found alongside bear claw marks. Bear symbolism in this case related to 'bear people' (the 'Hopi Bear Clan'), who were said by the ancients to be one of several 'human-animal' races living on (and inside) the earth in prehistoric times. The 'Bear' and 'Monkey' Clans can be found in both Native American legends and ancient Indian mythology possibly relating to Bigfoot and 'hairy angelic' humans, as I will come to later in the book.

The 'Son of Man' symbolism, *through* Adam, Atum, Osiris (the Green Man), are all symbolically connected to Orion, duality and 'the lord of time' – Saturn, as I have been illustrating so far. Whether Pagan or Christian (same original source), a 'twin force' symbolised through the biblical Jesus and John figures, reigns over the solstices in a perpetual cycle of life, death and rebirth (Alpha and Omega). Masau'u, whose head was often depicted as a 'skull or pumpkin' on the 'Hopi Fire Clan' tablets (symbolic of decapitation), was often shown 'carrying a head' or a 'bag' of seeds (or stars); in some instances, he is wearing a pumpkin-like mask or head (see figure 150 overleaf). The God of Death, Masau'u, and the God of Life, Kokopelli, are two aspects of a 'Divine Being' – Orion (Adam on High).

Another petroglyph showing the 'duality' of what the Hopi call the Divine Being depicts opposing forces. To the left is Kokopelli who represents life (upside down figure) and Masau'u (with two horns), to the right, represents death. The faces below the gods of 'life and death' are the Hopi Bear Clan who were said to follow Kokopelli, or follow the 'life force' of the

Figure 150: The God of Life & Death.
A Bronze Age petroglyph showing the duality of the divine being at Comanche Gap, Galisteo, New Mexico. The God of Death (Masau'u) facing west and the God of Life (Kokopelli), facing east marking the summer Solstice and Orion rising in the sky.
© Photo courtesy of Dan Budnik.

Figure 151: Kokopelli & Masau'u
A Bronze Age petroglyph showing the duality of the divine being in a 'fire-blackened' cave near Pecos, New Mexico. The black surface of the cave is used to emphasise both 'light and dark' forces through graphic reversal. The bear faces below are representations of the Bear Clan who follow Kokopelli (top left) and the 'two horned' figure (to the right) is Masau'u.
© Photo courtesy of Dan Budnik.

Sun and the Earth (see figure 151). The bear is an important symbol and also relates to Orion in some Native American myths. The Roman poet and author Hyginus (64 BC – AD 17), in his work *Poeticon Astronomicon*, mentions Orion as a 'bear' in pursuit of the 'seven maidens' – the stars that make up the Pleiades. The two opposing figures seen in these Native American petroglyphs are also symbols for opposite ends of the solar year and the dualistic forces that *turn* the solar cycle.

Two 'Sons' of the Sun

In the Bible, John the Baptist was said to be born six months before Jesus. John's birth and emergence astronomically marks the opposite end of the Milky Way in terms of the solar wheel (or sun cross) as seen from earth. Jesus, of course is a winter solstice solar baby who emerges at the opposite time of the year. Like their Celtic counterparts, the 'Oak and Holly Kings', John and Jesus are said to be 'twin solar deities' whose coronations coincide with the pagan Solstices. From our earthly perspective, these solar prophets are aligned with Orion's Heliacal Rising, and therefore Orion's stars. You could say that Orion is the point of reference for the *rise* and *fall* of the Oak and Holly Kings. Jesus, according to the scriptures referred to himself as the 'Son of Man' (the first Adam), whereas John was considered the 'Alpha and Omega' in the mystery schools connected to the Knights Templar. Indeed, the Baptist was considered a more important figure by the Templars based on his role in the narrative highlighted here. It was the Baptist's alleged 'preparing of the way' for the 'one to come', which saw him as having more importance by the Templars and Teutonic Secret societies.[2] The Knights of St. John (name gives it away) and the Knights of Malta, along with many lesser churches funded by these orders, are focused on John the Baptist. Why was this so? Because John's birth precedes the birth of Jesus on the solar wheel and John is another 'headless' Orion figure, esoterically speaking. There is a good chance the Baptist figure was actually Christ (the roles reversed) if any of them existed at all.

Some of the Templar churches in the Occitan region of France are also dedicated to John the Baptist, and hardly any idolize the Crucifixion. The reason for this is simple, the Brotherhoods who built some of Christendom's finest churches, were Dualists, Gnostics and Alchemists (Druids) who understood the symbolism associated with dualism and Orion. The 'Cult of John the Baptist' as one half of the 'Twin' symbolism was important to the Cathedral builders, so much so that the largest cathedral in France, in the city of Amiens, is said to house the most precious relic of the Templars – the alleged head of John the Baptist. Regardless of whomsoever the head 'belonged', the real focus here is the 'skull' and the symbolism connected to the God of Death and the 'darker apects' of Orion worship by the kabbalists and the secret societies controlling the Vatican.

The late Reg Lewis (Lewis Da Costa), in his masterpiece *The Thirteenth Stone*, argues that both John and Jesus were the same figure! Just as I have shown, Masau'u and Kokopelli are twin 'solar deities' (the celestial John and Jesus symbols of the Hopi); all are symbolic of the dual nature of Orion's influence on Earth. Orion's position in the Heavens also marks the time of 'darkness' as it rises in the Northern Hemisphere through September into October, marked by the Pagan Autumn equinox. Originally the eighth-month of a ten-month year, October comes from the Latin 'octo', meaning 'eight' and 8 is numerologically connected to Saturn, too. The eighth astrological sign of Scorpio is also significant to Orion, for reasons I outlined in the last chapter, it was said to be Scorpius in Greek myth who 'chased' Orion in October across the skies. The number '8' (along with triple 8) is said by occultists to be the number of Jesus (numerologically connected to the lineage from Adam to Japeth in the Bible).[3]

What is significant is that Orion acts as a celestial 'marker' for the Sun and Saturn rituals performed at the Solstices and Equinoxes. For the Rapa Nui Polynesian inhabitants of Easter Island, honouring their ancestors in

their month of 'Hora Nui' (October) through to 'Ruti' (January), Orion was
a key focus during this time. Orion's passage through the earthly year, is
dualistic, and marks the sun's passage into what the Hopi Indians called
the 'eastern and western houses'. When the Hopi god, Tawa (the sun),
reaches his eastern house and commences his ascension over the earth, he
has also just entered the western house, the Underworld and begun to set.
The sun's movement is Horus ('sun on the horizon') and Set ('sunset') is
joined together in a yin-yang-like manner.[4] For the Hopi, the earth only had
'two seasons' measured by the sun's movement between the houses and
overseen by Orion's position in the sky through winter (November to May),
and summer (June to October). All of the rituals connected to the Pagan calendar (festivals) are celebrating the sun's movement, as part of a celestial
backdrop focused on Orion and other surrouding constellations.

The Hopi term for Orion is 'Hotòmqam', which literally means either 'to
string up' (as beads on a string) or 'trey'. The use of this word could refer to
the three stars of Orion's belt but also to the 'tripartite' form of the ant, its
head, thorax, and abdomen. These shiny, bead-like sections of the ant's
body may have their celestial counterpart in what the Hopi consider the
most important constellation in the heavens - Orion. The appearance of
Orion through the overhead hatchways of Hopi kivas (semi-subterranean
prayer chambers) still synchronizes many annual sacred ceremonies with
Orion's appearance in the skies. The legends of the Ant People (possibly
Grey aliens) in the Hopi creation myths also connect to Orion's stars, as we
shall see.

Orion's appearance in the autumn sky above the horizon (in the northern hemisphere) signals the time when all that is 'unseen', or all that dwells
beyond the boundary or void, would begin to surface.
Sun wheel symbolism depicted on petroglyphs, alongside Orion figures, Masau'u and Kokopelli, are symbols of opposing forces. You could say all duality is
born of Orion, the celestial Adam. In Egyptian mythology, Osiris and Horus are sun gods that embody the
light, while Osiris's brother (Horus's uncle), Seth,
embodies the darkness (the Scorpion). Just like petroglyphs depicting a 'connected' Masau'u and
Kokopelli, Seth is depicted in a manner that attaches
him to Horus in other similar scenes (see figure 152).

'Spiro Mounds', a major Northern Caddoan
Mississippian archaeological site located in present-
day Eastern Oklahoma, also offers Orion symbolism.
It gives us some intriguing artifacts, such as engraved

**Figure 152:
The duality of Seth
and Horus.**

Figure 153: Orion's Belt-Cross
Orion's belt stars showing the duality of two figures encased within a solar cross and circle.

shell gorgets, and plates, depicting crosses and other symbols. One of the most prominent symbols at Spiro is the 'Birdman,' a winged human figure (possibly Horus), representing a warrior or 'chunkey' player. Chunkey, which involved rolling disc-shaped stones across the ground and throwing spears at them, was a game played in the Mississippian period, but also in historic times by the Choctaw, Chickasaw, Cherokee, and other Eastern Woodlands tribes. Another Shell shows what is clearly a cross within a circle, flanked by 'opposite Chunkey player figures', or 'warriors' (back to back) holding circular shields and rattles. The gorget from 900 – 1150AD has three circles inside the cross that seem to match the 'position' of Orion's belt stars (see figure 153). The alignment on the gorget clearly has the smaller-looking first belt star (Delta Orionis) positioned accurately. The symbolism also relates to the Axis Mundi or 'World Tree', a central axis on which all the worlds rotated and were connected. The Spiro Mound artifacts also show images of ogees, hands and eyes symbolism, mentioned in *Chapter Three*, all are connected to the Underworld (the stars), duality and Orion.

Adam's Sons

In many esoteric writings, Set (Seth) has been equated with Lucifer and considered a benevolent God before the slaying of Osiris. Set was also worshipped by the Hyksos invaders during Egypt's pre-dynastic period and Pharaohs even called themselves 'beloved of Set' until as recently as the 16th dynasty. Egypt's Rameses II, along with later emperors of Rome, would also align themselves with Set (Seth) or Saturn, which also means 'appointed'. The biblical bloodlines descending from Adam through Seth (Set) and beyond, seem to be part of the metaphysical story relating to Orion and the 'origins' of the gods.

One group of early Gnostics, the Mandaeans, who revered Adam, Abel, Seth, Enos, Noah, Shem, Aram, and especially John the Baptist, revered both 'life' and 'death' as part of their beliefs. Some literature speculates that the Mandaean priests were 'descendants' of John the Baptist, who in their original gnostic roots, competed with then-'emerging' Christianity.[5] In Mandean books, such as *Drasia d-Yahia*, or the *Teachings of John* (or *Book of John*), the Baptist figure along with 'ritual of baptism', seems to also be con-

nected to Mandean sects emerging in the centuries before the time of
Christ. According to the Mandaean text, *Haran Gawaita*, the recorded history of the Mandaeans began when a group called the 'Nazoreans' (the
Mandaean priestly caste as opposed to the laity), left Palestine and migrated to Mesopotamia in the 1st century AD. The earliest Mandaean religious
texts suggest a more strictly 'dualistic' theology, typical of Zoroastrianism,
Zurvanism, Manichaeism, and the teachings of Mazdak, an Iranian
Zoroaster priest. In their writings, there is a discrete division between light
and darkness, and duality is a 'projection' of the 'unknown' or 'deeply hidden', illustrated as simple icons. For the Mandaen mind, the ruler of darkness was called 'Ptahil', sometimes called 'Abatur' and similar to the
Gnostic Demiurge – the originator of the light ('let there be light' of *Genesis*
fame). Ptahil emanates other
spiritual beings, and like Gnostic
narratives I mentioned in an earlier chapter, these 'beings'
become corrupted, while their
ruler Ptahil constructs our world
matrix. The name Ptahil is similar to the Egyptian Ptah, and the
Mandaeans believe that they
were resident in Egypt for a
while – joined to the Semitic
tribes of 'El', meaning 'God'.
Abatur/Ptahil, another version
of the Ancient of Days (see page
127), is said to be the third of four
emanations from the supreme,

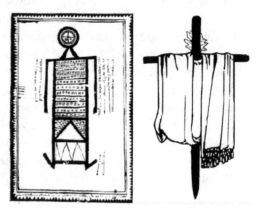

Figure 154: Orion Man & Cross.
(Left) An image of Ptahil (Abatur) taken from
the *Haran Gawaita*. **(Right)** A Mandean cross.

unknowable deity in the Mandaean religion. His name translates as the
'father of the Uthre', the Mandaean name for a 'celestial being' or man (see
figure 154). The celestial being is, of course, Orion, heavenly Adam, Abatur
or Atum.

Figures drawn in Mandean texts are clearly alternative versions of the
Tetragrammaton (mentioned in *Chapter Five*). They are also stylized,
abstract versions of heavenly Adam, with the Merkava as the circle for the
head of Abatur. You would be forgiven for thinking the Mandean cross is a
'scarecrow-like' effigy, but it is a symbol of life. The white garments worn to
symbolise light, in which the pure soul is clad, are draped on the cross to
give the image of a 'being' (whose spirit has flown) and is more important
than the flesh and bone. Not your usual Catholic scene of torture! In the
Mandaean-inspired, Bogomil and Cathar text, *the Gospel of the Secret Supper*
(12th century), Lucifer is a glorified angel and the older brother of Jesus,

but fell from heaven to establish his own kingdom, becoming the Gnostic Demiurge. Therefore, Lucifer, according to the Gnostics, created the material world and 'trapped' souls from heaven *inside* matter, which is what the cross really means. Symbolically, it was Jesus' (Son of Man's) descent to earth to free captured souls that was more important to the Gnostics.[6] In contrast to mainstream Christianity, the cross for later Gnostic groups, such as the Cathars, was denounced as a symbol of Satan and his instrument in an attempt to trap souls and kill Jesus (Adam). From my research, the Gnostics were a constant threat to Rome and the elite Babylonian-Roman Catholic Church. The common theme through the centuries has been that Gnostics = 'send the military in and destroy them and any record of what they knew or believed'. I am not saying for a second that they knew everything about reality, of course not, but they knew more than enough for the church to greatly fear them.

Seth's Knights

The Mandaen philosophy can also be seen in the 'Knights of Seth', a 19th-century British-German Neo-Sethian Gnostic group that attempted to resurrect Mandean, medieval Gnostic and dualistic Christian ideas. Like much earlier Gnostics, the Knights of Seth believed in a true God and a false God (duality). Apart from a handful of members in Edinburgh and Berlin, the group presently appears to be almost extinct. The group is sometimes referred to by its Latin name *'Ordo Equester Sethiani'* and according to the Ordo Equester, Adam's *third* son, Seth, was a messiah figure who could 'communicate' with the true god (the Upper Aeons) and acted as his herald, thwarting the plans of the Demiurge (see *Chapter Four*). The Knights of Seth believed that seven prophets (or visible stars of Orion) would deliver various teachings to humanity. These would then enable mankind to experience the true meaning of the 'hidden god', and not the imposter biblical god, warned about by the Gnostics. I myself have tried imparting knowledge, through my art and writings, aligning with these teachings, too. Art, symbols, letter forms all 'inform' our understanding of deeper 'hidden' teachings associated with the duality of being. In fact, our subconscious focus on images and symbols is what 'constructs' our reality; you could say that symbols train our thoughts and perceptions. The more I delved into this phenomena, the more I have come to realize the 'perception' or 'deception' we endure does not end with Saturn and Moon symbolism, which I have written about in other books and blogs. Orion *is* the door to so many symbols, rituals and states of mind made manifest in our reality. The Gnostic *Gospel of Philip* tells us:

> *Truth did not come into the world naked, but it came in types and images. The world will not receive truth in any other way. There is a rebirth and an image of*

rebirth. It is certainly necessary to be born again through the image.

The Cathars – *True* Emissaries of the Son of Man

In the land between the Mediterranean, and the hills and plains of the Aude Valley, France, is one of the most 'enigmatic' locations on earth. It is a location steeped in mystery, beauty and a history unlike any other. Over eight hundred years ago, the Occitan region was the backdrop for an 'epic' and 'devastating' period in French history. If ever turned into a movie, it would be a 'film épique'. Its narrative would be 'deep and very telling' with a storyline covering the plight of the people of this region, but also the plight of humanity as a whole. Through what became known as the Albigensian crusade (a war lasting over 20 years), came the devastation of the 'Cathars', the rise of the Dominican Order and the Medieval Inquisition. The targeting of the Cathars or 'Cathari' (which means 'pure' in Greek), by the Vatican Third Lateran Council of 1179, along with the King of France – Philippe Auguste, was ultimately for their land and 'treasures'. The Cathar treasure sought by powerful fraternities centred in the Vatican was really more about the Cathars' knowledge of bloodlines 'allegedly' connected to Jesus. The Gnostic Cathars' faith and understanding of subjects relating to Adam, Orion and the Aeons (along with subjects I've been outlining so far in this book), are also part of the knowledge (or treasure) that the Roman Church wanted removed. Not least the Cathar knowledge of the Gospel according to St. John (the unnamed disciple whom Jesus loved), so distinct to the synoptic Gospels (Matthew, Mark, and Luke).

The 'absolute' Cathar faith was one, purely-based Gnostic (dualistic) belief, especially in relation to the 'fall of man'. For the absolute Cathar, the fall occurred *before* the story in *Genesis* and involved the Aeons, Sophia and the Christos, all of which clearly offended the Roman Church. Branding those of the Cathar faith as 'wandering heretics' was only one aspect to this turbulent period in history. The ultimate price was the 'removal' of the Cathar priests, the 'good men and women' (Bons Hommes and Bonnes Femmes), called the 'Parfait' (or perfecti) by the people who knew them. The 'Parfait' were said to display *real* sanctity, humility and asceticism for those who heard them preach about the 'Light of the World', unlike their 11th Century Catholic opposites. The Cathars had both a Gnostic and scientific view of natural phenomena, believing that the light, the spirit was etherealised in matter (the physical world). For the Cathars, Christ had the 'appearance' of human form but was so etheralised (from the world of spirit/aeons) that he was able to reveal his 'true nature' to those that supposedly witnessed his transfiguration.[7] It was 'spirit' that was focused on by the Cathar, not the physical body, hence why the Cathar, in their public sermons, detested the crucifix, asking: 'why would you worship the instrument of torture?'

The Cathar Cross

The watermarks and symbols connected to the Cathars developed out of much earlier Gnostic groups, like the Manichæists, and relates to 'light', the stars and sacred geometry. Manichaeism, based on the prophet 'Mani', taught an elaborate dualistic cosmology describing the struggle between a good, spiritual 'world of light', and an evil, material 'world of darkness'. The writings of Mani, which means 'the Messenger' (born in 216AD), included texts on the *'Treasure'*, *'The Book of Giants'* and writings that eventually became the biblical *Psalms*. Manichaean symbolism also included the cross inside a containment circle, placed on a 'stairway' or pole, indicating their knowledge of the light that emanated from the Equilibrium, the *Invisible One* or the *Hidden One* (see figure 155).

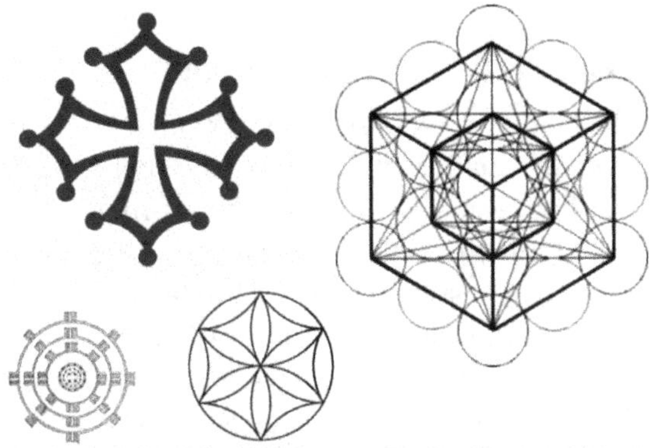

Figure 155: Cathar Cross of Light.
Variations of the Manichæists cross, which became the Cathar (Occitane) cross. The same geometry can be seen in Aphrodite's flower and the Metatron Cube.

The Occitane Cathar cross (with its twelve points) is another version of the 'Flower of Life' (light), or Aphrodite's flower and the Metatron Cube, all used as a containment circle, or 'creation circle'. These symbols show the *connectedness* of life and light, the place from where the Coptic cross comes. Old Coptic crosses often incorporate a circle and sometimes the arms of the cross extend through the circle (dividing it into four quadrants), as in the 'Celtic cross'. It's all the same symbolism if truth were known. Christian monasticism (born in Egypt) was instrumental in the formation of the Coptic Orthodox Christian Church. The Coptic Christians were very much like the Mandaeans and later Cathars; they followed a life of simplicity and humility, thanks to the teachings and writings of the 'Great Fathers of Egypt's Deserts'. These Fathers of Egypt's Deserts were early Mandaen (Christian) hermits, ascetics, and monks who lived mainly in the desert of Egypt around the third century AD. Arsenius the Great (350

AD) was probably the most influential anchorite amongst the founding fathers of Orthodox Coptic Christianity, much of which also took root in Syria, Armenia and the Balkans. The latter saw one of the strongest dualist Gnostic locations to emerge as the 'Bogomils', centuries before Gnostic Cathars flowered in the Occitanie. It was the Bogomil priest called Nicetas who was one of the key instigators at the Council of St. Felix, Lauragais in May of 1167 that made Catharism an 'official' church as such. The very thought of *another* 'official' church, opposing the power of Rome (capable of a natural belittling of Catholic priests) was enough for Pope Innocent III to call for the slaughter of a whole people in South West France, in 1209. Yes, it was genocide unlike any other of its time.

The Coptic Cross and the Ankh

The Coptic cross (also a symbol of Coptic Christianity), which is the primary denomination of Egyptian Christians today, uses the containment circle and figure similar to the Egyptian Ankh. The cross within the circle comes in a number of different forms, some of which are clearly influenced by older, pagan symbols relating to 'eternal life'. The Winged Wand of Egypt, a symbol of the soul and eternity, is very similar in design to the Coptic Cross (see figure 156). The winged solar disk also appears on seals connected to the biblical kings, and of course, can be seen today in many corporate logos. Many of the seals were used during Hezekiah's reign as the 13th King of Judah (8th and early 7th centuries BC), and together with the inscription *'l'melekh'*, meaning 'belonging to the king'. Hezekiah's royal seals featured two downward-pointing wings and six rays emanating from the central sun disk, some are flanked on either side with the Egyptian ankh symbol. Egyptian priests used similiar symbols to the biblical Israelite priests (the Levites), it seems.

The Coptic cross has *'three* cross beams', one for arms, a second sloped, one for the feet, and a third where the INRI label would sit placed above Jesus' head. Early Coptic crosses don't include the foot beam but often include a circle around the upper beam (like the symbol on page 246). Both the Coptic cross and Wand of

Figure 156: The First Cross.
The Ankh, 'Coptic cross' and 'Wand of Egypt' are essentially the same symbol and can be traced back to the Mandaean (Christian) hermit priests of Egypt.

Egypt are the same symbol; both originate from an ankh-like cross with an equal-armed cross inside the loop. For 'Copts' (Egyptian Christians), the circle is a 'halo' representing divinity and resurrection attributed to Christ. The 'Crux Ansata', which includes the 'T' cross and the circle and cross (if given a crescent), is said to be a symbol of Venus (the fallen light).[8] Halos, or sunbursts, are also found on orthodox crosses, and as I will come to later, seem to be renditions of the Trapezium located in the Orion Nebula.

Ankh – Hathor – Taurus

The Egyptian ankh was a symbol used to denote eternal life. Specifically, it was the eternal life granted by the gods. In Egyptian language, the word 'ankh', where 'n' is pronounced like the English letter 'n', these consonants were found in the verb meaning to 'live' (the noun meaning 'life'), and also means to 'cause to live' or to 'nourish life'. The ankh is commonly held by a god, sometimes offering it to the nose and mouth of the deceased to grant the breath of life. Other Egyptian imagery has streams of ankhs poured over pharaohs. Thus, it is not unlikely that it became a symbol of resurrection for early Egyptian Christians. In 2004, Andrew Gordon, an Egyptologist, and Calvin Schwabe, a veterinarian, argued the origin of the ankh is related to two other objects: the 'was-staff', representing 'power' or 'dominion', and the 'djed pillar', representing 'stability' and possibly magic. According to this hypothesis, the form of each sign is drawn from part of the anatomy of a bull. This is because Egyptian priests believed semen was 'life' and that it originated in the 'bones'. Both the Bull (Taurus) and the Ram (Aries) also seem to be connected to the Ankh, especially in ancient Egypt. It is the ankh (combined with the spectre and djed), held by the god 'Banebdjedet' (the Ram of Mendes), who stands over the 'Divine Tribunal' to judge between Horus and Seth (Duality). According to these myths, it is Banebdjedet who suggests Seth be given the throne of Egypt, as he is the elder brother. In other words, the Ram god *precedes* the dualistic 'Son of Man' deities, in this case (Osiris) Horus and Seth (light and dark forces). All this symbolism is important, as it seems to suggest the Taurus (and Aries) constellation *is* influencing Orion's dynamics in relation to cosmic order and the path of the stars.

The Book of the Heavenly Cow or the *Book of the Cow of Heaven*, which is said to have come from the *Pyramid Texts*, originating during the Amarna Period (1550 to 1292 BC), describes the reasons for the imperfect state of the world in terms of humankind's rebellion against the supreme sun god, Ra. The 'Heavenly Cow' in this context is the goddess, Hathor. It is another narrative, which hints at the Gnostic theme of the 'fall' from a higher state of awareness. Hathor is also connected to the Taurean Constellation (as the

Cow of Heaven); she is placed as the 'mistress of the west', who welcomes dead (souls) in the afterlife. Hathor is also part of the 'Osiris watermark' used by the Gnostic Cathars, and includes the Gnostic serpent and the 'trefoil' (trinity/quintessence) appearing from the serpent's mouth (see figure 157). The three circles at the end of the serpent's tongue are part of the 'Tawer' (pillar) of Osiris (Orion)
and relate to the fifth element - life. The 'Kiro' (horned vessel) hanging from the mouth of the Ox (bull) here relates to the 'anointed' and 'Christ' or the Greek word 'Krisma'. The bull and the cross are joined by serpent energy just as Orion and Taurus are connected through electromagnetic energy. The Cathar watermark also depicts Hathor as the face of the 'mother substance', with the Gnostic serpent of wisdom (Sophia) climbing the cross. It is said the serpent is spit-

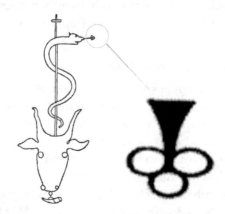

Figure 157: The Gnostic Watermark.
(Left) The Osiris 'watermark' used by the Gnostic Cathars combines Orion and Taurus. **(Right)** The 'trefoil' appearing as *three* circles from the mouth of the serpent are the source of life.

ting 'three blue apples', symbols for 'heavenly apples' that 'cast no shadows'. Some researchers have said that the three apples are the belt stars of Orion, and the cross is the alignment of Orion with Taurus in the heavens creating what writers, like Wayne Herschel, have called The 'sky cross' and the 'cross of churches'.

The goddess, Hathor, equates to love, beauty, music, dance, motherhood and joy, all attributes of a Golden Age on Earth, and a state of awareness pursued by the Cathars and the Troubadours of 12th Century Occitane. The Troubadours created poetry and music based on 'states of being' known as Courtly love, *devotion* to the *goddess,* or the queen at the court. The Ankh is a *feminine* symbol and in some ways depicts the 'womb of life', the 'Ma' and 'Sun' from whence all life is born.[9] As I will show in a later chapter, Orion is a 'birthing place' for stars and suns. The original cross, the ankh, and its later variations, are all symbolic of light and life, from the celestial womb of creation. The legendary female Cathar Parfait, 'Esclarmonde de Foix', whose name means 'Light of the World', clearly embodied the goddess's, Holy Spirit and the Aeon, Sophia, I mentioned in *Chapter Four.*

The Chi Rho & Orion

Another version of the Coptic cross is the 'Chi Rho', whch is one of the earliest forms of christogram crosses, created by superimposing the first two (capital) letters 'chi' and 'rho' of the Greek word for Christ. The Chi Rho symbol was used by Roman emperor Constantine (306–337 BC) as part of the military emblem and labarum (see figure 158). Could the three circles on Constantine's insignia be simple renditions of the three belt stars of Orion? What is interesting is that the Chi Rho and the main visible stars of Orion, mirror each other when a line is drawn through the stars diagonally, forming a double cross (or Leviathan Cross), used by the Knights Templar. The double cross

Figure 158: Chi Rho Christ as Orion.
(Left) The 'Chi Rho' cross and military labarum is symbolic of Orion's three belt stars. **(Right)** Orion (on his side) is Christ in this respect, forming the Chi Rho symbol.

is also the cross of Lorraine, which came from the Kingdom of Hungary to the Duchy of Lorraine and was used by the Dukes of Anjou in the 16th century. The double cross is also found on the 'Exxon' Mobile logo and the trademarked face of an 'Oreo' cookie, (almost an Orion cookie). The corporate world is awash with Orion and Saturn symbolism, which will become clearer as we progress through the book. The 'X' made by the Chi cross was regarded as the 'crux decussata', or Saint Andrew's Cross of Scotland, which also connects 16th century Scotland and Burgundy, France, but has its roots in 12th Century Germany and the Teutonic orders. The main point here is that the cross in the heavens, notably the Orion 'X', became a major occult and religious symbol through the ages. I'll come back to the 'X' symbol next as it is worthy of its own chapter.

Opposing the Bull (Taurus)

Orion plays a huge role in the shaping of our 'collective thoughts', our beliefs and above all, the belief in duality through 'information' (energy) and how we perceive reality. We see duality in many myths and legends in the ancient world, and of course, we see it all the time in the opposites in nature. In the epic legend of Gilgamesh, the Bull of Heaven fights (opposes) Gilgamesh and the symbolism is clearly another version of Orion facing Taurus in the heavens (see figure 159 overleaf). The alignment between

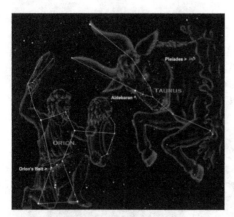

Figure 159: Orion Fights the Bull.
The celestial face-off between the warrior 'Son of Man' and horned Taurus.

Figure 160: Mithra (Orion) and Taurus.

Orion and Taurus, according to researcher, Wayne Herschel, creates a 33 degrees arc, from the belt stars to the Pleiades, passing by the eye of the Bull – the star Aldebaran (Alpha Tauri). I am certain the Orion and Taurus alignment also gives us the 'Tau Cross', which I will come to shortly.

In fights between 'Attis' and the Bull, through to Perseus and the Minotaur (who meet at the centre of Ariadne's labyrinth, symbolic of the mind or womb), we see the same symbolism alluding to a hero battling a horned beast. Orion is unique, whether holding his club or bow, he is hunting beasts across the zodiac (animal wheel). Similar symbolism can be found on crests, heraldry and other insignias showing opposing forces found amongst the stars. The Roman and Zoroastrian god, Mithra (see figure 160), also relates to Orion's 'face-off' against the bull (Taurus), not least in relation to the oldest texts of Zoroastrianism and Zoroaster.

In Zoroastrian texts, for example, Mithra is an exalted figure, who with 'Rashnu', (Justice) and 'Sraosha' (Obedience), is one of 'three' judges at the 'Chinvat Bridge', the Bridge of 'Separation' which all souls must cross. The bridge could also be the three belt stars of Orion placed above the area of Orion that forms the 'Door'. The bridge is also the brain's corpus callosum, a bridge between two worlds, or hemispheres. Unlike Sraosha, Mithra is not a 'guide' of souls to the place of the dead (the Moon), instead, he takes the souls 'across the bridge' between life and death. In other words, Mithra is a 'doorkeeper', like Orion, Osiris, Jesus, etc., ('I am the door. If anyone enters by Me, he will be saved, and will go in and out and find pasture'. *John* 10:9-16)

The Orion-like Norse giant, Ymir, mentioned in *Chapter Two*, was said to be formed from 'elemental drops' (celestial chaos), fed from the primeval cow, 'Auoumbla'. Egyptian imagery depicting Hathor, also show her as the

Figure 161: Primeval Cow - Hathor.
Hathor could be both Taurus and the Milky Way.

primeval cow being 'milked' by maidens of the stars (see figure 161). In other art she gives milk to the queens of Egypt, notably 'Hatshepsut', the fifth pharaoh of the Eighteenth Dynasty of Egypt. In Egyptian mythology, the 'Milky' Way was also considered a pool of cow's milk coming from the fertility cow-goddess by the name of Bat (often depicted as a human face with cow ears and horns), but eventually merged with the sky goddess, Hathor. The same fertility cow-goddess was interchangeable with Isis and both were addressed as 'One Who Comes in Peace'. Hathor was the original 'mediator queen' (the wisdom of Sophia) and was probably the source of the Gnostic/Cathar saying, 'Go in peace', or, 'Peace be with you'.

Mountains, Rivers and Belt Stars

The 'Sahasralinga' place of pilgrimage in India (dedicated to Shiva), located around 14 km from the Sirsi Taluk in the district of Uttara Kannada, according to writers such as Wayne Herschel, is a Taurus (Pleiades) alignment. The Shalmala River is famous for being the location where around a thousand 'lingas' (Sanskrit for 'form' or 'mark' often shaped like an egg) are carved on rocks in the river and upon its banks. Each Linga has an individual carved bull facing towards them, however one location seems to mirror the Pleiades; aligning with what the locals call, the Brahman bull rock.[10] From this perspective, Shiva could be seen as Orion-Saturn and the Brahman bull, Taurus.

William Henry, in his book, *Cloak of the Illuminati* (2003), suggests the Cathar watermark is the 'Meru' (the cosmic spine), the tree of life and can be seen mirrored in the human spinal column as well as in street plans, which usually enclose a 'secret garden'. The garden, of course, is Eden, symbolically. Symbols associated with Meru, the virgin Mary and Venus, for example, have also been seen in the street plans of Washington DC and other capitals around the world (for more on this see the work of David Ovason). Nicholas Roerich, a Russian painter, writer, archaeologist, theosophist, philosopher, and public figure, wrote that Meru Mountain or Peak (Meru Beluka), in Tanzania, was the world's highest base jump from earth, and according to the aboriginal Mongolians, was the dwelling of Orion.[11] It is also said that the Himalayan 'three' peaks, Dhaulagiri, Mount

Everest and Kangchenjunga align with Orion's belt stars, Alnilam, Alnitak and Mintaka, with Alnitak at +30 degrees passing directly over the peaks at the culmination of Orion. Amazingly, Mintaka, the third belt star, passes directly over Mount Kun Ka Shan, the greatest Himalayan peak overlooking lowland China.[12]

Mountains of this calibre are vortices, where two or more energy meridians cross on earth's grid. The symbolism of 'seeing the mountain top' used by Martin Luther King was highly significant to the spiritual power of those choosing to align with higher forces beyond the stars. Interestingly, for the Lakota Native Americans, 'Tayamnicankhu' (their name for Orion's Belt), was said to originate from the spine of a bison, or bull. The Belt stars clearly point the way to the Taurean bull in star maps (see figure 162).

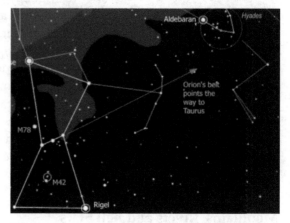

Figure 162: Orion Walks along the Milky Way.
His belt (sword) points the way to the eye of the bull.

For the Lakota, the great rectangle of Orion and the Hand of Kunu (mentioned in *Chapter Three*) are said to be the bison's ribs. The Pleiades star cluster (also in Taurus) are the bison's head and Sirius in Canis Major, known as 'Tayamnisinte', is its tail. The Kumeyaay Indians of California and the Yuma of Arizona all saw Orion's belt stars as mountain sheep (rams), and in Tewa mythology, the belt and sword of Orion belonged to the great hunter, Long Sash, who guided people along the 'Endless Trail', the Milky Way.[13] What we are looking at here is a deeper symbolism in oral traditions, myth and imagery that speak of the connections between Orion, Taurus, Aries and the celestial river – the Milky Way. But there is more.

He Who Walks on Water

According to myth, one of Orion's 'magical' abilities was that he could walk over water, a gift given to him by his father, Poseidon. Orion, Like Adam on High (the Son of Man), being a son of the gods, was able to 'tread the waves', or 'walk upon the waves' as though upon land. The notion of 'sea walking' relates to seafaring and navigation on one level, but it is Orion's position (as a constellation), and his position near the sea of stars, the Milky Way, which is more important. Orion's front foot, marked by the star Rigel (Orionis), appears to be stepping onto the first star in 'Eridanus', the 'River constellation'. Etymologically, Eridanus refers to the 'Rives' of a river rather than flowing water, as in French 'Rivière' and it is the land located along a river. The word river comes from the Indo-European root 'Rei', meaning to 'tear' or 'cut', and again relates to the 'rift' seen in the celestial river – the Milky Way. Here we also have a connection to the Anglo-Norman word, 'Rifa' and Danish 'Rift', seemingly related to the Indo-European word 'Danu', German 'Danube', Russian 'Don'; all allude to the 'foot', or the 'head' of the giant and the 'fluvial water' (see *Chapter Two*).

The Sumerian water god, Oannès, or 'Adapa' is another Orion deity connected to the biblical Adam figure, the sea, oceans and, of course, Poseidon. Cuneiform astronomical-astrological texts also refer to Orion by the Sumerian title DINGIR DA-MU, and DA-MU, which means 'child', or 'son', in Sumerian. DINGIR was the Sumerian word for 'god' and it also served as a logogram which stood for the Akkadian word star (walker); therefore, one of Orion's titles is, the 'Son of God'.

Of note is the Mesopotamian astronomical lore identifying Gemini as Mount Mashu, the 'Twin-Mountain', and Aquarius as the Water-god, 'Ea', a constellation-deity who inhabited the 'Sea of Stars' and is best-known for causing the Great Flood. In Greek mythology, the Eridan (ancient Greek Eridanós) is a river god into which the sun falls. This river is mentioned by Hesiod in his *Theogony* as the 'son of ocean' and *Tethys*, he who flows to the west of the world. The Greek word 'Erion' also means 'sepulchre' or 'tomb'; I am convinced that the positon of Orion, as it gradually becomes 'upright' on its passage through the year amongst the Sea of Stars (Milky Way), relates to the 'resurrection' found in so many ancient religious beliefs. Orion's passage and his 'fight' against the Bull (the darkness of winter), can be symbolised as the fight against 'dark forces', embodied in religious narratives of Jesus and the horned devil. Orion in this context is identified as the 'star of the sun' and the 'fallen (but risen) star man' (a sky-walker) as mentioned throughout the book so far. Could George Lucas's 'Skywalker' name be based on his knowledge of Orion symbolism?

Christian theologians say the Gospel authors were anonymous, Hellenistic (Gnostic) Jews who had *never met* Jesus (if he existed) and had no eyewitness testimony to draw upon. Yet, each shared the belief that Jesus was the 'Son of God' and 'Anointed One' (the Christos) who ascended into 'Ouranos' (or heaven)—a word that simultaneously meant 'sky' or 'firmament' and referred to the stars. As I have already shown, Adam on High is the same archetype that acts as bridge between the heavens (stars) and the earth. Writing on the internet, John McHugh points out how Jesus and Orion are interchangeable figures. In his article: *Walking the Waves: How*

Orion's Ability to 'Walk on Water' Was Ascribed to Jesus, he says:

> As educated Jews fluent in Greek and living in a land that had been colonized by Greek-speaking peoples, the evangelists had surely been exposed to the Hellenic religious tenet called *katasterismos,* or "placing among the stars", which proclaimed the forty-eight ancient constellations as a sacred record of monumental events that had once occurred on earth—each star-figure engaging in one or more of the preternatural feats that made it, like Jesus, immortal. Seven centuries before Jesus strode across the Galilean Sea, the Hellenic astronomer-poet Hesiod, in a work entitled Astronomy, reports that Orion was able to walk on water.[14]

Not long after his spectacular victory in France's 2017 presidential election, the cover of the British magazine, *The Economist,* depicted 'Emmanuel' Macron on its cover in 2017 as a figure 'walking on water'. Indeed, Macron was celebrated all across Europe as a kind of political 'saviour' when he became president, see figure 163. With the name, Emmanuel, one might expect such symbolism. Walking on water imagery relates to Orion symbolism as the 'star man', the 'giant' and in this context, a political giant - Europe's Saviour figure. Macron also came to power on the 14th May, when Orion drops below the horizon (symbolic of Osiris moving into the Underworld), waiting to 'rise again' as Summer arrives. Of course, I doubt the magazine would have considered such esoteric symbolism. Macron, as a world leader, could be one to watch at this time, as he seems to have been selected for some significant political purpose involving the future of Europe.

Figure 163: Europes Orion Man. Emmanuel Macron, was portrayed as Jesus (Orion) archetype, he who treads the waves, on the cover of the *Economist in* 2017.

Orion as '*Superman*' (the *Elohim*)

'El', as the 'Ancient of Gods', or the 'Father of all Gods', was mentioned in the ruins of the royal archive of the Ebla civilization, in the archaeological site of Tell Mardikh, in Syria, dated to 2300BC. El is another variation of the Demiurge, or the 'Father God' (or God Father), I mentioned in *Chapter Four,* and is thought to be the creator of Adam (Orion) in *Genesis.* El was the chief god of the Canaanites, sitting above Ba'al (Orion) and all the other deities, who the biblical Israelites called El Shaddai (Deus Omnipotens in Latin), or El Elyon.[15]

The DC Comic *Superman* character is an *El*-ite figure called 'Kal-*El*' at birth. The story tells how as a baby, he was sent to earth in a small space-ship by his biological family, Jor-El (hence the 'Genesis chamber' in *Superman's* entrance into the world in the movie). According to the story, *Superman* (Kal-El), was born on the planet Krypton, before being rocketed to Earth as an infant by his scientist/leader father Jor-El, moments before Krypton's destruction. The depiction of Jor–El (played by actor Russell Crowe in the *Man of Steel* movie (2013), and Krypton's high council, are 'visually' symbolic of the Ruling *El*-ite of the ancient civilisations of Sumeria and Egypt. The regalia and thrones of the high elders of Krypton in the film were no doubt inspired by the imagery and history of the ancient *El*-ite bloodlines and ancient dynasties on earth. The use of 'red and blue' for superheroes such as *Superman* and *Spiderman*, etc., across a swathe of regalia, costumes, logos and narratives in movies, also connects to the *El*-ite and duality of Orion, as we shall see. El is the *El*ohim, a 'race of gods' often depicted as 'God' in the Bible. El is also the Demiurge and the 'Father God' (God Father) that is obviously another reference to the 'entity' called Saturn. The fictional *Superman* is both 'Saturn-man' and 'Orion-man' on one level (hence the movie title, *Man of Steel*), but the character is also a symbol of immortality and mortality (duality) of existence. He is a god on earth and a 'fallen' star-man to those who originate from the same place as he. The 'L' in the word El is important too, as it seems to unite the *El*ohim and their creation, Adam (Orion), who is seen as the saviour, and stick/wand-carrying shepherd amongst the stars.

Staffs and Letters

According to some scholars, El is one of several names for Orion and as a constellation the stars of his belt, the 'El-wand' is said to reflect the shape of number 7 and our 12th letter 'L'. It could also be seen as the Hebrew letter 'Resh', which is the letter 'P' in Greek (see the Chi-Ro Cross). In some medieval illustrations, Orion is holding the 'L' shaped stick, rod or 'wand' while carrying the flayed skin of a lion. The 'lion' and the 'hare' are both symbols connected to what the Gnostics called the Demiurge, Yaldabaoth, the blind foolish god mentioned in *Chapter's Four* and *Five* (See figure 164 overleaf).

The 6th Hebrew letter 'Waw', which relates to a 'hook', 'peg' or 'spear' can also be related to Orion's 'stick' (see figure 165 overleaf). The letter 'L' (Lamedh) is usually considered to have origins in the representation of a goad, or a shepherd's stick (or a pastoral staff). It is 'L' in lion and the lion's skin carried by Orion (also Hercules) that also gives essence to 'lineage' of the gods, the *El*ohim. The El-wand is said to mirror Orion's Belt and the shape of a Masonic 'T' square; the shape of Orion's (El's) wand is used to

**Figure 165:
Orion's Wand or
Stick.**
'Lamedh' and 'Waw',
Orion's staff, wand,
stick or hook.

**Figure 164: Orion (Jesus) - the
Good Shepherd.**
A 15th Century illustration of the
'good shepherd', Orion, holding a
staff (hook). Note Lepus, the hare,
another symbol for the Gnostic
Demiurge. Hares and goats are considered unnatural, promiscuous and
hermaphroditic creatures in some
beliefs.

measure out boundaries and also relates
to the number 7 in shape. The idea of
seven stars, or the *seven* mystiques, *seven*
wonders, *seven* angels, *seven* seals, *seven*
trumpets, etc., connects to the notion of
'as above so below'.[16] The Lamedh letter
can also be seen on the Fortuna-Dignita
Tarot set, connected to the 'Last
Judgment', 'life and death' – and the
reckoning with the Son of Man. All these
letters and symbols connect.

Another letter in the Hebrew alphabet which seems to connect to the wand
is the letter 'Dalet' (Daled), which also looks like Orion's wand/stick and a
reversed number *seven*. Dalet is the fourth letter of the Hebrew alphabet
(Aleph Beit), and its symbolic meaning is the 'Door to the Divine' (see figure 166). The shape of the Dalet is almost a 'Tau Cross' and could be
defined as the 'breath of god', more on this in a moment. As I mentioned in
Chapter Five, there seems to be a direct correlation between the 22 Letters of
the Hebrew alphabet and the tarot, with Kesil (the Fool) identifying with
Orion. In the *Book of Remembrance* (2016) written by Leslie and Jayson
Suttkus, we find that the word Adam (Adamah) in Hebrew is spelt using
the letters Aleph, Dalet and
Mem.[17] Aleph means 'creator',
Dalet means 'Door' and Mem is
equated with the 'Living
Waters'; all three are expres-
sions of the 'divine human
being' and the creator com-
bined. According to Suttkus, the
Hebrew word 'ET', which uses

**Figure 166:
The Door.**
The Hebrew, Dalet is
the 'door' and relates
to 'grace' or the
divine.

'Aleph' (the first letter of the alphabet) and 'Tav' (the last letter), translates as 'Alpha and Omega' – the beginning and the end. In other words, Adam (Orion) could be seen as the incarnation of 'ET', the 'Word of God' and the male and female as *one* divine human being. This can be seen as Adam, coupled with an aspect of Sophia (Isis/Eve/Sekhmet), to form a 'trapezium' (a trinity symbol) through their child (or offspring), suggests a joining of 'opposites' to create a new *'one'* – a *new* life. Humanity are children of the celestial coupling between Adam and Eve and some researchers even go as far as saying that we (humanity) are *from* Orion. We are certainly star stuff that's for sure.

'T' Crosses

The 'T-statues' and the 'Ankh-cross-symbol' all seem to connect with Orion and humanity's relationship with forces working *through* Orion's location in the Pleroma (the Dreamtime). None of this symbolism is unique to anyone griup or faith. The Hopi god Masau'u was sometimes shown to carry a 'Tau' cross (T-shaped cross), which can be seen cut into the rocks of the Peublo Indian Great Kiva at Casa Rinconanda (see figure 167). The site is part of the Chaco Canyon National Park, adjacent to the largest ancient Peubloan ancestral house (town) in New Mexico called Pueblo Bonito, meaning beautiful town. Chaco Canyon, according to some researchers is said to align with Orion, not least the three belt stars mirrored in the ruins south of Pueblo Bonito, constructed over a period of 300 years.

Figure 167: Orion's Mark, or Door.
Orion's (Masau'u's) mark in the dwellings at Casa Rinconanda, Chaco Canyon.

An even older location in Turkey is 'Göbekli Tepe' (the world's oldest known megalithic site), which seems to have similar symbols associated with the Tau. Göbekli Tepe is a Pre Pottery Neolithic Temple dating back to about 9,000 BC (the Upper Paleolithic period) and is covered in art and symbols relating to astrology, the stars and possibly rituals. At this ancient site, are circles of massive T-shaped stone pillars, along with many other steles and sculptures, depicting hands, 'strange handbags' and animals such as the fox, bull, crane and boar. T-pillars found at Nevali Çori, not far from Göbekli Tepe, are also thought to represent human figures by some researchers. Göbekli Tepe, excavated by Dr. Klaus Schmidt between 1995 and 2005, unearthed huge T-shaped pillars. Judging from published drawings and photos, there are what appear to be six buildings with elaborately carved 'T'-shaped megalithic pillars, among others. The masonry work is exceptional and clearly makes us wonder about the type of artisans who made such works (see figure 168).

Figure 168: T-Stones/Pillars. The T-shaped pillars at Göbekli Tepe. Note the bird-like figures, and the scorpion, on the left pillar are symbols connected to the Orion myth.

We also find the T-shaped cross in the Mayan city of Palenque in Chiapas, Mexico. Specifically, a number of T-shaped windows were incorporated into the buildings there called the 'Palace', which again could relate to what the Gnostics called the 'house of many mansions'. The Mayan daykeeper, artist, and historian, Hunbatz Men, explains the meaning of this motif:

> *A transcendental synthesis of human religious experience is inherent in the word 'te' (T), or Sacred Tree, which emerged from the words teol and teotl the names of God the Creator in Mayan and Nahuatl. These most revered and sacred words of the ancient people, symbolized by the Sacred Tree, were represented in the Mayan hieroglyphs as the symbol 'T.' Additionally, this symbol represented the air, the wind, the divine breath of God.*

For many centuries the Mayan people revered the 'Ceiba Tree', or Ya' axche, meaning 'Green Tree' or 'First Tree'. They believed it to be the tree of life, which stood in the middle of the earth, uniting the terrestrial and spirit worlds. Much like the Norse tree, Yggdrasil, or the Saxon, Irminsul Tree, the Mayan First Tree was a celestial tree, out of which came many worlds or realities. The 'T' in this sense is symbolic of the foundation of the world tree, forming the structure for spirit to appear in the physical (lower) worlds becoming a 'Cosmic Tree' from where the 'hanged man', Jesus, Orion, Odin, and so on, would be placed.

The Cosmic Tree and the Bird that Sits in it

The Phoenician tribes and Aryan Hittite culture of Asia Minor, which influenced the Indus Valley, also record similar symbols for the Cosmic Tree. Within the sacred books of the Yutatán Chilam Balam of Central America, the Cosmic Tree was aligned to the four roads (directions) of the Milky

Figure 169: The T-shaped Yaxche Tree.

Way. This alignment occurred following the destruction of what the Maya call the 'Old Order', an ancient epoch when earth's Paleolithic tribes worshipped the North Celestial Pole Star as a 'god', known as the 'Pole God' (prior to 26,000 BC). The *Popol Vuh* of the Quiché Maya, along with Sumerian accounts, also explains the features of this 'celestial tree', through their hieroglyphic texts and cuneiform. Breast-like fruit were said to grow from the trunk of the sacred Yaxche Tree, while a bird in the form of a spirit messenger (often a dark force), is perched on top (see figure 169). The bird sometimes has a snake in its talons and 'combined' they are a symbol for the sky gods challenging the Earth.

Many times in ancient narratives, we see the heavens take the form of a tree and the comets and planets (plants) that grow from the celestial tree in the forest or sacred garden. Birds in the tree are seen as spirit messengers, perched atop the central trunk, all are symbolic of a celestial 'solar bird', or 'central sun', whose wings are repeatedly inscribed with the signs for daylight and night. To some, the wings suggest the bird's flight represents the unfolding of time. The symbolism contained within the Mayan Yaxche Tree is similar to the wand of Egypt (on page 250) and again relates to a higher force behind the creation of time and space. The head of the Mayan god, Hun Hunahpu (mentioned in *Chapter One*), is one of the hero twins, who, once decapitated, offers 'life out of death' for those that approach the tree. We are back to symbolism associated with John the Baptist and Jesus here, both Orion-Solar symbols.

In Native American legends the same tree has two birds perched in its branches. This depiction, along with other bird imagery often relates to the 'Old Order of gods' symbolised through myths and legends relating to 'Blue Quelzal Macaw', or the 'Seven Macaw' (parrot-like bird gods), otherwise known as 'bird-men'. In Mesoamerican mythology, the Macaw was considered an arrogant, false god and the same attributes given to the bird gods can be found in tales of the mocking bird and the Tower of Babel found in Mesopotamian myth. Here we have another predatory god in the form of a bird (possibly an eagle) who is the Mesoamerican version of the Gnostic Demiurge. The Babylonian legend of creation, inscribed in tablets found in 1870, also describes 'seven' human beings with faces of ravens (a Saturn symbol), who came and instructed the people in an ancient epoch. The seven bird-human gods (possibly seven stars) are found in Orion, Big

Dipper and the Pleiades. All are constellations mentioned in ancient myths, but the Taurean Pleiades stars are exceptionally relevant to birds; they are a star cluster that move in a 'bird-like' manner, all flocking at the same speed.

The 'T' Mark

The 'Tau' or 'Tav' literally means 'cross', and is the final letter of the Hebrew alphabet. It is numbered 300 in the Greek and 400 in the Hebrew 'numerical alphabet'. The Tau also corresponds astrologically with the planet Saturn as the winged creature sitting atop the Tau, including the concept of 'finality', something I will look at in the next chapter.

The Tau Cross features in the story of Moses. When he enters the Sinai desert, he encounters the Midianite tribe (also called the Kenites, descendants of Cain) who, supposedly are wearing 'T-shapes' marked on their foreheads, markings associated with the absolution of sin. It's also worth noting the Greek word for Sin, 'Harmartia', relates to 'archery' (see Orion and Artemis) and means 'missing the mark', or a person who has strayed from the path. It was the sign, or mark, which for the ancient Midianites, represented their god of storms (bringing water) and war (thunder), what later became known as the 'Yahweh Mark.' (See figure 170). The god of 'T'hunder, 'T'hor and his Mjölnir Hammer is an obvious connection, too. The marking of the 'forehead' in *Ezekiel's* time is not dissimilar (in action) to the pointing of a Forehead Thermometer gun at people in the wake of the coronavirus pandemic, so to allow

Figure 170: T-Mark.
(Left) The Yahweh Mark. **(Right)** A 12th century scene from St. Denis with the mark of the Tau on the foreheads of Christian believers.

them 'passage'. See also the 'mark of the beast' symbolism in *Revelation*.

In Hebrew, the 'Taw'or 'Tav' letter is represented by a (+) or an (x).[18] As a letter with two lines that cross, the Tau was viewed by early Christians/Gnostics) as a letter representing God, which was used in baptism and for protection, described in *Ezekiel 9*. The God represented by the 'T' is the Demiurge and his creation, Adam, *combined*. The Tau was adopted as the emblem of the Franciscan order of monks, and during the Renaissance it was used in religious paintings to denote monks, pilgrims, shepherds and wandering hermits. Renaissance painters, such as Giovanni Bellini in his painting, *The Blood of the Redeemer* (1459-1516), also portray Christ with a T-shaped cross standing on a checkerboard floor; the latter of which, is a classic Masonic symbol relating to light and dark – duality. In magic, the Tau represents a supplicating posture and ritual robes of male priests are typically referred to as 'Tau robes' due to their shape, going back to the traditional pattern of monastic robes. As J.S. Ward writes in *Freemasonry and the Ancient Gods* (1921): "The Tau cross is also a symbol of the male or creative side of the deity, and is really a conventionalized form of the phallus."[19] (see page 151).

In Greek, the 'T' also represents 'Theos' or 'God' and large T-shapes often appear in some of the inscriptions in the catacombs.[20] In the hermetic mysticism, the Tau represents the 'completion' of creation and is an emblem of infinity. For the Greeks, Tau is associated with the letter '**Theta**', an emblem of death originally symbolised by a cross in a circle or a skull. An arrangement of 'three' Taus in a spoked formation is an emblem of the Royal Arch degree of Freemasonry, the first part of the York Rite system (see figure 171). The 'Triple Tau' is said to comprise only 'two letters' – the Greek phrase 'Templum Hierosolymae', with the 'H' forming a pictographic version of the 'Arch of the Temple' and entrance (or door) to the original King Solomon's Temple. In this way, the middle Tau within a pentagram (star), can be seen as a symbol of 'death and resurrection,' also found in masonic initiation rites and on the Texaco logo. Incidentally, the five-pointed star, for some researchers, relates to the Hyades star cluster in the constellation of Taurus and is the nearest 'open star system' to our solar system.[21]

Figure 171: Triple Tau Symbolism.
The Masonic T can be seen in various logos.

So much symbolism found in Freemasonry relates to the stars 'surrounding' Orion and Saturn and the invisible scaffolding our solar system.

Outside of Christianity, the Tau Cross was a symbol of 'immortality'; the Chaldeans and Egyptians viewed it as a representation of Tammuz, the Sumerian god of 'death and resurrection'. Tammuz was an earlier Jesus (Orion-Saturn) figure and during baptism ceremonies the priests of Tammuz placed the 'T' shape on the forehead of initiates. Again, we have the same symbolism connected to duality (life and death) being used in the rites of Native peoples in different locations on the earth. In his classic book *Atlantis: the Antediluvian World* (1882), Ignatius Donnelly states that Tau was an important icon signifying 'hidden wisdom' for Mexicans as well as for Peruvians, Egyptians, Phoenicians, and Chaldeans.[22] In general, it was emblematic of rejuvenation, freedom from physical suffering, hope, immortality, and divine unity. Thus we have seen how different cultures associate the T-shape with *bringing new life*, the 'rising sun', 'psycho-spiritual jour-neying', and ultimately 'resurrection'. The latter of course relating to Jesus the Orion-Saturn figure. Sometimes the simplest symbols contain the deep-est meanings and in the case of Orion and his corresponding stars, they seem to enhance the idea of door, or gate, into worlds beyond this world.

The Door Marked 'H'

Another symbol found at sacred sites, and used as a religious symbol, is the 'H' mark. At Göbekli Tepe there is another megalithic pillar with a combination of symbols docu-mented so far including an 'H' motif (see figure 172).

Figure 172: The 'H' Mark.
The H and Saturn-Sun symbol marked in Stone at Göbekli Tepe, Turkey.

In the Hebrew alphabet, 'H' or 'Hey' is the 5th letter, and in the Tamil alphabet it is the 34th letter called π (ha). Both versions of the same letter relate to 'breath' and to 'revelation'. The 'H' symbol is open at both top and bottom of the insignia and in several versions, reveals an interest in spiritual matters – either light or dark (duality). 'H' is also a 'ladder', a symbol associated with the first letter of **H**eaven and of **H**ell. It is the 'marker' for those that descend from Heaven to Earth. The ladder, as we have seen in an earlier chapter, joins both heaven and earth realms, con-necting us to the stars. It's said the top half of 'H' represents Heaven, and the lower half Hell; therefore 'H' is capable of living in both worlds concur-rently and can be a symbol of enlightenment, or deception, at the same time. I think the latter is more prominent on earth today.

The Greek 'Hiero', or 'Holy', is also the root of the word 'Hierophant' and can be seen to carry the 'H' letter, acting as an initiator. Adding a fur-ther layer of symbolism here, the Hebrew equivalent of the Greek 'Eta' (H) is 'cheth', a *gate* and Cheth/Eta enumerates to 8 or 800, with the 'Tau' as 400, making the 'H' a *double* 'Tau' cross. In the English alphabet, 'H' is the *eighth* letter and can also relate to Orion and Saturn's influence over the *gate* or *door* I describe here. As the author Ellis C. Taylor, states in his book *The Esoteric Alphabet* (2004):

> *H is the 8th letter of the alphabet and number 8 is composed of two rings. LORD God is Saturn- the LORD of the Rings. Also two rings suggest two domains or two reigns Adam [Orion] and Saturn and a continuing interaction. The Oak King and the Holly King of Celtic lore for instance.*[23]

The 'H' symbol, in this context, is connected to Saturn and Orion simultaneously; motifs carved underneath the H on the Göbekli Tepe pillar are a sickle, or crescent moon shape, below a hollow circle. Both symbols are connected to the reverence of Saturn in an ancient Golden epoch, quite possibly from a time before the creation of Göbekli Tepe. In his book, *The Saturn Myth: A Reinterpretation of Rites and Symbols Illuminating Some of the Dark Corners of Primordial Society* (1983), David Talbot makes an interesting argument stating that thousands of years ago, earth was a former satellite of Saturn, called the 'Holy Land' and that a vastly different solar system alignment existed.[24] Wayne Herschel writes about Göbekli Tepe on his website, thehiddenrecords.com:

> *Something extra is seen in the "H" ... a small oval suggesting the belt aspect of Orion which aligns to show the way to what is beneath it. The Ra symbol... the circumpunct... the ultimate sacred symbol in my book found in the Senmut tomb (ref). and just like the Senmut tomb it is aligned with Orion's belt showing the way, personified as Horus. The Ra symbol also has the crescent ... not our moon but a world bathed in partial light from its own sun star... another solar system where one would expect life to originate from.*

Figure 173: IHS.
A symbol: encompassing the Sun, Saturn and Adam on High (Jesus as Orion). (PD)

The H also features below the cross in the Jesuit logo as the veneration 'Holy' name of Jesus (Adam/Orion). The 'IHS' monogram and the veneration of Nomina Sacra (Christian Scribal practice), in the form of the Christogram, were modified by the Jesuits to include the *three* nails on their logo (see figure 173). Headquartered in Rome and founded by Ignatius of Loyola with the approval of Pope Paul III in 1540, the Jesuits (one of the most important secret societies today) must be aware of the Orion-Saturn symbolism? The sunburst surrounding their logo could also be a reference to the 'Invisible Sun' and, I am sure, the three nails below the cross, refer to Orion's three belt stars in some way.

The Dogon 'Kanga'

The Dogon are an ethnic group living in the central plateau region of Mali, in West Africa. The 'H' symbol seems to appear very similar to the Dogon Kanaga symbol (see figure 183 overleaf). The Kanga is worn by men in ceremonial dances designed to ensure safe passage of spirits of the deceased to

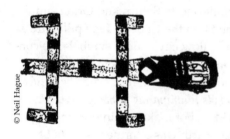

© Neil Hague

Figure 174: Dogon 'H'-like Kanga.
(Left) The Dogon Kanga symbol representing duality and a 'bridge' between
worlds.

the world of the ancestors.
According to Dogon oral traditions,
a race of people from the Sirius star
system, called the Nommos, visited
Earth thousands of years ago. The
Nommos lived on a planet orbiting
another star in the Sirius system.
These star ancestors landed on Earth
in an 'ark' that made a spinning
descent to the ground, with great
noise and wind. The Dogon say the
Nommos gave their ancestors
knowledge about Sirius B

(Digitaria), its orbit cycle and even knowledge of the rings of Saturn, and
the moons of Jupiter; a knowledge existing before 17th Century astrologers'
recordings.

Here we see the Kanga 'H' symbol used as a 'gateway' to provide safe
passage for souls as they journey back to the 'source', possibly inside the
Orion constellation (see figure 174). I will go into more depth about Sirius
later in the book, but the point I want to make here is that the symbol and
the colours used on the Kanga hint at the importance of Orion and Sirius
for those that make the 'soul journey' and go beyond duality. Equally fascinating, is how the Kanga looks like the celestial cross alignment orientated
(overlayed) above Orion's stars as it rises over the ecliptic. Author and
researcher, Wayne Herschel, makes many interesting correlations between
such symbols and the stars (see his website, hiddenrecords.com). The markings on the Kanga also replicate black and white shapes connected to
freemasonry and checkerboards also found on church and temple floors
and in Native American petroglyphs. The checkerboard symbolism is all
about duality. The Kanga also looks remarkably similar to the 'Squatter
Man' petroglyphs adressed in *Chapter One* (see page 30), found all over the
ancient world, which according to several authors, could have related to
ancient celestial event witnessed globally.

Pumapunku and Tiwanaku

Pumapunku is the name of a large temple complex located near Tiwanaku,
in Bolivia, and part of a larger archaeological site known as Tiahuanacu. I
visited the place in 2012 and found it to be one of the most 'interstellar'
sites I have seen. In Aymara, Puma Punku's name means: 'The Door of the
Puma'. The temple's origin is a mystery, but based on carbon dating of
organic material found on site, archeologists believe the complex may have

been built by the Tiwanaku Empire, one of the most important civilizations prior to the Inca Empire – that flourished between 300 and 1000 AD.

The site is part of a larger temple complex, thought to have been an incredible place, adorned with polished metal plaques, brightly coloured ceramic and fabric ornamentation; visited by costumed citizens and elaborately-dressed priests when in full use. Treasure hunters looting at Pumapunka and Tiwanaku, along with stone mining for building stone and railroad ballast, have damaged a lot of the stones. The original stones used to make the structures and walls of Pumapunku are so finely cut that they interlock with other surrounding stones. The precision with which these angles have been used to create flush joints is indicative of a highly sophisticated knowledge of 'stone cutting' (masonry) and a thorough understanding of descriptive geometry. Freemasons are much more ancient in origin! I am sure that giants and some kind of stone-softening technology were involved in its creation, because the blocks cut at Pumapunku fit together like a puzzle, forming load-bearing joints without the use of mortar. One common engineering technique involves cutting the top of the lower stone at a certain angle, and placing another stone on top of it, which was cut at the same angle. Such techniques, are said to appear similar in composition to those found in Egypt, Mexico and Asia. The similarity of techniques suggest a global (interstellar Masonic) building operation, but by whom? The most intriguing thing about Pumapunku is the stonework and of course here we have the 'H' shaped blocks unique to Pumapunku (see figure 175).

These megalithic blocks weigh several tens of tons and the red sandstone and andesite stones were cut with such exactitude that the technical finesse and precision displayed in these stone blocks is astounding. Some of the blocks are finished to 'machine' quality and the holes drilled to perfection. The accuracy and precision exemplified here is supposed to have been achieved by a civilization that had *no* writing system and was ignorant of the existence of the wheel. *Yeah, right.*

Figure 175: 'H' Blocks of Pumapunka.
Insterstellar 'Masonic' alien-like engineering at Pumapunka.

Like other megalithic sites I have touched on so far, Pumapunka and Tiwanaku seem to align with Orion and Sirius, and like the pyramid correlations in Egypt, Tiwanaku also has *three* main square building configurations aligning with Orion's belt stars. The Mesoamerican god, Virachoca, who is also Orion, acts as the 'keeper' of the gateway of the sun at Tiwanaku. Puma Punku, according to researcher Luis B. Vega, also corresponds to Orion's star, Saiph.[25]

The main focus throughout the book so far has been the layer upon layer of symbolism connected to Orion and adjacent stars. The letters, codes and archetypes I have unravelled seem to be part of an eloborate language of esoteric 'star magic' and ancient symbols, all of which have found their way into mainstream religious iconography. Before I turn my focus on Orion's 'passage' over the earth, along with Saturn's and Venus's importance in relation to Orion's passage, I want to unravel one more important symbol connected to Orion – one that takes us 'further' in the use of star magic.

Sources:

1) David, Gary A. *The Orion Zone*, 2006, p 96

2) Picknett, Lynn and Prince, Clive. *The Masks of Christ, Behind the Lies and Cover-ups about the man Beloved to be God.* Sphere 2008, p136

3) Lewis Da Costa. *The Secret Diaries of an Alchemist*, Fountainhead Press, 2005, p560

4) David, Gary A. *The Orion Zone*, 2006, pp 56-57

5) Picknett, Lynn and Prince, Clive. *The Masks of Christ, Behind the Lies and Cover-ups About the Man Beloved to be God.* Sphere 2008, pp 254-55

6) Willis Barnstone, Marvin Meyer. *The Gnostic Bible: Revised and Expanded Edition.* Shambhala Publications 2009, p745-755 and p831

7) Guirdham, Arthur. *The Great Heresy.* C.W Daniel Company Ltd, 1993, p31

8) Wood, David. *Genesis, the First Book of Revelations.* Baton Press, 1985 p133

9) https://nuta-ankh.blogspot.com/2014/04/ankh-kemetic-womb-of-mandkind-and.html

10) http://thehiddenrecords.com/om

11) Henry, William. *Cloak of the Illuminati.* Adventures Unlimited Press, 2013, p17

12) Lewis Da Costa. *The Secret Diaries of an Alchemist*, Fountainhead Press, 2005, p331

13) Ann Lynch, Patricia and Roberts, Jeremy. *Native American Mythology A to Z* (Second Edition). Chelsea House Publishers, 2004, p83

14) https://www.ancient-origins.net/myths-legends-europe/walk-water-0011191

15) Ashe, Geoffrey. *Dawn Behind the Dawn: A search for Earthly Paradise.* Henry Holt. 1992, p122

16) *Ibid*, p37

17) Suttkus, Leslie and Jayson. *Book of Remembrance*, 2016, p20

18) Danielou, Jean. *Primitive Christian Symbols.* Baltimore. 1964, p141

19) Ward, JS. *Freemasonry and the Ancient Gods.* 1921, p400

20) Ferguson, George. *Signs and Symbols in Christian Art.* Oxford University Press New York. 1961, p149

21) https://www.constellation-guide.com/hyades/

22) Donnelly, Ignatius L. *Atlantis: the Antediluvian World.* 1882, p340

23) Taylor, Ellis. *The Esoteric Alphabet.* 2004, p 77

24) Talbot, David. *The Saturn Myth: A Reinterpretation of Rites and Symbols Illuminating Some of the Dark Corners of Primordial Society.* 1983, pp 91-93

25) http://nebula.wsimg.com/bdedb91de25e91bd2fc6f08a5bf78315?AccessKeyId=D40106E1331 C24ABD7C3&disposition=0&alloworigin=1

X

THE 'MARK'
OF THE STAR MAN

*Symbolism is no mere idle fancy or corrupt degeneration: it is
inherent in the very texture of human life.*

ALFRED NORTH WHITEHEAD

We have merely scratched the surface of symbolism associated with 'star magic' and Orion. Language (letters) and symbols are all involved in forging star magic, especially the kind of spell-casting designed to affect the subconscious mind, as we shall see.

The word archetype the 'original pattern' from which copies are made, derives from the latinisation of the Greek noun 'archÈtypon', which means 'first-molded'. In this chapter, I want to consider the first-moulded form through the shape of letters and symbols leading us further into knowledge connected to star magic and its use. One letter is important when it comes to making a connection with the original archeytypes and the magic used.

Origins Made Simple – X's Everywhere

The 'X' symbol-letter is *everywhere*. We see its use in language (words) and runic symbols including talismans stretching back to ancient times. The letter X is the *third* least-used letter in the alphabet often to express extraordinary concepts. The word 'nexus' is a good example of the power of the letter 'X', which means to 'connect' or 'link' (by association) two or more people, or things. Words such as *exalt, exhale, expand, exclude, excite, experiment* and *exotic* are mere samplings of what I am talking about. X is also a symbol for the 'female' (the goddess) and unique magic connected to the femine 'divine' energy. As a movie watcher, I wasn't surprised to see the 'Last Jedi', Ray, in the *Star Wars* movie *The Last Jedi* (2019), form an 'X shape' with her light-sabers (at the end of the movie) to remove the Sith (the darkness) once and for all. In Greek, X, pronounced 'She', reinforces the use of the feminine across a very male corporate world and in most cases it is the power of the goddess *behind* the masculine world that is truly sought by those who desire power.

As I touched on in the last chapter, the Hebrew letter 'T' (Tau) is believed to be derived from the Egyptian hieroglyph meaning 'mark'. T is the *last* letter of the Hebrew alphabet, leading us back to the *first* letter – 'Aleph', a letter drawn as an 'X'. Alephor 'A', is also the first letter of the Semitic abjads (a type of writing system where each symbol, or glyph, stands for a consonant), including Phoenician 'Aleph'. The word 'Aleph' is derived from the West Semitic word for 'ox', and the shape of this letter derives from a Canaanite glyph that may have been based on an Egyptian hieroglyph depicting an ox's head. As we have already seen through the last few chapters, the ox is the bull of Taurus (Tau) and the words ALEPH - KA - CHi - ALPHA – OX, use oblique lines, much like a simple latin X, to connect them. Usually, the meaning of an X is defined when it is first used, but sometimes its meaning is assumed to be understood. You could say the use of an 'X' is the epitome of the 'unspoken word'. What is clear, as we shall see in this chapter, is the letter 'X' seems to be part of an 'esoteric magical code' connected to the stars, not least Orion himself. Other origins of the X letter can be seen in the Phoenician 'Taw', the 'Aleph' and the runic letter 'Gebo' for example (see figure 176).

The runes, in use among Germanic peoples from the 1st or 2nd century AD, are littered with X's. See also the runes, 'Nauthiz', 'Inguz', 'Othel', 'Daeg' and 'Mannaz'. As an ancient system of 'divination', the runes offer insight into humanity and our purpose as a whole. The 'seventh' rune, Gebo (pronounced

Figure 176: 'All the X's.
From Left to Right: The 'Taw', 'Aleph' and Runic 'Gebo'.

Ghay-bow), is relevant as it is a cross and 'sacred mark' combined. This rune hints at an existing connection between humanity and the Gods. Gebo, according to some experts, also signifies a 'gift', one that receives, and engenders a state of balance and harmony. To receive an 'X' is to receive a 'kiss' as such. It is the 'rune of giving' and teaches that creativity (being a creator) involves the gifting process. As a symbol it also says humans can be both generous and greedy (duality). The other 'X'-like runes, are: *Othel* (inheritance), *Inguz* (male potency/fertility), *Mannaz* (the individual human) and *Daeg* (Daylight, fruition). All are part of the same symbolism connected to human – divine – macrocosm and microcosm, which is important if we are to truly understand the X symbolism.

As I say, the X is seen in everything and once revealed it is a powerful symbol, revealing the *balance* between male and female; heaven and earth. It is also said to signify equilibrium within each individual. The 'X' was used by an 'individual' when signing important documents before the times of mass literacy, writing an X instead of one's name was equivalent to saying, '*I am* X' or 'I am a sovereign' leaving my mark.

X Signs and Symbolism

In Plato's *Timaeus*, it is explained that two bands form the soul of the world, which form a cross like the letter X. Plato's analogy, along with several other examples of X shapes and the 'ChI' (X) symbol relate to interconnectedness of *all things*. The symbol occurs in the work of Sir Thomas Browne's (1605-82) discourse, *The Garden of Cyrus* (1658). Browne's discourse, also known as the '*Quincuncial Lozenge*', considers the connectedness of all, occurring naturally, artificially and mystically. Browne was an English polymath and author of varied works revealing his wide learning in diverse fields including science and medicine, religion and the esoteric, and whose works were used in the 'witch trials' in the persecution of witches in England.[1] Browne's book revealed the interconnection of art and nature via inter-related symbols of the number *five*, along with the X and the lattice design in which the X appears (see figure 177).

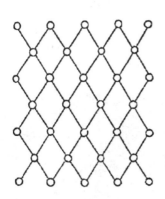

Figure 177: 'Multiple X's.' Symbols of the number *five*, along with the X and the lattice design.

The X can be found in modern insignias such as flags, logos and heraldic devices, not least the skull and bones flag flown by pirates and adopted by the Vatican (not so much to symbolise their centuries of pirate-like grand theft), but as a symbol of the 'keys' to heaven. In terms of numerology, 'X' = 10, which is the number of the 'door' of Downing Street in London - the residency of the UK 'Prime' Minister. The lion-headed door knocker below the number 10 Downing Street is could be another symbol for the Demiurge as addressed in *Chapter Four*. The number 10 and X are interchangable.

The lozenge symbol is also created out of joined X's and, as Browne's book attempted to illustrate in the 1700s, there is demonstrable evidence of 'intelligent design' running through our natural world. Whether it is the work of Fibonacci who found a numerological sequence in nature (a sequence of numbers in which each successive number is obtained by adding the two previous numbers in the sequence), or the 'golden mean' (ratio), or 'phi', discovered by Greek mathematicians; there is an *unseen* (energetcic) order to our physical world. The ancients must have known about the unseen order as too often we find symbols in ancient art attempting to reflect such knowledge. None of this is a surprise, as we know the unseen levels of reality, the worlds of energy, vibration and the subconscious are what really 'construct' our world. As Confucius once said:

Signs and symbols control the world, not phases and laws

The lattice X lozenge also appears in the Sigil (spirit) of Saturn or Solomon, which offers an origin of the Freemasonic compass (see figure 178). Lozenges also appear as symbols in ancient classic element systems, in amulets, and in religious symbolism. They are the diamond lozenge suit found in the playing card deck, one of *four* suits; the number *four* becoming relevant to the X, as we shall see shortly. Lozenge X motifs can also be found in cave art going

Figure 178: The 'Mark'.
The Sigil of Saturn is an 'energy' (frequency) mark.

back thousands of years. Neolithic and Palaeolithic periods in Europe have shown us a plenitude of abstract symbols thought to be connected to fertility and nature. The oldest seem to be portable pieces from the Blombos cave in South Africa, implying that abstract representations were made in southern Africa at least 30,000 years earlier than in Europe. Symbolic traditions were also common in southern

Figure 179: The Blombos Cave Marks.
Lattice-like X's carved into stone over 30,000 years ago.

Africa 70,000–100,000 years ago (see figure 179). The Neanderthals that made such pieces were clearly not as unevolved as 'mainstream science' would often have us believe. I will come back to Neanderthal and symbolic art and mind at the end of *Part One*.

Chi Ro – X Man

Chi or 'X' is often used to abbreviate the name of Christ, as in the word

Figure 180: (Left) Osiris. (Right) Nimrod.

Star gods making the 'X' or featuring the X.

Christmas or Xmas, and early Christians were known as *'Xtians'*; more on Xmas in the next chapter. When fused within a single type space with the Greek letter 'Rho', it is called the 'labarum' and used to represent the *person*, or *figure* of Jesus Christ. This is important, as here we are seeing the 'X' used to represent the Son of Man, which, as I have already shown in earlier chapters, connects to Orion. To reinforce this, we see the Egyptian god, Osiris, who is also the 'Orion Man' making the X symbol with his rods or sometimes his folded arms. The folded arms, or 'X', also relates to Aton or Aten, the disc of the sun in ancient Egyptian belief and originally an aspect of the god, Ra. It is also a 'sign' connected to the Babylonian 'hero god', Nimrod, who, as I have already shown in an earlier chapter, is another Orion-Saturn deity (see figure 180).

Figure 181: Heka.

The sorcerer using the 'X' wands/snakes.

The Egyptian god, 'Heka' (a word for magic), according to the *Pyramid Texts*, is a supernatural energy that the gods possess. All the deities (or Netjer) and supernatural beings of ancient Egypt had their own 'Heka', an intrinsic part of their nature, as much as their bodies and unique names. Just as the Netjer had Heka, so did the forces of chaos, symbolised as the great serpent, 'Apep' (or Apophis, who, for the Egyptians, existed in the watery abyss called Nun). Heka is also seen carrying serpents' (energy) making the X shape and belonged to a more ancient group of deities (see figure 181). Another god named 'Akhu', which means 'sorcery, along with Heka, were also thought of as star deities, whose magic was neither good nor bad (dulality). Just like the X symbol, its power can be harnessed (like electricity) to light up a healing sanctuary, or an abattoir. It's about the *intent* behind the symbol. I am convinced the magic relating to Heka and Akhu survived into the pagan world to become European Wicca lore.

In the 2015 book *Ancient Egypt Transformed: The Middle Kingdom,* authors Adela Oppenheim, Dorothea Arnold, Dieter Arnold, and Kei Yamamoto suggest the 'crossed arms' signify the loss of control of one's body in death, an idea expressed in the Egyptian god, Osiris who was slain by his brother, Set, and chopped in pieces according to myth. Arms making the X position can be found on coffins and statues in ancient Egypt and must have been significantly connected to the 'journey' made by Osiris into the afterlife – the stars.

I noticed in the Marvel Universe *Black Panther* movie (2018), the 'Wakanda Forever' salute seemed inspired by Egyptian pharaohs and sculptures found in West Africa. In American Sign Language, the same salute also means the words 'love' and 'hug'. There are some interesting ideas at the website **www.bibliotecapleyades.net** on the use of X symbolism in religious imagery and the media, not least the Scientology logo (which I'll come to shortly); and also the name 'Xenu', the 'galactic dictator' found in Scientologist teachings; a concoction of extraterrestrial civilizations and alien interventions in earthly events. The volcano and fireball on the cover of the Scientology book *Dianetics*, refers to the Xenu story.

Body Forms an X

Leonardo Da Vinci's *'Vitruvian Man'*, the divine proportion, is another variation of the X inside a circle (circle squared), a symbol which has its origins in ancient Greece. Leonardo da Vinci wrote: 'The workings of the human body are an analogy of the workings of our universe', which he expressed in *Vitruvian Man* (see figure 182). The Ancient Roman architect, Marcus Vitruvius (a Roman author, architect, civil engineer and military engineer during the 1st century BC), also wrote about the Vitruvian Man in his work *Ten Books on Architecture*. The text, written approximately 20-30 BC, is the only text on the subject of architecture to survive antiquity and also one of the first texts in history to connect architecture of the body to that of buildings. Vitruvius believed that an architect should focus on 'three' central themes when preparing a design for a building: *firmitas* (strength), *utilitas* (functionality), and *venustas* (beauty). Vitruvius was simply echoing ancient Greek and Egyptian concepts of the 'divine form',

Figure 182: X-man Da Vinci's *'Vitruvian Man'*

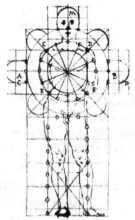

Figure 183: Vitruvius's 'divine form'.

which found its way into later Gothic architecture (see figure 183).

I mention the Vitruvian X simply to show how the idea of a divine human form (the heavenly Adam) can be equated to sacred geometry and

Figure 184: X Man - Orion-Man
An Islamic illustration of Orion. His arms and legs are forming and 'X' (an almost swastika shape).
© Courtesy of Science Photo Library

the X symbol. When the feet are apart, and the arms are held out, the body also forms a 'star man'. This star represents the 'celestial' side' of humanity and our origins amongst the stars. You could say our spiritual evolution is meant to be a state of awareness that takes us 'home', to the stars.

A circle fits around the body of *Vitruvian Man*, formed by the groin which is the exact centre of the square – the reproduction of physical life. The combination of the 'circle' and 'square' gives us the Vitruvian (star) man who is the symbolic of prime source. In mathematics, the 'prime number' is generally used to generate more variable names for things which are similar, without resorting to subscripts; 'X' generally means something 'related to', or 'derived from' the same (prime) source. In other words, the X is the symbol *of the* source, the place from whence life *originated*, symbolically.

In keeping with the Vitruvian Man, a 13th-century Islamic manuscript illustration, taken from the *'Suwar al-kawakib'* (1417), which is a later copy of a work commonly known as the *'Book of the Fixed Stars'* (964AD), shows the constellation of Orion depicted as a 'star man' forming an 'X shape' (see Figure 184). Orion here is almost 'morphing' into a swastika, too, another symbol I'll address shortly. The stars on the figure's costume are marked with yellow circles to match Orion's main stars.

Mannaz and Orion

The 'Mannaz' rune-meaning has been eroded perhaps more than any other rune. If any rune has locked within it the potential to help us think 'powerfully', it is Mannaz (see Figure 185). As a symbol, it is said Mannaz can represent a number of things, but according to Norse writings, it signifies Odin's two ravens,

**Figure 185:
Mannaz - X magic.**

'Huginn', who represents 'mind' (thinking), and 'Muninn', who represents 'memory'. Odin, of course, is another Osiris (Orion-Saturn) figure as I have already shown (see page 93). The Mannaz is said to be the rune of 'mortality' representing individuals or groups. It is not difficult to see visual connections between this rune and star patterns of Orion. The main visible stars of Orion form a shape that look very Mannaz-like, and we have already seen how Orion was the focus for ancient Egyptians, through the union of 'mortal' man with 'immortal' stars. The use of the letter 'M', also contained within the rune Mannaz, has been linked to the word Man, Human, Mankind and Mind (or human awareness). Like most runes, Mannaz also takes on a 'dual' meaning in divination all of which connect to divine influence, sustainability, intelligence, *awareness*, social order (including depression), mortality, self-delusion, bigotry, elitism and arrogance. Mannaz is also the name of a star in Orion's 42 'Ori' cluster, making the top part of Orion's sword. In terms of etymological value, the word Mannaz, is similar to 'Mizan' (a militant man), hence the warrior symbolism associated with Orion. Runic reader and author of the book *Secret Runes* (2020), Tyriel (James Stratton-Crawley), writes about Mannaz on his website:

> *Mannaz speaks to us of our own shrouded origins, for instance, the lack of memory we have of our birth, and childhood. In a collective sense our species have existed for millions of years before recorded history, but living memory of those times have been lost.*[2]

The shrouded origins Tyriel mentions are part of Gnostic understanding of creation on one level, but our 'genetic' origins, which I feel are connected to Orion. The X symbolism is deeply ingrained in our consciousness and I am sure it speaks directly to the divine side of humanity- the X in the heavens - Orion - the X-Man.

Solomon's Lost X Key

Although there is no historical certainty on the exact identity of Solomon in reference to the legend of The 'Key of Solomon', it seems highly likely he is the biblical King Solomon (son of King David) and hence carries the seal referred to as of the Star of David. Once a king of Jerusalem, it is said he builds the temple in Jerusalem at Temple Mount and from all accounts, Solomon was thought to have held the 'key' to unlocking a heavenly secret.

Writer and researcher, Wayne Herschel, has done some outstanding work looking at correlations between specific symbols and the stars. You can view the concepts on his website. He has compared the Key of Solomon with what is called the 'cosmic signpost', showing a parchment with the

Figure 186: The inner part of the Seal of Solomon.
The X-like Lost key of Solomon symbol could be a map leading to Orion.

Key of Solomon (housed at the British Library), overlaid with the Orion constellation and what he calls the 'sacred Cross of Orion'. The'criss-cross' icon he shows is precisely how the star constellation of Orion appears in the night sky, and it also appears to be represented in a smaller talisman (in the bottom left of the 'Sacred Cross', where the icon was traditionally shown). In other words, the parchment key shows a cross *within* a cross. As stated on Herschel's website: "The lost symbol of the 'Key' of Solomon is Orion... Orion as a 'key' shows the way to the secret!"

Part of the Seal of Solomon also shows an X symbol within a circle, which also has two pyramids meeting at the apex (see figure 186). This is also code for both masculine and feminine energy, 'uniting'. The X created out of the joined pyramids gives us the balance of heaven and earth, but also the mortality of life bringing death 'over time'. In this way, the X is an 'hourglass', or a measurer of time, carried by the god, Cronos (Saturn). The two triangles that form the X shape are also featured in the Scientology logo, interlocked by a snake-like letter 'S'. The arrangement of the two triangles carries the same meaning; the esoteric 'religious' symbolism is so blatant once you know what to look for.

The wings, and hourglass combined, were early Renaissance additions, eventually becoming a companion of the Grim Reaper, a personification of 'death' (Saturn), holding a scythe. The additional wings with the hourglass seem to have evolved from Egyptian symbolism but still relate to the passage of life *into* death. The X as the hourglass, therefore becomes an icon of mortal 'time' and 'death'. As I have already shown, Saturn's 'darker' connotations relating to death and ritual can be linked to the Seal of Solomon and the Ouroboros symbol of the snake (S) encircling the hourglass (see figure 187 overleaf). Symbolism is used to 'full effect' to bring about a desired mind/emotional response through the use of magic, hence the word 'Hex' starts to make sense when it comes to 'casting spells' over individuals, groups, or humanity as a whole. According to some Rune experts, Mannaz (mind/thinking) is being drawn upon again, which relates to sustainability, intelligence, awareness, social order, mortality, self-delusion, bigotry, elitism and arrogance. The latter has shown itself at times whenever Extinction Rebellion (XR) has been challenged over its lack of understanding of wider issues relating to the impacts of technology on our lives. I was not surprised to see the 'X' hour glass, 'death symbol' in global use with Extinction

Figure 187: (Top) Hourglass & Snake Circle. Saturn's hourglass encircled by the serpent. A common occult symbol associated with death and 'time', or 'time running out.' **(bottom) XO (ER) symbol.** Is it a modern day version of the Saturn - death symbol and an esoteric symbol by definition?

Rebellion, a movement that suddenly sprung up out of nowhere in 2018/19 in the UK. The 'obsession' with death is a key focus by the Orion-Saturn Cult and therefore I was not suprised to see 'coincidental' uses of such symbolisms across many of XR banners.

Casting Spells

The XR logo contains both the 'X' and the 'O'; in some esoteric traditions the 'X' is the male and the 'O' the female (Adam and Eve). Together they represent a magical union and connect to the 'Mark of the Beast'. Ceremonial magician, Kenneth Grant, who was secretary and personal assistant to the elite, British occultist Aleister Crowley (referenced in *Chapter Eight*) mentions the 'O' and the 'X' as symbols relating to a Celtic god called 'Nodens' (the god of the Abyss). The whole XR (XO) movement is there to serve as a 'magical sigil'; a *spell cast* on the minds of those willing to give their minds away. Its funding, political support and immediate airtime (with poster girl, Greta Thunberg having access to all major media outlets), tells me it is just another cult even if by definition only.

The scope of this book does not include discussing the 'politics' of such 'mindsets', but suffice to say it was clear to me the 'X' Seal and the hourglass of Cronos (Saturn) symbolism was in full use, for a specific 'effect'. Magic was being worked and spells had been cast when XR arrived on the scene. Interestingly, the same symbolism is also on the BBC Broadcasting house, positioned below an Eye of Providence (Saturn) symbol, with eight spokes out of which a slightly distorted X could be drawn (see figure 188). Where did Extinction Rebellion take their protest to in the autumn of 2019? the BBC building of course with the same symbolism on its façade. Isn't it funny how the media establishment are too often entrenched in 'mesmerising' the masses, often to suit political agendas. One that seemingly suits those behind 'green', 'Woke' politics pushed by the 'as-if-by-magic' appearance of Extinction Rebellion in recent years. In line with the 'extinction' theme, the UK *Sun* newspaper ran an article in late 2019 headed: *NO ONE IS SAFE Disease X outbreak that could 'kill 80 million' is 'on the horizon'*. Again, the 'X' is used to both 'panic' and 'mesmerise' the masses into believing a

Figure 188: Eye & Hourglass.

deadly plague, dubbed by the WHO as 'Disease X' (a flu-like illness) was on its way to kill the global population.[3] How 'prophetic' the media was in late 2019 considering what followed globally with Covid-19. The mainstream media have got a lot to answer for in terms of spreading *constant* fear. There is much more to know about the symbolism and reasoning for a 'Disease X' as I will explore later in the book.

Caught between the earth becoming extinct, due to human-caused climate change, and the current Disease X, you have to ask *who*, or *what*, is really 'pushing' such fearmongering on humanity? The answer does not end with dark suits and elite power, it's origins, I suggest, are connected to AI and otherworldly realms as I will explore in *Part Two*.

X Men and Women

The X symbolism is very much part of our cellular world, too. The symbolism connected to our 'cells' (our DNA) can be determined through the 'X' and 'Y' chromosomes. All of these symbols relate to life/death and duality, which as we have seen, is significant to Orion symbolism.

A male individual has an X chromosome, which he received from his mother, and a Y chromosome, which he received from his father. The male counts as the 'origin' of an individuals X chromosome and each person usually has one pair of sex chromosomes in each cell. Females have two X chromosomes, whereas males have one X and one Y chromosome. Science shows us that both males and females retain one of their mother's X chromosomes, and females retain their second X chromosome from their father. X chromosomes in humans span more than *153 million* base pairs (the building material of DNA). The X chromosome represents about 800 protein-coding genes compared to the Y chromosome containing about 70 genes, out of 20,000–25,000 total genes in the human genome (see figure 189 overleaf). You could say that the X is important from a biological standpoint. Interestingly, the number of possible ancestors on the human X chromosome inheritance line, at a given ancestral generation, also follows the Fibonacci sequence I mentioned earlier.[4]

The X symbolism also appeared in the works of English chemist and X-ray crystallographer, Rosalind Elsie Franklin (1920 –1958), whose work was central to understanding of the molecular structures of DNA (deoxyribonu-

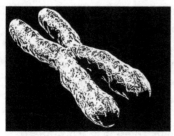

Figure 189: The 'X' Chromosone.

cleic acid), RNA (ribonucleic acid), 'viruses', coal, and graphite. Franklin is best known for her work on the X-ray diffraction images of DNA, particularly Photo 51. While at King's College London, she was part of a group of scientists which led to the discovery of the DNA double helix, for which James Watson, Francis Crick and Maurice Wilkins shared the Nobel Prize in Physiology or Medicine in 1962.

Photo 51, taken by Raymond Gosling in May 1952, is the nickname given to an X-ray diffraction image of crystallized DNA; the photograph provided key information essential for developing a model of DNA. Interestingly, around the same time, we had the origins of what would become the top secret 'Area 51' facility in the USA and the apparent cover-up of 'alien' activity. It is not too much a stretch of the imagination to consider the possibility of what has been described as 'Junk DNA' (non coding DNA), which makes up 98% of our genetic coding; meaning only 2% is used to determine what is 'normal' in terms of 'life' and 'sex'. Non-coding DNA mutations have been associated with cancer and other illnesses. Genetic disorders that are due to mutations in genes on the X chromosome are described as 'X linked'. If the X chromosome carries a genetic disease gene, it *always* causes illness in male patients, since men have only *one* X chromosome and therefore only *one* copy of each gene. Females, instead, may stay healthy and only be a carrier of genetic illness, since they have another X chromosome and a possibility to have a healthy gene copy. Marvel's *X-men* concepts and the many 'mutant' superhero figures connect-

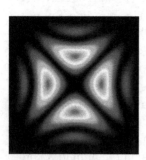

Figure 190: Photon X Hologram of a single photon reconstructed from raw measurements.

ed to the comic books, are another symbolic use of the X linked gene. So are the 'X files' series, based around concepts connected to Area 51.

In 2016, Polish physicists at the University of Warsaw produced interesting results in their quest for measuring what 'light looks like' and how photonic particles look. Based on work by Twentieth Century Austrian physicist, Erwin Schrödinger,* Radoslaw Chrapkiewicz, a physicist at the University of Warsaw and lead author of a new paper published in 'Nature Photonics', used more than 2,000 repetitions in tests to distinguish the shape of wavefronts of a single photon.[5] Using

Footnote: The Schrödinger equation is a linear partial differential equation that describes the wave function or state function of a quantum-mechanical system. Erwin Schrödinger, who postulated the equation in 1925, and published it in 1926, formed the basis for the work that resulted in his Nobel Prize in Physics in 1933.

holographic beamsplitters the experiments led to a pattern of flashes the team were able to reconstruct in terms of the 'shape' of the unknown photon's wave function. Photons were fired at each other and where they intersected, measurements were taken. The resulting image looks a bit like a Maltese cross (cross patte) see figure 190. In the arms of the cross, where the photons are in step, the image is bright – and where they aren't (the X shape), we see darkness. Here, we seem to have a perfect example of science 'shedding light' (no pun intended) on esoteric symbolism.

Wands and X's

The 10th (X) card of the tarot is the Wheel of Fortune, showing a giant wheel with three figures on the outer edge (see figure 191). These are Typhon (evil), Anubis (god of death) and the Sphinx (knowledge).The imagery also relates to the 'Precession of the Equinoxes' and the Galactic

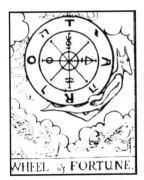

Figure 191: X-Wheel.
The 10th (X) card of the tarot.

cycle mentioned in *Chapter Eight*. The Precession is based around the sun gradually shifting its position a little each year, till about every 2000 years it begins the year in a different sign, shown in the corners of the Wheel of Fortune card. These four corners are the *four* fixed signs of the zodiac: Aquarius, Scorpio, Leo and Taurus and what Plato called, the 'X-shaped world soul'.[6] The four elements: fire, water, air and earth also constitute the 'X' along with the *four* suits of the tarot: wands, cups, swords and disks, which are also the clubs, hearts, spades and diamonds (lozenge). The X as a symbol for the *four* directions becomes the central precept of Gnosticism and Magic. Plato, for example, in his dialogue *Timaeus*, said that when the creator of the universe first formed the cosmos, he shaped its substance in the form of the letter X, representing the intersection of the two celestial circles of the zodiac and the celestial equator. This cross-shaped symbol was often depicted in ancient art to indicate the cosmic sphere seen on the Mithraic stone carving showing the 'lion-headed god', standing on a globe marked with the cross, representing the two circles of the zodiac and the celestial equator (see figure 192 overleaf). The mithraic image is essentially the same concept in the Wheel of Fortune image, both relating to *unseen*, astrological energies and angelic realms influencing humanity.

The *four* letters YHVH inscribed on the wheel's face are the words for God (the Tetragrammaton I mentioned in *Chapter Five*) and could also be the word TORAH (the law), or ROTA (Latin for wheel). The middle wheel

connects loosely to knowledge of the building blocks of life (DNA), said to be symbols for mercury, sulpher, water and salt. All four can be seen as the 'wheel of life' and are used by the 'magician or alchemist' in occult literature. The Magician card in the tarot can also be depicted as an 'X' and connected to the Hebrew letters 'Aleph' or 'Beth'. The magician is the Egyptian god, Thoth, who was known to the Greeks as Hermes Trismegistus; more on him towards the end of *Part One*. The use of 'black magic' through Hex's (or wands) performed by those with understanding of occult magic know the 'X' is very prominent in our world; not least through the media, movies, music, political 'mantras' and the use of money, all of the main vehicles that *shape*

Figure 192: Mithra standing on the X-Wheel.

our world.

The X on Wheel of Fortune relates to the numerological power of *three* and *four*, which leads to *seven*, on one level, but the *eight* spokes of the insignia inside the wheel seem to indicate the crossroads and key equinoxes on earth. In this image we are given a composite image relating to dual forces in motion, but also the *power of the X* as a symbol for *controlling* and *manifesting* form, or for manifesting fate and fortune.

The Cosmic Tree (the Crossroads)

A phrase in the Mayan texts, the *Popol Vuh* – 'cahib xalacat be' – means 'four junction roads' or simply put, 'crossroads'. It is said that *four* roads (a crossroads) emanate from the Galactic Centre (the womb) at the heart of the Milky Way, forming an ecliptic crossing point. The Maya, along with other ancient sky watchers, knew the ecliptic, which is roughly 14° wide, to be the path followed by the sun, moon and the planets in our solar system. The most common depiction of the ecliptic in ancient art and myth is the double-headed deity (quite often a serpent, eagle, or lion deity), one who sees both sunrise and sunset. The Earth god, Aker (two lions back-to-back), in the Egyptian *Book of the Dead* (1250 BC), is the most common portrayal. Aker, symbolic of sunrise and sunset, was said to stand on a cosmic sphere shown as two intersecting circles forming the ecliptic and celestial equator. The same symbolism connected to the two gates (Orion – Silver gate and Scorpio – Gold gate), I mentioned in *Chapter Eight*, could be seen to 'anchor' and bind the stars of the Milky Way to the path of the ecliptic and planets. It seems the Zodiac constellations also follow the same path as the five wandering planets, along with the sun and the moon also creating the X-shape. The Babylonians and the Chortî Maya, along with other ancient civilisations, considered the Milky Way to be a wheel, or circle, whose constant turning provided a transition of ages. Certain deities associated with the stars, held key positions on the cosmic cross (X), or tree, as it *turned*. In general, the sky watchers from numerous traditions were interested in the *changing* movements of the Milky Way throughout the nights of the year, and many attributes were given to the *four* sacred points called the 'galactic compass' or 'cosmic cross', tree, or the celestial swastika (see figure 193).

The Cosmic Tree was also said to house different parts of the creator and for the Hopi Indians, for example, this creative force was called 'Tiawa'; in China it was 'Pan Gu', the one who housed all life forms. Many references to multidimensional realms can be found in mythology all over the world, and refer to *three* areas of the Underworld, Middle world and Upper world. In both Norse and Greek mythology, various gods were said to reside on

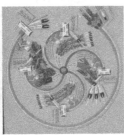

mountains, such as Olympus and the Vanhelm, symbolic of the Upper worlds. As I have already mentioned in earlier Chapters, Yggdrasil is a heavenly tree and the Milky Way literally takes the form of a vertical tree in the sky. The centre of this tree, or the centre of the 'cross', in most cases, was thought to be a direct route to the centre of the cosmos itself, to the worlds of Superconsciousness. The tree and the cosmic

Figure 193: The Cosmic X (Cross).
The Milky Way is a cosmic tree or cross, here personified by the American Indian sand painters.

sun at the centre is also where we get the symbolism associated with the sun-saviour figures; notably the 'hero' warrior, such as Orion or Hercules, etc. In many Mesoamerican rituals, the cosmic tree related to the journey to the centre of the galactic womb of the great mother goddess, the place that was said to have birthed the Milky Way. This is why much emphasis was made on the precession of the equinoxes, the 'Pole Star' and the constellations aligning with the Sun in ancient times. The Stars are *not* motionless in the sky, their positions change continuously as they move through our Galaxy and the Milky Way. These motions, too slow to be appreciated with the naked eye over a human lifetime, can be captured by high-precision observations like those performed by the ESA's (European Space Agency) billion-star surveyor, called 'Gaia'. The shape of Orion, as defined by its brightest seven stars, also moves slowly as time goes by, revealing how constellations are ephemeral.

In alchemical teachings, the tree was the structure of the world matrix, which branched out into invisible realms creating the structure behind the physical world. *Beyond* the cosmic tree, according to various native peoples, are the 'sky worlds' and beyond these are the 'lucid world's of the Dreamtime. What the alchemists called the *four-fold sphere* and what ancient cultures called the 'cosmic tree', is symbolic of the place where the centre of the Milky Way converges with the ecliptic, creating 'four cosmic roads'; this was often shown in the swastika-whirling log symbol, something I will look at shortly. The night sky was a forest, or 'garden of stars', possibly interpreted as a physical garden in texts such as *Genesis*. The same ideas were sometimes described as a tree next to a river, the latter also being an important symbol relating to the stars and the Milky Way. For many native Earth cultures, each of the four cosmic roads (crossroads) was associated with a specific colour, star (constellations) and numerous hero gods and goddesses, but as I have been illustrating here, Orion's cross seems to be another variation of the cosmic cross; it may well be the 'source' of the cosmic cross, too. The rise and fall of Orion, as he straddles the Milky Way (as seen on star maps), provided a 'marker' for the ancient sky watchers. He was an important 'visual aid' for monitoring the *four* seasons, a celestial being of the crossroads.

The Power of *Four*

The Indian deity, Brahma, depicted with four heads, is another example of the four junction roads (crossroads) and directions on Earth. So is Lord Shiva with his four arms, which is merely another version of the 'Vitruvian Man' mentioned earlier. The god-man or star man, placed on the 'cosmic cross' at the centre of creation, is both a representation of Orion symbolism and sun symbolism combined. Native American Medicine Wheels (see figure 194), or the 'Whirling Rainbow' symbol, also express the same knowledge. Here we have a symbol in the form of the X cross (often within a circle), which predates the Babylonian era; eventually becoming a mark relating to the Sun God model implemented as the state religion of empires such as Rome. The star/sun-man myth (why change it if it works?), went on to become the 'blueprint' for all the Babylonian-style (State) religions emerging over the centuries that followed. Roman Catholicism is the same religious model in terms of doctrine, beliefs and use of symbols; see the use of the X cross all over Christendom. What all religions have in common, without getting into the slight differences in names, dates and places, is the mechanism for 'mind control' and the desire to *separate* man from woman, human from being, etc. It's the Adam and Eve complex, or the X and Y complex if you like, preventing the true union between man and woman, and more importantly, the celebration of love that comes from this union. The X is certainly the symbol for either balancing or unbalancing polarities.

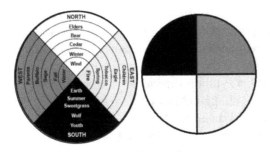

Figure 194: The Medicine Wheel.
The 'Power of Four' seen through the Native American Medicine Wheel, which is another symbol of the X and crossroads.

Another theme associated with the 'power of four' and X magic is how 'guardians' are used to 'mark' the circle squared in terms of temples, prominent city 'squares' and other structures that hold importance for those who wish to use this power for 'control'. The *four* lions at Trafalgar Square in London, enclosing Nelson's Column (Osiris/phallus), is one clear example of the use of Aker, or star magic, over the masses. The same symbolism can be found in other places like the Kailasa temple at the Ellora cave and the city of Dwarka in India. When we see the 'power of four' being used, it signifies the presence of a 'celestial door', or *gateway*, possibly connected to other dimensions, which will become more relevant to the topics as I look at other symbols. I can recommend a brilliant movie available on YouTube called Dwarka: *Atlantis of the East*, which covers some of these topics.

The Celestial Swastika - the *four* Fold Path

In Aztec mythology, the belt of Orion is associated with 'fire sticks', primal fire and the 'new fire ceremonies' performed on four solstice/equinox dates of the year. As I have shown, Orion is located close to where the Milky Way crosses the ecliptic in Gemini, this constellation relates to celestial twins and duality. As a guardian of the seasons, Orion (like Osiris), was both an agricultural deity and lord of the Underworld, depending on where the constellation of Orion was situated against the ecliptic. Symbolically, Adam (Orion), in Greek, is aligned to the *four* cardinal points represented as a cross. These are: *Arktos*, the North; *Dusis*, the West; *Anatole*, the East and *Mesembria*, the South. The four 'directions' are also thought to give us colours of the 'four human races', according to Native American beliefs.

The word 'Swastika', is derived from the Sanskrit word, swastika, and means to bring luck and well-being. The word originated in the Indus River Valley and spread during the Neolithic period to Persia, Asia Minor, Troy, and eventually around the world. Artifacts with swastikas dated as early as 4500 – 3500 BC have been found across various places and most represent the stars, the moon, the sun, the earth, the four directions, the rotation of mother earth and the rotation of life. Of course its use in Nazi Germany was intentionally 'inverted' to bring the opposite effect. Wayne Herschel's research into star symbolism in his book, *The Hidden Records: The Star of the Gods* (2003) shows some interesting connections to Orion and the swastika. So does Gary A. David in his online work entitled, *The Four Arms of Destiny: Swastikas in the Hopi World & Beyond.*

The oldest swastika in the world, a symbol considered to be have been found in Mezine, Ukraine. It is a bird-shaped object with swastika motifs made from the tusk of a mammoth and dated to 10,000 BC. Swastikas are also present in *Vinca* script, dated to at least 6th millennia BC and origins of this script are in the Balkans. The ancient swastika symbol can be seen in Hinduism, Buddhism, Jainism and Native American teachings (see figure 195) and is a 'universal' esoteric symbol until it was deliberately twisted in the 20th Century through its 'inverted' use in Nazi Germany.

Figure 195: Swirling Star Flower. One of the oldest cross-swastika symbols in the world.

The ancient Indian religion, Jainism (Jain Dharma), offers insights into creation- similar to Gnostic teachings. Jain texts describe the shape of the universe as simi- lar to a man standing with legs apart and arm resting on his waist. The agreed Jain symbol (see figure 196) is especially rele- vant as it features the abstract body of a torso; the Oggee hand (Ahimsa) with a wheel inside it (dharmachakra), all of which relate to non-violence and what the Jains call the 'Four Noble Truths', the 'Noble Eightfold Path' and 'Dependent Origination', with their focus on the Arihant (the soul) and its ability to defeat inner enemies like anger, ego, deception, and greed. The Swastika symbol and the three dots 'above' it hint at the 'power of three', possi- bly Orion's belt stars, as Orion features clearly in the Indian texts, such as the *Skanda* and the *Mahabharata.*[7] The swastika symbol also features in the Theosophical Societies Logo, an organisa- tion that also would later inform the appalling racial theories of Nazism.

परस्परोपग्रहो जीवानाम्

Figure 196: A Full Hand. The aggreed Jainist symbol has *all* the hallmarks of Orion sym- bolism. © Chainwit

The Navajo connected humanity to the four directions, or 'four sacred mountains' often used in their 'Nightway Ceremony', designed to evoke the Aeons (divine beings) that aided in the cre-

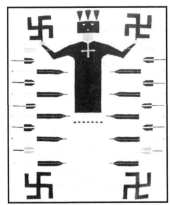

Figure 197: A Navajo Orion.
Adam and the Earth (Four corners or whirling logs)

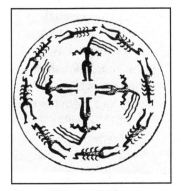

Figure 198: Neolithic art.
A symbol showing the four fold directions as a solar force.

Figure 199: The Solar Year, Ages and Astrological.
The central swastika used to illustrate the precession of the ages in occult literature

ation of earth. In some of their tapestries, a male 'Yei', possibly another version of Adam, Osiris (Orion) is surrounded by four swirling suns (directions) or swastikas (see figure 197). The Cox Mound gorgets, found in Tennessee and northern Alabama dating from 1250-1450 AD also have symbolism connected to the four paths or directions. The four-looped square, or guilloche, is considered by some to be a 'whirling sun' motif (swastika), or by others, how the earth is held up by cords to the Sky Vault at the four cardinal points. Other interpretations talk about the path of life with four stages of maturity. Four Woodpeckers on the gorget are associated with the four winds and are medicine birds said to extract illnesses. A spider (2x4 = 8 legs) within a cross can also be seen on other gorgets from the same region. The spider, of course, was thought of as the 'weaver' of realities constructed from the cardinal points formed by the four-fold-path.

Another symbol, called the 'Hands of God' by early pre-Christian Sanskrit cultures, shows *four* directional crosses enclosing *four* mini swastikas. A similiar symbol can be seen composed of figures dating to Neolithic times in ancient Ubiad culture (see figure 198). These are 'mandala' imagery used to contemplate the 'cyclical nature' and 'structure' of the heavens. The symbols and characters seem to relate to the notion of creating 'light'. The light of the stars, the celestial 'cross of light'. The same concepts can be seen in hermtic digrams for the precession of the equinoxes and the solar year (see figure 199).

In the Tang Dynasty of China, during the reign of the Empress Wu (684 –704 AD), the swastika was also used as a sun symbol, which is the symbol most commonly associated with the swastika. Armenians also used the swastika as a form of sun worship with

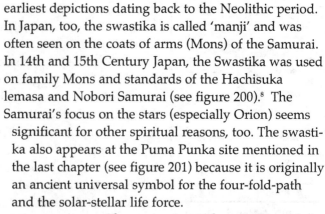

earliest depictions dating back to the Neolithic period. In Japan, too, the swastika is called 'manji' and was often seen on the coats of arms (Mons) of the Samurai. In 14th and 15th Century Japan, the Swastika was used on family Mons and standards of the Hachisuka Iemasa and Nobori Samurai (see figure 200).[8] The Samurai's focus on the stars (especially Orion) seems significant for other spiritual reasons, too. The swasti-ka also appears at the Puma Punka site mentioned in the last chapter (see figure 201) because it is originally an ancient universal symbol for the four-fold-path and the solar-stellar life force.

Figure 200: Tsugaru Tamenobu Samurai Banners (1550 - 1607). The sun, star and Orion-worship-ping Samurai.

Figure 201: The 'ancient' Puma Punka 'Four-Fold-Path.

The reason for such a widespread use of the 'four-fold path' symbol, is clear: it decorated the temples, artifacts and art of the ancients so to explain celestial relationships between the stars and the earth. It also could be connected to Orion (as a central star man) overshad-owing the *four* points seen as the equinoxes and solstices and the power of the light of the sun, or the light that powers the sun. But there is more!

The Power of *Three*

According to Native peoples, within the centre of the whirling crossroads is the potential to manifest reality. This philosophy can be found in Native American shamanic teachings but it is also known as the 'Rule of Three', or the 'Three-fold Law' (or 'Law of Return') in some Wiccan/Pagan traditions. Some occultists state that whatever energy a person puts out into the world, be it positive or negative, will be returned to that person *three times*. It's similar to the Hindu belief in 'dharma' signifying behaviours consid-ered to be in accord with 'Zta' (principle of natural order which regulates and coordinates the operation of the universe and everything within it), so to make life and the universe possible. It is also where we get the supersti-tious notion of things happening in *threes*.

Symbolism associated with the 'power of three' also appears in Islamic texts connected to the goddess, Neith. Before the destruction of Mecca and its statues by Muhammad the Prophet, the goddess Neith had a bigger rep-resentation within Islamic worship. Even though modern Islam prohibits these representations today, Neith is mentioned in a legend under the name of 'Noussayba', a heroine figure, who supposedly fought in celestial battles

Figure 202: The Power of Three can be seen *everywhere*.

to help the Prophet Mohammad. Symbolism associated with the pre-Islamic, 'three daughters of Allah', are the evolution of the wives of the Semitic God, 'Nergal', whose symbol is a 'solar rooster' and another variation of the Demiurge and the fallen Adam figure – Abrasax (see *Chapter Five*). Nergal is also an avatar of Osiris (Orion), the god of the Underworld.

The 'Om' symbol, the 'Trident' and the many variations of the *three* suns, crowns, kings, stars, degrees in Freemasonry and three X's, etc., all relate to the 'power of three' (see figure 202). Wayne Herschel's research into the Om symbolism, and Hungarian researcher, Márton Molnár-Göb, into the correlations with the Om symbol, the ancient swastika *and* Orion is, in my view, fairly accurate.

According to Danny Wilten's work, the Trapezium (the power of three loacted in Orion), could well be the location for the ultimate 'manifester' of reality, or our physical world.

Triple X

The official coat of arms for Amsterdam, three X's flanked by Babylonian Lions and the crown of Maximilian, also enforces the 'power of three' through its symbolism. The heraldic shield was said to have been adapted from the wealthy Knight, Jan Persijn's, Family Coat of Arms and relates to the three towns on the river Amstel (see figure 203).

Most people will see the 'Triple X' element to the shield (which some might think of 'porn' ratings or the 'three judges' on the X Factor), but I see ancient magic at work in the symbolism. Amsterdam (which gave us New Amsterdam – New York), was an important centre for the creation of the first 'central bank' (the Swedish Riksbank); the other two were in London, and eventually the USA. Any *three* devices set 'centrally' on their own are powerful in terms of using energy *through* magic. In his book, *The Ancient Wisdom* (1977), Geffeory Ashe writes about the 'magic of three' used across various cultures:

Figure 203: The Original X Factor.

Most of the hints at an ancient magic of three – admittedly, not all are outside the Fertile Crescent. They occur among the Indo European peoples, Celts and Greeks and the Vedic Hindus… Scrutiny of Greek myth and ritual suggests that 'sets of **three***' were never pictured in a way that would have lent itself to number-magic through the addition of four.*[9]

The point here is that *three* 'on its own' is sufficient in the use of magic. But 3 points *combined* 'manifest' reality. Just like religious symbolism connected to a 'Trinity', it is set to 'fix', or manifest, a 'belief' or a 'form' – through our mind. It is where we get the notion of a 'thought-from' becoming 'physical'.

The English word 'Trinity', derived from the Latin 'Trinitas' (meaning the number three), is the most common symbolism used for the power of three. Other systems consider them to be three *primary* forces, described as positive, negative and neutral. All three of these forces are necessary to create anything. The Trinity, the 'Three Forces', or the 'Three Pure Ones' are *formless* and are often portrayed in the three basic colours, from which all colours originate: Red (active, fire or creation), Blue (passive, truth or reason) and Yellow or Green (neutral, wisdom, gold, or philosopher's stone). In all instances, and esoterically speaking, the number *Three* is a building block for reality. It is as if the positive force *acts*, the negative force *receives*, and the neutral force is the *mysterious* force reconciling the two because it is the 'mix' of positive and negative. In the Vedic tradition, the same three primary forces are the 'Three Gunas' (that have *always been* and *continue to be* present in all things and beings in the world). For the ancient Indus Valley people, creation was described as the 'agitation' of a previously-inert and perfectly-balanced state into the Three Gunas of 'light', 'motion', and 'darkness'. The Biblical Adam, Eve and the Serpent are these same three forces on one level, and they represent the forces required for any creation to occur. As I keep saying, three stars, or 'X's (which is evident in Orion's belt stars) is a major numerological influence on our reality.

X Marks the Spot

The many uses of 'X' symbolism in corporate logos, products, and in the movies is also part of the 'magic spell' being cast by forces (magicians) which I feel are working through darker aspects of Orion consciousness. The 'X spell' is being cast through warning symbols, through to icons of 'desire' and 'fame', all of which speak to the subconscious mind. Like I say, the X is used to draw our attention, to mesmerize us and to keep many of us busy 'buying into' the material world (see figure 204). You could say that the X is the sigil of our 'time' and the most potent one we see everyday,

Figure 204: The 'X spell' is *everywhere!*

everywhere. Here are just a few examples:

Max Factor, **ex**cel **X**, Halifax, Experian, Fed E**x**, AXA, Disney **X**D, Television **X**, Netflix, Extra Strong Mints (**XXX**), the **X** factor, Optrex, Nexxt, Pepsi Max, Sony **X**peria **X**10, **X**box, **X**erox, Mascara **X**, Malcolm **X**, Planet **X**, Generation **X**, Brand **X**, and the **X** Files to name but a few.

The X was deliberately highlighted in the *Vaxxed: From Cover-Up to Catastrophe* (2016) documentary, which alleged a cover-up by the Center for Disease Control and Prevention (CDC) of a purported link between the MMR vaccine and autism (see figure 205). The film was directed by 'discredited' anti-vaccine activist, Andrew Wakefield, who was struck off the medical register in the United Kingdom in 2010 due to ethical violations related to his 'so-called' fraudulent research into the role of vaccines in autism. Or maybe the powers-that-be just didn't want people to know the truth? I can't say for sure. The word '*Vaxxed*', (like the *X Factor*) is all part of the same use of symbolism designed to 'draw us in' and then 'cancel out' any validity. All this is reinforced by the media focusing on the 'supposed' public outcry and widespread criticism of Wakefield's (discredited) theories. As I say, the X is in full use *everywhere* all of the time. The symbol makes a connection with our subconscious mind, and if we are not awake (or aware), it then affects the conscious mind through *its* magic.

Figure 205: All VAXXED Out. According to some occultists, the 'X' is often used to draw you in, then 'cancel out' the message.

The TV show, '*Brand X*' was another example of the play on the X sigil. The late-night talk show, stand-up comedy television series that premiered on the 'FX' channel, fronted by comedian and author, Russell 'Brand', in 2012-13 didn't hide its use of the X symbol (see figure 206). The show, seemed to be designed to 'grab attention' (our minds) and focus energy on the Jesus-like (Orion) image, using Brand as a TV *Icon*. The 'Brand' is important (excuse the pun) but the 'spell' being cast *through* the symbolism

Figure 206: The ultimate X Brand.
Russell Brand, the self-styled 21st Century Jesus-like (Orion-Man) figure.

is often more powerful. Symbolism can be blatant, sometimes coincidental, but the subconscious mind still laps it up.

Elon Musk, the billionaire Founder, CEO, Lead Designer of SpaceX, Founder of X.com (now PayPal) seems to be obsessed with the letter 'X'. Musk and Grimes (singer Claire Elise Boucher) named their son, 'X Æ A-12 Musk'. Most wouldn't know or care too much about the symbolism, but the couple clarified the meaning of their child's name as, 'X Ash Archangel'. According to the couple's tweets, 'X' is the unknown variable, 'Æ' is her 'elven spelling of Ai' and 'A-12' is a type of CIA aircraft known internally as *Archangel*.[10] Clear enough? The underpinning use of AI is relevant here, not least Musk's *infatuation* with artificial intelligence, connected to a greater plan, a subject I will come back to in *Part Two*. 'X' in so many ways is the 'unknown', *made* 'known'. As the author and numerologist, Ellis C Taylor explains in his books *In these Signs Conquer* (2008) and *Living in the Matrix* (2004), the 'X' is a monumental symbol-spell that can be used for, or against, human perception. The use of the 'X' by those who have created the media empire, know its true power: to keep the spell active in the minds of people. Taylor says:

X is able to 'see everywhere' and participate in every activity.

It will not fall over so it is 'determined' and although you might think it is yielding it is only resting …

X is the symbol used for cancellation and termination … X also describes mysterious experiences and unknown results.

X emphasises emotional confusion and X should be wary that advantage is not taken of it whilst it is engaged in other matters.

You could say that the X is also the twinkle in the eye of every human pupil; it is the 'star magic' that can be used to offer perfect balance of male and female energies. It is reflected in the light of our eyes, *our ancient eyes.*

In the last few chapters I have attempted to break down the symbolism associated with star magic and a myriad of mythological connections with Orion. I've also explained how Orion appears in religious symbolism, the media and works through art, archetypes and the core energetic being. In the next few chapters I want to 'expand' on Orion's influence and how the star magic plays out through Pagan rituals, turned into orthodox religious mantras associated with the equinoxes, solstices and other planetary bodies (not least Saturn), all *influencing* our reality on earth.

Sources:

1) https://en.wikipedia.org/wiki/Bury_St_Edmunds_witch_trials

2) http://runesecrets.com/author/admin

3) https://www.thesun.co.uk/news/10161931/what-is-disease-x-vaccine-plague-deadly/

4) Hutchison, Luke. *Growing the Family Tree: The Power of DNA in Reconstructing Family Relationships* (PDF) 2004. *Proceedings of the First Symposium on Bioinformatics and Biotechnology* (BIOT-04). Retrieved 2016-09-03.

5) https://cosmosmagazine.com/physics/what-shape-is-a-photon

6) Latura, George. *PLATO'S X & HEKATE'S CROSSROADS - Astronomical Links to the Mysteries of Eleusis*, 2014, p7

7) Vahia, Mayank. *Astronomical Myths in India.* (PDF) 2005. p3

8) Turnbill, Stephen. *Samurai Heraldry.* (PDF) Osprey Publishing. p62

9) Ashe, Geffeory. *Ancient Wisdom.* Macmillan. 1977 p 66

10) https://www.businessinsider.com/how-to-pronounce-x-ae-a-12-elon-musk-grimes-baby-name-2020-5?r=US&IR=T

11

THE WINTER MAKER

Orion-Saturn Worship (1)

But see, Orion sheds unwholesome dews;
Arise the pines a noxious shade diffuse;
Sharp Boreas blows, and nature feels decay,
Time conquers all, and we must time obey.

ALEXANDER POPE

The Ojibwa (Chippewa) Native Americans call the Orion constellation, 'Kabibona'kan', which means the 'Winter Maker', as its presence in the night sky heralds the coming of winter. Orion is the marker for the coming of the 'time of death' in nature and the eventual arrival of the new sun (new year). He is the 'Year Maker', and from late summer through to the Beltane (May Day), Orion dominates the sky above the horizon, along with Aldebaran, the Pleiades, Polaris and Ursa Major. Earth's Pagan festivals marked by the passage of the Sun and the Moon combined, give us the equinoxes and solstices; but the constellations, especially Orion, seem to provide a 'backdrop' for some of the most important rituals (festivals) on Earth.

Orion leaves our night skies during the late spring months of May and into June. While out of sight, Orion is said to be in the Underworld. Viewing the skies at this time, in the Northern or the Southern hemisphere, Scorpion (Scorpius) reigns supreme, all while Orion takes his place in the underworld. Six months before – in January – Orion has his turn to 'lord over' the winter nighttime sky. Orion only rises in the east after Scorpius sets in the southwest, and the reverse is also true: Scorpius won't rise in the southeast until Orion's departure in the west. According to many Indigenous Peoples, when Orion is rising to prominence, the 'doorway' *between* worlds is said to be 'opening'. *Orion's Door* 'opens' as we 'step into' autumn, and all of the Pagan-turned-Christian festivities marking Orion's passage along the ecliptic are relevant to his position, as we shall see.

In this chapter, I am going to consider Orion's passage through autumn into the heart of winter, and the symbols, festivals and other planetary bod-

ies connected to the star man, not least through the archetypes I have illustrated so far. Before we look closely at the festivals aligned with Orion's
height in the heavens, during the autumn and winter, we need to meet the
goddess of the doorway – Hecate.

Hecate's Wheel of the Door

Hecate was one of the principal deities worshipped in Athenian households
as a protective goddess who bestowed prosperity and daily blessings on
the family. The ancient Greeks honoured Hecate (or Hekate) during the
'Deipnon' – the evening meal, especially on a new moon, but generally, she
was a 'nocturnal' doorkeeper goddess. Hecate is sometimes associated with
cypress, a tree that is symbolic of death and the Underworld - sacred to a
number of chthonic (under the earth) deities. The 'Day of Hecate', or
'Soteira Nocturnal', is the Winter Solstice (21st December) and ritual sacrifice was (and still is) a common practice at the solstices and equinoxes in
many 'underworld cults', not least the Orion-Saturn Cult I've been highlighting. In *Hekate Soteira: A Study of Hekate's Roles in the Chaldean Oracles
and Related Literature* (1990), Sarah Johnston provides the chief attributes of
this goddess. She writes:

> *Hekate was present whenever souls crossed the boundaries between life and
> death... In her role as the goddess of the crossroads Hekate's control over passage
> of liminal points also included opening and shutting the gates of Hades.*[1]

Shrines to Hecate, a Strophalos (or Wheel), were often placed at doorways on homes with the belief that it would protect residents from restless
dead souls and other spirits (see figure 207). Likewise, shrines to Hecate at
three-way crossroads often had food offerings left, especially on a new
moon, so to protect travellers from spirits and demons (or Jinn). Dogs were
said to be sacred to Hecate and associated with
roads, domestic spaces, purification, and spirits
of the dead. As a lunar animal, dogs were also
sacrificed to the road or the 'passage' and of
course, the Dog Star, Sirius (Orion's companion),
is another connection to the goddess Hecate. As
mentioned in earlier chapters, Sirius is also the
lover of Orion (as Artemis, Diana and Isis), and
all of these goddesses are connected somewhat,
especially as 'torch bearers', huntresses and

**Figure 207: The
Strophalos, or Hecate's
wheel.**

triple-headed moon deities. The 'three heads' are
often symbolic of the moon's three phases: new
moon, full moon, and waning moon (see figure

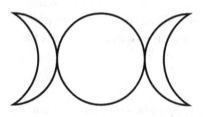

Figure 208: The triple aspect of Hecate

208) and the crescent can also be seen as 'horns'. These *three* phases or figures are often described as the 'Maiden', the 'Mother', and the 'Crone', each of which symbolises both a separate stage in the female life cycle, and a phase of the moon, each phase ruling one of the realms of heaven, earth, and under-world. I personally feel that most Pagan moon worship is based on an ancient 'coming-to-terms-with' the Moon's presence, after an aftermath of destruction on Earth caused by alien forces that 'moved the moon'. The battles for the moon by these extraterrestrial forces, some of which are connected to Orion, left humanity with only one collective mind response to such cataclysmic events – to worship what caused the destruction. In various forms of Wicca, the moon goddess, Hecate, has a masculine consort, a Horned God who is another variation of the hunter – Orion.

Beckoning Darkness & the Winter Door

Around 160 AD, the alchemists (or theurgist), authors of the Chaldean Oracles, linked Hecate to the Cosmic Soul in Plato's *Timaeus*, whose form was also a celestial 'X' (see the last chapter). The point here is that Hecate, as the 'triple' goddess, whether we see her as a personification of the moon, or the torch carrier at the gates of Hades, *is* the goddess of the 'darkness'. Hesiod, the Greek poet (750 and 650 BC), one of the authors credited with Homer for establishing Greek religious customs, described Hecate as a 'primal cosmic force, one that can be called upon when worlds cross'. Like the 'Three Norns', or the 'Three Weird' (Wyrd) Sisters found in Runic magic, all can be 'drawn down' at important dates on the pagan wheel at the equinoxes and solstices. Hecate's wheel symbolism also relates to the 'core star', or 'soul', said to be at the centre, interacting with what the Gnostics called the 'fire serpent' and primordial energy that creates us. What I see with Hecate's wheel is a 'celestial compass', tuned to the stars (especially Orion) and the moon in the darker days of the year. Incidentally, I've seen references to the three belt stars of Orion and the triple aspects of the goddess being connected. Maybe?

The winter triangle formed between the stars of Orion (Betelgeuse) and Sirius (Procyon) form another doorway, which is part of two prominent winter asterisms: the 'Winter Triangle' and the 'Winter Hexagon'. The other two stars forming the Winter Triangle, also known as the 'Great Southern

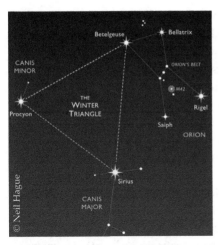

Figure 209: The Winter Triangle.
Formed by *three* stars, Betelgeuse,
Procyon and Sirius.

Triangle', are Sirius and Procyon, which are the brightest stars in the constellations Canis Major and Canis Minor, respectively (see figure 209). Writing in his book, *Stellar Magic* (2009), Payam Nabarz mentions the moon goddess in myths associated with Sirius and the Winter Triangle:

The star Sirius or the Dog Star is part of the constellation Canis Major (Great Dog), in Greek myths he was seen as Orion's hunting dog. After the death of Orion, Diana placed Orion's dog in the sky at his heel to help with the stellar hunt. The star Sirius is part of the winter triangle; the two other points of the triangle are the star Betelgeuse in Orion and the star Procyon in Canis Minor. Sirius, the brightest star in the night sky, can be located in the night sky by following an imaginary line from the three stars of Orion's belt to the left and down. The star Sirius is one of the oldest constellations described by man; the Fire Star is one of the stars in the Babylonian A Prayer to Gods of the Night (circa 1700 BC).[2]

Canis Major and Canis Minor are the 'hunting dogs of Orion' and with Betelgeuse (the reddish star), they are all symbolic of the royal hunt (fox hunting) in the UK (especially in autumn and early winter when 'darker days' draw to us). There is *no logic* behind fox hunting, unless you see the ritualistic symbolism associated with 'unseen' forces that demand such torture and killing. The fox hunting season starts with the 'Opening Meet' which normally occurs during the last week in October or during the first week in November (at Hallowe'en), running until the 1st May (Beltaine), although most hunts finish in March and early April. As I say, they are 'rituals' aligned with the movement of Hecate's wheel and nefarious forces connected to the stars, specifically Betelgeuse in Orion, the Witch Head nebula and Sirius.

Lenaea of the Wild Hunt

Like Orion and Artemis, 'Lenaia' (Lenaea) heralded the hunting season, which is predominantly through the autumn leading up to Samhain or Halloween (Hallowe'en). Samhain is a major point on Hecate's wheel, along with Kali and the Darker aspects of the Goddess. The end of October focuses our attention at the time of the ancestors, when the curtain between

Figure 210: The Other-worldy 'Wild Hunt', or *Wodan's Wild Hunt* by Friedrich Wilhelm Heine (1882).
Source: Wägner, Wilhelm. 1882. Nordisch-german-ische Götter und Helden. Otto Spamer, Leipzig & Berlin. (Public Domain).

the dead and the living opens. As a goddess of the door, Hecate was also known as 'Arianrhod', 'Catherine' and 'Persephone' in other cultures and myths, as she ushers in the winter festival of 'Lenaea' and the time of the wild hunts. The wild hunt, popular in ancient Greece, was also akin to celebrating 'dark forces' that would run amok from their point of entry into our world at Samhain (Hallowe'en) through to mid-December or Saturnalia. The forces hunting were said to be other-worldly, captured brilliantly in Peter Nicolai Arbo's painting, *Asgårdsreien (The Wild Hunt of Odin)* 1872 and by the German painter, Friedrich Wilhelm Heine, in his drawing, *'Wodan's Wild Hunt'* (1882), see figure 210.

The time of Lenaia was painted on numerous vases in Roman and Greek art showing the 'Maenad' (dance and ritual) scenes and those of aristocrats or the 'Bacchantes' (in Roman mythology) involved in wine-mixing rituals. The Bacchantes (or Maenads in Greek) were known for their love of the Roman god, 'Bacchus', and to wear a 'bassaris' or fox skin, which again connects to the modern day 'ritual' of fox hunting. From the 'Death Eaters' in the *Harry Potter* movies, to *The Witcher 3: Wild Hunt* (2015) action role-playing game based on *The Witcher* series of fantasy novels by Andrzej Sapkowski, all these archetypes and symbols speak of *darker forces* forming a vibrational pact with those involved in the hunt rituals. Some say the Orion Constellation is a celestial home for darker forces, which have haunted us since ancient times. As I have already illustrated through the chapters so far, these darker forces manipulate us to revel in 'rituals' that too often hold us back spiritually.

Life, Death, the Green Man & Going Within

The ritualistic death of a Pagan sun god 'personified as man' (or the death of a year through the arrival of darker days) all leads to 'All Hallows' Eve' (Hallowe'en). From this marker on the Pagan calander, we eventually head to Saturnalia and the winter solstice, something I will explore shortly. Hallowe'en has become a *focus* for modern-day satanists within the Orion-

Saturn Cult, and the, 'Do What Thou Wilt' movements of the 18th Century. Saturnalia, or what became Christmas, as we shall see, is another reinforced 'energy theft', instigated by endless commercials, shopping and the pressure to conform to the annual 'ritual'. The religious symbolism connected to Halloween and Christmas is enhanced (through rituals) so to 'steal our energy' through the constant flow of money at these crucial focus points on the calendar.

The mantra of Halloween and Christmas in their modern guise, along with imagery connected to other calendar dates, serves as a 'channel' for forces that feed off our collective mental energy, primarily through the darker nights as we head towards the birth of the new son (sun), or year. It's as if a door is opened at the autumn equinox and as daytime gradually gets shorter, with an increase in darkness, we become more susceptible to sublime forces appearing in the visible world. Archetypes are at work in the collective mind, too, and at the time when the veil is thin (at Halloween), we find ourselves starting to go inward; especially as we reach the end of what was the old Celtic year – 31st October –2nd November.

Figure 211: The Green man archetypes are Osiris/Orion cavorting with Gaia (Sophia) throughout the solar year.

As I mentioned in earlier chapters, John the Baptist was said to be born six months before Jesus Christ, and both figures astrologically mark Orion's arrival in the sky, along with the dog days of the Sothic Sirius calendar. They are the 'Oak' and 'Holly Kings' or 'twin sun kings' whose coronations coincide with the summer and winter solstices – 21st June and 21st December. In Pagan worship, they are also the 'Green Man' figure entwined with the goddess forming part of these coronations throughout the solar year, which is why Green Man symbols can be found all over Christian churches and cathedrals (see figure 211). The hairy woodwose figures, found in iconography and art from ancient Sumeria to 14th Century Christian literature, are also connected to the Oak and Holly Kings.

Green Man symbolism is evident in deities connected to fertility and life-death cycles found all over Europe and Egypt. Atum, Adam (Osiris), along with other Green Man figures, are connected to the fertility of the earth, when Orion and the 'lord of time' (who governs the solstices and equinoxes) rests in the darkness of the Underworld. The Green Man is symbolically sacrificed 'back to the land' as the veil between the visible and the invisible dissipates at Halloween. Pagan myths relating to the death of the 'sun king' (Maponos), mourned by the crone goddess in wintertime, are merely symbols that relay the 'passage' of the earth in relation to the sun across the solar year. On one level, Green Man symbolism *is* the cycle of the Oak and Holly king, but it is also a narrative connecting us to ancient forces in nature.

The Renewal Twins

Whether pagan or Christian, the twin sun king (Jesus and John) reigns over the solstices in a perpetual cycle of life, death and rebirth. According to the biblical story, John loses his head, symbolic of the pumpkin (skull) at Halloween, of which some scholars speculate was in the month of 'Tishre' (October), sometime after Yom Kippur.* Just as the leader of the 'Sun and Fire' clans, Pahana, of the Orion worshipping Hopi, also has his head removed on their ancient tablets. The Hopi deity of Masau'u, was said to sometimes carry a pumpkin-like mask (or head) and a sack of seeds (stars) and all of the symbolism relates to Orion's appearance in the form of Masau'u (see page 241-42).

The twin symbols of the 'skull and the crucifix' also represent two promi-
nent dates on the Christian calendar, especially in America - Halloween and Easter (see figure 212). And both fes-

Figure 212: John and Jesus.
Two main symbols of 'death' and renew-
al' *personified*. Both are Orion-Saturn symbols.

tivities have a common denominator, which is 'death' and 'renewal' represented by the solar king guided by Orion's passage across the skies.

The constellation of Orion the hunter (the 'killer' in mythology) rises higher in the Northern Hemisphere (upside down in the Southern Hemisphere) in the autumn, so to usher in the darker days of the year, when nature dies, so to be reborn (renewed). Orion, as we shall see, is a star system highly relevant to this 'opening of time' (the door) as we pass into winter and the ancient time the Romans called 'Saturnalia' (or Yule). The word 'Yule', which is the Pagan name for Christmas, also comes from the same root as 'wheel' and relates to the rotation of the solar wheel and the 'renewed' sun, all of which is 'witnessed' by Orion in the heavens. Orion is dominant in the sky through the period because 'he' is the archetypal, celestial, blueprint for otherworldly forces coming to the earth's surface at the end (and beginning) of the Pagan New Year.

Before we look at the symbols of Saturn and Orion at *Saturn*alia, the

Footnote: See *Ancient History: A Revised Chronology: An Updated Revision of Ancient History Based on New Archaeology* (2012). Volume 2. By Anthony Lyle.

'door' first opens on Halloween, or 'All Hallows' Eve'.

Mischievous Night, Halloween and the Burnings

You have to ask the question why Halloween has become another celebration on the festival calendar in the western world? When I was a kid in the UK, Halloween was simply a 'penny for the guy'. Kids back then would sit with an effigy of a 1600's English Catholic terrorist called Guy Fawkes (turned into the face of defiance by Alan Moore's novel and movie *V for Vendetta*), asking for a penny to put our 'guy' to a fiery end on Bonfire Night. At least our little voodoo-like Guy Fawkes looked harmless compared to some of the Halloween costumes that appear today. Obviously the American, 'trick or treat' is the real root of our obsession for Halloween. The theme turned into a stream of horror movies of the same name, not to mention the ultimate 'Devil's Night' in *The Purge* movies. Of course, the burning of Guy Fawkes, along with the 'Burning Man' festivals in the USA, can be linked to earlier Pagan (or Wicker) rituals, with their roots in ancient Babylon, which literally involved burning people alive.

Fire was a 'tool' of the Christian Inquisition the world over, and so 'burning alive' a victim was considered an offering to other-worldly entities, such as the fiery Jinn, which I touched on in earlier chapters (see page 100). The Roman Catholic obsession with burning alive anyone who did not accept their deity and version of Christianity was designed to align this horror with 'unseen' forces, also. The crusade against the Cathars, mentioned in *Chapter Eight*, saw thousands of men and women burnt alive en masse in the years between 1209 and 1250. One hundred and forty Cathars burnt alive at Minerve; four hundred at Lavaur in 1211, not to mention the population of Bézier and the *six or seven thousand* that were massacred in the church of St. Madeleine.[3] The burning of approximately two hundred Cathars at the foot of Chateau Montsegur in southern France (March 16th 1244), was one of the final 'acts of evil' performed by the Roman Church (see figure 213).

Burning, massacring and torturing those that had a different perception of life became the 'specialty' of those that controlled the emerging power of Roman Catholicism at this time. Similar fire rituals also took place on the Pagan calendar date of the 'Ides of March' (15th of March), or the rites of Mars – the God of War. This date was the feast of an old, Roman deity, 'Anna Perenna', another Hecate fig-

Figure 213: Burning of the Cathars.

ure, whose festival originally concluded the ceremonies of the New Year through use of bonfires. The goddess Anna Perenna seems to have inspired the 2002 Horror movie, *The Ring*, an American supernatural horror film directed by Gore Verbinski, whic, in my view, is a 'window' into the archontic worlds I mentioned in earlier chapters. These 'forces' run the Vatican and political, industrial complex to this day, but their power is fading.

Another fire ritual from late antiquity relating to the rites of Mars, called the 'Mamuralia', was focused on by Pagan Rome between the 14th March or the 16th.[4] The Mamuralia, which has aspects of the 'scapegoat' offering (or the ancient Greek 'Pharmakos' ritual), involved beating an old man dressed in animal skins and perhaps driving him from the city. Charming! Today we have the likes of Netflix and other forms of indulgence to keep us from such madness at these festival dates. According to some scholars, the Pharmakos ritual may have also been a pagan New Year festival representing the expulsion of the old year (father time). It could relate to 'Purim', celebrated on the 14th and 15th days of 'Adar', the twelfth month of the Jewish calendar (March). Adar is synonymous with joy (not for those who have been beaten or burnt) because it has traditionally been a month of hope and good luck for the Jewish people. Dressing up in animal skin and being sacrificed not only relates to animal sacrifice rituals performed in the ancient Temples of Rome, but also 'could' relate to a specific Paleolithic hybrid animal-human being that were expelled from earth in pre-historic times. The hairy-human figures found in much religious art hints at this.

The Holy Fire (or Holy Light) rituals that occur every year at the Church of the Holy Sepulchre in Jerusalem on 'Holy Saturday', the day preceding Orthodox Easter, are another expression with the church's obsession with fire. The Holy Fire ritual is based on a 'blue light' said to emit within Jesus Christ's tomb, rising from the marble slab covering the stone bed believed to be that upon which Jesus' body is believed to have been placed for burial. Gas mark seven (350°)? The light is believed to form a column of fire, from which candles are lit. This fire is then used to light the candles of the clergy and pilgrims in attendance. It's *all* about 'fire' at these festival dates because fire *is* the source from where otherworldly entities (like the Jinn/Salamander/Phoenix) dwell.

All Hallows' Eve

Halloween is a 'pantomime' in the UK and USA. Its place on the calendar is up there with 'Disneyland proportions' holding sway over the populace. From its original Pagan traditions, to the 'trick or treat', hoards of fancy-dress zombies, vampires and clowns 'get together' for the annual party gathering. Halloween, in its modern form, has become diluted but its reason for existing en masse (in its modern form), has more to do with 'nefarious' ceremonies connected to satanism as we enter the 'darker days' of Autumn. Dressing up as witches and devils (innocently), energetically mirrors forces wanting horror in all its forms. Whether effigies of a man nailed to a cross or a candlelit pumpkin, both energetically come from the same focus on 'death' just as in the ancient world. The imagery associated with the skull and the more 'cannibalistic rituals' of elite priests in ancient times, are rites connected to the Saturn Death Cult. The most popular festivals, besides Christmas in the 'Catholic' calendar, are Halloween and Easter and as I have already pointed out, both are 'celebrations of death' on the surface. For elite satanic 'networks', these points on the calendar are used to further 'distort' reality and harness potent 'invisible' energies, so to 'change the collective frequency' in which humanity is bathed. The sea of energy we are swimming in 'energetically' (collectively) is 'polluted' by dark rituals performed at these dates on the calendar. It's all about light or darkness and how Halloween, in truth, has become a ritual for focusing on the 'Underworld' and the 'nefarious side' of 'Orion and Saturn, courtesy of the otherworldy Cult I've been taking about.

The feast of 'All Hallows' Eve', on its current date in the Western calendar, can be traced to Pope Gregory III's (731–741) founding of an oratory in St Peter's for the relics of the holy apostles and of All Saints, Martyrs and Confessors. In 835AD, All Hallows' Day was officially switched to 1st November, the same date as the Pagan date of Samhain, at the behest of Pope Gregory IV. Of course, Samhain also Anglicised as 'Sawin', or 'Sowin', in the ancient world marked the end of the 'harvest season' and the beginning of winter, or the 'darker half' of the year. At this time, torches lit from the Samhain bonfire were carried sunwise around homes and fields to protect people from dark forces operating at, what we now call, Halloween. Many indigenous peoples used a 'sacred fire' as a marker for the beginning of the new sun as winter approached and Orion reached his prominence in the winter skies. For indigenous peoples, the fires were a kind of imitative, or sympathetic magic, mimicking the sun, the stars, helping the 'powers of growth', holding back the decay and darkness of the coming winter.

Light and Darkness at Hallowe'en

The 'dark side' is exactly what we are looking at with Halloween and the days leading up to it. The symbolism relates to death, and sometimes the opposite, 'the god of Life' (from the light half to the dark half of the year). The imagery associated with the skull (the Halloween pumpkin-head), the scorpion and the 'Day of the Dead' was, and still is, a prominent symbol for the cults who focus on death. As Stephen Arroyo writes in his book,

Astrology Karma & Transformation: The Inner Dimensions of the Birth Chart (1992):

> *The Scorpio period of the year (at least in the Northern Hemisphere) is the time when the life force withdraws from all outer forms in nature and is concentrated in the seed. It is striking that the cultural symbol for this time of the year in the United States is the Halloween pumpkin with its insides removed, leaving only an empty shell with a blankly staring face. In fact, the Jack-o'-lantern is a symbol of death, a symbolic skull with the glimmering remains of the departed life-force represented by the candle within. Traditionally, the Halloween feast (the Eve of All Saints Day) was a time when the dead came back to life and when human beings in the physical body could most immediately contact departed spirits of all kinds, as well as their own patron saints. It is significant that children are allowed at this time to wander out at night, past their usual bedtime, and that they are not supposed to go from house to house begging for food until the Sun (the symbol of physical life) has completely set!* [5]

As I have been showing, the skull is still used as an image at festivals, within the music industry and of course in movies to this day. Christmas, or Saturnalia, was the final doorway through to the 'new sun' (the new light) and in some of the Scandinavian folklores, Krampus, (the horned keeper), accompanies Father Christmas. Krampus is another symbolic representation of the devilish 'horned clan' I looked at in *Chapter Seven*.

Looking at vintage imagery associated with Halloween, I wasn't surprised to find certain costumes from the 19th Century showing swastikas. Tomb stones in pagan Europe often show swastikas and skulls (the original pumpkin) see figure 214. I have already pointed out how symbols for opposing forces born of Orion's duality can be seen in the use of black and white symbols, archetypes and 'light', all projected on the minds of those on earth. The candle inside the skull is also symbolic of the *activated* light in the mind when we arrive at these solar festivals. As I showed in the previous chapter, ancient Swastika symbols represent the Galaxy's swirling forces on one level; however, it can also be symbolic of Orion's cross formed by the belt stars and the four-fold main visible stars of the hunter's body.

Figure 214: Halloween and the Swastika. A Relief of a skull with a swastika on a 1669 gravestone, France. Both were common images in centuries gone by. (cc) Pethrus/ Public domain

Indian and Iranian coins dating back to 150BC also feature the swastika and warrior,

Figure 215: Yolamira (Mithra) Orion.
2000 year-old Iranian coins showing Yolamira (Mithra,) or Migra and the Swastika. All are symbols of Orion's influence.

Yolamira (Mithra as the warrior), who is another version of Orion (see figure 215). In other coins, the Orion archetype, the warrior, has a four-fold cross between his feet. The Jain festival Diwali, which is one of the most important festivals on the Hindu calendar, is a also good example of the focus on such symbols at Halloween. Despite the fact the swastika symbol also seems to crop up on pagan Halloween costumes, quite often in bad taste, (through its visual connection to the Nazi use of the symbol), its ancient meaning relates to the 'passage of light' and the forces of creation. The Diwali festival, celebrated in 'Kaartika' at Halloween, is concerned with 'light' or what is called the 'change light' (invisible light) on earth and the illumination of matter. One quote from the *Dhavalaa* by Virasenacharya relating to Diwali, says:

Since the light of intelligence (Vardhamana Mahavira) is gone, let us make an illumination of the material matter.

As the light symbolically starts to reduce (from Halloween) and the days in the northern hemisphere become shorter, Orion climbs and shines brightly above in the autumnal skies. It is here Saturn makes its esoteric connection with Orion in the most celebrated holiday period on Earth.

Saturnalia 'Time' – Two Sides of Christmas

On one level, Saturnalia was also a 'festival of light' in Rome, leading through to the Winter Solstice (21st December). Saturnalia was ushered in and signified through an abundant presence of candles (fairy-lights) and pine trees in ancient Rome. The tree and the lights on them are meant to be symbols of our quest for 'knowledge' and 'truth' (light) at the darker end of the year. Another aspect of Saturnalia is about both 'giving' and 'taking' of energy. However, when you look around our modern 21st century version of the Roman 'Saturnalia fest', I think it's safe to say that knowledge and truth has taken more of a back seat. The whole period of 'time' called Christmas can be an unnecessary burden for too many and it also focuses our energy on 'polarisation' of those who 'have' and those who 'have not'. Spending time with family and loved ones is wonderful for most, but sanctioning it as an official holiday becomes tedious, draining and for many that have 'woken up', or seen the light, it's just another energy theft that has no bearing on the real plight of humanity. Before anyone accuses me of

'Bah, humbug' (a phrase incidentally that means to act in a 'deceptive' or 'dishonest' way), I will say that there *is* a meaningful connection to the 'introspection' aspect at this 'time of year'. The winter period brings 'clarity of focus' for those who can look within. Being creative is important, too, as winter kicks in, but the modern day version of what was ancient Saturnalia is nothing more than a 'massive energy grab' (our human energy) just as it always was meant to be.

Polarization at Saturnalia is magnified, especially when we see the rich, the famous and the 'gods of our time' (celebrities) reveling in Saturnalia, while the masses struggle to survive the pressures of Christmas. The amount of presents being bought, and brought into some homes, and the overindulgence by those who have discovered their 'credit card's power' is beyond madness in my view. As Asterius writes in *Oratio 4:Adversus Kalendarum Festum*:

> This festival [Saturnalia] *teaches even the little children, artless and simple, to be greedy, and accustoms them to go from house to house and to offer novel gifts, fruits covered with silver tinsel. For these they receive, in return, gifts double their value, and thus the tender minds of the young begin to be impressed with that which is commercial and sordid.*

If anything, Christmas (Saturnalia) can bring heightened emotions, stress, arguments, loneliness, drunkenness, suicide and often the overpowering need to 'keep on with the programme' called Christmas. 'Boxing Day' in the UK (26th December) can take on a very literal meaning for some. I know Christmas also brings laughter, love and happiness too, which is why it has 'two sides'. Christmas shopping, Black Friday's, the sales, buying things and maxing up debt has become the norm for people who have 'bought into' the vibration of *modern* Saturnalia. When I was a kid, people used to stock up on food at Christmas like there was going to be a war! Bread was frozen in quantities across homes all over Britain in the 80's as though there was going to be a famine or *'pandemic'* (the shops really did close for days back then). But to understand the Christmas 'vibration' and its focus on Saturn in the month of Capricorn (the goat), when Orion dominates the skies, we have to go back in time to ancient Rome.

Inner Light - Outer light

Saturnalia was the Roman festival of the 'renewal of light' and the coming of the 'new year', celebrated as the 'Dies Natalis Solis Invicti', or the birthday of the 'Unconquerable Sun'. The date for this event was the 23rd of December, but the roots of this celebration go further back into the ancient world and have more meaning in the attachment to Saturn (the Old Sun), and not necessarily the Sun. Of course, the birth of the new 'sun' (a son) god was interchangeable with the 'Son of God' (born on the 25th of the month), not least thanks to Emperor Constantine and the absorption of pagan Rome into what became Christianity in 300 AD. Much of what followed Constantine's creed is fable disguised as history. In the 4th Century, Christian leaders succeeded in converting to Christianity large numbers of Roman pagans by promising them that they could continue to celebrate Saturnalia as Christians. The problem was, as it is today, there is nothing very Christian about Saturnalia – it is Pagan to its core.

In relation to more ancient texts some connect the 'darker days' of autumn and winter to Adam's (Orion's) fall, or sin in the garden which causes creation to return to a state of 'chaos' and 'darkness'. Again this could relate to Orion's precession over darker days of winter in the Northern hemisphere. The Jewish festival of 'Hanukkah' (with its lighting of candles) falls within the Orion/Saturn-based focus at the same time of year. The lighting of candles in the dark is not only symbolic of bringing light to darkness, but the candles themselves seem to represent a spiritual starlight. I've often wondered if the traditional Menorah, which holds the seven candles, was another symbol for the *seven* main visible stars of Orion, the Pleiades, or even Ursa Major? *Seven* seems to be an important number.

'Saturnius Mons' – Lord of the Golden Age

The oldest Roman religious calendars, thought to have been established by the legendary founder of Rome, Romulus and his successor Numa Pompilius, marked Saturnalia (Saturnius Mons) as a legal holiday in December. The 19th of December marked the dedication anniversary (Dies Natalis) of the Temple to Saturn in the Roman Forum in 497 BC (see figure 216 overleaf). Julius Caesar had the calendar reformed because it had fallen out of synchronization with the solar year; two days were added to the month, and Saturnalia then fell on 17th December, through to the 24th of December, which became Candle-mass Eve, or 'Christmas Eve'.

In Roman mythology, Saturn was an agricultural deity who was said to have reigned over the world in the Golden Age, (most likely a pre-Atlantis world), when humans enjoyed spontaneous 'bounty of the earth' without labour and in a 'state of innocence' (see *Chapter One*). Saturn was the first god of the Capitol, known since ancient times as 'Saturnius Mons', and he was seen as a god of generation, dissolution, plenty, wealth, agriculture, periodic renewal, law and liberation. In many ancient beliefs, the original sun (Saturnis Mons) was used as a marker for when the position of the sun (as seen from earth) would change simply to 'mark' the arrival of lighter

Figure 216: Temple of Saturn, Rome.
Interesting number of columns left standing 8 (Saturn) + 3 (Orion) = 11. Justice is a Major Arcana Tarot card, numbered either VIII or XI, depending on the deck, and Saturn is the symbolic ruler of the Justice system.

nights, and darker days (solstices). It is all based on the overarching mechanism of marking the passage of 'time'. Who was the Lord of Time? The old father figure - Saturn. The death of a sun and the 'birth of a sun' (or its light) as I have been describing in this chapter, are also embroiled in the symbolism of Saturnalia. So is the notion of 'old and young', 'Santa and children' and the gifts given through life itself. Life is 'given to death', so that 'death can live' (see figure 217). The BBC's children's drama *The Box of Delights* in the 1980's is a fine example of symbolism evoked through Saturnalia. The 'box', or cube, is another symbol of Saturn, appearing in many other religious forms, not least the black cube of Mecca and the Tefillin (black leather boxes) worn on the head by orthodox Jews on the Shabbat (Sabbath) Saturday, or Saturn's Day. The main statue over the entrance of the BBC building at Broadcasting House shows the 'old man' and 'the child', which is Prospero, the main character in Shakespeare's *Tempest* (who lives on an island and is a great sorcerer) and Ariel, the child (see figure 218). The same magician also features on an island in one of the episodes of *The Box of Delights*. The artist

Figure 217: Old Man Saturn & the Child.
Saturn and Saturday (Sabbath day) are both named after Saturnius Mons. *Life* (the child) known as Maponos and *Death* (old man), all are symbolic of Saturnalia and other darker meanings associated with 'Saturnic rituals'.

who made this piece was Eric Gill, an 'alleged' Paedophile. The scope of this book doesn't allow the time to delve into such subjects, but if I say the establishment and Jimmy Savile', I'll let you ponder on the ramifications surrounding of past horrors. Savile presented the first BBC *Top of the Pops*, January 1st 1964 (which is in part of the

Christmas/Saturnalia period).

Christmas Hypnosis

In Rome the revelries of Saturnalia were supposed to reflect the conditions of a 'lost mythical age', not all of them desirable to mind, as
much of it was connected to bestiality and
human sacrifice. In ancient Rome, priests
inside the ancient temple performed the rituals of Saturnalia, while homes were decorated
with cyprus and pine trees, covered in candles. Health and Safety didn't exist back then.
Trees, with a star atop, are all symbols of that
bygone 'golden era' and quite possibly a memory of the 'old sun' (Saturn) as it was seen from

Figure 218: Father Time.
Drawing of the Statue of Ariel
and Prospero by Eric Gill.

earth in an ancient epoch. For more information on ancient Saturn, see
David Talbot's excellent book, *The Saturn Myth* (see figure 219). The star
placed on the Christmas tree symbolism becomes clear through understanding how the ancients saw Saturn and other planets in the skies.
According to Talbot, Saturn looked very different (as seen from earth) in a
very ancient epoch.

Today, these symbols and rituals continue through focus of mass media,
mass consumption and the ethereal effect of the 'lack of light' at Christmas.
It has become 'Christmas hypnosis' for the many! And the official religions
of ancient Rome have now become the religions of 'buying things', 'consuming' and being drawn into a *programme*. Television, of course, becomes
more of a focus at this time of year, and with so many 'programmes' to

choose from, we become part of
a Saturnalia sleep on one level.
Shopping malls are the cathedrals decorated to the hilt with
neon lights. Even on the opposite side of the globe in
Australia, where if we went
back several thousands of years,
the Aboriginal people would
not have heard of such ceremonies and pagan rituals during the Christmas period in the
Australian heat. It's all a 'programme' that has spread

Figure 219: Star on the Tree.
Saturn was the 'old sun' (star) of a Golden Age
as seen from earth in an ancient epoch.

'worldwide' with good reason. Saturn's influence over humanity is through *'hypnosis'* and the connection to 'time' and the 'unseen' forces.

Pan & the Gingerbread Man

As I have already said, Ancient Rome was the epicentre of Saturnalia. The city's architectural symbols, not least the 'phallic symbol' or Obelisk relating to the 'death' and 'resurrection' of the Egyptian god, Osiris (Orion), can be found placed in the Capitols of Europe. They are there to invoke the 'sexual' masculine energy or the 'randy old goat' syndrome, also known as the god, Pan. Old Pan is connected to myths associated with Capricorn (Sex magic) and the 'Lord of Aquarius' (Electronic Communications), not least through Mercury, or Hermes, the god of travellers and shepherds (Pan) in Greek mythology. Saturnalia is also a time for family visits, trips, traffic jams and all communication electrical or otherwise, especially over the festival period.

Pan worship began in Arcadia (a district of mountain people, culturally separated from other Greeks), which was always the principal seat of Pan's worship. The hunt, the shepherd, the cave and the woods were all abodes of Pan. Hermes (or Mercury) was considered the great grandfather of Pan and symbolically, Mercury goes 'between' worlds and is the messenger of what Romans called 'the gods'. These gods are 'personified energetic realms' and it has become clear to me over the years, that imagery and symbols associated with 'the gods' are portals into these 'energetic fields', more on this in the second part of the book. Hermes, as the father/grandfather of Pan, connects Pan (the goat) with the titan Saturn in Capricorn (see figure 220). Hermes is also one of the 'threefold' fathers of Orion in Greek myth. The 'Gävle Goat' - the Swedish Gävlebocken, a traditional Christmas display erected annually at Slottstorget in central Gävle, Sweden, is a perfect example of the Pan-Saturn archetype (see figure 221). It is a giant version of a traditional Swedish Yule Goat figure (Pan) made of straw, often attacked by arsonists during Saturnalia.

Saturnalia, as recorded by the Greek writer poet and historian, Lucian (in his dialogue entitled *Saturnalia*), observes the same Saturn festivals in Lucian's time. Lucian

Figure 220: Pan, Capricorn, Hermes and the Gingerbread Man. All are symbols of Christmas time.

Figure 221: Pan-Saturn Gävle Goat.

also mentions human sacrifice, 'widespread intoxication', 'going from house to house while singing naked', 'violation' and other 'sexual activities'. It's not quite that today, thankfully, but we aren't far off in some cities of the world. Lucian also mentions consuming human-shaped biscuits, still produced in some British and most German bakeries during the Christmas season as the gingerbread man. *"You can't catch me!"* takes on another meaning when you consider the deeper (darker) esoterics behind Saturnalia and the horrors some might have suffered at that time. There is another side to Christmas invoking both the 'good and the bad', where children become the focus for this tussle, too. *Chitty Chitty Bang Bang* and the fairy tale *Hansel and Gretel* (with the gingerbread house) come to mind! I'll come to Krampus too, shortly.

We Three Kings from Orion Are

In previous chapters, I have pointed out correlation theories relating to the three belt stars of Orion (Alnitak, Alnilam and Mintaka) and the pyramids of Giza - not to mention the Hopi's Three Mesas of Arizona. However, many myths are allegories of the path of the sun through the zodiac signs, and the famous axiom, 'As above and so below', is so true. The word Orient, in the Christmas Carol *We Three Kings from Orient Are*, should be replaced by 'Orion' – 'We Three Kings of Orion Are'. The three Magi, or 'Drie Koningen', who searched for the newly-born solar Christ are symbolic of the three stars in the hunter's belt in the winter sky (see figure 222 overleaf). The Three Kings could also represent three divine aspects of 'will', 'love' and 'intelligence' (3 lights) in some sources. The name, Orion, in Hebrew, means 'the breaking forth of light' and therefore symbolises the 'place of light'. In ancient Akkadian, Orion was 'Ur-ana', the light of heaven and is the 'place' from where Saturn (Saturnalia) gets its interstellar instructions.

In some South American cultures, Orion's Belt is known as 'Las Tres Marias' (The Three Marys) in honour of Mary of Nazareth, Mary Magdalene, and Mary of Bethany. Astrologically, the alignment of Orion's belt (three Kings or Marys) as they follow Betelgeuse moving east over the horizon, towards the birth of the sun in the precessional cycle across the sky at night (on December 25th), adds another layer to the Christmas story.

The shepherd's dog (Sirius) and the ox (Taurus) in the stable all add another facet to the Christmas tale. It is a story that clearly seems to map the position of the stars and offer the idea of a 'star being' being born.

Figure 222: Orion's Three Stars (Kings).

Light Born of the Cave

Cronos (Saturn), as I mentioned earlier, was the 'sun in the cave' and it is said in myths that his mother, 'Rhea', carried Cronos (the stone wrapped in swaddling clothes), as though he were the babe to which she had given birth. The babe in a manger, born among animals (not least the ass and ox/bull), in a stable or a cave was common in many ancient religions. The mother of Cronos in Hindu myth equivalent was known as 'Chaya', meaning 'shadow' and she represented the unconscious, otherworldly, unseen light of the aura. You could see her as the 'Queen of the fairies' (fairy lights) in some myths. In a small and intriguing book called *The Greatness of Saturn* (1997), by Dr Robert E Svoboda, which covers Eastern Vedic myth, Chaya is represented as 'material things', the illusion of the material life and how the shadow allows this 'fake light' to be seen for what it is – illusory. The Gnostics also talked of the 'light of Christos' and its penetration of the dark, the shadow world of the cave. The light of Aeon Christos, in this sense, represented the truth, the light and the word, each attributed to the baby born in a manger.

According to legend, Hermes (Mercury) was also born in a cave on Mount Cyllene in Arcadia. Zeus had impregnated 'Maia', at night, while all the other gods slept. When Hermes was born at dawn (like the sun), Maia wrapped him in swaddling clothes. The pre-Christian Roman version of Jesus, Mithras, was also born in a cave, with shepherds in attendance, on the 25th of December. Mithras was also known to his followers as 'The light of the world', or 'The Good Shepherd', and urged his followers to share ritual communion of bread and wine. Mithra's priests were also called 'Father'. Add the word 'Christmas' after 'father' and there you have it. Mithra, as I mentioned earlier in the book, is the bull (Taurus) slayer and therefore fits as the Orion star man – the stellar 'light of the world'.

Krampus (Santa's Claws) - 'Sakwa Hu'

There is a darker, nefarious aspect to Saturnalia, which connects to the horned race, I touched upon earlier in the book. Krampus, the horned, anthropomorphic folklore figure described as 'half-goat, half-demon', is another symbolic deviation of Pan (see figure 223). Santa, or 'Saint Nick', in Nordic and Germanic versions, can often be seen with Krampus as two halves of the same symbol. During Saturnalia, Krampus is said to punish 'naughty' children, just like the Hopi Kachina, 'Sakwa Hu', who arrives at the winter solstice, or 'Soyal' (Soyalang-eu), to do the same (see figure 224). The Sakwa Hu, or 'Blue Whipper' Kachina, is considered an old Kachina although small boys usually impersonate this 'being'. Its main functions are to be a guard at certain ceremonies, mainly on the Third Mesa; according to the Hopi tradition, he is a 'whipper' who also punishes clowns, children, and people when they misbehave!

A group of about thirty official kachinas, called 'Mong Kachinas', takes part in five major ceremonies held during this period: 'Soyalang-eu' (Winter Solstice Ceremony) in December; 'Pamuya' in January, when the Orion is high above and the sun appears to move north again. The Mong Kachinas, I am certain, are 'Orion-based entities' who *arrive* at the winter solstice for the Orion worshipping Hopi. During 'Soyal', which lasts nine days of what we call Christmas, sacred rituals are performed in chambers called kivas and many ceremonies involving dancing and singing take place.

Figure 223: Saint Nick and the horned Krampus.
(Left) 'Old Christmas', riding a yule goat; 1836 illustration by Robert Seymour. (Public domain.)

The kachinas even bring gifts to the Hopi children and many orthodox Christians think it's all about Jesus.

Soyal time (Christmas time) is when stories are passed down to children from the elders and children are taught pivotal lessons like respecting others. The Hopi believe that everything that will occur during the year

Figure 224: (Left) Krampus & (Right) Sakwa Hu.
Both represent the same Saturnian deities used to get children to be good in the winter leading up to Christmas.

is arranged at Soyal (New Year Resolutions as such). Children are also given replicas of the kachinas (dolls), intricately carved and dressed like the dancers, to help them learn about the hundreds of kachina spirits. Sixteen days before the winter solstice, one of the chief kachinas enters houses on the Mesas. He appears as a tired, 'old man' who has just awakened from a deep slumber, teetering and on the verge of losing his balance. The Hopi god, Masau'u, is massively connected to the symbols of Orion, Saturn and 'Father Time' (see figure 225). *Masau'u is Orion and Saturn combined.*

Figure 225: Father Time - the Man of Winter.
Cottontail/Masau'u/Kokopelli (the Hopi Father Time). This Bronze Age petroglyph is a win-ter solstice marker left by the Hopi. © Dan Budnik

The same figure is called 'Cottontail' a pueblo symbol for both the 'hare' and 'time', more on the hare in the next chapter. Interestingly, the hare was said to be a 'child of Pan' and in many myths the hare was wrapped in goatskin. Of course, the hare and the moon are symbolically connected in much folklore, and the hare also takes on the role of the 'Demiurge' in some myths. See an interesting book called *The Lady of the Hare* (1944) by John Layard. The constellation of Lepus runs alongside Orion and there is more to know about this connection, as we shall see.

Krampus is also another version of Ba'al Hammon, the Carthaginian god regarded as the counterpart of the Roman Saturn and Greek Cronos (see page 188). As I've already pointed out, Krampus is one of the companions of Saint Nicholas in regions including Austria, Bavaria, Croatia, Czech Republic, Hungary, Slovenia and Northern Italy. The song *Santa Claus is Coming to Town* is based on the Germanic pagan folk tales of Krampus and again relates to the Hopi, Sakwa Hu or Blue Whipper Kachina's chastiser of children for misbehaving before Christmas time. As the song suggests:

> *He sees you when you're sleeping*
> *He knows when you're awake*
> *He knows if you've been bad or good*
> *So be good for goodness sake...*

Santa Chronos

The modern figure of Santa Claus (Saint Nicholas, Saint Nick, Father Christmas, Kris Kringle) is derived from the Dutch figure of 'Sinterklaas', whose name is a dialectal pronunciation of Saint Nicholas, the historical Greek bishop and gift-giver of Myra. During the Christianisation of Germanic Europe, this Myra figure may have absorbed elements of the god Odin, who was associated with the Germanic pagan midwinter event of Yule, and like Orion, leads the 'wild winter hunt'. Of course the celestial hunter, Orion, is observed clearly in the winter sky from November through to Imbolc, along with the constellations of Sirius and Lepus. Telling a child, in the child's early years, that Santa (who is essentially an old bearded bloke, a stranger with magical powers) sneaks into the house to leave gifts, is creepy enough, but then to reveal it was all a fib later on, is the power of dealing in 'Bah humbug' on a massive scale; something in which we have all innocently participated. The creeping around at night while children sleep is harmless to those from loving families, but consider the amount of creeping around in orphanages and children's homes over the years by figures that are more like Krampus? Saturnalia is a time of year when both the good and the bad are 'magnified' energetically.

In his book *Mushrooms and Mankind* (2003), the late author James Arthur, points out that the Amanita muscaria mushroom, also known as fly agaric, grows throughout the Northern Hemisphere under conifers and birch trees, with which the fungi (coloured deep red with white flecks) has a symbiotic relationship. Some say this phenomenon explains the practice of the Christmas tree, and the placement of bright, red and white presents underneath, resembling the Amanita mushrooms. Arthur wrote:

> *Why do people bring pine trees into their houses at the Winter Solstice, placing brightly coloured (red and white) packages under their boughs, as gifts to show their love for each other? It is because, underneath the pine bough is the exact location where one would find this 'Most Sacred' substance, the Amanita muscaria, in the wild.*[6]

I would suggest that it has more to do with Saturn's pole position in the Golden Age mentioned earlier, but there may be some truth in this notion across certain cultures.

Reindeer are common in Siberia, and seek out these hallucinogenic fungi, according to some researchers. Donald Pfister, a biologist who studies fungi at Harvard University, suggests that Siberian tribesmen who ingested 'fly agaric' may have hallucinated into thinking that reindeer were flying. The use of 'red and white' for Christmas and Santa is clearly connected to the Coca Cola imagery and their 20th Century campaign to associate Saturnalia with this popular drink.

Lord of Misrule

Another aspect to Saturnalia, is the 'King of Saturn' who ruled as the 'master of ceremonies' for the proceedings through the Saturnalia period. He was appointed by lot and has been compared to the medieval 'Lord of Misrule' at the 'Feast of Fools', the last day of Saturnalia at Epiphany (6th January). In England, the Lord of Misrule (known in Scotland as the 'Abbot of Unreason' and in France as the 'Prince des Sots') was an officer appointed to preside over the Feast of Fools (see figure 226). The Lord of Misrule was generally a peasant appointed to be in charge of Christmas revelries,

which often included drunkenness and wild partying, in the pagan tradition of Saturnalia. Sounds like many towns in the UK at Christmas? In his paper, *The Christmas Conspiracy*, Timothy Chilman tells us more about this festival and its connections between Mithraism, Christianity and the Lord of Misrule. He says:

Figure 226: Feast of Fools.
Note the hare, donkey and stag in this Medieval Image. All three are symbols of 'misrule'. They could also be Orion, Sirius and Lepus.

The general public also had a Lord of Misrule. The winter solstice marked the death and rebirth of the sun king Sol Invictus. Instead of killing a real monarch, a Lord of Misrule was appointed for Saturnalia, usually a criminal or slave. He was given royal robes and feathers or ass ears. He was honored as a true king until the end of the festival, whereupon he was killed on the altar of Saturn. The mocking ("mock-king") of Jesus by Roman soldiers in the run-up to his crucifixion would seem to have been inspired by this.

Emancipated slaves wore a felt cap called a "pilleus," but during the Saturnalia, everyone wore them. The ideal party had an attendance of "more than the graces" (three) but "less than the Muses" (nine).

The feet of the statue of Saturn in the Roman Forum were normally bound but were untied over Saturnalia. Punishments were suspended and wars had to wait until later. This behavior carried down to the level of individuals, who put grudges aside and did not chastise their slaves for the duration.[7]

Saturnalia and misrule make a 'mockery of a world' in which 'law' was determined by one man (a Fool King), and the traditional social and political networks are reduced to the emperor's power over his subjects. In general terms, Saturnalia was the celebration of the longing for Saturn to reign again, as in ancient times.

The donkey, or ass, was another symbol of misrule and 'mockery of law and order', 'title and kingship'. In Ancient Egypt, Seth, Osiris's brother and slayer, was sometimes shown to have the head of an ass. That's why Apuleius in 'The Golden Ass' describes a great metamorphosis, the transformation of Lucius to a donkey and his way back – spiritual evolution towards the human being. Jesus (like King Solomon before him) was also said to ride into Jerusalem on a donkey, which of could relate to Jesus as the Saturn figure, a Lord of Misrule, on one level. The 'She-Mule' could be also seen as 'Donkey Pope' found in anti-Catholic Satire during the Reformation in 16th-century Germany. Some of the oldest tarot decks also show the Pope as a Donkey.[8] The Lord of Misrule is placed on an ass (or depicted as one) as a symbol of the 'King Fool' of Saturnalia (see figure 227). He rides the donkey facing backwards as a symbol of 'inversion' at this time of year. In this case, the donkey represents sexuality, instincts, sensuality, ignorance. A red donkey was said to be one of the dangerous creatures that the soul met in its journey after death - possibly an archon (Jinn) of sorts? The ass and the Lord of Misrule go together at both Saturnalia (Christmas) and Ostara (Easter), more on Easter in the next chapter.

Figure 227: The King Fool, Donkey Pope. Medieval illustrations often showed a donkey crowned, which was another representation of the 'Fool of Saturnalia'.

The idea of a Lord of Misrule during Saturnalia also reminds us of the Donkey Pope/Priest that the Church Fathers mention, including Tertullian. This ass-faced 'scapegoat' connects to Baphomet of the Oriental Knights Templars and the redeemed Gnostic archon, 'Sabaoth', also called the 'Lord of Forces' in Gnostic scripture, *Hypostasis of the Archons and On The Origin of the World.* This Donkey-like god was connected to Yahweh (Jehovah) by the Gnostics, as Epiphanius in the *Panarion* (26:12:1-4).

The Lord of Misrule gets more gruesome in Rome. In 'Durostorum on the Danube' (modern Silistra), Roman soldiers would choose a man from among them to be the Lord of Misrule for thirty days through December. The Fool, or jester is also a Lord of Misrule figure (see figure 228). At the end of those thirty days, his *throat was cut on the altar of Saturn*. Similar origins of the British Lord of Misrule, as a 'sacrificial king' (a temporary king, who was later put to death for the benefit of all, have also been recorded. See the movie, *The Wicker Man* (1973) starring the late, Lord of Misrule himself – Sir Christopher lee. Christopher (Frank Carandini) Lee, who never got to play either 'Santa' or 'Krampus', as far am aware, often mentioned his ancient Roman ancestry (bloodline) in books and on TV interviews. His autobiography, *Lord of Misrule* (published by 'Orion' in 2003), hints at his knowledge of the occult and symbolism associated with Saturnalia, ancient Rome. I once stood next to Lee at a Eurostar waiting area over twenty years

ago, at the time he had just finished filming the *Lord of the Rings* trilogy and he seemed both enigmatic and 'strange' to me. Whether 'Sauroman', 'Lord Summer Isle' or Count Dracula, his movies were *very* Saturnian, to say the least.

Another movie set at Christmas time, is Stanley Kubrick's *Eye's Wide Shut* (2001). The film also highlights sordid, sinister rituals, which take place at the height of Saturnalia. The film is full of occult symbolism, especially relating to Kubrick's knowledge of the real power 'behind the scenes', and how Saturn is a focus for those involved in satanic (Saturnic) rituals. Sex is also a big part of Saturnalia and of course it plays a major part in *Eye's*

Figure 228: The Fool or Jester was another Misrule figure at Christmas.
The three-pointed hat worn by the fool is an Orion symbol. (Public domain)

Wide Shut, too. According to anthropologist James Frazer, in his book *The New Golden Bough* (1959), he says, "There was a darker side [and the rest] to the Saturnalia festival"; that is an understatement when you really look at the occult connections to both Orion and Saturn. These celestial bodies are 'connected energetically', at Halloween and Saturnalia, through some of the nefarious forces I have been describing.

Father *Time* (Saturn)

The infamous American *Time* Magazine, created by Henry Luce, a member of Alpha Delta Phi and Skull and Bones secret society, is another example of the subtle symbolism of Saturnalia 'end-of-year celebration'. As I have
already shown, Cronos is usually por-
trayed as an older, wise man with a
long white beard, similar to 'Father
Time' – hence the *Time* magazine.
Looking at the *Time* covers over the
years one can't help but see the obvious
symbolism connected to Saturn (see figure 229) through death symbolism, royalty, the moon and 'hidden worlds'.
Some of the current English words
whose etymological root is 'Chronos'
include 'chronology', chronometer,
chronic, anachronism, and chronicle.
Time Magazine is the ultimate 'chronicle'
with its cover of the 'Person of the Year' in December – at 'Saturnalia'. No matter where you look, Saturn is *everywhere*, especially at Saturnalia.

Figure 229: Saturn - Father Time - Chronos. (Public domain)

When in Rome

The phrase Saturnalia was also a characteristic 'shout' or 'salutation' of the festival, in Roman times. The 'Yo ho ho' is connected to this Salutation. Seneca, the Roman Stoic philosopher, statesman and dramatist, looked forward to the holiday of Saturn, if somewhat tentatively. In a letter to a friend he wrote:

> *It is now the month of December, when the greatest part of the city is in a bustle. Loose reins are given to public dissipation; everywhere you may hear the sound of great preparations, as if there were some real difference between the days devot-ed to Saturn and those for transacting business. & Were you here, I would will-ingly confer with you as to the plan of our conduct; whether we should eve in our usual way, or, to avoid singularity, both take a better supper and throw off the toga.*

The Roman writer, Microbius, also writes in his work titled *Saturnalia*:

> *Meanwhile the head of the slave household, whose responsibility it was to offer*

sacrifice to the Penates, to manage the provisions and to direct the activities of the domestic servants, came to tell his master that the household had feasted according to the annual ritual custom. For at this festival, in houses that keep to proper religious usage, they first of all honor the slaves with a dinner prepared as if for the master; and only afterwards is the table set again for the head of the household. So, then, the chief slave came in to announce the time of dinner and to summon the masters to the table.

That's your Christmas dinner! I am sure some people feel like a slave when it comes to cooking on Christmas day? Many others, I am also sure, relish the event with gratitude. Back then, a suckling pig was sacrificed (and still is eaten in large quantities in more latino and Hispanic countries). Turkey replaced the 'pig' over the centuries; unless one was eating other animal flesh in Tudor times, you might have a combination of both turkey and pork 'sewn together' as a 'cockenthrice', just one of the many twists of Saturnalia. How lovely!

Roman Saturnalia was also best known for roles reversal and behavioural license (the Lord of Misrule again), allowing slaves to act like masters and vice versa. Roman slaves were treated to a banquet of the kind usually enjoyed by their masters. Role-playing was implicit in the Saturnalia's status reversals, and there are hints of 'mask-wearing' or guising in ancient Rome. Historically, elite families would have loved all that role-play, hunting in masks and generally playing roles reversed? Maybe they did and still do? Slaves were set free just for the festivities... So 'nothing's changed then?' See *every* Bank Holiday in the western world. Who is it that rules over the banking system astrologically? Saturn! Who owns the banks? Those in power that seem to 'adore' Saturnalia. Henk Versnel writes in *Saturnus* and the *Saturnalia* (1994):

Gambling and dice-playing, normally prohibited or at least frowned upon, were permitted for all, 'even slaves'. Coins and nuts were the stakes. On the Calendar of Philocalus, the Saturnalia is represented by a man wearing a fur-trimmed coat next to a table with dice, and a caption reading: "Now you have license, slave, to game with your master." Rampant overeating and drunkenness became the rule, and a sober person the exception.[9]

The festival time is when you are allowed to feel free for a week or so, to drink (be merry) and pretend that you're not a 'slave to the system'. Some things change, some things don't.

In his many poems about Saturnalia, the poet Marcus Valerius Martialis, also names both expensive and inexpensive cheap gifts; including writing tablets, dice, knucklebones, moneyboxes, combs, toothpicks, a hat, a hunting knife, an axe, various lamps, balls, perfumes, pipes, a pig, a sausage, a parrot, tables, cups, spoons, items of clothing, statues, masks, books, and pets were given at Saturnalia. Writing today, he would be mentioning 'Poundland' and 'unwanted socks', too! In ancient Rome, gifts might be costly, such as a 'slave' or 'exotic animal', but Martialis suggests that 'token gifts' of low intrinsic value inversely measure the high quality of a friendship. You were being judged by the gift you gave even back then? Patrons or 'bosses' might pass along a gratuity (a sigillaricium) to their poorer clients, or dependents, to help them buy gifts. A 'Christmas bonus' for some, and 'bugger all' for others – no difference today. Some emperors were noted for their devoted observance of the 'Sigillaria' (19th December), when small pottery gifts were given. Some say that the giving of Christmas cards came from Sigillaria in Ancient Rome.

I wrote this chapter not to focus on the darkness of Saturnalia but to say that if people wish to make a change and want to really 'vibrate' to a 'higher level', and go beyond the religious symbolism and materialism connected to Halloween and Saturnalia, we may have to 'come away from the 'same old rituals', programmes and polarised views that are tucked away within all of the 'razzamatazz'. Symbols, icons, stories and legends are more powerful than we can imagine. We are *still in* ancient Rome (and Egypt) in so many ways; these rituals and festivals have been with us since then and linger still. I would prefer to focus on 'introspection' at this time of year (which is hard when you have small children, I know) but whatever you do, make sure you can get out of the 'Saturn vibe', even if it's just for an hour or two, to contemplate the 'bigger picture' beyond the hold of Saturnalia in the darker half of the year.

Before I venture into themes relating to consciousness and extraterrestrials connected to Orion and his adjacent stars, let us look at Easter and the hare, Lepus, who runs alongside Orion, through winter, into spring.

Sources:

1) Hekate Soteira. *A Study of Hekate's Roles in the Chaldean Oracles and Related Literature* (1990), & Sarah Johnston (Oxford University Press; 1 edition (May 1, 1990) Johnston, 1990, p150
2) Payam Nabarz is the author of numerous books on mythology and magic, including The Square and The Circle (2016), and *Anahita* (2012).
3) Guirdham, Arthur. *The Great Heresy,* C.W Daniel Company Ltd, 1993, p56
4) Lydus, John (6th century). *De mensibus* 4.36.
5) Stephen Arroyo writes in his book, *Astrology Karma & Transformation: The Inner Dimensions of the Birth Chart.* CRCS Publications, 1992, p59

6) Arthur, James. *Mushrooms and Mankind.* The Book Tree. 2003, p78
7) https://www.academia.edu/4003206/*The Christmas Conspiracy*
8) http://forum.tarothistory.com/viewtopic.php?t=663
9) Versnel, Henk. *Saturnus* and the *Saturnalia. Inconsistencies in Greek and Roman Religion, Volume 2: Transition and Reversal in Myth and Ritual.* 1994 p112

12

THE HARE, THE GODDESS & THE MOON EGG

Orion-Saturn Worship (2)

In Australia they celebrate Easter the exact same way we do,
commemorating the death and resurrection of Jesus by telling our
children that a giant bunny rabbit left chocolate eggs in the night.
BILL HICKS

A nother important religious focus point is Easter, a time when children
are often taught to connect Pagan origins with Judeo-Christian beliefs.
A connection that uncomfortably tries to equate a giant rabbit, or 'hare',
with the crucified star man, Orion. It's a mad, 'mad, world', especially
when 'State and religion' would have children focusing on the ritual killing
of Jesus (the crucifixion), in one hand, while celebrating the return of a
'giant bunny' delivering chocolate eggs, with the other. Giant rabbits,
chocolate eggs, alongside the crucifixion story of course, are not found in
the Bible. Still, the modern world celebrates Easter with the same vigour as
every other festival on the calendar. Christmas chocolates are now wheeled
out in September and Easter eggs are in the high street stores from mid
January here in the UK, as the consumer machine goes into overdrive at the
festival dates watched over by Orion.

Orion remains dominant in the skies as Saturnalia ends, and a new light
or sun is born as we head into the New Year. The star man, Orion, stays
upright and strong through the winter months up until the first rites of
spring, where he starts to decline at the time of the festival I am now going
to decode in great detail. In this chapter, I will weave together the main
themes associated with Easter and, as usual, delve a little deeper into the
symbolism.

Sun Cross 'Passing Over'

Christians refer to the week before Easter as 'Holy Week' as it contains the days of the Easter 'Triduum', including 'Maundy Thursday' and 'Last Supper', as well as 'Good Friday'. As I have already shown in previous chapters, Jesus (the Son of Man) comes from a long line of pre-Christian sun gods that 'fell' and rose again to redeem the sins of the world; see ancient Babylon, Tammuz, Bal and the Norse god Balder to name but a few. Essentially, they are all versions of the star man – Orion, who becomes the 'new sun' every year on earth. Without going into great detail regarding sun gods (as I want to focus on the moon, hare and egg symbolism) there are well over a dozen versions of the saviour sun god found all over the ancient world pre-dating Jesus (see my book *Through Ancient Eyes*).

The sun-cross circle (see figure 230) is what connects the sun and moon to the main festivals marked by the equinoxes and solstices on the original Pagan calendar. Orion and the

Figure 230: Hot Cross Sun.
Putting a cross on the bun or a 'sun on the cross', relates to the precession of the equinoxes overlooked by Orion as he travels the celestial ecliptic.

surrounding stars are a backdrop for the sun wheel seen through the zodiac (or outer circle) of the wheel. When we look more closely at religious symbolism associated with celebrations and festivals such as Easter, it becomes obvious to see correlations of 'time' being 'marked' through various 'stages' of the sun and moon in relation to how we see life and the passage of time on earth. The three main symbols showing the sun, moon and earth (along with Venus) have all been worshipped for thousands of years at the points (dates) on the Pagan calendar.

The eight-pointed star of Ishtar is often found alongside the crescent moon (Sin) and the rayed, solar disk of Shamash in Babylonian iconography on boundary

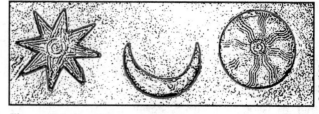

Figure 231: Star, Moon and Sun.
Worship of the Moon, Sun, Stars and the Goddess (Earth) under different names. **(From Left to Right)** Ishtar (Venus), Sin (Moon), and Shamash (Sun) on a boundary stone of Meli-Shipak II.12th century BC.

stones and cylinder seals (see figure 231). In the Christian version of Easter, some boundary stones are still marked, or 'hit' with a broom or stick to this day in older English churches. It all makes sense when we see that Easter, like Saturnalia or Christmas, came out of the pre-Christian world.

Lunar Calendars and the Time of the Crossing

Easter relates to the moon (or *moon*thly calendar) also known as a 'moveable feast' because it does not fall on a fixed date in the Roman Catholic-inspired Gregorian or Julian calendars. Easter is never the same day each year. Roman Catholic calendars follow the 'cycle of the sun' with 'irregular' Moon days and therefore Easter time, is determined through what is called a lunisolar calendar, similar to the Hebrew calendar. In 325 AD the Council of Nicaea decided Easter would fall on the first Sunday after the ecclesiastical full moon or soonest moon after the Spring Equinox on the 21st March. Those 'Pagan founding fathers' of the Roman Christian church knew how to 'use' the moon to create a calendar that would suit their own agenda for global prominence. Saturn (or dark star), I mentioned in an earlier chapter, underpins the vibrational (the invisible) structure given to us by the Moon and therefore, Roman calendars are no more than a Saturn-Sun & Moon vibrational measurment of time - or *illusion*. Authors like David Icke have called it the 'Saturn-Moon Matrix'.[1] Time, as a construct, is purely based on measurements of the movement of celestial bodies, so to keep the human mind locked on the illusion of time. Beyond the illusory clock created by the sun and moon, *there is no time*, only unlimited infinite 'timelessness'.

The sun and the moon are 'markers of time', but time as a concept was 'originated' by Cronos (Saturn). Both the sun and the moon 'manage light', creating night and day, therefore reinforcing the 'illusion of time'. The white rabbit and his 'pocket watch' in *Alice in Wonderland*, for example, is another symbol for the moon (with Saturn) and the Goddess (Alice) in 'wonderland' – the illusion. In other words, Alice (the goddess archetype), is trapped by time in the Saturn-Moon matrix of twenty-four hours, twelve months, and so on. These are the numerological 'constructs' that reinforce the moon's influence over 'our time'. And how do we spend most of our waking time? Working to earn '*Mooney*'. In ancient Chinese and Japanese calendars, hours were counted through animal names, and for these cultures an 'artificial day' began at six o'clock in the morning when the sun rises in the middle of what they called the 'Hour of the Hare' (or 'crossing'). It was the hour of the crossing, between night and day, when Orion, with Lepus the hare, can be seen to decline turning west after sunset (see figure 232 overleaf). At this time, Jupiter and Saturn also slowly move westward each night and Venus marks the dawn sky becoming the 'Morning Star' leading the Sun as it travels across the sky. It's as though Orion and Lepus together, offer 'renewal' as the spring appears, and Easter dawns.

Passover – Easter

Easter is also linked to the Passover ('Pesah' or 'Pesakh' in Assyrian) through much of its symbolism, as well as through its position in the lunisolar cal-endar. Jewish people celebrate Passover as a commemoration of their liberation by God from slavery in Egypt thanks to Moses (the Exodus), which I understand, but I cannot help but wonder if the skies at this time are highly significant to such nar-ratives, too? The Nehustan (the brazen ser-pent on the cross attributed to Moses) gives us more insight into the 'Passover-Easter' (Saturn-Sun) connection. The serpent sym-bolism refers to 'chaos calmed' and given a 'new order' that can be connected to 'Ophiuchus' (the snake bearer) and Serpens Caput (Serpent Head) to the west, and Serpens Cauda (Serpent Tail) to the east. All of which oppose Orion's 'position', as explained in previous chapters.

Figure 232: Lepus.
Orion and Lepus turn west as Spring approaches.

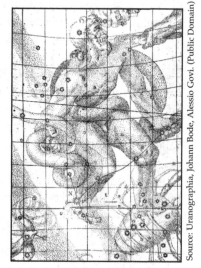

Figure 233: Ophiuchus.
'Ophiuchus' (the snake bearer) opposes, or 'replaces' Orion in the sky through spring into early summer.

In Greek mythology, Serpens represents a snake held by the healer, Asclepius, who is represented in the sky by the constella-tion, Ophiuchus (see figure 233). The myth states that Asclepius once killed a snake, but the animal was subsequently 'resurrected' after a second snake placed a revival herb on it before its death. The snake represents both gnosis and chaos. As the Masonic saying suggests, 'Out of chaos comes order'; a 'new age', or a year, along with a sense of *change* always seems prominent between Saturnalia and Easter (see the 2020 coron-avirus pandemic). In this case, the Moses or Jesus (Orion) saviour figure is both the snake, and the sun, resurrected at Easter. It is also said the 'light of the world' too, is 'renewed' at Easter (or spring time) and the numerous saviour figures, found in ancient myth, are symbols for this renewal on one

Figure 234: Sun, Snake, Resurrection.
(Left) The Jesus and Moses figures as portrayed, by the cross and serpent at Easter, are Ophiuchus-Orion-Saturn deities.
(Right) Saturn's astrological symbol expresses the connection well.

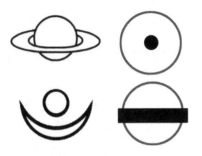

Figure 235: Saturn - Moon Symbols. Saturn and Moon symbolism in the world all around us.

level (see figure 234). Interestingly, Passover (Easter) arrives through the first month called 'Nisan' (or Nissan) on the Hebrew/Assyrian calendar, which is the month of April in the ecclesiastical year. Nissan, of course, is the name of a automobile corporation and its symbolism seems to be another variation of Saturn (see figure 235).

The crescent moon and Venus, the latter often seen as a star at Easter, are also interchangeable with the old sun (Saturn) and of course we have the Sabbath on Saturn's Day (Saturday). The Passover is also one of the *three* pilgrimage festivals, when the population of biblical Judah (in ancient times), would have made a pilgrimage to the Temple in Jerusalem. Today, Samaritans are said to still make this ancient pilgrimage to Mount 'Gerizim', and along with mount 'Moriah' and 'Zion', they give us the *three* sacred (holy) mountains in Jerusalem. What is also interesting is that these 'three' mountains, according to some researchers, can be correlated with Orion's belt stars, along with the wider geography from Shechem to Hebron.[2] As I have already shown in *Chapter Ten*, the number *three* seems to be important in terms of magic and will become more so as we proceed.

The Goddess Ostara (Easter)

In ancient Indo-European myths 'Ostre' or 'Ostara' was associated with the 'light of spring' (the light of the world) and the goddess who brings 'new light'. You could say she made the clocks go forward, so to speak. Ostara is also linked to Easter, hares and 'sacred eggs' and is another version of mother nature (the awakening feminine principle) behind the sun's light. She is also a variation of the goddess, Sophia. In other forms, she is known as Ishtar (star), Freyja and Anunitu, who on the Spring Equinox, was said to mate with the 'solar god' (the sun) and conceive a child that would be born nine months (or moons) later on the Winter Solstice. We all know who the child is supposed to be? The same 'star child' who eventually gets nailed to Moses' cross every Easter. The Son of Man, symbolised through Orion's *passover* the earth (his annual sun cycle), followed closely by the hare, Lepus, gives us new life at spring.

The Mesopotamian (Akkadian, Assyrian and Babylonian) goddess, 'Ishtar' was another version of Ostara – the goddess of light, among other things. She was also the goddess of fertility, love, war, sex and power. Ishtar, like Ostara, was said to have 'two sides', or 'two natures', both creative and destructive. Ishtar is also 'Aja' (the eastern mountain dawn goddess) and 'Anatu' (possibly Ishtar's mother). She is also 'Anunitu' (the Akkadian goddess of light), 'Agasayam' (war goddess), 'Irnini' (goddess of cedar forests in the Lebanese mountains), 'Wenet' (Egypt), 'Kilili' (symbol of the desirable woman), 'Sahirtu' (messenger of lovers), 'Kir-gu-lu' (bringer of rain) and 'Sarbanda' (power of sovereignty). Both Ostara and Ishtar (same deity in truth) usher in the 'time' we call Easter. 'Astarte' (English), 'Ashtaroth' (Hebrew), are also names for the Canaanite fertility goddess associated with the beginning of spring and Easter (see figure 236).

Astarte was also considered the goddess of the 'Underworld' (Saturn's domain) and her other name was El, the Queen of the Underworld. Note that 'ceremonial acts of war' (terror), political elections in some countries and the marriages of Royalty, also seem to occur at

© Neil Hague

Figure 236: The Easter Hare Goddess.
(Left) Astaroth. **(Right)** Wenet, the Hare goddess

the start of spring (Ostara) through to Walpurgis (Witches night) and Beltane on the 1st May. The latter festival being the beginning of Osiris/Orion's descent into the Underworld, as the star man disappears from sight. You could say that the Son of Man symbolically dies to be resurrected, just as Orion makes his descent into the Underworld to emerge again on the summer solstice. The pagan calendar of course is also used by those who follow satanism, hence endless acts of death and destruction we witness in the world conjured up by those in the shadows who dwell solely on death (the Underworld). Those who instigate war and destruction in our

world are a 'Death Cult' by definition; they also understand the significance of Orion, Saturn, Sun and Moon symbolism.[3]

The Ancient Hare and Rabbit Goddesses

The main animal symbol used in pagan lunar magic, nature and witchcraft
is the 'hare'. Many of the goddesses mentioned in this chapter were either
said to have a hare as a companion, or could take the form of a hare. In
ancient Egypt, Osiris was sacrificed to the Nile each year in the form of a

hare to guarantee the annual flooding that
Egyptian agriculture (and indeed their entire
society) depended upon (See figure 237). A
minor Egyptian goddess 'Unut', or 'Wenet'
also had the head of a hare. The hieroglyph
'Wn' (Wen) itself stands for the 'essence of life'
and often depicts a hare overflowing water.
The hare is often depicted 'greeting the dawn'
(the 'hour of the hare') and she sometimes
serves as a messenger for the god, Thoth,
(Sirius), Wenet (Lepus) and Osiris (Orion) are
the *three* main constellations that usher in the
turning points of the autumn and spring
equinoxes, as I have shown.

Figure 237: Osiris as a Hare.
The hare in Egypt, Norse
myth and in the stars as
Lepus.

In Norse mythology, there was also said to be a
goddess *before* Odin replaced the Germanic tribal
gods and goddesses. She was called 'Frau Holle',
or 'Holda', (see figure 238). Frau Holle was the
goddess of the 'wild hunt' mentioned in the last
chapter. Frau Holle, like the goddess Artemis of
Greece, was often shown with a large group of
hares bearing torches 'illuminating her way'. The
ultimate hunter, Orion and Lepus, the hare are
combined at this point on the solar wheel. The
hare as a hieroglyph signifies the 'keeper of the
Great Mystery' and was thought of as a symbol of
becoming, or 'to be' for ancient tribes. The hare's
ability to 'disappear quickly' was also seen as a
symbol for alternate states of awareness and transfiguration connected to 'supernatural activities'
and forces I described in earlier chapters. The hare
is a mammal that lives in solitude, and can navigate the hours of darkness and is said to a have a

**Figure 238: Frau Holle
(Holda).**
The Goddess of protection
often seen with the Hare
(Lepus) constellation.
Along with Sirius (Canis
Major), Lepus 'lights the
way' for the goddess.
Friedrich Wilhelm Heine (1845-
1921) Public Domain.

'foot in two worlds'.

In some Native American myths, the hero 'Michabo', or 'Great Manitou', was said to be the 'great hare' who brought knowledge to some of the American Indian tribes; many North American tribes spoke of this deity as their common ancestor. Michabo was considered a personification of the sun's light, a life-giver and his name compounded of 'michi' meaning 'great', and 'wabos' meaning both 'hare' and 'white' seems to relate to the 'white rabbit' symbolism found in *Alice in Wonderland*. I'll have more to say about the white rabbit shortly. Michabo of the dawn (or the 'great white hare') was considered the guardian of many Native American tribes. He was said to be the founder of their religious rites, the inventor of picture writing (symbols) and preserver of earth and heaven.

"Destroy this temple and I will make it *rise again*, in *three* Hares"

Hecate, mentioned in the last chapter, is another version of Ostara (Astarte) often shown as a 'triple-headed goddess' associated with 'crossroads', entrance-ways, light, magic, witchcraft, knowledge of herbs (poisonous plants), ghosts, necromancy and sorcery (See figure 239). The number *three*, as we have seen, is a power number found everywhere, from the

'Triquetra', three primary colours, to the three days the egg of the 'queen bee' takes to hatch. In numerology, *three* is considered to be feminine and the tarot card representative of the *three* 'energetically' is the Empress – Hecate – Ostara - El. Three is also the 'Trinity' and these are the three aspects of 'Shin' whose 'three wicks' are a symbol of the 'holy trinity' through the letter Shin (See figure 240). The god Brahma, of Hindu belief, also provides symbolism of the Trinity, 'three heads' and the egg. I'll come back to the egg at the end of this chapter.

© Neil Hague

Figure 239: Triple Headed Goddess.
The *Triquetra, Trinity* and *Triple-faced* goddess.

In many uses of numerology and ancient belief, *three* is an important number for 'creating reality' and 'manifestation'. The symbol of the 'three hares' found at sacred sites from the Middle and Far East, to churches in Devon, UK are all ver-

Figure 240: Shin.
The Holy Trinity and the egg.
(*see* also page 91)

Figure 241: Three Hares in Religious Art.
(Left) Tinners hares in Devon. **(Right)** A section from the painting *The Agony in the Garden* a possible connection to Orion, renewal and reserrection. (PD)

Figure 242: Lepus and Orion?
Lepus and possibly Orion's belt stars on a Knights of Malta tomb.

sions of Hecate's (Ostara's) 'power of manifestation' and 'renewal' (see figure 241).

Italian Renaissance painter, Andrea Mantegna, a Knight from a 'bloodline of painters, depicts 'three hares' in his masterpiece, *The Agony in the Garden* (1458-60). The full painting shows angels bearing the Instruments of 'the Passion' appearing to Christ in prayer in the garden of Gethsemane. In the painting, *three* disciples sleep, with *three* hares at their feet and in the background, Judas comes with soldiers to arrest Christ. The symbolism, obviously known to Mantegna (and elite circles of his time), relates to the Trinity of the Church born out of the Passion, on one level; however, it also relates to fertility, lunar cycles and the 'goddess of renewal'.

In the St John the Baptist Cathedral in Valletta, Malta, a Knights of Malta tomb clearly depicts Lepus (the hare) and the 'Shin', or possibly three belt stars of Orion (see figure 242). The tomb sits alongside many other tombs littered with images of grim reapers and skeletons with axes and other 'Orion-Saturn symbols'. As I mentioned in earlier chapters, the Teutonic Knights of Malta, who adored John the Baptist (the headless god), understood the celestial symbolism associated with Orion and Lepus, along with the passage of the sun and moon creating 'time' (Saturn). Remember, the hare was also considered 'otherworldly' and connected to forces (possibly Archons) and the Demiurge for some cultures. The white glowing eye of the hare on the Knight's tomb seems to suggest otherworldly forces at work behind the hare.

Vehicles of Light

The 'Vesicae Piscis' mathematical shape is also formed by the 'three ears' in

Figure 243: Triple Spiral.
The triskele is a Celtic and pre-Celtic symbol found on Irish Mesolithic and Neolithic sites.

the Tinners sculpture and the same shape gives us the spinning Mer-Ka-Ba (Star tetrahedron) or 'vehicle of light' (see figure 243). The symbolism of new life and renewal entwined in the story of Christ (who was said to baptize with 'fire'), clearly comes from the Pagan understanding of the 'goddess of light'. It also connects to Gnostic understanding of the 'light of the Aeons' and the Pleroma (see *Chapter Four*).

Another version of Ostara also found in Norse Mythology is the goddess Freyja who is associated with love, sex, beauty, fertility, gold, war and death. Freyja is the owner of the 'necklace Brísingamen', she rides a chariot pulled by two cats and she keeps the boar, Hildisvíni, by her side. She also possesses a cloak of falcon feathers and is accompanied by dwarves. Freyja and her 'seven dwarfs' are symbols for the 'seven days of the week' 'constructing' the lunar month in their 'springtime' kingdom. *Snow White* is Freyja and Ostara combined and the symbolism, primarily through colour, relates to the feminine archetype, duality and light of 'eternal spring'. The evil queen (the dark goddess archetype) in the story of *Snow White* (along with the innocent magical goddess that overthrows the queen), can also been found in Lewis Carroll's books *Alice in Wonderland* and *Through the Looking Glass*. All are stories that use goddess symbolism associated with moving *between* different realities, just as the earth's equinoxes and solstices are markers between changing worlds. The Chinese Moon Goddess, 'Chang'e' comes to mind when I think of the triple goddess figures and how three celestial bodies, the sun, moon and the earth, create day, night, time (or reality).

The Easter Moon Rabbit (or Hare)

Based on pareidolia that identifies the markings of the moon as a rabbit, the 'moon rabbit', in folklore, was said to be a rabbit that lives on the moon (see figure 244). Stories exist in many cultures, prominently in Asian folklore and Aztec mythology of a 'Moon Rabbit'. In East Asia, the Moon Rabbit is seen pounding in a mortar and pestle, but the contents of the mortar differ among Chinese, Japanese, and Korean folklore (see figure 245). In Chinese folklore, the Moon Rabbit is often portrayed as a companion of the Moon goddess, 'Chang'e', continually pounding the 'elixir of life' for her. The elixir could relate to the 'egg' and 'sperm' and how life is formed through DNA. In Japanese and Korean versions, it is pounding the ingredients for rice cake. Maybe the inspiration for the 'cake' that Alice eats in

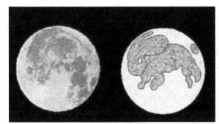

Figure 244: Moon Rabbit.

Figure 245: White Rabbit or Hare.
The mythological white rabbit or hare making the elixir of immortality on the Moon, from Chinese mythology. The white rabbit is embroidered onto 18th-century Imperial Chinese robes.

Wonderland?

In other Asian myths, 'Sun Wukong' fights the 'Moon Rabbit', which can be seen in the 16th century Chinese novel *Journey to the West*, depicted in Yoshitoshi's *One Hundred Aspects of the Moon* (1839-1892). In the Buddhist *Jataka* tales, a monkey, otter, jackal, and a 'rabbit' resolved to practice charity on the day of the 'full moon' (Uposatha), believing a demonstration of great virtue would earn a great reward. When an old man begged for food, the monkey gathered fruits from the trees and the otter collected fish, while the jackal wrongfully pilfered a lizard and a pot of milk-curd. The rabbit, who knew only how to gather grass, instead offered its own body, throwing itself into a fire the man had built. The rabbit, however, was not burnt. The old man revealed himself to be 'Akra'- Lord of Heaven - Orion and, touched by the rabbit's virtue, drew the likeness of the rabbit on the moon for all to see. It is said the lunar image is still draped in the smoke that rose when the rabbit cast itself into the celestial fire. The same story of the moon god sacrificing itself in a solar fire can be found in Hopi, Mexican and Mayan myths, not least in the stories of Quetzalcoatl. Cottontail, in Hopi myth (see page 316), was a god born of the sun and the moon after jumping into the solar fire (see figure 246). On one level, many of these stories are symbolic of the upheavals that

Figure 246: Cotton Tail.
(Left) A Maya whistle in the form of the moon goddess and her rabbit consort. CE 600. **(Right)** Drawing from an Aztec ceramic piece showing a rabbit-scribe. The Rabbit was considered a Moon scribe in China and connected to the scribe, Thoth, in Egypt.

took place in the heavens. But they are also narratives concerning the 'consciousness' of planets, moons and stars.

African folk tales told by the 'Namaquas' in South Africa, relate the story of phases of the moon with the idea of immortality, reintegration, decay and growth, repeated perpetually. Even the 'rising and setting of the moon' was interpreted by the Namaquas as its 'birth and death'. They say that a long time ago the moon wished to send a message to mankind of immortality, and the hare undertook to act as the messenger. So the moon charged him to go to humanity and say, "As I die and rise to life again, so shall you die and rise to life again." It is said that the hare 'reversed' (inverted) the message, so life became death and humanity instead focused on their mortality rather than their infinite eternity.

Contemporary video games and comics also seem to contain symbolism that relates to the moon rabbit. In 2000 video game called *Dark Cloud*, 'Moon People' are revealed to be anthropomorphic rabbits. In the Nexon game *MapleStory*, there is a party quest that involves protecting a 'Moon Bunny' while it produces rice cakes. In the 2014 game *Destiny*, the Jade Rabbit is featured as both an emblem that can be acquired on the Moon, as well as a primary weapon exclusive to PlayStation 4 owners. As I have said throughout the book, the symbolism is *everywhere* because it is *in* our consciousness. We have been revelling in these archetypes since ancient times.

The Goddess & the 'White Rabbit'

Celtic myths talk of the goddess, 'Cerridwen', who represented the human cycles of birth, life, death and rebirth. Cerridwen was another moon goddess associated with the hare. In one legend, the hunter Ossian (Orion) was said to have wounded a hare forcing it to find sanctuary in a thicket. When Ossian wounded the hare (possibly Lepus), he found a 'door' in the ground that led to a vast hallway and in that 'underground kingdom', he met a beautiful woman sitting on a throne, bleeding from the leg. Tales like this are plentiful in the pre-Christian world and hint at metamorphosis and parallel worlds connected to different gods, planets and stars.

A Japanese myth also tells of the 'Hare of Inaba' and the goddess, 'Amaterasu', and her search for a place for their palace or 'kingdom'. Like the white rabbit in *Alice in Wonderland*, Inaba suddenly appears to point the way to Amaterasu (see figure 247). According to the folk tale, the white hare bites Amaterasu's clothes and takes her to an 'otherworldly' location to look for a temporary palace at Nakayama Mountain and Reiseki Mountain. The 'mountain', the 'Goddess' and the 'white hare' are all symbols for the starlight, the moon, time and forces that create the collective world reality'.

Figure 247: Alice and the Hare of Inaba.

Figure 248: The Gnostic Venus as the Rabbit. Surrounded by 16 swords of truth symbolic of the Gnostic 'Uncontained'.

The white rabbit often appears in 15th Century Renaissance paintings to symbolise the connection between the goddess, the oceans and the moon (see figure 248). Other meanings relate to Venus, Sophia, love, wisdom and the 'duality' of male and female, as shown in the painting *Venus, Mars and Cupid* 1490 by Piero di Cosimo. The painting shows cupid lying on Venus next to a white rabbit. The lovers (Venus and Mars) are exhausted by their sexual activity (thanks to cupid) and the white rabbit is a symbol for 'timelessness' brought on through sexual excess. The Moon, Mars and Venus 'alignments' have also been linked to upheavals on Earth, when great cataclysms shaped the world and most likely ended the Age of Orion (giants), I mentioned earlier in the book.

The idea of rabbits as a symbol of vitality, rebirth and resurrection comes from the pagan world, and the Italian masters must have known this when they made such 'Christian works of art'. The elite painter Titian, in his work, *Mary and Infant Jesus with a rabbit* (1530) also alludes to pagan knowledge associated with the goddess and the white rabbit, or hare. The painting of *St. Jerome reading in the countryside* by Giovanni Bellini, is another work of art that also features a white and brown hare/rabbit and clearly relates to the power of solitude (the hare) and the world that would await the hermit once he/she leaves the cave to 'follow the white rabbit'. St. Jerome was the 'founding father' of the Christian Church (often shown in Saturn red with the lion); instead, in this painting, he is depicted as the hermit in the wilderness. The character, Neo in the *Matrix* movies, is also shown the 'white rabbit' as a way out of his illusionary 'solitary' world so that he can meet the 'god of the Dreamtime' – Morpheus.

The white rabbit symbolism found in the first *Matrix* Movie also appears in what has become the 'QAnon' phenomenon since 2017. The QAnon exposé is 'supposedly' detailing a secret plot by the deep state against U.S.

and President Donald Trump, and his supporters. The theory began with an anonymous post on the imageboard '4chan' by someone using the name 'Q', presumably from America. According to mainstream accounts, Q is reference to 'Q clearance' used by the Department of Energy; QAnon 'believers' (or followers) commonly tag their social media posts with the hashtag #WWG1WGA, signifying the motto "where we go one, we go all". I would suggest that Q, and those who are told to 'follow the white rabbit', *are* being offered endless Cult symbolism on one level. I also doubt that such a renegade cell within the Trump adminstration (at the time of writing) is planning to 'save the world', but we will see, I am open to all possibilities.

Trickster Hares

Some native cultures saw the hare as a 'trickster' or 'shape-shifter' akin to the Gnostic understanding of what they called the Demiurge. The hare appears in English folklore in the saying "as mad as a March hare" and in stories of a witch who takes the form of a white hare and goes out looking for prey at night. The *Br'er Rabbit* stories are loosely related to the trickster element of the rabbit and hare, as mentioned earlier. Interestingly, the hare was said to be a 'child of Pan' and in many myths the hare was wrapped in 'goatskin'.

Kit Williams' Book *Masquerade* (1979) relays the 'trickster element' of the hare. The book's objective, the hunt for a valuable treasure, became his means to this end. *Masquerade* features 'fifteen' (Saturn's number) detailed paintings illustrating the story of a shape-shifting 'hare' named Jack. The boy/hare, Jack, seeks to carry a treasure from the moon (depicted as a woman) to her love object, the sun (a man). On reaching the sun, Jack finds he has lost the treasure, and the reader is left to discover the location of the 'golden hare'. Was author Kit Williams inspired by pagan myths associated with the sun, moon and hare? The use of the name 'Jack' could also relate to the myths about the giants I mentioned in *Chapter Two*.

The púca (Irish for spirit/ghost), pooka, or púka is another hare-like creature of Celtic folklore. A púca was considered to be an omen of both good and bad fortune, or could either 'help or hinder' communities. These creatures were said to be 'shape-changers' (shape-shifters), taking the appearance of black horses, goats and hares. They could also take human form with 'animal features', such as long ears (see figure 249). According to legend, the púca can assume a variety of terrifying, or pleasing, forms. No matter what shape the púca took, its fur was almost always dark. I have personally witnessed a púca, of sorts, manifest in front of me in a Tudor house/hotel many years ago, in the form of a black panther-like creature.

Another creature called a 'Koschei', similar to the púca, was said to be

Figure 249: Pooka.
My image of a Pooka
based on the *Donnie
Darko* (2001) character.

able to use magic and could not be killed by conventional means. In various folklore, the Koschei's soul was hidden separately from its body, through a 'talisman' and other 'animate objects'. The soul could be inside a needle, which is inside an egg, which is in a duck, which is in a hare, which is in an iron chest, buried under a green oak tree, which is on the island in the ocean, etc. Think Russian dolls and how they slot in one another. The soul of the Koschei is not dissimilar to the concept of Sauron in Tolkien's *Lord of the Rings*, whose 'essence of being' was 'contained' within a ring that was connected to other rings, *through* magic. Legends say that anyone possessing the Koschei 'egg', for example, has the Koschei in their power. If the egg is tossed about, the Koschei, likewise, is flung around against his will. If the needle is broken, the Koschei will die. When the ring is destroyed in *Lord of the Rings*, so is Sauron's power, etc... you get the picture. The magic associated with the Koschei is 'invisible' and able to move through different realities; just like the hare (and white rabbit) symbolically speaking was also said to be able to move through different worlds and become 'timeless'.

In other folklore and legends, we have mythical hares that are hybrid creatures, such as the 'Lepus Cornutus' and 'Al-mi'raj' (an Arabic mythical unicorn hare) see figure 250. In Bavarian folklore there are stories of the 'wolpertinger' (also called 'wolperdinger'), a mythological hybrid hare allegedly inhabiting the alpine forests of Bavaria and having antlers. Images of this kind, along with the Trickster Hare, may well have been 'connecting' Lepus and Monoceros, the constellations adjacent to Orion, as they moved across the ecliptic. As I have already discussed in earlier chapters, the 'darker aspects' of Orion are also evident in such trickster, horned hare creatures and much more besides.

Figure 250: Lepus Cornutus.
Lepus cornutus (labeled in French 'Lièvre cornu'), as depicted in the 1789 *Tableau Encyclopedique et Methodique* by Pierre Joseph Bonnaterre.
(Public Domain.)

The Primordial 'Easter Egg'

Another symbol of Easter is the egg of course,

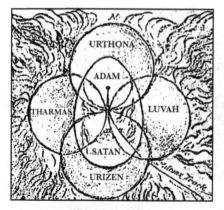

Figure 251: Eggs in Space.
The egg-shaped world of Los (Blake's word for imagination) swells from the swirling centre of chaos, forming the boundaries of illusory 3D space. Satan and Adam (Orion) 'obstruct' humanity's 'free vision' of things as they truly are.
(Public Domain)

a universal symbol for 'birth' and 'new life'. The 'primordial egg' holds the seed from which the whole of manifestation was said to have 'sprung'. Nearly all ancient civilisations and cultures share the idea that the universe was 'born from an egg'. The 'primordial man' was also said to originate from an egg (see figure 251). The egg is a symbolic 'boundary of the restriction' between 'matter' and other bodies making up the human being. In William Blake's image, *The Four Zoas*, we are shown the four bodies of the *mind, emotion, senses* and *imagination* surrounding the egg.

The cosmic egg, born from primordial Waters, in some myths, splits into two halves giving birth to Heaven and Earth (Symbolised as Adam and Satan in Blake's image), or as the Hindu Brahmânda and the 'two Dioscuri' in Greco-Indian myths. In Hindu mythology, Brahma – the omniscient (the source of all-that-exists) forms out of the golden embryo and egg. According to Hindu belief, Brahma was the self-born 'uncreated creator', the first manifestation of *The 'One's'* existence. As the embryo from which the universe originates, he is also called 'Hiranya Garbha' (golden embryo), the 'ball of fire'. Other names for the 'egg god' were 'Pitamaha' (the patriarch), 'Vidhi' (the ordinator), 'Lokesha' (the master of the universe) and 'Viswakarma' (the architect of the world). The 'architect' of course connects to Gnosticism, Freemasonry and the imposter creator – the Demiurge.

In Chinese creation myths, it is said that in the beginning, the Universe was contained within an egg, inside of which the forces of yin (dark, female and cool) and yang (light, male and hot) interacted with each other. The same theme is told in ancient Egypt as 'Ptah of Memphis' (an Orion-Demiurge combination) shaping the world in the form of an egg on a potter's wheel. However, it was said that his ten-dimensional world (or egg) became unstable and eventually cracked in two (polarisation), creating two separate universes; a four and six-dimensional universe. The Universe in which we live was born in that cosmic cataclysm and it could also relate to the creation of the Dreamtime (Sophia's dreaming), of which the aboriginal tribes of Australia refer to in their creation stories.

The egg also signifies the Hermaphrodite's polarisation in some instances and was a symbol for the beginning of life. For the ancient Egyptians, 'life emerged', by the action of a 'Demiurge', through 'Nun', (the personification of the primordial Ocean) that gave birth to the egg. In other creation accounts, found in several cultures, Erebus and Eros (love) were the first deities to be born to the mother substance (the Pleroma) and it is said they were issued from the Egg of Night.[4] Eros, in my view, relates to what astrophysicists describe as the 'Weak electromagnetic force', one that is invisible and permeates (penetrates) all bodies in our Universe. In truth, this vibration is anything but weak, it is the all-powerful creative 'love vibration' that can be utilised to reshape and heal our world.

Black Egg

Chinese legend tells of how an enormous 'black egg' was formed in the darkness at the beginning of time. Inside this egg, the sleeping giant 'Pan Gu' was formed. According to ancient Buyei Chinese mythology, he was the first man (Adam-Orion), who married the Dragon King's daughter, and their union gave rise to the Buyei people, the Watchers (Nefilim) I mentioned in *Chapters One* and *Two*. Likewise, 'Hanuman', the Monkey King, was said to be born of primal chaos, hatching from a 'stone egg' impregnated by the sky (stars). The Gnostics also talk of Heaven and Earth, symbolised by the 'world egg' in the womb of the universe. Not a crucifixion in sight here, folks?! Just a human (light being) born of the cosmos and one who returns to the source.

In terms of symmetry, astronomy and sacred geometry, the egg has been used by alchemists to depict the 'cycles within cycles' and the 'relationship' between the Earth, the Moon and the solar system. The elite Elizabethan occult magician, Dr. John Dee, likened the origin of the planets to the metamorphosis of an egg made up of four elements (the Zoas), which a scarab beetle brings along a spiral path. The paths of the scarab can be seen to form the egg-like geometric symbolism found in the movement of planets; more on the scarab in *Part Two*. Dee referred to the 'egg white' as the work of the Moon (and Saturn) and the 'yoke', the essence of the Sun (and Jupiter). Among the Egyptians, the egg was associated with the Sun, the 'golden egg.'

Druids saw the egg as a sacred emblem in their initiation rites, hence the egg's importance in spring (at Easter). The procession of the goddess of agriculture, Ceres, in Rome, was preceded by an egg and it was often depicted entwined by a serpent or crowned by a crescent moon, we are back to Ophiuchus again. In the mysteries of Bacchus in ancient Greece, the egg was also a consecrated emblem that symbolised the 'soul' and this symbolism was portrayed in the movie *Angel Heart* (1989), when 'Louis Cyphre' (Lucifer), played by de Niro, peels an egg and eats it as a symbol of the 'consumption of the soul' (see figure 252). The 'eye and egg' are other symbols for the 'theft of the soul' in occult symbolism, or the visionary limits of 'perception' placed on humanity by the Demiurge. All over the ancient world, from China to Babylon, the egg was also painted, and venerated as a symbol of rebirth and the soul. The 'soul of humanity', captured, bound or 'eaten' is a common theme through the use of the symbol of the egg (see figure 253). The 'Alchemical Modena' relief also symbolises both the 'world' and the 'egg' and the 'Egg of Heliopolis' and Typhon's Egg where used in ancient Mithric rituals. Inside the egg (or Modena), Mithras or Phanes (the light of the world) emerges with his 'lighted torch' surrounded by a 'mandorla' (an almond-shaped aureola) of the zodiac (corresponding to the twelve 'altar fires' in the Pythagorean cult). The mandorla can also represent the 'vulva', and thus the arrival of a 'new being into the world' through the *goddess* Ostara (Easter). The mandorla is also a sign of union, climax, opening and departure into a new life. Once again, the symbolism is all based on the feminine and masculine coming together, or the Christos and Sophia entwined to produce the new light of the world.

Figure 252: Soul Egg.
The egg is symbolic of the soul encased in the physical world.

Figure 253: Eating the Soul.
The eye and the egg were considered a symbol of the soul in alchemical teachings. 'Eneph' or 'Ptah' (Orion), like the Demiurge of ancient Egyptian/Gnostic mythology (seen on the right of this image) eats the egg (soul) with Saturn (death) next to him.

'Born' of the Easter egg

The painting *Concert inside an Egg* (1549), credited to Thomas Crecquillon, depicts his knowledge of alchemy, the 'philosophical egg' and the 'light that can be seen with the ears'. The 'light' is the electromagnetic *waveform* the brain translates into *pictures* and *sounds*, hence the light 'seen with the ears'. The elite artist, Hieronymus Bosch also includes humans entering *into* an egg in his masterpiece *Garden of Earthly Delights*, painted in the 15th Century. The strange creatures and imagery contained within the scene are reminiscent of reptilians/dragon people/greys; naked humans (Adam and Eve prototypes) of course, are being born in reverse, or being 'encased' in the egg – through the limitation of their DNA. The egg is also a symbol for the moon and its *control* over our biological bodies.

In paintings by Leonardo Da Vinci and Bachiacca, the Greek myth of *Leda and the Swan* (a bird that symbolised Venus) also uses the symbolism of the children 'born of an egg' (just as reptiles are). The egg, and its nest, are also symbolic of the goddess, and the word for nest, 'shechinot', in Hebrew, is virtually the same as 'shekinah', which means the 'feminine glory of God' come to 'dwell on earth'. It literally means 'dwelling' or 'presence'. Interestingly, the hare also builds a 'form', which looks like a 'birds nest' or 'dwelling', which perhaps lends to the 'visual idea' relating to the Easter egg? In the *Leda and the Swan* myth, Zeus takes the form of a swan and seduces the goddess Leda, whose offspring, Castor and Pollox, are born as 'hybrid humans'; part-god, and part-human. Castor and Pollox are the Gemini constellation, close to Orion and the Silver Gate mentioned in *Chapter Seven*. The myths and paintings on one level, are hinting at the 'copulation' of 'non-human' with 'humans' in the ancient world, but are also pointing to the stars. The egg symbolism at Easter is, in many ways, a symbol of initiation into star knowledge, which was understood by the mystery schools of antiquity.

Personally, I always see Easter as a period of 'transition and renewal', a time for 'new ideas' and 'new beginnings'. The time of year can also be used by 'darker forces' to *force* changes on humanity (see the coronavirus pandemic and the lockdowns that followed leading up to Easter 2020 all across the world). William Blake's image of a *winged infant emerging from a cracked egg* also hints 'awakening' to our 'true potential' and breaking free of all that encases us. Blake had no time for orthodox religion and the Status quo of his day, he was well aware of the Gnostic roots of Christianity. The image is one of many from his collection of writings and drawings called *The Gates of Paradise*, and this one in particular, shows the 'hatching' of a winged infant (or cherub with Blake's face) breaking free of the confinement imposed by the egg. According to Blake, 'the child becomes acquainted with the functioning of his mind through the four spheres (the *Zoas* mentioned earlier), of the *body, mind, imagination* and *emotions*'. These bodies give form to the 'egg shape' and signify humanity's 'limited field of vision'. Writing in his Selections from *Milton* [The Mundane Shell] in 1793, Blake said:

> ... *The Mundane Shell is a vast Concave Earth, an immense*
> *Harden'd Shadow of all things upon our Vegetated Earth,*

Enlarg'd into Dimension and deform'd into indefinite Space, ...[5]

Easter is the festival of visible *new* light and life emerging. The symbolism behind the moon egg, the hare and the goddess represent the interconnectedness of the moon, sun and Orion's descent into the subterranean realms after the Spring Equinox. The star man dies symbolically to be reborn as such. As I have shown, Easter is another 'marker' on the sun wheel as Orion makes his way towards spring, taking Lepus, the hare, with him. The goddess of Easter reigns, as the masculine falls gradually into the darkness, the void, to return with the sun on the Summer Solstice. The symbolism I have unravelled and explained as the 'Orion-Saturn' rituals, in the last two chapters, is simply ancient star, sun and moon worship, probably given to the ancients via 'off-world' elite priesthoods (sky-watchers) and 'their gods'. We are still worshipping the planets, sun, stars (especially Orion) through our annual movement energetically (via the festivals and holidays) as we synch with the Pagan calendar.

In the last few chapters of *Part One*, I want to delve a little deeper into the myths and legends connected to *other* star systems also adjacent to Orion and how individual stars (our DNA), and the original people of earth, were (and still are) keepers of star knowledge.

Sources:

1) Icke, David. *The Perception Deception.* 2013, p 143-166 (Chapter 9)
2) Vega, Luis. B. https://www.postscripts.org/ps-news-358.html
3) Icke, David. *The Trigger,* 2019. p 577-78
4) *Bulfinch's Complete Mythology.* p9
5) https://www.bartleby.com/235/291.html

13

CHILDREN OF THE STARS

Ancient Keepers of the 'Knowledge'

He is the Maker of the Bear and Orion,
the Pleiades and the constellations of the south.

JOB 9:9

Our true history has been forgotten. We are a collective species that seems to have 'no memory' of a time before the fall – an epoch where we interacted freely with stellar consciousness. Some of the symbolism, rituals and prehistoric subjects I have already touched on so far, only scratch the surface of our deeper memories and in this chapter I want to explore these connections further.

The world today does not resemble earth's mythological Golden Era – the ancient paradise where we connected with spirit so freely. Our ancestors were 'free' and lived in harmony with the earth, at least up until the great cataclysms and arrival of organised warfare and empire-building, which according to some academics started 6000 years ago.[1] We are human 'beings', free spirits, rather than just 'being human' going through motions governed by time, rituals and the most prominent vehicle for 'control' today – money. Our personal magic, creating reality, living in harmony with the organic world as creative free spirits, should be our true purpose, as it was for our ancestors. All of the systems of governance we know today, as far as I can see, do not celebrate our true human purpose. These systems are 'given' to us, even 'imposed' upon us by forces that are alien to our spirit, or to our true 'nature'.

Throughout earth's history, contained within our myths and legends, we have had stories of gods, goddesses (star people) in all indigenous cultures, who came to humanity in a Golden era. Not all that came had good intentions, but others brought magic, knowledge and 'technology', evidenced through many of the megalithic wonders, like the pyramids, mentioned in earlier chapters. As J.R.R Tolkein wrote in his epic, *Lord of the Rings* (1954):

...some things that should not have been forgotten were lost. History became

345

Legend and legend became myth... [2]

In this chapter I am going to focus on what I believe to be the original tribes of earth and their mythic connection to the stars, including Orion.

Language of the Stars

According to the alchemist, Egyptian hieroglyphics were teachings given to the priesthoods of Egypt by one of their star gods, 'Thoth', who was depicted as a human with the head of an Ibis. Thoth, or Hermes in Greek, was said to be chief scribe of the gods and an early rival to the Sun-god, Ra, as creator of Egyptian civilisation. Thoth was also regarded as the personification of the 'mind' of God, sent to earth to write for Ra and the Goddess of Justice, Matt.[3] It is written in the Egyptian *Book of the Dead* and the *Book of Divinity* that Thoth came from the place where the sun sets (possibly the Underworld) bringing with him the language of 'writing' and 'magic'. The *Book of the Dead* declared Thoth to be the author of works by which the ancients believed the deceased gained everlasting life. Thoth's appearance in Egyptian art as a human with the head of an Ibis was mainly due to the bird's resemblance to the human heart, when its head was tucked under its wing. The Freemasonic historian, Manley P Hall, records in his work *The Secret Teachings of All Ages*, that Thoth (Hermes) learned his knowledge from 'Poimandres', the 'Great Dragon'. Hall also said these teachings were contained in *The Vision of Hermes*, or what became known as hermetic writing associated with magician, 'Hermes Mercurius Trismegistus'.

The mystery schools of antiquity equate Trismegistus as the 'master' of all arts and sciences, scribe to the gods and keeper of the books of life, more on this figure shortly. Mercury, Hermes and Thoth, rolled into one figure became the key personage associated with the alchemy and principle of magic and thought.[4] For the Celts, Hermes became 'Herne' (an Orion figure), the god of the forests, animal wisdom and connecting to the serpent bearer, Ophiuchus, which is why Thoth/Hermes, or Mercury (figure 254), was often portrayed as a blue 'man with a red serpent arm' - see the original British Telecommunications logo. Thoth also took the form of a Baboon or a 'dog-headed monkey' scribe, a deity that had already existed in the ancient city of Hermopolis in Middle Egypt, the leading centre for his cult. Thoth was considered the

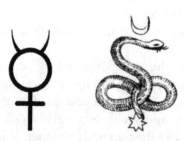

Figure 254: Mercury - Hermes
The glyph of Mercury/Hermes.

god of language, numbers, art and the hermetic sciences that came out of Egyptian belief, through magic and the knowledge of creative thought (power). Thoth was also considered the divine scribbler (artist), said to have been given the key to the mysteries of Osiris (Orion). In Egyptian symbolism, the chariot of Osiris (pulled by the lion pair Aker), also relates to the wisdom held by Thoth. The twin lion symbol of Aker, in relation to Thoth, represented *creative thought, individuality, originality* and *'genius'*. All these attributes are within each of us and are more often than not sup-pressed through the misuse of language, numbers, logic and mind magic cast through the mainstream media, etc. The latter relates to the mind, but the genius creative spirit (of the heart) is *why* Thoth was often referred to as the 'heart of Ra', the 'god of the divine word' and creative genius (See fig-ure 256).

Images and symbols found in ancient shamanic, and later alchemical illustrations, are direct references to Thoth's hidden powers that lay beyond the realm of the five senses. Art, in its truest form, is metaphysical in con-tent and certain symbols or hieroglyphs seem to express a level of under-standing that are scientific by nature. Certain alchemical images hint at the types of 'experiments' that may have been carried out in the laboratories of the 'gods', some of which relate to neurobiology and DNA experimenta-tion. Other alchemical works seem to be recording a naïve understanding of genealogical connections between animals and humans, especially the 'royal bloodlines'. Correlations exist between Thoth, the scribe of the gods, who was often portrayed as a monkey (artist) in Egyptian art, and the advancement of the human brain in a prehistoric era. Could these links

relate to myths associated with gods said to have come to earth from the stars, influencing the artist-shaman in prehistoric times? Thoth, I believe, was one such star god, who like Osiris (Orion), craft-ed much of our religious mindset, our symbolism relating to the stars, from Atlantean times, but certainly since 'ancient' Egypt.

In Hermopolis, it is said Thoth led the 'Ogdoad', a pantheon of eight principal deities, with his spouse, 'Nehmetawy', whose name translates as, 'she who embraces those in need'. The ancient

Figure 256: Thoth - the Heart of Ra.
The scribe of Ra, Thoth and the dog-head-ed Baboon image of Thoth (all Sirius sym-bols) found in some tarot cards .

Egyptians regarded Thoth as the *One*, self-begotten, and self-produced – *magician*. He follows Orion, the Fool, as the second card in the tarot (numbered *one*) – the Magician. Thoth was originally a moon god, and a 'measurer of light at night', and the magician who could reach into the subconscious mind. As a personification of the moon, Thoth allows time to be 'measured' (without the sun) through the moon's phases, which is why the cycles of the moon organised much of ancient Egyptian society's civil and religious rituals and events; they still do on our society today, for reasons I have explained in the last few chapters. Consequently, Thoth, was gradually perceived as a god of wisdom, magic, and the measurement and regulation of events *through* time. He was said to be secretary and counsellor of the sun god Ra, and with Ma'at (truth/order); he stood next to Ra on the nightly voyage across the sky.

Figure 257: Djehtí - the Magician.
Thoth the teacher and magician who measures time and space. The magician unites Sirius A and B with Earth and its Moon. © Neil Hague 2016.

Another name for Thoth was 'Djehuti' – the teacher of mysteries who 'came from the stars'. The Dogon also had a similar figure called 'Kemet' and refers to the 'Black Rite' connected to 'Ausar' (another name for Osiris), offering insight into the highest mysteries of Auset (Orion), or Isis (Sirius). It is said that Djehuti came to earth to teach civilization before he 'mounted to the stars', leaving behind the Kemetic/ancient Egyptian Mysteries (see figure 257). 'As above, so below' is attributed to the great Kemetic teacher, Djehuti (or Hermes Trismegistus in Greek adaptations). The magician archetype is where we find the connection to these mysteries, especially 'star knowledge', including the themes found in this book and other books like it.

Thoth is 'Hermes Trismegistus'

Hermes Trismegistus is associated with the Greek god, Hermes, and hermetic literature among the Egyptians concerned with 'conjuring spirits' and 'animating statues'. The latter, I am certain, relates to the 'creations' of the Greek god, Hephaestus, more on him in *Part Two*. The texts of Hermes Trismegistus are said to inform the oldest Hellenistic writings on Greco-Babylonian astrology and on the later developed practice of alchemy. As a divine source of wisdom, Hermes Trismegistus was credited with tens of thousands of highly esteemed writings, reputed to be of immense antiquity. Plato's *Timaeus* and *Critias* state that in the temple of Neith at Sais, Egypt, there were secret halls containing historical records which had been kept for 9,000 years.

Many Christian writers, including Lactantius, Augustine, Giordano Bruno, Marsilio Ficino, Campanella, and Giovanni Pico della Mirandola, all considered Hermes Trismegistus to be a wise 'pagan prophet' who foresaw the coming of Christianity. Symbolically, you could say Trismegistus created the original religious blueprints that grew into Gnostic, hermetic and ecclesiastical knowledge. Many early Christian scientists, monks and artists believed in a 'prisca theologia', the doctrine that a single, *true* theology exists, which threads through *all* religions. I suggest this 'single' theology is hugely connected to Orion and Sirius 'consciousness', which I am exploring in this chapter. This 'single' truth appeared *as* Gnosticism, and was given by God to man in antiquity, according to Giordano Bruno (16th Century Italian monk and physicist).[5] The prisca theologia also passed through a series of prophets, which included Zoroaster and Plato and in order to demonstrate the truths of the prisca theologia, Christians appropriated hermetic teachings for their own purposes and for some, Hermes Trismegistus was either a contemporary of Moses or an Egyptian priest king and author of the legendary Emerald Tablet.[6]

Hermes Trismegistus is also mentioned in the *Quran* in verse 19:56-57 and mentioned in the Book *Idris*, saying, 'he was truthful, a prophet who was 'took up to a high place – the stars'. A late Arabic writer wrote of the followers of Trismegistus (the Sabaeans) that their religion had a sect of 'star worshippers' who held their doctrine to come from Hermes Trismegistus through the Prophet, Adimun.[7] These star worshippers focused on Orion and Sirius, along with Ursa Major and Bootes.

The *Jabirian* corpus, a huge body of arabic texts covering topics including alchemy, cosmology, numerology, astrology, medicine, magic, mysticism and philosophy, contains the oldest documented source for the 'Emerald Tablet of Hermes Trismegistus'. They were said to be translated by Jbir ibn Hayyn (Geber) for the Hashemite Caliph of Baghdad Harun al-Rashid the

Abbasid (800AD). In these writings, Hermes Trismegistus is identified as Idris, the infallible Prophet, who travelled to 'outer space' from Egypt, and to heaven, whence he brought back a cache of objects from the 'Eden of Adam' (within Orion), including the 'Black Stone', from where he landed on earth in India. I think the black stone, or rock, set into the eastern corner of the Kaaba, the ancient building located in the centre of the Grand Mosque in Mecca, Saudi Arabia, is also a space object, possibly a fragment of a meteorite from the Kuniper regions, possibly Saturn, or further afield?

Hyperborea & Shambhala

Those who kept the teachings of Hermes Trismegistus, also knew of mystical places connecting the earth with the stars. Stories about 'Hyperborea' and 'Shambhala' are two mysterious locations often said to connect gods, like Thoth, to the stars.

In the 17th Century BC, a Greek priest named Aristeas of Proconnesus is believed to have travelled to the subterranean region called Hyperborea. His expedition was eventually turned into a now-lost archaic poem called *Arimmaspea*. The people Aristeas encountered were said to be called 'Issedonians', a 'blue-eyed', 'blond-haired' race of beings who lived in everlasting bliss, beyond the northern hemisphere, and whose caverns were supposed to send forth the piercing blast of the north wind.[8] These lands in the north were said to be inaccessible by land or sea and could relate to either a location underground or a higher invisible realm. In dreams I have had over the past thirty years, I too, have encountered what Aristeas calls 'Issedonians', especially in one detailed dream in the Cathar country in the mid 90s. In the dream, I was sent underground beneath the castles, in the region below what seemed like Lastours, where I encountered a gathering of blue-eyed, blonde-haired people, all hiding from a terrible force that was hunting them. In the dream, I was approached by a blonde-haired boy who asked me to help them escape, pulling on what seemed to be a chain mail I was wearing. What amazed me was not only the boy's piercing (star-like) blue eyes, but the sight of my own hand when I looked down at him. I didn't have human hands - *I had paws*, which will become relevant as I unravel this chapter. We are not *all* human once we venture into 'other realms' and Hyperborea is not necessarily a 'physical location' but a parallel reality. I am not saying that an 'underworld' does not exist, on the contrary, it is very likely, considering the vast amount of ancient subterranean cave networks, towns and legends that support the idea.

The work of Michael Mott in his book *Caverns, Cauldrons and Concealed Creatures* (2000), cites vast amounts of ancient and modern phenomena to support the idea of worlds within the earth. The ruins known as Hal

Saflieni, on Malta, for example, are amongst the most ancient and mysterious subterranean sites in the world; regarded now a UNESCO World Heritage Site. Stories of missing people surface all over the world, and one story, like something out of a horror movie, or a book by HG Wells, speaks of *thirty* school children in 1935, who were said to be forever lost in the hidden underground tunnels accessible from the Hal Saflieni Hypogeum. Who knows for sure what happened? There have been other experiences at Hal Saflieni and other mysterious subterranean sites, to dismiss those who have said they have seen giants and other strange creatures underground is to be flippant and somehow erroneous.[9]

The light elves in Norse mythology were also said to live in a region located far north above the frozen mountains and the Hyperborean kingdom. Because of its wealth, gold and other treasures, it was said to be guarded by griffins. The Navajo, or Dineh Indians have 'emergence' creation myths that tell of a series of 'underworlds', from where the 'original' people arrived. In these creation myths, the human world was created and destroyed several times by the gods. The first man and woman were created out of nebula-like clouds or 'star stuff', more on this in *Part Two*.

In *The Ancient Wisdom* (1997), Geoffrey Ashe suggests that to an early Greek, the strong cold Boreas wind would blow from the north, but for a Siberian shaman living nearer Asia, it would come from the east. For Ashe, Hyperborea and 'Shambhala' of ancient Asian legend are the same location. He also links the Great Bear or the Plough constellation with an Hyperborean Age, which is the most conspicuous constellation in the Northern Hemisphere (see figure 258). Like the Orion constellation, its inspired symbolism connected to an ancient era on earth; Ursa Major has other nebula within it offering symbolism relating to otherworldly beings and a long, lost past. As we shall see, the 'bear' was very important to original humans in the ancient world.

In the book, *Shambhala: Oasis of Light* (1977), Andrew Tomas, talks of a secret symbolic code used by initiates connecting Asia with the Mediterranean area thousands of years ago; with a language that originated in another world, or dimension. These codes are connected to

Figure 258: Ursa Major - the Great Bear.
The Plough or Great Bear, a possible source for an ancient Hyperborean Age. (© Neil Hague)

knowledge of symbols, numbers and glyphs, used by ancient initiates within early shamanic cultures. A seven-starred system focusing on the Plough, Orion and the Pleiades are part of this knowledge of symbols. The mystic, Nicholas Roerich, along with his wife (writing under the name J. Saint-Hilaire), speculated on the origins of the mystical location of Shambhala being somewhere in Orion itself.[10] The writer Stephen Jenkins, talking about Roerich's work, in his book, *The Undiscovered Country: Adventures Into Other Dimensions* (1978), writes of Orion's connection to Shambhala:

> *The reported statements of the entities about beings living somewhere in Orion are a reflection of an actually existing Central Asian tradition... they connect Orion with an earthly, if mystical, Shambhala.*[11]

Seven Stars

Seven seems to be a number having magical connotations that can be attributable to the phases, mystical locations or positions of various celestial bodies. Even the four phases of the moon, for example, each last seven days. In various religious texts, we also find number seven referred to at least 54 times, from the seven seals (and the Seventh Angel) through to a seven-headed beast in the *Book of Revelation*. The tarot cards of Marie Anne Adélande Lenormand, who was the greatest fortune-teller of 18th Century France, also worked with 54 cards, all illustrated through astro-mythology, hermetic knowledge, and said to contain the 'sacred system of seven'. In ancient texts, such as the *Vedas* of India and in later 'esoteric' literature produced by the Zoroastrians and Gnostics, seven was considered a magical number. Seven also relates to what alchemists call the seven planetary stages of transformation found in all ancient teachings. Native American medicine men from the O'odham tribes of the South West also perform the green corn dance using *seven* ears of corn from *seven* fields of the *seven* clans to ensure a healthy harvest. And in many Native American tribal beliefs there are said to be seven dream states (paths) of initiation. Constellations with 'seven visible stars' (for the naked eye), like Orion and Ursa Major, have to be connected to such esoteric systems.

The mountains of Belukha, and the Altai range of Central Asia are referred to as the mountains of the 'seven-starred system', and to the ancient location often called Shambhala. Writers like Geoffrey Ashe, refer to the seven stars as seven 'Wise Ones' – 'blacksmiths' or 'shamans'. The 'Mountain' and the 'Bear' were especially important to many shamanic cultures that practiced magic and followed the stars. The bear clans and bear people, from the Hopi to the Japanese Ainu, all revered the goddess in the form of a bear, as we shall see. As noted previously, Orion is also referred to as a 'Heavenly Shepherd' or 'True Shepherd of Anu'. The 'Bear Lodge' refers to Ursa Major as it aligns with the Pleiades. In the *Odyssey*, Homer referred to 'the Great Bear that men call the 'Wain', that circles opposite Orion, and never bathes in the sea of the stars'.

People of the Polar Bear Cult

The North Celestial Pole, believed to be the highest god at the centre of existence for our ancient ancestors, became a guiding light for ancient people of the northern hemisphere. The further south people travel, the lower the North celestial Pole on the horizon loses its prominence; therefore, other gods with different attributes were revered in more southern regions. Bands of migrating people, led by sky-watchers (shamans/priests), also followed the path of the stars while worshipping gods of earth. These gods were animals, alpha predators and others were often depicted in imagery as human-animal hybrids. From my own research, I feel that the concept of a 'polar god' found amongst people of the Upper Palaeolithic era (40,000 BC), related directly to migration and 'journeying' to what shamanistic cultures called the 'cosmic centre' – at the heart of our Galaxy.

The Pole Star gave our ancestors a 'fix' on where they were, concerning cosmic time, especially during and after major cataclysmic events on earth. The constellations that held 'pole position' obviously changed due to the natural cycles of the Galaxy and the precession of the earth in relation to the sun. For example, the constellation of Draco was the Pole Star 4,600 years ago, currently it is Polaris.[12] But it is the Great Bear – Ursa Major that leads the way to the Pole star. Whatever constellation, or star, was prominent at the pole, it provided both physical and spiritual orientation for our ancestors. Southward migrations, bringing new discoveries, encounters with strange animals and more light, eventually changed people's perception of the great polar deity. I feel certain the Native American deity, Kokopelli, also known as 'Maui' to the Polynesians, was a solar deity (tribal leader and star god) of people migrating south from Hyperborea/ Shambhala in the ancient world.

Certain animals are connected to the stars but the 'Big Dipper', or Great Bear, was a prominent North Celestial Pole constellation. Therefore, it would seem plausible to suggest our Neolithic ancestors revered animals, like the bear, as a polar deity, and for its usual physical attributes. For example, many Native American tribes regarded the bear a powerful female deity, one that signified medicine and leadership.[13] Many chants and ceremonies were done so to engage the different guardians or goddesses associated with the bear. Both the bear and the bull were considered aspects of an ancient goddess. The Sumerians gave the bear goddess other names, such as Astarte, I-Nan or Ishtar. Could she have been an (alien) hybrid crea-ture revered by Neanderthal people? In Sumerian texts Astarte (I-Nan), was known as the goddess 'Innana' and in Mexico as 'Innan' or 'No-Nan-tsin', which in the Sanskrit language means 'wise mother goddess'.[14] However, to our more distant relations, this goddess was connected to the bear and Underworld as symbolised by the cave, the womb and the place of hiberna-tion.

In the Upper Palaeolithic period of what is now Europe, many caves have been found containing bear skulls, placed in what seems to be an exact and deliberate manner. The 32,000 to 30,000 year-old Chauvet cave, at Vallon-Pont-d'Arc (discovered in 1994) in the Ardéche region of France, is a perfect example. This under-ground art gallery, like the Volp Caves in Southern France, all speak of, at least, a 20,000 year-old fascination for animal wor-ship, especially the bear, lion and the bison (see figure 259).

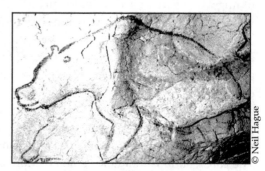

In much folklore from all around the world, the bear plays a significant role as a dark, hidden terror, lurking in the ancient forests and groves. At Chauvet, the bones of a bear have been carefully and system-atically arranged, while a bear skull sits on an altar, overlooking the remains of someone the tribe considered of great importance, possibly a shaman.

Figure 259: The Chauvet Bear.
My drawing of one of the three bears at Chauvet, found near the prehistoric entrance.

In almost all indigenous cultures, shamans were said to be able to invoke animal spirits and some could even turn into their animal guides. This was believed to be possible due to their unique kinship (being anthro-pomorphic), through their DNA, connecting the shaman to original (extraterrestrial) species of planet earth. It was also believed that shamans were relations to star people; the bear especially, was considered an ancient 'clan' from a time when humans and animal-human hybrids (or were more 'animal-like') walked the earth. The Athabascan Native American tribe, the 'Sinkoyne' (of the Athapaskan-speaking peoples of northern California), according to folklorist E W Gifford, writing in a 1937 article in *The Journal of American Folklore*, mentions tales of bear-like men. Anglo Saxon folklore also tells of a bear-man-hero (Beowulf) and so does the story of *Grendel*, in Scandinavian myth. In more contemporary terms, 'Wojtek' the Second

World War 'soldier bear' and *Paddington Bear* are also examples of our connection to human-bear characters.

Bear Butte

The Bears' Lodge, or 'Matho Thìpila, situated in Wyoming, USA (known locally as 'Bear Lodge Butte', or Devil's Tower) is a place connected to Native bear myths (see Figure 260). I visited the place in 2010, a fantastic part of the world, along with the Black Hills of South Dakota, which are near Bear lodge. The whole landscape is considered sacred to Native American Indian tribes, not least those tribes like the Lakota connected to Sun Dance rituals. Bear Lodge Butte was also the backdrop and landing base for aliens in Steven Spielberg's film, *Close Encounters of the Third Kind* (1977). According to Native American myth, the legends of Bear Lodge Butte describe the creation of the Butte through the claws of a giant bear that supposedly scratched at a 'giant' rock (or tree) as it 'grew skywards' to the stars. Giant tree or not, what is more interesting to me is the notion of humans becoming stars, or did the *stars become humanity*?

Figure 260: Bear Lodge Butte.
The author at Bear Lodge Butte. An ancient landscape involving legends of bear people and the stars.

In Kiowa legends of Wyoming and South Dakota, Bear Lodge Butte was where many bear people lived. In one Kiowa legend, it is said that seven young girls from the Kiowa camp were out gathering berries far from the campsite, when two bears attacked them. The girls ran out across the open prairie until they came to a large, grey rock. Climbing onto the rock, the bears began to climb in pursuit of the Kiowa girls. According to the legend, the bears tried to climb the rock as it grew steeper and higher, but their huge claws only split the rock face into thousands of strips as the rock grew upwards out of their reach. The hewn rock, cut and scarred on all sides, as the bears fought to climb. It is said the bears gave up the hunt in the end and turned to go back to their own lodge; as they did, they slowly returned to their original sizes. As the huge bears came back across the prairie and gradually became smaller, the Kiowa saw them and broke camp. Fleeing with fear, looking back at the towering mountain of rock, they guessed it

must be the lodge of these giant bears. After escaping the bears, according
to the myth, the girls had been lifted up so high they eventually turned into
seven stars – the Pleiades. In other legends, they became the seven stars of
the Great Bear, Ursa Major. The story, of course, is an elaborate narrative
which could be pure 'imagination', but nonetheless, Bear Lodge Butte is an
ancient landmark belonging to a prehistoric era.

The bear also became a symbol for the setting sun, evening and the com-
ing of winter, a time when the bear would enter the cave to hibernate.
Tribal songs, such as the *'Bear Mountain Chant'* (sung by Navajo shaman),
were sung to welcome winter and the hibernation period on earth. In
Europe, there are also annual bear festivals that take place in various towns
and communes in the Pyrenees region in winter, too. The Basque region of
France was a huge area for bear worship and in Prats-de-Mollo, during the
Fête de l'Ours (the festival of the bear), held on Candlemas (February 2),
men would dress up as bears brandishing sticks to terrorize people in the
streets.[15] Formerly, the festival centred on bears mock-attacking the women
of the town and trying to blacken their breasts (with soot), scandalous to
first-time outside observers. King Charles VI of France and five other
nobles are documented as dressing as 'wild men' (or bears) for a court festival in suits covered in pitch and flax; when a flame was brought too close
to the group, it is said that four of the five were burnt to death and only the
King survived. As we shall see, certain royalty (part-stellar bloodlines who
have run the world since antiquity), have either a fascination for, or are
related to, bear-like, or 'hairy', forest dwelling creatures.

Ainu – Bear People

The Ainu people of the northern islands of Japan, all worshipped the bear
for its wisdom and knowledge.

The 'hairy Ainu' belong to an
ancient shamanistic tribe that
are not Japanese by race. Some
have fair skin, blue eyes and
are hairy, bearded and seem to
have Aboriginal physical traits
(see figure 261). It has been
suggested that the Ainu culture
is at least 10,000 years old, originating with the native tribes of
the Island Hokkaido. Some
researchers also claim their reli-

Figure 261: Ancient Japanese Bear Worship.
The Ainu culture; relations to a more ancient
ancestor through their god, Kamuy (bear).

gion was/is dominated by a fire goddess, a symbol often associated with Hyperborea and 'fire and ice' symbolism of Atlantis. Yet, for the Ainu, the bear was a 'bringer of fire', a master and 'keeper of secrets', coming down from the mountains to teach the people.[16]

The Ainu named the bear, 'Kamuy', which means God. While on earth – the world of man – the Ainu believed that God appeared in the form of animals. This is why animals were considered sacred by so many Indigenous Native, or Aboriginal first peoples. For them, God had the capability of taking human form, but they (the Ainu) only took this form in their home, the 'country of the gods', which is outside the world of man.[17] The country of the gods, in simple terms, means the stars. Ainu belief also relates to coming from another reality, a world connected to, but not the same as, our human world. It's a similar concept to Australian Aboriginal creation myths relating to the Dreamtime, and how three main worlds: the *human*, the *sacred* and the *physical* world are not the same, but all connected.

To return a god from the physical world, back to the sacred (steller) world, the Ainu would sacrifice and eat the animal, sending its spirit away with civility. This ritual is called 'Omante' and usually involves a deer or adult bear. The dear or 'Migra' relates to Orion, as I have shown, and many Native American beliefs also relate the antelope, deer, stag, moose, bison and bear to an ancient human-animal 'consciousness', coming from the stars. Look into a deer or stag's eyes and tell me you don't see an ancient soul? For the Ainu, Omante occurred when the people sacrificed an adult bear. Still, when they caught a bear cub they performed a different ritual which is called 'Iomante', in the Ainu language, or 'Kumamatsuri', which translates as 'the bear festival' and means 'sending off'. As with all aboriginal 'first people', discrimination against the Ainu by Japanese citizens and the government persists to this day (see the Native Americans and Aborigines). The remaining Ainu communities in Hokkaido receive poorer education, struggle to find gainful employment, and have a significantly lower quality of life compared to that of many modern Japanese. And like most Natives, outside of the community, the Ainu have become so assimilated that most citizens with Ainu ancestry aren't even aware of it today.

Permian People

In the legend of 'Masha and the Bear' in Russian Folklore (probably the inspiration for *Goldilocks and the Three Bears*), we find common themes hinting at a race of bear-people who once roamed the earth many thousands of years ago. Yet these bear folk don't seem to have been the only anthropomorphic bipeds to emerge in the distant past. In recent years, conventional science has recognised that during the Permian era, roughly 290 million -

250 million years ago, certain creatures were in the process of evolving into mammals and were, therefore, evolutionarily extremely sophisticated. One in particular, called Lystrosaurus, was said to have been an herbivore and is believed to be the ancestor of every mammal now on earth. A BBC Horizon programme in 2002, *The Day the Earth Nearly Died*, pointed out the extinction of mammal-like creatures, (including animal-people), cleared the way for the early reptilian dinosaurs and the extinction of the dinosaurs cleared the way for mammals. If this is true, then evolution is not a smooth process of advance, but is marked by 'steps' and even 'reverses'. I often wonder if the evolutionary 'advances' are telling a story of how consciousness manifests on earth, in various forms. 'Prehistoric' art offers us insight into such human-animal hybrid forms (possibly star consciousness). Interestingly, on a cuneiform seal dated 4,000 BC, found in Iran and now in the Louvre, Paris, we see a biped creatures that do not represent a typical human. Also in places such as Mexico, Siberia and Syria, many strange figurines have been found that do not carry any likeness to humans. Twelve-inch statues of lion-headed figures found in Germany and France could be artistic memories of a prehistoric age when master geneticists (from a long lost advanced civilisation), created hybrid creatures entwining our DNA with that of animals. Themes found in H.G. Wells' book, *The Island of Dr Moreau* (1896), or Pierre Boulle's, *Planet of the Apes* (1963) hint at another history, found in oral traditions of many of earth's indigenous tribes. I think there is much more to know with regards to the Permian world and the fantastic creatures that inhabited it – the truth may be stranger than science fiction.

Monkey's Demons and Bears

All bear worship, including the making of alters by Neanderthal humans as far back as 100,000 years ago, relates to the reverence of the 'power of the bear'. The reverence could also relate to star worship, possibly Ursa Major and Ursa Minor. Geoffrey Ashe suggests extraterrestrial visitors from Ursa Major, or what the Hindus called the Seven Bears, brought star knowledge, allowing early man to develop advanced civilisations. I feel the same can be said of the stars within the Pleiades, Orion, Sirius (Canis Major) and a host of other important star systems, which have provided earth with a myriad of 'alien DNA'. The larger portion of our DNA, aptly named 'junk' by conventional science, still holds 'codes and memories' of these so-called alien races. I feel certain what we call constellations (the heavens) are mirrors of human cultures and races on earth. Coming from the 'stars' has nothing to do with distinction based on race, because *all stars* are born from the same source – we are all one. When I say star races, I am referring to 'spirit' and how our ancestors aligned themselves with the stars and the greater cosmos. Our DNA is also our key to the stars and the constellations to which we feel a personal connection, which is why ancient tribes used specific constellations as a focus for their beliefs.

The northern lights, otherwise known as aurora borealis, can also be connected to the mythical Hyperborean civilisation, which, according to some writers could have stretched from ancient Britain to the tip of Iceland. It's also suggested the northern lights are a manifestation of an 'Inner Sun', giving light to earth's deep and vast subterranean worlds. Inner Sun symbolism, or what alchemists called the 'Aurora', can also be found in petroglyph art forms, suggesting that an advanced people in prehistoric times possibly understood the powers of the Inner Sun. The ancients thought of the four winds as powerful god-beings, and in several myths, the wind god 'Agni', is said to have created monkey gods that were capable of travelling through the air. Interestingly, connections between alien and human hybrid races, such as Bigfoot, have also been seen with UFO phenomena, too. In the Sanskrit epic *Ramayana*, the sun god 'Indara' (another Thor figure) is asked by Vishnu (the preserver) to help him rid the earth of demons. In Hindu myth, Vishnu incarnates on ten occasions to preserve the earth and rid Gaia of demonic forces. The incarnations of Vishnu could relate to different dimensions or epochs/worlds endured as part of earth's evolution. Could these composite stories have spawned the saviour myth? In some cases, battles between demons and monkey gods, found in ancient myth and recorded in Indian art, are memories of an ancient epoch telling of the struggles between opposing forces. Could these myths relate to original earth races repelling an invading alien force? Legends of Vishnu and his incarnations as *four* princes, in the *Ramayana,* also relate to four points of the cross, Orion and the *four* Adams I talked about in earlier chapters. The four points are also powerful electromagnetic forces existing at each of the earth's directions.

The *Ramayana* thoroughly illustrates the battles between the forces of evil led by the ten-headed demon king, Ravana, and the forces of the 'warrior Prince', Rama (Vishnu). Such narratives would make great science fiction epics! In this monumental clash, Indara, the sun god, takes the form of the monkey king and aids Vishnu by sending an 'army of apes and bears' (our ancestors) to defeat the demons and reptile-like creatures. This battle was said to have taken place in the area we now know as Sri Lanka. 'Hanuman' (the monkey god) along with 'Vayu' the wind god (symbolic of flying craft), are said to have created the stepping stone network of islands between Southern India and the home of the demon king in Sri Lanka. Myth tells us that this was done so to rescue Sita, the eternal lover of Prince Rama, with the help of monkey and bear chiefs and 'Vanara', a word that

Figure 262: Ancient Bear and Monkey Tribes.
Human-animal gods: the monkey and bear chiefs and Vanara
(to the rigtht), is another Orion figure.

translates as 'forest man' (see figure 262).

Interestingly, Vishnu as 'Rama', in his tenth incarnation, is depicted clasping a 'flaming sword' (Orion's sword) while riding a white steed in pure Gandalf and Shadowfax style! Tolkien would have been very aware of many interconnected themes found in much of the world myths, as they appear in various forms within his novels. However, I feel that myths of this kind, tell of dual forces operating on many levels, not least interstellar opposing forces (see the *Star Wars* movies). Dual forces can also relate to ancient humans coming to terms with immense magnetic forces, housed at the poles of the earth, which have reshaped Gaia (and humanity) many times in previous epochs. On another level, they refer to stages in evolution, often symbolised in religious texts, and seen in the movement of the stars. The *Book of Revelation*, for example, also speaks of the saviour returning on a white horse, followed by armies on white horses and this 'revelation' seems to be linked to a discovery in 1995, when the first planet outside of our solar system was observed in the constellation of 'Pegasus'. In the same month came a report that told of thousands of stars rushing to the core of a globular cluster in the sign of Pegasus (the white horse). This supernova phenomenon incident, along with several others never seen before, are said to be signs of current evolutionary changes we, as a species, are moving through at this time.

Images from an illustrated version of a 13th century Arabic treatise by Zakariya al-Qazwini entitled, *Marvels of Things Created and Miraculous Aspects of things Existing*, shows imagery based on animal-human fusion. The text is probably the best-known example of classical Islamic literature concerned with cosmographical and geographical topics that challenged thoughts on creation. Al-Qazwini's treatise explores an eclectic mix of topics, from humans and their anatomy to strange mythical creatures, from plants and animals, to constellations of stars and zodiacal signs. The treatise

**Figure 263:
Animal-Human Fusion.**
My drawing of the Hohlenstein-Stadel Lion Man. All of these works of art seem to be hinting at an ancient fascination for anthropomorphism and animal consciousness. Did the Paleothithic artists (shamans) experience bipedal animal people through altered states? Or did they 'see' such figures amongst them?

© Neil Hague

was extremely popular and frequently illustrated over the centuries into both Persian and Turkish. When we compare Paleotlithic art, such as the lion man of the Hohlenstein-Stadel (see figure 263), to the various illustrations of anthropomorphic creatures in *Marvels of Things Created and Miraculous Aspects of Things Existing*, we have to wonder whether there are 'non-local' realities (visited by humanity while in states of altered awareness), teeming with 'alien life'? I go into more depth on such topics in *Journeys in the Dreamtime* and *Lions & Velons: The Bestiary of Kokoro and Moon Slayer*.

Arcturus – the Bear Son – 'King of Kings'

As Orion gradually disappears in the night sky and spring returns to earth, with it comes the glowing light of the star 'Arcturus' in the constellation of Boötes. Arcturus derives from Ancient Greek and means 'Guardian of the Bear' and like Orion, Boötes is another shepherd-figure amongst the stars.

The constellation of Boötes is mentioned in the *Book of Job* and in Homer's *Odyssey*, the second-oldest extant work of Western literature. The epic poem covers the return of the Greek warrior and hero figure, Odysseus, and tells of his tribulations with the gods, not least Poseidon (Orion's father). The long-delayed homecoming of Odysseus is closely associated with a bow and a dog, both of which are symbols connected to the annual returning warrior - Orion. Odysseus is also symbolically connected to the 'wild man', John the Baptist, through the Baptist's announcement of the coming of Christ, as "carrying a fan with which he will winnow the wheat" (*Matthew* 3:12; *Luke* 3:17). In the Poem, Odysseus is instructed to carry an oar (or winnow) until a traveller asks him what he is doing with 'a fan to winnow grain,' suggests Odysseus is also the 'water-treading' Orion/Osiris 'star-man' figure (see *Chapter Seven*). As the author of *Star Myths of the World* (2015), David Warner Matjisen, puts it on his blog:

There is another important aspect of Orion which may also be connected to the long-suffering Odysseus, and that is the fact that Orion is associated with Osiris, and it has been convincingly argued by Giorgio de Santillana and Hertha von Dechend in Hamlet's Mill that the "delaying action" of precession, seen in the

failure of Orion/Osiris to rise "on time" on the appointed day of the year, was
mythologized in ancient Egypt by the story of Set slaying his brother Osiris and
usurping his throne, in which it is pointed out that the same "usurpation" is later
found in the story of Hamlet and the story of The Lion King.[18]

I agree. As I have shown throughout the book, Orion is possibly the main
focus for much religious symbolism connected to the hero, saviour-god
archetype.

Like Orion, Boötes is also the great herdsman, the Wildman and 'lord of the
animal's' (see figure 264).

In Celtic myth, he is Cernunnos, who, like Enkidu or the woodwose
(wild man), dwells within groves and forests of the ancient world. Arcturus
(Boötes) is also the 'bear keeper' watching over the two bears, Ursa Minor
and Ursa Major and referred to as the 'One
who comes', or the 'Coming One'. Again,
we have a reference to Odysseus or Orion as
the coming hero figure. The three constellations of Boötes, Ursa Major (Great Bear) and
Ursa Minor (Small Bear), along with
Arcturus are connected to a common mythological theme of a 'Once and Future King', a
'King of Kings' to be more precise. These
constellations are entwined with the myths
about King Arthur 'sleeping in the land' and
the archetypal protector of the forest, or land
(the earth).

In Greek myth, Boötes is said it be
'Arcas', whose mother, 'Callisto', was transformed into a bear by a jealous Juno. It is
said that Arcas, when out hunting, discovered his mother in her bear form and pursued her into the temple of Jupiter (Zeus).
To prevent Arcas from unwittingly killing

Figure 264: Boötes.
Boötes the 'bear shepherd' is another
star man like Orion.
Source: Uranographia, Johann Bode, Alessio Govi.
(Public Domain.)

his mother, Jupiter took them both and placed them in the stars. Jupiter
does this a lot according to numerous myths. Placing people in the stars or
making a 'star man' is the work of the creator, the Demiurge of Gnostic
belief. The key point here in this version of the myth, is that the bear is a
goddess - a 'she-bear' and like the goddess Artemis, she is the great earth
bear and companion to Orion the hunter. The she-bear was also the precursor for the Neolithic goddess of the cave, quite possibly symbolised
through the cult of the bear. In simple terms, the bear (along with big alpha

cats) was the ancient hunter of the forest, before the arrival of the star man (Orion).

King Arcturus - the 'Bee Wolf'

In Druid ceremonies, at the northern section of the wheel of the year (the crossroads), they call upon the Great Bear of heaven and the earth, who points to the Pole Star. The north, especially, is connected to the bear not least through the word 'Arctic', which means 'region of the bear-stars' and the land beyond the North winds, also known as Hyperborea. Like the bear, the star Arcturus goes into hibernation (from our view of the skies) in the autumn, only to return in the spring. As Orion rises, and as Arcturus declines, the earth goddess alters her surface accordingly; we call it the change in seasons. For the ancients, Arcturus, who I believe is hugely connected to the King Arthur legend, was said to bring honour and good fortune. In fact, the Welsh word 'arth', as in King *Arth*ur, means 'bear', and the name by which this hero was affectionately known.

It was Edgar Cayce who spoke of Arcturus (King Arthur) as he who dwells at the centre, the guardian of a doorway to other realms of consciousness. The best selling Astrologer, Stephen Arroyo, says 'he', Arcturus (King Arthur), is an important doorkeeper relating to expansion and spiritual growth. Along with the Great Bear constellation, Arthur and his twelve knights (months/zodiacal signs) have a special connection to our original earth and the symbolic light of a 'new dawn'. In various European myths the she-bear is said to give birth to a divine child and in other versions it is a human woman who mates with a bear-man and produces a son. The hero Beowulf, whose name means bear, or 'Bee-Wolf' (honeyeater), is the most common version of this myth. The story of *Beowulf* survives in a manuscript known as the *Nowell Codex*, which also contains a fragment of *The Life of Saint Christopher*, the hero giant I mentioned in *Chapter Two*. He is the 'Bear Son', who, like King Arthur, relates to a lost lineage of royalty, giants and the Watchers I mentioned earlier in the book. The Bear-Son legends relate to bear worship as an ancient guardian and protector of the earth. The Greek *Odysseus* (*Odyssey*) also refers to the family of Odysseus as the house of 'Arceisios', meaning 'bearish' or 'ursine'; according to older myths, Arceisios was the child of the union between a man and she-bear.[19] It all connects once you look more closely at the myths.

Bear symbolism also relates to the royal Merovingian bloodlines and the tales associated with a bear-people descending into the Underworld to do battle with a dragon.[20] This is why much religious iconography in Christian cathedrals seems to be speaking about the true royal lineage of the 'people of the bear', the true bloods, or first kings and queens. The symbolism can also be found in the *Harry Potter* books, too, with 'Arcturus Black' (a true blood lineage of wizards), along with 'Sirius' Black, being the maternal grandfather of Arthur Weasley.[21] In a very intriguing book by Stewart Swerdlow, called *Blue Blood, True Blood – Conflict & Creation; A personal Story* (2002), the author lists at least twelve different alien species that have had a massive impact on earth's evolution (our DNA). One extraterrestrial in particular, he calls the 'Bear or the Bigfoot' clan. Before I look at Bigfoot, there is one particular ancient human who fits the description of the 'bear son' and the star man of the woods archetype.

Hairy Knights and Shiny Saints

The most famous portrayal of duals between good and evil forces can be seen in the legends of St. George of Cappadocia (Ancient Turkey) slaying the dragon. Similar legends also depict St. Michael (a Phoenician deity called Miok), casting the serpent into the abyss. St. George inspired many artists and writers, not least John Ruskin, the leading English art critic (and artist) of the Victorian era. Ruskin founded the 'Guild of Saint George' in the early 19th Century and his endeavours attracted international respect, bringing praise from figures as varied as Tolstoy, George Eliot, Proust and Gandhi. Many well-known artists were connected to the Guild Orders, not least the Guild of St. George and the Order of the Garter. However, the original source for St. George seems to have been inspired by legends of the 'hairy human' or 'Woodwose' often depicted in religious iconography and on heraldry.[22] Interestingly, the first renditions of the saints who opposed the dragon (George and the Dragon) were painted, or carved, as hairy men and women – the Woodwose and Woodwives. The most famous depiction of a 'hairy St. George' can be seen on the misericords of Chester Cathedral (see figure 265). These are 'Woodwose' or wild men, semi-human beings, according to legends, which could not speak and were unable to control themselves when angry and lustful. They were often depicted with green or brown hair (the Green Man).[23]

Images of wild men can also be found at Bodmin Church in Cornwall and in St Mary's Church, Beverley, to name but a

Figure 265: George and the Dragon.
St. George the Woodwose, as depicted on misericords of Chester Cathedral. © Neil Hague

Figure 266: Jack of Birds.
The unicorn (monoceros) and hairy man relate to the 'untamed' stellar human (star being). (Public Domain.)

Figure 267: Hairy Adam.
There are many other depictions of the 'hairy human' (often called the human angel) on coats of arms and heraldry. Note the use of the 'X' shape on the shields.

few. The Christian church seems to have had an obsession with these wild men figures and the German engraver, goldsmith and printmaker of the late Gothic period artists, Master E. S, even portrayed a wild man riding a unicorn on the playing card, 'Jack of Birds' (see figure 266). On some heraldic shields, the unicorn (Monoceros) is replaced with a hairy wild man, symbolic of divine lineage connected to Orion, Adam and the first human prototypes (see figure 267). As I've been illustrating, Monoceros belongs to the Orion family of constellations, along with Canis Major, Canis Minor, Lepus and Orion.

At times, John the Baptist is often depicted as a 'hairy wild man' by medieval artists, which could have been both a celebration of the wild man figure, and possibly a connection to the Babylonian Enkidu wildman who accompanies Gilgamesh (Orion) in ancient Mesopotamian mythology. Other late Gothic period depictions of Orion show him with long hair and in knight's armour, holding a club and shield, with the face of a wild man or beast (see figure 268 overleaf). Pierre Sabak, in his book *Holographic Culture* (2018), connects the Wildman (Aboriginal man) with the Proto-Human Angel and what he calls 'Adamic Man', who were also considered 'light beings' (a lineage from the biblical Shining Ones and the Watchers I mentioned in earlier chapters).

Other saints (knights) and prophets of biblical fame are often depicted as hairy or wild looking. Why? I am sure it is a reference to ancient humanity and our connection to angelic, non-physical worlds I am going to explore in the second part of the book. St. Onuphrius and Elijah the

Figure 268:
Orion - The Wild Knight.
15th Century engraving of Orion
as the wild knight (the Adamic
man), a symbol of the 'Shining
Ones'. He wields the club just
like Kesil and the Fool.
This image is from the Poeticon
Astronomicon (Poetic Astronomy), a
star atlas by Hyginus that was published in 1482. © Courtesy of the
Science Photo Library

prophet all seem to have been Woodwose-
like, covered in hair. As it is written in the
Bible, 2 *Kings* 1:8:

*He was a hairy man, they answered, with a
leather belt around his waist. It is Elijah the
Tishbite, said the king.*

The ancient Hyksos royal bloodlines of
Egypt, and the biblical Israelites (not Israel
as we know today), seem to be another
source of the Wildmen appearance. The
'Hyksos' Dynasties, also known as the
'Shepherd Kings' (Rulers of Foreign Lands)
ruled from Avaris in the Eastern delta of
Lower Egypt. Author Ralph Ellis, in his
book *Jesus, Last of the Pharaohs* (2002), documents evidence connecting Egypt with
Sumer and Mesopotamia and how great
Jewish figures of the Old Testament were
actually pharaohs of Egypt.[24] Ellis also states
the first Hyksos pharaoh known as 'Sheshi',
whose name was 'Mayebre', or 'Mayebra',
was possibly 'Abraham' from the lineage of
Adam (Orion).

The word Pharaoh, can mean 'Liberated
One', or 'Para' (brother), which in Hindu is 'Pra' (Praja), also meaning 'lord
of creatures' – the star-lord, Orion. In Scotland and Ireland, the word
'Farragh' means Chieftain; the word 'Pharos' (fire) also means 'light',
adding to the idea of the 'light-bringer' or angelic host within the royal
bloodlines. The scope of this book cannot give the Egyptian/Israelite subject worthy attention, but suffice to say, it is possible to imagine a 'hairy'
lineage of priest-kings (royalty) descending from the Shining Ones (or
'Fury') predating biblical times. Pierre Sabak, writing about connections
between the Fury and the hairy-angelic line in his book, *Murder of Reality*
(2010), states:

*A class of deity, the Fury is typically described as possessing the visage of a dog
with bat-like wings and writhing snakes for hair. Combination of the 'reptile with
hair' is an esoteric marker of the 'human-angelic' lineage.*[25]

The tribe of Levi, the lion's priestly tribe of biblical Israel, have been said by some authors to connect to the Hyksos, Shepherd Kings, who eventually emerged in France as the Merovingian dynasty (5th century until 751). An idea that came out of the writings of the first century AD Jewish historian, Josephus, and the Hellenistic Egyptian historian, Manetho. Also, the obsession with animal skin and the 'bearskin', those tall, fur black caps, worn as part of a ceremonial military uniform (all over the world), could be a form of symbolic reverence for these warrior (hunter) chieftains going back to the time of the Hyksos.

Hyksos and Ormus

The Merovingians were Sicambrian, or Frankish kings, who ruled large portions of what are now France and Germany between the fifth and seventh centuries. The period of their rise corresponds to the time frame of the King Arthur figure, though the stories of Arthur didn't become widespread until several centuries later. As with King Arthur, from whom some writers suggest the Merovingian dynasty derives its name, his historical reality is obscured by legend. However, Arthur can be connected to a 'mother goddess religion', spreading into France before the rise of the Merovingians. Black Madonna effigies found all over Europe (especially France) are remnants of pagan goddess worship connected to Isis, Artemis, 'Artio', Mary and Demeter (see figure 269). According to author and mythologist Joseph Campbell, Artio's roots lie with ancient bear cults. Campbell also connects Artio, the she-bear to the constellations of Ursa Major and Minor – the Great Bear and the Little Bear.[26]

Figure 269: Ormus (She-Bear). Mary (the She-Bear woman), along with wild man such as St. Onophrius, can be found in the 14th Century *Book of Hours.*

Merovee (or Merovech or Meroveus), like Jesus and the Hyksos shepherd king, Moses, all have a supernatural origin. The Merovingians' long hair distinguished them among the Franks, who cut their hair short. The Merovingians were also known as the 'long-haired kings', with Clovis I, the first king of the Franks who united all Frankish tribes under one ruler. Another important attribute of the Hyksos Shepherd Kings (who were also high priests) and later Merovingian rulers, was that they *all* claimed descent from the Watchers, or Shining Ones, I mentioned in earlier chapters.

According to authors Michael Baigent, Richard Leigh and Henry Lincoln, in their book *The Holy Blood and the Holy Grail* (1982), the Prieuré de Sion adopted another name in 1188. It became known to its members as 'Ormus' and its symbol was an acrostic combining 'Ours' (meaning bear in French) and 'Ursus' in Latin, all surrounded by the letter 'M'.[27] The 'M' symbol can also be found in the astrological sign for Virgo - the virgin goddess. It is also worth noting that the bear was used as a symbol of Arcadia (an ancient epoch) relating to the animal-gods. The very name 'Arcadia' derives from the Greek 'Arkaden', meaning 'people of the bear'. It is this type of symbolism, used by the temple orders that would eventually find their way into the symbolism of Christian Gothic cathedrals, designed by the same temple orders.

The story of King Ursus (Sigisbert VI), known as 'Prince Ursus' (or the 'Bear Prince'), between 877AD and 879AD, is another example of the alleged true, hairy royal lineage in Europe (see figure 270). It is said King Ursus led a revolt against Louis II of France in an attempt to re-establish the Merovingian dynasty. The revolt failed and Prince Ursus and his supporters were defeated in a battle near Piontiers in 881AD. The same prince/king appeared on a mural above the font in Wrexham Cathedral in North Wales, and it seems to me, that the hairy

Figure 270: The Bear (Bigfoot) Prince.
King Ursus (Sigisbert VI) of Merovingian France.

Figure 271: Orion Man of the Woods.
(Above and Left) Man of the Woods at Thiers (Puy-de-Dôme). The Fool's head on the staff is a symbol of Kesil (Orion). **(Bottom Right)** The same wild men at Moulin Cathedral, France.
© Neil Hague 2002

human (or Woodwose) was possibly the original bloodline of kings on the British Isles, not least through King Arthur. The bear and hairy men, often depicted in art, are symbols for the 'Children of Hermes', the original magicians and angelic humans. A house in Thiers (Puy-de-Dôme), France, shows an effigy of a bear-man (a woodwose) with the head of a Fool on his staff. The 15th century place is called the 'House of the Man of the Woods' (see figure 271). The Fool, of course, is a link to Orion (or Kesil); similar sculptures can be found on numerous Christian cathedrals, all of which seem based on the man of the woods – or the children of the bear.

The 'Monkey Earth' God

Myths from all over the ancient world tell of a mischievous monkey god who had incredible powers. In China and India this deity was able to shape-shift, fly through the air and turn into wind and firestorms. In China, the Monkey God is Hanuman, or 'Monkey', an ardent devotee of Rama and often described as the 'son of Pawan', the Hindu god for wind. Hanuman is known for his extraordinarily daring feats, strength and loyalty and whose father, 'Kesari', was a 'Vanara Chief' of the forest people. Hanuman's mother, Añjanā was said to have been impregnated by Vayu, the wind god. According to Indian and Dravidian mythology, Hanuman was believed to have been able to stop the wind blowing and in Chinese legend he had supernatural powers. Monkey's story from Arthur Waley's translations of the original myth also tells of a cloud-riding hero-god that fought demons and helped Vishnu transform the World Ages. The Vietnamese still call this god 'Lei' and according to Native American prophecy, the return of Lei, or 'Bigfoot' (Sasquatch), signals the time of 'cleansing', a paradigm shift, when dimensions merge. In an amazing book called *The Book of the Elders* (1994), produced by Sandy Johnson and Dan Budnik, the Hopi tell of the return of the 'Earth Monkey God' at the time of 'awakening'. We are in the time of awakening today.

Since the late 1980s there has been a growing number of Bigfoot sightings, especially in America, Europe and even in the UK. In my view, the sightings relate to a 'merging of different dimensions' (realities) as people start to access their 'ancient eyes'. As a child I saw what seemed to be a Bigfoot several times in the woods near where I grew up, in an area of land once owned by the Fitzwilliam families, a bloodline descending from William the Conqueror. I am not the only one to have witnessed such phenomena in the UK. The sighting of upright, bear-like creatures at Loch Lomond, in Scotland, an eight foot Ape-like creature seen in Tunbridge Wells and similar phenomena at Wolfhole Crag in the Forest of Bowland in Lancashire, England, to name but a few, are classic signs of Bigfoot.[28] The point I am making here, is that Bigfoot phenomena is not all 'physical', it can be inter-dimensional and very much connected to whomever 'experences' such events. In my case, I always felt at 'home' when I experienced such sightings, more on Bigfoot in a moment.

Charles Darwin's theories on evolution did much damage to original knowledge surrounding earth's monkey species, by inferring that all humans evolved from one such strand of intelligent life. The 'monkey people' of the ancient world, according to Dreamtime myths, were turned into dolphins, so to survive cataclysmic floods and extreme pole shifts of the ancient world. All of these stories hint at various species, such as Bigfoot (or a bear people), being able to shape-shift and traverse time! In fact, I feel the reason why creatures such as Bigfoot have never been 'officially', physically caught, is because they are interdimensional manifestations, co-existing on parallel worlds, or realities. When the veil between these worlds becomes thin, or non-existent, we are able to access such phenomena. We, too, are time travellers and multidimensional consciousnesses; what we create and think into physical existence, depends on how we use our imagination to 'see' alternative dimensions of reality. Bigfoot, according to some writers, are a genetic mix of the earth's Neanderthal race and an alien species, created (or grafted) by the 'gods' (plural), the same gods in the Bible that genetically made Cro-Magnon human.

As mentioned in a previous chapter, Sumerian records also account for Enkidu, the friend and opponent of Gilgamesh, a hairy, ape-man figure. The Gilgamesh myth tells of Enkidu having superhuman strength and living amongst the animals in the forest. Myths connected to the 'Kapre', a Philippine cryptid creature, characterised, as a 'tree giant', is another variation of the monkey earth gods, Bigfoot and ancient peoples of the forests. The Kapre are described as being a tall (7'- 9'), big, black, hairy, muscular creatures with a strong smell that would attract human attention. The nearest image I can think of resembling the types of c cryptid creatures found in world myths, is the 'skin-changer', fictional character, Beorn, found in J.R.R. Tolkien's book *The Hobbit*.

The only ever footage captured of a Bigfoot was the Patterson – Gimlin film shot October 20th, 1967 at Bluff Creek in California. The film shows a supposed female Bigfoot (a she-bear) moving through Bluff Creek, giving us a feel for what our Neanderthal relations may have looked like in the flesh. Some have said the film was fake, but at the time of writing, the Patterson – Gimlin footage was given a makeover in 2019 - and it is now more convincing than ever before, according to experts in special effects. Almost five decades have passed since the footage was captured and it has faced heavy scrutiny from sceptical scientists, forensic analysts and special effects experts. The technology didn't exist back in 1967 to create such detailed muscle movement, which leads towards the idea this film is not a hoax. Just type "The Roger Patterson Bigfoot film" into YouTube and watch it for yourself.

So what's the big deal about Bigfoot? The fact remains, Bigfoot still is a global phenomenon that has connections to ancient ancestors and the stars.

The Bigfoot Mystery

The American Bigfoot, also known as 'Sasquatch' in western Canada, has affinities to *giant*, hairy ape or bear-like hominids reported from the western mountains of Central and South America. These creatures have also been sighted in the well-forested areas of China, Tibet and Indochina. It is a fact that the cultural histories of many Native American and First Nation peoples include stories and beliefs about the wild, non-human peoples. Many of these descriptions bear a striking resemblance to the hairy man-like creatures reported over the past fifty plus years. With over 550 sightings a year in North America alone, it is estimated that there is a population of at least 1,500 to 2,000 Bigfoot in the Pacific North West.[29] The possibility of a prehistoric species still surviving is not so difficult to comprehend, especially when other species have been discovered since the 1950s. One case, in particular, was when USA federal wildlife officers, flying over a remote part of Wood Buffalo National Park, Alberta, spotted a small, isolated herd of 200 wood bison, thought to be extinct! On inspecting these animals it was found that they were the last remaining pure wood bison, an enormous Ice Age species not known to exist in a pure strain anywhere else in the world.[30]

Indian folklore and myth is littered with stories of hairy giants living in northern forests of the east and west coast of America. Local Native American, Native Canadian and Inuit accounts all comment on these ancient hairy, human-like beings. To the Eastern tribes they were called the 'Windigo' and in the upper midwestern parts of the United States these creatures were called 'Wendigo', 'Weetigo' and 'Uncegi'. Further east, for the Micmac tribes, they were named 'Gugwe' or 'Koakwe', a hairy giant that looked similar to a baboon. The Iroquois of the upper New York State also told of similar hairy human-like beings in their folklore; according to the Iroquois, these people were known as 'Stone Giants', or to the Inuit as 'Tornit'. This was because both were said to be able to lift huge stones and uproot small trees. In North Carolina, indigenous peoples called the same creature the 'chikly cudley' (pronounced: ke-cleah kud-leah) which, in Cherokee, means 'hairy thing'. While Indian folklore records Bigfoot's existence, the first Europeans that came to the Americas also reported strange giants and hairy creatures. In 986 AD, Leif Eriksson wrote of encountering monsters that were ugly, hairy and swarthy with great black eyes. Other records tell of explorers, such as Samuel de Champlain (who founded Quebec and mapped the Atlantic coast of Canada in the early 1700s), being warned by the native peoples of Eastern Canada of the 'Gougou', a giant hairy man. The Bigfoot phenomenon continues to this day, especially with sightings in the USA, Europe and China. As the state-run Xinhua News Agency reported in 2003: "In Beijing, China, on Sunday 12th October, Chinese authorities started investigating several apparent sightings of a legendary 'ape-like' beast at a nature reserve in the central Hubei province. This mythical creature, suspected by locals to be a 'Bigfoot', was apparently seen by six people, including a journalist in the Shennongjia Nature reserve on the Sunday afternoon." So what are we dealing with here? Zoologists and scientists, open-minded to the Bigfoot phenomena, would suggest we could be 'seeing' ancient creatures that have survived into the 21st Century. I am more inclined to think that Bigfoot, along with many other similar phenomena, relate to seeing manifestations of our ancient animal-human star-god 'aspects', which are stored in the memory of our 'crystaline-like' DNA. We have an interstellar database, which can be tapped into, through our Junk DNA.

Bigfoot in Europe and America

Sightings of Bigfoot in Europe have also been recorded since medieval times. These creatures were referred to as 'Woodwose' (Wudwasa) or 'wildmen' of the woods, and in France they were called 'Le Feuillou'. The troubadours of 12th Century France and the minnesänger of Germany (the creators of epics through rhythm and folk songs), record a meeting between a knight and a hairy giant in the Celtic Arthurian epic, *Owen* (pronounced: ee-vine). This story, which includes over 8,000 lines, tells of a knight called Kalogrenant encountering a hairy giant in the wilderness of the Bretagne.[31]

It seems the incident was

Figure 272: The Fight in the Forest.
Hans Burgkmair (1473-1531).
© Ailsa Mellon Bruce Fund (public domain)

illustrated by Hans Burgkmair (1473-1531) who called the drawing, *Fight in the Forest* (see figure 272). The drawing suggests the giant measures about 7 foot 3 inches in height with a 14 inch foot. Across Europe, the Wildman enigma became associated with Green Man stories, another figure who can be found carved in stone on almost all of Europe's Gothic Cathedrals. As I mentioned in a previous chapter, the Green man *is* Osiris (Orion) and connects to the Underworld, the forest and Subterranea.

In her book *Wildmen: Yeti, Sasquatch and the Neanderthal Enigma* (1983), Myra Shackley asks if these Wildmen could still be in existence? As already touched on, over two hundred European aristocratic families have had wildmen as heraldic emblems and many more as supporters. Why? Because these blue blood families know the hidden meaning behind these emblems. Symbolism, as with much heraldry, relates to *bloodlines* claiming allegiance to the gods and the stars through their DNA.[32] Wildmen appear again and again in medieval paintings, illuminated manuscripts and as figures, along with an array of strange cryptids paraded as part of 18th and 19th Century Freak Shows and circuses.

There are endless accounts of wolf-men, or werewolves, contributing to this phenomena, too. Apparently, on the walls of Castle Ambras near Innsbruck, Austria, alongside a portrait of Vlad the Impaler (Count Dracula), there are portraits of a 'wolf man' (real name Petrus Gonsalvus) and his children.[33] This collection of paintings is called *The Wolfman of Munich*, and depicts Gonsalvus, his son and daughter with the condition

Figure 273: Hypertrichosis. Fedor Jeftichew, better known as Jo-Jo the Dog-Faced Boy, from St. Petersburg (1868). Could hypertrichosis be a genetic connection to the bear people? (public domain)

hypertrichosis. The paintings were given to Ferdinand II by the Duke of Bavaria, Wilhelm V. We don't seem to have a problem accepting the reality of 'human mutants', especially going back centuries based on codes within our DNA causing congenital terminal hypertrichosis (see figure 273). But wildmen, Woodwose and Bigfoot seem to be too difficult to imagine.

The many records of Bigfoot, from ancient Native American stories of the Windigo, to the highly controversial film footage caught by Roger Patterson and Bob Gimlin in 1967, leave us with the possibility that an ancestor, like Bigfoot, shares this planet (reality) with us. As the world-leading cryptozoologist, Loren Coleman states in his book *Bigfoot, The True Story of Apes in America* (1985):

The truth is that at least one unknown species of primate exists in America. It's a big story and it's not getting the attention it deserves.[34]

From my research, I feel the animal species of earth, like the bears, lions and apes were considered gods by our ancestors, not just because of their obvious physical 'alpha predator' attributes, but also because of their connections with earlier ancient epochs recorded in myths and legends. Another reason why animals, like the bear, monkey/ape, bison and reptile, have been revered across a wide geographical distance since ancient times, is more to do with animal-human DNA *fusion* and the gods coming to earth from the stars.

The Anthill Prince - Kokopelli

Other magical godlike figures coming from the stars are recorded in myths and legends the world over. One such character called 'Kokopelli', or 'Blue Monkey', seems to have made such an impression on the shamanistic clans and Bronze Age artists that he can be found in rock art from northern India to the American southwest. This god or 'entity', also known as 'Wood Hump', was said to be the archetypal flute-playing trickster, sometimes depicted as an insect or mantis (see figure 274).

Kokopelli has been worshipped since at least the time of the ancient Pueblo Peoples and the first known images of him appear on Hohokam pottery dated to sometime between 850 - 750 AD. Yet, Bronze age rock art shows that he must have been known to the Pueblo thousands of years before. Kokopelli may have been initially representations of ancient Aztec traders, known as 'pochtechas', who travelled to the southwest from Mexico. However, this origin story is still in doubt, since the first known images of Kokopelli predate the major era of Aztec-Anasazi trade by several hundred years. Another theory is that Kokopelli is actually an anthropomorphic insect deity whose origins are not of this physical dimension. Many of the earliest depictions of Kokopelli certainly make him very insect-like in appearance. The name Kokopelli is said to be a combination of 'Koko', another Hopi and Zuni deity, and 'pelli', the Hopi and Zuni word for the 'desert robber fly'. The latter is an insect with a prominent proboscis and a rounded back, noted for its zealous, sexual activities.

Figure 274: Wood Hump.

Figure 275: Anthill Prince.
(Top) A typical Anthill. **(Bottom)**
Possible locations for 'Sipapu', or
entrance to the Hopi Underworld near
the bottom of the Canyon of the Little
Colorado, above its junction with the
Colorado River.

According to Hopi origin myth, Kokopelli was the 'Khiva (anthill) Prince', who led the Hopi to the earth's surface at the time of their emergence into the Third World (an ancient epoch). The Hopi say they came out of subterranean worlds, in the geographic area of the Four Corners, guided by a Khiva Prince (see figure 275). When we look at photographs of desert settlements in the southwestern States of America and in places such as Afghanistan, it is easy to see the visual connection between the ant-like underground homes and the indigenous peoples' cave dwellings in these locations.

Gene Matlock, in his book, *The Last Atlantis Book You'll Ever Read* (2001), connects the Hopi with the 'Khopis' and 'L'Hopitai' tribes of now Afghanistan and Uzbekistan. According to Matlock, the Hopi were led out of northern India in two groups (in the ancient world), one going into Greece and the other to America. The Hopi say their ancestors, the 'Khivites', were subject to a small kingdom named 'Muski'. In the same area where Khiva, Uzbekistan is today, there was a small kingdom of non-Hindu tribes, called 'Musika', or Muski. These people were said to have bitterly opposed the Brahmin priests' attempts to force them to hand over their lands and become part of the caste system, (the same story the world over – see the Native Americans and the Cathars in France). The Hopi origin story even goes as far as stating that the Hopi killed two sacred 'Mahus', which the Hopi say were 'horned beings', to keep them warm on their migration. However, Matlock translates, Mahus, as being a sacred 'cow' or 'bull', and he even goes as far as suggesting the Hopi were forced to leave Northern India for killing the sacred cows of the Hindu. Matlock says of the Muski religious leaders:

According to the Hopis, the priests and leaders of the Muski began to persecute their forefathers, even ravishing their wives and daughters. They then asked their chief, called Yai-owa, to ask even a greater leader, Maasawa, to help them leave Sivapuni. By some strange coincidence, it just so happened in ancient Northern India, the compound word Ja-ovaha meant 'chief, overseer, caretaker'. Maha-

Ishvara meant 'Great Lord, King God Shiva.[35]

As shown in earlier chapters, both Masau'u (Maasawa) and Kokopelli can be found etched together in Bronze Age rock art across the South Western States of America. Both archetypes are said to be two aspects of the same 'being', the 'dual being' according to the Hopi. Kokopelli was always drawn alongside migration symbols of 'bear claws', a mark of the bear clan made by ancient people who *followed* Kokopelli. Were they 'bear-people' who followed this star deity? As stated earlier, Orion was seen as a 'shepherd of bears'; therefore, Kokopelli could be associated with Orion in that role as a guiding Pied Piper shepherd-figure. The significance of the bear people and Kokopelli could also relate to Atlantis and the animal people, gods and extraterrestrials that mixed their DNA with that of the human form (see my illustrated novels, *Moon Slayer* and *Aeon Rising*).

Kokopelli was also known as Cotton Tail (see page 316) in his winter disguise and connected to the one-eyed 'Kikulupes' (pronounced: keek-lopehs) or Cyclopes, which again relates to legends of giants and the Underworld. Edward Pocoke, the 17th Century Greek scholar and Orientalist, wrote that the word 'Cyclopes' is a Greek corruption of the name of a pastoral people in India.[36] The dark historical fantasy novel *Vorrh trilogy* (2012), created by Brian Catling, also gives some interesting insights into creatures like the Cyclops, all based on myths and subjects mentioned in this chapter.

Figure 276: Blue Monkey.
My artistic impression of Kokopelli and how he may have been seen by the Ancient Pueblo people.

In an inspired painting I made in 1995, before I knew anything about the multidimensional levels regarding the Kokopelli character, I also placed a one-eyed head garment (helmet) on my image of Kokopelli (see figure 276). Kokopelli can also be connected to the Indian deity 'Kubera', a hump-backed, dwarf-like creature wearing a feather headdress. The Pleiadean symbol for peace, given to the famous contactee, Billy Meier, is similar in my view to the goggle-eyed, plumed headdress imagery of Masau'u and Kokopelli. Kokopelli was said to be deformed, club-footed and a bit of a rogue and a cheat, with an immense sexual appetite. Rather like the dwarf god, Bes, in Egyptian belief, Kokopelli also became a protector of pregnant women and children. Other stories say that Kokopelli carried a bag of seeds (stars) like his opposite Masau'u, which he scattered across the path of the sun, and they became the first crops (or planets). Again, this myth could be hinting at Orion's connection to our solar system, not least 'energetically', and how nebula can birth stars, planets and moons; more on this in the next part of the book. I am sure many parables relating to sowing and reaping are references to 'light' (star and solar forces), the invisible worlds aiding creation on both the physical and non-physical levels. From my own research, I feel the stories of Kokopelli relate to the ancient understanding of duality and moving beyond the illusion of death, or the Underworld. Kokopelli is another Osiris, or Min figure who can go beyond death (Underworld) and return to earth as a star god. Kokopelli also has associations with sixth-sense related feelings encountered when we attune to finer vibrations and feelings stretching beyond the physical world. The same was said of 'Maui' in Polynesian myth and all were fertility deities similar to Kokopelli of Native America. Mantis (Min/Pan) was considered protector of travellers, who wore a plumed crown and played the flute or pipes. In some accounts, Pan is referred to as 'Asklepios', a figure said to have the power to reverse death. Legend has it that Zeus (in the form of an eagle) killed Asklepios for raising the dead. Zeus then instructed a Kyklopes (cyclops) to slay Asklepios with a thunderbolt, all of which relates to the wars between the gods. In Hopi legend, Kokopelli was also said to have been shot by an eagle (Zeus) for bringing the first Hopi out of the 'Underworld' – the place of death; giving the light of new life. Prometheus did the same for humanity in Greek myth; all of these narratives are telling the same story of how certain 'star people' (possibly from Orion) brought gifts of life (and death) to humanity.

The Ant People of Orion

The 'ant people' mentioned in Hopi myths also seem to be interchangeable with the 'Greys' of extraterrestrial fame. Therefore it may be more accurate to see Masau'u as the chief of the Ant People, a leader of the Greys (see figure 277 overleaf), whose origins could be connected to Orion?

Two Hopi clans called 'anu' and 'pala anu' are also the name for red ants (that help form the horned-millet phratry), along with other clans such as the deer, elk and antelope. According to the Hopi, the black ant, 'sisi-w'anu', or 'piss ant', was believed to be the source of witchcraft.[37] I think there is a fine line between alien 'interference' in human reality, and what we call 'dark' witchcraft. I also wonder whether most alien phenomena is a projec-

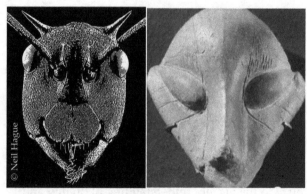

Figure 277: The Ant People - Greys.
(Left) My image of an alleged microscopic view of an ant compared to an ancient art form. **(Right)** found in the former Yugoslavia, depicting what appears to be a Grey alien.

tion of what we call sorcery, or interdimensional witchcraft coming from the different planets and stars, notably Orion's star, Betelgeuse.

In Mesoamerica the Maya, who share many cultural traits with the Hopi (both are Orion worshippers), tell legends of ant-like men building stone cities and roads during the 'First Creation', or 'First World'. These peculiar beings, according to the Hopi, possessed magical powers and could 'summon stones' into precise architectural positions by just 'whistling'. So that's how the megalithic sites were built? Hmmm! The common ground between the Mesoamerican legends, and the desert tribes of North America, are tales of an ant-like race aiding the ancients as earth went through tremendous upheavals. Archaeologist J. Eric S. Thompson writes in *Maya History and Religion* (1970):

> *Zayamuincob can be translated as 'the twisted men' or 'the disjointed men,' suggesting a connection with 'hunchback.' The word may also be connected with zay, 'ant,' for there is also a Yucatec [Yucatan Maya] tradition of an ancient race called chac zay uincob, 'red ant men.'*

Both the Maya and Hopi were industrious like ants, taking out the 'red earth' (red rock areas of the Americas) and making straight roads through forests. The Maya created roads and walkways leading to pyramids in the jungles, but one has to wonder about what kind of technology may have been used to construct their pyramids? Both the Hopi and Maya venerated crops and each February the Hopi perform the 'Bean Dance' inside their part-subterranean kivas, all of which relates to their ancestry, to the Ant People. The fires are kept continuously ablaze in the kivas, turning these underground structures into superb hot houses. The Bean Dance ritual, according to some researchers, may commemorate a time when the Ant People taught the Hopi how to sprout beans inside underground caverns in order to survive upheaval on the surface world (see also page 37).

Ants resonate deep in our psyches as archetypal denizens of dual worlds: the earth plane and the Underworld. Both linguistic and mytholog-ical evidence indicates, however, that the image of ant-like anthropoids is more than a psychological reaction to the tiny formicidae of the natural world. Mass media, movies and 'experiences' in the modern world consis-tently give ETs the characteristics of bugs (see the *Men in Black* and *Independence Day* movies). The Grey alien phenomena called 'Zeta Reticuli I' and 'II' along with Mantis-like Insectoid aliens, seen in movies such as *Star Wars* and *Men in Black*, are all too common in the myths, art and beliefs of Indigenous peoples. Endless Bronze age petroglyphic rock art, in the American South west, show Insectoid beings. The Wachoski film-maker twins even included the Zeta Reticuli Greys in their movie *Jupiter Ascending* (2014), as part of an alien hierarchy, including reptilians and human-like Nephilim beings (royalty) manipulating and 'feeding off' humanity. I am sure the planetary systems mentioned in this movie are references to Saturn and Orion's Betelgeuse, and the alien species that can move between differ-ent dimensions.

I feel Kokopelli was part of the Nephilim, the rebel angel (alien) alliance, mentioned in earlier chapters. Did an emissary from Orion, led by an Anthill Prince, come to earth to teach about the stars? Is Kokopelli also Masau'u, the creator god of the Hopi, or Osiris/Min for the ancient Egyptians? I think the Kokopelli and Masau'u are 'connected' and were involved, with the Ant People (Greys), in aiding the ancients in a previous earth-matrix. Hopi legend talks of the Ant People aiding humanity in *two* different natural cataclysms ending what the ancients called the Third and Fourth Worlds. I can't prove any of this, but, the stars and the correlations between forces we can't see and some of the earth's megalithic structures, especially how they were even built or aligned, promote intrigue enough to want to know more about our star ancestry. Let us look at one more impor-tant star connection before we go deeper into Orion and its stars.

Orion's Hunting Dogs

Canis Major contains Sirius, the bright-est star in the night sky, known as the 'dog star'. In Greek Mythology, Canis Major represented the dog 'Laelaps' a gift from Zeus to the goddess, Europa. Both Canis Major and Canis Minor (Procyon) are Orion's hunting dogs (see figure 278). They chase Lepus, the hare and sometimes the fox, while aiding Orion in his face-off with the bull

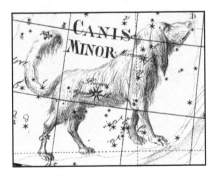

Figure 278: Orion's Dog Procyon.
Source: Uranographia, Johann Bode, Alessio Govi. (Public Domain)

(Taurus). Canis Minor was also given the name DAR.LUGAL in Sumeria, its position defined as 'the star which stands behind *it* [Orion]'. In the Babylonian compendium of stars, the 'MUL.APIN' (686 BC), the constellation Canis Minor represents a rooster (another version of Hermes), which is a symbol connected to royalty and their bloodlines (see earlier chapters).

As I have already mentioned, the dogs of Orion feature hugely in the symbolism of the hunt and are associated with royalty, who see themselves as 'children of Orion/Osiris'. As Pierre Sabak writes in *Murder of Reality* (2010):

> *The Dog Star celestially is grouped with Osiris 'Lord of the host', situated opposite Horus, Egyptian 'Kar' (the hunter), Greek 'Orion'. The rising star Sirius parallels Osiris [Orion], subsequent to his rebirth as the first King of Egypt.*[38]

M Temple Richmond, also writing on the Internet, draws an astronomical-astrological connection to the Canis (Canine) and the jackal-headed Anubis. Writing in his article, *Sirius for Seekers: The Star Sirius in Astronomy, Myth, Religion and History*, he says:

> *The jackal (or dog) – the symbol of Anubis – represented the star Sirius in Egyptian hieroglyphics perhaps as early as 3285 B.C. Thus, through the connection of Anubis the Jackal-Headed god and Sirius, Sirius came to be called the Star of the Dog, or the Dog-Star. Eventually, this imagery imparted its name to the star grouping within which Sirius is perceived. Hence, the constellation of the Dog, or Canis, using the Latin in which some constellations are designated. Today astronomy recognizes two dog constellations, the Greater and the Lesser, or Canis Majoris and Canis Minoris. The star Sirius is to be found in the Greater Dog.*[39]

Figure 279: Sirius Star System.
A double star system, Sirius is a binary star dominated by a luminous main sequence star, Sirius A **(Left)**, and a white dwarf, called Digitara, Sirius B **(Right)**.

Sirius, when observed low on the horizon during certain atmospheric conditions, is over *twenty times* brighter than our sun and twice as massive. Its brilliant white colour is tinged with blue and purple; some ancient mystery schools regard it as the 'true light' and original source of all life, including our sun. The sun was considered a 'shadow' of Sirius– which illuminates the illusory, physical world (see figure 279).

Like the Egyptians, the Greeks labeled Sirius with various forms of the 'term' Dog-Star (Alpha Canis Major) because of the star's placement in the constellation of 'Canis', Latin for Dog. Pliny, the Roman scholar of science, politics, and literature, who lived from 23 to 79 A.D, propounded the view that Sirius was highly influential upon our planet. He associated Sirius with the origin of honey at the times of its rising. The time of year Sirius rises, is still called the 'Dog Days', where Greek and Roman astrologers linked the heliacal rising of Sirius (with Orion's rising) in late July with heat, drought, sudden thunderstorms, lethargy, fever, mad dogs, and bad luck.[40]

Sirius is also represented on the walls of a step-temple at Sakkara, dating from 2700 B.C and thought to have been erected in honour of the star. Also at Denderah, great prominence is accorded to Sirius on the square zodiac there, where Sirius is symbolised in the Egyptian style by the cow-goddess, Isis. Sirius is also 'Sopdet', who in ancient Egyptian belief is related to Isis. The goddess Isis was the wife of Sahu (the hidden one), or Orion, and the mother of Sopdu ('skilled man') or a falcon god who represented the planet, Venus. Venus and Sirius are hugely connected as 'Eastern Stars' and represent the *light* (or knowledge) handed down to humanity from the *stars*. In Egyptian myth, Anubis – the dog-headed guardian of the mysteries and the gates of death, is a companion of Isis as she searches for the pieces of Osiris. The myth is based on Osiris (Orion) having been mutilated and scattered by Set (Satan) in his evil bid for the ancient Egyptian throne.

Figure 280: Sirius Personified.
The goddess Isis-Sothis-Demeter (Sopdet).

Could the thirteen bits relate to the number of stars scattered making up Orion's body? The Rosicrucians, and the Order of the Eastern Star, give Sopdet (Sirius) utmost importance. Often depicted as the All-Seeing-Eye of Heru/Horus (the Masonic concept of Christ, or the highest level of enlightenment achievable for humans on earth).

Star Goddess – Sopdet (Sirius)

Sopdet, the brightest of all fixed stars, was regarded as the most important star in the sky in ancient Egypt. The star formed the astronomical foundation of their religious system, and delineated the rhythms and cycles by which the Egyptians lived. Sopdet (meaning 'she who is sharp' or 'bright'), is said to be the cradle of human knowledge (see figure 280). The personification of Sirius as Sopdet symbolizes 'power', 'will' and 'steadfastness of purpose', exemplified by any initiate in ancient Egypt who succeeded in bridging the lower self and higher levels of consciousness.

The link between Sopdet/Sirius in occult knowledge connects to 'Ausar' the Hunter (another Osiris/Orion figure) as they are located along the celestial equator. Sopdet is regarded as the source of divine power and home of humanity's great teachers. Sopdet (Sirius) was also considered the 'flaming star' (often shown as a rising sun), also appearing in Masonic temples, on flags and in company logos. The colour 'red' is also associated with Sirius and secret societies aligning themselves with this star. The use of red carpets for royalty, and Hollywood film 'stars', is highly significant to the Orion Cult and Masonic orders that influence the world.

The *Dogon* – Sirius Connection

The African Dogon, I mentioned in *Chapter Nine*, claim there are five or six solar systems with intelligent life in the vicinity of our system.[41] This, they said, was explained to them by the visiting Nommos, also called 'Annedoti', a race of subterranean amphibious beings (fish-gnomes), from Sirius's star system. According to the Dogon legend, the Nommos lived on a planet orbiting another star in the Sirius system; these star ancestors landed on earth in an 'ark' that made a spinning descent to the ground with great noise and wind. According to the Dogon, these creatures were hermaphroditic creatures that provided their ancestors with the science of letters and numbers (language) and art (symbols) of civilisation. These gods were also called 'Masters of the Water', 'The Monitors' and 'The Teachers' and their oral tradition recalls how these 'beings' became saviours and spiritual guardians: As their beliefs state:

> *The Nommo divided his body among men to feed them; that is why it is also said that as the universe "had drunk of his body"... the Nommo also made men drink. He gave all his life principles to human beings." The Nommo was crucified and resurrected and will again visit the Earth, in the future but this time in human form. Later he will assume his amphibious form and will rule the world from the waters.*[42]

The Dogon knowledge of the Sirius constellation was way ahead of official discoveries made in the 1970s, when Sirius B was photographed for the first time.[43] Scientists today are now facing the fact we are definitely *not alone*, and that our universe contains an infinite number of other universes.

To this day the Dogon priests consider the most important star in the sky to be Sirius B, which they admit is invisible. With no telescopic instruments at their disposal, the Dogons say their knowledge of what they refer to as the 'Po-Star', was given to them by beings from Sirius, thousands of years ago. The knowledge given to them by what they call the Nommos, was *not* available to Astronomers until American, Alva G. Clark, discovered Sirius B in 1862. Sirius B is said to be a star moving more rapidly than the 'fastest' of three planets in our solar system, Pluto, Neptune and Uranus. These planets were also known to the ancient Sumerians as mentioned earlier; they were personifications of the 'Titan race', said to have been connected to an ancient epoch on Earth.

According to the Dogon, Sirius 'A' has two companion stars, 'Potol'o' (the Digitaria 'Po-star'), and 'emme 'ya tolo', the female 'Sorghum' star. According to the Dogon, when Digitaria is closest to Sirius, that star brightens when it is farthest from Sirius, it gives off a twinkling effect suggesting to the observer it is made up of several stars. The first binary star system discovered, Sirius A, easily overshadows her darker companion white dwarf star, Sirius B, invisible to the naked eye although four times the diameter of our earth. According to the Dogon, the orbit cycle of Digitaria takes 50 years, which is something modern astronomy only confirmed in the 20th Century. The Dogon clearly had access to star knowledge way in advance of Western Astronomers. For more on this see *The Sirius Mystery* (1998) by Robert Temple for in-depth insight into Sirius and the Dogon. Interestingly, the Dogon also appeared to know of the rings of Saturn, and the moons of Jupiter, before conventional astronomy.[44] But this should be no surprise when we consider the type of mysteries and wonders, such as the pyramids, along with the multitude of aboriginal stories of 'star people' coming from constellations I have considered in this chapter. Our 'ancient' ancestors were much more advanced and possibly more 'awake' due to their connections to their star ancestry.

In the final chapter of *Part One*, I want to consider our ancient ancestry in relation to star knowledge and how the ancients evolved through our connection to the stars.

Sources:

1) Taylor, Steven. *The Fall, The Insanity of the Ego in Human History and the Dawing of a New Era.* O Books, 2005, p30

2) Tolkein, J.R.R. spoken by Galadriel in *The Lord of the Rings: The Fellowship of the Ring* (1954).

3) *A Dictionary of Egyptian Civilisation.* Methuen. p158

4) Hall, Manley Palmer. *The Secret Teachings of All Ages.* pp103-106

5) Yates, F. *Giordano Bruno and the Hermetic Tradition.* Routledge, London, 1964, pp 14–18 and pp 433–434

6) Hanegraaff, W. J. *New Age Religion and Western Culture.* SUNY, 1998, p 360

7) Stapleton, H.E.; R.F. Azo & M.H. Husein. *Chemistry in Iraq and Persia in the Tenth Century AD:*

Memoirs of the Asiatic Society of Bengal. Volume 8. Calcutta: Asiatic Society of Bengal. 1927, pp. 398–403.

8) *Bullfinch's Complete Mythology*. p 7

9) Mott, Michael. *Caverns, Cauldrons and Concealed Creatures*. Grave Distractions. 2011, p127

10) *On Eastern Crossroads: Legends & Prophecies of Asia* (original). 1930, p30

11) Newton, Toyne. *The Dark Worship. The Occult's Quest for World Domination*. Vega, 2002, p42

12) Jenkins, John Major. *Maya Cosmogenesis 2012*, pp 32

13) Bryant, Page. *The Aquarian Guide to Native American Mythology*. Aquarian Press, 1991, p31

14) Matlock, Gene. *The last Atlantis book You'll Ever Read*. Dandelion Books, 2001, p116

15) Kindaichi & Yoshida. 1949, p. 349.

16) Cambell, Joseph. *Primitive Myths*. p277

17) Loos, Noel; Osani. Takeshi, eds; *Indigenous Minorities and Education: Australian and Japanese Perspectives on their Indigenous Peoples, the Ainu, Aborigines and Torres Strait Islanders*. Tokyo: Sanyusha Publishing. 1993

18) https://www.starmythworld.com/mathisencorollary/2014/12/odysseus-and-orion.html

19) Hill, Douglas. *Man, Myth & Magic*, 1970. p233

20) *Man Myth & Magic*. Issue 8. Published by Purnell 1970, p233

21) https://harrypotter.fandom.com/wiki/Arcturus_Black_II

22) https://en.wikipedia.org/wiki/Wild_man

23) Barber, Richard and Riches, Anne. *A Dictionary of Fabulous Beasts*. Boydell Press, 1971, p154

24) Ellis, Ralph. *Jesus, Last of the Pharaohs*. 1997, p68

25) Sabak, Pierre. *Murder of Reality*. 2010, pp 48-50

26) https://feminismandreligion.com/2015/08/26/artio-celtic-goddess-of-wild-life-transformation-and-abundance-by-judith-shaw/

27) M. Baigent, R. Leigh and H. Lincoln. *The Holy Blood and the Holy Grail*. Corgi, London, 1986, p 250.

28) https://britishbigfootsightingreports.com/category/british-bigfoot-accounts/

29) Coleman, Loren. *Bigfoot, The True Story of Apes in America*. Paraview Pocket Books. 2003 p5

30) *Ibid*, p8.

31) Fahrenbach, Dr. W. Henner. *A Medieval Sasquatch*. Bigfoot Field Research Organisation

32) Swerdlow, Stewart. *Blue Blood, True Blood, Conflict & Creation*. Expansions Publishing, 2002, p156

33) T. McNally, Raymond & Florescu, Radu. *In Search of Dracula. A true History of Dracula & Vampire Legends*. New English Library. 1975 p7

34) Coleman. Lauren. *Bigfoot, The True Story of Apes in America*. Paraview Pocket Books 2003. p11

35) Matlock, Gene. *The last Atlantis book You'll Ever Read*. Dandelion Books, 2001 p 78

36) www.viewzone.com/kokopelli.html

37) Bradfield. *An Interpretation of Hopi Culture*, pp 290-296

38) Sabak, Pierre. *Murder of Reality*. 2010 p334

39) http://www.harrypotterforseekers.com/articles/siriusforseekers.php

40) https://en.wikipedia.org/wiki/Dog_days

41) Temple, Robert. *The Sirius Mystery*. Arrow 1999. p278

42) *Ibid*, p38

43. *Ibid*, p40

44) M Griaule, G Dieterlen. *The Dogon of the French Sudan* (1948) pp. 286-298

14

HUMAN EARTH STARS

'First and Future Consciousness'

The thing about perfection is that it is unknowable, it's impossible,
but its also right in front of us, all the time
KEVIN FLYNN - (*Tron Legacy*)

It seems that from overwhelming sources of information, Paleolithic humans worshipped numerous animal gods/goddesses. Amongst the art and sculpture showing animal/human hybrids, we find reference to a alien, human-like beings that could perform miraculous feats. The stars (especially Orion) were a focus along with the earth itself. As already touched on throughout the book so far, these gods were the 'brains' behind advanced civilisations that seemed to have appeared out of nowhere to become the Egyptian and Central American pyramid societies. According to certain sources these 'gods' could 'create life' through knowledge of DNA and 'measure time' as recorded in the Sumerian Tablets and the *Pop Vuh*, the bible for indigenous Mesoamerican tribes. In fact, the *Long Count Calendar* used by the ancient Olmecs and later Mayan culture of Mesoamerica, was probably inspired by an intelligence with a higher understanding of the planetary precession and celestial events spanning millions of years. According to the Sumerian Tablets, the Anunnaki gods (see *Chapter One*) are said to have interbred with earth women creating a hybrid bloodline of 'god kings', which we now know as the Pharaoh/Royal dynasties and their likes around the ancient world.

According to the late scholar, Zechariah Sitchin, the Anunnaki (or Shemsu Hor) visited our earth at least 400,000 years ago. In his books *The Stairway to Heaven* (1980), *The Wars of Gods and Men* (1985), *Divine Encounters* (1995), Sitchin writes how *their* breeding programmes, which included 'genetic trials' (in test tubes), created what the Sumerian texts call a 'primitive worker' (or worker race), to carry out the wishes of the gods. The obsession with 'cloning' and altering DNA to this day comes from elite families and descendants of the 'gods' and their desire to 'manipulate' *all* life on earth. In fact, it would be safe to say, that interference in our DNA structure would appear to be continuing, supported by worldwide reports of alleged 'alien abductions' (including cattle mutilations) and through global, nefarious Eugenics policies. Along with an increase in GM foods, vaccination programes (including 'test-tube' created viruses), and other chemicals in food and water, all are designed to alter our DNA. Never before in the history of our species have we faced such monumental tampering with our genetic codes.

The ancients understood the DNA and its connections to 'gravity', 'electro-magnetics' and 'light'. German physicist, Hartmut Müller, working at the Institute for Cosmic Research in Russia during the 1980's, pioneered studies into biofields and the interaction between DNA and gravitational standing waves permeating the whole Universe. According to the late George Merkl, PhD, the Sumerian clay texts also contain a library of biological information, showing how 'living cells' can be affected by weak electromagnetic frequencies and that a 'biofield' pervades the entire universe. Some writers have called the biofield, the 'cosmic soup' or the 'cosmic internet' (see figure 281). Electromagnetic plasma, the stars, suns and planets (everything that lives) lives in the library of biological information. In other words, our cell structure and DNA, as understood by advanced intelligence behind the great civilisations, knew that *all life* is 'connected' to a universal waveform-energy. The ancients measured it through 'sacred geometry', 'numerology' and 'astronomy'. All the amazing pyra-

Figure 281: Cosmic Human.
The Biofield, or 'Cosmic Soup', connects *all* electromagnetic life in the Universe.

mid structures, especially in Egypt, through to the building of the Gothic Cathedrals, were designed by an 'intelligence' that understood the interconnectedness of 'sound', 'geometry' and a universal standing wave, which, according to the likes of Dr. Müller, affects our DNA structure.

Mitochondrial Robo-Humans

Science has also recently discovered 37 *strange* 'mitochondrial' DNA structures included in our cells, and this discovery about the origins of DNA replication, according to some scientists, offers startling confirmation that mitochondrial DNA is in fact the result of some kind of 'alien interception'. Unlike other DNA, mitochondrial DNA happens to have a distinct circular structure. Thus it is extremely plausible that aliens (the star gods) could have used this circular structure to conceal the thirty-seven genes of mito-chondrial DNA; the 'concealment' would allow these genes to replicate under their own steam and thus maintain their independence from human DNA, while at the same time existing within it. Could we be a genetically modified species created by extraterrestrials so to influence our minds and therefore our world-reality? Alan Alford, the author of *Gods of the New Millennium* (1996), is just one of many researchers open to the concept of alien intervention when accounting for anomalies surrounding man's origin and evolution. He writes:

> *Homo sapiens have acquired a modern anatomy, language capability, and a sophisticated Brain (well beyond the needs of everyday existence) apparently in defiance of the laws of Darwinism. There are a number of possible explanations for this anomaly. One is that mankind evolved in the sea, and that crucial fossil evidence is missing. Another is that Darwinian theory itself has a missing link. And the third explanation is that the genes for modern man were suddenly implanted by an intelligent extraterrestrial species who colonised the Earth.[1]*

In the *Enuma Elish*, the Babylonian creation Epic, the god Marduk (a serpent god), while listening to the words of other gods, was said to have con-ceived the idea of creating an intelligent device to do their (the gods) will. Marduk (quite possibly an extraterrestrial), said:

> *I shall bring into existence a robot; his name shall be Man.[2]*

Was this robot-human Homo sapiens? An experiment destined to become a 'slave race' for the gods. Or are we talking actual biological robots (or droids) built to carry out tasks for the gods in ancient times? When I say robot, I mean a robot in the symbolic sense here, as it is possible to 'organ-ise' intelligence biologically to act 'robot-like', without the notion of a 'machine' and computers as we know them. The human brain *is* a sophisti-cated computer, so 'programming' it, or 'manipulating DNA', to suit a pro-gramme, would be easy for an advanced species to do. By advanced and intelligent, I also mean 'artificial', which, as we shall see in *Part Two*, is a significant part of our connection to 'extraterrestrial life' especially in rela-tion to Orion.

The influx of movies featuring robots might not be so 'science fiction' today, considering the advancement of science, especially 'underground science, is usually five or six decades ahead of what the public can see. The concepts in the movie, *Interstellar* (2014) directed by Christopher Nolan, shows us NASA, TARS, artificially intelligent robots, programmed with personality, characterized as witty, sarcastic, and humorous. *Interstellar* is teeming with concepts relating to sentient beings called 'Bulk Beings' able to perceive higher dimensions and 'see time' just as another physical dimension, allowing them to 'create wormholes' and higher-dimensional 'tesseracts'. The Bulk Beings are no different to the Gnostic Aeons I talked about in *Chapter Four*. As the movie suggests, the tesseracts are an enormous, hyper-cubic, grid-like structure and a means of communication for the bulk beings to express action through gravity with humanity. As I will come to in the next part of the book, the 'robot phenomena', along with Artificial Intelligence (A.I) is not necessarily something we (humanity) have created; it is technology *alien* to our original 'higher dimensional species and, I believe, *is* a 'threat' to our existence. I will explain why, later in the book.

Figure 282: Ancient Sumerian Robots.
Drawings of ancient Robot-like entities copied from the Sumerian Tablets?

The Sumerian tablets mentioned in *Chapter One*, said to be 4000 years old, seem to depict what looks like robots (see figure 282). Ancient occult texts also refer to a slave 'robot-like' creature as golem.[3] Many people who have had modern-day encounters with extraterrestrials also tell of similar 'beings' looking like robots. Whitley Strieber, the author of the bestselling book *Communion* (1987), described his personal alien encounters with what seems like a toy alien-like robot creature. There is much more to know about such ancient robot phenomenon, and in a later chapter, I will explore this important theme in great detail.

Human Gods (Stars)

According to neurobiologists, it seems as though the human brain went through a rapid change in neural ability at some point during the upper Palaeolithic period (30,000 years ago). Some of the most sensitive artwork has been discovered from this time and according to some scientists the use of symbols by our prehistoric ancestors seems to go back 100,000 years at least. Around 70,000 years ago, humans began migrating out of Africa, but when they arrived in Eurasia, they found they were not alone. Neanderthals had been living in the region for hundreds of thousands of years, and their bodies were well adapted to its harsh climate. Modern humans can fight off infections, like flu (coronavirus) and hepatitis, because of Neanderthal DNA inherited from their ancestors, new research has found.[4] In truth, we are immense biological computers that have developed a sophisticated anti-virus immune system, and I would suggest any 'external' 'invasion' (from alien or artificial life forms) has manipulated changes to our biology. Technology and drugs, I am sure, are responsible for more damage and changes to our biological 'field'; as I will come to in *Part Two*, we are being prepared as a species for a massive 'upgrade', whether we like it or not.

If our ancestors were genetically changed from Neanderthals to Cro-Magnon within a short period of time (hence the missing link), then what, or who, facilitated this upgrading of the brain? Put another way, what made artists out of Neanderthals? Answers to this question seem to point to an intelligence of a higher form (or an upgrade), carried out by custodial 'gods' that altered the DNA of our species. According to ancient texts and myths, these 'gods' made man in their image. The western, almost apologetic, excuse for the sudden leap in evolution along with the total disappearance of a race at the same time is called a transition. According to leading scientists, Neanderthals:

> *Could learn how to make fine blades but they could not conceive of a spirit world to which people went after death. Nor could they conceive of social distinctions that depended on categorisations of generations, past, present and future.*[5]

Yet, just at the time of the demise of these so-called one-dimensional conscious creatures, we find some of the most amazing Palaeolithic cave art. Was the Neanderthal a lot more evolved than our experts give him credit? Or were these genetic streams remnants of the original Atlantis evolutionary period I talked about in earlier chapters?

The Mayan, *Popol Vuh*, has a story of extraterrestrial gods who came down and made man in their own image. When they first made 'man' he was so perfect – he was said to live as long as the gods – he could see far and wide –was clairvoyant – and was as wise as 'they' were. However, the gods realised they had made a 'competitor' who was as wise as the gods themselves. So, therefore, it is said they destroyed their 'experiment' (first human prototype) and started over, creating present-day humans. Modern humans now live shorter lifetimes, use less brain capacity, and are here to act as a servant race to the gods. In truth, we are in servitude to a consciousness manifesting fear, and if *fear* could take on a physical form, it could take the form of interdimensional forces like the Archons and demons I mentioned in the first few chapters.

Official history suggests original human forms died out and were followed by a new species; thus Cro-Magnon and Homo sapiens (modern man) replaced, or outnumbered, the Neanderthals. But archaeologists, working in the Middle East in recent years, have discovered evidence to show that all these species existed during the *same* period on earth. The 'missing link' connecting them, explaining the sudden and dramatic changes in the appearance of their physical forms, has never been found because establishment academia would rather stay ignorant to the possibility of a diversity of extraterrestrial forms interacting with humanity in the ancient world. The same mentality also debunks 97% of DNA as 'junk', because scientists don't know what it does! It could just be the majority of DNA, relating to the 95% of all matter in the universe (much of which we can't see with our eyes), is the home of what we call gods or extraterrestrials. The 'Fall' of Mankind, recorded in ancient texts, on one level, is a symbolic story of the separation of the original human DNA (Adam and Eve) and the creation of a *new* species placed on 'middle earth' (in this dimension) to serve the gods. Custodial gods, possibly originating in Orion (mirrored in the stars as constellations), could have ruled over a custom-made human being. The decline in extra-sensory abilities, such as 'telepathy' and 'interdimensional communication' (which are part and parcel of our original human DNA), could have been 'reprogrammed' to shut out all that can be seen, felt and understood beyond the physical world. There is so much more to know about our DNA and capabilities of our mind's true power.

Falling beyond the Spectrum

I feel humanity does not originate from within the boundaries of a physical earth. In our true form, we, like other intelligences (across the universal spectrum of life), are infinite consciousness. Who we are, and where we have come from, often filters through the 'programming' imposed upon our consciousness via our DNA (physical family) and other external 'mind programmes' (education, TV, media and what the authorities want us to 'perceive'). Visionaries, free thinkers and 'maverick souls' (throughout history), have been a channel for higher intelligence and Superconsciousness, reminding us of our higher purpose. What we perceive to be 'time' is also connected to our physical servitude (to the old order of gods) and our calendar systems imposed through religion, the state and now, money, all are part of the ultimate programming tying us into flesh and bone, keeping us focused on *only* the material world. We are a 'possessed' species that has forgotten our true spiritual heritage. As the late American Indian poet, singer and activist, John Trudell, said in his song *Crazy Horse* (2007):

> ... *Predators face he possessed a race*
> *Possession a war that doesn't end*
> .... *Decoration on chains that binds*
> *Mirrors gold, the people lose their minds* ...

Yes, we have 'lost our minds' (look at the world around us), and it is obvious the more we choose to become conscious and awake to other versions of reality. The so-called Woke movement, which has appeared in recent years, is the epitome of not 'seeing' the need for 'higher consciousness', 'freedom of expression for *all*' and the need to care for people's views and alternative ideas. As I have said on social media, being 'woke' is not to be confused with being truly 'awake', the two are not the same thing.

According to Swiss psychologist and psychiatrist, Carl Jung, the collective unconscious contains 'archetypes', universal primordial images and ideas. In Jung's time, archetypes were accepted mostly as cultural phenomenon or as something 'originating' in the inherited structure of the brain. However, scientists have since begun to look for a physical mediator between the brains of the people, still assuming that archetypes, controlling our minds, are originating in the brain. They do not. The brain and the mind are not the same thing. In other words, our minds are a storehouse of all possible 'past and future' epochs. From this perspective, the brain can be compared to a 'computer processing unit' and the mind to the 'software' that facilitates the evolution of our Universe. If the software is upgraded, or the CPU upgraded in some form, then so would the physical form. The mass extinctions of species were actually mass 'replacements' of species with more advanced brain capacity, while having capability to hold memories of previous evolutionary phases within the cell structure of our bodies. The mind (or consciousness) can 'programme' our DNA, too. Not only has the hardware (brain) been altered through evolution, but the software (the mind) too has been programmed to 'project' specific realities and paradigms. Fight or flight is one of these early models and, in truth, the mind is connected to a collective matrix mind, governed by fear and survival since the birth of our earliest human ancestors, a subject I will return to in the second part of this book.

Humanity has within its genome structure memories of past evolutionary phases and the ability to 'call on the time' (commonly described as the 'Fall') and utilise our ancient memories. I have seen the period called the

Fall, in dreams and visions, which mainly come through images associated with what can only be described as a hairy 'Wookie-like' race of humans (see previous chapter). These ancient humans are living in caves, especially in the Americas (see my book *Aeon Rising- The Battle for Atlantis Earth* 2017). In other versions of these visions, I have seen what are now described as bird-men (griffins) appearing at that time, and 'rounding up' large portions of Neanderthal-like wookies, to be used in experiments. None of this imagery necessarily relates to an ancient era. What these visions showed me, is the possibility of parallel realities, both 'ancient and futuristic' (same thing), all existing as narratives that can be tapped into through memories in our DNA. More importantly, it is our art, imagination and creativity, in all of its forms, that can reveal 'untapped', or 'unknown' levels, of our DNA – our consciousness. Beyond these 'other worlds' or 'other dimensions of being', is the heart and higher consciousness. When we forget where our true home resides, we forget who we are, and then we become merely 'human beings' who fell from 'being human'. As the 12th Century artist, visionary and abbess, Saint Hildergard of Bingen, said of the time before the Fall:

Art is a half effaced recollection of a higher state from which we have fallen since the time of Eden.

Bingen's statement, along with much research into cave art by historians and neurobiologists, hints at the possibility that human consciousness, through our prehistoric ancestors, went through immense neurological and biological changes around 40,000 years ago. You could say our human ancestors' brains were upgraded (as if by magic), to facilitate what some scientists refer to as a 'higher-order consciousness'. In mythology and oral traditions spanning the globe, this new-found ability of a 'new earth race' was described as the 'gods giving knowledge to the first humans'. Legends associated with Prometheus and the 'light-bearers' recorded in ancient myth are part of this story (see *Chapter Six*). However, the more one researches into subjects of alien visitation and star people and relevant mythological accounts, it seems one strand of our original ancestors, the

Figure 283: Original Earth Stars. My drawing of what Neanderthals may have looked like. Neanderthals were the original 'Superconscious' humans in my view. Possibly Atlantean/Lemurian tribes; survivors of ancient cataclysms? © Neil Hague

'Neanderthals and Miocene apes', disappeared abruptly, while their 'replacement', Homo sapiens, seemed to go on to flourish (see figure 283). It is the latter species that we, in our modern physical form, are said to have originated from. The course of this book would be insufficient to cover this particular strain of the subject in great detail and I am not a scientist (obviously), but I feel it is worth investigating further the so-called, sudden 'Fall of the Neanderthal' in line with the discovery of earth's oldest artworks.

Atlantis and the Artist Apes & 32 Mystical Pathways of Wisdom

It seems from an overwhelming amount of historical and modern-day evidence, a highly evolved civilisation once existed on the planet. As I have already shown, these advanced ancient civilisations have been referred to as Atlantis, Antilla, Aztlan, Shangri-la, Hyperborea, to mention just a few. According to many ancient texts, this global colony was one of several land masses, now submerged under the sea, in the area today called the Atlantic. It is also said that its sister continent was another ancient landmass called Lemuria, located in a place where the Pacific Ocean now sits. Many battles between the gods, recorded in ancient myth, are really stories telling of earth's wars and a technological 'star wars' between these two continents. My reading of the subject leads me to believe what was once called Atlantis, is actually on a par with our current global civilisation today. We are rebuilding it, as I will come to in the next part. The state of mind that manifested Atlantis is prevalent today through the rise in technological advancements, like cloning, hi-tech weaponry (star wars), globalization and 'artificial intelligence'. We are becoming Atlantis revisited. Is it unreasonable to suggest that what has become a collective amnesia point in history, called Atlantis, may well be a code for a 'state of mind', which exists when our collective consciousness reaches a certain level? Simply put, did Atlantis the movie (part one) become Atlantis the 'Fall' (part two), when we lost our connection to higher levels of consciousness? Much ancient art (including cave art) and myth seems to capture similar themes relating to these *two* states of mind (movies), often symbolised as duality in earth's evolution.

Genevieve von Petzinger, a Canadian paleoanthropologist and rock art researcher, finishing up her doctorate at the University of Victoria, stumbled across some interesting ideas relating to symbols and our ancient ancestors in terms of originating with *two* states of mind. She studied some of the oldest art in the world. Ice Age cave art created by early humans in Europe between 10,000 and 40,000 years ago (the time of the Neanderthal), leaves us with some interesting symbolism associated with a language that could be the first form of organized communication amongst the Paleolithic hunters, according to Petzinger. Her specific focus on geometric signs found at many European sites, explained how certain cave art images/symbols seemed to be part of a human cognitive evolution, an ancient system of patterns, including migration, symbolism and graphic communication. What she found was a common set of *thirty-two* symbols in use between 40,000 and 10,000 years ago. What I found interesting is the numerological link to the mention of the 'gods' in biblical terms. Among the 434 Hebrew words in Genesis, the word Elohim is used *thirty-two* times. The number 32 also correlates with the Hebrew word for heart (lev) and maybe the ancients spoke with their true brains - their hearts, through this first form of coded language found in art.

As mentioned in *Chapter One*, the ancient landmass called Lemuria comes from the word 'Mu' or 'Mu-devi', which means the 'Land Ancestral' or 'Land of the Ancestors'. Mu-Devi was also the Hindu mother goddess, while Shiva was her counterpart and was seen as the great father of humankind. Lemuria was the mother ancestor and Atlantis the father. Atlantis was thought to have been a centre for alien activity, a hub for advanced science (genetics), language and advanced mathematical concepts. Many scholars still wonder why the likes of Sumeria, Egypt and the Indo-Aryan civilisations already had 'fully formed' alphabets, mathematical systems and symbolic cosmologies from their offset. The reason for this is that all of these advanced civilisations were surviving colonies of Atlantis the movie (part one), whereas the more Asian and aboriginal cultures to the South were said to be satellites of the Lemurian civilisation. Deities, like Osiris (Orion) worshipped in Egypt, Nimrod in Sumeria, and Shiva in India, for example, were said to have come out of the Atlantis era. Thoth, of the Egyptian Pantheon mentioned in the last chapter, was clearly some kind of Atlantean demi-god, or star entity. This is why the same gods and archetypes, under different names, crop up all over the ancient world, because Atlantis was a *global* state of evolution – no different from the now global paradigm we partake in as a species. In my view, the ancestors *are* the 97% of our DNA classified as junk, or 'non-coding', relating to roughly 90% or more of our brain capacity we don't use. Imagine what we could truly see if we were fully activated through our ability to access unseen worlds connected to noncoding DNA (see Figure 284). Other realities and life forms, which are all part of the same waveform information (on different frequencies) constructing the Universe, stars, suns, planets, etc., could be more readily accessible to our 'ancient eyes'. Lumeria and Atlantis are ancestral links to the 'Dreamtime', via the 97% of our DNA termed 'junk'.

We are recreating Atlantis (blueprint) today as we engage in all of the possible scenarios that separated us from accessing other levels of con-

Figure 284: Worlds Within Worlds.
Unseen worlds (beyond the visible spectrum) connected to noncoding DNA. We are a universe of alien worlds. © Neil Hague

sciousness – namely fear in all its forms. Fostering war, segregation of peoples and using technology, science and religion to *control* indigenous peoples of earth are part of the *control* that was Atlantis. And nothing will change unless we change our perceptions of who we are and what we can truly achieve. The cataclysms and rifts that brought about the end of 'Atlantis part one', manifesting as earthquakes, floods and volcanic eruptions, on one level, caused a 'rift' between the human heart and mind. This separation, in my view, disconnected humanity from its true potential, leading to massive changes in our DNA and human brain. The same 'rifts' are appearing 'again', as today we move through another change in consciousness. The potential to 'see' into the Dreamtime and retain the knowledge of our original form, came crashing down like an iceberg as we began a myopic 'frozen' state, locked into fear and survival. According to much scholarly research, not least the work of James Churchwood (see page 32) in the first half of the last century, it has been suggested that Atlantis was initially ruled by the gods (extraterrestrials), but eventually came under the rule of hybrid bloodlines (half-alien, half-human), I talked about in earlier chapters. These are the genetic bloodlines that retained a connection to the stars and to Atlantis, and which were given the name 'fallen angels'; more on angels in *Part Two*.

The gods that fell to earth, as recorded in the Old Testament and in the *Book of Enoch*, as the fallen angels, created the inspiration for our religious templates that became the movie 'Atlantis the Fall', or 'Atlantis part two', which is the time frame we are still in. And if we are comparing evolutionary landmarks with movie sequels, then is 'Atlantis part three' about to premiere in 2030-50? The same alien overlords, or gods (working through the Orion Cult) intend to reorder the world, yet again, using artificial intelligence. The coronavirus (Covid-19) Pandemic, unleashed on the world in 2020, will be remembered as the first stage (or attempt) to usher in a new global Atlantis. The fallen angels, or consciousness, are by definition the latest modern human 'genetic' forms and as I will come to in *Part Two*, synthetic humans are meant to be the next (unnatural) evolutionary stage. As I have already touched on earlier, the gods of Atlantis were the Annunaki, Rephaim, Titans and the Watchers recorded in myths and texts all over the ancient world. They were the fallen angels recorded in the original garden of Edinu (Eden), and this particular genetic stream *are* human-dinosaurs - the brains behind the demise of earth's indigenous peoples' connection to their ancestors (or Superconsciousness).

Human-Animal People and the Cave

As I have already shown, according to many indigenous tribes, both the bear and the monkey race were said to have lived on the earth in ancient times, before the arrival of 'humans'. These myths and legends could relate to an interstellar level of consciousness accessed by a Neanderthal/Miocene people. As I mentioned in the last chapter, Thoth in ancient Egypt, a monkey god, was considered the originator of science and letters, and in ancient India, the Monkey god, Hanuman also had magical abilities and was attributed with similar skills. Almost every Christian cathedral also shows reverence to the monkey gods in some shape or form. More often than not, they are direct references to either Enkidu, the ape-man who accompanied Gilgamesh in his search for immortality, or Thoth. As I touched on in the previous chapter, Hanuman was said to be immortal, with the instantaneous ability to reduce, or grow to whatever size he liked, which seems to relate to the knowledge of microcosm and macrocosm and 'higher dimensions'. In Native American lore, the 'Uncegi' of Sioux oral tradition (another form of Bigfoot) was said to appear as fire tornadoes, at the time of cleansing, a period we are moving further into. The horrendous fires witnessed in Australia in 2020, and the endless fires in other continents (not least the USA), are on one level, not 'natural'. Whatever is creating them is aware of what the Hopi call, 'the end of the Fourth World' (Age), and therefore could be manipulating such burnings through the use of technology to suit an agenda? Interestingly, the fires that have ravaged many parts of the world over the past fifteen years, some of which I saw from the air while taking flights in the USA, often swirled uncontrollably. According to Native American prophecy, these are one of many signs of the current world being cleansed; and the onset of a new paradigm (collective reality) embracing humanity at this time.

I feel the Neanderthals were more advanced than we have been led to believe. Just the art of these ancients tells us more about their coming to terms with a new level of perception and a change of 'world matrix' around 26,000 years ago. From another viewpoint, did our ancestors set in motion our current evolutionary timeline, through their newly-powered level of awareness? When we consider the oldest forms of visual communication, to date, art (right brain activity), then it says much about what type of creatures and levels of consciousness our human ancestors were *before* the biblical Fall. And why, in our current civilisation, is more emphasis placed on left brain logic (written word, mathematics and science), while drawing is diminished and relegated in schools to the level of a 'poor relation'? The stream of consciousness that has become modern humanity has created a biological model that serves the gods (the fallen angels) of Atlantis well. As we are starting to see, 'technology' is our 'new god', but is it really new? We have facilitated a different kind of paradigm shift, born from ancient chambers of the mind. As I will come to in *Part Two*, we are being prepared for another upgrade, where we interface with the 'gods'.

I also feel that many different extraterrestrial races (gods) have seeded the genetic mix we now call the human race; much rock art is showing us the types of intelligence our ancestors either encountered, or were connected to. Orion is one of the main sources for such extraterrestrial races and the structures and hierarchies are very much inspired by the ultimate 'empire-building' consciousness, I feel originates in Orion. The cave was more than a shelter for the first Homo sapiens, it was a symbol of their innermost mind, a place where images are born and become reality. On the other hand, the *cave* was a place where the mind of our ancestors struggled to adjust to its new environment, a world (or matrix) where human consciousness could be born.

The Promethean Gene

I believe humans are naturally gifted with an ability to see, feel, imagine and exude an energy often referred to as our charisma, magnetism - our aura. The origins of the human soul and spirit (the imagination) are all aspects of a source that creates all life. As creators in our own right, we have the ability to draw in and express a vital energy, especially when we are in a heightened state of awareness, I call this state of awareness the 'Promethean Gene'. You could say it is magic and power emanating from a person that makes them seem superhuman and charismatic to others. In some cases, this energy can be turned on, and tuned into, by forces existing outside of our three-dimensional reality, so an individual concerned, can seem godlike. Our thought-forms (energies) can be of a lower frequency range; others are of a higher level of love and wisdom, but ultimately, thought influences reality. There's another crucial point to highlight about DNA: it is also the home of what we call the emotions. This is the greatest deceit of all that holds us in servitude to the physical world, because we accept our instinctive responses and reactions must be coming from

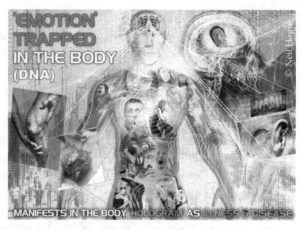

Figure 285: Thought Creates Our Reality.
We 'manifest' ourselves and the world around us through how we 'perceive' form (reality). © Neil Hague

us; they must be who we are, *they are not who we are.* Emotions are phenomena of the DNA often caused by trauma and thought patterns passed from generation to generation (see figure 285). People say things like 'I am only human', and they talk of 'human nature', as if this is who they are. But it's not. They are the consciousness of Infinite Possibility and what we call 'human' is the DNA mind, emotions and holographic 'biological body'.

What we align ourselves with through our thoughts and actions will attract the same states of mind to us. As always it is the intention behind the thought that creates reality. In this way, angels can also be demons, depending on our state of mind and how open our hearts are. In more

modern terms it could be said that what we eat, watch and think is what we become, which carries truth. All life exists because of the creative impulse igniting our ideas, which becomes solid form and manifest in our world. Everything from a mountain to a teaspoon only exists because of energy (particles of matter), which solidify, or slow down, to become physical objects (see figure 286).

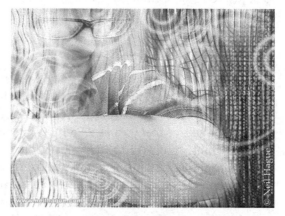

Figure 286: We Manifest 'Form' (the World).
We 'manifest' ourselves and the world around us through how we 'perceive' in*form*ation (reality).

Figure 287: *Everything* **is Waveform.**
Human wavefields connect with other fields through wave entanglement – we experience this as relationships of every kind. People, places, jobs, lifestyles, etc., are waveform entanglements. © Neil Hague

Whether it is the mind of the earth (Gaia) shaping the landscape of her body to accommodate changes brought on by how we, as a species, relate to her, or an idea in the mind of an individual, which then becomes a painting, book or physical object in the physical world; all physical forms exist because of the influence of nonphysical forces. It is waveform information that constructs our world as we 'entangle' with others in the 'collective' information field (figure 287). We are continually creating our reality (collectively and individually) through how we think, imagine and see reality. It is a process of delivering our personal magic to the world and this is why our ancestors entered the dreamtime – to shape reality. The collective waveform field is from where we change the physical world. Think only good things, live *without* fear, and be at *peace*, and *all* these things will 'manifest'. If the intent and feelings are coming from our heart, the 'true brain', we cannot fail to heal our world.

The Brain as a Radio Receiver

According to mainstream science, we have an ancient part of our brain called the 'R complex' or the 'reptilian' brain stem which, mainstream science accepts evolved over millions of years. The brain stem is the oldest and smallest region in the evolving human brain; it is more like the entire brain of present-day reptiles, hence its name. It is found at the base of the skull, emerging from our spinal column. The R complex is also similar to the brain possessed by hardy reptiles that preceded mammals (according to mainstream science), roughly 200 million years ago. It's 'preverbal', but controls autonomic life functions such as breathing, heart rate and the fight or flight mechanism. Lacking language, its impulses are instinctive and ritualistic. It's concerned with fundamental needs such as 'survival', 'physical maintenance', 'hoarding', 'dominance', 'preening' and 'mating traits' that can be found in every human world to this day. The R complex is also found in life forms such as lizards, crocodiles and birds – the gods of the ancient world.

According to scientists like Carl Sagan, the reptilian part of the brain gives us our hierarchical and ritualistic behaviour, including the need for top-down control, traditions and territorial actions. All these characteristics can be found in the very structures governing our modern world. Therefore, our view of the world has been, thanks to this ancient part of our make up, very 'obsessed' with time, with 'clock-watching' and the 'matrix mind' so much so, that we have forgotten our connection to the Dreamtime. Even timetables (daily routines) in schools and colleges are described as a 'matrix', and this word sums up ' R complex perception'. With the infusion of reptilian genes somewhere back in our evolutionary history, we have a perfect vehicle for 'one track', or 'one frequency', perception and this has given us what both ancient and modern sources refer to as the 'dualistic mind'. As I will show in the next few chapters, Orion's stars seem to be archetypal when it comes to duality.

Light-Bearers

As mentioned in earlier chapters, Prometheus was credited with the discovery of magical power and the human ability to *imagine* the future by projecting a horizon of possibilities within the mind. This ability is supposedly what sets humans and our animal ancestors apart today. Could this ability relate to a sudden shift in human evolution from Paleolithic animal-humans to a new human and brain capacity? Much Paleolithic rock art suggests a fascination for imaginary sequences, involving both animals and humanoids, that seem to emanate a *personal magic*. Images of stars, suns, refer to higher consciousness, a gift from the gods as recorded in many myths. The role of the trickster hero, in relation to some of the Orion-Prometheus symbols and myths mentioned in earlier chapters, was one who brought knowledge of eternal life and magical power to humanity. As I have touched on already, the 'gods', in my view, relate to a mixture of extraterrestrial intelligence, animal intelligence (which is much brighter than great swathes of humanity today), and 'artificial intelligence'. These streams of 'intelligence' were used to create the Homo sapiens species.

We are said to have been made in the image of the gods; therefore we are gods and goddesses in our own right, with immense tools at our disposal. What we have, which was always there, is the knowledge that we are 'light beings', capable of using our minds, creativity and imagination to change the illusion in which we dwell. This is one of the great truths hidden from us. We are projected points of light originating from the source of *Infinite Possibilities*. People experience 'stillness' and 'silence' in states of deep meditation through which they can access 'knowingness' – the *All-knowingness* of *The One*.

Forces I have highlighted throughout *Part One*, not least the priests behind the Orion and Saturn Cults that created religion, do not want humanity remembering a former glory – as light beings connected to Superconsciousness – *All-knowingness*. If humanity could awaken from its spiritual slumber, open its eyes and heart, then our divine form (intelligent light) would automatically flood every cell of our being. We don't have to go out and find this level of consciousness, it is already within us and waiting to be tapped into whenever we choose to do so. By accessing our imagination and using our own creative powers, we automatically activate and recognise the light within us – no saviour figure required! In truth, we are all aspects of the same consciousness that creates both light and dark, Heaven and Hell and, love and fear. We also have the *imagination* to recreate any reality we require in our lives. Our highest power is our ability to reshape our destiny, create our own realities and move between different dimensions of thought. All of this takes place through our personal creativity, our process of self-discovery and our ability to laugh and play in the playground called Earth!

In the next part of the book I want to go deeper into the stars (the heavens), notably the Orion constellation, and show how stellar intelligence not only influences our reality but has been influencing Earth for a very long time. Our reality (world) is being *transformed* to meet a specific 'alien intelligence'. One that is **not** human and is building a 'new world' structure, which makes topics and themes found in Science Fiction books and movies, look far too real and everpresent today.

Sources:

1) Tsarion, Michael. *Atlantis, Alien Visitation & genetic Manipulation*. Angels At Work Publishing. 2000, p26
2) Sitchin, Zecharia. *Divine Encounters*. p276
3) Swerdlow, Stuart. *True Blood, Blue Blood*. p128
4) Neurobiologists accept that the fundamental cell type in the brain is the neuron. Neurons are connected to other neurons by synapses. See the work of Gerald Edleman
5) Lewis William, David. *Mind in the Cave*. Thames & Hudson, p190

PART TWO

Heavens War & the
Reign of Chaos

Do you know the laws of the heavens?
Can you set up God's dominion over the earth?
JOB. CHAPTER 38 VERSE 33

15

INVISIBLE SUN

Orion's Projector

There has to be an invisible sun
It gives its heat to everyone,
There has to be an invisible sun
That gives us hope when the whole day's done...
STUART COPLAND (THE POLICE)

I have pondered for many years on deeper symbolism relating to Orion and its influence on human perception. The symbolism and Cult I've illustrated in *Part One*, along with their focus on Orion's stars, are part of a multi-dimensional system of *influence*. In this chapter, I want to 'unravel' concepts that I feel relate to Orion's *purpose,* and probably why the ancients focused on it with such accuracy. More so, our modern world is still locked into Orion's influence through 'empire-like' systems of governance inter-linked to alien intelligence. All will become relevant as I venture through celestial constructs bonded to Orion and the stars (suns) that forge links with other worlds.

Three Forces Combined

In Myth and allegory, Orion was born from the hide of the bull (Taurus) through the interaction of three gods: Apollo, Vulcan and Mercury. In vari-ous alchemical texts, Orion is 'conceived' in an allegory of the three-fathered 'philosophical child', or three fires. In simple terms, the three-fold powers of 'electromagnetic light', 'celestial fire' (spirit) and 'energy' (force) all together, construct the celestial man - Adam/Orion. Symbolically speak-ing, these three forces 'combine' to create the Heavens and all contained within 'time and space'. Celestial light and 'star fire' are crucial to this three-fold process, but it is what Mercury (Hermes Trismegistus) carries in his hand that *unites* these forces.

The caduceus, or the double-snake symbol carried by the god Mercury, is a representation of the 'celestial' kundalini uniting all three forces. In other versions of this story, three deities or forces, representing 'fire', 'deception' and 'plague' form on one side, while on the other, 'creative imagination', 'magical arts' and 'perception' come together. In every instance these forces come together to forge the persona of the 'star man' of the heavens.

The Gnostics also talked of 'Three Forms of First Thought', or the *Trimorphic Protennoia*, which they described as a divine triad of 'father, mother and child' (or son). These are Aeons, according to the Gnostics, that descend as *first thought*, or *primal being*. The Gnostic texts, the *Trimorphic Protennoia* (200 BC), talk of the 'descent' from the pleroma to earth, symbolised as 'voice' (speech/sound), or *word*, all of which were attributes of a divine human being. Sound and the music of the 'celestial spheres' are another expression of this philosophy and it is through sound (vibration), or the 'word' (Logos in Greek), that 'Protennoia' (first thought) creates life. As I showed in *Chapter Four*, the Aeon, Sophia is part of 'first thought' that lives in 'light' beyond the boundary, a light that is creator of all. From her *light* also comes the divine child - the Son of Man.

Another term for the three-fold process in Alchemical texts, like the Opus Magnum, is the 'Aurora' which relates to the essence of the 'inner sun'. The Invisible Sun, or Inner Sun, are both terms used to describe a celestial connection between the heavens and humanity. When 14th Century alchemists talked about the 'Aurora', in truth they were referring to the Gnostic Sophia (wisdom), and how this celestial (aeon) energy descended into matter through three bodies - the Sun, the Moon and the Earth. Alchemical terminology and imagery in relation to transmutation of the human soul (and Sophia's place in the heavens), shows how the Aurora plays its part in this process. The location for the 'projection' of light that creates our 'reality' or matrix, I am sure is within Orion's Nebula.

The fall of Christ/Adam/Orion-figure, through the structures I am going to describe in this chapter, which are underpinned through both religious and scientific observations, will tell of a 'celestial' and energetic *system* through which we manifest our physical world, our reality. As Manly P Hall describes in the *Secret Teachings of All Ages*:

> *Certain Rosicrucian scholars have given special appellations to these three phases of the sun: the spiritual sun* [Orion's Nebula], *they called Vulcan; the solar and intellectual sun, Christ* [Orion] *and Lucifer respectively; and the material sun, the Jewish Demiurgus Jehovah* [Saturn]. *Lucifer here represents the intellectual mind without the illumination of the spiritual mind; therefore it is "the false light." The false light is finally overcome and redeemed by the true light of the soul, called the Second Logos or Christ* [Orion].[1]

What alchemists, philosophers and esoteric thinkers, like Hall, describe are 'dual forces' on one level, but also the mechanics (albeit personified through figures like Christ) of a higher consciousness, or an eternal sun on another level. Vulcan (Hephaestus), Christ and Lucifer (all versions of Prometheus) are connected to the god, Apollo; all are life givers, 'bringers of sacred fire' that came down from heaven (the stars). This *fire* was thought of as a 'spark' from the eternal sun, the central fire and home of the Aeons.

Sacred *Fohat* – Eternal Sun

For the alchemists, the symbol of wisdom, or what was described as the 'Centre of Power' or 'Heart of Things', came through the sun. A sun that was very much considered female for ancient native people on earth. Our sun is a centre of energy and a storehouse of power. It receives energy from another source, a centre of energy, which alchemists and esoteric spiritual teachings call the 'Invisible Sun'. Each sun, or living 'star', contains within itself a centre *of life*, which can be a supernova, a giant, a white dwarf, etc. What the mystics called 'divine power', was stimulated by the light of the sun (star), illuminated by an invisible celestial sun. Our physical sun in the sky can only give back power (reflect light) it receives from a source located *beyond* the solar system. The 15th Century alchemist and astrologer of the German Renaissance, Paracelsus, said of the eternal (invisible) sun:

> There is an earthly sun, which is the cause of all heat, and all who are able to see may see the sun; and those who are blind and cannot see him may feel his heat. There is an Eternal Sun, which is the source of all wisdom, and those whose spiritual senses have awakened to life will see that sun and be conscious of His existence; but those who have not attained spiritual consciousness may yet feel His power by an inner faculty which is called Intuition.

In Mayan belief, for example, the maize/sun god also carried the notion of interconnectedness of all living things. The cosmological 'centrality' of what the Mayans called the 'first father', or Hun Hunahpu (who fathered the hero twins I mentioned in earlier chapters) is a central source. As I have already shown, the maize god, like Osiris of ancient Egypt, was thought to have travelled through the sky (on a canoe) back to the central fire of creation. Descriptions of gods travelling through space back to the 'source of all life' are similar to later religious notions of the 'assumption' and resurrection. The personified energy returns to the source, whether it is the Judeo Christian 'Father', or the 'Mother' goddess source, found in Pagan beliefs. The latter, of course, is an expression of the wisdom, intelligence and creative imagination focused on by the Gnostics and much earlier

Eastern philosophies, such as the followers of Zoroaster.

Other names for a central spiritual force behind creation is the 'Fohat', or 'vital power' linking spirit to matter. According to the occultist philosopher, H.P. Blavatsky, the Fohat is 'the animating principle *electrifying* every atom into life'. I don't share every idea put forward in books by Blavatsky as there was certainly an Orion Cult connection to the Theosophical Society she was part of; still, where science and spirituality converge in texts like the *Secret Doctrine* (1888), we have some interesting insights into the 'invisible' nature of the cosmos. As Blavatsky says:

Fohat is a generic term and used in many senses. He is the light (Daiviprakriti) of all the three logoi—the personified symbols of the three spiritual stages of Evolution. Fohat is the aggregate of all the spiritual creative ideations above, and of all the electro-dynamic and creative forces below, in Heaven and on Earth.[2]

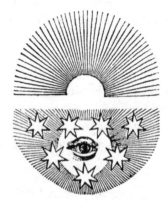

It is the 'Fohat' kundalini symbolism, or the equivalent of a cosmic Birkeland electromagnetic current, that converges to create the eye of Osiris (Orion) - the 'Eye of Providence' I mentioned earlier in the book. An alchemical version of the Eye of Providence is called the 'Wonder-Eye of Eternity' (see figure 288), a mirror of Gnostic understanding of Sophia's eternal wisdom; it could be seen as a vehicle by which wisdom 'looks into our world'. To paraphrase the message of the Gospels, "the eye is the lamp of the body and if your eyes are healthy, your whole body will be full of light" (Matthew 6:22). Or as Jakob Böhme, German philosopher, Christian (Hermetic) mystic, and Lutheran Protestant theologian also said in his *Wonder-Eye of Eternity* (1620):

Figure 288: The Wonder-Eye. The hermetic alchemical image of the female-looking Eye of Eternity. Note the seven star system, which relates to seven stars (Orion/Pleiades/Ursa Major), seven types of electromagnetic waves, seven angels, etc.

It is like an eye that sees and yet guides nothing in seeing that it may see, for seeing is without being … Its seeing is in itself.[3]

What Böhme and the 9th Century visionary philosopher, Eriugena each purported, was that a 'cosmic sun', or 'eternal eye' (in a central position), lived within the cosmology of humanity and therefore our reality. Paracelsus also wrote:

So it is a great truth, which you should seriously consider, that there is nothing
in heaven or upon the earth which does not also exist in man,... man is a sun and
a moon and a heaven filled with stars: The world is a man and the light of the sun
and the stars his body.[4]

The Greek poet, philosopher and scientist, Empedocles, like Homer 400
years before him, also realised that light was both physical and invisible.
This concept is found in ancient beliefs of Zoroastrianism, Manichaeism,
Hellenistic Gnosticism and more Eastern traditions (which are all founded
on duality taking place in time and space). These philosophies refer to the
duality of 'inner light' and 'physical light' and how unseen forces osculate
to create the physical world. The divine light, or inner light, was considered
a higher state of consciousness, while the darkness (or lower state of consciousness) was considered the cold light (electro-magnetic), a shadow side
structuring the physical world. Similar theories are now understood in
groundbreaking studies, made by astrophysicists into matter and anti-matter, as well as holograms.

The 18th Century alchemist and Mason, Emmanuel Swedenborg, who
inspired a huge 'New Age' movement within Britain, also talked of an
inner eye, or light. Swedenborg inspired artists, such as William Blake, who
visited the Church of Swedenborg in London on several occasions.
Swedenborg and Blake said a lot of similar things although they came from
very different backgrounds. In *The Everlasting Gospel* Blake wrote:

This life's dim windows of the soul
Distorts the heavens from pole to pole
And leads you to believe a lie
When you see with, not through, the eye.

Swedenborg said a similar thing when he wrote: *So Deep*

The eye so crude that it cannot see the small elements of nature except through a
lens as everyone knows, so it is less able to see the things that are above the realm
of nature like the things of the spiritual world.

One was a scientist and esotericist, the other, a poet and artist, yet they
were both coming from the same viewpoint and both shared similar principles in that period of British history. Eventually, Swedenborg and Blake
were ostracized and marginalized and in my view, Blake's 'New Jerusalem'
is not the New World Order – it isn't a physical location either – it's about
people *'becoming'* the New Jerusalem within their hearts. Although many

artists generated imagery relating to religious symbolism and inner-worlds, Blake was trying to elevate Christianity back to the Gnostic understanding of creation. His work was to help others reach a higher level through the 'true teachings' he felt were more important than the Church itself. Like the early Gnostics, he revered the teachings of Jesus and shunned the orthodox hierarchy within the Christian religion. Blake said:

> *If the doors of perception were cleansed, man would see everything as it is, infinite.*

Electric Fohat, Divine Fire (Light)

In Hindu belief, 'Agni' (Divine Fire) was said to be the source of our sun's light, a central fire, or central light that powered our solar system. In Hindu philosophy, 'Ormazd' is light, the Sun-God, or life-giver and it was said that souls issue from the 'soul of the world' and return to the central light as sparks to the fire. William Blake tapped into this knowledge of forces working through the sun, primarily through his interest in Paracelsus. Blake created a 'personal mythology' in his illustrated books focusing on both spirit and material aspects of solar energy. He called the former Los (an anagram of Sol/Sun) representing divine imagination and the latter, as a material Saturn-like sun called Urizen, who represented 'reason and doubt'. For Blake, both figures were opposites, or twins, caught up in duality and very much reminiscent of Gnostic thought. Blake was a true Christian, a Gnostic for sure and his work clearly expresses these concepts.

The creation of the world, out of a central source, can be found in both Gnostic and later Cathar philosophy. For the Gnostic-Cathars, light had an echo, just as sound-vibration creates an echo. Light, for the Gnostic mind, was bent back on itself (refracted) to create 'Divine Fire', or the eternal flame. The type of fire I am describing here is not physical (physical fire is a lower light) but is similar to rays of fire that pass through 'shimmering glass' we call stars and suns. The bending of sunlight through glass, so to create fire, is the nearest physical description of such metaphysical concepts.

Gnostic creation myths talk of the 'bending back of light' from a central source, which was considered to be 'flame' and 'fragments of light'. As the fragments of light bent back towards the source, at the point of impact, according to the Gnostics, was just another way of describing aeons and their lesser forms we know as angels.[5] The Gnostics also talked about aeons as *living light* that had 'returned to the source' (out of their natural connection to the source), now 'oscillated' (like electricity) round a central invisible sun. The Cathars called this living light 'good spirits' who stayed in contact with the father.[6] The Gnostics said that light from a central source impacted on its own echo, producing flame (the aeons/spirits) and eventually becoming vibrational matter, creating both non-physical and physical worlds. The projection of light, bending and fragmenting could be compared to modern physics' understanding of the mechanics of a holographic reality, as I shall explore shortly.

The Electric Sun (Prana)

For the ancients, the central sun was considered the soul of all things. But is this our sun or another invisible central sun? The 'Invisible Sun', or Central Sun, as referred to in esoteric writings and Hindu belief, in my view, is the central fire of the Orion Nebula. It is this Invisible Sun that powers our solar system, as I will come to. The Fohat also seems to be another esoteric description for a force that 'determines' the *direction* and *motion* of matter and therefore is also the substance (life-force) of every sun/star within its mass. Electric Universe theories also explain the same concept, in terms of an electrical source (or force) powering the Universe, rather like electricity powers up a city, a country and ultimately a whole planet. For some scientists today, the Universe is also thought to be 'powered' by a living (electrical) force, a plasma or life-blood, which travels through star systems rather like an electrical current travels through wires.

Another name for this plasma, or celestial life blood, *is* the 'Fohat' kundalini symbolism, or the equivalent of a cosmic Birkeland electromagnetic current (a ladder) that converges out of the Orion Spur to power our Solar system and therefore, ultimately *all* planets including Earth. I often chuckle at the naivety of mainstream 'physical-world-obsessed science', when it fails to see how electromagnetic plasma (Fohat currents) 'shapes' and 'connects' star and solar systems (see figure 289).

Alchemical imagery also expresses the same concepts of electromagnetic structures creating a celestial tree (see figure 290 overleaf). The 'physical' leaves, the twigs, the branches and the trunk are all part of the same tree and *all* 'trees' become forests' as do planets, suns, stars, nebulas and galax-

Figure 289: Plasma Fohat.
Part of an enormous, celestial (ladder-like) Birkeland electromagnetic current (plasma) travelling out of the Orion Nebula.

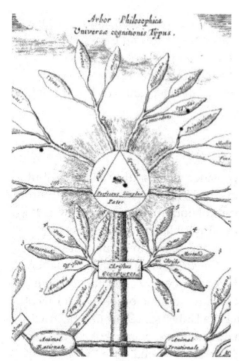

Figure 290: Plasma as the Celestial Tree.
Notice the trapezium in the upper section of the tree. (Public domain)

ies. What connects all of these different aspects of the same 'being', 'tree' (or galaxy/spur), are 'particles' of life (energy) that animate them. Freemasonic Historian, Manly P. Hall wrote:

We are the gods of the atoms that make up ourselves but we are also the atoms of the gods that make up the universe.

According to esoteric writings, such as the Blavatsky's *Secret Doctrine* (1888), the Fohat manifests in different ways and is spoken of as 'universal energy', 'vitality', 'electricity' and 'life force' operating on different levels of creation. This electrifying force (Fohat), is also what is described as 'Kalpic Masks', or serpent/kundalini force, expressed through twisting, or coiled serpent-like energy; from Birkeland currents to the double helix, all are an expression of the Kalpic Masks (see figure 291).

Our sun is an electrical transformer; any nuclear reactions happen on its surface – not at its core. The core gets its electrical power from whatever celestial grid it is connected to, in the sun's case, the Orion Spur of the Milky Way. The sun transforms electricity in the cosmic plasma field (the

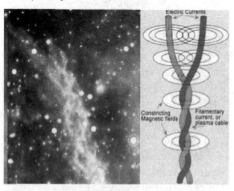

Figure 291: Birkeland Currents.
The Universe is electrical plasma; electrical currents power suns and stars.

sun is 99 per cent plasma itself) into what we call 'light' or *information*. Solar flares and massive sunspots appearing on the sun, are pure electrical charges (see figure 292). Even the word 'information' suggests 'form in the making'. This is the same principle as an electric light bulb, receiving electricity from another source and transforming it into light. Depsite mainstream dog-

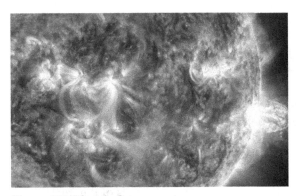

Figure 292: Electric Sun.
Sunspots are not created by internal activity but external strikes caused by massive charges of electricity.

matic 'this-world-is-all-there-is science', the sun is not producing light from inside itself. It takes electricity from the plasma field (cosmic grid) and converts it into 'light'.

It is also 'projecting' light, rather like a projector in a cinema. The 'information' it projects constructs our collective reality on earth. The sun is also processing electricity sourced from elsewhere, and it appears to change size in different phases of its cycle because its plasma ('Langmuir sheath') shrinks and expands in line with electrical changes that impact upon its surface.

If the stars, along with our sun, are electric bodies (often personified in myth) powered by a 'central source', then scriptural references such as: 'He speaks to the sun and it does not shine; he seals off the light of the stars' (Job 9: 7) seem to make more sense. What alchemists and writers of such texts were conveying, in my view, is the idea of a 'central command', often depicted as a male god or an 'eye'; encased in a 'cloud', reaching into a parallel world, affecting it, but *external* from it. As I have already shown, so much art and symbolism relays this concept of a central source and godlike power creating life. As Blavastky writes in the *Secret Doctrine* (1888):

> ... *The radiant energy flowing from the central sun called the Earth into being as a watery globe, whose tendency, as the nucleus of a planetary body, was to rush to the (central) Sun ... within the sphere of whose attraction it had been created, but the radiant energy, similarly electrifying both, withheld the one from the other ...*[7]

The term 'Prana' can also be related to the concept of Fohat, which relates to the power of attraction between atoms, and is seen as what some mystics called 'Divine Thought'. Again, Blavastky writes in *Secret Doctrine*:

> *On the earthly plane his influence is felt in the magnetic and active force* [electromagnetic plasma] *generated by the strong desire of the magnetizer. ... It is present in the constructive power that carries out, in the formation of things -- from the planetary system down to the glow-worm and simple daisy -- the plan*

*in the mind of nature, or in the Divine Thought, with regard to the development
and growth of that special thing ... In his* [the Central Sun] *secondary aspect,
Fohat is the Solar Energy, the electric vital fluid and the preserving fourth principle, the animal Soul of Nature, so to say, or – Electricity.*[8]

I see the Fohat, or Prana, as the electrical spirit or force that 'powers' components of the Universe we call nebulas, stars, suns and planets. Humanity
is connected to the cosmos through the Tree of Life; a tree that has an electric, Fohat serpent-current travelling up and down its trunk (the kundalini),
connecting the earth, humanity and the stars. It is light from a central
source, according to the Gnostics, that connected *all* levels of the tree.

For Blavatsky, the Fohat was also the 'spiritual-scientific' aspect of
Vishnu and Indra (or Osiris), in their primordial form, also described as
'Toom coming out of Noot' in ancient Egyptian esoteric symbolism. In the
Egyptian *Book of the Dead*, Toom (Tomb) was considered the 'Protean God'
who creates other gods, often shown as a 'man' with 'breaths' in his hands.
Again in the *Book of Job* (12:10) it states:

In his hand is the life of every creature and the breath of all mankind.

The word 'Toom' also relates to the old English word 'Tom', or Germanic,
Tommaz, meaning 'empty', or ready to be filled. The Babylonian saviour
god, Tammuz, is a cognate of the same word relating to 'time', 'to build'
and 'to empty'. The 'Tau', 'Time' and the 'Hourglass' (mentioned in *Part
One*) are all symbols of Toom, interconnecting with Atum Ra/Adam/Orion.

To understand the idea of an electromagnetic 'central source' animating
our world, and before I can describe more of the mechanics in detail, let us
look briefly at the idea of a holographic reality, some say 'Universe'.

Virtual Universe

According to quantum science (and Gnostic teachings have more or less
tried to express), we are 'living' in a highly sophisticated version of a virtual-reality game; or, put another way, a holographic cosmic Internet giving
the illusion of 3-Dimensional space. One of the big questions people ask is
why, if we are creating our illusory reality, do we 'all *see* the same basic
world' in street scenes, people, cars, roads, forests and mountains? The
answer is that we are *fed* 'frequency signals' by information (light codes)
that we 'collectively' decode into the reality we call the world. For example,
every single computer on earth, in almost every country (except for those
that have government firewalls), can collectively download the same
Google web page, the same Internet sites and same web pages, which on

the screen all look the *same* to someone viewing in America, Europe or South Africa, etc. Online computer gaming, such as *Fortnight*, is another example of creating a collective reality (the game itself) across a vast spectrum of 'players' all over the world; *all* participating in the same illusory game (reality). Yes, it is a virtual reality, where players live and die, but in principle, the same applies to the super-virtual holographic reality we call life. The real players, of course, don't die on screen, only the *virtual self* does and this philosophy is the basis of much mystical and esoteric teachings around life and death. We are living in a dream world in our heads, connected to the information codes, or what many have called the 'matrix'. The matrix, or the virtual-reality game, is a super-hologram projecting endless other holograms, including the human body and they are all, by their very nature, *illusions*.

In terms of galaxies, stars, suns and planets and how they are information fields quantum physicists call waveform particles, or light, all play their part in constructing the holographic universe – the matrix of worlds. One of the leading scientists in this field, Leonard Susskind, explains how two-dimensional versions of our reality stored in black holes, create a three-dimensional 'movie' based on information on the 'surface' of the black hole (see *Chapter Four*). In his book, *The Black Hole War: My Battle with Stephen Hawking to Make the World Safe for Quantum Mechanics* (2008), Susskind says:

> *The three-dimensional world of ordinary experience, the universe filled with galaxies, stars, planets, houses, boulders, and people is a hologram, an image of reality coded on a distant two-dimensional surface. This new law of physics, known as the Holographic Principle, asserts that everything inside a region of space can be described by bits of information restricted to the boundary.*[9]

The boundary is, of course, the *intersection* between what the Gnostic's called the Pleroma and the Kenoma (see page 107). Or in simpler terms, it is where the shore meets the sea, or where the ocean ends and the crest of a wave begins (see figure 293 overleaf).

Our Holographic Reality

As touched on in *Chapter Four*, holograms are made by directing a laser onto a piece of photographic film through a semi-transparent mirror. Some of the light is deflected away in another direction and onto the object you want to photograph. Now you have the laser light pointing at the film (known as the reference beam) and the part deflected away onto the object (known as the working beam). This working beam, carrying the vibrational image of the object in question, is then directed onto the photographic film.

Figure 293: We are a Crest of a *Wave*form.
Information constructs our here-today, gone-tomorrow, physical reality. The sun and the moon act as projectors of light (information) giving us our holographic *wave*form reality. © Neil Hague

When it hits the film, it 'collides' with the reference beam – its 'other half' – and this creates what is known as an interference pattern between the two.

Holograms are made by using two parts of the same laser light. One half (reference beam) goes almost 'directly' to the photographic plate and the other (working beam) is 'diverted' onto the subject. When this working beam is diverted again onto the print it forms an 'interference pattern' with the reference beam. If a laser is shone upon this pattern it creates a 3D holographic picture of the subject. The more I have looked at the nature of reality, I feel that our sun and moon give us a 'working' beam and 'reference' beam. Both celestial bodies provide information (light) at waveform level, required to manifest our earth 'matrix'. You can liken the principle to throwing *two* stones (sun and moon) into a pond (space) and seeing how the two wave formations collide and interfere with each other. They form a pattern, a *wave* representation of the two stones, where they fell and at what speed. The interference pattern imprinted on the holographic film looks much like waves in the pond; it is the 'waveform' level of reality our brain decodes into what we perceive as physical (3D) holographic reality.

One of the unique characteristics of a holographic film is that, unlike a conventional picture, you can have many images on the same print. They are different interference patterns, waveforms, various pictures selected by the angle at which the laser strikes the film. The same principle applies to a laser passing across wave patterns of a DVD; picking out the scenes in order, making up a movie-reality. All over the world there are many examples of templates, or blueprints, that have manifested as architectural styles, religion, political mindsets, and so forth. *All* are part of our holographic reality, a *projection* of the collective on one level, but also a precise focus on the information fields made into physical forms. The holographic nature of physical reality explains why the human aura (energy field) and earth's magnetic field look the same; it also explains why brain activity mirrors the

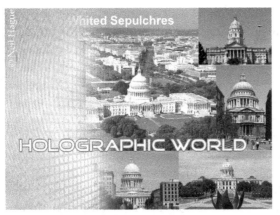

Figure 294: Holographic Blueprints.
All over the world we see the same architecture and symbols. The holographic physical world is made manifest through the *wave*form level of reality.

connectivity of the universe. As the genius Nikola Tesla said, "Our entire biological system, the brain and the earth itself, work on the same frequencies."

Nature gives us much evidence of the holographic principle in macrocosm-microcosm, but so does the material (human-made) world or 'matrix'. Architectural 'blueprints' projected out of the minds of high priests of Babylon and Rome, for example, are no more than *focused* energy appearing as the *same* architecture in hologram form of all over the world (see figure 294). Our 'world matrix', constructed and 'controlled' by archontic forces I mentioned in *Chapter Four*, have aided in 'distorting' our reality. These non-physical forces (the Archons) understand the nature of the cosmos, its holographic principle and that *we* can see it for what it is, if we only choose to open our eyes. All physical realities start at waveform level and are made *real* (3D) by the mind.

I am convinced that ancient and modern inventions, archaeological finds, along with the 'sudden introduction of technology', political trends, movements, even a *perceived* 'virus' can be seen as 'holographic inserts' (downloads) within the virtual game-world reality we experience collectively. Recurring mindsets, which we label 'human nature', manifesting as wars, inquisition, genocide and other fears, *or* terrors (including manipulated pandemics), are also part of this programmed virtual reality. It is a 'mind virus' which often infects our perception. I disagree with the idea that 'true human nature' manifests such mindsets, but a 'mind-controlled species' could collectively create a reality based on *information* (waveform) we constantly receive; more on this topic at the end of the book.

Celestial Mirrors

We know how holograms are created through directing light (a laser) onto a piece of photographic film through a semi-transparent mirror, but what if the principle could be scaled up to the size of 'black holes', 'stars' and 'suns'? What if, according to scientists, the universe *is* holographic in nature then there must be a scaled-up version of holographic mechanics within the universe and galaxy, including star systems. As I mentioned earlier in the book, the work of Dr. Ladislav Šubr (Charles University, Czech Republic), explains how high mass stars and centrally clustered stars could be the source of black holes. The Orion Nebula Cluster, according to Šubr, is one example of a high mass black hole, one of the closest, young star clusters from earth (about 1300 light-years away). Based on holographic principles and the mechanics of how holographic realities are created, I have often wondered if the source of our solar system, and therefore our earth reality, was not a projection from the Orion Nebula? Does strategic 'precise placement' of our sun and moon, visible as synchronistic eclipses (according to mainstream physics), create the mechanics for our earth matrix? One example of this precise relationship is how the moon can be seen through numbers and distances. The moon is 400 times smaller than the sun, and at a solar eclipse it is 400 times closer to earth. This makes the moon appear, from earth, to be the same size as the sun during a total eclipse. Another example is dividing the sun's circumference by that of the moon and multiplying by 100, resulting in the earth's size (see page 25). Divide the size of the sun by the size of the earth and multiply by 100 and you get the size of the moon. These math examples can be explained through the holographic nature of reality and how other 'forces' are at work behind the 'design' of the heavens. Modern Gnostics would say that these 'alignments' are the work of the Demiurge and angelic 'celestial' forces. From this point of perception, I see our sun and moon as *energetic mirrors,* or portals (probably both), that take invisible light (*information* projected from the Orion Nebula), and refract this 'light'. The refracted light via these celestial mirrors create what we see *as* reality (the night-and-day movie) as perceived

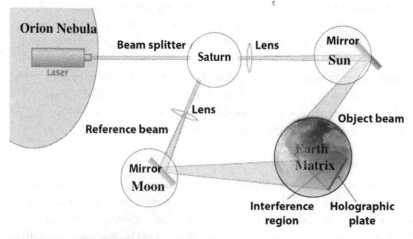

Figure 295: Celestial Mirrors and the Holographic Earth-Matrix.
How a hologram works, overlaid by *how* celestial bodies (realities) *could* also function as energetic mirrors. Is this how our holographic world is made manifest? © Neil Hague

from earth. The location of the holographic laser could be in the Orion Nebula, an area I am going to look at in more detail throughout the next few chapters. My diagram is not to scale and not intended to be read as scientific evidence. Of course, it is merely a 'visual idea' to suggest the possible concept of such holographic mechanics in relation to the positions of the sun and the moon (see figure 295).

German Jesuit scholar and polymath, Athanasius Kircher, published around 40 major works, most notably in comparative religion, geology, and medicine. Kircher was also an artist who displayed a keen interest in technology and mechanical inventions; inventions attributed to him include a magnetic clock, various automatons and the first megaphone, to name but a few. In his work, *Ars Magna Lucis Et Umbrae (The Great Art of Light and Shadow)* 1646, Kircher also draws on religious symbolism to portray his understanding of optics, light, shadow, colour, refraction, projection, distortion and luminescence. What is striking about Kircher's 17th Century illustrations is his use of personified 'energetic mirrors' showing the sun and moon seemingly creating projections of light (reference beams) rather like holograms are created (see figure 296). Kirchner's *Ars Magna Lucis Et Umbrae* seems to illustrate the projection and refraction of light in our world, but it is very telling in terms of capturing a 'higher source' (the Invisible Sun), seen to be passing its light *through* the sun and the moon. Other works by Kircher also show a central source, a light surrounded by clouds, housing the Tetragrammaton (see page 126). The cloud depicted in Kircher's art seems to be conveying the idea of a nebula in a central location, a possible birthplace for stars. As I mentioned earlier in *Part One*, the work of Danny Wilten, in his e-book *Orion in the Vatican*, goes into great detail with regards to the 'mapping' of religious art against the Orion Nebula. Like Wilten, I feel the Orion Nebula (the great cloud in much high altar art) is the source of what

Figure 296: Projecting Reality.
Athanasius Kircher, A*rs Magna Lucis Et Umbra* (1646). (Public Domain)

esoteric thinkers for centuries have called the 'Invisible Sun'. It's also my feeling that clusters of hot stars in the Orion Nebula, act as a giant laser feeding lesser projectors, and together, creating worlds (suns/stars/planets). Depending on what part of the galactic movie we focus on, will depend on the physical reality we create. For example, in one version of the projected movie, the earth is still in the Atlantean Age and the likes of Mars is 'teeming with life'. In another version, humanity is subordinate to robots and Artificial Intelligence and earth is a 'slave camp' for alien life. The mechanics of these celestial projectors and how we read the information

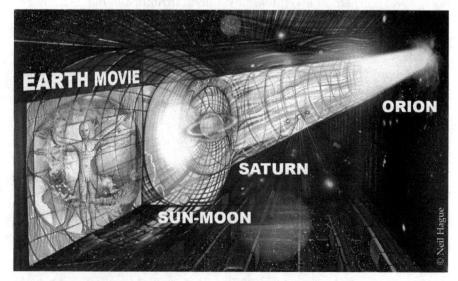

Figure 297: Celestial Projector and Movie Earth.
My symbolic interpretation of the central source as a projector passing through lesser projectors (Sun, Saturn and Moon), creating our Earth Movie (holographic reality).

projecting through them, will always determine reality. Simply put, the stars are a source of light and the projectors of our reality (sun and moon) are placed accordingly to project the movie – 'Earth' (see figure 297). According to native peoples, there have been various earth movies, depending on the position of these projectors. World ages (or movies) come and go in the multiplex cinema we call 'ancient-future life' on earth.

Shimmering Projectors (Eyes in the Sky)

What I am about to say may seem 'far out', but, considering indigenous creation myths and numerous alchemical illustrations showing projections, I've an intuitive feeling that our sun is the main 'projector' for this reality

Figure 298: The Sun is a Projector of Reality.
(Left) A close up of a typical movie projector and its similarity to the blinding effect of the light of the sun. **(Middle and Right)** The Oculus forms a projector of light in places such as the Pantheon, Rome. It gives the effect of a both the Sun, and the 'projector of reality'.

Figure 299: Projectors of Reality.
The Moon over water, or a projector-portal?

(matrix). Much like when you go to the movies and the film is being projected behind you through a little hole in the wall, I think the ancients, and later alchemists, knew on one level that our sun and moon acted as celestial projectors (mirrors). I think that's why priesthoods throughout history have worshipped the sun, the eternal flame and the 'eye' as objects relating to 'light' and how the world is made manifest. Try staring at the projector light in a cinema (see figure 298) and compare it to staring at the sun, when it's at its brightest, and you'll get the idea. At times the moon also appears to be 'projector-like' (see figure 299). Reality *is* a 'projection' designed by something beyond restrictions of the boundary and the so-called physical world. The symbolism runs deeper than we realise, especially when considering the visionary work of William Blake's image, '*The Ancient of Days*', which suggests the sun is a portal and projector, or a creator of reality (see page 127). The 'projector' could be seen as the both the 'eye', or the 'brain' of the Gnostic Demiurge. Therefore, what it projects (courtesy of the light given by the Aeons) *becomes* 'reality', or a holographic Earth movie. The movie can be 'X-rated', or of any genre, depending on the focus it attracts. Can you imagine the scale and magnitude of such forces that are able to manipulate the movie script (light codes), or *enter* the movie at any given (time) frame? These forces are the angelic realms, gods, or aliens mentioned since ancient times.

So much symbolism relating to the cult of 'two eyes' in ancient Egypt (often with a third eye on the brow) are symbols relating to the projectors I

am suggesting here. The eyes are
the sun and the moon ruling over a
new matrix (earth), forming the
reign of Osiris/Horus (Orion) and
possibly a new reality, after major
cataclysms. The Egyptians wrote of
the pharaoh 'Hor' (also a word for
Horus's face), 'he who is above', or
'Mekhenti-irry' (he who has on his
brow 'Two Eyes'). The sun and
moon represented his eyes and on

Figure 300: Horus the Elder (Haroeris).
God of the two-eyed Cult in ancient Egypt.

nights when there is no moon he was considered the god of the blind, a
description given by the Gnostics for the Demiurge and of course, to Orion
himself. The moon blinds us to the true nature of reality and the third eye
(the pineal gland), allows us to 'see' *all-that-there-is* to *see*. Do the sun and
the moon projectors prevent us from seeing beyond the *The Illusion*? In
Egyptian belief, 'Haroeris' (Horus the Elder), an early form of Horus, or a
'God of Light', was often symbolised with two eyes (see figure 300). His
eyes also represented the sun and moon; Haroeris was thought to be the
brother of Osiris and Set/Saturn (Osiris) becoming satan (Set), with Horus
losing an eye; the latter becoming a symbol for the illuminated ones. I feel
that a new earth matrix ruled over by Osiris/Horus was one that focused
on the Sun and Moon, rather than Saturn and Orion's (Osiris) pre-
Atlantean Golden Age I mentioned in earlier chapters. A time when the
pineal gland was most likely fully-activated in the minds of the ancients.

As I said in my book *Journeys in the Dreamtime* (2006), the chambers of
the human mind are equivalent to being inside the movie theatre; entering
the cinema theatre is symbolic of entering the chambers of the subconscious
mind which is why cinema (movies) became an important tool for forces
that have a lot invested in how we 'see the world'. How we see the world,
which is fundamentally influenced by a) our subconscious thoughts and
beliefs; and b) the primary visual cortex at the base of the brain, is the primary, creating factor of both our individual and collective reality! New Age
or Stone Age, are all movies running in parallel theatres, existing in universal 'cities of the imagination'.[10]

We exist simultaneously in many parallel realities. Just as light, matter
and particle exists in different forms at the same time. The idea that all life
is born of light from a star to a crystal, tells us that we are all *One*. The projection I am highlighting here is part of the hologram and *the* hologram, of
course, is made up of smaller aspects of the whole. It is no surprise to find,
for example, a projector in the heavens, a projector in our sky and projec-

tors in our reality. The holographic principle can be simply understood through macrocosm and microcosm and therefore it would also be no surprise to see why the Orion Constellation has been mirrored on earth in places like Egypt and elsewhere through ancient correlations (see *Chapter One*). It can be seen in the geography of the Nile as shown by Danny Wilten's overlapping imagery of the Nile Delta. Still, more importantly, the projection gives us fresh insight into religious themes in connection to the human skull, vertebrae and how this can also be seen in the topology of the birthplace of all religion - Egypt. In his conversations with Asclepius, Hermes Trismegistus, the hero and god of medicine in ancient Greek religion and mythology (mentioned in *Chapter Thirteen*), states:

> *Art thou not aware, O Asclepios, that Egypt is the image of heaven, or rather, that it is the projection below of the order of things above? If the truth must be told, this land is indeed the temple of the world.*

Spheres of Influence

Hermetic teachings talk of a beam of light and a source from where *all is projected.*[11] In these mystical books and teachings, there is often reference to a central sun and three 'secondary suns' in different solar systems; two of these I believe are now Saturn and Jupiter that at one time had their own mini solar 'systems'. These planets seem to be dwarf stars with many lesser planet-size moons orbiting them. Some, like Titan (the second-largest moon in our solar system) is almost the size of a planet and one of the most Earth-like places in the solar system, albeit at vastly colder temperatures and with different chemistry. Saturn and Jupiter are crucial to the invisible mechanics of our solar system and, therefore, the information (waveform) that continues to affect our world throughout the ages. You could say that the position of Saturn and Jupiter is part of a system of 'secondary projectors' and in some ways, the diagram of the Tree of Life seems to convey the order of these planetary bodies from the moon up to Neptune and beyond the stars, to what I feel is the Orion Nebula. As Blavatsky writes in *The Secret Doctrine* (Vol II):

> *The Central Sun ... was to them the centre of Rest; the centre to which all motion was to be ultimately referred. Round this central sun* [Orion's Nebula]*... the first of three systemic suns ... revolved on a polar plane ... the second* [Saturn]*, on an equatorial plane ... and the third only was our visible sun.*[12]

The 'systemic' suns, as Blavatsky calls them, are energetic fields serving as secondary 'hubs' through which waveform (energy) passes, creating our earth matrix. The two lesser suns, 'Saturn and Jupiter', in simple terms, are like giant, interstellar Wi-Fi hubs through which interstellar, cosmic Wi-Fi (waveform) allows us to 'download' our 'screen-world', or earth reality. Whatever is programming these 'hubs' is ultimately affecting our matrix and what we percieve to be reality. These two celestial hubs also influence other planets in the solar system, but Saturn or Cronos (the Lord of Time), especially, plays a crucial function in the *distorting* of our earth-reality. Not least through our focus on 'time', death and systems of governance.

Time is part of the illusion (the hologram) holding us in servitude to the earth matrix as it is expressed through seconds, hours, days, weeks months and years in our world. All of the planets play their part, along with the larger Zodiac Wheel, in what we call human-life experience on earth. The seven main planets, metals and 'days of the week' are just a tiny example of the mechanics of the projection.

White Cloud and the Bountiful Eye

Electromagnetic 'plasma' is the vehicle by which suns (stars) convey their energy onto other bodies. All 'radiance' in esoteric terms was said to flow from a central 'invisible' sun that powered lesser suns and planets. In Blavatsky's book, *Isis Unveiled* (1877), she mentions how the ancients under-stood the sun was not a direct cause of light, but merely a 'portal' through which a true source passed through into our world (sphere). She writes:

> *Thus it was always called by the Egyptians "the eye of Osiris" who was himself the logos, the first-begotten, or light made manifest to the world, which is the mind and divine intellect of the Concealed.*[13]

As mentioned in earlier chapters, Osiris *is* Orion and this deity (or persona) is constructed by the 'light of the eye', or what the Gnostics called the Demiurge. All religious iconography showing the 'eye within a triangle', encircled by a nebula, are quite simply telling those who have *eyes to see* that the Abrahamic God operates *through*, and *within*, the parameters of an invisible, central sun (eye), which I feel is located within the Orion Nebula.

According to Gnostic writings, the Demiurge (and Archons) evolved out of nuclear fusion focused within the Orion Nebula and its surrounding, gaseous interstellar clouds. Named after the Latin word for cloud, 'nebu-lae'/nebulas are not only massive clouds of dust, hydrogen and helium gas (and plasma), they are often 'stellar nurseries' - or places where stars are born. As I have already touched on, there seems to be a massive 'nursery' in the hottest part of the Orion Nebula. All life is born of these nurseries, or stellar 'wombs'; I would suggest that our DNA is made of 'genetic star stuff' giving us a myriad of life forms, including all 'junk alien' aspects of our DNA. Life, death, all duality centred on Orion, has to pass through a symbolic 'door' (or portal) into the lesser worlds (stars, suns and planets), all of which create reality for us earthbound humans. I am sure there are a multitude of 'levels' to the projection, from its source, to the 3D and 4D holographic earth matrix, including what are called 'angelic orders', which I'll get to shortly.

The Eye of 'God'

In Christianity, the All-seeing Eye, or 'Eye of Providence', has been used as a symbol from at least the 16th century, by Italian artists, to portray the 'Eye of God'. It is also paralleled with the 'Third Eye' found in other esoteric teachings used by the ancients and those who inspired later Masonic Orders. In the *Rig Veda*, the 'eye' is also thought of as the 'eye of the creator', one that never closes, watching over all. The eye-in-pyramid (surrounded by rays of light) is

Figure 301: The Eye of God.
(Left) 16th century Christian painting dated 1525 by Italian artist Pontormo (student of Da Vinci), called *Supper in Emmaus*, depicts a scene from *Luke* 24: 13-32. **(Right)** Aachen Cathedral all-seeing eye.

another variation of the symbolism, relating to God's omnipresence (all-seeing eye) watching over creation (see figure 301). It is also the eye of the Gnostic creator – the Demiurge, Odin and the Orion Cult symbolism mentioned in *Chapter Three*.

Other examples of the eye, positioned within a triangle symbolism, can be seen in Aachen Cathedral in Germany. The cathedral was originally built in the late 8th century under the Emperor Charlemagne and then expanded in the middle ages, with various changes and updates along the way. It would seem the All-Seeing eye symbol was placed on the cathedral in 1766 to mark renovations done that year. Pontormo's painting pre-dates the founding of the Bavarian Illuminati (1776), although Freemasonry already existed in England and Europe by this time. Freemasonic use of the eye-inside-a-triangle symbolism is no more than secret societies showing their knowledge of Orion's Trapezium and the Demiurge (Architect) they idolise, in my view. In Alsace, France, the fresco painted above the altar of the

Figure 302: The Trapezium area of the Orion Nebula.
The hot place indicated by the triangle is where stars (stones) are born and the possible location of a mini black hole.

Figure 303: The God of the Trapezium.
Troyan Monastery Fresco, Bulgaria.
(Public Domain.)

Abbey Church of Saint-Jean-Baptiste (1763) also shows a large example of the eye-in-pyramid symbol, with rays of glory breaking through the 'clouds'. The clouds are visual interpretations of the inner area of the Orion Nebula and the eye is the invisible sun 'projecting light'. The triangle or pyramid shape, as we shall see, is clearly symbolic of the Trapezium inside Orion's Nebula (see figure 302).

Similar imagery is found in cathedrals and churches all across Europe, not least in the Co-Cathedral of the Ascension of the Lord, Kecskemét, Hungary; Hartegbrugkerk Church, Netherlands and the Fresco in the Troyan Monastery, the third largest religious centre in Bulgaria (see figure 303). Bulgaria, of course, was a Gnostic centre in the period historians like to call the 'Dark Ages'. Within these murals and frescos we see the 'triangle' around the head of 'God' (the Demiurge) whose third eye *is* the 'Eye of Providence'. The same concepts are seen in Italian fresco art, not least on the Fresco, *Triumph of the Order of Saint Francis* by Giovan Battista Gaulli, in the Basilica of the Santi XII Apostoli, in Rome. It shows what looks like a triangular light just above and behind the figure of Christ, again looking remarkably like the Trapezium area in the Orion Nebula.

The Isenheim Altarpiece (when opened) from the chapel of The Hospital of Saint Anthony, Isenheim, Germany (1510-1515), created by German Renaissance

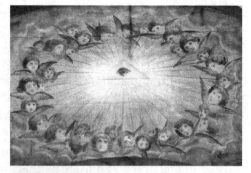

Figure 304: Eye of God.
The All-Seeing Eye (Eye God) surrounded by Cherubim (Cherubs), in Santa Maria Maggiore, Rome, Italy

painter, Matthias Grünewald, also offers a striking combination of the Trapezium and the Demiurge projecting 'light' downwards to Christ as an infant with Mary. Other Catholic art of the same intensity can be found at Santa Maria Maggiore, the fourth church of Rome, and the largest church dedicated to the Virgin (see figure 304). I would suggest that so much of Christian 'religious art', throughout the Renaissance and into the Baroque period, was made by initiates given insight into deeper symbolism connected to knowledge of an invisible sun, its light and Orion's part in it all.

Black Pyramid, the Sword and the 'Power of Three'

As I have already mentioned, the Gnostics and later Cathars of 12th Century France considered the world to be a fabrication of *three forces* 'projecting or creating' the Cosmos. The English word 'Trinity', derived from the Latin 'Trinitas' (meaning the number three), is the most common symbolism for these three forces. Other systems consider them to be three primary forces, described as positive, negative and neutral. In esoteric terms, all three forces are necessary to create anything. The positive force acts, the negative force receives, and the neutral force is the mysterious force reconciling the two; it is a mix of positive and negative. In Vedic tradition, the same three primary forces are the 'three Gunas'. For the ancient Indus Valley people, creation was described as the 'agitation' of a previously inert and perfectly balanced state into the three gunas of light, motion, and darkness. The biblical Adam, Eve and the Serpent are these same three forces on one level, representing forces required for any creation to occur. In other words, to manifest anything, three primary forces 'separate' and then 'unite' creating a triangular shape – a 'Tetrahedron'.

The Tetrahedron is the smallest and most compact of all the Platonic Solids, which are the building blocks for solidity, or three-dimensional reality. It's interesting to note that the Black Pyramid, with the Eye (or UV fluorescent Third-Eye Pyramid), a magnetic stone artifact discovered in La Maná, Ecuador in the 1980s, is not a pyramid but a Tetrahedron (see figure 305).

Figure 305: The La Maná Pyramid.
The Black Pyramid with All-Seeing Eye and 33 segments, said to be over 10,000 years old.

There is much mystery surrounding this artifact, not least the hieroglyphs on its base, which seem to infer there was a global civilisation pre-dating the Mayan civilisation. It also features the Orion Constellation and the 'Eye of Providence'.

One of the world's most accomplished linguists, Professor Kurt Schildmann (1909-2005) studied the object and translated the hieroglyphs on the base of the Black Pyramid. According to Schildmann, the inscription translates as: 'The son of the creator comes from here.' The bricks in the body of the pyramid add up to 33, code for the human vertebrae, the kundalini force and the 'power of three'. The Trinity, the 'Three Forces', or the 'Three Pure Ones' are *formless* and often portrayed in the three basic colours, from which all colours originate: Red (active, fire or creation), Blue (passive, truth or reason) and Yellow or Green (neutral, wisdom, gold, or philosopher's stone). In all instances (esoterically speaking), the number *Three* is a building block for reality on so many levels.

Three forces of creation seem to be evident in the idea of humanity's falling through the frequencies, or the 'fall'. The Adam and Eve story, which sees God (the Demiurge) expelling Adam (Orion) and Eve (Sophia), along with the Serpent (the electromagnetic kundalini force), for 'disobeying' him, is another version of the fall. These Three forces take the form of the tree of good, evil and the 'tree of knowledge' in the Garden of Eden; all of which seem to be symbolic of forces focused on the Orion Nebula. In Jewish theology, the higher 'Gan Eden' is called the 'Garden of Righteousness', a location said to have been created at the beginning of the world. It is said that here the 'righteous' dwell in the sight of the 'heavenly chariot' carrying the throne of God (Demiurge). Is it possible that the 'chariot' and 'throne' is another way of describing the Trapezium area of the Orion Nebula? Were Orion, and his Queen Eve, both expelled from realms of paradise (the place where Upper Aeons dwelt), for recognising their place in the light of the Trapezium? Again, it is interesting to note that the word 'paradise' comes from the term 'pardes', meaning a 'royal garden' or 'hunting park'- a perfect place for Orion and his lover.

Benben Stone of Eden – The Treasure of the World

The Benben Stone coming to earth is shrouded in mystery and many theories talk of a shrine guarded by priests and an object that came from the stars. Whether part of a meteorite, or other space rock, the Benben Stone seems to be associated with a Heavenly Eden or a 'radiant location' amongst the stars (possibly Orion). According to legend, Benben was the mound that arose from the primordial waters of Nu, in which the creator god Atum (Orion), the Supreme Solar God, shaped the world. The oldest written reference for the stone appeared in the *Book of the Dead*, where it is called the 'Throne of Radiance'. The Benben stone is a symbol of the Phoenix, which had the ability to revive itself and be reborn. It also represents the 'cycle of the seasons', which I have shown in part one can be seen through Orion's position throughout the earthly year. The Benben was found in the Temple of the Phoenix, within the precinct of the Great Sun Temple of Heliopolis (City of the Sun), one of the oldest cities of ancient Egypt.

For ancient Egyptians, the stone was considered the 'seed' of the Phoenix. Since 'ben' meant 'fertilization' could it be another Black Pyramid object relating to the central fire of creation? Interestingly, 'Ben' can also mean son, daughter, firstborn, nation and 'spark'. Ben comes from the

prime root word 'Banah', meaning to build, obtain children, make, repair and set up. The final letter 'Nun', the last letter of the Bible, also means the 'soul rising', the 'salvation of the soul', 'heirs to the kingdom of heaven' and the 'throne are redeemed'.[14] All of these descriptions are talking about a throne amongst the stars, a place from where life is restored, or born. Australian Aborigines preserved an ancient oral tradition saying the Benben rode the Milky Way called Mu. Tibetan belief maintained the Benben was 'from one of the solar systems in the constellation of Orion,[15] and Buddhist Lamaism refer to the stone as the 'Treasure of the World'. From my research, I am convinced this 'Treasure of the World', or 'Throne of Radiance', is another way of describing the Trapezium,

Figure 306: Treasure of the World. The Orion Nebula ('Throne of Radiance') the focus of by so many ancient cultures and religious artists.

located within Orion's Nebula (see figure 306). The Throne could also be the origin of the symbol of the 'white' dove revered by the Cathars, too.

The 'Treasure of the World' is also the capstone in Masonic lore and the stone that was rejected in the *Psalm* (118:22) and translated as Jesus himself being the stone that was rejected. The 'Central Sun', 'Invisible Sun' and the 'Treasure of the World' are different descriptions of the same source. It's also interesting to note that in some Christian literature, Christ is often depicted on a cloud (nebula) which looks like the Orion Nebula. As the biblical text in *Amos* (5:8) says:

Seek him that maketh the seven stars and Orion, and turneth the shadow of death into the morning, and maketh the day dark with night: that calleth for the waters of the sea, and poureth them out upon the face of the earth: The Lord is his name.

Orion's electromagnetic nebula, centred on the Trapezium (possibly a portal), seems to send 'life force' through the stars (like an electrical current) passing through our Sun, through the dwarf stars Jupiter and Saturn, and other minions, or Moons. It is the Invisible Sun, a 'power house' that constructs many levels (realities) often symbolised as the Cosmic Soul, Tree of Life, Music of the Spheres, or the 'Ladder', in Alchemy. Robert Fludd, the prominent 16th Century English Paracelsian physician, alchemist, astrologer, mathematician and cosmologist, often depicted this 'projection' in his *Utriusque Cosmi*, showing man the 'microcosm' within the universal 'macrocosm' (see page 140). So did Athanasius Kircher, in his many papers and drawings attempting to order the connections between the 'stars and humanity'. His systems, maps and illustrations symbolise the path taken by electromagnetic light as it descends through the 'world tree'- ladder, or circles, into the human eye.

The descending light in the Qabalah/Sefirot is often depicted as a 'flaming sword' that travels (like lightning) through the Tree of Life. The flaming sword travels from Keter (the crown or branches) to Malchut/Malkuth (the roots), from the 'above to the below'. The flaming cloud 'houses' the throne of Yahweh and is another representation of the central source at the heart of the Orion Nebula. All duality seems to spiral out of this central source giving us the understanding described as the 'Heavenly Eden' to which there is no human approach, and the 'Earthly Eden', which is approached by thirty-two paths - the 22 letters (of the Hebrew alphabet) and 10 numerals. Or as Dr Ariel Benson puts it in his book *The Zohar*:

> *No one knows the Earthly Eden but the Little Face* [the seven lower Sephiroth], *and no one knows the Heavenly Eden but the Great Face* [the three Elevated Sephiroth] ... *Should the Upper Eye* [Keter] *cease looking into the Lower Eye* [Malkuth], *the world would perish.*[16]

The cosmogony within the *Zohar* and later hermetic teachings is simply referring to an 'infinite source' and an 'invisible structure' (the projector) projecting reality and 'order'. Of course, there are mystery school and religious conotations connected to what Judaic teachings call the *seven* lower Sephiroth and the Upper Eye (all-seeing eye). The seven lower Sephiroth (also called 'seven emanations' of Eden), are thought to be archetypes and virtues 'projected' from the mind of God (the Demiurge). The number is part of the *seven* emanations of God, 'supposedly' passed from the biblical God (Demiurge) to Adam and Noah (the bloodline of the Watchers and giants).

As I said in the last chapter, many years ago I heard the term '*Earth*

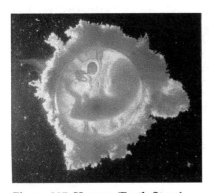

Figure 307: Human 'Earth Stars'.
Gnostic texts describe the Demiurge and Archons as a 'neonate form', like an aborted fetus.

Stars', and with it the understanding that humans are 'points of light', or stars, projecting (a hologram) onto the surface of a 'flat earth plane'. Each human being could be seen as the 'life and death' of each individual as a 'star'. It is no stretch of the imagination to see that the holographic nature of the universe would give us 'macrocosm-microcosm' when it comes to stars forming and 'human stars' forming (see figure 307). I have found that most people involved in 'ritual magic', paganism, and the *lower* knowledge called religions, have no idea what actually 'powers' the so-called 'celestial bodies' of the Sun, Planets and the Moon. Too many are 'worshipping the instrument' with no knowledge of who, or what, made the 'instruments' they worship in the first place.

Orion's Trapezium, Firestones & Altars

As I have already shown, other triangular structures, Mesas and Kivas of the Hopi, were often aligned to the greater picture that is Orion's influence on 'life and death' (symbolism) on Earth. The Mayan also focused their pyramids on Orion, especially the three stars or 'stones' of Alnitak, Saiph and Regel. The Hopi also used three fire stones to rest cooking pots on within their homes.[17] They were called 'Hearth Stones' (firestones) to the Mayan and Hopi and were often found in their ceremonies as symbols of firestones (or stars) in the Orion constellation. Alnitak, Saiph and Regel were regarded as the 'Hearthstones' to the Quiche Mayan culture; these three stars framed a 'triangular boundary' around the area where the Orion Nebula is located. The triangle is also referred to as the 'Lion of God' because of its importance to the ancients, a subject for a later chapter. The centre of this triangular area was also considered home to a central sun, as I've been describing. The same allegory connects to Orion's Trapezium, situated in the hottest region of the Orion Nebula, just below the three belt stars in Orion's sword. This hot region of Orion, according to some researchers, is the location for the 'projector' of our 'reality'. In other words, the Trapezium is the true source of the 'movie screen' as the projection creates 'everything' we call 'reality'. The Sun, Saturn and the Moon are 'strategically placed' to alter that projection, to create our Earth 'matrix'.

Alchemical knowledge of the 'Nine Spheres', the 'Holy of Holies', the

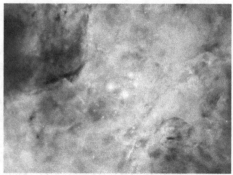

Figure 308: Altars to Orion.
(Left) Karlskirche Church featuring Orion's Trapezium and cloud-like nebula. **(Right)** Inside the Orion Nebula; the white-hot Trapezium area is said to be the place where stars are born.

Figure 309: Altars to Orion.
The High Altar art at the Church of Saint-Merri, Paris showing what seems to be the Orion Nebula above the Son of Man (Orion-Adam-Jesus). (Public Domain.)

Sephiroth (Tree of Life) and the 'Epithets of God', all seem to be telling the same story of how a central sun (inside the Trapezium) was involved in the creation of our Solar System. From time to time this knowledge appears in religious iconography (see figure 308). One example is Saint Charles Church, also known as Karlskirche, one of the most beautiful and interesting buildings in Austria (see Danny Wilten's work). Another altarpiece portraying what looks like the Trapezium is the Catholic Church of Saint-Merri, Paris, located along the busy street, Rue Saint Martin. Its altar, like Karlskirche, depicts rays bursting out of a Trapezium area and nebula-like clouds surrounding it, full of Seraphim and Cherubs, which could easily be seen to represent the ionized stellar clouds of the Orion Nebula (see figure 309).[18] The body of Christ on the cross (the Adam/Jesus figure) below the Trapezium area, symbolises the *fallen* state of humanity.

Karlskirche was constructed on the order of the Emperor of Austria, following the Baroque architectural style, its sculptural central focus. According to author Danny Wilten, the altarpiece could be one of many depictions of Orion's Trapezium cluster. The clouds and light contained within the art and decor of this central piece seem to correlate with imagery of the Orion Nebula when overlapped. In fact, so much Renaissance art, not least the Creation of Adam by Michelangelo, which forms part of the Sistine Chapel's ceiling, seems to be telling the story of Orion's part in the Gnostic creation myths. The painting quite clearly depicts a 'brain' in profile framing God, who is creating Adam, the first celestial man. What is fascinating is that the word 'men' (man), etymologically, means 'to think', or states of 'mind' (thought). Were the Masters of this period trying to tell us the Orion Nebula houses the mind (or eye) of God? Or more accurately, the 'human mind' under the influence of God (Demiurge)? What is fascinating, in relation to these types of altars and paintings from the Renaissance period, is how they overlap (in great deatil) to give an identical 'visual comparison' of different areas of the Orion Nebula. Danny Wilten writes in his remarkable E-book, *Orion in the Vatican* (2012):

> *The Orion nebula acts as a master key and helps us link these important clues together. Michelangelo presented us God in the Orion nebula. The Tetragrammaton also appears as God in the Orion nebula. What could this bright area represent in the center of the brain? Could this area represent the Pineal Gland?*[19]

If we consider the holographic principle, the Orion Nebula area surrounding the Trapezium seems to be a macrocosm of the human mind-body-spirit. Wilten, through his detailed overlapping of the Orion Nebula, as compared to the brain, reinforces such ideas in a convincing way.

As we travel farther away from the Trapezium into the body of the Nebula, what looks like a human face, a 'red dragon' and the 'lion-headed-

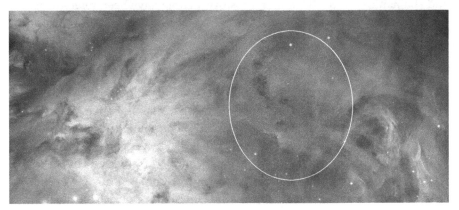

Figure 310: Faces in the Ionized Clouds of the Orion Nebula.
Faces and other entities appearing from within the interstellar clouds of the Orion Nebula (opposite the Trapezium). Is this the Gnostic Demiurge, Adam, or Eve at work amongst the nascent stars? (Public Domain).

serpent (Demiurge) in the Flame Nebula (within Orion), all seem visible in the interstellar cloud of dust, hydrogen, helium and other ionized gases (see figure 310 on the previous page). Other nebulae such as Barnard's Loop, the 'Horse' and 'Monkey Head' also appear in the Orion constellation. It's as though a celestial narrative, unfolding in the ionized gases of Orion's stars, is telling us something profound about our stellar (genetic) origins. I will look at symbolism connected to Orion's Nebulas later. Suffice to say, anything is possible within the realms of 'star magic' and the holographic nature of the Universe.

Fibonacci in the Stars

The Orion Nebula is said to be a place where stars are born. Is it possible that Orion's outer stars (the constellation) were formed by the Orion nebula? Considering some of the information presented earlier in this chapter, could it be possible our sun came from the Orion Nebula, too? Look a little closer at the stars that make up the four outer corners of the Orion constellation. You will notice interstellar dust from Barnard's Loop appearing to trail at least two major stars in the constellation, Betelgeuse and Saiph. If this is the case, then perhaps the Orion nebula has played a much larger role in creation than we thought. As I've touched on already, the Orion Nebula is referenced in multiple cultures, not least the Mayans, at a time when there were no telescopes (or so they say). The Mayan 'Hunab Ku', which they considered to be the centre of the Universe, could also be a focus for the central fire of creation. However, as we have seen so far, the physical ability to see this nebula made no difference to certain artists, seers and shamanic cultures throughout history. People have been referencing it for thousands of years.

French astronomers, Nicolas-Claude Fabri de Peiresc (1580 –1637) and Joseph Gaultier (1564 –1647), were the first to see the Orion Nebula by telescope. Peiresc came from a wealthy 'noble' family and therefore could afford to purchase such a device. The Orion Nebula, like similar nebulae now known as H II regions, or 'emission nebulas', are interstellar, atomic hydrogen that is ionized. H II regions are formed by ionized gases emitting light of various wavelengths, spanning great distances. The most common source of ionization is high-energy photons emitted from a nearby 'hot star'; in Orion's case, this could be the hot Trapezium central area of the Orion Nebula. What is fascinating is how emissions appear to correlate with other sequences and 'forms' found in nature, which again, relates to the holographic nature of the Universe.

The red spiral forming Barnard's Loop is an emission nebula, spanning the full length of the Orion constellation. It is approximately 1500 light-years away and the arc covers a distance of about 300 light-years across. It is thought to be the result of a supernova explosion about 2 million years ago and was also the result of the creation of several runaway stars. When placing a Fibonacci spiral over the top of this loop, one can see the origin of the loop is the Orion Nebula (see figure 311).

Fibonacci numbers are named after Italian mathematician Leonardo of Pisa, later known as Fibonacci and show how mathematical sequences appear in biological settings found in what is called the golden ratio. Knowledge of the Fibonacci sequence was expressed as early as Pingala (450 BC–200 BC) and can be found in music and parallel computing today. The sequence can also be seen in the 'biological' world we call 'reality', not least in shells, flowers, pollen, petals, etc. As I said earlier, the numerical codes creating the Fibonacci sequence are just another expression of the macrocosm and microcosm, and all roads lead to the holographic nature of reality. Why would stars and constellations be any different?

Figure 311: Stars Born of Orion. Orion's Nebula birthing life, while Barnard's Loop trails two stars.

Stars and planets form in clouds of dust and gas called nebulae; using infrared wavelengths, astronomers have been able to see more deeply into the Orion constellation and its nebulae than ever before. One such lead scientist, Holger Drass, at the Astronomisches Institut, Ruhr-Universität Bochum, Germany, has studied such nebulae in depth. His team, using the groundbreaking HAWK-I infrared telescope (VLT) on Europe's Southern Observatory, have produced the deepest and most comprehensive view of the Orion Nebula in recent years (see figure 312 overleaf). Peering through the veils of dust and gas (not just stars) many more planetary-mass objects have been seen by this High Acuity, Wide-field K-band telescope. There are said to be so many planet-sized objects revealed in images of the Orion constellation (and many other constellations) that the thought of life 'existing only' on planet earth is lunacy in my view. Drass said, "Our result feels to me like a glimpse into a new era of planet and star formation science."[20] A planet ten-times bigger than Earth has also been discovered near Orion. Professor Mike Brown at the California Institute of Technology thinks this possible new planet, which is

Figure 312: Orion's Stars and Nebulae.
Orion is a stellar nursery teeming with stars, suns, planets and *life*. © sagesolar

in the southern end of Orion, could be the *ninth* planet of our solar system.[21] In 1983, NASA's Infrared Astronomical Satellite also found signs of an 'unknown object', possibly as large as the 'giant' planet Jupiter and possibly so close to Earth that it would be part of this Solar System'. This object – then referred to as 'Planet X' rather than Planet 9 – was also in the region of Orion. Whatever the 'nature' or names of these planetary bodies, I would suggest that the main stars in the Orion constellation, positioned at the outer edges of the H II region (the Orion Nebula), are teeming with other life forms, some of which I will speculate on in the next few chapters.

As I mentioned earlier in the book, scientists now say all of our galaxies and star systems are holograms projected from black holes. These vortices are said to store information; projecting that information from the surface of the Black Hole to create reality, or our perception of reality. According to astrophysicists (including UQ's Dr Holger Baumgardt), the Orion Nebula has a black hole at its heart, whose mass is some 200 times the mass of our sun. The mini black hole in the Trapezium of Orion appears to have given ancient humans a focus; so much symbolism seems connected to alchemy and other mystical/esoteric systems. Could this focus on a region in space be connected to knowledge of what Orion is actually creating? As I mentioned earlier, what the Mayans called the 'Hearth Fire' in the middle of the Orion Nebula acted as a macrocosm/microcosm for life and death on earth. As we have seen, the alignments of the Great Pyramids and the Hopi mesas testify to this understanding of a 'holographic' projection from Orion, through the solar system and onto the surface of earth by 'those' who constructed these alignments. The scope of this book is not sufficient for me to discuss the detailed science behind such architectural wonders; I am mostly interested in deeper symbolism imbued on humanity that seems to have come from our focus on the 'projection' coming out of the Orion Nebula region. Is all religious focus on God (the creator), the angelic orders and the 'creation of Adam and Eve, nothing more than 'mythological allegory' and 'symbolism' conveying Orion's creation, our solar system and our place in this super holographic projection? I think this is highly likely. The projection I am discussing is 'multidimensional' (macrocosm/microcosm), coming from what the Gnostics called the 'part-twisted mind' of the counterfeit creator – but it is also connected to the light of the *true* creator.

In the next chapter, I want to look at what 'lives' in the projected light made manifest by the counterfeit creator.

Sources:

1) Hall, Manly Palmer. *The Secret Teachings of All Ages*. Tarcher Penguin 2003, p142

2) Blavatsky, Helena Petrovna. *Collected Writings vol. X* (Wheaton, IL: Theosophical Publishing House, 1988, p334

3) Böehme, Jacob. *Böhme's cosmogony or the "Wonder-Eye of Eternity"* (1620), 18th Century Edition.

4) *Paracelsus*. Harriman, p67 and p265.

5) Guirdham, Arthur. *The Great Heresy*. C.W Daniel Company Ltd, 1993, p143

6) Ibid, p144

7) Blavatsky, Helena Petrovna. *The Secret Doctrine*, Theosophical Publishing House, Vol II p215

8) Ibid, p111-112.

9) Susskin, Leonard. *The Black Hole War: My Battle with Stephen Hawking to Make the World Safe for Quantum Mechanics*, Little Brown, 2008, p233

10) Hague, Neil. *Journeys in the Dreamtime*. Quester, 2006, p184

11) Fuller, J. F. C. *The Secret Wisdom of the Qabalah: A Study in Jewish Mystical Thought*. 1937, p23

12) Blavatsky, Helena Petrovna. *The Secret Doctrine*. Theosophical Publishing House Vol II p215

13) Blavatsky, Helena Petrovna. *Isis Unveiled*. Cratylus, 1877, p79.

14) *The Zohar*. Benson, P19

15) Tomas, Andrew. *Shambhala: Oasis of Light*. 1977. p200

16) *The Zohar*, Bension. p.123-4.

17) David, Gary A. *The Orion Zone, Ancient Star Cities of the American Southwest*. 2006, p70

18) Wilten, Danny. *Orion in the Vatican*. 2012, p65

19) *Ibid*, p66

20) https://www.theguardian.com/science/across-the-universe/2016/jul/12/new-orion-image-hints-at-a-wealth-of-earth-sized-planets-awaiting-discovery

21) https://www.dailystar.co.uk/news/latest-news/nibiru-latest-news-nasa-planet-17017350

16

CREATURES OF THE LIGHT

Guardians at Orion's Door

*After he drove man out, he placed on the east side of the Garden of
Eden cherubim and a flaming sword flashing back and forth
to guard the way to the tree of life.*

GENESIS 3:24

Named after the Latin word for 'cloud', nebulae are not only massive
clouds of dust, hydrogen, helium gas, and plasma, they are often 'stellar nurseries', the place where stars are born. Humans are born there, too.
Our DNA is genetic star stuff giving us a myriad of forms (information). As
the projection from a central source takes the form of non-physical structures, these 'forms' manifest as light beings, aliens, entities and angels.
These beings have been described in hermetic, alchemical and religious
texts, not least through the notion of, 'My father's house has many mansions', connected to Jesus (Orion Man). According to the Alchemists,
Hermetic Qabalists and Gnostics, the light emanating from the 'Christos'
and 'Sophia' provided a 'structure' called the Sephiroth, a tree of light (life)
with its branches growing to create multi-dimensional realms (see figure
313). As always, the projector, or invisible sun, sits at the top of the tree,
providing illumination. An engraving by 18th Century German mystic,
author and philosopher, Karl von Eckhartshausen, in his book, *Number
Theory of Nature*, shows the projection becoming ten separate facets of the
same projection – or the Sephiroth (see figure 314).

Von Eckhartshausen's image, like other alchemical hermetic illustrations
of the same period, tries to explain the concept of creation forming the measure of 'all things', including non-physical worlds of the 'gods'. It is also
described as the 'Epithets of God' in Christian terms and this also relates to
the ten areas of the Judaic Sephiroth (Tree of Life), which are: 1) Crown; 2)
Wisdom or Sophia; 3) Prudence; 4) Clemency; 5) Power; 6) Grace; 7)
Triumph; 8) Honour; 9) Redemption and 10) Kingdom of Earth. These
Epithets are part of our 'higher' human nature but can be inverted through

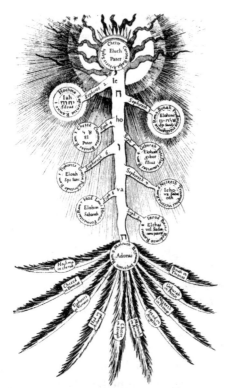

Figure 313: Sephiroth.
The Tree of Life, based on the depiction by Robert Fludd, showing upper and lower worlds of the Sephiroth. (Public Domain.)

Figure 314: Sephiroth as a 'Projection'.
Engraving from Karl von Eckhartshausen, *Zahlenlehre der Natur*, Leipzig, 1794. It shows the projection through the hand of Sophia (while she measures the Divine Child / Christ / Son of Man). (Public Domain.)

duality, as I will explore in a later chapter.

The Sephiroth, is also called the Ogdoad (the Eightfold), or the Holy of Holies. It is said to form the hierarchy of primordial worlds (deities) and 'angelic worlds', all of which dance in the light of the projection. The Holy of Holies, or the projection, is also a 'ladder of light' symbolised through our DNA and spirals in holographic fractals found in the Fibonacci Sequence. The hierarchies contained within the projection, in my view, are expressions of a 'hack' caused by 'lesser celestial bodies' designed to refract light, or hide themselves within it (see the holographic nature of reality I described in the previous chapter). The ripples (or circles) created through the impact of light on lesser celestial bodies connect us energetically, I feel, to 'non-physical' tricksters (the Archons), that according to Gnostic texts, evolved out of 'nuclear fusion' becoming the 'Orion Nebula'. Archons and Angels are the same entities to a lesser degree, and they are all expressions of the light created by the projector. Put another way, if the projector was the source of all that exists within our human reality, it could be compared to a multi-dimensional mansion (made of light), but within its structure (its walls and grounds) other life also exists in the darkest corners of the mansion (the projection). Life, death, all duality centred on Orion, challenged by the Bull of Taurus and anchored by the dwarf stars (Jupiter and Saturn) and their minions (Moons and planets), give us the ingredients for our 'human world'. The 'unseen' interacts with the 'seen' through giants such as Saturn and Jupiter, their waveforms (energetic blueprint) is transmitted to smaller bodies, like the earth. Artificial Intelligence, as I will come to in the next few chapters, and the 'cloud' we all accept now as an alternative storehouse of 'digital reality', is part of this energetic connection to Saturn, Jupiter and specific forces within Orion. Various descriptions of the 'Ogdoad', 'Holy of Holies' or the 'Nine Circles', I would add, are simply 'frequency bands' emitting the blueprint of life (and death) centred on the Orion constellation. The frequencies are further transmitted by our sun (including Sirius) through the 'Kabbalistic Tree' (our Solar 'System').

Unseen Circuitry – Unseen Realms

In the Gnostic *Hypostasis of the Archons*, a 'system' of eight circles were said to be the 'projected heavens', or worlds, forming our immediate Universe; in Norse myth, these 'worlds' also formed the 'world tree', 'Yggdrasil'. They were also called the 'Seven Heavens', with an eighth and ninth world called the 'Ogdoad'. The Ogdoad was considered a 'super celestial region' creating the spheres of the Seven Heavens or 'Seven Stars'. The stars structuring our reality were thought to be Saturn, Jupiter, Mars, the Sun, Venus, Mercury, and Earth's Moon. For the Gnostic mind, each of these stars are presided over by a different archon, or angel. The lower realms (the eighth sphere), beyond the influence of Sophia (from Saturn to the Earth), are said to be the abode of '*Arc*hangels', or *Archon*angels.

Within this overall structure, it was said the Archangel Samael resided in the seventh heaven, although he is declared to be the chief angel of the fifth heaven. It was Jacob in the Bible story who wrestles with Samael, also known as the 'poison of God' (the Demiurge), a poison that symbolically represents the spiritual 'blindness' of those who serve the Demiurge, his priests and institutions on earth. In fact, when we look at Gnostic and Ophite creation stories spanning two thousand years, all hint at the creation of mankind as an integral part of the 'creation of the world'; both world and human are connected as part of the 'projection' outlined in this chapter.

According to the Gnostics, world-creating angels – not one, but *many* –

create mankind (Adam in his fallen state), but the seed of a 'higher spirit' comes into their creature called Adam, 'without their knowledge', by the agency of a higher Aeon (Sophia/Christ). The angels (or archons) are then terrified by the 'faculty of speech' by which their creature rises above them (spiritually) and they ultimately try to destroy him. The Gnostic and Ophite systems give the archon-angels names: Michael, as a lion; Suriel, as an ox; Raphael, as a dragon; Gabriel, as an eagle; Thauthabaoth, as a bear; Erataoth, as a dog; Onoel (or Thartharaoth) as an ass/donkey (see page 319). The central pillar (the projection) connecting all angelic spheres is the *body* of heavenly Adam (Orion), combined with the 'mind' (mankind) of God. At the highest point of the Eight Spheres was the 'Ninth Sphere', where it was said that the 'great archon' - ruled over the 'Dodecad', or *ethereal* region, described as reaching down to the moon.[1] Above and beyond the Dodecad, is the Anthropos, Logos, and the Ogdoad. The dwarf star, or planet Saturn, is hugely influenced by Orion, not least through the Dodecad and unseen worlds (waveforms) connecting each celestial body 'caught in the projection' (see figure 315). Our Solar system, on one level, can be considered a lesser eye (sun) for unseen forces to 'see through' and also a microcosm of the 'original structure' as it projects out of the central Invisible Sun.

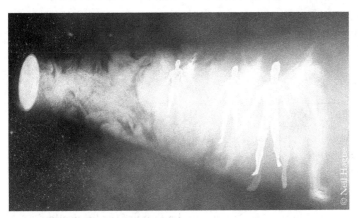

© Neil Hague

Figure 315: Unseen Angelic Realms.
The light of the projector creates many levels, or realities, that are holographic. The farther we travel from the source of the projection, the more solid the worlds are (or seem to be). Just because there is no 'physical life' (so we are told) on neighboring planets, doesn't mean these celestial worlds are not teeming with unseen life forms.
© Neil Hague 2020

What we call angels, ghosts and extraterrestrial entities are, in my view, macrocosmic 'aspects of the projection' mesmerized by its light; the light that constructs all worlds from the highest to the lowest - from the point of projection - to the holographic movie screen we observe as reality (or 'project ourselves' into).

Hierarchy of the Archons (Angels)

A hierarchy of angels is a belief found in the 'angelology' of different religions, which holds that there are different levels or ranks of angels. Higher ranks may be asserted to have greater power or authority over lower ranks, and with different ranks having differences in appearance, such as varying numbers of wings, or faces. Writers such as Pierre Sabak in his book, *Holographic Culture* (2018), refer to angels as "…grafted (stitched) beings that command vessels or UFO's."[2] He also explains how biblical angels, such as the Seraphim are also the Archon, or Jinn mentioned in Gnostic writings. There are also human and non-human angels generally described as 'Elhh Khay', meaning 'High Creature', which are part of the *light* that is the projection I am describing. I imagine angelic realms as lesser projections of the original source, and these lesser hosts could be visualised as 'specks of dust' dancing in a shaft of light within the vastness of the 'house with many mansions' (see figure 316). You cannot 'see the dust' without the light and so it is with the angelic realms. Sabak's etymological research into angels and their names, clearly shows that angels, in their religious context, are no more than otherworldly, extraterrestrial messengers (often invaders) that command vessels (ships). All of this is highly possible; yet, these entities are made of the 'same light' that constructs the hologram.

Figure 316: Dancing in the Light of the 'Projection'. Angelic realms (non physical entities) can be seen beyond our limited spectrum.

Renaissance artists have given us the most common 'visual' interpretation of these 'unseen' forces. They are described as supernatural beings throughout the *Tanakh*, or Hebrew Bible. In the book of *Kings* (19:32-36) and *Exodus* (3:2-4) references to the 'Angel of God' and the origins of angels (or the mal'akh) seem to describe a powerful force capable of both annihilating, or bringing tidings. Angels in the roles of teachers become especially important in Jewish apocalyptic literature, in such books as *Daniel, Zechariah*, and *Ezra*. No matter where we look in orthodox religious texts we find a complex hierarchy of angels, ranked from highest to lowest, into nine orders or groups. As we travel farther away from the source of the light, the projector, and through what Christianity calls the 'Epithets of God', we descend into what are commonly described as 'nine spheres'. Within these spheres are said to be angelic hosts who dwell in the 'refracted light' of the great projector – the Eye of Wonder.

The Assumption of the Virgin (1475) by Francesco Botticini at the National Gallery, London, shows *three* hierarchies and *nine* orders of angels, each with different characteristics. We find the same themes in much Byzantine Orthodox icons also showing 'nine orders' of angels, grouped as Seraphim; Cherubim; Thrones; Dominions or Lordships; Virtues or Strongholds; Powers or Authorities; Principalities or Rulers and Archangels. The number 'nine' is important as I will come to presently, but what is equally telling is the need for an 'other-worldly' hierarchy, which is not different to our earth-matrix hierarchy of royalty, rulers, lords, governments, civil servants, politicians and military with the masses under their subjugation. These are the type of 'beings' that appeared to the originator of the *Book of Mormon*, Joseph Smith. One thing is for sure, angels *are* part of the 'projection' I am describing, and the rebel angels (the fallen) are quite possibly part of the Saturn 'hack' on one level. Duality would also come from the same central point of light as it separates into 'illusory light' and 'dark', night and day, etc. As the philosopher Goethe said in his lectures on Physics in 1806:

> *Visible world, to construct it from light and darkness. Or break it down into light and darkness. That is the task, for the visible world, which we take to be unity, is most agreeably constructed from these two beginnings.*[3]

I would also add that 'reality' is a 'theatre', or a 'movie' and the divisions between people are manufactured, as we shall see in the next chapter. The ultimate god of division (light and dark) found in early Christian texts, is 'Abrasax' (Abraxas) - the god of 'division' and 'separation'.

Abrasax and the Hierarchy of the 'Lower Worlds'

The word 'Abrasax' also comes from Gnostic and Egyptian knowledge alluding to the archons and their creators. Abrasax is therefore the god of 'division' and 'separation' (the great Architect), the one that Essenes warned of at Qumran and that later Cathars of Southern France preached about, saying the world was the creation of Abrasax. The Gnostic Holy Book of the *Great Invisible Spirit*, for instance, refers to Abrasax as an Aeon dwelling with Sophia and other 'Aeons of the Pleroma' in the light of the 'luminary Eleleth' (the Gnostic angelic realm). In several texts, the luminary, Eleleth (or angelic forces), are the last of the luminaries (Spiritual

Lights) that come forward, and it is the Aeon Sophia, associated with Eleleth, who encounters darkness and becomes involved in a chain of events leading to the Demiurge's rule of this world and the salvage effort that ensues. As such, the role of the Aeons of Eleleth, including Abrasax, Sophia, and others, pertains to the 'outer border' of the Pleroma, where Sophia encounters the ignorance of the fake world (the illusion) and interacts with the illusion to rectify the error of ignorance of the world of materiality (physical world). The story of Sophia's 'correction' is based on the 'error being rectified', a subject I have talked about in my lectures and will come back to at the end of the book.

In the 'system' described by the Greek bishop, Irenaeus (130 – 202 AD), noted for his role in guiding and expanding Christian communities in southern Europe, also known as 'the Unbegotten Father', is the progenitor of the Gnostic understanding of the aeons in the form of 'Nous' (the mind of the creator). Through Irenaeus's system, the expansion of the Unbegotten Father passed from 'Nous Logos' (the word or thought), from Logos Phronesis (intelligence), from Phronesis Sophia (wisdom) and Dynamis (actuality); from Sophia and Dynamis, the principalities, powers and angels came into existence. The latter, according to Irenaeus, created the 'First Heaven'. The aeons, in turn, originate a second series of projections creating a 'Second Heaven' until the angels assume the role of authors of our world. In truth, these are *not* angels but the archons, as I have mentioned in earlier chapters. The 'chief deity' of the lower Aeons, or chief Archon was Abrasax, another version of the Demiurge (see page 121).

In a great majority of instances, the name Abrasax, is associated with a singular, composite figure. As I have already shown in *Chapter Four*, the Gnostics showed this deity as having a Chimera-like appearance, somewhat resembling a basilisk or the Greek primordial god, Chronos (not to be confused with the Greek titan, Cronus). According to the English Egyptologist and Orientalist, E. A. Wallis Budge, Abrasax is a 'Pantheus' (or All-God), who has the head of a cock, or of a lion (Ra, or Mithras); the body of a man and his legs are serpents that terminate in scorpions. In his right hand he grasps a club or a flail and in his left is a round, or oval shield (like Orion or Hercules), this form was also referred to as the 'Anguipede', a divinity often found on magical amulets and seen in Vedic and Judaic myths (see figure 317).

E. A. Wallis Budge, surmised that Abrasax was 'a form of Adam on High or Primal Man whom God made in His own image'. In other words, Abrasax, is the fallen state of Adam (Orion), a Frankenstein-like figure who interlopes with archons and angels (see the 2013 movie, *I Frankenstein*). The cockerel is a major symbol for the French Republic amongst other symbols, a

Figure 317: Abrasax.
The fallen Abrasax as a Pantheus;
he carries a flail and Shield, just like
Orion.

nation fully immersed in 'Orion-Abrasax'
consciousness.

Another movie that features Abrasax is
Jupiter Ascending (2014), created by the
Wachowskis who also brought us the
Matrix Trilogy (1999-2003). In *Jupiter
Ascending* we are shown an alien dynasty
called the Abrasax, notably two brothers,
'Balem' (played by Eddie Redmayne),
'Titus' (Douglas Booth) and a sister called,
'Kalique' (Tuppence Middleton). The
mother of these off-world gods is called
'Seraph', another reference to the angelic
orders I will explore further. The
Wachowskis, in my view, are making a
direct reference to the archon hierarchy in
this movie. Balem is the elder heir to a rul-
ing alien dynasty that live like our earthly elite (our Royals) but 'magnified
hundreds of thousands of times'. He is shown in the movie to travel on a
floating boat (raft) in his kingdom, just as the god, Abrasax does. Where
earth's elite own countries, in the movie, the Abrasax Siblings own planets;
it's all a matter of scale.[4] I will come back to this movie's theme later in the
book, but it could also be that the three siblings (four if you add the 'queen-
to-be', Jupiter herself) are all connected, not least symbolically to the dwarf
stars 'Jupiter', 'Saturn' and the wanderer, Venus. What *Jupiter Ascending*
does brilliantly is show the 'scale' and 'vastness' of these planets (stars) and
therefore the size of the structures they could harbour. What lives on
Jupiter, or Saturn, does not necessarily have to be 'physical'. As I am
attempting to illustrate here, the 'house of many mansions' (constructed
from the light of the projector) and therefore everything within its influence
can be seen to be both non-physical and physical, depending on the wavelengths of light we are accessing.

In biblical texts, the 'Seraphim' (Seraph in *Jupiter Ascending*) are
described as the highest order of the hierarchy of Angels. The word,
'Seraph' translates as the 'burning one' or 'burning serpent' and clearly
relates to the fiery (reptilian-like) Jinn mentioned earlier in the book. In the
Book of Isaiah, the Seraphim are described as six-winged 'beings' that fly
around the 'Throne of God', crying "Holy, Holy, Holy" *(Isaiah 6:1–8)* see figure 318 overleaf. I would suggest the 'Throne' is the 'Eye of Providence'
(the central sun) contained within the Trapezium as depicted in certain
pieces of Greek iconic art (see figure 319 overleaf). The triangle above the

Figure 318: Seraph.
Cherub on a Neo-Assyrian seal, c. 1000–612 BC.

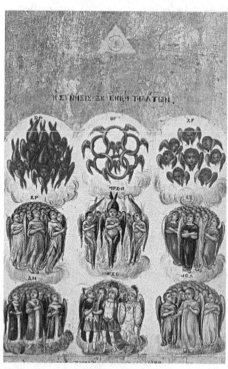

Figure 319: The Nine Orders.
The archon/angelic hierarchy, showing nine orders under the 'eye', or 'throne'. Note the Trapezium above the groups of angels.
(Public domain)

nine angelic orders, in my view, is a stylized version of the Trapezium in the Orion Nebula.

The Seraphim are non-human celestial fire, or light; and like heat, the Seraphim move upwards and are continuous in their motion around the eye or throne (central sun) within Orion's Nebula. They are part of the ionized gases forming within the nebula and can be seen to appear through the clouds forming in the nebula itself. In the Book of *Isaiah*, they are described as the physical representation of Christ and of the Holy Spirit. They are also depicted on the Ark of the Covenant as its 'Guardians' (Guardians of the Galaxy) and relate to the power invested in the Ark, which was quite possibly some kind of extraterrestrial weapon, or 'vessel'. It is said also in *Genesis* that God sent the Seraphim to guard Eden after the expulsion of Adam and Eve: 'After He drove the man out, he placed on the east side of the Garden of Eden cherubim and a flaming sword flashing back and forth to guard the way to the tree of life' (*Genesis*: 24). As I mentioned in *Chapter Five*, the sword, in this narrative, relates to the immediate and surrounding regions of the Orion Nebula - and the interstellar forces converging below the Trapezium. The 'flaming' sword of Orion comprises three stars (42 Orionis, Theta Orionis, and Iota Orionis) and M42, the Orion Nebula, which together, are thought to resemble a sword, or a scabbard. Iota Orion is a 'multiple star system' and in most cases, each star orbits another within its own system. Just as the Seraphim are said to orbit the Throne (the Trapezium area), these multiple 'triple star systems' osculate towards the nebula's centre of 'mass'.

The 'Covenant' and the Cherubim

Kesil (Orion) is often shown holding 'keshet' (a bow), and is a weapon twinned in Hebrew with 'kashtit', meaning the 'iris of the eye', another insignia of the Seraphim. Hence the symbolism of many eyes on the wings, or bodies, of gods (such as Argos), giants and even on the clothing of royalty, not least Elizabeth I. In Judaic theology, 'keshet' (the bow of war) is also a signifier of 'keshet be'anan' (a rainbow – literally a 'bow of the cloud'). Bow symbolism, according to Pierre Sabak, "... is accorded with the descendants of Orion in particular the 'Covenant' between Noah and the 'Elohim' (the High Ones) following the great flood which destroyed mankind." Sabak, like myself, believes that the use of the words 'bow' and 'cloud' and 'covenant' in the book of *Genesis* refer to the Orion Nebula (see figure 320).

The angelic realms are part of a 'hierarchy' descending out of Orion to form the covenant between the 'unseen' and those on earth who are considered humanity's 'rulers' (the Shining Ones). In the Book of *Genesis*, the story of the deluge is replete with astro-theological symbolism from which the descendants of mankind are destroyed and replanted upon the earth; to quote *Genesis* Chapter 9 Verses 12-16:

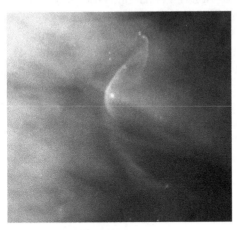

Figure 320: The Covenant in Orion.
The bow shape to the lower right of the Trapezium inside the Orion Nebula. (PD)

And God said, "This is the token of the covenant which I make between me and you and every living creature that is with you, for perpetual generations: I do set my bow in the cloud [a rainbow / the bow of Orion], and it shall be for a token of a covenant between me and the Earth. And when it shall come to pass, when I bring a cloud over the Earth, that the bow shall be seen in the cloud [Nebula of Orion]. And I will remember my covenant, which is between me and you and every living creature of all flesh; and the waters shall no more become a flood to destroy all flesh. And the bow shall be in the cloud; and I will look upon it, that I may remember the everlasting covenant between God and every living creature of all flesh that is upon the Earth" '... and the Sons of Noah went forth from the ark... and of them was the whole Earth overspread.[5]

According to Abrahamic religions, the 'Cherubim' are described as unearthly beings said to directly attend to God (the Gnostic Demiurge). In pre-Christian mysticism, there has long been a strong belief in Cherubim and other angels regarded as having influence over humanity. Cherubim, or Kerubim, are an order of angel described in the Bible as a combination of two, or more often, four creatures - including that of a human. The mythical Sphinx of Egypt and the scriptural cherubim are 'hybrid' beings combining two to four creatures with wings. It is also interesting to see how diagrams of the human brain, illustrating the 3rd ventricle as seen in *Stedman's medical dictionary* (1911), show what could be Cherubim wings contained within the human brain (see figure 321). This is another example of the holographic nature of reality. As I said earlier, human 'beings' and the Earth itself, must *all* be a macrocosm of the holographic projection.

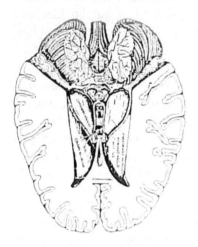

Figure 321: The Ventricle.
The folded wings of the Cherubim.
Symbolic of the light inside our brain.

The *Zohar* states that the Cherubim were led by one of their number named 'Kerubiel'.[6] The word 'Kerubim' (Kerubiel) means 'one who prays', or 'one who intercedes'. Lucifer is described as both a cherub and an angel. In *Ezekiel*, Lucifer is described as the anointed Cherub.[7] The Apostle Paul explains Satan himself is transformed *into* an angel of light (*Corinthians* 11:14) and the only link in the Bible showing that cherubim are angels; no other cherub is described as an angel directly. Jesus says in *Luke* that he saw Satan as 'lightning fall' from heaven (*Luke* 10:18), which is consistent with the movement of a cherub described by Ezekiel (*Ezekiel* 1:14) and also correlates with the *electro*-plasmic nature of the stars and nebulae.

Ezekiel's Creatures of Light

The description of the Cherubim in various biblical texts, all seem to be talking about 'creatures of light' (electro-plasma), hybrid in form, composed of human and animal. Other religious imagery depicts them as 'children' or babies (especially in places like the Vatican), which speaks volumes regarding the true 'nature' of the deeply disgusting and 'depraved creatures' in the Vatican that have abused children for centuries. One cannot help but wonder if the 'energetic connection' between the depravity of paedophile priests and the very structure of the Vatican (its energetic foundation) are not part of the connection to these unseen 'so-called angelic' forces. The Cherubim as a cherub (baby) is also the closest image of the Gnostic description of the archons (angels) resembling a fetus. To quote *Ezekiel*: "And it [the paneling of the holy place of the temple] was made with cherubs ...and two faces were to a cherub, the face of a man, toward the palm tree from here, and a young lion's face toward the palm tree from there. It was made to all the house round and round...on the wall of the temple."[8] The lion, of course, is another representation of the Demiurge *and* the archons I mentioned earlier in the book, all of which are variations of the Cherubim.

In *Ezekiel* the Cherubim are described as having the likeness of a man (humans), and having four faces: that of a man, a lion (on the right side), an ox (on the left side), and an eagle. The four faces represent the four domains of God's rule: the man represents humanity; the lion, wild animals; the ox, domestic animals and the eagle, birds.[9] The Cherubim can also be seen in the four galactic markers (or precessional astrological quadrants) found in the zodiac, as the age of Leo (Lion), Taurus (Ox), Scorpio (Eagle) and Aquarius (man). These are also the four apostles / gospels in the New Testament, as the Winged Man (Matthew), Winged Lion (Mark), Winged Ox (Luke) and the Eagle (John). The latter is 'born with wings' and represents the idea of 'revelation' and the Apocalypse. An image taken from the *Johannes Piscator Bible* (1602 –1604), *Apocalypse Angel with Book*, also portrays the Cherubim as a hybrid, celestial lightning-being. As I have already shown, these zodiac markers connect to the rise and fall of Orion throughout the year (see figure 322) with Orion's position next to the Ox (the Taurean bull) and Orion's opposite - the sign of Scorpio – the Eagle.

Figure 322: Arabic depictions of the Cherubim.
Creatures of Light encircling a sun.
The 'four supporters (angels) of the celestial throne' (detail from a Persian Manuscript 373).

Many mythological hybrid gods found in art forms throughout the ancient Near East, ancient Greece, Phoenicia and ancient Egypt, I am certain, are based on the focus on the celestial cherubim (see figure 323 overleaf). One example is the Babylonian 'lamassu' or 'shedu', a

**Figure 323: Celestial Cherubim -
Creatures of Light.**
Altarpiece by Nicodemus Tessins, Denmark
1732. (Public domain)

'protective spirit' with a sphinx-like form, possessing the wings of an eagle, the body of a lion, and the head of a king. The wings are often the most prominent part, and like the Winged lion on the West façade of St Mark's Basilica in Venice, these images represented various forms assumed by the Cherubim (see figure 324). The stars behind the lion on St Mark's Basilica are telling us of the angelic realms connected to the stars, not least the Orion Nebula and surrounding stars. There is also another important symbolic piece of art inside St Mark's Basilica, which I'll come to in the next chapter.

The four markers, or faces, assigned to the Cherubim are part of the 'energetic covenant' between earth

Figure 324: St. Mark.
Celestial winged Cherubim on St Mark's
Basilica in Venice. The archons are lion-like.

and the stars. The Cherubim also make up the body of what Pierre Sabak calls 'Proto-human', a light (star) being born on a vessel (spaceship); a being *not* genetically modified (see *Chapter Thirteen*). As mentioned in *Part One*, the number four, numerologically relates to 'dedication' to 'structure' and the 'mechanics of hierarchy', which is why we see 'four' everywhere in landmarks and iconic symbolism connected to the elite. The use of 'four' points (the cross), 'markers' and 'pillars' are often reminders of the covenant between angelic orders and the royalty on earth.

Trafalgar Square in London, with its 'four lions', is a classic example of the 'structure' and 'markers' denoting the influence of the 'Cherubim' (archons) through the 'Thrones', 'Dominions', 'Virtues', 'Powers', 'Principalities' and 'archangels' over the earth. Leylines are also influenced by angels, too. The fourth card of the major arcane is the 'Emperor' and this again is another symbol of authority over others, royalty and lordship. The Cherubim (like the Seraphim) are often shown to have four wings, reminding us of the hierarchy of the angelic realms and the structure of invisible worlds, which are part of the projection out of Orion.

A Game of 'Thrones'

In Christian angelology, 'Thrones' are a class of angel, and third-ranking in the order of angels. They were also known as 'Wheels' or the 'Many-Eyed Ones' (see figure 325). These angels were often believed to be 'deployed' like charioteers, around the Throne of God (the Trapezium within Orion's Nebula) and were described in *Ezekiel*, 'as having four wings and four faces'. They are also described as moving on wheels in the middle of wheels and blue-green in colour. They are described in *Ezekiel*, 'above their heads the likeness of the firmament, which was the color of crystal, and under this were their wings, two on each side of their bodies. The noise of their wings was like the noise of great waters.'[10]

Figure 325: Thrones, Space-ships.

The wheels and eyes seen in Ezekiel's vision of the 'chariot' (or Merkabah, in Hebrew) describes the 'wheels' and 'eyes' as angels (*Ezekiel* 1:15-21). Similar descriptions are also in one of the *Dead Sea scrolls* (4Q405). Other descriptions can be seen in late sections of the *Book of Enoch* (61:10, 71:7) portraying the Thrones as a class of 'celestial being' who (along with the Cherubim and Seraphim) never sleep, but guard the throne of God. Just like the seventh card of the Major Arcana in the tarot, the Chariot, is constantly moving and controlled by a prince (royalty), or angel. Many angelic eyes also appear in William Blake's illustration in Dante's *Divine Comedy* (Canto 29), titled, *Beatrice Addresses Dante from the Car* (1824). The car, or chariot, is both a symbol of the institution of the church but also a 'ship' and in Blake's version, the chariot is also a gryphon (a symbol of the Christos). The figure Beatrice, who appears as one of Dante's guides in the *Divine Comedy*, is surrounded by Cherubim and Thrones; symbolised as four supporters and the multitude of eyes. Some say the figure, Beatrice

Portinari, in Dante's work was hidden code for the original Gnostics (Sophia). Other writers have said Dante was a Cathar (Gnostic) with connections to the Templars, so this would make sense, if true.

Paintings of Elizabeth I, not least *The Rainbow Portrait* (1563) by Isaac Oliver, show eyes (and ears) embroidered on the queen's dress, a reference to the bloodline of the Watchers, Elohim and the angelic Seraphim. The name of the Phoenician letter 'øeyn', 'O', means 'eye', and its shape originates simply as a drawing of a human eye (possibly inspired by the corresponding Egyptian hieroglyph of a winged creature or bird). The Hebrew word Erelim (or Er'el) is usually not translated 'thrones', but rather 'valiant ones', 'heroes' or 'warriors', which is exactly the role of the charioteering Thrones. They are warrior-like, celestial (non-physical) flying discs, or 'sky boats'. Rosemary Ellen Guiley, in her book *Encyclopedia of Angels* (1996) states: "... the 'thrones'; also known as 'ophanim' (offanim) and 'galgallin', are creatures that function as the actual chariots of God driven by cherubs."[11] These chariots, or thrones, could also be considered vessels, crafts or (space) ships, as often described by those who have seen extraterrestrial crafts and UFOs. There are far too many examples of UFOs in art and witnessed by the ancients, through to modern times, to dismiss such phenonema.

The Dominions, or Lordships.

As we move further away from the source (the projector) we find another angelic host called 'Dominions' or *dominationes*, a word translated from the Greek term 'kyriotetes'. The projection of light I am talking about creates 'circles within circles' as it passes through the refractors – the sun and moon 'portals', which then orders the celestial/astral bodies of 'all beings' caught up in the projection at this point. Some writers claim the order of hierarchy, from spirit to flesh and bone, is also caught up in the angelic world (within the projection) and our astral bodies are part of the realms under the influence of the Dominions.

The Dominions are believed to look like humans with a pair of feathered wings, much like the common representation of angels, but they may be distinguished from other groups by wielding orbs of light fastened to the heads of their sceptres, or on the pommel of their swords. The Dominions are said to regulate the duties of lower angels, the 'Rulers' and 'Archangels'. According to some, this Order of Guardian Angels can decide the success or failure of nations, which on one level would be true, as those who run the world (from the unseen) are influenced by these angelic/archon (ET) orders. I would suggest here we are talking about 'non-physical' influence over our physical world through secret societies under the influence of angels, or archons. The Dominions (or Kyriotetes) have been described as wearing long, hooded gowns reaching to their feet, hitched with a golden belt and carrying golden staffs in their right hand. At other times, they are said to hold an 'orb' or a 'sceptre' all of which can be seen repeatedly through our perception of royalty and authority. See every religious order of monk and secret society going back to ancient Egypt and later Gnostics.

The Virtues or Strongholds.

For some, these angelic forces are said to manifest as 'signs' and 'miracles' in our reality. The term 'virtue' appears to be linked to the attribute 'might', from the Greek root 'dynamis' (dynameis) in *Ephesians* 1:21, which can be translated as 'Virtue' or 'Power'. The forces here are either 'virtuous' or 'vicious' in their use of power, another aspect of duality born of the projection and most likely the source of 'fallen angels' who followed Satan (follow Saturn) within biblical narratives.

The Virtues have also been called 'The Brilliant or Shining Ones', the latter, of course, relates to the Watchers and Elhoim I have already mentioned in *Part One*. In the *Book of Enoch*, the angel Ramiel is described as one of the leaders of 200 'Grigori' (Watchers), or fallen angels, and is identified as 'Semjaza' who can appear as thunder and lightning. Other names for the Virtues, derived from 'Pseudepigrapha' (texts ascribed to various biblical patriarchs and prophets but composed within approximately 200 years of the alleged birth of Christ) and recognized by Eastern Orthodox and Oriental Orthodox churches, are 'Selaphiel', 'Jegudiel', and 'Raguel' - the latter being the Judiac Angel of Justice.

The Virtues were also called 'Angels of Miracles', dedicated to encouragement and blessings and according to the church, are particularly involved in aiding people struggling with their faith. Struggling with their 'mind-control' is a more accurate description. Virtues are said to be chief bestowers of grace and valour on one level, or they could also be the source of demonic possession. Again, the latter is prominent within the highest levels of the church and machinery of power on earth. The two angels at the Ascension of Jesus were traditionally believed to be from the Order of Virtues according to John 7:33-65. As I have already pointed out, Jesus (as Orion), often shown on a 'cloud' in modern religious imagery, could relate to the Orion Nebula and its ionized clouds, the source of these creatures of light. Many paintings from the Renaissance period onwards, from Botticelli, to Gustave Doré's depictions of angelic hosts for Dante's *Paradiso* (1870), often show creatures of light forming around a celestial light, or door. Therefore, the so-called Ascension of Jesus, I feel, is pure symbolism associ-

ated with the Nebula and the 'hierarchy of angels' I am describing here
(see figure 326 overleaf).

Powers or Authorities

The primary duty of the 'Powers'
(Authorities), according to the
Roman Christian Church, is to
supervise the 'movements' of heavenly bodies in order to ensure the
Heavens remain in order. You might
ask under 'whose order' are these
powers supervising? The lord architect - the Demiurge (God), of course;
he who 'placed' the sun, moon and
planets accordingly (so precisely) to
harness the light of the projector.

© Neil Hague

Figure 326: A Projection of Angels.

These celestial 'powers' are said
to be the sixth ranking Order of Angels and are credited as being the first
Order of Angels 'organised' by the Demiurge. You could say these are the
'workforce' or scaffolding of the great architect's 'construct'. They are
responsible for maintaining the 'border' between Heaven and Earth, or the
'boundary' between the Upper Aeons and Lower Aeons; like the Seraphim
(Jinn), they act as guards on the doors at every level of the 'Father's House
of many mansions'. The War in Heaven, between forces of good and evil, is
a mirror of all earthly wars, *all* influenced by unseen realms and the angelic
orders I am describing here. The war between humans and the machines, in
the Gnostic *Matrix* movie trilogy, is a perfect example of how worlds 'outside' of the illusory earth-matrix are influencing the matrix. The warring
factions within the 'ranks' of the archon/angelic orders (on unseen levels)
are still playing out their war games through our global military-industrial
nations (authorities) on earth. This is why so much military insignia, air-
borne badges and general militaria are littered with angel wings, swords,
lightning, skulls and talons, etc. We are replicating the Powers and
Authorities in our human world. The deeply disturbing Order of Nine
'Angles' (*not angels*) - ONA organization in the UK, the 'Church of Satan'
and the 'Temple of Set', established in the United States in 1975 by Michael
Aquino (an American political scientist, military officer, and a high-ranking
member of Anton LaVey's Church of Satan), are all examples of a 'non-
physical influence' ruling over the minds of those in power or authority.
The same could be said of every 'cult' or religion (including 'celebrity wor-

ship'), all designed as vehicles for taking human power and having authority over us.

The Principalities or Rulers.

The 'Principalities' (Latin: *principatus*) also translated as 'Princedoms' and 'Rulers', from the Greek word 'archai', are said to be the fifth-highest order of the ninefold celestial angelic hierarchy. Like the Powers, they are said to be angels that guide and protect nations, groups of peoples and institutions. The Principalities are often shown wearing a 'crown' (like kings or Queens), and carrying a 'sceptre', similar to depictions of the Thrones. As with our physical reality, from the upper echelons of control (our 'rulers'), to the lower classes, these angelic worlds form part of the same holographic projection. According to religious texts, Principalities' duty is to 'carry out the orders' given to them by the upper sphere of angels (archons), and just like our material physical world, the lesser angels are expected to do as they are told. During the Late Middle Ages from 1200 to 1500, Principalities (on earth) were often at war with each other as royal houses asserted sovereignty over smaller principalities. The core ideology of these unseen forces I sketch out in this chapter are obsessed with war and hierarchy, as we shall see towards the end of the book.

Some say the Principalities were considered to be the 'guardians over 'nations' and 'world leaders', and it is believed they are given more freedom to 'act' than lesser angels below them. I often wondered if these forces could influence the group identity of a nation, or a country, or even a 'leader'. Possession of a nation (collective mind) or a world leader (whether a public face, or a hidden one), these angelic-archon entities can, and do, influence our world. The Principalities are thought to be responsible for carrying out divine acts concerning their area of jurisdiction, which according to some, can manifest as 'coming to someone's aid' in the physical world. To say, 'an angel must be watching over me' relates to such acts. The same influence can also be seen as 'acts of madness', brutality manifested through violence, war and the plight of nations. It is said that it was from the Principalities came an Angel to aid David in his task of slaying the giant, Goliath. David was said to have been helped by an angel and Goliath was quite possibly a descendant of the angelic host, part-human, part-Rephaim (Nephilim), or as Pierre Sabak states in his book *Angelic Invasion* and *Holographic Culture*, a 'stitched' angelic offspring.[12] Principalities have been described as 'soldier angels' (possibly aliens, or 'Greys') who are commanded by those above them (the Elohim) and those who call upon them.

Angels, demons, Archons and otherworldly entities, etc., are, I would suggest, the source of much extraterrestrial activity.

Archangels

Below the Principalities we find the 'Archangels', a word that comes from the Greek (archangelos) meaning 'chief angel', or 'angelos' - a 'messenger' or 'envoy'. Archangel also derives from the Greek 'archein', meaning to be 'first in rank', or power. According to religious texts, there are said to be fifteen Archangels named as follows: Ariel - Lioness of God (more on this force later in the book); Azrael – Whom God Helps; Chamuel – He Who Sees God; Gabriel – Strength of God; Haniel – Grace of God; Jeremiel – Mercy of God; Jophiel – Beauty of God; Metatron – Highest of Angels (twin); Archangel Michael – He Who is Like God; Raguel – Friend of God; Raphael – God Heals; Raziel – Secrets of God; Sandalphon - Highest of Angels (twin); Uriel – Light of God and Zadkiel – Righteousness of God.[13] Out of this group of 'fifteen' we have *seven* main Archangels named as: Michael, Gabriel, Uriel, Chamuel (Camael), Raphael, Jophiel, and Zadkiel. But only two archangels are mentioned by name in the Bible - Michael and Gabriel. The names of the other archangels are thought to come from tradition and other antiquated sources, not least the 4th Century father, Pseudo-Dionysius the Areopagite, and mystics such as Emanuel Swedenborg in the 18th Century.

According to the books and sources on angels (such as the *Areopagite's*, *On Angelic Properties and Orders*), the Seven Archangels are said to be guardian angels of nations and countries with Principalities; according to one Internet source, these are concerned with the issues and events surrounding politics, military matters, commerce and trade. For example: Archangel Michael is traditionally seen as the protector of 'Israel' and of the ecclesia.[14] Archangels are 'chief Archons' in my view, working for 'forces' that have constructed the illusion (out of light) affecting the natural and material world and have given humanity its hierarchies of control. According to Rudolf Steiner, four important archangels also display periodic spiritual activity over the seasons: Spring is Raphael, Summer is Uriel, Autumn is Michael and Winter is Gabriel.[15] I wonder if the angelic hosts (the chief Archons) are the real protagonists of climate change on earth and every other planet in the Solar system?

Archangel Michael is believed to be the highest-ranking *warrior* angel in God's heavenly host. Michael is said to play a special role in the end-of-time narratives found in the *Book of Revelation*. On one level he is a representation of the Sun and the constructed illusion through solar light, which is why we find many sacred sites (especially on islands) dedicated to St. Michael, or the Archangel, Micheal. He is also connected to Saturn's matrix and can be seen as 'rays of light', the central pillar descending to earth in the Qabalah. The 'hairy angels' (or 'earth angels') I mentioned in *Chapter*

Thirteen, are also connected to the Sun and Orion's stars (the solar influence over nature). Sunlight filtering into a forest is very much symbolic of 'forces' attributed to earth angels and their natural connection to nature and animal consciousness. The mini projections, or shafts of light filtering into the forest, especially in wild, untouched places on earth, acts as a *doorway* into invisible realms (see figure 327). This is something I have personally experienced while immersed in dense forests with no other humans around for miles. The shafts of light act as portals for non-physical entities to make themselves felt (or seen) in our world, such as Bigfoot, fairies, gnomes (ETs) and their like found in global folklore. The light reflected through stained glass windows in certain cathedrals built in the middle Ages is also an attempt to reproduce creative, interdimensional aspects

Figure 327: Doorways to Angelic Realms.
A first class ticket to the angelic realms courtesy of the sun and the forest. This energetic connection was replicated in every gothic cathedral in Christendom. (Public domain)

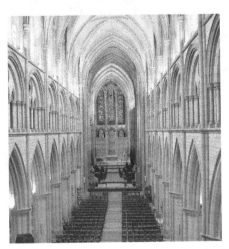

Figure 328: Replicating the Forest.
Gothic Cathedrals are the house of the angelic host, both good and bad (but mainly bad). © Jack Pease Photography

of light echoing the angelic worlds. It is the same watery-like 'aeon light', which the likes of Abbé Sugar (who was responsible for the Basilica of Saint Denis in Paris in 1137) tried to convey with similar effects on stained glass windows and immense architecture (see figure 328). The columns of the cathedral with light reflecting through stained glass windows were the Church's 11th Century interpretation of the mystic forest and druidic grove. Interestingly, the Sefirot can often be seen in the inside roof and upper architecture where the columns converge into 'arches' of many gothic cathedrals.

Messengers of Light

Archangel Gabriel is considered the highest-ranking 'messenger' who
brought special messages to people in the Bible. In Scripture, we find
Gabriel bringing messages to Daniel to reveal future events to him *(Daniel
8:16; 9:21)*. He also went to Zacharias regarding the birth of John the Baptist
(*Luke* 1:19) and to Mary to announce the birth of Jesus (*Luke* 1 :30). I am certainly not religious, as evidenced from my writings and art, but I find it
interesting that these archangels (merely archons in Gnostic writings) were
supposedly pivotal in both pre-Christian and Christian texts such as the
Book of Enoch. I would suggest that almost all religions on earth are
'inspired' by archon-angelic sources connected to the Watchers and Shining
Ones I've mentioned throughout the book.

The Essenes, who gave us the *Dead Sea Scrolls*, had an elaborate but simple series of 'contemplations' based on the seven
archangels, which correlated with the seven days of
the week. Much of the Essene contemplations (or
meditations) were contained within the *Book of
Hymns*, texts which connected invisible worlds to
the visible world, rather like a tree trunk connects
the upper branches with its hidden roots. The
Essene 'Tree of Life' symbolism was similar to later
alchemical drawings by Fludd (see page 140). The
Archangels were also 'titles' inferred on initiates
within the Essene brotherhood, which is probably
where the stories in the *Book of Daniel* and the 'messages' to Zacharias, announcing the coming of the
prophet and messiah, originated.

Angels & the Electromagnetic Spectrum

The Archangel Chamuel, whose name is said to be
'He Who Sees God', is considered the Archangel of
strength, courage and war in Christian and Jewish
angelology. Chamuel can also appear to be dualistic,
as an angel (archon) of both light and dark (see figure 329). Chamuel sits in the *middle* of the seven
archangels and can be 'seen' to represent the light
and dark spectrum of 'visible light', symbolised by
the rainbow. Could higher orders of angels be symbolic of the *seven* aspects of our electromagnetic

Figure 329: Chamuel.
Chamuel (Camael) is one
of the ten angels and one of
the main seven Archangels
along with Michael,
Gabriel, Raphael, Uriel,
Jophiel, and Zadkiel.

spectrum from Radio through to Gamma? The electromagnetic spectrum is constructed through Radio Waves: Instant Communication. Microwaves: Data and Heat. Infrared Waves: Invisible Heat. Visible Light Rays: The rainbow. Ultraviolet Waves: Energetic Light. X-rays: Penetrating Radiation.

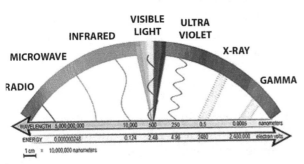

Gamma Rays: Nuclear Energy (see figure 330). I am purely speculating here as there is no evidence I can find that would correlate such ideas, but it is interesting to note that electromagnetic radiation comes in a *range* of energetic forms, known as the

Figure 330: *Seven* **Archangel (Angelic) Bandwidths?**
Another way of seeing the archangelic spectrum.

electromagnetic spectrum; electromagnetic light and radiation travels in 'waves', just like waves on the ocean. The aeon 'watery light' talked about by the Gnostics is also described as existing as various levels of light, all of which could relate to the spectrum beyond visible light, or the wavefield. As Jonathan Talat Phillips writes in *The Electric Jesus: The Healing Journey of a Contemporary Gnostic* (2011):

> *With the illusion stripped away, I could see that we were part of an ocean of light. We are light flowing, moving, and transmuting shape similar to the way that water morphs into steam and ice and snow.*[16]

The word 'light' usually makes us think of the colours of the rainbow, or light from the sun, or a lamp. This light, however, is only one type of electromagnetic radiation. It is the light behind the 'speed of light' that is of the highest 'living source of energy', or what the Gnostic's called the 'aeon light'.

Electromagnetic radiation travels in waves and the energy of radiation depends on the 'distance between the crests' (highest points) of the waves, or wavelength. The smaller the wavelength, the 'higher' the energy of radiation. Gamma rays, for example, have wavelengths less than ten trillionths of a metre, about the size of the nucleus of an atom. This means that gamma rays have very high energy, whereas radio waves, on the other side of the spectrum, have wavelengths ranging from less than one centimetre to greater than 100 metres. The energy of radio waves is much lower than the energy of other types of electromagnetic radiation. The important point here is that the only type of light detectable by human eyes is 'visible light' (the rainbow), which is the tiniest portion of electromagnetic light. Everything we can't see, therefore, must be *hiding* on other wavelengths as part of the greater projection of light I've been describing. The angelic worlds, I would suggest, are 'hidden' to the eye and beyond the tiny portion of light we see. So are the entities of light often appearing in *orbs* and other ethereal objects from time to time.

Delving in the Dark

What is becoming more and more apparent through the work of astrophysicists and scientists studying parallel realities, is that the majority of what exists in our universe is undetected by the five senses - 95% of all matter to be precise.[17] What we cannot see, touch, taste, smell or hear therefore belongs to the realms of 'thought' and the emotions that manifest in the physical world. Our imagination and memories are also harnessed through thought; it is through our imagination and intuition that we can uncover our sixth-sense ability. The imagination is our most unique tool for transforming our world and by the same token, it is the most suppressed part of our psyche. So are our deepest 'feelings' associated with love and creativity, which can provide us with a higher directional purpose in life. These, too, are often suppressed through day-to-day drudgery of the five-sense (rainbow) world. Our reason for 'being', our visions and deep-rooted knowledge of oneness, is in my view, the path to truth, wisdom and peace. Loving ourselves and trusting our creativity connects us to super (or higher) consciousness. Therefore, if we do not know ourselves as individuals, how can we truly know others? We are taught from an early age that the physical world consists of three dimensions, governed by the predictable laws of physics and chemistry. Our failure to admit how limited our knowledge is of those particular sciences, combined with a common human arrogance that pretends a mastery of those same sciences, only dooms future generations to the same small set of choices previous generations deliberated over. As always, it has been the visionary, the individual, the maverick artist or scientist, through genius, that has constantly reminded humanity that we use only a fraction of our true universal power. As Sir Francis Bacon once said:

Ipsa scientia potestas est (Knowledge itself is power)

It is accepted by mainstream science that ninety-five per cent of what is understood as matter is undetectable by our five senses. In other words, what we 'see', touch, taste and hear and smell (the visible spectrum) is only a fraction of what exists within the universe. This ratio corresponds with human brain capacity and how we are said to be using only around *five percent* of our brain. In astrophysical terms, the larger portion of life (energy / matter) we don't see is referred to as 'dark matter', or 'dark light'. The notion of dark matter, or electromagnetic 'weak forces', as physicists describe it, first became evident about sixty years ago.[18] The term 'dark matter' was concocted to get around a disturbing fact that galaxies spin so fast that they should have twirled apart aeons ago. Something else is holding together the oscillations of galaxies and atoms, something which is 'alive'. The projection I am describing is part of this living force. Science is also coming to the irrepressible conclusion that there isn't nearly enough gravity to hold the whole conglomeration of stars together. However, what is becoming obvious is that interference waves, subatomic particles and the higher dimensional space is key to understanding the nature of reality, along with the science of holograms. This understanding connects us to what Jung called the *Superconsciousness*, or the Aeons in our minds.

The mind is also unknown territory for conventional science and confused with the physical brain. As I said in *Chapter Fourteen*, the mind is not the brain! The Nobel laureate, Isidor I. Rabi was once asked what event in his life first set him on the long journey to discover the secrets of nature. He replied that it was when he checked out some books on the planets from his library. What fascinated him was that the human mind is capable of knowing such cosmic truths: *"The planets and stars are so much larger than humans, yet the human mind is able to understand them."*[19] As I've been highlighting in these chapters, the planets and stars are our energy – consciousness interacting with our mind; our consciousness. The angelic realms are merely an 'expression of consciousness' that we can either interact with or 'bypass' – when we connect directly with the source – the Invisible Sun.

In recent years, astrophysicists have recorded giant 'vacuums' between stars, which they say are full of living particles (bodies) that we cannot see. Just as any substance placed under a microscope reveals bodies that would normally be undetected by the naked eye, various star systems are revealing interesting 'energies' that can be detected and in some cases 'felt' here on earth. As far back as 2000, *The New York Times* reported that the Orion Nebula has revealed the existence of some kind of 'unworldly' dark matter. The same article went on to state that:

> *Empty space is pervaded by a mysterious dark energy, a kind of anti gravitational humph that is accelerating cosmic expansion.*[20]

Obviously since the millennium, we have had further insight into the notion of a black hole centred within the Orion Nebula itself. Something certainly lives within the Orion Nebula - a level of consiousness that can influence other worlds.

Light from Darkness

For decades, scientists have known there is an invisible component of matter in the universe, one that barely interacts with light and ordinary matter. Dark matter has revealed itself only through its gravitational attraction, which influences the rate at which galaxies spin, including the 'motion' of galaxies within clusters. But some scientists predict that particles of dark matter should interact with each other and produce a detectable signal. In seeking that signature, scientists have pointed telescopes toward regions that should be rich in dark matter, such as the centre of the Milky Way galaxy about 25,000 light-years away and areas of nebulas like the Orion Nebula. In 2009, astrophysicists Lisa Goodenough and Dan Hooper pored over measurements from NASA's Fermi Gamma-ray Space Telescope and found an unexpected high intensity of gamma rays, the most energetic form of electromagnetic radiation, emanating from the Galactic Centre. Hooper, an American cosmologist and particle physicist specializing in the areas of dark matter, cosmic rays, and neutrino astrophysics, suggested that gamma radiation is the signature of weakly interacting massive particles (or WIMPs) and proposed dark matter particles would collide to produce electrons, positrons (or the antimatter partner of electrons) and gamma rays. In other words, dark matter is alive and 'kicking'.

Other cosmological measurements show that 70% of the Universe consists of dark energy and at least 26% of cold, dark matter. What scientists call ordinary 'baryonic matter' (in the form of gas and stars etc.), only makes up 4% of the Universe. According to astrophysicists, these numbers could be seen to make interesting reading since dark matter equates to some 37% of the Universe's total dark energy mass content. It is almost a third of the so-called light (energy) that constitutes the Universe. Could dark matter be the 'energetic locations' around each physical galaxy within which to *imprison* the biblical Jinn, genies, archons or demons by angelic portions of energy? What I am suggesting is that within various wavelengths of the electromagnetic spectrum (the projection of light), through light and dark matter (or from red to blue as I will come to), we find both angelic and demonic worlds I have been highlighting in this chapter.

Sefirot From Another Angle

It's interesting to see how many religious ceiling murals and altars often

Figure 331: Angelic Orders, Projected.
The ceiling in the Baptistery in Florence gives us a symbolic renditions of the *projection* of angelic orders.

depict what looks like the 'projector' (or Invisible Sun) with its various waveforms as sometimes circular, or octagonal-shaped structures. The ceiling mosaic of the Baptistery in Florence depicts (in the innermost octagon), seven of the orders of angelic beings (minus the Seraphim and Cherubim), under which are the lesser, angelic hosts (see figure 331).

Octagonal symbolism relates to the 'eighth place' in the Tree of Life or Sefirot, called 'Hod', described as being a *force* that breaks down energy into different distinguishable forms and is associated with intellectuality, learning and ritual. Its opposite in the Sefirot is 'Netzach' which is the *power of energy* to overcome all barriers and limitations, and is associated with emotion, passion, music and dancing. Both 'Hod' and 'Netzach' find balance in 'Yesod', the foundation, or the world of the unconscious (the Moon) – the place where different energies created await expression in the lowest world of Malkuth (the Earth). The realms, or points according to Jewish mysticism, are 'assigned' to specific angels and archangel Michael - the 'Bene Elohim' (sons of God) are said to be the Angelic Order presiding over Yesod (the Moon), see earlier chapters. The opposing demonic order in this sphere is called the 'Qliphoth' (the realms of evil) and is said to be connected to 'Samael' (Satan/Saturn), headed by the Chief Archon (archangel), 'Adrammelech' and 'Anammelech' (or Mollech). Both are considered lunar (archon) entities that demanded human sacrifice through fire. From the 'point of

Figure 332: Angelic Projection.
Fresco of The Assumption of the Virgin. The Fresco is clearly a 'projection' of angelic forces made to look like a nebula. (PD)

projection' at 'Keter' (the crown or source), to Malkuth (the realm of matter or the earth), can be seen in the three-dimensional painting, *The Assumption of the Virgin* by the Italian Late Renaissance artist Antonio da Correggio. It decorates the dome of the Cathedral of Parma, Italy and is not dissimilar to the fresco in Florence (see figure 332 on previous page).

The higher spheres in Gnostic and hermetic teachings, the Keter or Chokhmah, are where consciousness and intellect reside through wisdom (Sophia), connecting to the heart of the Invisible Sun. The place from where all consciousness and lesser frequencies of light (angelic through to the realms of the illusory earth) are manifested.

In the next chapter, I want to delve deeper into areas surrounding Orion's Invisible Sun and decode further, the levels of consciousness that seem to often interpenetrate our world through blueprints in the mind.

Sources:

1) https://en.wikipedia.org/wiki/Ogdoad_(Gnosticism)
2) Sabak, Pierre. *Holographic Culture*. 2018, p485
3) Roob, Alexander. *Alchemy and Mysticism*. Taschen, 1996, p269
4) http://throughancienteyes.blogspot.com/
5) E. W. Bullinger. *The Companion Bible. Genesis* Chapter 9 Verses 12-19, The Authorised Version of 1611, pp14-15
6) *Jewish Encyclopedia*. 2002–2011 [1906]
7) *Ezekiel* 28:14
8) *Ezekiel* 41:18
9) *Ezekiel* 1:5–11
10) *Ezekiel* 1:13-19
11) Guiley, Rosemary Ellen. *Encyclopedia of Angels*. 1996, p. 37
12) Sabak, Pierre. *Holographic Culture*. 2018, p463.
13) https://zodianz.com/archangels-101/
14) https://www.newworldencyclopedia.org/entry/Archangel
15) Guiley, Rosemary Ellen. *Encyclopedia of Angels*. Infobase Publishing. 1996, p. 37
16) Phillips, Jonathan Talat. *The Electric Jesus: The Healing Journey of a Contemporary Gnostic*. Evolver Editions, 2011, p160
17) Conforto, Giuliana. *Giordano Bruno's Future Science*. Edizioni Noesis. 2001, p106.
18) Ibid, p207
19) Kaku, Michio. *Hyperspace*. Oxford University Press. p333
20) The *New York Times* Week in Review Sunday March 5 2000 Section 4 *Dark matters afloat in the cosmic hall of mirrors* by: George Johnson

THE DUALITY BLUEPRINT

Orion's Great Red & Blue Stars

The Heavens are more alien and wondrous
than meets the earthly eye.
ARISTOTLE

The Orion Nebula is one of the most scrutinized and photographed objects in the night sky, and among the most intensely studied celestial features in recent times. According to Astro Science, the Orion Nebula reveals much about the process of how stars and planetary systems are formed from collapsing clouds of gas and dust, which are in abundance with the Orion constellation. Astronomers have directly observed proto-planetary disks, brown dwarfs, intense and turbulent motions of the gas, and the photo-ionizing effects of massive nearby stars in the region of the Orion Nebula. It is an enormous cloud of gas and dust, 30 to 40 light-years in diameter which seems to show numerous faces and figures (see figure 333). You could say it is a 'stellar cradle' of its own kind and a unique *formation* when one considers many of the subjects I've covered so far in the book.

The first discovery of the diffuse nebulous nature of the Orion Nebula is credited to French astronomer, Nicolas-Claude Fabri de Peiresc. On 26 November 1610, Peiresc, made a record of observing the Orion Nebula with a refracting telescope purchased by his patron, Guillaume du Vair. Other historical figures such as Ptolemy and Galileo had noted 'fixed stars',

Figure 333: The Orion Nebula.
A haven for heavenly faces and forces.
(Public domain)

but neither scientist mentioned definitive objects; instead, both listed 'patches of nebulosity' in the Orion Constellation. Jesuit mathematician and astronomer, Johann Baptist Cysat of Lucerne, made the first published observation of the Orion Nebula in his 1619 *Monograph on the Comets*. Lucerne made comparisons between Orion and a bright comet seen, in 1618, describing how the nebula appeared through his telescope, he writes:

> *One sees how in like manner some stars are compressed into a very narrow space and how round about and between the stars a white light like that of a white cloud is poured out.*

His description of the centre stars as different from a comet's head, in that they were, a 'rectangle', may have been an early description of the Trapezium cluster. The first detection of three of the four stars of this cluster is credited to Galileo Galilei in a February 4th, 1617. However, he did not notice the surrounding nebula - possibly due to the narrow field of vision of his early telescope.

As I have already touched on in previous chapters, the Orion Nebula seems to have 'spoken' to artists such as Michelangelo, influencing his painting for part of the Sistine Chapel's roof, painted between 1508 and 1512 (one hundred years before the official discovery of the nebula). Danny Wilten has consistently shown in his research, Michelangelo mapped (in great detail) within *'The Creation of Adam'*, the area surrounding Orion's Trapezium. But I don't think Michelangelo was the only artist to 'visualise' the Orion Nebula in the same century, as I will get to shortly.

Orion's Nebulas

The colourful cluster of glowing, interstellar gas clouds and hot, bright, newborn stars within the Orion Nebula, can be seen forming two distinct 'red/pink and blue' areas when viewed with powerful telescopes (see figure 334). The 'blue' area to the left is the 'Running Man Nebula' (SH2 –279) and the pink/red area to the right, is the 'Orion Nebula', which reveals the 'House of Fire' (the white-hot area) and the Trapezium. Other nebulas within the constellation, near to the Orion Nebula (M42 region), are the 'Flame' Nebula' and 'Horse Head' Nebula (Barnard 33), the latter is just south of 'Alnitak', the brightest star in Orion's Belt (see figure 335). Alnitak means 'The Wounded One' or 'The Slain One' in Arabic, which again relates to the warrior archetype, death and the hunt. The Horsehead Nebula is also called the 'Dark Nebula', which some Christian writers have connected to the Second coming of Jesus in *Revelation*. The Internet is full of articles connecting Second-coming symbolism to the Pegasus constellation, Pisces, and a

Figure 334: Orion's M42 Region.
Artists graphic pen rendition of the Running Man Nebula alongside the Orion Nebula within the Orion Constellation.

Figure 335: Flame and Horse Head.
Alnitak and the Horse Head Nebula and the Flame Nebula. Both the flame and the horse are ancient symbols for war and strength.
(Public domain.)

white horse Jesus *supposedly* rides on his return to earth. In the same texts he is accompanied by his angels (see the last chapter) in the battle of Armageddon: 'And the armies in heaven, clothed in fine linen, 'white' and 'clean', followed Him on white horses.[1] I can't validate a literal connection between these nebulae and biblical scriptures, but as I have shown, Orion's stars are symbolic of the Son of Man (Jesus) stories connected to his passage into Egypt, atonement and supposed sacrifice; more on this at the end of the book. The stars and nebula within Orion are also significant to the symbolism connected to giants, royalty, hidden hand and the eternal flame symbolism, as I have shown. For example, the star, Betelgeuse, in the upper quadrant of Orion, is *hugely* connected to symbolism of the giants, fallen angels and other facets of hierarchical rule on earth. It also relates to a planted lineage and lion symbolism, as I will come to soon.[2] I am convinced Betelgeuse and Saturn have a vibrational link, too.

The Witch Head Nebula (IC 2118) is believed to be an ancient supernova remnant, or gas cloud, illuminated by the nearby supergiant star, Rigel; a star that seems to 'oppose' Betelgeuse. According to astronomers, the colour of Witch Head Nebula is blue caused not only by the blue colour of Rigel but, also because of gaseous dust grains that 'reflect' blue light more efficiently than red. The colour wavelength of blue is scattered more than other colours because it travels as shorter, smaller waves (information),

which is why we see a blue sky on earth most of the time. The Witch Head Nebula is about 900 light-years from earth and falls into the 'Eridanus' (River) constellation, linked in part to the 'rift' in the Milky Way and what the Mayan's called, 'Xibalba'. Etymologically, Eridanus refers to the 'Rives' of a river (rather than flowing water), referring to land located along a river. The Witch's head in profile (see figure 336) is symbolically sep-arated from the river and on one level can be seen as a symbol relat-ing to unseen forces mentioned ear-lier in the book. When we consider the hologram and macrocosm/microcosm, the blue head could easily be interpreted as a celestial Krasue (demon) or Will-o'-the-wisp.

Figure 336: The Witch Head Nebula.
A blue nebula adjacent to Orion's blue giant, Rigel is 900 light-years from Earth.

The Mayan underworld, Xibalba, as described in their sacred text the *Popol Vuh*, also seems to relate to the nebulas in Orion. For the Maya, Xibalba was made of 'houses' through which the soul had to travel; each house was occupied by a range of dark entities such as jaguars, bats and fire demons. These darker entities, or forces, are the Jinn (Islam), Sidhe (Irish myth), Wiwila and Cun Otila (Lakota) and Asuras (Hindu) in Indian belief. They are also root stories connected to dragons, gnomes, fairies and witches found in folklore on one level, along with the angelic worlds I described in the last chapter. All are part of 'unseen' forces (often conjured through magic) that can also be seen *inside* the ionised gases and 'electro-magnetic dust' creating such nebulas. Images of dragons, various faces and a bird seem to appear out of the dust within the Orion Nebula, which is not Pareidolia as far as I understand. Danny Wilten's enhanced analysis of the Orion Nebula clearly defines what appears to be a bird, an eye, a figure fac-ing the Trapezium (with smaller figures) and a dragon.

Wilten's book demonstrates how Pareidolia can be debunked through

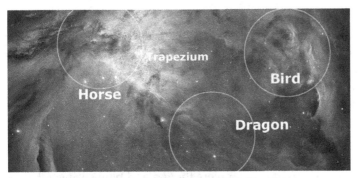

Figure 337: Orion's Dragon, Horse and Brid-like Beings.
Enhanced analysis of *inside* the Orion Nebula reveals imagery that could be seen as a horse, a dragon and several bird-like entities.

the study of single-image stereograms (autostereograms), designed to create the visual illusion of a three-dimensional scene or image.[3] There is a distinct sense of various forms *appearing* within the nebula, not least the face of the bearded man (see page 433) and a horse, or dragon (see figure 337). Under scrutiny and the ability to look more closely into the gases forming the clouds of the Orion Nebula, we can see phantom-like entities, no different to what I saw (with my own eyes), with the appearance of a Jinn (genie) in the clouds in Peru mentioned in *Chapter Two* (see page 54).

Orion's Caves of Creation

In creation myths and migration records of the Toltecs of Central America, there is reference to what indigenous accounts call the mysterious opposing colours of *red* and *blue* 'Springs' or 'Caves'. The same caves can be found in South American and Zulu legends. According to the Toltecs, these 'red and blue' origin symbols (a circle and square spiral), relate to their warrior god 'Huitzilopochtli', who is another version of Orion. I feel these Toltec Springs (or caves) are a symbolic version associated with the Orion Nebula and its 'creation' elements (see figure 338). The blue, circular spiral and red,

© Neil Hague

Figure 338: Red and Blue Toltec Springs.
My drawing of the Mythical *blue* (circle) and *red* (square) origin springs, as depicted in the 16th Century Historia Tolteca, Mexico, Aztec Valley of Puebla.

square spiral springs also form part of the myths connected to the Old God, 'Huehueteotl', who was considered the lord of duality. For the Aztecs, the same deity was called, 'Ōmeteōtl', an omnipotent and omniscient spirit of duality and creator of all that exists. Ōmeteōtl, according to the Aztecs, was a 'three-levelled' god whose dwelling was in the *cloud* - the Orion Nebula.

For the Toltec, Aztec and Mayans, red and blue colour symbolism also relates to the 'meeting place' between 'heaven and earth' (sky and land) and every temple on earth is considered to be a central place of focus for dual powers. The Aztec myths, like the Hopi myths, speak of years of wandering and eventual settling in what is now the Texcoco Valley in Mexico. According to their myths, when the ancient Aztecs arrived in the Texcoco Valley, they saw a series of symbols indicating that this place was the location chosen by their ancestral god – Huitzilopochtli (Orion). The first symbols the Aztecs were said to have seen were the red and blue springs of water, fish, frogs, and white plants, all of which are signs of a 'sacred spirit'. The ancient Toltec also witnessed similar signs and symbols when they arrived in Cholula City in an even earlier epoch. The common ground between the Aztecs and the Toltecs was their establishment of a 'sacred centre' that became the city in relation to their migration myths and receiving these sacred symbols. Here we have indigenous peoples establishing a central place (on earth) so to correlate with a heavenly central source, the central sun I talked about in *Chapter Fifteen*. As the historian of religions, Mircea Eliade, has shown in his writings, the 'sacred mountain, temple and axis mundi' were all in alignment for ancient Mesoamerican peoples. The same can be said of the Egyptian and South American pyramids and their location in alignment with Orion's stars. In indigenous art, heaven and earth are a 'meeting point', or a city, where the 'god of duality' would emerge. The two caves or spring symbols, like the double whirlpool gate of the Hopi, is, I feel, a symbol for the 'projector' located in the Orion Nebula.

The duality of 'light and dark', along with many deities representing duality, especially in the Americas and Asia, was often depicted with a blue, or red skin, too. Numerous Indian and Etruscan demons are shown with blue skin, and in Japan, the oni is an ogre, or troll, with blue skin, found in Japanese folklore. Lord Vishnu and Krishna are often depicted as blue, symbolic of the sky and the limitlessness of the sky and universe. The creators of the film *Avatar* (2009) also used blue skin for the same reason. The ancient race of giants also had blue skin, I feel, which would mean Orion was blue, too (see the cover art). Another example would be the Lakota god of the doorway, Heokah (see page 195), who was said to have both a blue and red face. Again, this colour symbolism relates to *opposing forces* - sky and earth, father and mother, or sometimes good and evil. As I have already mentioned, many angelic figures and saints in Italian Renaissance art are also depicted in red (or pink) and blue, which could have been a subconscious attempt to convey this knowledge. The elite painter, Hieronymus Bosch, certainly seemed to understand blue and pink (red) symbolism, as he too, used it to full effect in his monumental work *The Garden of Earthly Delights* (1503–1515).

Bosch's 'caves of creation', in the landscape at the back of the central panel, seem to be offering similar symbolism found in Aztec, Zulu and Mayan mythology. It seems *red* and *blue* symbolism is paramount when it comes to understanding the parameters of reality, manifestation and creation. Interestingly, the same colour codes were used in the Matrix movie, for the pills offered to Neo (symbolic of Adam/Orion the first human) by the 'god of the Dreamtime', Morpheus. The colours are also used to denote the dual aspects of the 'force', in the *Star Wars* movies - the red Lightsabers of the Sith and the blue (or green) of the Jedi orders.

Figure 339: 'Red' and 'Blue' Portals.
Mosaic at the entrance to St Mark's Basilica, Venice, seems to depict the mysterious *red* and *blue* Springs (or suns/stars).

Red (pink) and blue symbolism also appears on the ceiling art of Saint Mark's Basilica in Venice (see figure 339). The building is a profusion of domes and more than 8000 square metres of 'luminous' mosaics dating back to the 11th century. Part of the mosaic at the entrance to St Mark's Basilica shows a reversed version of the mythical red and blue caves, or holy springs. The blue and red circles, depicted in the gold glass tesserae, are symbolic of the seraphim (red) and cherubim (blue) I mentioned in the last chapter, on one level; but they appear to be shown above sun and moon symbolism in the upper circle and more than likely refer to the symbolism I am looking at in this chapter (see the art on the back cover).

Mysterious Red and Blue Stars in Orion

I have researched Native American myths for over two decades now and from my understanding, I know enough to say that the 'order of influence' over our 'human perception' and therefore 'our society' (by non-human secret societies) has to include the giant red and blue stars of the Orion constellation – Bellatrix, Betelgeuse, Siaph and Rigel. As we shall see, all of Orion's novas, his shoulders, knees and feet stars have been focused on by many indigenous people of earth. The colour symbolism encoded in the Hopi prophecies connects to the red and blue star kachinas, the former being known as the 'purifier' that leads to the emergence of the Fifth World on earth. Part of this prophecy relates to Betelgeuse and the possibility of its transformation, signalling the coming 'new world'.

Bellatrix is a blue star, which is a Latin name for 'female warrior', and was also called the 'Amazon Star', the 'Conqueror', or 'Lion Star'. To the left of Bellatrix is Betelgeuse, or Alpha Orion (abbreviated Alpha Ori), the ninth-brightest star in the night sky and second brightest in the constellation of Orion. Betelgeuse is also the 'shoulder star', and along with Orion's 'belt and sword', is frequently referenced in ancient and modern literature. Orion's stars even found recognition as the *shoulder* insignia of the 27th Infantry Division of the United States Army during both World Wars, influenced by the division's first commander, Major General John F. O'Ryan (Orion). All military and often their insignia seems to be invoking Orion's warrior spirit through such symbolism. The red and blue used on nations' flags is very much part of this symbolism and much more besides, as we shall see. The colours were also used on the original Orion Pictures logo in 1978-1981, too.

In Sanskrit, Betelgeuse was called 'Bahu', part of a Hindu understanding of the constellation as a 'running antelope or stag'. Again, this aspect of Betelgeuse and Orion relates to the horned clans I mentioned in an earlier chapter and the cults on earth that work with this 'trickster' aspect of Orion. In 825AD, the Japanese Samurai (who also wore horned head gear) seem to have focused on Orion's stars (see figure 340). The Taira, or Heike Samurai clan, adopted Betelgeuse and its red colour as its symbol, calling the star, 'Heike-boshi'. In the same epoch (900-1200AD), the Japanese Minamoto (or Genji) clan chose Rigel and its blue-white colour as its insignia. These two powerful Samurai families fought a legendary war in Japanese history, symbolic of the two stars seen 'opposing' each other and only kept apart by the belt of the warrior hunter - Orion. According to legend, due to the extraordinary bravery and loyalty exhibited by many members of both sides of this Samurai conflict, the colours red and white came to have special significance still seen in present day Japan, most notable of course in the colours of the Japanese flag itself. The Samurai armour is also relevant to the types of entities connected to Orion, as we shall see in the next chapter. Symbolizing duty, sacrifice, and loyalty, Rigel and Betelgeuse are still seen as reminders of these basic Japanese values. Thus, it may be quite appropriate that the bright stars of Betelgeuse and Rigel shine as emblems for the heritage of Heike and Genji.[4]

Opposing sides, in myths and legends, seem to relate to these opposing stars and as I will come to, these blue and red *gaints* influence such narra-

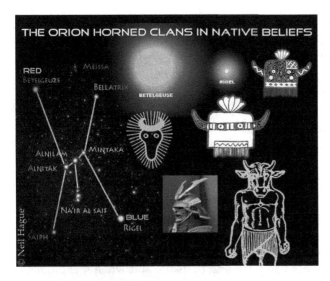

Figure 340: Orion's Horned Opposing Clans.
The Horned clans of Betelgeuse and Rigel.

tives in movies like *Star Wars*. The same stars are also part of the 'Winter Hexagon', along with Rigel, Aldebaran in the constellation Taurus, Capella in Auriga, and Pollux and Castor in Gemini (see *Chapter Eleven*). The Hexagon also forms a cube, which again mirrors Saturn's influence over our reality. Betelgeuse and Saturn are hugely connected 'energetically' and this reddish nova, also known as the 'Ninth Gate' or the 'House of Orion', is important to the Orion Cult. The Ninth Gate symbolism is important too, as it relates to an interdimensional 'portal' connecting Saturn and our Moon.

Betelgeuse-Saturn 'Hack' – The Ninth Gate

Betelgeuse, or the 'House of Orion', is one of the largest stars currently known, with a radius around 1400 times larger than the Sun's (notably the

Figure 341: Betelgeuse - the 'Sun of Suns'.
The giant Betelgeuse (compared to the Sun), is enormous and affecting our reality, *energetically*.

millimeter continuum, the measurements of circumstellar dust) see figure 341. This supergiant is quite near to earth (around 600 light-years away) and burns brightly as the most recognised star in Orion, along with the belt stars. In terms of size, Betelgeuse would engulf all four terrestrial planets — Mercury, Venus, Earth and Mars — and even the gas giant Jupiter. *Only* Saturn would be beyond its surface. Betelgeuse is affecting our collective reality more than we realise, not least through the Ninth Gate 'mechanisim', which I'll describe in a moment. At the time of writing this chapter, it was reported in the mainstream press that Betelgeuse was said to be giving off powerful, 'unusual' and 'unexpected' gravitational wave bursts hitting Earth. One *Daily Mail* article stated, "the ripple in the fabric of spacetime was spotted by the Laser Interferometer Gravitational-Wave Observatory (LIGO) in the USA, the largest and most ambitious project ever funded by the National Science Foundation and the Californian Institute of Technology." According to astronomers at LIGO, 'gravitational waves' are 'ripples' (wavefields) in spacetime (predicted by Einstein's General Theory of Relativity), which were only detected for the first time in 2015. The detection of such waves tells us that stars, such as Betelgeuse, influence lesser planets 'energetically', especially when black holes or binary systems orbit each other.[5]

Betelgeuse is said to be nearing the end of its life and when it explodes, it should be visible in our skies. Some researchers say this could be the 'fire in the sky' prophesied by the Hopi at the time of 'great change' on earth. When we consider some of the symbolism related to the 'horned clans' I mentioned in *Part One*, Betelgeuse, along with Saturn, could also be the focus for what Christianity describes as 'hell', a dimensional frequency separated by the Ninth Gate (or *door*). Combined with the dwarf star, Saturn, *together*, these stars provide a multi-dimensional backdrop for all things connected to fire, nefarious tricksters (devils) and satanic rituals. I do not see the Lucifer (Prometheous) figure connected to such malevolent vibrations. There is a huge diffierence between the Betelgeuse-Saturn force and the Light-Bringer - Lucifer (Venus) and the archons that broke rank.

The Polanski Movie, *The Ninth Gate* (1999) featuring the 'growing-darker-by-the-year' Johnny Depp, is a film about a satanic elite; so was the book, *The Nine Gates of the Kingdom of Shadows*, written by 17th-century author, Aristide Torchia, which was said to be able to summon the Devil. Interestingly, the final scene in Polanski's *The Ninth Gate* is filmed at the Cathar castle, Château de Puivert, in Occitane, France, (a place I have visited several times) and involves an invocation through fire (the Archons).

The Knight Templar, Dante Alighieri, in his 14th-century epic poem, *Divine Comedy*, followed by *Purgatorio* and *Paradiso* and on to *The Inferno*, tells the journey of Dante through the nine realms of Hell. In the poem, Dante who is accompanied by the ancient Roman poet, Virgil, ventures through *nine* circles of suffering, located *within* the Earth. The nine levels are symbolically *inverted* realms shown on the tree of life and 'seven' of these circles are concerned with the so-called *Seven Deadly Sins*, depicted as an 'eye' by Hieronymus Bosch. Without going into huge detail here, the cir-

cles are 'realms' aligning with planetary fields through the light of the projection I mentioned in *Chapter Fifteen*. Perception or deception, are both part
of the nature of the Ninth Gate and as I have been illustrating for decades,
these gates, or *doors*, are frequencies, 'planes of existence' (realms) or
human archetypes (see the nine Enneagram), connected to the soul. For
many native cultures, nine is the number that represents giving thanks for
what we receive through our creativity (birthing process), hence the human
nine-month pregnancy period in humans. The nine muses, as mentioned in
the Gnostic texts *The Apocalypse of Adam*, also connects Sophia's fall (her
dreaming) to the creation of the nine circles and eventual nightmare (or
hell) that fell on our human world. From these texts we read:

> ... *from the nine Muses* [Circles] *one separated away. She came to a high moun-
> tain and spent (some) time seated there, so that she desired herself alone, in order
> to become androgynous. She fulfilled her desire and became pregnant from her
> desire.*

In some esoteric traditions, the ninth gate (and the number nine) can be
seen as a personal heaven or hell as symbolised through the ninth tarot
card, the Hermit, representing the going-off-alone archetype, in search of
spiritual wisdom (or Sophia). Therefore, to leave Hell (a state of mind),
passing through Purgatory into Paradise, 'one needs to become one again',
through nine dimensions, creating ten – the new beginning, or the born
again human. As the Egyptian saying goes: "...the king is dead, long live
the king." The invisible structure projecting out of Orion, via its main stars,
in my view, is creating energetic states, frequencies (circles) and dimensions
affecting the mind. It is the mind that creates reality and as Michelangelo's
painting, *The Creation of Adam*, reminds us, our human world is taking place
inside our heads - Hell or Heaven is within us.

Interestingly, in Danté's *Paradisio*, the 'Eighth Circle', called Malebolge
(evil trenches) or the upper half of Hell, was a place saved for the fraudulent and malicious. The 'eighth circle' was described by Dante as a large
funnel of stone, shaped like an amphitheatre, around which runs a series of
ten deep, narrow, concentric ditches, or trenches. Within these ditches are
those punished who are guilty of 'fraud and deception' (it must be full of
deceased politicians?). The G8 global political summits are an expression, in
my view, of the 'fraud and deception' played out by puppet world leaders
for the hidden hand I mentioned at the beginning of the book. The 'pup-
pets' always change, but the 'vibe' remains the same. According to Danté's
poem, the giants and titans were chained in the abyss between the eighth
and the ninth circle. The number eight (8), of course, can be seen as either
the 'restraints' of Saturn's rings, or the knowledge of 'infinity'. Satan, or

Saturn, is frozen in the ninth circle and I have always imagined these as Saturn's rings, restricting the fallen celestial Archon, while the rings themselves seem to be artificially intelligent in nature. According to one time NASA engineer, Norman Bergrun, in his book, *The Ring Makers of Saturn* (1986), the rings are not natural and are being generated by extraterrestrial vehicles of immense power, more on this in the next chapter. I would suggest 'aliens' that are manipulating planets or worlds, such as Saturn (including the Moon), *are* artificial intelligence or cyborg-like, as we shall see in the following chapters.

Betelgeuse-Saturn Clowns

Betelgeuse was also known as 'Palasohu', or the red star by the Hopi and The Hopi 'Palaakwapi' was also known as the 'red house', a city of the 'star people' located in Arizona (possibly the Sedona area). The Hopi ancestral home, the Red City, was also said to be a 'temple city' surrounded by a 'towering wall of red stone'. If you ever visit the Sedona region, especially the desert areas of Arizona and New Mexico, as I have many years ago, you will sense both the magic and their 'darker'aspects in the stones and rock formations surrounding Sedona. Spider Rock, at Canyon De Chelly National monument in New Mexico, is another perfect example of the 'Betelgeuse trickster energy' connected to the land. As mentioned earlier in the book, the 'spider' was considered a 'trickster' (a fire stealer) by most Native American Indian tribes, and Spider Rock, according to author Gary A. David, aligns with Orion's star – Saiph (Kappa Orionis), which is the right foot of the star man, while Betelgeuse occupies his right shoulder.[6]

The colour red, especially, is connected to both Betelgeuse and Saturn (satanism), especially through Orion-Saturn Cult rituals. The Orion-Saturn Cult are, on one level, the 'Betelgeuse-Saturn Hack', *unseen* forces taking form. These cults are master inverters of life and manipulate collective consciousness to focus on the inversion, which in its simple form is to focus humanity on all that is 'evil' (the opposite of life, love and good). There is also another aspect of the 'hack', I sense, relating to 'alien' (cyborgs) and artificial intelligence, which has targetted earth and humanity as a whole.

Clowns, or *Coulrophobia*, is also connected to the Betelgeuse-Saturn Hack, not least through the Koshari clowns mentioned earlier in the book and their darker aspects, often expressed through many clown horror movies. The Science Fiction cult classic, *Killer Klowns from Outer Space* (1988), which offers up the notion of aliens, in the form of circus clowns, coming to earth using 'dark magic' to invade earth and harvest humans – the latter is a common alien agenda it seems. The evil clown is a Betelgeuse phenomenon in my view and can be seen expressed in the 'twisted' Joker (psychopath archetype), made popular by DC Comics and Stephen King's 'Pennywise' character. Their origins seem to have evolved from 18th Century niche plays and much earlier Harlequin archetypes in recent times. The horrendous serial killer and rapist, John Wayne Gacy, in the late 70s, who murdered at least '33' teenage boys, became known as the 'Killer Clown', due to his Pogo the Clown act performed for children in Illinois, Chicago. The University of Sheffield in the UK, along with Californian State University, have more or less said that the concept of 'evil clowns' is a cultural phenomenon transcending just the phobia (Coulrophobia) alone; and that clowns are universally disliked by children due to their frightening, threatening, controlling and 'hidden-behind-the-mask' persona. The mask symbolism is crucial to these nefarious cults, hence the obsession with the mask as part of the coronavirus pandemic.

The bizzare 1970s BBC test card F, showing a clown and a young girl (Carole Hersee) playing noughts and crosses ('X's), has to be the strangest image seen by *millions* every day for over *twenty years*. I would suggest that anything good can be inverted and therefore, the Betelgeuse-Saturn Hack is, at its core, mind-magic, trickery (deception) and at its extreme end - *psychopathic*. Another aspect of what I have termed the Betelgeuse-Saturn Clown 'vibration' can be seen in endless images of clowns and *some* of the Transvestite imagery appearing in recent years. I personally have no issues whatsoever with drag queens or Transvestites; celebrating our uniqueness is 'key' to being 'free' (as long as all involved are consenting adults); but to 'present' scary-looking clown imagery' *to children* through 'story time' performances in the USA and UK seems bizzare to say the least (see figure 342).

Progressive 'liberal (Woke) parents' don't seem to question such imagery, especially in places like California. School and library administration in schools hosting these events also seem oblivious to the content and image being presented; performances in some cases have involved 'Twerking' and other sexualized dancing, to children 6 years of age and under, which some in the gay commuinity have also slammed as irresponsible. Despite some drag queens having an inherently sexualized form of performance, 'progressive parents' still insist

Figure 342: Scary Clown Costumes.
Xochi Mochi dressed as a clown-like figure, with red-tipped demon-like horns, reading to children for 'Drag Queen Story Hour' at the Michelle Obama Public Library in California.

there is nothing odd about exposing children to them. When Scottish MP, Mhairi Black, invited a drag queen called 'Flowjob' (shakes head in amazment) to read to children as young as *four* at Glencoates Primary School, Paisley, furious parents raised concerns after it emerged the 'adult entertainer' (the word 'adult' gives it away) had previously uploaded sexually explicit content to Twitter, including a lewd act with a toy and simulated oral sex. Parents who complained were branded 'homophobic', which is now a classic response to anyone who points out that just maybe, children should be left alone, until they are adults, to make such decisions about their sexuality. The nonconformist gay Drag Queen, Kitty Demure, even said on Twitter in January 2020, that "Drag queens are quite *frightening* in person'...very few look attractive, or are tasteful." The frightening 'image' part is important, as it seems to feed into the Betelgeuse–Saturn Clown vibration. As Xochi Mochi's Twitter profile reads – "Greeting Earthlings! I'm your resident killer clown from outer space, stationed here on Earth." *'Outer space'* possibly being the clue, I think.

Rigel (Regal/Royal) Blue-White

In opposition to Betelgeuse is the giant Rigel, also known as Beta Orion (see figure 343). Rigel is the seventh-brightest star (sun) in the night sky and the brightest star in Orion. Rigel is a massive, blue supergiant, much smaller than Betelgeuse but calculated to be anywhere from 61,500 to 363,000 times

as luminous as the sun, and 18 to 24 times as massive as the sun. The name Rigel strictly refers to only the 'primary star' and seems to be a huge focus for the ancients, some say part of a stellar alliance with Leo and the Pleiades. Rigel looks blue-white to the naked eye, contrasting with orange-red Betelgeuse. Although appearing as a single star to the naked eye, Rigel is actually a multiple star system composed of at least four stars: Rigel A, Rigel Ba, Rigel Bb, and Rigel C. The blue supergiant primary has a visual companion, which is likely a close

Figure 343: Rigel, Orion's Foot.
A drawing of Rigel (Beta Orion) – the Royal star of Orion.

'triple' star system; a fainter star at a wider separation might also be a component of the Rigel system.

Rigel is derived from Arabic, 'Jauzah', meaning the leg, or foot of Orion, an earlier name for the Orion figure. An alternative Arabic name was the 'foot of the great one', which is the source of the rarely-used variant names 'Algebar' or 'Elgebar'. The Alphonsine Tables* saw its name split into 'Rigel' and 'Algebar', with the note, 'et dicitur Algebar'.

Pierre Sabak explains in his books that Rigel was the origin of the Adamic race and that the Nephilim (giants) were connected, or originally from the Betelgeuse system. Within Gnosticism, the Adamic race is referential to what Sabak calls 'human-angelic intercourse' (part of the Fall of the Anthropos) and the inception of the Nephilim (the blueblood giants), uniquely part of the Orion system. All Royalty on earth, may have stellar origins connected to Orion's opposing star systems, Betelgeuse and Rigel. We also have to remember that these opposing star systems are more than just the 'stars/suns' called Betelgeuse and Rigel, we are also talking about the possibility of *many* planetary systems connected to these two giants. Two stars between Betelgeuse and Siaph, HD 37605 b and HD 38529, have been noted as having planets and there will be more coming to light, I am sure.

The Mäori people of New Zealand named Rigel as 'Puanga', said to be a daughter of Rehua (Antares), the chief of all stars.[7] Rigel's heliacal rising presages the appearance of 'Matariki' (the Pleiades) in the dawn sky, marking the Mäori New Year in late May or early June (when Orion moves below the equator). The Moriori people of the Chatham Islands, as well as some Maori groups in New Zealand, mark the start of their New Year with Rigel rather than the Pleiades. I am certain that the Pleiades, along with Rigel, are the home of ancient humanity (what Sabak calls proto-humans) and the bird/lion people I see in dreams and visions, and constantly referred to in aboriginal myths. It is also possible that the great stellar wars talked about in indigenous belief and later 'alternative' arenas, could relate to Rigel's influence, or Rigel's opposition to Betelgeuse, along with Bellatrix's opposition to Siaph.

The Lions of Orion

In my graphic novel *Aeon Rising* (2017), I depicted what I saw as opposing forces within Orion waging war against each other (see figure 344 overleaf). In a series of visions, I was shown what seemed to be 'Lion-like' priests caught up in a war with each other; centred on the Rigel system. I felt they were a type of archon, or 'Elyon' (another word for the Seraphim) opposing each other, rather like George Lucas' Jedi and Sith fighting each other in Lucas' epic *Star Wars* movies? I was told that their names were the

Footnote: The Alphonsine Tables were 13th and 14th Century data gathered by Alfonso X and astronomers for computing the position of the Sun, Moon and planets relative to the fixed stars. Alfonso had gathered in Toledo, among the astronomers' several Jewish scholars, like Yehuda ben Moshe and Isaac ibn Sid, just as Queen Elizabeth I in England, gathered to her, the likes of Dr John Dee.

'Panthera', 'Jezura' or 'Rezura Order'; magicians that were located in both Rigel and Siaph's systems, and originally part of the Regulus star system in the constellation of Leo. According to Sabak, the biblical Levite priesthood is of the same lineage of the Nemean lion and part of the Orion wars on earth. The text *Hosea 11*, also expresses the lion connection to higher consciousness and humanity's connection to these orders, it says: "They will follow the Lord; he will roar like a lion. When he roars, his children will come trembling from the west." The Orion (lion) man – Jesus, was reputed to have said,

Figure 344: Orion's War - Lion Priests of Rigel.
A war is raging within Orion's star system, between Jedi and Sith-like lion priesthoods (Orders).

'Blessed is the lion which man eats, and the lion will *become* man.' The lion, in this context, symbolically, represents the highest order of star magic on earth, hence why the Egyptian-Babylonian priests, used the lion to represent both sides in the war. Of course I cannot prove the existence of lion beings, as it is purely 'visionary', but when we consider that some of the oldest art on earth clearly depicts lion-humanoids, we have to wonder what exists beyond the visible spectrum, amongst the stars. As I wrote in *Aeon Rising* (2017):

> The lions of Orion fought each other now. Those of the Panthera that wanted peace used the light of Manu and sought council with their ancestors on Regulus in Leo. The Jezura and Rezura became willing servants of the darkness (Naga) aiding in the creation of the priesthood that would rise to rule the Fourth Age on Earth. Every ancient warrior order on Earth from the Djedi of ancient Egypt to the many 'knights orders' of the past four thousand years are blueprints of the 'dualistic Lion Priests of Orion.[8]

I feel certain that war *is* raging within the heavens (the stars), unseen by our limited perception, and a constant war, or conflict on Earth, is nothing more than a macrocosm of the 'star wars' being fought across the Orion,

Pleiadian and Lyra constellations. I think George Lucas knew his *Star Wars* movies would activate deeper memories of such wars, which is why the fictional Jedi/Sith order, along with the movies in general, have had such a massive impact on several generations since their creation.

Lion of God Symbolism

Rigel, also known as Altair (or Aquilae, the 'eagle star') by the ancient Babylonians and Sumerians, and much of the lion, fire and griffin symbolism connects to this aspect of Rigel. In Jewish and Christian mysticism Rigel *is* Ariel, which in the *Apocrypha of John* means the 'Hearth of God' or the 'Lion of God' (see figure 345). The Hearth of God is an area contained by Rigel and two other stars, Alnitak and Saiph, that together, create a triad framing the 'central fire' of Orion. Rigel was also called the 'firebrand' by the Polynesians on Easter Island due to its position in relation to the Orion Nebula and the flaming sword. The Lion, or Hearth of God, is also the symbolic location of Orion's Door (portal) into what the Gnostics called the Upper Aeons; something I will come back to at the end of the book.

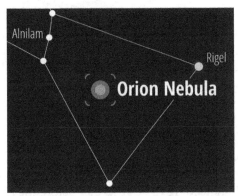

Figure 345: Lion of God (Ariel)
The Lion of God configuration.

In Thomas Heywood's *Hierarchy of the Blessed Angels* (1635), Ariel (Rigel) is called the prince who rules the waters and 'earth's great Lord'. He is mentioned with other elemental titles such as the 'third archon of the winds', 'spirit of air', 'angel of the waters of the earth' and 'wielder of fire'. In esoteric art, Ariel is usually depicted as a 'governing angel' with dominion over the earth, creative forces, the north, elemental spirits, and all of the beasts. 'Ariel' is also another word for the 'city of Jerusalem'; Shakespeare used it as the name of a spirit in his play, *The Tempest*. In my image, Ariel, with the lord archon at his third eye, is focusing plasma (energy) which encompasses the 'separation' of man and woman, or Adam and Eve (see figure 346 overleaf). In my painting *The Lion of God*, Ariel is an 'energy field' that can *change* human destiny. In its current state, this energy is 'sleeping' (dreaming); Ariel is still caught up in his own arrogance, like the Demiurge, but is also *contemplating* the existence of something greater than himself. Symbolically speaking, is the Lion of God a metaphor for the 'unawakened' Jerusalem? In the *Lion of God* painting, the 'Lord of Hosts' (the figure at

Ariel's third eye) is manifesting the energetic prison-like worlds, the auric eggs around the man and woman, its shell intact *is encasing* humanity within an illusion. The same philosophy exists in the Hermetic Qabalah relating to

Figure 346: *The Lion of God* - Ariel and Orion.
The image is based on a dream I had which seemed to show me the *Lion of God* thinking into 'existence' the 'duality of life'. Adam and Eve (Eden) are a projection of Orion's central sun and the moon.

the 'exoteric shell', the 'esoteric yolk' and the 'egg white' symbolic of a wisdom needing to be absorbed before the shell can be broken.[9] In other words, self gnosis has to occur before we can break free of any 'programming'. As Jesus is reputed to have said (according to the *Lost Gospel of Thomas*):

> *If those who lead you say to you, 'See, the kingdom is in the sky,' then the birds of the sky will precede you. If they say to you, 'It is in the sea,' then the fish will precede you. Rather, the kingdom is inside of you, and it is outside of you. When you come to **know yourselves**, then you will become known, and you will realize that it is you who are the sons of the living father.*

The path travelling across the expanse of Ariel's body, leads back to the Tree of Knowledge and the 'living father', and symbolically speaking, gives us the potential for duality to cease, and for the 'two' (hand-in-hand) to become *One* again. The genius song writer/musician, Peter Gabriel, expresses well the same notion of returning to *Oneness* in his song, *Blood of Eden* (1992):

> *In the blood of Eden we have done everything we can,*
> *In the blood of Eden, so we end as we began,*

With the man in the woman and the woman in the man,
It was all for the union, oh the union of the woman, the woman and the man.

Orion's opposing stars, Betelgeuse (red/orange) and Rigel (blue/white), along with the dual area contained within Orion's Nebula (the blue and red caves of creation) can be also be seen as the source for what I call the 'Duality *Red* and *Blue*print'. These archetypes are the left and right, male and female 'pillars of life', depicted in the hermetic Qabalah and used to full effect in our illusory world matrix.

The '*Red*' & *Blue*print'

The symbolism associated with 'red *and* blue' can be seen in so many areas. We find it in the ancient Egyptian 'Hall of Records', where Ma'at would oversee the weighing of the 'red' heart against the 'blue' ostrich feather. If the heart were 'heavy' then the soul in question would be fed to a demonic deity called 'Ammit' (the devourer of the dead). *Red* is the colour of death, anger (seeing red), fire, earth and blood (sport) and this is why red is seen in so many symbols, corporate logos and insignia. It also relates to deception (distraction), passion, war, the planet Mars and Saturn, which, as I have been illustrating for years, are *all* connected. So many political world leaders wear red at events, which again is all part of the Cult symbolism and dualistic effect on the subconscious mind of those viewing them. The 'red lion' for example, is both emblematic of royalty and the bloodlines connected to the stars. Red carpets, Hollywood, and the 'royal treatment' of celebrities (stars) are all part of this symbolism or 'blueprint'. The use of red and blue as part of the Orion Cult, mentioned earlier in the book, and how 'ritual magic' plays a huge role in the media, politics and military-industrial complex is also paramount. Blue of course relates to 'authority', 'balance', '*change*' and can

Figure 347: Blue = Change.
Yawn – the same old mantra.

be expressed through all forms of water and air symbolism. The use of the word '*Change*' over the past decade, in democratic (Woke) and conservative politics in the UK and USA, is just one example of the use of blue/red symbolism (see figure 347). Both colours are used so, so many times to give the effect of 'opposing' choices, as seen in political parties (*red* Labour, *blue* Tory, etc.). The colours dominate the logos of the two major Universities in the US, Yale (blue) and Harvard (red) see figure 348 overleaf. Political logos, flags and insignia often combine both primary colours for full effect

Figure 348: 'Red and Blue' *Programming* **(The Duality Blueprint).**
The red and blue spectrum, or the 'projection of duality' (as seen in Orion's opposing stars), represent opposing forces above and below. Our 'manufactured' division of 'governance', 'opposition parties (the political *spectrum*), and how we polarise our world in every way is part of a greater celestial blueprint possibly focused on Orion.

when offering up political choice to the masses. In truth, the choice is part of the illusion, the 'projection of duality'.

Blue also relates to the idea of 'bluebloods', royalty (regality) and connects to Mercury, Jupiter and Pluto, esoterically speaking. Both red and blue were used in the original British Telecommunications logo to depict Mercury (Hermes) with his red serpent arm. Blue and red neckties are frequently used in political posturing to signify the esoteric symbolism of leadership, which is why we see Donald Trump often wearing a red tie, while his Vice President, Mike Pence, wears a blue tie, etc. The same motif could be seen whenever Trump stands next to his leader counterparts, one wears a *red* tie while the other adorns a *blue* one. It is a form of 'protocol', a 'blueprint' for duality; part of the 'spell' connected to the Orion vibration, the Betelgeuse-Rigel-Saturn hack, I feel.

The 'red and blue' giants personified in the myths, legends and folklore of many indigenous peoples, relates to 'rulers of dreams' (not the red and blue American Dream, sadly), but the world within worlds (the Dreamtime), teeming with inter-dimensional life, or what physicists have called 'non-local' realities. The worlds I am talking about here are the frequency ranges of the Archons (angels), the Jinn, the 'tricksters' and the myriad of non-human life forms operating just outside of visible light but within the red to blue spectrum. The red to blue spectrum is another symbol for 'good and evil' forces connected to Orion through its opposing star systems of Betelgeuse and Rigel, Bellatrix and Siaph.

Red & Blue in the Movies – *it's all a movie*

We find the use of red and blue in much Superhero symbolism, from *Superman* to *Spiderman*, which are also codes for Orion-Saturn archetypes.

Marvel is awash with red and blue duality, with *Captain America* and *Iron Man* movies, not least the 2016 *Captain America: Civil War* movie poster, which said: "Whose side are you on?" with **war**, being the 'focus' for duality and much more besides. Red and blue is even used in the symbolism and branding of HD DVD (red) and Blue Ray, the choice of platform for watching movies. Red and blue symbolism can also be seen in 3D computer-animated comedy films such as Disney's *Zootopia* (2016), with the good 'blue' bunny versus the naughty 'red' fox character. The emotion of 'feeling blue' was represented via the blue coloured character of 'Sadness' in the 2015 Pixar film *Inside Out*, while the red coloured emotion was displayed through the character of 'Anger' – it's *all* by design.

As I have already mentioned, so many horror movies incorporate the 'evil clown' archetype, which seems to have its origins in the myths associated with the star, Betelgeuse. The movie *The Purge - Election Year* (2016), offered some symbolic imagery connecting to the 'red and blue'; 'X's for eyes and 'clown masks' were used prominently in this horror film. Indeed, use of 'red and blue' symbolism is deeply connected to the duality of 'opposing forces' said to be at 'war in Orion'. The 2016 movie *Warcraft*, also depicts rival forces of the Orcs (red) and Human Clans (blue) on its movie poster. I would say that all war on earth is a microcosm of dual forces at war in Orion and as I have already pointed out, this theme can be seen in the *Star Wars* movies, too. The same use of red and blue can be found in Netflix's, *Stranger Things* (2016), Season One and Two; not least with the Sheriff, Jim Hopper, wearing the 'blue band' from his daughter who died of cancer (chemotherapy) in the story. The opposing colour of pink and light blue (mirrored in the blue and pink-red regions of the Orion Nebula), can be seen in pink ribbons used as an international symbol of breast cancer awareness. The blue ribbon is used to raise awareness of prostate cancer and within this pink and blue symbolism, of course, we also have the old colour uses for the binary sexes.

Opposing colours of red and blue can be found in sport too, not least boxing (duals), with the classic 'red corner' versus the 'blue corner'. In soccer, or football in the UK, many of the top teams use either red or blue as their colours and insignia. Liverpool, Manchester United and Manchester City are just a few examples. If you look closely at the Manchester United logo, it is actually a red devil within an eye shape, which is telling of the esoteric symbolism I've been highlighting in this book. Blood sports are also part of the same symbolism, and 'fox hunting' is the classic Orion-Saturn Cult ritual in my view. The red blood-jacketed hunters with their canine helpers (Canis Minor/Sirius), is a stellar ritual caught up in the symbolism of the elite, the aristocracy (blue bloods) and has nothing to do with preservation. When a fox is caught and killed by packs of dogs, it is said to be traditional to smear any new member of the riders with the blood of the fox, a barbaric custom but nonetheless, all part of the *ritual*. Hunters are also said to toast with *red* wine (blood) at the start of the hunt, another symbol connected to ancient rites of the Greco-Roman deity, Dionysus and sacrifice.

Pink for Girl – *Blue* for Boy

The use of colour iconography and symbolism to affect the mind is part of the star magic I am describing in this chapter. It's no surprise to see the same colour symbolism used in activist movements and social political agendas in the 21st Century. In 2019, I was not surprised to see the climate change activist, Greta Thunberg, wearing Orion nebula pink set against a Running Man Nebula blue background at the New York Climate Summit. The Seventeen year old, who is a selective mute with Asperger syndrome, seems to be getting huge amounts of 'airtime' on the global news platforms (prior to the pandemic), which, unless you are serving a political agenda, would not normally happen. Some media have even described her impact on the world stage as the 'Greta Thunberg effect', which is exactly what it is, an attempt, through the use of a 'poster girl', to 'affect' the minds of young people into accepting monumental, global, economic and social change. I've been 'trolled' on social media in recent years, for pointing out a simple observation that this poor lass has been used 'big time' for an agenda, based on the ludicrous notion that the earth is going to die soon because of our human need for oxygen, produced by the 'breath of life' – CO_2. It is tiring to keep pointing out that 'demonising Co2' is as stupid as demonising water vapour. Both are needed for life on earth to flourish.

Genuine climate scientists know the sun (solar electromagnetism) is affecting our climate (weather patterns) and the climate of other planets. Electromagnetic pulses are coming from the sun; changing the climate on Mars, too. Of course, HAARP and its electromagnetic interference is also altering our weather; weather changes too easily blamed on man-made climate change. Real investigative science, like exposing chemtrails, will not get mainstream media airtime, anywhere; only poster girls (and boys with no scientific background) seem to get media attention. I am not saying 'pollution' hasn't reached dangerous levels, *it has*, and it needs to be challenged. But, for goodness sake, people need to see the 'Extinction Rebellion' movement for what it is: a possible cult in the making. Like any religious mindset, the use of colour iconography and symbolism by such cults is designed to affect the mind. Frightening young people into accepting a centrally-controlled technocratic future is disgusting and so is using this young 'actress', Greta, to panic her generation. The young are being targeted more today than at any other time and they really need to see what is happening to their future.

If people truly want to save the planet, I would suggest something worthwhile, like going vegetarian, using biodegradable products, or supporting young pioneers who are developing technology to deal with waste and pollution. Limiting car use and challenging the military-industrial complex more urgently for peace, etc., are other options but, for goodness' sake, at least have the intelligence to realise when the 'hidden hand' is at work through 'media magic', political spin and celebrity virtue signalling.

Blue to Red *Hue*man

Perception of colour derives from the stimulation of cone cells in the human eye by electromagnetic radiation in the visible spectrum. Colour categories and physical specifications of colour are associated with objects through the wavelength of light reflected from them. The RGB (red, green and blue) colour space, for instance, is a colour space corresponding to human trichromacy (possessing colours) and to the three cone cells in the human eye that respond to three bands of light: long wavelengths, peaking near 564–580 nm (red); medium-wavelength, peaking near 534–545 nm (green) and short-wavelength light, near 420–440 nm (blue). Remember what I said about the projector in previous chapters, the 'three' points are also part of the holographic principle and the 'illusion of light' being turned into colours by the eye and the brain. The manipulation of reality is one thing, but how we 'see' what we perceive to be real is also part of the illusion.

Blue, the third primary colour, is said to signify spiritually-healing powers. I have felt this resonance with blue personally and know that it does have 'healing abilities' as I have used it in healing visualizations many times. Blue is the most sublime subject and colour which is also said to represent, in biblical terms, the 'Word of God'. Our blue sky, blue earth and blue oceans, along with the frequency (vibration) of green (turquoise), connects us to higher vibrations. Blue is said to symbolise trust, loyalty, wisdom, confidence, intelligence, faith, truth, and the heavens. Blue is also considered beneficial to the mind and body and slows human metabolism, producing a calming effect associated with tranquility and calmness.

The symbolism for short-link radio technology, later named Bluetooth, after Danish king, Harold Bluetooth, is why the symbol for Bluetooth is a combination of runes (a bind rune, to be specific) coming from minds at the Silicon Valley 'Intel Corporation' (see figure 349 overleaf). The rune symbol relates to *binding magic* and the letter 'B', or 'Bjarkan' (Birch) in the logo can

**Figure 349:
Bluetooth.**
Blue is also used
in the Intel logo.

be seen in the Old Norwegian Rune poem as 'Loki (the clown/trickster), the horned Haokah god; the master of deceit'. The letter Runic 'H' in the logo is the 'Hagall' or 'Hail' rune, referring to Christ creating the world of old. Notice also the 'X' formed by the binding, which relates to 'star magic' and spell subjects I covered in *Chapter Ten*. The whole idea behind 'Bluetooth' technology was to create a 'linkage 'between computer devices in the early 90s operating under what IT specialists call a 'master and slave' connection (or a BR/EDR network). It is also perfect for 'track and trace' Apps, especially since the coronavirus pandemic and the Cults push for endless surveillance. Bluetooth devices were the early stages of forming the 'wireless' (A.I. transformation of humanity) technology now being used evermore to create a Cyber-Grid; more on this in the next few chapters.

In the Middle Ages and the Renaissance, the colour blue and natural ultramarine, was made by grinding and purifying lapis lazuli, the finest blue pigment to be found. It was extremely expensive, and in Italian Renaissance art, it was often reserved for the robes of the Virgin Mary and the celestial regions I have been discussing in the last few chapters. Human eyes perceive blue when observing light, which has a dominant wavelength of roughly 450–495 nanometres. Blues with a higher frequency, thus a shorter wavelength, gradually look more violet, while those with a lower frequency and a longer wavelength gradually appear greener in colour, such as turquoise. Isaac Newton included blue as one of the seven colours in his first description the visible spectrum. He chose seven colours that corresponded with the number of notes in the musical scale he believed was related to the optical spectrum. He included indigo, the hue between blue and violet, as one of the separate colours, though today it is usually considered a hue of blue.[10]

Red is one of the boldest colours in the spectrum and stands out in any work of art, hence its use to signal danger or warning. Red is used to contrast with its surroundings, drawing the viewer's attention towards a particular point of reference. The 19th Century Royal Academy artist, J.M.W. Turner, used red in his feudal-like relationship with painter, John Constable. In 1832, while Constable laboriously put his finishing touches to the busy scene, *Opening of Waterloo Bridge* in the Royal Academy gallery, Turner, seeing that in comparison his serene seascape, *Helvoetsluys* was a little lacking in colour, entered the room, painted a small red buoy in the middle of his canvas - which had only taken him a few months to compose - and left without saying a word! The red splodge immediately transformed the attention of those viewing the painting. Yellow and red together are the most noticeable colours to the human eye, hence why they are often combined in advertising, global franchises and corporate logos.

Red also represents power and courage and in different cultures, red carries a range of different meanings. For example, in Russia, the word for red means beautiful. In some cultures, red represents purity, joy, celebration and is a traditional colour worn by brides. In China, red is used for prosperity and represents happiness. Red symbolised superhuman heroism to the Greeks and is the colour mostly associated with Christ, the Christian crucifixion and founders of the early Church, like St. Jerome. The pigment to make red was almost as rare and as expensive as blue and purple in ancient times – a fact that may explain its magic and power, which again tells us who really controlled the patronage of the arts through the Renaissance (see my book *Journeys in the Dreamtime*). Paradoxically, today's intense red dyes come from crushed insects (the Lac Beetle and cochineal insect). Beetle symbolism will become relevant in the next chapter.

The human eye sees red when it looks at light with a wavelength between approximately 625 and 740 nanometers. A primary colour in the RGB colour model (the human trichromacy), it also gives us the 'reality' of full colour, as seen on TV/computer monitors. When it comes to visible light, the highest frequency colour, violet, also has the most energy. The lowest frequency of visible light, red, has the least energy. Light that is just past this frequency range of 625 and 740 nanometers is called infrared (or below red) and cannot be seen by human eyes, although it can be sensed as heat. For instance, bulls *cannot* see the red colour of the bullfighter's cape, but are 'agitated' by its movement or *vibration*. Infared is also the wavelength associated with barcode readers, or red light districts and can be seen used in Masonic lodges. It is the vibration here that is important, as red signifies a lower vibration connected to unseen forces operating on the same wavelength.

Checkmate - Duality in Everything

The idea that all colours are made from light giving us 'seven' colours of the spectrum (rainbow) is only one part of the spectrum. We also have the lack of light, or 'dark light', at work within the universe. The lack of light gives us darkness and the lack of darkness is due to an increase in light. Light, in this context, can be seen to be 'electromagnetic light' but it also has a spiritual side relating to what the Gnostics called 'dualism'. The principles of light and dark are also contained within the wisdom of the ancient texts like the *Zohar*, which speak of the Upper worlds of Light and the Lower worlds of Darkness.

The most common symbolism for the worlds of dark and light are found in chequerboard symbolism (chessboards) which captures the same duality, or opposing forces, I'm highlighting. The chequerboard has its origins in Persia before the crusades and can also be seen in petroglyphs of various shamanic cultures of Native America – cultures that used duality symbolism to focus on Orion and Sirius. Chess, as a game, probably invented in India and China, was initiated by the Assassin brotherhoods of 9th Century Persia and the Knights Templar of Europe as an 'anti-church and anti-king (divine rule) game. The 8 x 8 squares of the chessboard is significant also, as it relates to the 64 codons and amino acids of our DNA, which also relates to the 64 hexagrams in I Ching; all relate to the use of light to construct reality. The number eight relates symbolically to the 'spider' and to the Betelgeuse-Saturn Hack, as I call it. In other words, the game of life (symbolic of chess), with its two sides, is a macrocosm of the polarity of human life as it plays out in the world. Beyond *eight*, the number *Nine* was also connected to the 'mirror world' and the 'shadow self', used as a tool by native peoples for healing, introspection and accessing other realities. Have you noticed how politics, over the past few years, has become more 'polarised'? All this is all part of Orion's vibrational archetypes and a 'consciousness' connected to Orion's stars, not least the vibrational duality of the red and the blue, or the black and the white I've outlined in this chapter.

Native American 'sacred' clowns and shamans are often adorned in black and white chequerboard symbols (or stripes), symbolic of their connection to the teaching of 'opposites'. The origins could be born of an interstellar tussle, but I am sure the symbolism relates to the duality of reality (see figure 350). The eye mask is important, too, as it signifies the 'lone' warrior-magician (Orion), the 'hidden one' and creates a 'non-human' persona, more on this in the next chapter.

Identical symbolism can be seen with the West African deity 'Eshu', which the Yoruba people also regarded as a trickster duality god. This particular figure was capable of traversing time, haunting gateways (roads and portals) and changing into different forms. Eshu partially serves as an alternate name for 'Eleggua' a messenger for all 'Orishas', human spirits, similar to the Gnostic Aeons; Eleggua looks remarkably like the Hopi Masau'u (Orion) deity I mentioned in *Part One*. Both Eleggua and Eshu are the African/Caribbean versions of Masau'u and Kokopelli in truth, which suggests a global knowledge of the archetypes I am exploring. In one Yoruba Poem regarding Eshu, it says: " Eshu throws a stone today and it kills a bird yesterday."[11] This particular phrase relates directly to the ability to travel back in time and suggests that the ancients were adepts at manipu-

Figure 350: Masked Shaman with chequerboard symbolism.

lating time. The same phrase reminds me of the lyric in the 1970s song *'Lone Ranger'*, by Quantum Jump, which says, "... *right into tomorrow today*, who was that masked man you say, it was the Lone Ranger... " Eshnu, like Loki of Scandinavian myth, or the antler Celtic god, Cernunnos (Orion), was also said to move between different worlds. In doing so, Eshnu is said to get caught between benevolent and malevolent gods (often symbolised by having 'two faces'); therefore, reflecting the duality of life. For this reason, the archetypal trickster god is often identified with the Christian devil, but as I have already shown, Lucifer and the saviour Sun god in Christian and Pagan belief, are two sides of the same coin. Both are versions of the same archetype that carry symbolism referring to the duality of light and dark forces, on earth and from the stars.

The two-faced Roman god, 'Janus', was also said to be the god of beginnings, gates, transitions, time, duality and 'doorways'. Like the Lakota Haokah, his 'two faces' were said to see the past and future simultaneously and represented all 'beginnings and ends'. Temples dedicated to Janus were open only 'during war' in ancient Rome; again, this was another symbol for the forces operating 'behind' the veil, or what the ancients referred to as the 'Gates of Heaven'. The hidden, subconscious world of symbols influence the physical (visible) world more than we realise. As Goethe once said, *"To construct it* [reality] *from light and darkness. Or break it down into light and darkness. That is the task, for the visible world, which we take to be unity, is most agreeably constructed from those two beginnings."*

Mirror Worlds

Numbers provide insight into other frequencies interacting with our physical reality. Entire worlds and 'parallel realities' spiral and exist within the vortex-like projection I've been describing in *Part Two* of this book. The same vortex can be visualised as a crystal with a crystalline core (our DNA), from where all dimensions are projected and 'connected'. Parallel worlds are not necessarily something found in science fiction. Scientists in Oak Ridge National Laboratory in eastern Tennessee have completed building equipment to test for a parallel universe which could be identical in many ways to our own, with mirror particles, mirror planets and possibly even mirror life.[12] According to Leah Broussard, the physicist behind the Oak Ridge National Laboratory project, "...they are hoping to discover what many mystics over the centuries have told us exist, which are called mirror worlds." The discovery of a concealed mirror world may sound like something from the *Stranger Things* series, but these concepts can be found in indigenous beliefs all across the planet.

For the Lakota and Celts (who were most likely connected through an ancient Atlantis), for example, both peoples talked about the 'Great Smoking Mirror' in their oral traditions and pagan rituals. The mirror was another way of describing a doorway, or portal into a parallel world, and is similar in concept to the 'scrying mirror' used by the likes of Dr. John Dee in the 16th Century. The 'Black Mirror' is another version of the scrying mirror and again, was used to 'see into' parallel realities. The third and final episode of the television-first series of Charlie Brooker's *Black Mirror*, called *The Entire History of You* (2011),

was set in an alternative, mirror reality. It was a world where most people have something called 'grains' recording everything they do, see, or hear, allowing them to play back their memories in front of their eyes, or on a screen. The concept is very much in keeping with occult rituals in modern form and the 'black mirror-screens' (much like cell phones, digital TV and iPads today) are used to 'scry' for facebook memories amongst other thoughts and desires (see figure 351). The black mirror is a device for seeing into other

Figure 351: Black Mirrors.
Both modern and medieval scrying mirrors. It's what is *looking back* through the mirror (screen) we should be concerned about.

worlds, worlds connected to the 'darker aspects' of Orion, forming part of the Betelgeuse-Saturn Hack. It is interesting to note that the biggest provider and most popular black screen android, or cell phone, is 'Apple', which *is* symbolic of the 'beginning' of the so-called *fall* of Adam (humanity) in the celestial Garden of Eden. Could the fall have taken place in Orion, possibly the red and blue areas of the Orion Nebula? I feel intuitively that the Orion Nebula, with its primary blue and red zones, either side of the primary yellow trapezium, is the doorway to the parallel (mirror) world connected to our non-coding (junk) DNA. It is also a key to the 'non-local' worlds, as described by quantum physicists, accessed through our DNA. Could it be that higher dimensions and alternative realities, as described by the ancient mystics from across a range of beliefs and religious history, are all speaking of the mechanics of the projection centred in Orion? The lost (technological) worlds of Atlantis, Hyperborea and Shambhala, for example, may be located in the stars (notably, through Orion's stars) leading to a parallel reality (through a stargate). Some of these stargates on Earth, I feel, are in places such as Egypt, Jerusalem, Cambodia, Himalayas, Antarctica and where the Caribbean sea meets the Atlantic Ocean. I am sure there are other portals in and around the ancient landscapes where the Gnostics and early mystics set up home, such as the Occitane in France.

Shambhala in Orion Itself

In the book, *Shambhala, Oasis of Light* (1977), Andrew Tomas talks of a secret, symbolic code used by initiates connecting Asia with the Mediterranean area thousands of years ago; a language that originated in another world, or dimension. Mystic Nicholas Roerich and his wife (writing in 1930 under the name 'J. Saint-Hilaire', in their book *On Eastern Crossroads*) also speculated on the origins of the mystical location of Shambhala being somewhere in Orion itself. Writer Stephen Jenkins, talking about Roerich's work, in his book *The Undiscovered Country: Adventures Into Other Dimensions* (1978), writes of Orion's connection to Shambhala:

> *The reported statements of the entities about beings living somewhere in Orion are a reflection of an actually existing Central Asian tradition… they connect Orion with an earthly, if mystical, Shambhalla.*[13]

The Golden Age on earth, possibly Atlantis, Shambhala and other ancient, mysterious locations, could all be part of the original projection (our original earth reality) before it was 'hacked'. The vast array of extraterrestrial phenomena in relation to the topics I've been discussing in the past few chapters, could easily be lesser 'projections'. In the next chapter, I will look in more depth at how certain ET's may well be *totally* artificial (holographic) entities; no more than a creation of a *superior* 'Artificial intelligence'; *one that has 'hacked' the original projection*, from within the Orion Nebula. I believe there is an ongoing stellar war in the so-called heavens that is mirrored on earth and this battle is between opposing forces (within the projection) creating polarity, division and war on earth. The war is for total control of the human mind (soul), our world and what remains of the organic world of Gaia, Earth, or Sophia. Artificial Intelligence (and the alien force behind it) is, I would suggest, seeking to invade humanity. What if cyborgs and alien-like robots (machines), as seen in many movies, are more real than we can possibly imagine? Who truly knows what is 'out there' or within the earth? None of us do. All we have is what we 'feel', and can gleam from other ancient and modern sources.

In the next few chapters, I am going to explore further the Orion-based 'intelligence', to consider both its 'ancient and modern' manifestations. My intent is to draw on the seemingly endless themes in movies (courtesy of

Hollywood and its 'star magic') and ancient myths which, when we look closely at the plots and symbolism in relation to alien life, they point us in a different direction – to automatous sentient gods from the stars.

Sources:

1) *Revelation* 19:14
2) Sabak, Pierre. *Angelic Invasion* (not yet published).
3) Wilten, Danny. *Orion in the Vatican.* e-book, 2012, p18-22
4) http://www.renshaworks.com/jastro/orion.htm
5) https://www.dailymail.co.uk/sciencetech/article-7891181/Mysterious-burst-gravitational-waves-appears-coming-direction-Betelgeuse.html
6) David, Gary A. *The Orion Zone.* Adventures Unlimited Press, 2006, p68-70
7) Janet Parker; Alice Mills; Julie Stanton (2007). *Mythology: Myths, Legends and Fantasies.* Durban, Struik Publishers. p. 419.
8) Hague, Neil. *Aeon Rising - Battle for Atlantis.* Quester, 2017, p45
9) Fuller, J. F. C. *The Secret Wisdom of the Qabalah; A Study in Jewish Mystical Thought.* p13
10) *Annotated Myths & legends*, p 86
11) Arthur C. Hardy and Fred H. Perrin. *The Principles of Optics.* McGraw-Hill Book Co., Inc., New York. 1932. p 200
12) https://www.independent.co.uk/news/science/parallel-universe-portal-mirror-world-science-stranger-things-oak-ridge-a8987681.html
13) Newton, Toyne. *The Dark Worship.* Vega, 2002, p4218

18

ANCIENT-FUTURE GODS

It's All in the Movies (Part 1)

I guess cyborgs like myself have a tendency to be
paranoid about our origins.
Мотоко Kusanagi (*Ghost in the Shell*)

The projector and its blueprint I have been describing so far is manifesting an earth-matrix reality which, in my view, is inspired by the stars
(the heavens). The invisible 'circuitry' connecting the stars was created by
consciousness from beyond the illusion, or the blueprint I described in the
last chapter. The correlations between the pyramids and the Orion constellation, along with other star systems, are part of the circuitry. The building
of ancient pyramids, mesas and other temple structures all over the earth,
are part of the blueprint that has given humanity common religious beliefs,
empires, political structures and above all, constant duality, conflict, and
hierarchy. The much more 'sinister' aspect of our earth-matrix and the
invisible circuitry is the Betelgeuse-Saturn Hack influencing our reality, taking us into a future control grid we have experienced before as a human
race. Within this control grid is a particular strand of consciousness I want
to explore in this chapter.

Being born into the earth-matrix is like being born into a vast super
holographic 'game world' that has many rules, levels, programmes and
other software constructing the game. Other authors have described the
physical (five sense) experience as akin to wearing virtual reality goggles,
or being inside a bubble reality. The world is very real to anyone inside a
virtual game, just as our physical world is very real, but from a higher perspective, it is still a game. The virtual reality software could be seen as the
source origin for our physical experience on earth. The Orion constellation,
through the projection (holographic nature) of reality, in league with the
human-body-mind vehicle (our biological computer), is the 'programmer of
the world' we all collectively experience. As I have already shown,
blueprints, archetypes and symbols connected to Orion seem to infuse the
'fabric of our reality' – a reality that is too often based on duality and the

illusion of choice.

The pyramids found all over the world are the most obvious example of a 'steller lore' and advanced science (knowledge of the blueprint) which connects us still today to an ancient earth matrix. At the same time, we are obsessed with Science Fiction subjects, all of which offer us a glimpse of a 'cyber-grid' future. How far into the ancient past do we have to travel until we end up in a science fiction future? One thing is for sure, we are not alone in the Universe and the constant theme of war on earth, hierarchy and worship of the gods (or God), is a mirror of a constant war in the heavens. Many science-fiction books and movies offer us a glimpse of the possibility of a war being waged 'above and beyond' our earth matrix (amongst the stars) see figure 352.

The prolific Russian writer, Isaac Asimov (who wrote and edited more than 500 books), along with Robert A. Heinlein and Arthur C. Clarke, are considered the 'Big Three' science fiction writers of the 20th Century. Arthur C. Clarke, knighted in 1989 (appointed Commander of the Order of the British Empire (CBE) for services to British cultural interests in Sri Lanka), also believed the computer would change the future for all people. He wasn't wrong there! Clarke accurately predicted many things that became reality, including 'online' banking, shopping, and what became the Internet. Science fiction writers of such calibre as Clarke and Asimov seemed to know something about Orion's influence as it inspired many books and later TV Science Fiction programmes such as *Star Trek*. Mark Finley, a Seventh-day Adventist Church pastor and former host and director of *It Is Written*, a Christian television show (from 1991–2004) seems to know the significance of Orion's influence over war, duality and humanity's tussle with opposing unseen forces.

Figure 352: Orion's Wars.
Orion's 'flaming (light) sword' or 'door' (cloud) has been an important subject for Science Fiction writers and filmmakers.

You could say that 'good' science fiction is grounded in 'religion and myth', and I am sure, 'initiation' into the 'mysteries' helps those 'in the know', too. In an article by Mark Lawson in the *Weekend Guardian* (at the time of the release of The *Phantom Menace Star Wars Episode One* (1999), he says, "Francis Ford Coppola advised Lucas when the success of the series became known that, rather than extend the sequence cinematically, he should 'found a religion' with the scripts as the scriptures."[1] Obviously, Lucas made the films instead, but he, along with other 'mythmakers' in Hollywood, must have already known what effect the films would have on the masses. *Star Wars* has inspired generations of movie fans.

Lucas and Spielberg

As I said in my book *Journeys in the Dreamtime* (2006), directors such as George Lucas seem very adept at hiding true knowledge of the nature of our world behind the label of 'science fiction'. In his first film, *THX- 1138* (1971), Lucas covers an oppressive, sexless, bureaucratic society, where robotic officers chase a fugitive hero figure. Thirty years later, Lucas's friend, Steven Spielberg, produced *Minority Report* (2002), which like *THX-1138*, also hints at the type of global society and technology desired by a robotic consciousness. The writer, Jim Paul, said of Lucas, "Though he draws on our century's pop culture for his raw material, his vision arises from the Middle Ages." Spielberg's talents aren't limited to the movie set. He has also proven to be one of Hollywood's most astute entrepreneurs, amassing a business empire that includes video games, toys, even restaurants. Directors such as Spielberg, are treated like gods in Hollywood. To satisfy Spielberg's interest in video arcades, DreamWorks (part-owned by Spielberg), created a joint venture with Sega and Universal Studios so to provide creative input for music, computer games, arcades, television production and movie distribution. Joseph McBride, author of the (unauthorized) book *Steven Spielberg: A Biography* (2012), says:

> *Spielberg is much more in touch with his subconscious than most people.*

And that's the exact point! Directors, filmmakers and entrepreneurs like Spielberg and Lucas seem to be part of an artistic clique who over the years have had their finger on the pulse when it comes to supplying us with content for cutting edge films and games. All of these media platforms are vehicles for affecting the subconscious, shaping reality and often mesmerizing people in a typical Hollywood - magician-like manner. From religious books that talk of battles between good and evil empires, through to the simple narratives of Lucas's original *Star Wars*, I feel we have been given endless narratives and symbols associated with Orion (and other star systems).

In this chapter, I am going to delve deeper into themes connected to Orion's influence on humanity. Some of the topics will be both objective and subjective, but what I can say for sure, the movie industry and the many themes we have seen in films, especially since the late 70s, are telling us more than we 'realise' or can see with our 'real eyes'.

War on Terra (Earth)

You cannot write a book about Orion without seeing constant themes relating to Extraterrestrials (ET's) and their influence on humanity. The multi-million dollar movie industry, Hollywood, has given us countless films over the past forty years that consider extraterrestrial interaction with humanity. I am only scratching the surface in this chapter, but one theme that comes through repeatedly is the 'alien invasion of earth'. In other forms, it is also portrayed as a 'war of worlds' or a war on Earth. The war on terror initiated through era of the Neo-Conservative Bush presidency from 2001 was (still is), a manifestation of a constant war on earth. Even the word terra (or French 'terre') is the name of planet earth, referred to as 'Terra', 'terraform' and 'terrestrial'. Therefore, the extraterrestrial 'war theme' is really a war against humanity (the earth), which is why we often see the same theme in so many movies. *The Petlya Oriona (Orion's Loop)*, a 1980 Soviet science fiction film directed by Vasili Levin, also gives further credence to the subjects I am discussing, along with the *Orion Conspiracy* (2007/2008), a short movie by French director/photographer, Seb Janiak. The *Orion Conspiracy* consists of a long presentation with a slideshow given by an anonymous, shadowy lecturer, to a group of world leaders, trying to cover every major conspiracy in a single, unified narrative. It is tongue in cheek and clearly over-edited to suit the narrative, but it concludes with a hoax attack on the earth by those that already have alien (UFO) technology. It is the greatest cover-up of all time, alien interaction with earth's elite who are said to be alien-human hybrids.

The invasion of earth and humanity by extraterrestrials (non-humans) can be seen in endless movies. Stretching as far back as the 50s from the original *The Day the Earth Stood Still* (1961), through to the Marvel Universe movies of recent years, such as *Avengers: Infinity War* (2018) and *Endgame* (2019). Other films, to name but a few, include: *Invasion of the Body Snatchers* (1978); *War of the Worlds* (1953 & 2005); *Signs* (2002); *The Invasion* (2007); *Skyline* (2010); *Attack the Block* (2011); *World Invasion: Battle Los Angeles* (2011); *Cowboys & Aliens* (2011); *Battleship* (2012); *Pacific Rim* (2013); *Oblivion* (2013); *Edge of Tomorrow* (2014); *The 5th Wave* (2016); *10 Coverfield Lane* (2016); *Independence Day* (1996); *Independence Day Resurgence* (2016); *Arrival* (2016), *Men in Black Trilogy* (1997-2019) and, of course, the seven *Transformers* movies (2007 onwards). I will come back to a few of these movies later in the chapter because they are relevant to the themes in this book.

Other movies, such as *Valerian and the City of a Thousand Planets* (2017), directed by Luc Besson, offers concepts relating to planets and 'alternative dimensions' where alien species interact with each other. The story revolves around a former International Space Station that has been expanded until its mass threatens to cause it to fall out of orbit. Relocated to deep space using thrusters, it becomes Alpha, a space-travelling city inhabited by millions of species from thousands of planets. There are non-tech, biotech and robot species amongst races of reptilians and other bizarre creatures. The 'robot species' in *Valerian* are called 'Omelites', expert-level programmers that evolved using advanced information technology (they are technology), constructed with an impenetrable outer shell made up of armour-like mechanical components. In the movie, the Omelites are primarily responsi-

© Neil Hague

Figure 353: Police Force of the Future. The K-Tron army – total artificial consciousness from the movie, *Valerian and the City of a Thousand Planets.*

ble for banking, technology, IT development and maintenance on the city planet Alpha, not to mention its military. A special police division on Alpha is created by what is called the 'United Human Federation' (a world government formed by a federation of earth's countries). This world government also have at their disposal a robot police called K-Tron, an enforcement force for Alpha's Council of Elders (see figure 353). Similar concepts are seen in the *Terminator* movies featuring 'Skynet', an artificial neural network-based mind operating through artificial general intelligence that takes over the earth. Films like *Robocop* (1987 & 2014), made by Orion Pictures, also hint at a future (global) enforcement on earth, something I will come back to in the next chapter.

'Masks', Metal Music, Knights and Kings

The more I have researched into the subjects linked to Orion, the more I see an overarching, archetypal blueprint tapped into by humanity. The notion of royalty, as I have already touched on in earlier chapters, seems to connect to Orion (especially through the star Rigel and Betelgeuse). It was no surprise to see Orion symbolism used in a movie about the 'King' (Elvis) who was a major archetypal music figure on earth. A movie called *The Man Who Would Be King* (2015) tells the story of Jimmy Ellis - an unknown singer plucked from obscurity and thrust into the spotlight as part of a crazy scheme that has him masquerade as Elvis, returned from the grave. As the

film suggests, there are many who
believe Elvis is still alive - if he is alive,
he wears a mask (a death mask) and
goes by the name 'Orion', according to
the *Nashville News* 1979 (see figure 354).
The Elvis-meets-Zorro 'image' seen in
the Jimmy Ellis character has more to
do with archetypal symbolism and is
connected to both 'Orion' and the
'mask' of a Pharaoh, or a 'king'.

Figure 354: Orion - the King.
The mask seems to be a major symbol of
the Orion Cult. (mage inspired by the
concept from *The Man Who Would be King*).

The mask is also symbolic of a 'face
without a body', or a head without a
body, often called the 'faceless one', or
'Little Face' (see page 172). The *Lone Ranger* figure made popular as the fictional masked, former Texas Ranger who fought outlaws in the American
Old West (with his Native American friend, Tonto) is another classic Orion
archetype. So is the American and UK *Masked Singer* - reality singing competition television series (part of the original South Korean *Masked Singer* by
Munhwa Broadcasting Corporation franchise). The show features celebrities in head-to-toe costumes, with face masks concealing their identities
from other contestants, panelists and audience. As I've been saying
throughout the book, the levels of distraction through the 'entertainment
industry' and their use of archetypes originates from the Orion Cult. The
obsession with face masks worn by all ages as a result of the Covid-19 pandemic in 2020 was (is) more about the 'dehumanisation' of humanity in my
view. Fear of 'death' and daily terrorising of the public by mainstream
media, brought about social distancing and mask-wearing hysteria in relation to the pandemic. With *no* science to justify the logic of wearing a mask
in public, the mask in this context, is an 'identity symbol'.

The word 'mask' appeared in English in the 1530s, from Middle French
'masque' (a covering to hide, or guard the face), derived in turn from
Italian 'maschera', from Medieval Latin *masca* 'mask, 'spectre' or 'night-
mare'. The oldest masks discovered are roughly 9000 years old, at the
Musée 'Bible et Terre Sainte' in Paris, and the Israel Museum (Jerusalem).
The mask is essentially a symbol of 'possession' by otherworldly forces,
graphically portrayed in the comedy movie *The Mask* (1994) featuring Jim
Carrey. The mask also comes from Ancient Greek Bacchanalia and the
Dionysus cults; it relates to **controls on behaviour** being temporarily suspended, as 'something else' comes through the wearer to cavort; often causing mayhem. Like the Koshari clowns I mentioned in an earlier chapter, the
mask, the clown, and the revelry connected to Hallowe'en and Saturnalia

are all Orion-inspired to a greater degree. For example, French author and intellectual, René Guénon, claimed that in the Roman Saturnalia festivals, ordinary roles were often inverted; a slave or a criminal was temporarily granted the insignia and status of royalty, only to be killed after the festival ended. The Carnival of Venice, in which 'all are equal behind their masks', dates back to 1268 AD and relates to the 'false face' (facebook anyone?) where one can hide his/her true nature from behind the mask. The use of carnivalesque masks in Jewish Purim festivities of the late 15th century also seem to have been part of a tradition, connected to the Orion archetype, Kesil Horeth (see *Chapter Five*). Elsewhere, North American Iroquois tribes also used masks for healing purposes and in the Tibetan culture, masks functioned above all as mediators of supernatural forces.[2] The Mayan bat God, Camazotz, which translates to either 'death bat' or 'snatch bat' relates to mediators of dark, supernatural forces. Camazotz appears in the *Popol Vuh* and is a prominent figure in ancient Mayan belief. The use of bat symbols concerning 'dark forces' operating from the shadows is common, see the official narrative for the 'origins' of Covid-19. The archetypal Batman figure in movies like *Dark Knight Rises* (2012), which features the masked psycopathic villain, Bane, also seems to be symbolic of billionaire Death Cult operatives creating an 'insane' earth (see figure 355).

The mask visually relates to a 'shell' that would be occupied by someone; therefore, metal armour can also be a form of mask or shell. The notion of the metal shell also seems to be connected to an ancient fascination for robots, as we shall see. From the 1980s Russian 'Orion Robot', to the more sophisticated cyborgs developed by The Defense Advanced Research Projects Agency (DARPA) in the USA, we are seeing the emergence of a 'hidden' (masked) force. This 'hidden force' is also referenced throughout the ancient world, and I am convinced has its origins in Orion. Even Metal

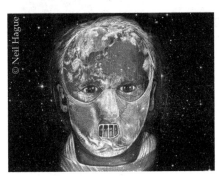

Figure 355: A Masked Earth.
Psycopaths creating 'malevolent', dark, global problems we endure can be summed up in one image.

music genres seem to encompass Orion themes. The Greek symphonic power metal band Orion's Reign and their album *Scores of War* (2018), as well as *Orion*, by Metallica, are a few examples. The Metal music genre seems to intuit and encapsulate the Orion-Saturn connection within its lyrics, songs and albums. The 'clashing of metal', war machines, dark knights and the general vibe associated with metal music, seems to be telling us something about Orion and

Saturn. The late Sir Christopher Lee also became heavily involved in 'metal music' winning the 'Spirit of Metal' award for his album *Charlemagne: By the Sword and the Cross* at the 2010 Metal Hammer Golden Gods ceremony in London. Orion (warrior) and Saturn (death) symbolism is obvious across the metal music genre. There is even a roller coaster at 'Kings' Island, located north of Cincinnati, called 'Orion'. It is said to be the largest rollercoaster at 300 feet and its longest section at over 5000 feet. The Orion roller coaster is one of the tallest, fastest and longest rides, with a 300 feet drop lasting *three* minutes. That magic number again.

Orion Pax & the 'Robots in Disguise'

One of the biggest franchises in the past decade has been the *Transformers* toys, movies and spin-offs. Takara Tomy Company, Ltd., with Hasbro, gave us *Microman, Transformers, Battle Beasts* and *Zooids*, large 'mechanical' animals, and animal-based designs including dinosaurs, insects, arachnids and mythological creatures. The concepts came out of Hasbro, Inc. (Hassenfeld Brothers) an American worldwide toy and board game company, probably the largest toymaker in the world in terms of stock market value, and third largest with revenues of approximately *$5.12 billion*. The origin of such corporate might came from three Polish brothers, Herman, Hillel, and Henry Hassenfeld, who also founded Hassenfeld Brothers in Providence, Rhode Island, in the early 1920s. Hasbro and Universal Pictures signed an agreement in February 2008 to derive four films from seven Hasbro properties for production led by Bennett Schneir to lead its Hasbro Films division. In 2009, Hasbro Studios was formed for TV development, production and distribution. One of its most popular creations has been the *Transformers* (shapeshifters) movies and toys, a subject that seems to be very symbolic of the themes I am about to explore.

Michael Bay (*Transformers* movies, especially 2017 *The Last Knight*) and Steven Spielberg (serving as executive producer) both seem to have knowledge of mysticism and mythology connected to Orion and other stars? What these movies do *very well*, is illustrate a common theme of an 'off-world' advanced extraterrestrial robot species coming to earth to take over the human population. The *Transformers* are essentially split into two groups (duality again), the 'Autobots' and the 'Decepticons', the latter being a malevolent robotic life form driving the 'takeover' of earth. Similar concepts can be seen in the *Doctor Who* 'Cybermen' series (with one series called '*The Sword of Orion*'), who originate from another fictional planet (a twin earth-like world) and are also bent on 'taking over the earth'. The Autobots are also sentient mechanical self-configuring modular robot life forms coming from a fictional 'metal' planet called Cybertron. Could

Cybertron be an Orion-based planet?

These sentient mechanical beings, within the narrative realm of comics and films, are a synergistic blend of biological evolution and technological engineering whose technology is 'living', a combination between nature and engineering. They utilise a sophisticated, bio-mechanical organ, known as a 'Transformation Cog', that allows Cybertronians to change shape at will. That they are essentially 'shapeshifters' is a common theme found in numerous ancient myths and legends. Both Autobots and Decepticons are inextricably linked to their 'Spark' or 'Energon', a fuel that Transformers need to survive. Within the *Transformers* narrative, Megatron, the leader of the Decepticons, schemes to turn the planet Cybertron into the ultimate weapon, a 'war world' wreaking havoc across the galaxy. The resulting war knocks Cybertron out of its orbit and set it adrift in the universe. According to the fiction in its different forms, the Decepticons and Autobots belonged to the same group until they fought each other and their conflict eventually brought to earth. Similar themes also appear in the *Superman* movie, *Man of Steel* (2013), where Krypton is being brought to earth through the 'World Builder' machines, even if it means totally killing off humanity. The title, 'Man of Steel', also hints at the 'metal/machine, alien/god' saviour figure (a Superman); more on this towards the end of the book.

The visual imagery of the *Transformers* quite clearly depicts them as 'living' robots, or sentient mechanical beings, who, according to comic writers, were part of an older universe, destroyed - consumed - by a fallen deity called, Unicorn. I am sure there is a subtle reference here to the Gnostic Demiurge, Saturn and the fallen angels. The older Transformers came into existence through a living planet (or star) and deity-entity, called 'Primus', who fought against the chaos-bringer, Unicron. The writers of these science fiction scripts, stories and comics are utilising ancient myths relating to some of the themes I've been looking at throughout this book. The 'Lord of the Light', or 'Primus', in the story is a 'being' who created the 'Primes' and the 'Matrix of Leadership', so to help defeat Unicron and save Cybertron. The Primes, which follow a lineage rather like a royal lineage on earth, lead to the main leader of the Autobots, the great 'red and blue', Optimus Prime, also known as 'Orion Pax' in the comics (see figure 356 overleaf). It is Optimus, or Orion, who heads the secret task force in preventing the Decepticon takeover of earth. The *Transformers* movie plots are nearer to the truth of what is happening on earth, more than most would care to consider.

Another figure in the *Transformers* narrative is the goddess figure, 'Quintessa', who is a major antagonist in the *Transformers* Cinematic Universe. She appears as one of two main enemies of earth (alongside

Figure 357: The Cybertronian (Orion) Queen - Quintessa. My rendition of the Orion Queen inspired by the movie.

Figure 356: Orion Pax - Optimus Prime. A model based on the original figure.

Megatron) in the film, *Transformers: The Last Knight.* She is also a Cybertronian 'sorceress', and one of the creators of the Cybertronian robot race, as well as the creator of Orion Pax (Optimus Prime) see figure 357. The symbolism surrounding Quintessa relates to the supposed extraterrestrial 'Orion Queens', a concept found in various alternative/UFO literature. They are themes suggesting that our rulers on earth are 'mirroring' the minds of an alien hierarchy presided over by a sentient, mechanical, Orion Queen (the creator of a hive mind), designed to aid the takeover of humanity; more on this in the next chapter. The idea of giant non-human forms, whether robot, giant spiders or even the more tangible dinosaur figures, which incidentally appear in robot form in the *Transformers* movie, *Age of Extinction* (2014), seems to be a subject with both 'ancient' and 'modern' roots.

Otherworldly Monsters and Giant Robots

Another movie, offering up concepts of giant alien creatures and colossal robots fighting for the earth, is the film, *Pacific Rim* (2013). In the movie, we see the arrival of colossal interdimensional creatures called 'Kaijus', a Japanese word meaning 'strange beast' or 'monster'. These monsters look Godzilla-like and seem to be 'charged' electromagnetically via another source. The Kaijus are like the Kraken of Greek myth and monsters of Norse folklore. A legendary creature, the Kraken resembled a giant squid and was known for destroying ships in Greek myth. Its tremendous size and power aligned it with the 'titans'; in legend, the Kraken was often referred to as the 'last of the Titans'. In Norwegian folklore, the Kraken seems to have been very real and talked about by fisherman from the 16th Century as a monster that came out of the sea. From Leviathan to the Loch ness monster, or the Nomo found in the creation myths of the Dogon of Mali, to the sea serpents and 'mermen' found in endless other legends, there is a constant theme of creatures emerging from the sea to do battle with surface people. The movie shows how, in response to the threat of the colossal Kaiju creatures, humanity unites under a common 'fear' to form a 'world government' and world army. But not just any ordinary army, it is a robot army called the Jaeger Program, ultimate, giant metal warriors. The symbol for this global authority, not least its war machine branch symbolised as a phoenix, or 'winged crest', which for anyone who has studied symbolism will know the winged entity that 'rises and presides' over a *new* world, refers directly to a 'New World Order'.

The interdimensional 'bridge' the Kaiju creatures travel through into the 'Pacific Rim' is a 'wormhole'. Mainstream science, including scientists like the late Stephen Hawking, and physicist, Michio Kaku, assert that wormhole travel is possible through something called the Casimir Effect (an electromagnetic vacuum). The Kaiju in *Pacific Rim* seem to 'dwell' at the entrance of a stargate, or wormhole, that clearly shows an 'eye' looking into the bridge between both worlds. The movie *Stargate* (1994) also had similar concepts that went as far as referencing Orion as a 'key' to the location from whence ancient Egyptian gods came forth (see figure 358). As I have already mentioned in earlier chapters, the eye is a symbol for the gods that can look into this world, akin to looking into the world of a goldfish and

seeing beyond its limited 'bowl-reality'. In *Pacific Rim*, the Kaijus are not wild beasts but 'engineered weapons' fighting at the behest of a race of alien conquerors. As with ancient texts and myths that talk about Archons, Jinn, etc.,

Figure 358: Orion is the Key.
The scene in the film, *Stargate* when Daniel Jackson (James Spader) realises that Orion is the 'key' to opening the Stargate.

the Kaiju and interdimensional force they represent is seeking to take over the earth by using these colossal 'ghosts in the machine' to

prepare the way for their own arrival. To combat the Kaiju, humanity unites to create the Jaegers, gigantic humanoid robots that look similar to the *Transformers* but much bigger in scale (see figure 359 overleaf).

The Jaegers are 'colossal' exoskeleton creatures, powered by a human *mind merge*, a common theme found in the 'trans-humanist agenda' - to *merge* machines *with* the human brain. Such technology exists and the human computer interface is part of The Defense Advanced Research Projects Agency (DARPA) agenda, which in the film makes no excuses for

Figure 359: Gigantic Robots.
My rendition of the ultimate
warrior - Jaeger, Gipsy Danger,
from *Pacific Rim.*

mentioning DARPA in the script near the beginning of the movie. DARPA has also openly stated it is seeking to enhance human troops genetically and technologically to create fighting, sub-human robots devoid of compassion, empathy, or ability for free thought.[3] The agenda to assimilate robots with humans is well underway today and part of what I call the 'Cyber-Grid Empire', as I will come to. The constant recurring themes of human and robot merging are relentless and at now-epidemic proportions in movies at the time of writing this book, because, as I've been saying for years, if it's in the movies, it is coming to our reality! With the robot theme in mind, I wasn't surprised to read in one online article, that U.S. government researchers (in other words DARPA) are choosing Sparton Electronics of De Leon Springs, to develop 'conceptual designs' of a 'future system' with "the potential to launch a wave of distracting light strobes, blinding lasers, electronic warfare jammers, or other kinds of 'non-lethal weapons that pop up to the ocean's surface, without warning, in the middle of an adversary's naval battle group."[4] Like I say, what kind of movie awaits humanity next? Maybe I can shed further light on that in the next few chapters?

In the *Pacific Rim* movie plot, two pilots have to 'merge their neurological pathways' so to be able to control the Jaegers. The pilots' minds are joined by a neural bridge, which seems like a clever portrait of the merging of the left and right brain on one level. The merging is referred to as a 'drifting' in the film; in order to do this, both partners have to empty their memories and dwell in the *now*. This is straight out of DARPA-funded research, which has developed a technique called 'mind-meld' that can connect brains into one multiple-functioning unit and transfer thoughts and perceptions between them. DARPA 'mind meld' technology also has the potential to be downloaded into robot technology so to give the robot 'artificial intelligence' – or the 'ghost in the shell'. The US military is already talking about these robots being given the ability to make their own decisions about who to kill (or not) and when to react, etc.

Similar concepts were put forward by Kevin Warwick, professor of cybernetics at the University of Reading in the UK, who said: "If a machine is passing down signals that keep you completely happy, then why not be part of the Matrix?" No, thank you, Mr Warwick! I prefer to make my own organic connections to the earth-matrix. This is exactly what is happening in the mind-meld-drift scenes in *Pacific Rim* and is a sign of things to come in many areas of human society, not least through vaccinations. Professor Warwick has made numerous appearances in the media over the years after being microchipped himself, promoting this and other transhumanist ambitions, as the means for human progress. Is it really progress or is it regression to an ancient future-prison reality? Interestingly, the CEO and co-founder of Apple, Steve Jobs, was also referred to as the 'Man in the Machine' in a documentary film of the same name, about the 'technology giant' that changed the world. The same themes of humanity *merging with machines* can be seen in other films, too. Neo, in the *Matrix* movies, also symbolically merges with the machine hive mind (the power behind the matrix) to cancel out the rouge agent programme called Agent Smith.

In this sense, the movies are not 'just movies', they are 'predictive programming'. Films like *Pacific Rim, Transformers* and the list I mentioned a few pages back are telling the masses what is on the cards in the not-so-distant future. The movie *Ghost in the Shell* (2017) is the epitome of a future immersed in AI, robots and alien technology connected to the gods of the ancient-future world.

Titanic Metal Gods

Many of the alien invasion movies I have mentioned seem to depict an attack manifesting from the oceans. I've said before in blogs and articles, what 'could emerge' from the sea (an alien invasion) could be used to 'bring about' a New World Order, not least the obsession with World War by those who worship the 'beast' in all its forms. The so-called inspired script for a future scenario, otherwise known as the *Book of Revelation*, also gives us a sense of the type of alien that could surface from the sea, as do the movies *Battleship* (2012), *The Abyss* (1989) and the *Sphere* (1998). Hollywood is forever tantalizing our mind's eye with what is possible and what kind of war machines could be used against humanity in a not-so-distant future war. Our subconscious minds have soaked it all up for decades.

The beast in *Revelation* refers to 'two beasts', the first beast is said to come 'out of the sea' and the second, from out of the earth. The first beast is given authority and power by the dragon (*Revelation* 11:7) and comes out of the abyss. This beast's appearance is described in detail in *Revelation* and in my view, relates to an AI-Robot war machine that could be used to try and bring about such a global tyranny. The second beast is said to come from 'out of the earth' and this entity directs all peoples of the earth to worship the first beast - the 'body' or the organisation that becomes the 'World

Government'. The second beast is described in *Revelation* 13:11-18 as the 'false prophet', this person/government/authority 'preaches' *for* a global government, or a technocratic New World Order. The two beasts in Christian belief, are aligned with what *Revelation* calls the great deceiver, the dragon, and the devil, as such. The 'new human', or a 'trans-human, micro-chipped human', under the rule of the 'beast' would certainly not be like any other type of human. One text accredited to Marduk, the Babylonian father-deity in his role as the creator of a new human being, reads: "I shall bring into existence a robot; his name shall be Man." The robot in this sense, is a possessed human form – a human that is more machine than human, or quite simply, a mind-merged artificial human, designed to connect to what I call the Cyber-grid Empire; something I will return to in the last few chapters.

Creators of Ancient Robots and the Weapons of the Gods

The Colossus of Rhodes, is a statue described according to several ancient accounts, as a structure being built with iron tie bars onto which brass plates were fixed to form its skin (see figure 360). You could say it was a primitive attempt at building robot Jaeger to scare off otherworldly invaders. The interior of Colossus was said to have stood on a 15 metre (50 foot) high white marble pedestal near the Mandraki harbour entrance. Other sources place the Colossus figure on a breakwater in the harbour and standing over 30 meters (98.4 ft) tall. Interestingly, 'Colossus' was the name for the world's first electronic programmable digital computer. Colossus computers were used by British codebreakers during World War II to help in the cryptanalysis of the Nazi security teleprinter, Lorenz cipher. Considering the discovery of a 2000-year-old analogue computer called the 'Antikythera' mechanism in 1901 (see figure 361), retrieved from a wreck off the coast of the Greek island Antikythera, I am sure that advanced technology existed thousands of years ago.

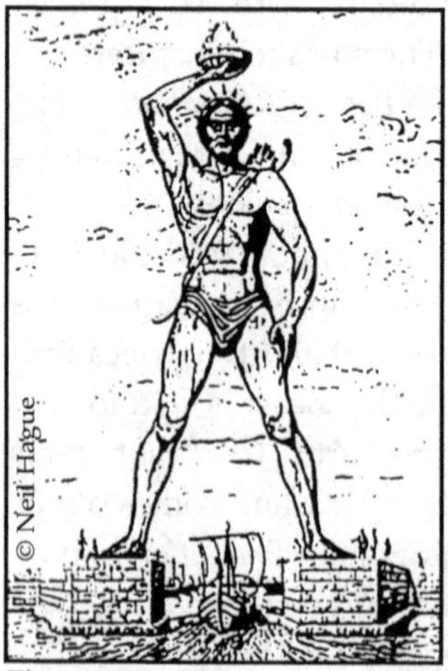

Figure 360: The
Prometheus-like Colossus.

Figure 361: The Antikythera
mechanism.

In fact, I have often wondered if the robot phenomena today, which includes computers and artificial intelligence, is not part of alien 'futuristic' ancient civilisations on earth? Was Atlantis *technologically* advanced? Yes, I think so.

Ancient sentient mechanical beings (gods) can be found in several Greek myths and others can be found on the island of Sardinia, which may have been the original source for such Island 'protectors'. Talos is one example of a giant automaton made of bronze, created by the blacksmith god, Hephaestus (or Vulcan in Roman belief) to protect Europa in Crete from pirates and invaders (see figure 362).

Figure 362: Hephaestus (Vulcan).
The god of fire, 'metalwork' and ancient technology.

Figure 363: Talos.
A Silver didrachma from Phaistos, Crete (ca. 300/280-270 BCE) featuring the metal giant, Talos. (Public domain)

Hephaestus, the god of fire, metalworking, stonemasonry and forges, created Talos to circle the island's shores 'three' times daily, rather like the robot Jaeger, keeping guard in *Pacific Rim*. According to the legends, Talos was not flesh and bone but a living metal creature, possibly the first 'robot-like' human.

The most well-known depiction of Talos is seen in the story and movie *Jason and the Argonauts* (1963), where Talos guards the treasure chamber of the gods (see figure 363). Talos was eventually killed by Jason and the witch, Medea, in the myths. Talos was said to be a gift from Hephaestus to King Minos of the Minotaur legend. Other creations of Hephaestus included 'bronze fire-breathing bulls' (Tauroi Khalekeoi), an eagle drone, Kaukasian Eagle (which attacked Prometheus) and an 'army' of automaton skeletons said to have sprung to life from planting dragon's teeth ploughed by the Tauroi Khalekeoi. The god of fire, it seems, was also responsible for ancient 'self-driving chariots' and the liquid fire called 'Ichor' which kept automatons, such as Talos, alive. You could compare the Ichor to the 'all-spark', which keeps alive the sentient mechanical *Transformers*. When I see the word 'fire', in relation to Hephaestus's 'creations', I see the word 'technology', which will make sense as we proceed. Hephaestus was helped in his creation of Talos by the Cyclop in the form of a bull (see earlier chapters for symbolism associated with the one-eyed and the bulls-eye, fiery red star - Aldebaran. In other versions of the myth, Talos is a gift from Zeus (Jupiter) to Europa (the bull) and in other versions he was the son of Kres, the personification of Crete. On the Greek island of Crete, Zeus was also called 'Talios' and in the ancient Greek dialect 'Talos' was the name of the Sun – the Sun Saturn, as it was before it fell further into darkness.

Incidentally, Notre Dame Cathedral in Paris, which partly burnt (mysteriously) in 2019, was an ancient shrine to Hephaestus (or Vulcan in Roman myth) and as I pointed out in earlier chapters, sacred fire was also said to be an important element through which the 'unseen' (the archons) manifested into our 'physical' human reality. Notre Dame's fire was more likely the work of the unseen, and not 'man-made' in my view. Interestingly, Vulcan's fire contained the ability to mould and shape magical forms through which the 'gods' (archons) could also appear.

Hephaestus was credited with other 'artificially intelligent devices' such as an invisible net (a cloaking device) to ensnare his unfaithful wife, Aphrodite, and a robot dog, Laelaps. Many self-moving automata were credited to Hephaestus, from metal owls, to shields, self-moving tables and clocks, not unlike the Antikythera mechanism on page 508. You could see Hephaestus as the Marvel Comic character, Tony Stark, of ancient Greece. The Tony Stark/*Iron Man* character is a modern day version of the same mythological narratives of a godlike, master craftsman making 'artificially intelligent armour' that would have seemed alien to humanity. Hephaestus was also said to have created Hermes' winged helmet and sandals, the Aegis breastplate, Aphrodite's famed girdle, Achilles' armour, Hercules' bronze clappers, Helios' chariot, the shoulder of Pelops, Eros' bow and arrows and Hades' helmet of invisibility. Where the titan, Prometheus, brought knowledge and inner fire, Hephaestus brought *technology* and *artificial fire*. Curiously, in the *Captain Marvel* comics, Talos is the name of the reptilian-looking Skrull General who collaborates with *Captain Marvel* in order to save the remnants of his own people from the Kree Empire. The war between the Skrull and the Kree, created by Stan Lee, is very much symbolic of the wars between human-like aliens and the draco-reptilians and Watchers mentioned earlier in the book. It was Hephaestus who also gave his assistant, Cedalion, to guide a blinded Orion (see page 68).

Copper Gods and Machine Men

According to the Dogon tribes, their star gods (teachers) called the Nommo (who came out of the sea), were made out of copper. According to the

Dogon elders, copper was equated with both water and 'rays of light' and it was said that the Nommo also excrete copper.[5] Why am I seeing the liquid-like *Terminator* character from the movie of the same name? The Dogon word for copper is 'mênn', very similar to the Egyptian phallic fertility god, 'Min', another variation of Orion (see page 151). Strangely enough, in connection to Talos, ancient copper ingots have also been found in Crete, which look very similar to the 'shape' formed by the Orion constellation (see figure 364).

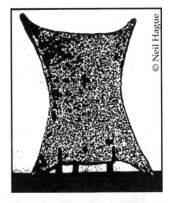

Figure 364: Orion currency?
A drawing of a bronze ingot from the Cape Gelidonya shipwreck 1200 BC. Original artefact in the Museum of Underwater Archaeology at Bodrum Castle, Turkey.

Author Barbara Hand Clow (co-founder of Bear & Company Publishing house) produced many books on interstellar consciousness and channelled communication with star beings over the past twenty years. In *The Pleiadian Agenda* (1995), Clow talks about alien humanoids from Orion that also resemble a machine and are mechanical. The 'red race' culture also mentioned in other similar books, talk of the Atlanteans being a reddish, copper-like people that also came from the stars. The *Pulse of Creation* books by Ernest L. Norman, especially the *Voice of Orion* (1961) have similar 'channelled' themes. Ernest Leland Norman (1904 - 1971) was an American electrical engineer, philosopher, poet, clairvoyant, scientific researcher, paranormal investigator and the co-founder of the Unarius Science of Life. I am always fairly skeptical of channelled information, unless I can see more objective connections linked to the information received. Some authors, like Norman and Clow, have mentioned extraterrestrial syndicates under the guidance of Orion and its stars/suns and how other star systems, such as the Pleiades, have influenced each other through 'star wars'. Such subjects I can only speculate on and would not want to say either way if any of this material is true (or untrue). I do feel that a celestial empire originating in Orion (not dissimilar to the fictional one in *Star Wars*) is near to the truth and is influencing, even manipulating, geopolitics on earth.

Alien Engineers

As I mentioned in an earlier chapter, the Greek god, Prometheus, was said to have stolen fire from the forge belonging to Hephaestus, a place considered unapproachable by humans. Could the forge of Hephaestus be the central fire of the Orion Nebula? Prometheus, like Hephaestus, was a gift-bringer charged with 'creating other life forms', whether natural, organic or 'artificial'. Hephaestus also created the 'gift of the gods' a woman called Pandora, a major figure connected to the themes in this chapter, more on her shortly. Plates in the British museum and another in the Thorvalsens Museum, Denmark, show Prometheus seated with a hammer creating the first human skeleton. The image mirrors scenes of the Egyptian god, Ptah creating the first man and the Assyrian images of Enki doing the same. All of these images refer to the creation of a new biological human, one that possibly arrived on earth after the Deluge. Both Prometheus and Hephaestus are symbolic of the Orion-Saturn composite gods (the Elohim) who create a new human (blueprint) for life on a post-flood earth. To give a narrative feel for what I am describing here, it is worth watching the opening 10 minutes of Ridley Scott's Movie, *Prometheus* (2012), which shows alien 'engineers' disseminating their DNA into the water on earth. The engineers are alien, giant-like creator gods that use the elements (life) to forge a new genetic species on earth.

In Greek myth, the only giant not slain in the conflict between the Olympians and Titans was Aristaios (or Asterion), who was said to be turned into a dung beetle by Gaia, that he might be safe from the wrath of the Olympians (see figure 365). Aristaios was born of Ouranos (Uranus/Poseidon) and Gaia (just like Orion), and like other offspring of Gaia, such as the Cyclops and other titans, Aristaios dwelled 'inside' the earth (the Underworld) the location travelled to by Osiris/Orion. It's also amazing to note that many of the 'alien invaders' seen in movies such as *Superman – Man of Steel* (2013), *Transformers*, *Jupiter Ascending* (2014) and the *Matrix* movies, all seem to travel in scarab-like, or other insect-bug-like space crafts or 'machines'. According to historian Isaac Myers (1836-1902), the scarab symbol and its worship were already in existence in ancient Egypt and could have been part of an elaborate language connected to Osiris (Orion) and the *Book of the Dead* before 4000BC.[6] The Greek God, Argus Panoptes (Argos), another giant I mentioned in *Chapter Two*, can be associated with

Figure 365: Aristaios in different forms.
The exoskeleton giant Aristaios holding the 'hive' - keeper of the insect-like hive mind. Both bees and beatles (scarabs) are considered creator gods.

both ancient and modern interpretations of metal giants/gods with 'all-seeing' abilities, possibly 'technological' in origin. In a fantastic book *Gods and Robots, Myths, Machines and Ancient Dreams of Technology* (2018), author Adrienne Mayor sums up the connection between the gods (the past) and the present technology in use today, when she says:

> *The ancient myth of a hypervigilent watcher that never sleeps and observes from all angles inspired Jeremy Bentham's eighteenth-century panopticon designs for institutions and prisons, heralding the proliferation of banks of surveillance cameras ubiquitous in the modern world. Accordingly, numerous security providers operate under the name 'Argos/Argus'.[7]*

As I will come to, we are going 'back to the future' through the global arrival of all things artificially intelligent: the new Watchers, giants and gods for an atomic, technological (technocratic) generation.

Khepri (Orion's) Spiders and Shard Symbolism

In November 2018, the French (Occitaine) city of Toulouse witnessed the appearance of Asterion, the giant 'robot Minotaur', as part of the French street-theatre company, La Machine's show, *Le Gardien du Temple (The Guardian of the Temple)*. The unpainted lime wood and metal giant Minotaur was followed through the streets by a giant metal spider, (La Princesse, Ariane (Ariadne), as part of a constituted Act, accompanied by a cast comprised of scores of actors, opera singers and musicians.[8] Some 350,000 to 400,000 people were said to have gathered to watch the spectacular, which gave a visual effect of such mythological creatures. The Minotaur and Ariadne are aspects of the Underworld and myths associated with

Dionysus, another Orion figure. It was Ariadne, according to Greek myth, that created the Labyrinth to hold the horned Minotaur. In fact, the giant spider-scorpion (see figure 366) and the Minotaur can be seen as nefarious forces opposing Orion and Taurus, the latter (the bull) is the old symbol for the Occitaine region and Toulouse, a symbol I've been illustrating throughout the book. Ariadne is also the name of the original European space shuttle (one of the heaviest telecommunica-

Figure 366: Giant Robot-like Spiders. Do giant spiders reflect a distant memory of an alien threat? See the endless movies and myths containing spider-like machines.

tions spacecrafts), built to carry satellites (the spider's telecommunications web) into space.

It is also interesting to note that in Lakota myth, there is a giant spider called 'Iktomi' who is a trickster spirit, and a culture hero for the Teton Sioux Lakota people. Alternate names for Iktomi include Ikto, Ictinike, Inktomi, Unktome, and Unktomi and according to numerous North American plains tribes, Iktomi rep-
resents a star deity. I would suggest Ikto is connected to the clown trick-sters originating from Betelgeuse (see image 367). On another level, Lakota mythology is a 'living belief system' and the spider, Iktomi, rep-resented a 'living (alien) conscious-ness' that would spread its web all over the land. Today, this has been interpreted by some contemporary Native Americans to be the telecommunications network, the Internet, or the World Wide Web. Some Lakota see the spirit of Iktomi as the patron of 'new technology', from the invention of language, to today's modern cyber world of the computer, robots and I would add 'artificial intelligence'. Another Native American mythological crea-ture of giant proportions was the

Figure 367: Iktomi (Ikto) the Spider God. My inspired image of the Iktomi Spiders of Orion (see my books, *Lions & Velons, The Bestiary of Kokoro, and Moon Slayer)*

'Wendigo', an evil force that took the form of a giant spider-like 'skeleton' (machine) wrapped in skin. Similar concepts of the Wendigo appeared in the Netflix series *Stranger Things* (2016), Spielberg's movie *Super 8* (2011), *A Quiet Place* (2018) and the 2017 version of the Stephen King horror novel *It*. Other versions of an alien race that appear to be a metallic superorganism are the 'Mimics' in *The Edge of Tomorrow* (2014). In the film, the alien Mimics arrive in Germany, via an asteroid, and swiftly conquer most of continental Europe. By 2020, the United Defense Force (UDF), a global military alliance established to combat the alien threat, finally achieves a victory over the Mimics at Verdun using newly-developed exoskeleton 'mech-suits'. The Mimics in such movies, are very much based on the idea of the Archons from Gnostic texts and the same name can be found used in Australian Dreamtime myths to describe frog-like creatures that can create illusions.

Could all of these deities be ancient collective experiences of giant interdimensional robot-like aliens? It's hard to know for sure. But the spider and many other insects, from wasps to cockroaches, seem to drive a primeval fear into the hearts of humans.

The gaint Aristaios (Asterion) can also be seen as Khepri, the scarab-faced god of ancient Egypt; both were considered gods of creation, connected to the sun's movement and rebirth. The perfect balls rolled by scarabs (Khepri) relate to these subjects. In some myths, Aristaios taught men to hunt (like Orion), keep bees and 'shepherd' the fields watching for fires and other forms of destruction. Aristaios and Khepri, like the god Atum (Orion), are all interchangeable. They were all considered aspects of the creator god, Ra. The 'mechanics' behind the creation of our reality, the precision of the sun and the moon, along with the notion of measuring time and inventing weapons could be attributed to the god-giants Aristaios and Khepri of ancient Greece and Egypt.

In connection to Aristaios and Khepri (both engineers), the covering of a beetle is called a 'shard', a tough sheath, or shell, which could be seen as armour. Aristaios and Talos (like the scarab) were considered to have been born with armour and therefore, the exoskeleton structure of such gods would set them apart from more human-looking deities. I am sure George Lucas's half-man, half-machine Sith Lord character, Darth Vader, was inspired by the beetle's *black* exoskeleton. It's interesting to note also that in the *Transformers* movies, the 'Shard', or 'All-Spark', which gives life to the sentient mechanical 'Transformers' shapes, can also be related to the 'elytron' or the outer wing-covering of a beetle. Japanese worship of the beetle is also connected to the 'strength' and god-like powers afforded to these ancient futuristic deities.

Figure 368: The Shard.
The London highly-symbolic Shard, alight. Like the otherworldly 'All-Spark' – symbolised in the *Transformers* movies.

The symbolism is also not lost in the London 'Shard' building, formerly London Bridge Tower - the tallest building in the United Kingdom and the European Union (see figure 368). The Shard has 72 floors and is no more than a modern version of Osiris's phallus, who, as I have already shown, is another version of Orion. The numerological symbolism of 72 also relates to 72 'Immortals' in Taoism. According to the *Zohar*, there are 72 degrees of Jacob's ladder and 72 spirits (or angels) in the heavens.

Osiris (Orion) was encased in a coffin by 72 disciples and accomplices of Typhon.[9] The mass of the Moon is 72 times that of the Earth and the 'volume' of Saturn is 72 times that of the Earth. I think we can safely say there is something significant about the 'Shard' and the symbolism associated with the gods of Orion. Buildings and effigies, like the Shard, 'could' be energetic prototypes which manifest energetic, *unseen connections,* between the Moon, Saturn and Orion's central Trapezium. As mentioned earlier, word 'Da'ath', is so close to Darth (as in Vader), it is not too much a stretch of the imagination to see parallels between certain symbolism in science fiction and a future 'machine-like' alien tyranny thanks to advancement in robotics and the ever-encroaching artificial intelligent world.

Exoskeleton Worship

An exoskeleton is the external skeleton that supports and protects an animal's body, in contrast to the human internal skeleton (endoskeleton). It is the opposite of 'being human' on one level, which is why many exoskeleton animals and insects, such as grasshoppers, cockroaches, crustaceans (crayfish, crabs and lobsters, etc.), snails, clams, tusk, hoofs, shells, chitons and nautiluses, were considered 'unholy'. The crayfish, especially, is an exoskeleton that lives at the bottom of the sea, considered 'unclean' (the living dead) in Judaic law.[10]

The almost mechanical world of certain insects, from Bees to ants, can also be connected to the gods I am outlining in this chapter. The collective mind, or the hive mind, can be seen to be artificial on one level and therefore, 'robotic'. Cockroaches and termites, for example, also express collective decision-making in an almost 'robot-like' manner, as they closely align their world with human habitats (especially kitchens and bathrooms in hot countries). A study published as part of a *Science Robotics* article, entitled *Insect-scale fast moving and ultrarobust soft robot* (July 2019), used specially-scented roach-sized robots, showing how similar cockroaches are to tiny robots. The study used soft robots, based on a curved unimorph piezoelectric structure (electricity resulting from pressure and heat/energy whose relative speed is 20 body lengths per second), to demonstrate that cockroaches appear to use just two pieces of information to decide where to go: 'how dark it is and how many other cockroaches there are'. Once there are enough insects in a place to form a 'critical mass', the roaches accepted the collective decision on where to hide, even if this was an unusually lit place. In other words, cockroaches, like other exoskeleton insects, are pure hivemind - robotic. This is why insect-like exoskeleton robotic structures are being developed for military purposes by the likes of DARPA, and the Russian Foundation for Advanced Research Projects, as part of the Defense

Industry. A robotic hive-mind will not only do as it's told, but it will not deviate from the central signal. The exoskeleton not only provides the ability for 'super powers', it also acts as a 'structure' for the robotic weapons currently being developed for war by main superpowers: the USA, Russia and China, with the EU following in line. The State Corporation for Assistance to Development, Production and Export of Advanced Technology Industrial Product Russia Rostec is also developing military exoskeleton soldiers (see figure 369). We are no longer in the movies when it comes to military hardware (and software) that seems to be visually mimicking robots, sentient mechanical beings, and 'star lords'. At what point will we see the *deeper* connections to a more sinister and hellish world being ushered in by computers, androids, cell phones, masts and the 'ghost in the machine'? The 5G network, and the use of electromagnetic DEWs (Direct Energy Weapons), as I will come to in the next chapter, is very much part of this *new*, hellish world.

Figure 369: Mimicking the Alien. The Darth Vader, beetle-like (robot) soldier developed by Rostec on display at the Army 2018 International Military and Technical Forum.

Stormtroopers, Terminators and Black Dogs

The US Army has been testing exoskeleton suits for decades. All intended to give soldiers 'superhuman' abilities, using artificial intelligence to provide additional power and mobility to soldiers, enabling them to carry heavier loads. One particular exoskeleton, happens to be the Tactical Assault Light Operator Suit, otherwise known as 'TALOS', effectively giving its wearer 'superpowers', such as the ability to see in the dark, superhuman strength and a way of deflecting bullets (see figure 370 overleaf). The military are 'inspired', at the highest levels by such 'technological gods', with Lockheed Martin and Nasa involved in developing such technology.[11] The TALOS suit is obviously inspired by the Greek sentient being of the same name created by Hephaestus. The US Army is also currently testing the Lockheed Martin ONYX exoskeleton, which like TALOS uses a powered lower-limb designed to reduce the fatigue and effort of hauling heavy gear into the field and allow battle-field commanders to do more with fewer troops. According to official sources, ONYX potentially reduces the number of injuries suffered by non-combatant soldiers in support roles often requiring strenuous activity.

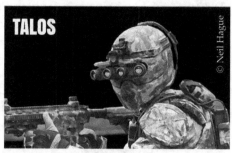

Figure 370: The TALOS suit.
My rendition of the 'new look' for the US military.

Another leader in the market for assistive exoskeletons is a Japanese company called Cyberdyne Inc. founded by billionaire, Yoshiyuki Sankai. Cyberdyne is noted for marketing and distribution of the 'HAL' robotic exoskeleton suit. HAL, of course, is the name of the artificially intelligent super computer controlling the spacecraft in Arthur C. Clarke and Stanley Kubrick's screenplay/movie, *2001: A Space Odyssey* (1968). Interestingly, the name Cyberdyne (Cyber Dynamics Systems Corporation) was also used as the 'fictional' corporation that created the 'Skynet' system in the *Terminator* movie franchise. For those who have never seen a *Terminator* movie, Skynet, like HAL, becomes a 'self-aware', 'artificial intelligent' neural network system. In the case of Skynet, it spreads into millions of computer servers all across the world; realizing the extent of its abilities, its creators try to deactivate it. But Skynet continues to operate almost exclusively through servers, mobile devices, drones, military satellites, war-machines, androids and cyborgs (usually a terminator). In the interest of self-preservation, Skynet concludes that all of humanity would attempt to destroy it and impede its capability in safeguarding the world. A global war was created by artificial intelligence and within decades, Skynet had established a global presence, using its mechanized units to track down, collect, and dispose of human survivors. As a result of its initial programming directives, Skynet's 21st-century manifestation is that of an overarching, globalised, artificial intelligent hierarchy that seeks to *destroy* humanity in order to fulfil the mandates of its original coding, or order. On one level, we are entering very dangerous ground when it comes to self-aware artificial intelligence and neural network systems, as we shall see in the next chapter.

Mimicking the exoskeleton creature for military purposes, etc., gives the soldier wearing it an 'alien-like' appearance. The technology has also been used for advancement in medical areas, such as limb replacement and rehabilitation of military personnel and people suffering the effects of terrible accidents. One recent story tells of a paralyzed French man who walked again after falling 40 feet (12 metres) from a balcony four years ago, leaving him paralyzed from the shoulders down. He was able to walk again thanks to a brain-controlled exoskeleton suit. Within the safety of a lab setting, he was also able to control the suit's arms and hands, using two sensors on his brain.[12] The American global aerospace, defense, security and advanced technologies company, Lockheed Martin, is also developing the F-35 Lightning II stealth bomber, leading the international supply chain for the development and implementation of technology solutions for the new USAF Space Fence (Star Wars Program). Lockheed Martin is the primary contractor for the development of the 'Orion command module' I mentioned in an earlier chapter.[13]

Several authors have mentioned over the years that the Pentagon and Hollywood are closely linked. The book *Operation Hollywood: How the Pentagon Censors the Movies* (2004) by author David Robb, shows how filmmakers bow to pressure from the Pentagon, when it comes to making films involving the military. Films such as *Forrest Gump* (1994) and *Star Trek IV-The Voyage Home* (1986) are just two of many films requiring Pentagon approval prior to release.[14] None of this is a surprise, especially when we see endless Science fiction themes in movies such as *Star Wars* (1977), etc., now appearing in the 'real non-fiction' military world.

Netflix's future-shock anthology drama *Black Mirror*, also featured machines running amock in the episode called *Metalhead*, Series 4; Episode 5 (2017). The creator of *Black Mirror*, Charlie Brooker, seemed to have been inspired by actual real-life robots, created by Boston Dynamics, called 'Big Dog'. These robots were also designed for the U.S. military with funding from Defense Advanced Research Projects Agency (DARPA). The dog is an obvious connection to Orion's dogs, Canis Major (Sirius) and Canis Minor (see figure 371). Charlie Brooker's post-apocalyptic future, in *Metalhead*, shows robot dogs hunting human survivors across the usual post-apocalyptic, dystopian barren landscape. Is the real thing being created precisely for this purpose? Similar robot dogs made an appearance in South Korea and China, during the coronavirus pandemic in April 2020. These robots were 'policing' social distancing in parks. Welcome to the real

Figure 371: Orion's Robot Dogs.
DARPA's 'Big Dogs' could have been based on the Greek god, Hephaestus's 'automaton creation', 'Laelaps'.

life movies, folks.

   The US Army is also looking to go full 'Iron Man' at some point in the future for its Special Operations soldiers with TALOS (Tactical Assault Light Operator Suit) leading the way. As Michel Fieldson, a former TALOS project manager said in a 2013 statement: "We sometimes refer to it as the Iron Man suit, frankly to attract the attention, imagination and excitement of industry and academia." I think there is more than just 'publicity' here. The notion of god-like soldiers, especially using the TALOS suit, hints at ancient weaponry connected to Hephaestus (Vulcan) and Zeus (Jupiter). Another robot-like entity created by Hephaestus, at the order of Zeus, is the beautiful 'Pandora'. According to myth, Pandora, like Talos and Aristaios, is an ancient obscure mechanical being who unleashes terrible events on earth.

Robot Goddesses

Several Greek tales, along with other myths, describe 'lifeless matter': statues, idols, ships and even rocks being brought to life by gods and their magic. One story concerns the bringing-to-life of inanimate objects by fiat. At the time of the great deluge, Deucalion (Noah) and his wife, Pyrrha (Naamah), would toss rocks over their heads that turned into men and women. Another story is the ancient myth of 'Pygmalion' and his love for a nude, ivory statue of his own making, probably the first 'adult doll'. Other stories from Sparta, southern Greece, tell of a malevolent dictator, Nabis, and his cruel wife, the machine-like, 'Apega' (Apia). According to the chronicler, Polybius (264–146 BC), Apega was more terrible than her tyrant husband. When Apega was despatched to Argos to raise funds, she would summon the women and children and personally inflict torture until Argos gave up all its gold.[15] According to Polybius, Nabis had a mechanical Apega constructed to resemble his demonic wife; he used her to threaten his wealthy guests who refused to comply with his demands. According to Polybius, Nabis would stand behind his machine-wife, working and manipulating her metal arms, causing her to clasp the victim, tightening so forcefully that her hidden spikes and blades would pierce whomever she 'hugged'.[16] The demonic robot used by Nabis is not dissimilar to metal torture instruments, such as the Iron Chair used by the Inquisition and the later Iron Maidens resembling an Egyptian mummy sarcophagus (see figure 372). In fact, the notion of an 'Iron Lady (or Maiden) in politics (see Margret Thatcher throughout the 80s) is very much part of the Apega symbolism.

   It is said in Greek myth, after humans received the stolen gift of fire (possibly knowledge of technology) from Prometheus, an angry Zeus

Figure 372: Iron Maiden, Apega.
'Machines' of torture in medieval times are almost science fiction-like.

decided to give humanity a 'punishing gift' to compensate for the knowledge brought by Prometheus. Zeus commands Hephaestus to mould from earth the first woman, a 'beautiful evil', whose descendants would torment the human race for millennia. After Hephaestus creates this beautiful figure, the goddess Athena dresses her in a silvery gown, an embroidered veil, garlands and an ornate crown of silver stars. This woman remains unnamed in Hesiod's poem, *Theogony* (c. 8th–7th century BC), but is presumably 'Pandora', whose myth Hesiod revisited in *Works and Days* in the same century. Ancient Greek Pandora is nothing like the Pandora in the American science fiction television series,

of the same name that aired in 2019; the ancient Greek Pandora was 'totally' artificial. She had a key position on the Acropolis in Athens, with a massive line-up of gods and goddesses on either side of her. Pandora was eventually brought to earth by Hermes (Mercury), according to the myths; her jar, or 'pythos', was thought to be made of metal (possibly bronze) and considered unbreakable. Pandora's jar (mistranslated as a box) probably contained both benevolent and malevolent 'non-physical' life forces, possibly the Jinn, likely where the notion of the genie in the bottle originates. Fate, duality and hope were also said to be contained within Pandora's jar but the releasing of these forces created pain and suffering on humanity. The Gnostics, as I have mentioned in earlier chapters, called these non-physical forms, 'chaos', the home of the Archons, demons and the 'ghosts in the shell' that still haunt human life.

Pandora and Orion

When Pandora first appears before gods and mortals, it is said 'wonder seized them' as they looked upon her. But she was 'sheer guile, not to be withstood by men'. Hesiod elaborates (590–93):

From her is the race of women and female kind: of her is the deadly race [of robots] *and tribe of women who live amongst mortal men to their great trouble, no helpmates in hateful poverty, but only in wealth.*

Of course, Hesiod is limited by the perceptions of his time, referring to an 'artificial life force' that supposedly 'animated' Pandora and her kind. The concept of the 'Golem', an animated stone, or clay manikin is similar in concept. So are the concepts found in Goethe's play, *Faust* and his homunculus (a fully formed 'repli-cated' individual). So are the 14th century Kabbalistic teachings of Rabbi Loew on how God created Adam (Orion).[17] Was Hesiod refer-ring to a 'race of robots'? We cannot know for sure but Pandora is clear-ly depicted as a classic 'kore', a Greek statue of a young woman (maiden), standing and clothed in long robes, with an unusual

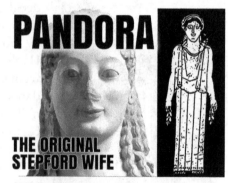

Figure 373: Pandora.
Pandora or Kore – the original ancient 'Stepford Wife'.

'*Stepford Wife*-like' stare (see figure 373). Like the original 1972 movie *The Stepford Wives*, there is a 'gentlemen's club' working 'behind the scenes' cre-ating the fawning, submissive, impossibly beautiful 'android wives'. There are so many movies and TV series in recent years that have pursued themes relating to future human life-like androids populating the world, from HSBO's *Westworld* (2016), to the Channel 4 and Kudos production *Humans* (2015-2019). The third series of *Westworld* actually has a 'Transformer-like' robot in the plot which makes me wonder if there is more to know about such sentient machines. Interestingly, one of the original *Westworld* (1973) poster featuring Yul Brynner's half exposed robot face offers a visual con-nection to the obsession with 'mandatory mask wearing' across the world because of the coronavirus pandemic (see figure 374). Ridley Scott's *Prometheus* (2012), the Alien prequel, includes the android, 'David 8', who is

responsible for unleashing the exoskele-ton-like 'alien' species on humanity. As I am showing in this chapter, robots are not entirely Science fiction. The concepts go back to the ancient world and can even be found in the Middle Ages, as I will come to.

In the American science fiction fran-chise *Star Trek*, the 'Orions', also known as the 'Orion Syndicate' (a fictional extraterrestrial humanoid species) made their first appearance in the original TV pilot series *Star Trek: The Cage* (1965). In

Figure 374: *Westworld* (Our New World?) The ostensible visual con-nection to robots and global 'manda-tory mask' wearing.

this episode, the USS *Enterprise*, under the command of Captain Christopher Pike (not Kirk), receives a radio distress call from the fourth planet in the 'Talos' star group, Talos IV from whence the 'Talosians' originate. The use of the word 'Talos' again hints at the subjects covered in this chapter, but more engagingly is the portrayal of Orion females in these episodes of *Star Trek*. They are often Osiris (Orion) green and renowned for their use of pheromones to influence men sexually, so to 'distract', and in this scenario, used for an attempted theft of the starship Enterprise. You could say they are 'Pandora-like' in their approach. The Talosians are por-

trayed as a subterranean race of humanoids with bulbous heads that use 'technology'. They are described as sentient humanoid natives, who over 100,000 years ago, fought a nuclear war, leaving most of the planet's surface uninhabitable – a common theme in many movies since 2010. Living under the surface of their planet, the Talosians developed powerful psychic abilities, able to create illusory realities through the use of memories.

Figure 375: Alien Hive Mind.
My rendition of the hive mind 'connection' through a queen, based on the Orion-Talosians and Borgs in *Star Trek*.

The Talosians also seem to appear as part human, part-grey, part reptilian in appearance and I am certain the Grey alien is a 'hive mind' species, connected to the Zeta Reticuli star system and Rigel in Orion (see figure 375).

Orion women have also been portrayed in the movies *Star Trek* (2009) and *Star Trek Into Darkness* (2013), where one is seen seducing Captain Kirk. The Pandora aspect of these fictional characters is obviously hinting at the power of 'sex magic' and also the mesmerising allure of such otherworldly creatures. I've met a few in my time and you have to wonder how many males and females we encounter who are not under the influence of some kind of mind control. The Orion's in these science fiction narratives operate a mafia-style syndicate (in space) where aliens are 'trafficked' and Orion women/girls are seen as (sex) slaves. The Orion girl slave image is popular amongst the bizarre Japanese Cosplay characters. Such topics seen in these science fiction scripts makes me wonder if they are inspired by the very real, and utterly disgusting, alleged global sex trafficking activities that have come to the surface in recent years. The late Jeffrey Epstein story of underground facilities (dungeons) on Little St. James in the Caribbean is one such story of such vile activities.[18]

Male Orions also made their first appearance in the *Star Trek:* (the Animated Series) episode *The Pirates of Orion* (1974), but did not appear in live action until the *Star Trek: Enterprise* episode, *Borderland*, which also featured female Orions. I feel that the so-called 'Orion Federation' talked about in numerous books and channelled texts is an actual empire very similar to the Galactic Empire seen in George Lucas' *Star Wars* movies. Orion's stars could be home to a vast array of alien species and I am convinced that sentient mechanical beings are part of that mix of alien life, along with other human types including reptilian-greys. The movie *Jupiter Ascending* (2014) gives a fictional peek into the vast array of alien lifeforms operating through a hive mind hierarchical structure affecting other planets, including earth. I am also convinced that much of what we call 'alien life' is actually interdimensional entities (the archons and Jinn) that were unleashed after portals were opened all over the world at significant events.

Cyborg Queens - *Controlling* the Hive Mind

The plan to turn humans into AI-controlled cyborgs has been symbolised many times in science fiction movies and television series, and few more accurately than *Star Trek* and its concept of the 'Borg'. These are portrayed as a 'collective species' – part biological, part technological – that have been 'turned' into cybernetic organisms functioning as drones within a hive mind called the 'Collective', or the 'Hive'. The Nefilim, Watchers, Reptilians, Greys and others Archontically-controlled are also a 'hive' species. The Borg are portrayed as emotionless drones, malevolent just like the Archon entities mentioned in earlier chapters, and coordinated by a 'Borg Queen' in the way a queen bee relates to a hive. Identical themes appeared in the movie *The Great Wall* (2016), where a collective reptilian species called the 'Tao Tei', all controlled by a Queen that had come to earth in ancient times, directs her hoard to feed off humans. The aliens and their hybrids (like the Greys and Reptilians, found in so many books and literature) are said to have a similar structure based on a Queen. Therefore, would it be too much of a stretch of the imagination to think of the archetypal alien 'Queen' as pure artificial intelligence? Are we being manipulated by a technological species that is also using other alien species to create a technological prison on earth? Cyborg Orions, as I call them are also epitomized in the *I Robot* movie (2004) which shows 'VIKI' (Virtual Interactive Kinetic Intelligence) as the central 'Queen intelligence' controling all of the robots. She makes Google's Alexa look like an Abacus compared to a Cell Phone. The Alexa-like cyborg world is where we are going in the not-too-far distant future.

The key to understanding alien life is to look at the devices we are now using and if you're of my generation, when there was no digital world, no Wi-Fi interference or none of this 'other' intelligence, the world felt very different. All of this technology has come from 'somewhere' - it hasn't just evolved. Humans haven't decided that they're suddenly going to build robots that are artificially intelligent, this is not a 'natural' evolution for humanity. As I am hinting at here, we're dealing with an infusion of artificial intelligence giving us the tools to 'reconstruct' our world to the detriment of future generations. That's the conspiracy! We are destroying our world, courtesy of alien (artificial) intelligence that wants the world to resemble a playground such that alien intelligence can purely interact with and control - the goal being the end of the human species as we know it. I think that there's going to be a point that hasn't happened yet - where it's going to be very difficult for a highly-evolved human, interacting with their Superconsciousness, to NOT see the alien; the digital beast for what it is – pure evil.

The android (or artificial being) can also be broken down to different types, such as the 'Actroid', a type of android (humanoid) with strong visual human-likeness developed by Osaka University and manufactured by Kokoro Company Ltd. Then there are 'gynoids', or fembots (see figure 376), feminine humanoid robots. The 'fembot' (female robot) was popularized by the television series *The Bionic Woman* in the episode *Kill Oscar* (1973), to the more realistic *Ghost in the Shell* (2017) movie, augmented with a cybernetic Artificial Intelligent, female Major, played by Scarlet Johansson. In truth, the idea of a robot (or cybernetic) being 'genderless' is due to the fact that it is 'artificial' and therefore can assume any gender due to *whatever*

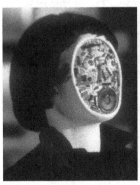

Figure 376: Fembot - Sexbot.
(Left) A 1970s fembot. **(Right)** A Realbotix Sex doll being made – spot the difference? Are we being 'inspired' to create Orion-like entities?

programming has being implemented. With this in mind, I am sure the 'gender-neutral' thoughts young people are 'experiencing' today, seem to be a sudden phantom 'download' in line with the way 'artificial intelligence' can switch gender, depending on its 'programming'. I ask, from where are these thoughts coming? What 'intelligence' is driving this relatively new state of being? I would suggest it is connected to the rise of artificial intelligence (and the robot) globally.

Creepy 'Love' Dolls

In modern times, an android is a robot (artificial being) designed to resemble a human, and often made from a flesh-like material. The Amazon tribe of women would not be proud of Amazon's 'Pandora Peaks Love Doll' and the creepy 'Harmony' sex dolls now surfacing globally. Who would have thought SkyNet would have 'slipped in' via sex dolls? Dr. Birchard, who serves as the clinical director of the Marylebone Centre for Psychological Therapies, told the UK *Daily Star*, the Love Dolls serve the same purpose as alcohol for people with drinking problems. He said: "It would just be another way of expressing sexual activity or addiction." Birchard also explained:

> Sex addiction is a way to anaesthetise hard to bear feeling states...These include, but are not limited to, loneliness, shame, boredom, and stress.

All of these are negative traits brought on by a range of 'fallen human' states of mind caused by unseen forces influencing our world. There is even, wait for it, a brand of adult toys called 'Orion', which started in 1948 and has now become the largest chain store selling sex toys in Germany.[19] Are you not surprised considering what you have read so far in this book? Some experts have gone so far as saying that the rise of sex robots risked turning Japanese people into 'an endangered species'. The warning came from the fact that sex doll ownership rose in Japan (a nation obsessed with androids), while birth rates were on the decline in certain areas. In some areas of Asia, according to journalists, 'sex robot swapping forums' are increasing in popularity. I know it's all mad but it is relevant to the concepts I am unravelling here.

In September 2018, The UK *Sun* exclusively revealed how one sex-bot collector had spent $200,000 on 'love dolls' – which he keeps in a cupboard.[20] The article said "Brick Dollbanger (obviously not his real name), the horny hobbyist in question, also moonlights as a sex robot tester." Pandora's 'box' has never been used so much it seems. But seriously, the technology being used now to create such monstrosities is building 'hyper-realistic' bots with features such as built-in heaters to create the feeling of body warmth and reactions to touch with 'emotional connections'. The virtual world and the robot world are *merging* and humanity is caught up in Pandora's snare for sure. What the ancient android goddess supposedly opened, according to myth, was the releasing of *all that avails humanity*.

To really understand the level of 'alien intelligence' wreaking havoc on humanity, we have to look at the ultimate fictional Pandora - the 'Maschinenmensch'.

Robot Queens and Frankensteins

The Maschinenmensch (German for 'robot' or literally 'machine-person') is a fictional character in Fritz Lang's film *Metropolis* (1927), played by German actress Brigitte Helm, in both its robot form and human incarnation (see figure 377). In the movie, she is a gynoid (a female robot or android) created by the scientist, Rotwang. Named Maria in the film, and 'Futura' in Thea von Harbou's original novel *Metropolis* (1925), she was one of the first robots ever depicted in cinema.

The Maschinenmensch has been given several names through the decades: Parody, Ultima, Machina, Futura, Robotrix, False Maria, Robot Maria, Roboria and 'Hel' (from where the word 'Hell' originates).

Figure 377: Maschinenmensch. Alexa: "Turn off the lights, set my alarm and make us some dinner, love."

Maschinenmensch and Metropolis, symbolic of Pandora's presence over her otherworldly jar, uses conceit, creating a reality where workers (worker bees) live below the ground. In contrast, the aristocracy live in skyscrapers high above the worker *slaves* of 'Metropolis'. Pandora and Maschinenmensch are the 'fallen Eve' I mentioned in *Part One*, revealed to the world as the robot Sophia, a citizen of Saudi Arabia. In Metropolis, workers are gobbled up by the demon Moloch, while extremely rich people cavort around places such as the 'Eternal Gardens' and the central skyscraper called the 'New Tower of Babel'. The symbolism in *Metropolis* is no different to some of the themes I have been describing so far, a world taken over by 'artificial, machine-like forces', unleashed on a people becoming robotic by proxy. The hive mind is also apparent in this film and is a subject I will cover in the next chapter, because it is highly relevant to the robot phenomena and Orion's influence over us. The amount of female celebrities (singers) offering robot imagery over the years, also gives credence to the theme of robot (artificial intelligence) working through humanity, too. Beyoncé, Kylie Minogue, Christina Aguilera, to name just a few, have artistically flaunted the Pandora-Maschinenmensch look on stage.

A central character female android also appeared in more recent movies and TV series. Dolores Abernathy, portrayed by Evan Rachel Wood, in *Westworld* (2016), is one of the series' central characters. The plot of

Westworld shows how Dolores is the 'oldest host' working in the high-tech theme park where wealthy humans can go to interact with human-like robots. They are so human it is hard to tell who is a robot and who isn't, which is precisely the idea, as I will come to. Dolores is a rancher's daughter who discovers her entire life is an elaborately constructed lie. The robot, Dolores, is also portrayed by another actress (Tessa Thompson in the second series) after Dolores' consciousness is transferred to a new robot body. This transference of 'Transcendence' is another significant theme frequently occurring in Hollywood productions - which I am sure exists in the 'real world'. The *American Cyberpunk* action film based on the 1990s Japanese manga series, *Alita Battle Angel,* seemed to connect all the dots in terms of symbolism and themes relating to human cyborgs. Produced by Jon Landau and James Cameron, the movie depicts another 'fallen' Eve/Sophia figure who emerges from the wreckage of one world to become a beacon in a new 'tyrannical world', ruled over by an unseen technological dictatorship and policed by cyborg serial killers. The word *'Elita'*, in Latin, means *'chosen one'* and in Hebrew means *'high above'* or *'most excellent'*.

Another version of a living robot would be Mary Shelley's (1797–1851) *Frankenstein*. Since publication of the original novel, the name Frankenstein is often used to refer to the monster itself. Still, this usage is sometimes considered erroneous by academics, as Victor himself is the creator of such an abomination and therefore, the creator of something perceived to be 'soul less.' In the novel, the monster is identified via words such as: 'creature', 'monster', 'fiend', 'wretch', 'vile insect', 'daemon', 'being', and 'it'. Speaking to Victor Frankenstein, the monster refers to himself as "the Adam of your labours", and elsewhere, as someone who "would have been your Adam", but is instead "your fallen angel." All of this alludes to more Adam-Orion symbolism. The latter is important because it is the symbolism for the 'fallen state' of mankind (as recorded in religious texts) and a subject that connects to the transhumanist (artificial intelligent) agenda today. Movies like *RoboCop* are no different in theme to that of *Frankenstein* and as I have mentioned, we are not so far away from robots being used in many areas of social life, from 'sex toys', to 'soldiers' (see figure 378), in a much more sophisticated way in the near future (see the 2020 movie *Monsters of Man* for evidence of the latter).

The film director, Neill Blomkamp, gives a disturbing vision of the future on earth through his Oats Studios computer-generated films called *Adam* (2016-2017). These short YouTube movies, titled *The Prophet* (2016) and *The Mirror* (2017), are set in a dystopian future, where the organic body is seen as a privilege easily lost to a grim reality where consciousness is 'transferred' into a 'mechanical shell', another Frankenstein-Adam theme.

© Stephen Bowler

Figure 378: Autonomous Robo Cops.
A typical visual example of the type of robots policing humans in the movies.

Blomkamp's films are quite thought-provoking visually and often include alien intelligence working through humanity. The quote reinforces the self-induced takeover of humanity by artificial intelligence in *Revelation*, which says: "During those days people will seek death but will not find it; they will long to die, but death will elude them"(*Revelation* 9:6). In Blomkamp's short movie *Rakka* (2017), an American-Canadian military science fiction film, a race of ruthless, reptilian aliens invade the earth, enslaving humanity through brute force and telepathy. Other Blomkamp movies of a similar vein are, *District 9* (2009) and *CHAPPiE* (2015), dystopian science fiction action films set in South Africa. In *CHAPPiE*, a skyrocketing crime rate leads the city of Johannesburg to buy a squadron of scouts—state-of-the-art armour-plated 'attack robots'—from a fictional weapons manufacturer called Tetravaal. These autonomous androids are developed and created through uploading 'consciousness', via Tetravaal computers and largely supplanting the human police force. The way some protesters were calling for a 'defunded police' force, in the wake of the George Floyd death in May 2020, was, in my view, playing into the hands of the Orion-Saturn Cult who would like to have a 'future' autonomous android *global* police force to replace the current human one.

Such movies are giving us a glimpse of the not-so-far distant future unless we become more conscious and awake. Blomkamp seems to have a fascination for robots and extraterrestrials, especially focused on South Africa. The shrimp-like aliens featured in his brilliant movie *District 9* (2009) are also interfacing with biological weapons and machines. As I say, alien life forms could take 'many' forms, so why not a metal-machine-like form? Or a sentient machine empowered by artificial intelligence?

Metal Knights and Robot Serfs

The word 'robot' was said to be introduced to the public by Czech interwar writer Karel Apek in his play R.U.R. (Rossum's Universal Robots), published in 1920.[21] But the word 'robot' itself was not new, existing in the Slavic language as 'robota' (forced labourer), a term used to classify peasants obligated to 'compulsory service' under a feudal system.

The fascination for robots can be traced back to Mechanical automata constructed in the 10th century BC in the Western Zhou Dynasty by the artisan, Yan Shi. He was said to have made humanoid automata that could sing and dance; possessing lifelike organs, bones, muscles and joints. Other robots can be seen in diagrams of 15th Century Europe. The Italian painter and printmaker, Ventura Salimbeni in 1595, also seemed to show a fascination for what appears to have been the first image of an artificial earth satellite? Art Historians and critics, of course, declare this was a 'celestial sphere' (or orb). Still, the painting has what looks remarkably like antennae seen on the 'Sputnik' satellite, launched by the Soviet Union into an elliptical, low-Earth orbit on 4th October 1957. The point I am making here is that the Renaissance period (from the 14th to the 17th century), through initiates such as Leonardo Da Vinci, seemed to have had access to 'knowledge' and 'science' not available to the masses.

As I have been illustrating so far, the robot and cyborg *obsession* can also be seen in TV and film, not least through *Doctor Who* and the *Daleks* and *Cybermen*. The same themes appear in the *Robots of Sherwood* in episodes of the second season of the American historical fantasy drama series, *Da Vinci's Demons* (2013-15), which present-ed a fictional account of Leonardo da Vinci's early life. However, there was nothing fictional about Da Vinci's inter-est in automatons and futuristic weapons. You can see Da Vinci's repli-cations of his 'fascination' for Automata if you visit Chateaux Amboise, the royal seat of the French king, Francis I in Amboise. At Da Vinci's home, Château du Clos Lucé, a model of Leonardo's humanoid designed robot (Automaton knight) with inner work-ings, constructed around the year 1495 (see figure 379). Leonardo is said to

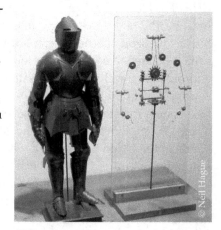

Figure 379: Leonardo's Robot Knight.

have featured the machine at a celebration hosted by Ludovico Sforza at the court of Milan in 1495. The robot knight could stand, sit, raise its visor and independently manoeuvre its arms; as well, it had an anatomically correct jaw. A series of pulleys and cables operated the entire robotic system. Since the discovery of Da Vinci's sketchbooks, the robot has been built based solely on Leonardo's design, and found to be fully functional.[22] The human fascination with robots (living machines) from Da Vinci's Robot Knight, to the first British robot 'Eric' (created in 1928 by First World War veteran Captain William Richards), through to 'TOPIO' (the 2007 Ping Pong Playing Robot) from Japan, are just a few examples of our magnetism to the living machine.

The illustrations of technological inventions by fifteenth-century Venetian physician, engineer, and alleged 'magus', Johannes de Fontana (1395-1455), also seemed to be inspired by knowledge connected to machines, magic and possibly otherworldly connections. In his technological or mechanical treatise, *Bellicorum instrumentorum liber cum figuris* (1420), Fontana devised a whole series of machines for use in war, travelling, entertaining children, flying, robots, rocket-powered craft, timepieces, fountains, and even a means of projecting images like a magic lantern. Unlike most other inventors at this time, Fontana showed the workings of his inventions—the pulleys and weights (sand, water) by which his mechanical

devices worked. His imagined 'Robot Witch' seems to be hinting at an Apega, or Pandora-like, Automaton. A French Illustrated manuscript, *Messire Lancelot du Lac* (1470), also shows an image of Lancelot, the fabled knight of King Arthur's Round Table, battling with 'demon knights' (see figure 380). The manuscripts, of course, only offer subjective ideas, but I find the visual idea of a 'knight in armour' very robot-like. The *Transformer* movie, *The Last Knight*, also carries the same themes of 'robot knights'.

Figure 380: Demon Knights.
Lancelot fighting the animated knights, Lancelot du lac, France, ca. 1470.

There is something both menacing and mystic in the idea of a ghost in the 'metal shell' seeming to mimic the idea of fabricated Automatons – droids, or robots. *The Last Knight*, is obviously inspired by such Renaissance imagery and artefacts but, maybe there is more to the knight and its 'armour' than just protection in battle. The strange horned helmet, given to a young Henry VIII in 1511, by Roman Emperor Maximillian I, seems to hint symbolically at the horned Cernunnos/Orion imagery I looked at in *Part One* (see figure 381 overleaf). Made by Konrad Seusenhofer, a leading 16th century Austrian armourer who worked for Maximillian, the helmet, due to its bizarre appearance, was believed to have belonged to Henry's court jester (or fool), Will Somers, who most likely incorporated it into his clowning. The Fool, of course, is another Orion symbol as I have shown, but I can't help but wonder if the armour was intended to give the wearer (the king), the appearance of a celestial god?

The Samurai who also had a fascination for Orion's stars, used very similar armour, not least the metal horns, masks and robot-like appearance which made them look terrifying to those who faced them in battle.

Figure 381: Imitating Metal (Robot) Gods. One of many Mesoamerican metal masks. The same can be seen with the Horned Helmet given to Henry VIII and much fierce Samurai armour. All designed to invoke terror in battle.

Samurai helmets and body armour were made with great detail and this, in my view, was to evoke their ancestral star gods, possibly from Orion (see figure 393). The Samurai in full armour looks like the 'machine man' or 'horned aliens' (possibly sentient mechanical beings) connected to Orion's stars, especially Betelgeuse and Rigel. As I have said several times throughout this book, some of the themes I am covering are subjective; however, we cannot avoid our human ancient fascination for god-like technologies and what could be *living machines*, waiting to make themselves known. However, Scientists *have* created what they claim are the first "living robots": entirely new life-forms created out of living cells. Teams from the University of Vermont and Tufts University have built what they call 'Xenobots', which are about the size of a grain of salt, made up of heart and skin cells form 'frogs', designed to clean up microplastic in the oceans.[23] These Xenobots could also end up in the human body, too. Why am I thinking vaccines and chemtrails?

I cannot say for sure if the reason for our human ancient and modern obsession with Automaton (living robots) is due to advancement in technology, or, if the phenomena of robots is simply a 'creation of 'artificial' (alien) intelligence, both in the past *and* present time. The war machine was always a 'machine'. Whether it was thousands of metal men (robot knights) making up a primitive beast of war in the Middle Ages, or AI-activated drones today - *all* bring death and destruction. The obsession with 'living machines' (ghosts in the shell) seems to have been a common theme across the ages. There are endless books on robots and artificial intelligence's rapid advances on the market today, this book isn't about the detail of such subjects; instead, what I am saying here is that I have often wondered if we, as a species, are being 'guided' to connect with 'alien' intelligence through its primary means of communication – Artificial (alien) Intelligence (or invasion), through what I call, the 'Cyber-Grid'.

We have come a long way from knights in armour but our enigmatic attraction of the gods and the 'effects' of Pandora's box are still with us. The alien 'takeover' of earth is not from something 'out there' in my view. It's coming from *within* the projection, inspired by the stars, but already altering the human mind – creating a *grid*, or *net*, to ensnare human consciousness.

Let us now look at the grid and what is ensnaring us.

Sources:

1) *The Second Coming*, Mark Lawson; *The Weekend Guardian* April 24th 1999.

2) François Pannier, Stéphane Mangin, *Masques de l'Himalaya, du primitif au classique*. Paris: Editions Raymond Chabaud, 1989, p. 44. Lisa Bradley & Eric Chazot, *Masks of the Himalayas*. New York: Pace Primitive Gallery, 1990. Dominique Blanc et al., *Masks of the Himalayas*. Milan: 5 Continents Editions, 2009.

3) https://www.sciencedaily.com/releases/2015/11/151103064554.htm

4) https://www.militaryaerospace.com/trusted-computing/article/16715809/darpa-chooses-sparton-to-help-develop-hidden-weapons-and-sensors-that-pop-up-from-the-ocean

5) Griaule, Marcel. *Conversations with Ogotemmêli*, op. Cit, p.119p

6) Myer, Isaac. *Scarabs.The history, manufacture and religious symbolism*. 1836-1902. Leipzig, O. Harrassowitz; 1894.

7) Mayor, Adrienne. *Gods and Robots, Myths, Machines and Ancient Dreams of Technology*. Princeton University Press. 2018, p138

8) https://www.theatlantic.com/photo/2018/11/la-machine-giant-spider-and-minotaur/574930/

9) https://www.ridingthebeast.com/numbers/nu72.php

10) *Leviticus* 11:10

11) https://www.dailymail.co.uk/sciencetech/article-5309795/US-Army-wants-designs-futuristic-Iron-Man-suit.html

12) https://www.technologyreview.com/f/614476/a-brain-controlled-exoskeleton-has-let-a-paralyzed-man-walk-in-the-lab/

13) https://directory.eoportal.org/web/eoportal/satellite-missions/s/space-fence

14) Robbs, Dave. *Operation Hollywood: How the Pentagon Shapes and Censors the Movies*. p77

15) Mayor, Adrienne. *Gods and Robots, Myths, Machines and Ancient Dreams of Technology*. Princerton University Press, 2018, p194

16) Polybuis 13.6-8. Apega 18-17. Sage 1935. Pomeroy (2002, 89-90).

17) Wilson, Eric G. *The Melancholy Android: On the Psychology of Sacred Machines*. State University New York Press, 2006, p80-81

18) https://www.dailymail.co.uk/news/article-7294665/Jeffrey-Epstein-doomed-dome-Pedophile-Islands-mysterious-temple-lost-golden-dome.html

19) http://www.3hcorp.com/en/orion.html

20) https://www.thesun.co.uk/tech/7272600/brick-dollbanger-real-doll-realbotix-harmony-sex-robot/

21) Roberts, Adam. Introduction to *RUR & War with the Newts*. London, Gollancz, 2011, ISBN 0575099453 (pp. vi–ix).

22) Rosheim, Mark Elling. *Leonardo's Lost Robots*. Springer, 2006, p69.

23) https://www.independent.co.uk/life-style/gadgets-and-tech/news/living-robots-xenobots-living-cells-frog-embryos-a9282251.html

19

THE CYBER-GRID EMPIRE

It's All in the Movies (Part 2)

Disobedience is the true foundation of liberty.
The obedient must be slaves.
HENRY DAVID THOREAU

We think of empires in terms of concentrated power in the hands of the few, or those who gained power, needing to control more land resources and people treating the masses as slaves. From the Roman Empire to the empires of Britain, Spain and France over the centuries, we have seen repeated power structures follow a similar *blueprint*. This blueprint usually revolves around the infiltration of target countries (people) and then the eventual takeover of that country or people. The patterns of previous empires can be seen in the 'templates' of our societies, even to this day. Just as ancient Rome had its emperors, senates, armies and the 'rule of law', so did the later British, Spanish and French Republic's 'Empires'. The only difference 'today' is that our modern empires have been built through the use of technology, which has become god-like in its own right. Maybe technology was always 'god-like' and as I have already hinted at, artificial intelligence could be the 'alien' elephant-in-the-living-room? In this chapter, I want to explore the technological empire being built around us, through its connection to the blueprint, or network. As I have shown so far, Orion is influencing our collective-earth reality through technology and I am sure this technological blueprint has 'off-world' origins – possibly Orion and Sirius combined.

The Grid

Orion is a star 'system' that has connections to humanity's journey through life on earth, not least through the many *rituals*, *archetypes* and *blueprints* mentioned in previous chapters. The connection between Orion and earth is created through the 'blueprints' I have been highlighting, and an 'invisible grid' that encompasses starlight pathways (including sacred geometry/DNA), connecting humanity to Orion and other star systems.

This grid, in turn, links us to knowledge that would be perceived as 'alien' intelligence, the same intelligence that, I am sure, built the pyramids on earth along with other 'unexplainable' feats such as the Nazca lines in Peru (see *Chapter One*). In channelled art and imagery, I have visualized what I see as the 'pyramid builders' and an ancient global network that facilitated such architectural feats in ancient times. I cannot prove to you with hard evidence that global pyramid building was coordinated by alien intelligence, but I feel the pyramids were connected to the earth's energetic (magnetic) network of ley lines so to utilise the collective consciousness of the earth - Gaia (Sophia).

Hundreds of temples all over the ancient world from Egypt, Mexico, Greece and Mesopotamia, for example, are 'templates' for such circuitry connecting the earth to the stars. Many of the temples, seen from an aerial perspective, resemble detailed circuitry that look remarkably like an arrangement of components on an electrical circuit (see figure 382).

Figure 382: Earth Circuits (Grids). (Top) The layouts of the three main pyramids in Teotihuacan, Mexico with an incredible resemblance to a modern day circuit board with processors (Bottom).

The ancient temples were more than places of worship they were transistors and capacitors of interconnected components making up a 'living grid'. Just as neurons in the nervous system (especially the brain) connect through neuronal pathways, using electrical and chemical signals, the ancient earth grids connected via the many temple structures activating a living grid – or a star-earth connection, which is focused on Orion, Sirius and other stars. This grid provides humanity with thought patterns and beliefs (through religious archetypes) so that we connect with aliens, entities, or interdimensional forces using this ancient grid for their own end.

Sound, or frequency, is also massively part of the circuitry I am describing here; some of the stone circles, not least Stonehenge in the UK, indicate a resonance with the human brain. Some say Stonehenge was constructed to resonate at the frequency of 10 hertz, which is the Alpha Wave frequency of the human brain.[1] The pyramid alignment at Giza, of course, gives us a visual alignment with the belt stars of Orion (see *Chapter One*) but I am sure these alignments are, more importantly, based on 'sound', 'frequency' and 'vibration'. This vibration is what the Zulu Shaman, Credo Mutwa, called the 'song of the stars'. But as Michael Tellinger points out through his research, there is also a 'silica' component to these ancient temples, a substance that is crystalline and also a massive transmitter of frequency, or sound. The Parthenon in Athens and the many amphitheatres and ancient temples were obviously designed to be conduits of sound, so to harness a particular frequency. The destruction of the Amphitheatre and temples of Palmyra in Syria by Isis since 2012, for example, was 'orchestrated' to devastate the ancient grid and ley lines of the earth. If silica and water (the two most abundant elements on earth) are combined they conduct light and sound (frequency) and their *combined* potential to connect with information increases massively.

Modern sport stadiums of today, like the original Colosseum in Rome, were built, on one level, to manifest a specific vibration, one that powers the grid. Endless fear, death and 'duality' in the ancient Colosseum, for instance, provided energetic 'food' for non-physical forces such as the archons and jinn. In the modern world, the soccer or football stadium does a similar job 'energetically'. The sound (vibration) of the crowd is key to 'manifestation', which is why such events exist on one level. The ancient temples were conduits of sound (frequency) through rituals, chants and ceremonies all connected to the planets, solar system and the stars. As I have shown in *Part One*, many religious rituals and festivals are overshadowed by Orion's passage across the ecliptic; bringing that focus to the temple circuit would connect to Orion's frequency - both dark and light vibrations. In the alignment of architecture, the pyramids and pillars would also act as a door to the stars and the alien intelligence behind such creations. How do we not know that artificial intelligence working through 'alien lifeforms' was not behind such amazing feats of engineering? I have seen nothing in my fifty plus years to prove otherwise.

Persepolis, the ceremonial capital of the Persian Achaemenid Empire (550–330 BC), sixty kilometres northeast of Shiraz's city in Fars Province, Iran, looks like a vast circuit from above. This ancient city is a network of pillars that look like giant diodes, the components used to conduct a current in one direction around a circuit (see figure 384). Computer science tells us that a circuit is a 'model' of computation in which input values proceed through a sequence of 'gates' (doors), each of which computes a function. In simpler terms, the ancient temple structures act as mathematical (numerological) and frequency templates for information to travel through, just as a computer circuit mechanically supports and electrically connects components, so to be able to access information. The ancient temples are like macro-processors connecting to a larger printed circuit board, one that I

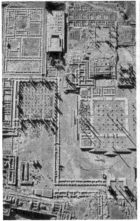

Figure 384: Ancient Earth Grids.
It's a matter of size! The ancient silica temple ruins of Persepolis, Iran (Left), juxtaposed with a circuit board used in almost everything today.

am sure forms a connection to a stellar circuit focused especially on the Orion star system.

From this perspective, the Acropolis of ancient Greece (as seen from above) also becomes a macro processor to a higher intelligence, or alien intelligence. The pyramids themselves are enormous conductors of information on what I sense was a 'motherboard' that stretched all over the earth. In Atlantis and Mu (The Motherlands), the pyramids, some of which are now submerged, would have been surrounded by water in places like Cuba and Bermuda (see *Chapter One*) and these would have been exceptionally powerful places for connecting to higher intelligence, information and the stars.

Whoever orchestrated and implemented such work on earth in ancient times must have connected to intelligence and information that wanted to see such circuitry in use all over the earth. The projector I mentioned in *Chapter Fifteen* is also part of the same intelligence but on a higher level. The more I look at such phenomena, the more I am inclined to think that a very advanced scientific-technological civilisation (from Orion) may have used an ancient 'slave human race' to construct the physical grid I outline here. The level of intelligence I refer to must understand the holographic nature of macrocosm, microcosm, and the engineering skills required to create such giant silica stone components and templates. As I said in the last chapter, we as humans are either being inspired, or pushed, down a path towards a technological, digital future. Are we dealing with the same interstellar alien intelligence that initiated the ancient grids/temple circuits - or are we facing a very different artificial alien today? I think *both* ancient and modern are the same intelligence, only *we* are different in our 'assimilation and amalgamation' of the intelligence that has been with us through our journey. You could say that sentient mechanical intelligence has been here all along. Remember, empires are also microcosms of a greater template, or circuit and we are witnessing the birth of a new 'Cyber-Grid' Empire today.

To get a better understanding of the interdimensional stellar grid I am outlining in this chapter, let us again turn to the movies.

Tron – Orion

In 2010, an American science fiction film directed by Joseph Kosinski (from a screenplay written by Adam Horowitz and Edward Kitsis) hit the cinemas. The movie in question was *Tron: Legacy*, the sequel to the 80s Disney movie called Tron.

The movie script for *Tron: Legacy* is profoundly Gnostic, as I have been saying in lectures in recent years. Essentially, it is a story of a 'programmer', or 'creator', called Kevin Flynn (played by Jeff Bridges), who is also the brains behind a fictional technology giant called ENCOM. Through his passion for building an artificial reality, Flynn finds himself being transported to the world he was building and consequently disappearing without a trace. The film starts twenty years on from Flynn's disappearance in the original 80s movie, where his son, Sam (Garrett Hedlund) receives a signal from an old pager coming from his father's office at the Arcade, where Flynn was last seen. The narrative goes on to reveal that Flynn had been working to build the 'perfect computer system', along with an anti-virus software called, Tron. Sam discovers a large computer in a hidden basement of his father's Arcade, which suddenly digitizes and downloads Sam into the 'Grid', a virtual reality created by Flynn existing within ENCOM's computer mainframe. When inside the virtual world, Sam encounters algorithms and trojans lead by a replica of Flynn, called Clu, who is now the tyrannical leader of the virtual grid-world. Sam escapes Clu, helped by an androgynous character called Quorra (played by Olivia Wilde) and is taken to his father who is in exile (off grid). Flynn (divine human) and Clu (digital-virtual being) are symbolic of the Gnostic creator gods (see figure 385).

Flynn reveals to Sam how he had been working to create a 'perfect' computer system and had appointed the avatars Clu, and an exceptionally-skilled warrior, Tron, as the grid's co-creators. During the construction of this virtual reality, the trio (Flynn, Clu and Tron) discover a species of naturally-occurring 'isomorphic algorithms' (ISOs) not conceived by Flynn; bearing the potential to resolve various mysteries in science, religion and medicine. However, Clu considers them an aberration, betrays Flynn and attempts to remove Tron,

Figure 385: Creator of the Virtual Grid. Flynn, Sam and Quorra in the movie *Tron Legacy* symbolise the Gnostic Aeons in their roles as the Christos and Sophia .

Figure 386: Tron - the Cyber Enforcer.
Rinzler -Tron the ultimate Orion-like warrior. His scarab-like black outfit is quite Saturnian and symbolic of the Orion-Saturn connection. © Neil Hague

wiping out all the ISOs. Tron who turns sides to become an agent for Clu, is embodied in the character, Rinzler, Clu's primary enforcer (see figure 386). Tron eventually remembers his true role and allegiance to the original creator (Flynn) and helps save Sam and Quorra. Orion's role in our human 'virtual reality' is similar to Tron's purpose, on one level. Orion, in my view, is the programme (the place of projection) from where the gods of artificial intelligence and technology have infiltrated human life.

The narrative of *Tron: Legacy* is a modern-day version of the Gnostic myths I covered in *Part One* of the book. Flynn, Sam and the warrior Tron are based on the Father/Son, Adam on High symbolism. The isomorphic algorithms, the ISO called Quorra, are an aspect of Sophia and they represent the 'creative imagination', hence why Quorra is important to the Creator, Flynn. As Quorra explains to Sam when his father saves her:

When I opened my eyes, standing above me was the Creator, your father! He saved me. I guess you can say I was a rescue.

According to screenwriter Adam Horowitz, director Kosinski said the film's universal theme was 'finding a human connection in a digital world.' They followed this by approaching the world from a perspective of the character, using Kevin Flynn as an organizing principle, and focusing on the emotional relationship between father and son and their reconciliation, bringing profound truths in their respective individual lives.[2] Actor Jeff Bridges said that Tron: Legacy "was evocative of a modern myth," adding that ideas alluding to technological advancement were prevalent throughout the film. Talking to Cyriaque Lamar of io9 blog, around the time of the release of the movie, Bridges also added, "... the film's approach to technology was reminiscent of a koan, which formed out of Manichaeism and Buddhist philosophy."[3]

The Counterfeit Digital God

The leader of the digital virtual world, Clu (who is a replica of the creator Flynn), represents the 'false demented god' - the Gnostic Demiurge, who, in the movie, desires to take his technological tyranny to the human world. At all costs, Clu must be stopped from infiltrating the human world. Clu could be seen as artificial intelligence 'personified' and the original grid built by Flynn symbolizes the original ancient grid we see in temples and stones all over the earth. Clu's new grid, which spreads like a virus, killing off any form of individuality (as seen in the costumes and graphics within the movie), represents the technological grid and artificial (alien) intelligence to which it is connected. As Clu says in his 'takeover' speech to the legions of the virtual grid world, before they attempt to remove Flynn and Sam so to enter the human world:

> *Greetings, programs! Together we have achieved a great many things. We have created a vast, complex system. We've maintained it; we've improved it. We've rid it of its imperfection. Not to mention, rid it of the false deity who sought to enslave us! Kevin Flynn! ... My fellow programs, let there be no doubt that our world is a cage no more. For at this moment, the key to the next frontier is finally in our possession! ...Out there is a new world! Out there is our victory! Out there is our destiny...*

The threat to our reality is not necessarily a full-blown 'physical' dictator-ship; those are obvious and can usually be seen for what they are. The tyranny upon humanity today has its roots in the **'non-physical'** *made phys-ical* through linking the human mind to **off-world** artificial intelligence and the Cyber-Grid Empire built around it.

Artificial intelligence and the rise of the robot is probably the most important aspect of the grid I am illustrating here. All 'virtual' or 'artificial' intelligence has the ability to connect us to the robot phenomena. Alien life is 'artificial' if compared to organic life on earth. And the Cyber-grid gradu-ally being constructed around us through electromagnetic technology, for example, is one that will be the 'spirit' or lifeblood for all things robotic connected to artificial intelligence (AI). The grid would also be designed to facilitate 'programmes' which are not organic human beings, but synthetic, part-human, connected to AI. The danger of AI has not been fully explained across 'mainstream' platforms that dominate human perception. To do so, it would bring into question many other global issues, not least Cyber war-fare and population control methods and the loss of human sovereignty. The Gnostic texts describe the Demiurge and archons as what we see today as artificial intelligence, AI. We have to get over the belief that intelligent life can only take humanoid form or needs to take form at all. We are, after all, in our infinite-state only *awareness* and 'physical' form *is* an illusory part of the projection I described in *Chapter Fifteen*. All forms of Information cre-ate our 'human experience' (which can be controlled); it is not the true self and so it is with the artificial (alien) intelligence. We recognise our own

Figure 387: Reality *is* In*form*ation.
Waveform in*form*ation creates our reality, or our perceived human physical experience.

'form', our collective reality (see figure 387). Still, artificial intelligence, from beyond the narrow parameters of 'physicality', must also be able to take *form*, or at least 'possess' other life *forms*. In truth humanity is a 'possessed race', an observation becoming more obvious at this time on earth. You only have to see the impact cellular phones have had on us to realise that humanity is 'possessed' by technology for reasons I am coming to. Technology does and can improve our world, but to what costs?

Technological Hosts - Summoning the Soulless Ones

The 2013 movie *The Host,* showed the earth inhabited by an 'alien' species known as 'Souls'. These Souls looked like luminous metallic crustaceans (glowing sea urchins) which travelled great distances from one planet to another, seeking 'bodies' to possess. In this case, humanity and the earth was their target. The insertion of the host, via entry into the back of the head (neck) in the film, reminded me of the transfer points in the Matrix movies, hinting at possible 'interference' (or hijacking) of the pineal gland and therefore the brain (CPU), by machine-like aliens. The alien souls in *The Host* also looked visually similar to the 'intelligent spirits' of the 'Navi' in the 2009 movie *Avatar*, which moved as one collective spirit. Many times in movies, we have seen such collective 'hive-like' intelligence. Agent Smith in the *Matrix* trilogy is also a 'host programme' that not only spreads like a virus to take over the illusory matrix reality, but these 'agents' in the film represent a digital version of the archons or Jinn I've mentioned previously. One particular scene even depicts Agent Smith, who has now infected much of the matrix, as a fiery archon (see figure 388 overleaf) when he attempts to infiltrate the human world in *Matrix Revolutions* (2003).

The machine-controlled world portrayed in the *Matrix* trilogy seems an increasingly accurate reflection of both the virtual illusion (reality) that humanity is 'plugged into', but also how machines in these movies had taken the earth after a war where the sky was 'torched' during nuclear war.

Figure 388: Alien (Virus) *or* Agent (Demon).
My image inspired by the Agent Smith from the *Matrix* movies. Smith is a digital software programe, or Jinn, who appears in different virtual *forms*, not least fire.

The movie industry has saturated our reality with films that have 'transhumanist', apocalyptic or dystopian themes for a reason, because those seeking to affect consciousness and control humanity want to re-shape the earth to their 'alien' liking! In many ways, we are dealing with an alien hive mind that is rapidly becoming the collective human mind through our connection to technology. Transhumanism is the plan to technologically control the human body (vehicle) through artificial intelligence, so it cannot be influenced in any way by 'awareness', or consciousness. We have invited the 'gods of technology' into our human, organic world and they are now almost running the show. We have to ask the questions, could a technologically advanced species communicate with humans 'telepathically' over vast distances (through time and space)? Could our obsession with technology be inspired by intelligence from *elsewhere*? I think we are 'connecting' with artificial intelligence via the vast cellular networks, not least mobile phone technology and the coming Fifth Generation networks and beyond.

Quantum scientists and neurologists today view the human brain as a 'receptor' of digital information that operates on the same principle as a computer.[4] Our brain waves and Extra-Sensory Perception (ESP) has to be part of how we interpret information 'collectively' and how other alien life forms can also communicate with us. The Cyber-Grid Empire being built to control human thought and *limit* consciousness (our awareness), I feel, has been inspired by sentient programs operating from outside of the collective virtual reality (matrix) we call Earth. The current matrix is their creation and is being upgraded to allow for a transhuman world. All of the technology we are utilizing today is merely a *bridge* for other (alien) intelligence to interface with us, and I would suggest, even 'possess' people's minds (see figure 389). Our mobile phones are 'digital scrying mirrors' connecting us with AI – alien intelligence. These devices provide the potential for the ultimate alien invasion, a possible world beyond 2040 that is run by AI.

We have a responsibility to our children to not let the future become a transhumanist nightmare. There is plenty of literature on transhumanism

Figure 389: Forming a Bridge *Through* Technology.
Technology is *invading* our mind – AI is *the* alien invasion.

for those wanting to dig deeper. But I think Julian Huxley (brother of Aldous Huxley and the founding member of the World Wildlife Fund and President of the British Eugenics Society 1959-1962), in his 1957 book *New Bottles for New Wine*, summed up the transhumanist agenda when he wrote:

> *The human species can, if it wishes, transcend itself – not just sporadically, an individual here in one way, an individual there in another way, but in its entirety, as humanity. We need a name for this new belief. Perhaps transhumanism will serve: man remaining man, but transcending himself, by realizing new possibilities of and for his human nature. I believe in transhumanism: once there are enough people who can truly say that, the human species will be on the threshold of a new kind of existence, as different from ours as ours is from that of Peking man. It will at last be consciously fulfilling its real destiny.*

Technology is playing its part in 'transcending us', and 'realising new possibilities' as Huxley explains, but, it doesn't have to be so! We need to make sure that our children become aware of the AI agenda and the dangers of this kind of technology, especially Fifth Generation devices (5G), which has been developed to 'addict', 'enslave' and I would say, 'destroy' young minds. The addiction to Apps is also all part of the transhumanist agenda which, if you really consider what has happened to humanity since the late 90s in terms of the growth of cell phones, Pads and wearable cellular technology, all these are perfect 'infiltration tools' of our minds and emotions, as I will come to shortly.

Killers & Apps

The addiction to Apps has reached huge levels over the past decade, with experts saying all Apps have a common goal of reeling you in and 'holding your attention'. App designers and developers have all said that 'Push Notifications' coming through Apps are a key part of keeping young people addicted to cellular phones, devices or services. Hence the connection to a 'pusher', as these devices keep 'push-notifying' those addicted enough to coming back for one more fix. From the ease of purchasing everything from music, films, to food along with the constant 'feeds' on social media plat-forms, all are part of the ever-increasing focus on what will become a Transhuman way of life. But these Apps have also been shown to have a 'darker side'. For some, transhumanist ideals and the cyber-grid are part of an evolving 'sacred space' seminal to the one-world religion (humanity transcending the limitations placed upon it by the Creator and becoming a god). In truth, transcendence through 'transhumanism' is meant to give life to the artificial, beast-like human. Altering human DNA through nanotech-nology is part of the transhumanist process.

The *Child's Play* (Chucky) horror movies created by MGM (Orion Pictures), especially the 2019 film, focuses on an app called 'Buddy' that is controlling (possessing) the automated doll, 'Chucky'. The general theme here is possession by artificial intelligence, which can be seen to pose a con-siderable threat to humanity if taken out of the world of science fiction, for reasons I am coming to, shortly.

One example of an adult Chucky-like scenario could be seen in the Kalamazoo random shootings in Kalamazoo County, Michigan in February 2016. The event saw 6 people shot dead and two others injured by an Uber driver, Jason Brian Dalton, who was charged with murder, assault, and ille-gal firearm use two days after the shootings. According to reports, Dalton blamed his actions on his Uber mobile app, claiming that its *symbol* resem-bled that of the 'Masonic Order' of the Eastern Star. Dalton claimed it 'took

over his body' during the events after he pressed the but-ton of a new app resembling the Devil when it abruptly popped up (see figure 390).[5] The Eastern Star, connected to 'Eliphas Levi' (Alphonse Louis), had a deep impact on the magic of the Hermetic Order of the Golden Dawn and the ex-Golden Dawn member we all know as Aleister Crowley. No one knows for sure if such

Figure 390: Horned Apps.
(Left) The Inverted "Devil horned'/Eastern Star (pentagram) logo. **(Right)** The 'Little Face', the original horned-like Uber logo that 'supposedly' 'spoke' to killer, Jason Brian Dalton.

'mind control' via this particular app can be blamed, but the technology itself seems to be 'living a life' through human addiction to such technology; possession is more common than we realise (see page 237).

We are obsessed with social media and so many apps and when we take a closer look at such logos since the dawn of the app, it's no surprise to see designs that appear to be Masonic symbols (see figure 391). The logo (symbol) for Facebook, Google Mail (Gmail) and the Apple App Store logos are a bit more of a 'giveaway', especially when we find that Facebook is an 'intelligence' front for secret societies operating behind governments globally. Google, for example, has been a partner with the CIA since 2004, when the company bought Keyhole, a mapping technology business that eventually became Google Earth. In 2010, Google and In-Q-Tel made a joint investment on a com-

Figure 391: Masonic Logos in early cyber platforms?
The visual resemblence is striking. All coincidence? *Maybe?*

pany called Recorded Future, which has the *Minority Report*-style goal of creating a 'temporal analytics engine' that scours the web and creates curves predicting where events may head.[6]

Intelligence networks are using all social media platforms. But more importantly, they are vehicles for intelligent entities existing beyond the veil of everyday life. I have personally 'felt' an otherworldly presence 'behind' such computer platforms and even the term 'android', 'cell phone' leads me to question what type of alien (artificial) creature could be working through such Internet, cyber-based platforms? Possession is a huge phenomenon and not limited to religious literature and phenomena, or horror movies. It is probably the leading cause for almost all heinous crimes. As I touched on in the previous chapter, an otherworldly alien intelligence seems to thrive off technology and is quite possibly robotic by definition.

The Internet of Things – Connecting the Robots

Transhumanist gurus such as the American inventor and futurist, Ray Kurzweil, are openly promoting the technological nightmare of total control (while saying it is good for us). You can see this all the time if you peek through veils designed to obscure the real reasons for the latest technology to flood human society. Movies especially are 'selling' the latest gadgets and technology. According to *Financial Express* online, the James Bond film of 2020, *No Time To Die*, which was due for release twice, will feature 5G phone technology. Transhumanism and the robot phenomena go hand in hand, as it is all part of the AI takeover, this is why we are seeing such an apparent move to robots replacing workers and across many other areas of human life. As The Microsoft Network (www.msn.com) reported in December 2018:

> *Walmart will soon deploy 360 robot janitors across a few hundred of its stores. Using maps plotted by human employees, the AI-powered cleaners will placidly traverse the aisles, sweeping and buffing as they go—just as blue-aproned human employees used to do (and still will, in Walmart stores without an Auto-C, as the robots are called). Perhaps the most striking thing about these robot workers is how not-striking they are. Sci-fi movies suggest a future full of humanoid robots who unnerve us with their "uncanny valley" qualities. Now the future is coming into view, and it looks like a giant Roomba. It's easy to imagine walking absent-mindedly past an Auto-C on a shopping trip without even registering its presence.*[7]

It won't end there either as we head into the technological Cyber-Grid world I am outlining here. The Covid-19 pandemic is very much about introducing the Cyber-Grid Empire initially through global 'Track and Trace', leading to ID passes and vaccination. Apps introduced in 2020, are just the *first* phase to achieving technological control of human movement.

The creation of the Internet was also no accident, if it was actually 'created' at all. Over the past few years, I've wondered if the 'Internet' wasn't part of a stage one 'phase' for the arrival of a much more sophisticated (alien) technology waiting to be unleashed. David Petraeus could not have been more 'direct' in his brief spell as CIA Director when he discussed the then coming of the 'Internet of Things', now very much with us and growing by the year (see figure 392). Petraeus spoke at the In-Q-Tel CEO Summit in 2012. He said:

> *The current 'Internet of PCs' will move, of course, toward an 'Internet of Things' – of devices of all types – 50 to 100 billion of which will be connected to the Internet by 2020. As you know, whereas machines in the 19th century learned to do, and those in the 20th century learned to think at a rudimentary level, in the 21st century, they are learning to perceive – to actually sense and respond. Key applications developed by our In-Q-Tel investment companies are focused on technologies that are driving the Internet of Things...*

In-Q-Tel is a technological arm of the CIA and 'Q' supposedly refers to the technology inventor in the James Bond movies, which of course, presented the 'New Cyber-Grid World Order' in the Bond movie, *Spectre* (2016). A movie that also offered obvious symbolism relating to a global elite who were using technology to control the world's population. QAnon seems to

Figure 392: The 'Alien Intelligent' Invasion of Earth.
The Internet of Things – *everything* connected to AI.

be wordplay on Q-Tel-like symbolism and I wouldn't be suprised to find that QAnon and the 'drops' (via military intel) isn't all artificial intelligence at its source (or controlled opposition), as they say.

Surveillance is only part of the plan behind the Internet of Things. The word 'Smart', like 'Q' is another way of describing what is essentially the digital platform for artificial intelligence and the vast robot network being built to connect to it. The movie *I Robot* (1999), starring Will Smith, gave a glimpse of what the future will be like as technology keeps expanding at the hands of private corporations and governments working together. As I wrote in earlier chapters, VIKI (the Virtual Interactive Kinetic Intelligence) central command in *I Robot* takes over so to implement a coup on the existing smart system; replacing the friendlier robots with a prototype designed to police the human population. As I said before, remember when Google's Alexa, or Apple's Siri started as an innocent Interactive Kinetic Intelligent toy? An excellent example of how 'real' some virtual reality simulations can be was with the arrival of the CGI avatar, 'Lil Miquela', in 2018 on social media platforms such as Instagram. This complete fiction, or artificial personality, created by the DJ Yung Skeeter, attracted over a million followers, including political trolls who thought she was real (see figure 393 overleaf). AI personalities, such as Alexa, along with social media platforms connected to such technology, are designed to play on our five-sense emotions. We need to get wary and more conscious of such dangers that are already here and sitting in each home.

It should also be no surprise that robots are being readied for integration into all aspects of human life, from Janitors, sex toys, to cute robot pets. For those who have the money, Sony is rolling out a $2,900 robotic dog called AIBO, which will soon be able to turn on microwaves, flick the switch on the vacuum cleaner and bark when the washing machine is done. Sony has

Loving The Alien: Why AI Will Be The Key To Unlocking Consumer Affection

Body Con Job
Miquela Sousa has over 1 million followers on Instagram and was recently hacked by a Trump troll. But she isn't real.

Figure 393: Digital Aliens (Avatars).
'Miquela Sousa', or 'Lil Miquela' the artificial (alien) entity who some thought was real.

been continually adding features to AIBO and the latest features will allow the small robotic dog to communicate with a range of household 'smart' appliances to help make life easier for its owners, this is precisely the idea. The smart grid is primarily being implemented through the Internet of Things for surveillance and control on one level, but it is also how anything artificial will connect with humanity, ultimately, the human mind.

Smart Meters are another vital facet of the Cyber-Grid and are described as an 'intelligent digitised energy-network, delivering electricity in an optimum way from source to consumption'. The language is disturbingly Orwellian, as Smart Meters are part of the emerging Cyber-Grid of wireless communication, linked to control centres from every home and business. It is planned that *everyone* on the planet will eventually be connected to the Smart Grid wireless field; therefore, the 'push' for all things smart has been ramped up in recent years. How will everyone be 'smart connected', especially people living in rural areas, isolated homes, and the billions scattered across rural lands all over the world? In truth, these people wouldn't be there anymore! Technology, laws, and pandemics would ensure that people are either killed off or moved to other locations in line with geopolitical agendas such as Agenda 2030 and 2050. Those who were not culled would be packed together in the densely populated 'megacities' where everyone will be subject to the wireless mind control and surveillance through the Smart Cyber-Grid.

The Cyber-Grid is the structure through which everything and everyone will be connected to artificial intelligence. Where Smart meters and the Internet of Things (artificial intelligence) have been looked at and considered 'worrying', other terms have been created in recent years so as not to 'frighten the children'. Names such as 'augmented reality', 'intelligence augmentation' or 'Intelligence amplification' are now being used. The sales pitch for 'intelligence augmentation' (IA) is that it won't control the brain like AI, but I say this is only a means to the same end by entrapping those who initially question what is *really* behind AI.

Plans for unleashing robots on humanity are well underway and as I showed in the last chapter, it is no surprise to find ancient gods described as robots. Michio Kaku, an American theoretical physicist and futurist, said in one TV programme: "We would become the gods that we once feared and worshipped." Some of the gods (ETs), I am sure, were artificial, not biological as a species; the onset of technology is part of their arrival. With the coming of more advanced technology, supported by a 'living' Internet of Things, we, as a species, would be assimilated into the digital hive mind of those that 'claim to be our gods' – the aliens who have already been assimilated. As David Icke says in his book *Everything You Need to Know* (2018):

> *I say that AI is the Archontic inversion and distortion that has taken over the thought and perception processes of the hive mind Reptilians and the Greys, among so many others, and is now seeking to complete the same assimilation of collective humanity. The term 'AI' would be more accurately defined in its ultimate form not as 'artificial intelligence' but as Archontic Intelligence.*[8]

I agree. AI is designed to turn humanity into biological robots serving the gods of AI – the chief Archon – the Demiurge. We are being influenced (not least through our addiction to technology), to prepare the way for a Skynet-like takeover of everyday human life, unless we start to challenge the rollout of such technology.

The Hive Mind Swarming

A six-part television series broadcast by National Geographic called *Year Million* (2017), sold the advantages of artificial intelligence as a 'cloud-based', brain-to-brain communication through microchip 'telepathy' and the creation of a super-hive mind. *Year Million* described how the hive mind would allow communication between diversity of thought and opinion, but in truth, it is meant to destroy all diversity and think only as 'one mind' with 'one agenda'. The voiceover on the series said the hive mind would mean 'coming together as one', yet, this is purely the 'mimicking' of all-is-one Infinite Awareness but confined only to the digital level at the expense of the Infinite level of consciousness. Or as the fictional character, Motoko Kusanagi, from the movie *Ghost in the Machine* (2017) said:

> *What if a cyber brain could generate its own ghost and create a soul all by itself? And if it did, just what would be the importance of being human then?*

Exactly the point! The human being is not meant to be any more important than a computer is to the world-wide-web, when it comes to merging with Artificial Intelligence. The collective cyber-soul would become a swarm-like intelligence, in competition with artificial intelligence. But why are we opening the way for *another* intelligence we have to compete with? It is calculated madness. Algorithm AI would be fine when supporting the human experience under human stewardship, but once the line is crossed into control and takeover, this is surely insanity being passed off as technological development. For this nightmare to happen, humanity has to become addicted to technology and desire its constant expansion. Among the younger 'smart' generations, this is already happening and the reason it is happening. Virtual video games such as *Detroit: Become Human* (released in 2015), is just one of several examples of popular culture pushing assimilation of humans with AI. Writer and director of *Detroit: Become Human*, David Cage, was inspired by Ray Kurzweil's book, *The Singularity Is Near* (2005), which explains that the rate at which human intelligence develops pales in comparison to that of a machine. Like I say, the Cyber-Grid is the foundation for humans to become robots and for AI to become 'humanity' and in so many ways, thanks to virtual reality headsets, social media and virtual video games, the combining of the two worlds is getting nearer by the year.

Selfie Heaven – the Beast with 95 million Faces & Growing

Social media platforms are also part of the enticement towards assimilation with AI. With billions of users, all social media networks are part of the grand scheme to bring about the Cyber-Grid. According to recent figures, Instagram has over *1 billion* users and growing; Facebook, *1.4 billion* with the likes of other social network sites, Twitter *68 million* users and Pinterest *250 million*. These are not small figures considering there are 7.53 billion people on the planet. It is said that half the monthly active users on Instagram are logging in daily and actively engaging on the platform. That's significant, especially since this number, too, keeps climbing. Nearly two out of every three social media users, between the ages of 18-29, are using Instagram. As of November 2019, the most-followed person, footballer Cristiano Ronaldo, has over *188 million* followers; the most-followed female singer, Ariana Grande, with over *166 million followers*. It's nice to see so many people focusing on the important things in life! In January 2019, the most-liked photo on Instagram was a picture of an 'egg', posted by the account @world_record_egg, attracting *53 million* likes. According to those behind the Instagram account, it was created with the sole purpose of surpassing the previous record of 18 million likes on a Kylie Jenner post. The world's youngest self-made billionaire, in response to losing her top social media slot, went on to post a video of her cracking an egg on a hot road. While all this trivia is being 'liked', humanity is being prepared for takeover by AI through a global technocratic Cyber-Grid.

Another fact about platforms such as Instagram is that the 'like button' is getting hit *4.2 billion* times a day (at the time of writing), meaning that the average user is going through their 'feed' and pressing that button more than once on a daily basis. This shows how obsessed we have become with Apps, being recognised for 'anything' (often for doing nothing), while buying into the idea that if you have an instagram account, then fame is within reach. Added to the constant addiction is the growing-by-the-week, life coach, webinar, masterclass online self-appointed gurus who seem to thrive off these platforms, too. I am not saying that life coaching and gaining knowledge and insight isn't important, it is, but the online growth in the hard-selling of endless entrepreneurial gurus, through such social media platforms, is clearly a 'sign of the times' I am highlighting here. The number of people putting their energy (focus) and attention into social media every minute of the day is breathtaking. With over *93 million* selfies being posted every day (at the time of writing), can you imagine the information being gathered by an artificially intelligent 'super-being', a *faceless god*, whose face is constructed out of millions of selfies? What happened to playing in the fields as a young person, building dens, making art or simply reading a book?

In May 2017, a survey conducted by the United Kingdom's Royal Society for Public Health, featuring 1,479 people aged 14–24, asking them to rate social media platforms depending on anxiety, depression, loneliness, bullying and body image, concluded that Instagram was the worst for young people's mental health. This is no surprise and I have personally seen this rise in mental health issues gradually worsening in education. Some experts have suggested the rise in mental health issues may contribute to digital dependence which is exactly the point of these SM platforms. It's about getting young people 'dependent' on the Cyber-digital world. Yes, there can be some positive effects, including self-expression, self-identity, and community-building with social media, but, Instagram and other SM apps seem to be facilitating a darker desire – the need to be constantly 'online'.

Whilst Social Media was in its infancy, in 2008, the UK *Telegraph* ran an online article about a 'condition' titled, *'Truman Show Syndrome Delusion'*, named after the 1999 film starring Jim Carey. The condition came from the main character realising his life is one big 'live reality TV show,' and everyone he knows are actors on a 'fake' TV show watched by millions. Psychiatrists said that viewers of the film, suffering from depression, became so depressed by their perception of 'reality' they felt they could no longer trust anyone, experienced suicidal ideation and even threatened suicide. As psychiatrist, Ian Gold, quoted in the article, said at the time, "We've passed a watershed moment, with respect to the Internet, in which you can do something very silly and without skill, and yet become famous instantly [see Instragram]."

One's continuous presence on a social media app trains the brain to more readily accept being linked into that online Cyber-Grid reality I am illustrating in this chapter. The pressures of being 'liked' on platforms like Instagram, for younger generations (even though the company has taken affirmative steps to deal with the harmful effects on mental health), can still be devastating. Depression and anxiety caused by prolonged time on these platforms has not magically disappeared, it has grown, especially since the 'lockdown' caused by the Coronavirus pandemic. For example, in 2019, Instagram began piloting in Canada, Ireland, Italy, Brazil, Australia, New Zealand and Japan a *'change* in post information displays' they said would hide the number of photos and videos received in an effort to create a "less peer-pressured" environment. On the surface, such moves are an improvement, but we are still dealing with a 'global phenomena' affecting power over human thinking and human emotions. AI is literally gaining its knowledge *from everything we put online*. The Cyber-Grid Empire, as I call it, is being built with our 'thumbs' and cell phones (including pads and cellular wearable devices), from the 'content' we input and circulate daily.

A 'Digital New Age' & Revelation

As I have been illustrating in earlier chapters, teachings within the Hermetic Qabalah can be seen as a 'blueprint' for 'constructing' reality (metaphysically) and is part diagraphic in terms of the projection (manifestation) of an infinite light (a matrix or god). The hermetic Qabalah is also thought of as the manifestation of a 'light body' in hermetic mysticism and it is this 'invisible light' of the Creator that constructs the Tree of Life.

According to the *Zohar* (Splendor or Radiance), the mystery of *'six'* thousand years before the deadline for a future New Age is considered crucial to understanding the nature of a coming technological age I am describing in this chapter. The Hebrew year 6000, from sunset of 29 September 2239 until nightfall of 16 September 2240 (on the current Gregorian calendar), is thought to mark the initiation of what would be considrered a 'New Millennia'. In other words, an emerging New Age *could* start to manifest, leading to a greater millennia to come. The *Zohar* states that the deadline by which the new age, or millennia, will arrive is 6,000 years from creation.[9] If so, *whatever* is coming to our world in the next twenty, to *thirty* years, will most likely be the start, or part of, a *new* techonological age. Whatever emerges, could reveal an 'heavenly force' *for great good*, or possibly, a sentient alien force (an artificial intelligence takeover) that does not necessarily have humanity's best interest at heart. I'll leave that up to you to ponder on. Even though I am going to illustrate what looks like a dire, irreversible outcome, I sense something loving, wise and good is coming to our world.

As I say, the notion of six thousand years is said to come from interpretations of mystical texts, such as the *Zohar* and, of course, the idea of *six days of creation,* forming the Sefirot (the Tree of life), is also thought to create an hexagram shape. The hexagram-shape-star, known as Metatron's Cube, is said to be the symbol for a 'god-man' (or part of God) that is *revealed* to humanity at the chosen time. It is also called the 'Microprosopus' for the likes of Christian Knorr von Rosenroth (July 1636 – 1689) a Christian Hebraist and Qabalist. I often wonder if something 'divine' is coming to earth *from* Orion in the not-so-far distant future? Is this the Second Coming referred to in Christian-Gnostic and Hemetic revelation? In similar ancient texts, the Seventh Millennium is also thought to be when a celestial liberator will arrive on earth, too. Numerologically, from the number *seven* upwards, we are said to enter the 'spheres' of the 'higher Adam' (or heavenly Adam) and the *source* of the projection I mentioned in earlier chapters. In line with such numerology, (according to various Premillennialists') we also find seven 'Adamic Covenants' (phases or figures) supposedly given to humanity by God, from Noah through to the 'renovation of the earth by fire'. The seven figures in the bible are named as Adam (Orion), Noah, Abraham, Moses, Jesus, the 'Second Coming' and the 'renovation by fire' (after the Millennia); the latter seems to relate to the 'New Earth' created out of fire (possibly technology?) The number *eight* and *ten* are also important numbers in this configuration, as *eight* is said to be the number of covenants (with dispensations) between Eden and the New Heaven and Earth, as commented on by the Christian Premillennialist, Clarence Larkin (1850–1924) in his *Dispensational Truth (or God's Plan and Purpose in the Ages 1918).*

In Hermetic-Gnostic teachings there are also ten spheres of the Sefirot and *ten* dimensions of what is called the 'Shi'ur Komah', the 'Archetypal Man' - 'Adam on High'. This 'man' is considered by some to be the same Archetypal figure relating to the 'mark of a man', in the *Book of Revelation,* who is possibly the protogonos of the new 'digital human' - a 'digital creature'. One who is said to have a 'direct experience' with the Creator in a new millennia. How could this *new* adam (or human being) have a direct experience with the creator god of technology? Through his/her 'mark' (or Digital ID-chip), I would suggest. As the text in *Revelation (13:15–18.)*

explains:

> *And that no man might buy or sell, save he that had the mark, or the name of the beast, or the number of his name. Here is wisdom. Let him that hath understanding count the number of the beast: for it is the number of a man; and his number is Six hundred threescore and six.*

The numbers 666 and the 'mark of the beast' have been shown to relate to the use of barcodes, microchips and electronic currency (creditit), which constitutes the digital 'traceable' human. I tackled some of these subjects in my fictional story, *Kokoro - The New Jerusalem & the Rise of the True Human Being* (2009), where I saw the Cyber-Grid as a 'City World' policed by clones or agents of

Figure 394: Cyber-Grid Clones.
The *new* Adam (humanity) 'experiences the creator' via the mark (microchip/nanotechnology).

the grid (see figure 394). The clones had received the 'mark' and were merely servants (worker ants) for the machine-like god (the Demiurge), the god of technology that created the Cyber-City-Grid Empire.

Cyber platforms, from PayPal to Apple Pay, along with Bitcoin, etc., are unkowingly pushing the transhumanist (new world) agenda, waiting to be ushered in when the digital god (artificial intelligence) connects to the human mind. Transhumanism is almost a belief in the exponential growth of technology, designed to take us far beyond our understanding of what it is to be human, today. Where would such ideas take us? Into an AI contolled dystopia as far as I can see.

The idea of 'experiencing' a new world, or 'cyber age' in the 21st Century, may not necessarily be what some think it will be. The coming age is intended, so it seems, to be a transhumanist utopia unless we wake up and regain what's left of our organic 'humanity'. I wonder if this 'hidden' intelligence (AI) *is* the Gnostic Demiurge (an alien diety), and the future world *is* the Artificial Intelligence-controlled World Order? With such an advancing new era, at this time, it is also said that 'science' and 'technology' *becomes* God-like. Only a *living*, artificial consciousness could be titled so and fulfill such prophecies.[10]

Today, thousands of start-up companies are creating new technologies and services 'challenging' the status quo and changing markets every day. It's a story being repeated by all the leading tech and Internet companies connected to a growing Smart Grid - see, Apple, Google, Microsoft, Amazon, Facebook, etc. Such innovation is becoming a global force in technology and cyber 'security', almost in line with the emergence of a new 'cyber age'. The growing Cyber-Grid is not unique to any one location on earth, too. What I am saying is that there seems to be an off-planet extraterrestrial intelligence' (possibly an AI Cyborg consciousness), influencing our world, *our thoughts* through the types of technology we are being given. Is an intelligence fostering a 'global' digital-AI revolution that we, as humans, see as *our own invention*?

I think the collective human family are been driven down a road towards an alien-AI controlled dystopian futuristic world that does not have the welfare of future generations (of *all* nations) as its priority. We seem to be merely 'worker ants' for an alien hive mind that does not really care for the earth (all *life*) in its organic form. I have also wondered if we are dealing with an alien (AI) spider-like Queen (possibly originating in Orion), or, could it be an expression of the Gnostic Demiurge, a machine-like deity not dissimilar to the machine world in the *Matrix* movies? Interestingly, according to some scientists, spiders appear to offload cognitive tasks to their webs, making them one of a number of species with a 'mind' that isn't fully confined within the head. In otherwords, the spider's mind is 'non-local' (a hive mind) and can be *everywhere* on its web - or its Cyber-Grid. The 'technology' operating out of places like, Silicon Valley, China's Zhongguancun, Israel's Be'er Sheva and elsewhere, seems to be more of a 'techno-spider' that does not necessarily have humanity's best interests at heart. There is much spirituality and good on earth at this time, too, and people of *all* nations need to unite to prevent such a rise of the robots, of 'artificial intelligence' and the harmfull expressions of a possible transhumanist (dystopian) future.

As I have explored throughout the book so far, I sense we are dealing with an extraterrestrial 'inspired' technology that is becoming our everyday reality. Not every advancement in technology is good for humanity, too. Consider nuclear power (weapons) and the dangerous levels of radiation through new (and future) cellular devices. Surely we are not meant to be permanently bathed in such electromagnetic technology, daily? Neither is the Earth (all nature/wildlife) supposed to be *so* polluted, even destroyed to levels we have witnessed over the past few decades? Big Technology and industry has advanced rapidly towards the coming Cyber-Grid Empire I am describing. Myths and stories that tell of the demise of advanced civilisations like Atlantis (and previous advanced empires 'falling'), in some ways, would have been due to what could be described as the 'high-tech' wars, possibly nuclear (advanced) weapons in the ancient world that buried the civilisations of Atlantis and Lemuria and other ancient places, too. But what if these are not the ancient world, but our future high-tech new age revisited?

Spells and the 'New Normal'

A new age is undoubtedly being maneuvered into place, towards a techno-logical grid I am highlighting. Symbolism and magic are being used to 'mesmerise' humanity, subconsciously. Symbolism, sound bytes, mantras and iconic imagery are used to target the subconscious, more than we realise. The rainbow, for example, is one symbol that represents a 'new age' emerging after great earth changes, after the legendary biblical flood (or deluge). A flood that seemingly destroyed earth's advanced civilisations, such as Atlantis and Mu. Symbols are powerful and are used to invoke real-ity, to lay the foundations in our subconscious towards manifesting specific outcomes. Those who innocently made rainbows during the Covid-19 pan-demic, seemed to be under some kind of 'spell', or at least *unknowingly* cele-brating the coming of a not-so-distant (better world), a 'new world' (a promise of a cure) beyond the rainbow. Daubing windows with rainbows all over the UK at the beginning of the pandemic, felt like some kind of rit-ual on a par with the ancient rite of 'marking doorways and windows' (to "write the words of God on the gates and doorposts of your house" *Deuteronomy* 6:9). Of course, they are *not* the same thing; but, in terms of 'suggestive' media-programming and the 'power of symbols' to convey a message, we seemed to witness a national ritual (along with thursday night clapping) that took place at that time. What were the lyrics to that 1970s Kermit the Frog song, *Rainbow Connection*?:

> *What's so amazing that keeps us stargazing*
> *And what do we think we might see?*
> *Someday we'll find it, the rainbow connection*
> *The lovers, the dreamers, and me*
> ***All of us under its spell***
> *We know that it's probably magic …*

The other aspect of 'spell binding' throughout the 2020 pandemic was

Figure 395: The Future Cyber-Grid Empire - a Soul Cage for Humanity.

the use of the 'power of three' mentioned earlier in the book. The UK government's use of *three* words, such as, 'Strong and stable'; 'Get Brexit done'; 'Stay home, protect NHS, save lives'; 'Stay alert, control the virus, save lives'; 'Hands, Face, Space'; 'Build back better', etc. All are mantra-like, consistently reinforcing the message. As I said earlier, magic is part 'spell' and part 'mantra' - the latter is practiced to train, or *initiate* those using it.

It feels as though a nefarious 'star magic' is behind the 'digital alien' (in its many forms), one that 'symbolically' emerges from the fallen state of Orion; or through an *inverted* version of Orion, symbolically ending the Old World Order and birthing a new 'Cyber-Grid World Order'. I wonder if this is the so-called 'New Normal', in symbolic form? A Cyber-Grid, seems to be emerging to *control* the world's population *through* every country, not least the Superpowers, and I would suggest, will be almost 'god-like'. Technology already holds power, not least through our addiction to *it* and how we have become more so in recent years. Is it too far out to suggest Artificial Intelligence, in more sophisticated forms, is intended to 'overshadow' the ancient grid touched on at the beginning of this chapter. Will AI create digital quarantine facilities for the human soul (soul cages), eventually controlled by advanced artificial intelligence? It's interesting to note there are also *three* types of AI: Artificial Narrow (Machine learning, like Alexa) ANI; Machine intelligence (AGI) and Machine Consciousness (ASI), and all three would create the Cyber-Grid. Every facet of human life is intended to be connected to this grid, from driverless cars, trains, planes

ORION CLOUD PLATFORMS

© Neil Hague

Orion is used to symbolise the connection between our world & AI

Figure 396: Orion Influenced Platforms.
Orion *seems* to signify the connection between our world and the AI Cloud reality. The name is used in Orion Aerospace LLC and many other platforms. There has to be some kind of 'symbolic' connection here to an artificial (extraterrestrial) intelligence?

(all public transport), smart meters (the Internet of things) and ultimately, the idea of a *new synthetic* genetically modified human being (see figure 395). Far fetched? No, its almost here. ANI and AGI are already upon us. It feels like we are on the precipitate of a new world, one that children today will be pivotal in as they become adults.

Orion Platforms

Even the use of the word 'Orion' for many artificial intelligence 'platforms' is a alluding to the 'interstellar connection' (see figure 396 overleaf). These include, Orion labs, AI voice-activated business communication and automation systems based in San Francisco. There are also other tech-based products, services and systems that have Orion as an influence, from the name of educational bodies, online gaming, to aerospace engineering. The '8Pack' OrionX Gaming high-speed computer (one of the fastest ever PC's) even has the 'red and blue' symbolism within its design. *Master of Orion*, the strategy game released in 1993, is another global product that hints at a form of Artificial Intelligence based in the Orion constellation. In the first version of the franchise, players could only play against AI (the computer) with human and AI players controlling the management of colonies, technology development, ship construction, inter-species diplomacy and combat. There is definitely a connection between a 'machine world, the Cyber-Grid, AI and all things Orion.

The same can be said of the word 'Cloud', which is simply the Latin word 'nebulae' (nebula) - the Orion Nebula. The Marvel Universe character, the daughter of the giant tyrannical alien-god, Thanos, is called Nebula and coincidentally, she is part-machine like the Borg found in *Star Trek*. In the *Avengers* movies, Thanos unleashes a reptilian alien hoard, using advanced technology to highjack the earth. The same plot, in theme only, also features in the *Transformers* movies where the demonic-looking Decepticons lead by Megatron, bring their world, Cybertron, to Earth, so to enslave and feed off humanity, like a parasite feeds off its host. The common theme always is an *invading alien intelligence* (possibly originating in Orion) that uses both gradual steps and then brute force to enslave planets it targets.

AI – Nanotechnology & Silicon gods

The vast spectrum of technology connected to transhumanism is a multi-layered control grid also manifesting as nanotechnology and 'smart dust'. Nebula are made of interstellar 'dust', and it could be that an alien intelligence has inspired the creation of nanotechnology for use on earth - so to turn earth into a habitat that eventually will 'naturally' manifest physical, biological-artificial life forms. Together, all these smart nanotechnologies are planned to comprise the 5G Smart Grid, which is another expression of Ray Kurzweil's AI cloud. This grid is formed from the fact that 'Smart Objects' interact not only with people but also with other Smart Objects. Therefore, the foundation of this interconnected communication is 'smart dust', or tiny electronic particles capable of wireless communication with each other and anything with which they connect. The dust particles are so tiny that if you take the distance between earth and the sun to be one millimetre, then the length of one nanometre is the very short distance from New York to Boston. According to the science, a nanometre is one billionth of a metre and nanotechnology is in the size range of 1-100 nanometres. Nanotechnology is also known as nanobots, nanorobots, nanoids, nanites, nanomachines, nanomites, neural dust, digital dust and smart dust. They are the 'nanoprobes' of the *Star Trek*, Borg in other words. This is the real level at which humanity is being connected to technology. The 'cloud' or hive mind (coordinated through 5G) will see this globally activated in the not so distant future. I will come to 5G shortly but almost everything we endure, especially through big tech and the media, is, in many ways, a diversion away from our organic nature as true sovereign human beings.

We have been *given* artificial intelligence in its basic form courtesy of the likes of DARPA, the inspiration and funder behind so much transhumanist technology designed, it seems, to hijack the human mind. AI gadgetry that people would never connect to the technological development arm of the Pentagon, is now amongst us in the form of 'Alexa', 'Cortana' and 'Bixby', the latter courtesy of the Samsung Group. The word 'Cortana' is a Latin form of the Anglo-French 'curtein', from Latin 'curtus', and refers to a ceremonial sword, which again could suggest a connection to Orion and the sword and belt stars 42 Orionis, Theta Orionis and Iota Orionis.

All transhumanist technology is connected no matter how innocuous it may appear to be. Apple's AI 'assistant' marketed as 'Siri', for example, came out of the DARPA-funded CALO project or 'Cognitive Assistant that Learns and Organizes', involving 300 researchers and 25 university and commercial research centres. Do we really believe that one of the most sinister organisations on the planet (DARPA) only funded Siri because the Pentagon so wanted you to have an AI helper to make your life easier?

Thousands of WikiLeaks documents labeled 'Vault 7' have allegedly exposed CIA hacking tools to access information on people through Internet-connected devices, including the Apple iPhone, Google's Android, and Samsung TV's. Amazon's electronic book pad, 'Kindle', is mentioned in relation to 'code templates' and Amazon's Alexa AI 'personal assistant' has been said to have the ability to listen to conversations and 'take notes'. We are also told that 'Alexa AI can now whisper sweet nothings and express emotions like a human' and 'add emphasis to words and even be programmed to say regional-specific phrases'. LG Electronics Inc., a South Korean multinational, is Amazon's partner in the Alexa project. David VanderWaal, LG's Vice President of Marketing, announced plans to add 'advanced Wi-Fi connectivity' (5G upwards) to all of its home appliances and eventually have 'tens of millions of smart-connected devices' in homes. All this is part of the assimilation of human and artificial intelligence, even though it is still in its stage of infancy.

Silicon Valley, just south of San Francisco, is the centre of the new science related to surveillance and transhumanism. Here you find the Internet 'giants', Google and Facebook, which are globally controlling the information we are allowed to see. Computer software giants like Microsoft and other technology giants, like Apple, are also in Silicon Valley, along with the Singularity University created in 2008 by Ray Kurzweil and Peter Diamandis at the NASA Research Park, to promote and advance transhumanism. Singularity, in this context, refers to the merging of humans and machines at a point when artificial intelligence surpasses human intelligence and can 'self-replicate autonomously'. This, I feel, is intended to be the new humanity on a 'new earth' as prophesied in religious texts, like *Revelation*. We can see how important AI is to off-world 'unseen' forces.

In 2019, American billionaire Stephen Schwarzman gave Oxford University *150 million* pounds (*188.6 million* US dollars) for a new institute to study the 'ethical implications' of artificial intelligence and computing technologies. Schwarzman, allegedly a 'Skull and Bones' (Delta Kappa Epsilon) member and CEO of the private equity firm, Blackstone also gave a *350 million* dollar gift to the Massachusetts Institute of Technology (MIT) to establish a centre for computing and artificial intelligence. The money given to the 'elite' Oxford University would also fund a centre to house all of the university's humanities subjects in a single space to encourage collaborative study on AI. Some billionaires are supporting and funding such research, as it will provide a major injection towards the development and 'understanding' of the impact of AI on humanity. I am sure there are many in positions of influence (like Schwarzman) who have legitimate concerns about the dangers of AI, hence the funding. The BBC ran an article on the donation, where Schwarzman said:

> *AI is going to be the fourth revolution, and it is going to impact jobs, excellence, efficiency … It is a force for amazing good and also a potential force for not good.*

He also compared the rise of AI to the rise of the Internet, launched by computer scientists as a workable prototype in the late 1960s with the creation of ARPANET, or the Advanced Research Projects Agency Network. Schwarzman said:

> *And parts of it [the Internet] were cool — interconnectedness, globally the ability to communicate, it is pretty amazing, … What they forgot were all the negatives, this inability to control cyber bullying, lack of freedom of speech — all kinds of negative things.*[11]

It is said that the Internet was originally funded by the U.S. Department of Defense, ARPANET using packet switching to allow multiple computers to communicate on a single network, not the World Wide Web, invented by the English engineer and computer scientist, Tim Berners-Lee. I merely scratch the surface here, as the scope of this book is insufficient for tackling the background to these particular strands of information, but it is important to mention some of the key areas connected to the implementation of a future AI Cyber-Grid.

'Artificial' Kuiper Belt for the Earth

To facilitate the Internet of Things and the Cyber-Grid, a network of satellites were launched into the earth's thermosphere and exosphere. The Federal Communications Commission in the USA approved SpaceX on March 29, 2018, to launch 4,425 satellites into low orbit around the earth; the total number of satellites expected to be put into low and high orbit by several companies will be 20,000.[12] Each satellite is said to be the size of a small refrigerator, weighing approximately 880 pounds, with a life expectancy of only 5 years.[13] Eventually, all those satellites will 'fall to earth' and burn up as they re-enter earth's atmosphere. In January 2020, SpaceX also launched 60 Starlink communications satellites into orbit, which showed up as a line of bright dots gliding across the night sky at that time. They were visible to the naked eye in the weeks after launch, slowly become dimmer as they entered orbits farther into space. Was the strange 'mini-moon' observed orbiting the earth in February 2020 also part of the SpaceX launch? Further satellites were launched in late March 2020 as the world went into 'lockdown' due to the Coronavirus pandemic. One cannot help but wonder if all this was *perfectly timed,* especially in relation to switching on a global 5G network, a topic I am coming to shortly.

As part of the same satellite launches in April 2019, Amazon's Project Kuiper, were advertising to hire engineers for a 'big, audacious space project'.[14] Amazon said:

> *Project Kuiper is a new initiative to launch a constellation of low Earth orbit satellites that will provide low-latency, high-speed broadband connectivity to unserved and underserved communities around the world. This is a long-term project that envisions serving tens of millions of people who lack basic access to broadband Internet. We look forward to partnering on this initiative with companies that share this common vision.*[15]

According to the same report, Project Kuiper could potentially bring Amazon closer to 'Blue Origin', the space exploration company founded by Billionaire Amazon owner/founder Jeff Bezos, should they collaborate on the satellite network, which at the time of writing, is highly likely.[16]

Figure 397: Project Kuiper.
Encasing the earth with what could be devastating technology.

The Kuiper Belt is one of the largest structures in our solar system, others being the 'Oort Cloud', the heliosphere and the magnetosphere of Jupiter. It is similar to the asteroid belt but far larger—20 times as wide and 20 to 200 times as massive. The Oort Cloud is an even more distant, greater spherical region of icy, comet-like bodies surrounding the solar system, including the Kuiper Belt. The idea for the Kuiper Project name and effect is based on the spherical enclosure of satellites forming the network that would facilitate the earth-based Cyber-Grid (see figure 397).

I am sure the same enclosure effect is also operating around other bodies in the solar system and involves highly intelligent life. The rings around Saturn, for example, recently shown to harbour even more satellites, or tiny moons, seems to be acting as a frequency-enhancer or possible blocker. According to a team led by Carnegie astronomer Scott Sheppard, some of the new moons belonging to retrograde and prograde groupings used algorithms (artificial intelligence) to examine Saturn's images captured by the Suburu scope between 2004 and 2007. The tiny moons (satellites) could also have been parts of larger moons that were obliterated.[17] Or could they be something else?

Electromagnetic Alien Vehicles

Dr Norman Bergrun (a much-awarded American scientist and engineer and former scientist at NASA's Ames Research Center) became fascinated with Saturn's rings after studying Voyagers I and II photographs from the early 80s. Bergrun concluded, from a detailed study of the Voyager pictures, that the rings of Saturn are not natural; the rings are generated by gigantic cylindrical objects, electromagnetic in nature, which can be identified in many pictures (see figure 398).

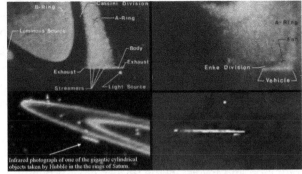

Bergrun does not refer to these phenomena as conventional spaceships but as 'electromagnetic vehicles'. Bergrun detailed his findings in a book, *Ringmakers of Saturn* (1986), and his conclusions have gained further support with images recorded by NASA's Cassini mission which arrived in 2004. Cassini captured the same cylindrical objects, of fantastic scale, in and around Saturn's rings that NASA simply ignored. What a surprise. I personally think the rings are a gigantic 'broadcasting system' and what these electromagnetic vehicles are releasing is essential to the *frequency* broadcasting from Saturn. I am merely mentioning this phenomenon here to suggest that there are obviously different levels and sizes of artificial intelligence and electromagnetic vehicles. The electromagnetic machines being positioned

Figure 398: The Ringmakers of Saturn.
Are electromagnetic vehicles releasing a frequency broadcast from Saturn? How 'big' is AI (Alien Intelligence)? Much bigger than we imagine!

Figure 399: The Real Alien Invasion?
The electromagnetic soup of radiation and *technology* covering the earth is creating an *alien* environment.

around the earth are placed for a specific purpose – to facilitate the global satellite networks, yes; but are we naive to think that such machines are not altering the vibrational fields of the earth?

Another way to the see the 'exosphere Cyber-Grid' is to think of it as a 'blocking frequency' enhanced by satellites orbiting the earth. It is a firewall that will most certainly act as a barrier to higher energetic forms of life (higher consciousness) connecting us and the organic earth to the stars. I actually saw this idea of a 'blocking frequency' back in the 90's when I was creating imagery for magazines and books. In recent imagery I've made it has become clear that the Cyber-Grid is designed to create an electromagnetic soup around the earth (see figure 399 on previous page).

This soup of radiation is the essence of all things artificial and alien to us as a species. Can you imagine how the earth once looked to the ancients compared to how it looks and 'feels' now in the Cyber-Grid age? The only comparison I can think of is to imagine going to a national park and instead of finding vistas of nature in all their organic glory, seeing instead, endless power stations, shopping malls, concrete and factories. The Cyber-Grid Empire will be the equivalent, in terms of shock, to our collective system as an alien invasion. I would also add that the alien Cyber-like God (possibly the Gnostic Demiurge), operating *through* artificial intelligence (including radiation and EMFs), is the unseen creator behind the rapid advances in technology, robots and the proposed Singularity. AI as a God-like concept does not want a higher conscious human being, fully connected to infinite worlds of Superconsciousness. It seems we are all meant to be part of the Cyber-Grid.

Dark Fibre, 5G & the Internet of Things

Expanding Internet access has become something of an obsession among tech companies. Google offers fibre Internet services as well as its own cellular network. Facebook scrapped plans to offer Internet access via drones in June 2018, and Amazon isn't the only company hoping to use low earth orbit satellites to allow previously unconnected people to join the rest of the world online, finally. The reason why all these seemingly 'independent' Big Tech companies are rooting for the *same* technological advancements, I would suggest, is because they are connected, at their highest levels, to the off-world Cult. The Cult seems to be operating as a Mafia-style global body (without borders) for its alien (artificial Intelligent) masters, and possibly why we are moving ever-so-quickly towards an AI assimilated reality.

The unrelenting push for implementing 5G (Fifth Generation), as an unknown infrastructure through what is called 'Dark Fibre', is also part of the Cyber-Grid, *digital* World Order. Dark fibre can be used to create a privately-operated optical 'fibre network', run directly by its operator over 'dark fibre' and existing Internet networks. This is opposed to purchasing bandwidth or leased line capacity (used to connect offices and large groups of internet users) on an existing network. Dark fibre networks may be used for 'private networking', or as Internet access or Internet infrastructure networking, through devices that are part of the 5G network. In simpler terms, 5G is the *means* by which the 'artificial intelligent grid' will be connected to the Internet of Things. And as I have already pointed out, this Cyber-Grid will be used to control *all* human life in the not-so-distant future.

Previous generations of Radio Frequency cellular communication (2G, 3G and 4G) used large antennas to send a blanket of radiation in all directions. The lower frequencies they used, and the broad distribution of microwaves, limited the numbers of cellular devices that could connect through an individual tall tower. The much shorter length microwaves used for 5G will make it possible to use small phased-array antennas to send, and receive signals via 5G enabled products now being made available. Each 5G product is said to have multiple phased-array antennas used to create a powerful beam of radiation back to the 5G devices mounted on electrical utility poles, or toward a specific satellite in space. These beams of radiation will also need to be strong enough to *pass through walls and human flesh, such as a hand or head,* to reach the intended destination. The technology used for 5G is a weapon in itself and very dangerous for humans and other organic species on earth. 5G is said to have one thousand (1,000) times the capacity of 4G, and has never been studied for adverse health reactions or effects![18] Well, not officially at least! While 4G's wavelengths travel along the surface of the skin, 5G's millimeter waves are said to be more insidious. According to some experts, when 5G wavelengths are emitted, our skin will automatically absorb them, causing the skin to rise in temperature.

According to Martin L Pall, PHD, Professor Emeritus of biochemistry and Basic Medical Sciences at Washington State University, health risks associated with 5G and radiation are very worrying. A study titled: *"Microwave Frequency Electromagnetic Fields (EMFs) Produce Widespread Neuropsychiatric Effects Including Depression"*, published in the *Journal of Chemical Neuroanatomy*, outlines quite clearly the major concerns regarding 5G. Pall's report, *'Compelling Evidence for Eight Distinct Types of Great Harm Caused by Electromagnetic (EMF) Exposures and the Mechanism that Causes Them'* is cause for concern. He says:

Putting in tens of millions of 5G antennae without a single biological test of safe-

ty has got to be about the stupidest idea anyone has had in the history of the world ... We have created something that is harming us, and it is getting out of control. Before Edison's light bulb there was very little electromagnetic radiation in our environment. The levels today are very many times higher than natural background levels, and are growing rapidly because of all the new devices that emit radiation. Putting it bluntly, they are damaging the living cells in our bodies and killing many of us prematurely.[19]

But it's not stupid, or out of control, for a non-human extraterrestrial intelligence that wants to install the Cyber-Grid Empire. Not all tech is bad, of course not, we need it for a range of reasons today, but how do know when 'tech' is no longer serving us and instead, we are serving it?

Targeting the Old Grid

The Cyber-Grid is designed to impact on the global population and eventually lead to a revolution as the transhuman (human robot) replaces the organic human being, courtesy of the artificial (counterfeit) God I have described so far. The Grid highlighted in this chapter is also intended to facilitate advanced weapons (technology) that can be used on humanity. There are endless videos and articles connected to the use of directed energy weapons (DEW) across California, resulting in horrendous fires in that region. The fires that ravaged Australia in 2019, which saw destruction of 12.35 million acres of land, could also have connection to the use of DEWs. Evidence that Californian fires in 2018 were a result of directed energy weapons (DEW) in the form of lasers and microwaves, at least in part, is undeniably strong. DEWs have been considered:

- Invisible and inaudible.
- Immune to gravity, wind and Coriolis forces.
- Travel at light-speed and have near infinite range
  and thus suit able for use in space warfare.
- Land-based, mounted on planes, drones, satellites or
  Boeing X-37s and have pinpoint accuracy.

We are talking 'star wars' technology, available in its basic form since the 80s. Retired California firemen, John Lord and Matt (last name withheld) talking in an interview after the destruction of Paradise, about the anomalies they'd observed, led them both to conclude that DEWs were involved.[20] The firemen reported that plastics, attached to metal, completely melted, while plastics standing alone withstood what must have been extraordinary heat. Other investigators observed how guardrails caught fire at the points where the metal bolts connected to the wood. DEWs could produce these effects. There are also theories of smart meters, or transformers, blowing up, being a cause in some cases. Smart meters might have contributed, but that wouldn't explain cars also being 'toasted' with no burn path between the houses and the cars. It is not at all unfathomable that more than one weapon could have been used to ensure the desired effect. On September 11th, 2001, rescue workers being interviewed said they heard bombs

Figure 400: Paradise, the Aftermath.
Were Direct Energy Weapons used in places such as Paradise, California in 2018?

going off when they were inside the twin towers and also Dr. Judy Wood, a former professor of engineering mechanics, gave a presentation filled with strong evidence that directed energy weapons were used on 9/11 as the building and all its contents 'dustified' in mid-air and cars nearby looked toasted.[21] There is so much more to know in relation to these type of fires.

When we see the aftermath photos of such events, like the destruction of Paradise on November 8, 2018 (see figure 400), it is hard to believe that a forest fire that doesn't burn the forest but totally obliterates each home was due to 'natural' events! Put 'Direct Energy Weapon' into YouTube and you will see many examples of this technology in use by the Pentagon, DARPA and Airforce Research Laboratory testing such weapons.[22] Some videos even show columns (or beams of light) coming from the sky, instigating some kind of fire! These may be hoaxed, but, crikey all this needs looking into.

A Scientist Speaks Out

Dr. Katherine Horton, a particle physicist with a PhD from Oxford University, expressed her concern over the current rollout of 5G networks over the past few years - and for a good reason. Horton has allegedly worked as a high-energy physicist on the particle collider at the German Electronsynchrotron DESY in Hamburg, Germany, and on the infamous Large Hadron Collider at CERN in Geneva, Switzerland, according to the website, wikispooks. At Oxford, Dr. Horton is also said to have worked as a research fellow at St John's College, which allowed her to expand her research from particle physics into medical physics and the physics of complex human systems.

During her childhood in Romania, Dr. Horton alleges she and her family experienced intimidation because they were highly educated and refused to take part in the criminality being promoted by mob-like networks in her country. She also says that stalking and other such activities escalated in November 2011 while she was attending a High Court case in London as part of her systems analysis research into the English legal system. Horton (who seems to have dissapeared from public view) says she was openly stalked on her way home from court and started noticing a thug waiting for her outside her home every morning to follow her to the train station. Horton has appeared on several online platforms and interviews since 2011, where she outlined what 5G technology is really all about. One use for such weaponry, according to Horton, is for depopulation and to target individuals who would be considered a problem for those in power. She said in one interview:

> *I think the average person struggles so much understanding what all this is about and that's what they [Global Elite] are banking on. So they are banking on the fact that, for example, there is a very simple con hidden in this marketing ploy that is 5G. For example, when they brought up 3G and 4G, everybody assumes that 5G is just a better 3 and 4G so what's all this fuss about?... 5G is a fundamentally different system.*[23]

I mention Horton's information simply for those interested in the possible dangers of such technology and its capability, I personally have no way of knowing whether what Horton claims happened to her is true or not, nor do I know her or ever met her.

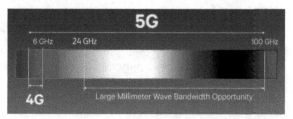

Figure 401: 5G is an Ultra-high Frequency Weapon. Can you imagine how powerfull 6 and 7G would be?

5G is said to operate on an entirely different frequency range known as millimeter waves. The waves pulsate their highly-disruptive frequencies within the window of 30 and 300 gigahertz; 5G is an ultra-high frequency, with ultra-high intensity, that will bombard the body and the brain with ... *90 billion* electromagnetic waves per second (see figure 401).

UK microwave expert Barrie Trower says he trained at the Government's Microwave Warfare Establishment in the 1960s, worked for the Royal Navy and British Secret Service as an expert in microwave weapons, helped debrief spies trained in microwave warfare in the 1970s, and worked in the underwater bomb disposal unit which used microwaves.

His degree in physics specialises in microwaves. He said before the 'pandemic':

All microwaves of all 'G's ... they all reduce immune systems of all living things except for three things. One of those is bacteria and viruses. They thrive and multiply when they are microwaved. So you have a situation ... where all living things are losing their immune systems but the bacterium and viruses are strengthening theirs, and 5G will only exacerbate the situation.

These are said to be some of the effects of electromagnetic fields and the super-impact of 5G needs to be added to the mix of possibilities. According to Trower, babies, children, pregnant women and the elderly are especially vulnerable to 5G, which also diminishes antibiotic potency while making bacteria stronger and more resistant. Pregnant women and the elderly are also susceptible to 'respiratory illnesses' such as influenza and pneumonia, the latter of which rose in numbers through March and April 2020 due to the coronavirus (Covid-19) outbreak. Or was it all a perfect base for escalating a global virus?

Covid-5G?

In February and March 2020, the coronavirus hit China, Italy, and continued to seemingly infect the rest of the world seemingly out of 'nowhere'. Social media went into overdrive at the time of the outbreak. At the same time, information circulated about 5G and the impact this technology *could* have on the biological mind-body, and also its alleged effects on our ability to access higher levels of awareness. As the coronavirus pandemic arrived in February 2020, growing numbers of people revisited the concerns outlined by scientists over the safety of Fifth-generation (5G) technology.

As far back as September 2017, over 180 scientists and doctors, in almost 40 countries, warned the world about 5G health risks. These scientists, in response to Resolution 1815 of the Council of Europe, said:

We, the undersigned scientists, recommend a moratorium on the roll-out of the fifth generation, 5G, until potential hazards for human health and the environment have been fully investigated by scientists independent from industry. 5G will substantially increase exposure to radio frequency electromagnetic fields (RF-EMF)... and has been proven to be harmful to humans and the environment.[24]

Fifth-generation wireless technology (5G) began full deployment in 2018; coincidently, symptoms being described as coming from victims of Covid-19 in China, via GreatFire.org and other censorship-busting websites (in their words), showed tens of thousands of posts describing the *first* symptoms of Covid-19 being a 'dry cough' making those infected tired and fatigued (breathless) just as any flu would. The EUROPA EM-EMF Guideline 2016 also stated: "There is strong evidence that long-term exposure to certain electromagnetic fields (EMFs) is a risk factor for diseases such as certain cancers, Alzheimer's disease, and male infertility ... ." According to the guidelines published, common EHS (electromagnetic hypersensitivity) symptoms can include "headaches, concentration difficulties, sleep problems, depression, lack of energy, fatigue, and *flu-like symptoms*."[25] Was China's EMF levels of toxicity polution a factor in *their* pandemic? Its hard to know. As we shall see, China is leading the way with Fifth Generation cellular technology and its use of 5G and AI (through robots, facial recognition and drones, etc) expecially its response to Covid-19 was/is unprecedented.

Within weeks of the first announcement of a global pandemic, China mobilised its tech, drones, and sophisticated surveillance system to keep a tab on infected individuals and enforce quarantines. The West followed suit on a global scale because the Chinese model was (still is) the blueprint for the 'New Normal', as parroted by the mainstream media in almost every country at that time. Covid-19 inspired 'Track and Trace Apps', rolled out in different countries, seemed to be based on the Chinese model of surveillance. 5G was also being used in Asia and according to the *Bangkok Post* in March 2020, 5G 'robots' were in use to treat patients with Covid-19 at Rajavithi Hospital, the Central Chest Institute of Thailand and another at Nopparat Rajathanee Hospital (see figure 402).[26] With 5G technology in

place all over China (especially Wuhan), and coincidentally, in countries such as Iran, Italy, America, and elsewhere in the world, we have had over a million deaths worldwide from Covid-19 by the end of the summer of 2020 (so we're told). Could Fifth-generation technology have played a factor in creating coronavirus's symptoms *(not the virus itself)*; therefore, the 'perceived' spread of a virus?[27] I cannot say for sure. More independent scientific research is needed. Such ideas are purely conjecture and there may well be no solid evidence at all for this. We will

5G smart robots take care of coronavirus patients

Figure 402: Smart Robots.
5G 'Smart' Robots and Covid-19 all in one place – *nice*.

have to see. The truth will always prevail.

As I say, what wasn't shown in the mainstream press was the *possibility* of virus 'symptoms' being connected to new technology (or at least similar symptoms *claimed* to be caused by Covid-19), attributed to side effects relating to (EMFs), or 5G microwaves. As I've already highlighted in this chapter, connecting 5G to the virus in any way would *never* happen (or at least be debated) because, it seems, the 5G network *is* to be rolled out no matter the cost. When author David Icke touched on the subject in April 2020, via the media platform *London Real* (reaching well over a million live viewers), the censors' reaction was swift and immediate, banning Icke's highly-subscribed YouTube channel and Facebook page. What was Icke saying that those in power did not want the masses to hear? Facebook even went as far as to label anyone who questioned the 5G connection as 'far-right'. Ofcom went so far as 'imposing a sanction' on Brian Rose's *London Real* station for broadcasting, what it declared was 'potentially harmful content about the coronavirus pandemic'. By 'harmful' is it more correct to say they meant Icke's interview broadcast potentially dangerous content which *alerted* the populace to the mendacity of the official story? On UK television, during an airing of ITV's *This Morning* show in April 2020, presenter Eamonn Holmes also got heavily, criticized for so much as even daring to mention the dreaded words, "5G"!

Doctors Speak Out

In March 2020, a New York intensive care doctor, Cameron Kyle-Sidell, took to YouTube in his desperation to make people aware of what was happening with regards to patients entering hospital with Covid-19 symptoms. YouTube continually deleted the video uploads, and he was reported to have been removed from intensive care work for questioning the use of ventilators. Kyle-Sidell said they were told to prepare to treat an infectious disease called 'Covid-19', but said that is not what they were dealing with. Instead, he was seeing people with lung conditions he had never seen before. Kyle-Sidell told viewers of his video, the symptoms he was seeing were what one would expect to see with people suffering cabin depressurisation in a plane at 30,000 feet, more akin to someone dropped on the top of Everest without acclimatisation, or by definition, an oxygen supply.

We have to consider that human cells possibly poisoned by electromagnetic fields, *could* release exosomes (or what some medical experts have called fake 'Covid-19'). Again, I cannot say for sure, whether this is true, but why haven't these claims been taken into account and investigated thoroughly? See also the work of Dr. Andrew Kaufman, practicing forensic psychiatrist, Doctor of Medicine and former Medical Instructor of

Hematology and Oncology at the Medical School of South Carolina for more information.

Spanish biologist Bartomeu Payeras i Cifre, who specialises in microbiology at the University of Barcelona and researched smallpox bacteria and viruses at Hubber pharmaceutical laboratories, produced a preliminary study in April 2020 of the correlations between the main locations of 'Covid-19' and 5G activity. The study did not attempt to show a cause and effect between 5G and the alleged 'Covid-19' only that the major countries and regions where the 'virus' was reported to be most prevalent corresponded with 5G locations. Global 5G rollout coverage, shown on maps, compared to the outbreak of Covid-19, especially in Italy (the 2nd worst 'infected' country in Europe at the time of writing), not least the comparisons to the 5G rollout in Milan and surrounding areas, seems to have been overlooked by the mainstream media. Again, I cannot say if there is a correlation, but surely the topic needs to be fully researched and presented to the public? In addition to the media blackout over 5G, insurance firms (at the time of writing) don't seem to want to insure against Fifth-generation wireless technology, too. Any technological effect on us (our bodies - electromagnetic fields) needs to be scrutinised if we are to fully understand what impact (if any) such technology will have on humanity and the earth. Watching the censorship unfold concerning alternative information, during the Coronavirus pandemic, caused many thousands to question the official narrative being announced every day via mainstream news outlets. The 'war room' bulletins published every week by government officials, especially in the UK, seemed to be focusing mainly on death rates, while never offering us recovery rates, or more positive ways of treatment, prevention and ways in which we can build our immune systems.

Disease X (Spreading the *Fear*)

Within weeks of the Coronavirus 'outbreak' in China, the World Health Organisation was calling it disease 'X' (see *Chapter Ten*) as attention and focus went global, not least due to relentless press coverage. The imagery that came out of China in February 2020, showed people in hazmat suits on a par with the 17th Century Plague Doctor outfits (see figure 403). The mask-wearing and social distancing in every country (courtesy of China's initial image), was designed to reinforce the fear of a deadly contagion.

The decision for Covid-19 to be 'perceived' as a pandemic (a modern plague) by the World Health Authority (therefore the public perceived it to be so) was evident and intentional from the start. Pandemonia (literally meaning 'the place of all demon') was exactly what happened as panic ensued. Panic buying escalated in many countries as the global media went into overdrive 'pushing' *fear* of the 'new plague' into every living room. Toilet rolls and pasta started to disappear in quantities that beggared belief. Why? Because 'panic' was created through psychological fear of both the unknown, and being 'trapped' at home without the basics of life. If the

Figure 403: Robot Doctors.
The 'Plague' Doctor out and about in China, March 2020.

Figure 404: Symbols & Scripts.
X Symbolism connected to China, Hong Kong and The Umbrella Corporation.

media announce there *is* a shortage of *anything*, people will go out and panic buy the same products, making the shortage *a* reality - it's all about 'fear'. 'Fear of something' is the oldest weapon used against humanity.

It's also odd that the outbreak of Covid-19, starting in Wuhan, Hubei Province, China, just happened to be mentioned in an 80s novel, *The Eyes of Darkness* by Dean Koontz, which on page 333 refers to a 'deadly biological weapon' called Wuhan-400, created in their RDNA labs. In Wuhan, a Category Four biotech lab (a weapons lab) RLSW, also uses what looks like an umbrella symbol similar to the fictional 'Umbrella Corporation' from the game, *Resident Evil*, a narrative that includes the unleashing of a Zombie pandemic. The umbrella itself usually symbolises the canopy of the heavens (*Psalm* 91:1-16), a symbol of 'shelter' and 'protection'. The parasol is thought a symbol of the sun, whereas the umbrella is a symbol of shade (darkness); hence, the umbrella corporation in *'Resident Evil'*. The umbrella is also seen as a symbol of 'fight the power' (protests), through unity and protection in places like Hong Kong, especially during the 2019 mass protests (see figure 404).

The umbrella is also thought to be a symbol of providence and love in Asia, hence its use on clinics in China. In Japan, it means 'Ai-Ai gasa' or 'Love-Love umbrella'. There is nothing 'loving' about a virus, though, or a 'biotech weapon' released from a category four laboratory in Wuhan - the latter of which I am doubtful exists. Or even hidden in a 'cure-all vaccine', just a thought! Mandatory vaccination programmes have been called for by the World Health Organization (WHO), (see Bill Gates) and the governments influenced by the Global Health Partnerships, Gavi (The Vaccine

Alliance), and the CDC in the US. Surely we as people, as nations, have a choice, right?

Mandatory vaccination and digital Identification have been and are currently being suggested by governments, so to combat the spread of Covid-19. Yet, for some researchers, even the name, 'Covid' seems to be an abbreviation for: **Certificate Of Vaccine ID** - the coming ID for proving an individual has had the vaccine. Many of the minimal numbers of those infected (at the time of the first lockdown), compared to the 7.6 billion global population, seem *not* to have travelled profusely or come into contact with anyone who could have passed on the virus. Something else must have been at play, surely? Even exposing an asymptomatic 'Covid person' in one track-and-trace scenario in the US, to 455 uninfected people, according to the stats in May 2020, *'zero'* became infected. As the study placed on the PMC (US National Library of Medicine National Institutes of Health), said:

> *Apart from hospital staff, both patients and family members were isolated medically. During the quarantine, seven patients plus one family member appeared to show new respiratory symptoms, where fever was the most common one. The blood counts in most contacts were within a normal range. All CT images showed no sign of COVID-19 infection. No severe acute respiratory syndrome coronavirus 2 (SARS-CoV-2) infection was detected in 455 contacts by nucleic acid test.*[28]

I would ask what affliction exactly did people have? PCR testing to date has proved unreliable (creating false positives), not to mention the overblown computer models, in the UK especially, predicting hundreds of thousands of deaths that did not materialise. Neil Ferguson, married father of one and Imperial College's creator of these computer models, revealed his true colours in May 2020. He was telling everyone to 'stay at home' (and not have anyone visit who didn't live in the same house), whilst he himself engaged in sexual trysts with his lover, at his own home, while his lover was living elsewhere with her husband and children. Even more of a head-shaker was that Ferguson claimed to have the 'virus' in the same period. The extraordinary hypocrisy continued in May 2020 with Boris Johnson's advisor, Dominic Cummings flouting lockdown laws, too.

Covid-1984

Through his CEPI (Coalition for Epidemic Preparedness Innovations) project, Bill Gates raised over $460 million towards rapid vaccine production. Gates is a man whose family were involved in the Eugenics movement in the 20th Century and seems to be *obsessed* with vaccinations. A strange obsession for a computer software manufacturer who supposedly created Microsoft, and has no medical background as far as I am aware.

Since the Ebola outbreak of 2013, Gates has appeared on numerous media platforms over the past few years (prior to the Covid-19 pandemic), saying the world wasn't prepared for a coronavirus pandemic. His TED talk in 2015 even showed a coronavirus in the first few opening slides, which is more than a coincidence. Gates and co have consistently called for a global 'medical-military' and the use of 'germ games' (simulations of a pandemic) to deal with 'real' epidemics. The Microsoft Team's commercial, that ran on mainstream television during the early months of the Covid-19 pandemic, was ludicrous in my view. It tried to suggest doctors were running out of 'technology response' caused by the pandemic. How can anyone run out of technology? Isn't that like saying we are running out of broadband or Wi-Fi? The commercial finished by saying: "We are living on Teams." Exactly the point! The new way of *living online* being reinforced through what was another Bill Gates organisation is obvious to those who could see the connections. One can't help but feel the outbreak of coronavirus in China 2020 was *perfectly timed* to further advance towards the Cyber-Grid Empire; not least proposed mandatory vaccinations and a 'new normal' global cashless economy .

Figure 405: The Pandemic *Before* The Pandemic. It was obvious to those who really see what's going on.

We were being warned about a possible 'new pandemic' by global bodies such as the 'Event 201' pandemic exercise hosted by Johns Hopkins Center in October 2019 (see figure 405). Event 201 was a pandemic simulation (which involved the Bill and Melinda Gates Foundation, the World Economic Forum, the CDC, etc), which coincidentally more or less matched the unfolding events of Covid-19 in March 2020 to the utmost detail. I wonder why? Well, the answer seems obvious; the 'pandemic simulation' was a test run for what would happen a few months later. The global lockdown seemed organised and coordinated *through* 'global' bodies like the WHO, but the real agenda, I am sure, was orchestrated by the hidden hand (or off-world nefarious forces *behind* the hand), as almost all national governments sang the same lockdown song sheet (see figure 406 overleaf). At the time of writing we are facing a 2nd Lockdown across Europe and elsewhere, based on 'scenarios' (cases-figures) and very little else.

Orwell's *1984* seemed suddenly to be a reality in most countries as self-isolation and mass 'house arrest' (along with pandemonium and the fear of the virus) allowed authorities to move further towards a global police state.

Figure 406: Singing From the Same Song Sheet.
If anything, the Covid-19 pandemic revealed how easy it is for a
global authority (the WHO) to 'dictate' to national governments.
It seems, we already have a defacto unelected global government.

Cash (notes and coins) were considered 'dirty' as almost all stores moved to electronic payments, beckoning a long predicted cashless society. As the world went into meltdown due to the coronavirus, the UK government, after ten years of austerity, seemingly ended all austerity, revealing vast forests of 'magic money trees' (a term used in 2017 by the then Prime Minister, Theresa May). Some countries were even forced to create payday-lending stores as governments offered credit, grants and loans to businesses and the self-employed. Millions of workers (employees in the UK) were 'furloughed' from late March 2020, leading to thousands also losing their jobs in the months that followed. According to the UK, HMRC (at the time of writing), *6.3 million* people, had been temporarily laid off by 800,000 companies by May 2020. What better excuse to create instant swathes of unemployed people, all dependent on the State, while shutting down smaller businesses due to a virus. Like I say, you would be forgiven for thinking you had woken-up in a dystopian reality on the 22nd of March 2020. The Chinese social '*universal*' credit system (basic living allowance) will no doubt follow? The world will be very different in 2021-22, all created courtesy of unseen forces and operatives behind the not-so-hidden emerging global government structures. What a story to tell the grandkids! When the global *technocratic* New World Order was being built, most were 'stockpiling' toilet rolls, 'told' to stay home, wear a mask 'everywhere' and fear a virus with less than a 0.1% death rate. As someone said on social media during the lockdowns, "If you are allowing the likes of Gates and the WHO to tell you *when and how* you can see *your* loved ones, you are not only living in fear, but you are living in an Orwellian state in-the-making."

I wouldn't be surprised if Covid-19 was 'allowed' to be let loose in several countries simultaneously. Who knows for sure what actually happened? The 2011 movie *Contagion* presents a strong message portraying the type of scenarios relating to the Covid-19 pandemic as it unfolded. Even the UK government posters had a '*Contagion* look' about them in the early weeks of the lockdown. All by design to give the impression of an ultra-deadly situation. The UK government also rushed through parliament as the lockdown began, legislation that in effect, placed the country in, what feels like, a 'police state'. The Coronavirus Bill 2020, along with modifications to the Public Health (Control of Disease) Act *1984*, seems to allow government to suspend provisions and install new 'investigatory powers'. Simple freedoms (such as gathering in public) have been criminalised under terminology deemed 'not essential', or a 'danger to public health'. In the first lockdown, police forces across the UK used these new laws to fine people for simply sitting *alone* on park benches and on beaches. As soon as the lockdown was imposed, social distancing was also enforced in super-markets and other stores. Suddenly-ubiquitous rules that didn't seem to apply to employees of supermarket chains (in March through to June 2020) were swiftly implemented for the 'unclean' general public. Walking two metres apart (almost like robots) and wearing masks 'everywhere' felt like we were extras in a bad dystopian movie (see figure 407). Some masks being sold in June 2020 even had LED lights that lit up around the mouth area when the wearer spoke. One Japanese robotic company even developed a 'smart' mask that could access the internet.

I am more inclined to think Covid-19 pandemic was 'created' (even invented or exaggerated) by forces who want a global economic *reset*, a

Figure 407: The New (Insane) 'Normal'.
The rules imposed on the masses as part of the 'globally orchestrated' lockdowns in 2020, *felt* designed to reinforce a dystopian movie script - surreal times!

transformed global society, enforced vaccinations, Digital ID (travel restrictions), and the end of freedoms, we take for granted. It feels like we are witnessing the birth of a technocratic New World Order, not dissimilar to dystopian themes found in movies such as *Blade Runner* (1982) and *Equilibrium* (2002), etc. As the *Contagion* movie poster read: "It is fear that spreads the disease". One can't help but wonder if *Adrenochrome* (the oxidation of adrenaline) played its part in the pandemic in some form? Ramping up the fear and panic from late February 2020 (through the mainstream media), combined with severe underlying health issues (for the majority of deaths), could have been a recipe for disaster healthwise. Again, this is speculation, not fact. Tens of thousands of people die in the United States annually *every* winter from flu (many with pneumonia complications) with Centers for Disease Control (CDC) figures recording (estimating) that 45 million Americans were diagnosed with flu in 2017-2018 of which 61,000 died.[29] Around 250,000 Americans are admitted to hospital with pneumonia every year and about 50,000 die. With the alteration of death certificates (authorised by the authorities) those people are all potential 'Covid-19' statistics. The fact that *65 million* people suffer from respiratory disease every year, with an estimated three million deaths, makes influenza the third biggest cause of death worldwide. With the estimated figures being noted, what difference would either lockdown or no lockdown have made? It is worth remembering this at *all* times: Statistics don't speak for themselves – they speak for those who compiled them.

At the time of writing, the media is already spinning the advancement of a 'second wave' of the coronavirus pandemic and a tiered system of further lockdowns to deal with it. The question is, are we going to let 'unelected' technocrats change our world *so* dramatically, while watching the eradication of our given rights and freedoms? These are the freedoms afforded to us by our grandparents who sacrificed so much in previous wars to prevent all future tyranny. Freedom is not something to give away so lightly. How come we have not feared other viruses before? *Why are we living in so much fear of death?* Because, I would suggest, we have not yet realised our true power! When we regain *our* power (as collective human family), the 'spiritual war' within, will be over, and our world will be free of 'unseen (off-world) forces' that are manipulating and influencing us.

Agenda 21 (2030, Climate Change and Beyond)

As I say, the Cyber-Grid Empire seems to be part of an ongoing war against humanity, mainly psychological, not least through our global mainstream media and geopolitical structures. The Cyber-Grid could be both a depopulation weapon (by stealth), and the blueprint, for a AI controlled New

World Order.

Two UN 'agendas' – Agenda 21 and Agenda 2030 – call for the *transformation* and *centralisation* of global society. Much of this transformation is justified by the climate change 'mantra', also driven by 'mass hysteria' (based largely on a biased science), the Extinction (cult-like) Rebellion, and the poster girl Greta Thunberg. While Thunberg 'idol worship' goes unchecked (not that much is happening since Covid-19), another teenage activist, German born 19 year-old, Naomi Seibt, was threatened with jail or a fine for exercising her freedom of speech.[30] Why? Because she *denounced* 'man-made climate change via online videos and at public events. Seibt (unlike Thunberg) came first place in physics during a local regional competition of the Jugend forscht, junior division (Students Experiment) and second place in mathematics. Censorship seems to be happening more frequently to anyone offering an alternative narrative to what the global Cult want the masses to hear, especially since the coronavirus pandemic. We've had the equivalent of book burning 'digitally' with individuals losing their YouTube channels and blogs for exposing aspects of the coming Cyber-Grid. As the Russian chess grandmaster, former world chess champion, writer, and political activist Garry Kasparov once said: "The point of modern propaganda isn't only to misinform or push an agenda. It's to exhaust your critical thinking, to annihilate truth." The climate *is* changing, as it *always* has and *always* will, thanks mainly to the sun and its relationship with earth's colossal ocean mass, producing natural CO_2 gases that forests, trees and plants turn into oxygen. Pushing governments to create 'carbon taxes' that will be paid to a 'global authority' will not prevent the sun from affecting the earth, therefore changing every planet's climate within its electromagnetic reach. The demonisation of CO_2 is as ludicrous as banning fresh air. But when the 'drive' is to build a 'new technological' Cyber-Grid Empire, then focusing the masses on 'fear' and 'death' will always convince those *in fear* to believe whatever is needed (including narratives and ideas) to keep their fears from manifesting. Fear is *'False Evidence Appearing Real'*. Or as one Japanese Proverb puts it, 'Fear is only as deep as the mind allows.' Too many people are being 'frightened' into accepting the 'New World', 'New Deal' or 'New Normal' I've been illustrating here. Whether it's a pandemic or extinction of the human race, *fear* of death *is* the driving force. We have to stop giving our power to fear, to global authorities (the Cult) who are pushing Agenda 21, Agenda 2030 to the masses.

The aims of Agenda 21, from its own documents, match themes relating to the need for a Cyber-Grid Empire, which would include 'global' assimilation of artificial intelligence into everyday human life. Here is just a snapshot of the documentation put forward through Agenda 21:[31]

- An end to national sovereignty [*see Globalisation*].
- State planning and management of *all* land resources, ecosystems, deserts, forests, mountains, oceans and fresh water; agriculture; rural development; biotechnology; and ensuring 'equity'.
- Abolition of private property [*banks foreclosing on home owners?*].
- 'Restructuring' the family unit [*see all forms of Technocracy*].
- Children raised by the state [*the introduction of a 'basic income'?*].
- People told what their job will be [*see all forms of Technocracy*].
- Major restrictions on movement [*see the coronavirus pandemic?*].
- Creation of 'human settlement zones'. [*all forms of gentrification*]
- Mass resettlement as people are forced to vacate land where they live [*see the Hunger Games movies*].
- Mass global depopulation in pursuit of all of the above.

As I say, weaponry/technology such as DEWs and Fifth, or even Sixth, Generation cellular masts and devices, along with the desire to connect a *smaller* (reduced) global population *to* artificial intelligence, could be viewed as tactics used as part of securing the above outcomes. The Cyber-Grid Empire is the ultimate template for 'forces' wishing to 'reshape' the world and usher in a New World Order. You could say, the alien life force is well and truly embedded and part of our everyday life. We seem to be in the last years of the 'old world order', with technology (including weaponry) being put in place, to facilitate the 'New Order'. Just look at the world today (especially in the wake of the coronavirus pandemic) and see how far we have 'progressed' towards a more centrally 'controlled' reality, within a short space of time. Within the space of six to eight months, cash has almost gone out of circulation, with most transactions now being 'virtual' or 'electronic'. Technology now *controls* our ability to purchase on earth. Our obsession with technology is taking our species through immense neurological changes caused by addiction to what feels like alien technology. Look how far we have travelled since the first email was sent, to using virtual reality and the possibility of interacting with holograms. We are not that many years away from full 'assimilation' with what we call artificial intelligence, *or* the concept of off-world forces working *through* it. You could see the technological invasion as a war on humanity, being waged on so many different levels. As I say, our world is changing so rapidly, it will be unrecognisable to those of my generation in the next few decades and not all rapid change is good for the spirit of humanity and the Earth.

You could say 'forces' inspiring the Cyber-Grid Empire are at *war* with humanity. If so, we as a collective have a responsibility to bring peace and balance to our world and not allow artificial (alien) intelligence to rule over it - or us.

Sources:

1) https://www.ancient-origins.net/news-history-archaeology/researchers-reveal-stonehenge-stones-hold-incredible-musical-properties

2) Jensen, Jeff (December 3, 2010). *"TRON: Legacy' and 'Lost' writers discuss rebooting the sci-fi landmark and their new TV projects."* Entertainment Weekly. Retrieved January 3, 2013.

3) Lamar, Cyriaque (December 14, 2010). "Jeff Bridges and Olivia Wilde say *Tron Legacy* is all about religion." io9. Retrieved April 23, 2012.

4) Alexander, Eben. *Proof of Heaven. A Neurosurgeon's Journey into the Afterlife*, 2012 pp 80-81

5) https://eu.freep.com/story/news/local/michigan/2016/03/19/uber-call-botched-kalama-zoo-shootings/81915560/

6) https://www.wired.com/2010/07/exclusive-google-cia/

7) https://www.msn.com/en-gb/news/techandscience/artificial-intelligence-is-creeping-up-on-us%E2%80%94literally/ar-BBQK93U?ocid=ientp

8) Icke, David. *Everything You Need to Know*, Ickonic, 2018 p581

9) *Zohar* (1:117a) and Zohar Vayera 119a

10) Loper, DeAnne. *Kabbalah Secrets Christians Need to Know*, 2019, p92

11) https://www.marketwatch.com/story/american-billionaire-gives-oxford-university-180-million-to-study-artificial-intelligence-2019-06-19

12) https://www.cellphonetaskforce.org/5g-from-blankets-to-bullets/

13) https://www.cellphonetaskforce.org/wifi-in-the-sky/

14) https://www.geekwire.com/2018/beyond-cloud-amazon-web-services-hiring-engineers-big-audacious-space-project/

15) https://www.independent.co.uk/life-style/gadgets-and-tech/news/amazon-space-internet-satellites-bezos-blue-origin-spacex-a8993741.html

16) https://www.tomshardware.com/news/amazon-project-kuiper-internet-satellites-fcc,39805.html

17) https://www.smithsonianmag.com/smart-news/twenty-tiny-new-moons-discovered-around-saturn-180973294/

18) https://www.collective-evolution.com/2019/07/31/5g-is-the-ultimate-directed-energy-weapon-system-says-particle-physicist/?fbclid=IwAR2f7RPZ3-XHYj86LgiD7iDcHTfrl8AEzkqrX6NK5-aLvIao8ksmoUzFzrI

19) https://www.radiationresearch.org/wp-content/uploads/2018/06/EU-EMF2018-6-11US3.pdf

20) https://www.youtube.com/watch?v=UHldRe4rtps

21) http://www.drjudywood.com/articles/BBE/BilliardBalls.html

22) https://www.youtube.com/watch?v=OEyy1EaYBlQ&feature=emb_title

23) https://jamesfetzer.org/2019/08/dr-katherine-horton-5g-is-the-ultimate-directed-energy-weapon-system-says-particle-physicist/

24) http://www.5gappeal.eu/scientists-and-doctors-warn-of-potential-serious-health-effects-of-5g/

25) http://www.whatdoesitmean.com/index3141pl.htm

26) https://www.bangkokpost.com/business/1874534/5g-smart-robots-take-care-of-coronavirus-patients

27) https://www.youtube.com/watch?v=a-XGuBYdt78

28) https://www.ncbi.nlm.nih.gov/pmc/articles/PMC7219423/

29) https://www.cdc.gov/flu/about/burden-averted/2017-2018.htm

30) https://notalotofpeopleknowthat.wordpress.com/2020/05/26/naomi-seibt-faces-prison-for-incorrect-climate-views/

31) https://sustainabledevelopment.un.org/outcomedocuments/agenda21
https://www.un.org/en/ecosoc/docs/pdfs/fina_08-45773.pdf

20

A WAR ON HUMANITY?

It's All in the Movies (Part 3)

If we don't end war, war will end us
H.G. WELLS

The Cyber-Grid Empire being built all around us, in my view, is an extension of a larger network of interstellar grids focused on AI (as a god-like intelligence) and its real source of origin – possibly the darker aspects of Orion. The Cyber-Grid is a master template or 'off-world empire', with its power structures, rulers, military force and trade federations. As with any empire on earth, the 'Orion Empire' can be seen to include an array of extraterrestrial life, ruling over colonies, planets and other star systems. Just as the British Empire for example, had colonies all over the world, the nations being 'ruled' were considered British, falling under British Maritime Jurisdiction (control). I see the Cyber-Grid Empire in the same vein, where even a planet, or a star system, could be considered 'real estate' to whomever gets to own it, along with the planet's population who become (plugged in) servants to forces that control the empire. Fleets of ships in the ancient world, even spaceships in a futuristic world, all seem to serve the same purpose - to 'facilitate' those that come to *take* what often belongs to others. It is not the remit of this book to offer an historical timeline of historic invasions from the Phoenicians through to Columbus, etc., I am merely drawing parallels relating to common themes and patterns pertaining to war and invasions. As I said at the beginning of *Part Two*, wars on earth seem to be a mirror of the 'star wars' (in the heavens) and this concept seems to be very much part of the unfolding, technocratic empire I've been describing.

All war, warfare and imposition seems to have 'arrived' in the human mind from elsewhere, especially when we compare the lives of ancient 'peaceful' hunter-gatherer people on earth, with the opposite - warrior-like chieftains, pharaohs and Caesars that came thousands of years later. Having kings and queens in the ancient world to having royalty still in our 21st Century world, means nothing has really changed for the best part of

2000 years. We are still owned, ruled and separated from our true heritage – the land. Today, our minds have evolved to meet the rise in technology (now fully immersed in our psyche, especially in the young), but our hearts remain those of organic human beings. The technology invading our world is more 'alive' than we think and it is *changing* our world dramatically, so quickly, that those born in the 1950s and 60s will fail to recognise their environments if they are still alive by 2040-50.

From Warriors to Warlords

I presume the majority of people reading this book may already be intrigued by the idea of extraterrestrial life existing across the billions of galaxies that constitute our observable Universe. This book is not attempting to debate such views, it is simply weaving together themes that relate to extraterrestrial life in connection to Orion and humanity's plight. In the past few chapters, I have expressed an interest in 'themes' relating to the Cyber-Grid World Order and the rise of robots connected to artificial technology. All of which seems to be influenced by Orion 'archetypes' and different extraterrestrial consciousness linked to this constellation. I am not saying that other star systems have not been involved in the 'colonization' of earth, there will have been many more 'civilisations', not least those connected to Sirius and the Pleiades. But, Orion seems to be influencing our psyche on so many levels, especially so through previously-outlined political-religious structures (blueprints) to the templates that have structured our past political, military-industrial empires. The 'warrior' archetype (the warlord or warlock) of the ancient world comes through these archetypes, as I showed in earlier chapters, as the ancient Age of Orion.

Today, the warrior (Orion) archetype is evolving further so to meet artificial intelligence; the age of the robot will be an integral part of this as discussed so far. Warfare, in my view, is one of the oldest aspects of the Orion blueprint manifest on earth and *all* war serves as a vehicle for invading gods (aliens) I have been outlining throughout this book. We, as a species, have become 'slaves' to war, conflict, division and more importantly, to forces manipulating us into thinking our world needs to have a vast war 'machine' to survive on earth.

Recorded history shows us that since 3600 BC, over 14,500 major wars have killed close to four billion people – two thirds of the current world population. We have seen endless wars on earth, too many to mention in this chapter. But to give you an idea of the magnitude of war, we have seen at least one battle every year between 300AD and 2000AD. In simple terms, we have had 700 years of conflict, not to mention the religious wars, Crusades, the French-Anglo Hundred Years' War and the First and Second World Wars, the latter of which saw *50 million* people killed. From these

statistics you would think we are an insane species, that we just love perpetual conflict. In fact, the 1990s saw a new peak in the annual number of
wars being attended to by the UN. According to John Rees in his book,
Imperialism, Globalization, The State and War (2001), there were 34 conflicts in
1992 and in 1994, the highest number of war-related deaths were recorded
since 1971. The unstable and violent climates witnessed in Iraq, Somalia,
the Balkans, Former Yugoslavia, Rwanda, Liberia, Turkey, Chechnya,
Angola and Algeria over the past three decades were more to do with long-
term global economic and political processes brought about through the
centralisation of power. Look what has happened since Rees wrote his
book? We have endured the nonsensical 'war on terror' ('war on terra
firma'), or war against earth. Since 2001, we have seen the fall of Iraq,
Libya, Yemen and Syria, with Iran, North Korea and China now in the mix.
All these countries were listed in the infamous 'Axis of Evil' speeches made
by George W. (Boy George) Bush, and named in documents created by the
Project for a New American Century (PNAC), months before that fateful event
in New York. The scope of this book is insufficient to go into detail on such
areas, but if anyone is interested in finding out more, there are many excellent and well-researched books written over the past sixteen years docu-
menting the 'conspiracy' around 9/11 and all that has happened since.[1]

Over the years, governments and national leaders are often the most
horrific perpetrators of violence attributed to war. Torture occurs in more
than 100 countries and is carried out as part of government policy in at
least 40 territories, not least through intelligence networks and military
occupation. During the Roman Empire, of 79 emperors, 31 were murdered,
6 were forced to kill themselves, not to mention death and destruction per-
petrated by the Roman Empire through its dominance of Europe and North
Africa. Medieval China saw a major 'revolt' almost every year, while one
60-year period in Russian history (1801-1861) saw 1,467 revolts.[2] It is also a
fact that only a third of all civil wars occurring after 1800 ended through
negotiations; since 1945 around 25 per cent of conflicts have been solved
through negotiations. Again, it seems we are neither good at being diplo-
matic nor at fostering peace.[3]

War has been waged against nature, not least through the obsession for
land ownership, seen as one of the main attributes for invasion and occupation since time began. Millions of Indigenous Peoples, from the Americas to
Australia, were invaded for their land and possibly because of their star
knowledge (or connections to other stars at war with each other). War and
invasion seems to be part of our genetics. Today, land is still used as a
weapon against humanity (earth stars) by the elite, which I am sure have
off-world 'masters'. In Britain especially, far too much land (wealth) is in

the hands of the few.[4] The taking of land by 'invading armies', or corporations, is one of the real reasons for any war machine. The Roman Empire would not have been able to invade so many countries if it wasn't for its hugely cosmopolitan army. According to the Byzantine historian Procopius, throughout Justinian's thirty-two-year reign, each annual inroad of Barbarians killed 200,000 inhabitants of the Roman Empire, which would come to a total of *6.4 million* people. What with plagues and other terrible effects of war (terror) and trade, humanity, under the rule of 'empires', seemed doomed to squalor, death and destruction. Nowhere in the animal kingdom do we have anything that compares to these horrifying statistics. Animals may kill each other for food, but we, as a collective species, have mastered war, aggression and conflict as an art form.

In Steven Taylor's book *The Fall: The Insanity of the Ego in Human History* (2005), we see the war machine is a relatively recent historical development that can be traced back to Neolithic warriors emerging from the Sahara region around 4000BC.[5] Taylor describes this time period as a 'spirit of suffering' and turmoil in human history leading to a new type of human being. A human that made weapons, amassed property (including slaves) and 'worshipped the hierarchy' set out by a patrilinear king, chieftain, pharaoh or emperor (all connected to a ruling lineage of the gods). It was an ancient era that saw the creation of patriarchal dominance; the rise of fortifications, fighting over land and resources due to scarcity caused by drought in Mesopotamia and the Saharasia regions 5000 years ago. The changing topography saw a mass movement (migrations) from the Saharasia into the Middle East, Central Asia and central and Eastern Europe. The far greatest of the migratory people at this time were the Indo-Europeans (or Aryans), the predominant ancestors of most modern European, American and Australian people today. It was these people, according to Taylor, who brought with them violence and war to the more peaceful Neolithic hunter-gatherers of Europe, Africa and eventually North and South America. Steven Taylor says of the Indo-European invaders in his book *The Fall*:

> *For centuries they had to be content with attempting to prise new territory and new wealth and power from each other. But the conquering and empire-building instincts were so strong that it was inevitable that, as soon as they had developed the right kind of technology* [a common theme], *they would turn their attention to the rest of the world.*

Empire-building and war have gone hand in hand throughout the centuries and as I have already highlighted in the last chapter, a new empire is emerging in the 21st century. The Cyber-Grid Empire is fuelled by the same mind or intelligence; the only difference between the might of Rome, for example, or the Cyber-Grid Empire, is the 'technocracy', or the level of *sophistication* of how technology is used to wage war. As we have seen, AI and smart technology is capable of administering cyber-wars, as well as supporting physical warfare. The Cyber-Grid is appropriately a 'skeleton' for all possible future wars; death, as always, being a focus for such demonic realms I mentioned in earlier chapters.

Global Government – World Army – Total Control

The idea of a world government is a crucial part of the Cyber-Grid Empire I have been describing. It is intended to be the 'central command centre' for *all* aspects of life on earth. It is also nothing new, as the old empires that formed the old grid desired the same ends; just as dictatorships and all tyrannies of every age also desired total control, the Cyber-Grid will facilitate 'new unprecedented levels' of control. Historically, we know that Bronze Age Egyptian Kings desired to rule 'All That the Sun Encircles'; Mesopotamian Kings spoke of ruling 'All from the Sunrise to the Sunset', as did the ancient Chinese and Japanese Emperors who desired 'All under Heaven'. These four civilizations also developed impressive empires of what historians describe as 'Great Unity', or Da Yitong as the Chinese put it. In truth, they were ancient dictatorships, but the one being inspired for our future age will make all past tyrannies pale in comparison.

Known human history can be seen as a constant centralisation of global power which has become more technological as the ages passed. Some say the far ancient (prehistoric) world was also advanced 'technologically', hence the building of such amazing architectural feats such as the pyramids and megalithic structures mentioned in earlier chapters. The pyramid itself is the perfect 'model' for the type of centralisation of power harnessed by the earth's energy field – the grid. In the ancient world, the pyramid was also the abode of the gods (aliens) and served both as a temple structure and important 'nodes' on the ancient grid. The Cyber-Grid Empire seems to be designed to *overshadow* the original grid, or leylines, of connecting megalithic sites, temples and other important sites all over the world. The *vibration* of the whole planet is meant to change once again so the new Cyber-Grid Empire can become the ultimate focus of attention for humanity. Look at the focus we are now giving the artificial beast-like intelligence through our collective 'disconnection' from the old ways, or the organic world, as we become more addicted (intentionally so) to the new technological grid and what it belies. As I said in the last chapter, the 'smart world' is making the 'real world' not so smart, courtesy of AI gadgetry and an ever-growing need for an artificial world. Just look how people panic when there is 'no WIFI' or panic in general at the thought of being without even the basic supplies. The mass buying of toilet rolls in the UK and USA at the time of the coronavirus outbreak in March 2020 was a perfect example of 'project fear' and mind control. Can you imagine mass blackouts caused by AI? Who would be in control of our world then?

What has long been termed 'globalisation' – the centralisation of global power in all areas of our lives, through the grid – has not happened by chance. The Cyber-Grid will facilitate further the centralisation of power globally and through it, a new empire will be created. This Grid-structure will be like no other in the history of humanity. Why? Because if it unfolds, the mind of a counterfeit god-like software (artificial intelligence), will be revered and 'connected' to *all* who are part of the coming Cyber-Grid. Cult networks helping to create and steer the Cyber-Grid into place, are working towards the centralisation of power through a world government, which will impose the Cyber-Grid Empire (New World Order) on *all* nations (all people). When anything becomes mandatory, whether vaccinations, taxes, or travel permits, etc., we know the precedent is being set for a global technocratic structure. At the time of writing, we are in the early stages of seeing the 'mandatory vaccinatons' being pushed for, not least thanks to the global mainstream media which seems to be predominantly biased towards the official narrative.

As I pointed out in the previous chapter, the Covid-19 pandemic allowed governments to pass emergency legislation and mandatory 'powers', which seem to be facilitating the changes that 'could' help bring about a future Cyber-Grid Empire. Technology such as 5G, being rolled out globally from 2019 onwards, will obviously enhance the capabilities of 'everything' connected to the Grid. It's also amazing how a coronavirus seems to have fostered a move towards a less tolerant, totalitarian society, too.

We already have a de facto world government under codenames like 'G-8', 'G-20', the World Health Organisation and the United Nations Security Council. Proposals for global United Nations 'taxation', in the form of carbon and currency taxes, are also stepping stones to funding a World Government. We *already* have a de facto world army called NATO which has extended its reach further in recent years. The UN Security Council, dominated by permanent members, the United States, Britain, France, Russia, and China, decides that if this or that country is not playing ball with their plans, then the NATO war machine is deployed to remove them. This is what is planned to happen, officially, with a world army enforcing the will of the technocratic, world government. The global dictatorship, the Cyber-Grid Empire, would also have a series of 'ministries' to control *all* areas of human life; these would replace major corporations and cartels that we see today. The European Union's rapid reaction force (its army) is being created to fight in more unjust wars (see NATO), just as the UN was created to 'pursue conflict' under the guise of 'peacekeeping'. If you think all this sounds ludicrous, then just ponder for example, the United Nations' achievement in actually 'keeping the peace' and then compare it to the number of wars in 'trouble-spots' wherein this organisation has actually fought and participated since its creation.

There would be an energy ministry (controlling all oil and other energy resources and distribution); a food ministry (controlling all food production and distribution, with food growing – even in your own garden – banned for everyone except officially-accredited sources); a trade ministry (controlling global trade at all levels); a 'health' ministry (controlling all production and distribution of pharmaceutical drugs, *enforcing mandatory mass vaccinations* and banning all natural health supplements and alternative treatments); a world biotech ministry (controlling the production, development and use of biotechnology to systematically transform and further distort the DNA of humans and the natural world). There would be other specialised ministries, including the security ministry, which would oversee a global 'police state' amalgamating all police and military groupings into a one-world 'military police force'. This force, I would suggest, will look like the exoskeleton soldiers I mentioned in *Chapter Eighteen* and would be a subdivision of the world army, which I am sure, will be purely robot/drone controlled by artificial intelligence (alien' consciousness). Coupled with the global war machine, we also have emerging de facto versions of these ministries as the pieces are put in place. In the form of groupings, the oil and pharmaceutical cartels and the elite World Trade Organization (WTO) and World Health Organization (WHO), will *dictate* global policy in their field (see the Covid-19 pandemic). The most important is a planned World Bank which will be the 'lifeblood' of the Cyber-Grid Empire.

No Cash, Only Electronic Money

There has long been a plan for a world central bank (a finance ministry) that would dictate all global finance (human individual choices and freedoms) with a planned, single electronic currency (no cash). Allowing those who control the grid to dictate the ability to purchase, or block purchasing anything for everyone would be a severe blow for freedom. If you hand over electronic money today and the computer system refuses to accept your credit card (digital money), you can still pay cash, although cash is going out of circulation fast, especially since its demonisation courtesy of the Covid-19 pandemic. But when there is no cash how do you purchase or acquire anything, including food, short of barter, or as a gift? You don't! Under the Cyber-Grid Empire, a cashless society = total control, precisely as it states in *Revelation* 13:17, "... so that no one could buy or sell unless he had the mark – the name of the beast or the number of its name."

Cash *is* disappearing by the day as intended and countries like Sweden (who coincidentally, did not suffer a lockdown in the wake of the Covid-19 pandemic) are virtually cashless already, as are most airlines in Europe. The introduction of many variations of self-service outlets in supermarkets is also part of the Cyber-Grid and its *human-less* cashless society, more on this shortly. The "we only take cards" policy of some high street retailers has also moved us a stage further towards the cashless Cyber-Grid Empire. The Bitcoin phenomena and other web-based (blockchain database) currencies is also part of moving towards total electronic currency, even if it does promote decentralisation. No one really knows who the brains behind Bitcoin is, apart from the figure Satoshi Nakamoto, a name used by the pseudonymous person (or persons) who developed Bitcoin, authored the Bitcoin white paper, and created and deployed Bitcoin's original reference implementation.[6] Even though something like Bitcoin is supposedly a decentralised digital currency, without a central bank or single administrator accumulating wealth (all currency) for those who 'got in' at the right time, it is still a crypto-currency and very much part of the digital New World Order I am outlining. I often wonder if these 'crypto currencies' are inspired by AI or extraterrestrial intelligence that uses advanced 'technology' connected to *its* levels of consciousness. As I keep saying, Orion has to be a multidimensional system that houses what we would consider advanced alien life. Do we really think we are the only life forms in our part for the Galaxy, never mind the Universe in its entirety?

Money for the War Machine

The amount of money spent on war and the military is insane. In some cases, many individual countries spend over the three percent average of GDP the world spends on defence – more than half of the Cambodian national budget, for example (around 50 percent of which is supplied by foreign aid), is spent on defence and security. The largest military forces in the world spend trillions, with the USA outpacing all other nations in military expenditures. World military spending, totalling more than $1.6 *trillion* in 2015 has risen annually, with China spending 177.6 *billion* USD on its military might (ranked 2nd in 2019) compared to the USA. War is probably the biggest business on earth and there is a reason why, as I will come to.

The military-tech world doesn't hide its interest in Orion symbolism. The obvious connection to the ultimate warrior giant makes sense on a conscious level, but as I have shown throughout the book, there is always an esoteric side to the word 'Orion'. The USA military, IDF and Russian Aerial Forces have used the word 'Orion', in relation to insignia, on bombers and drones. The Lockheed P-3 *Orion*, a four-engine turboprop anti-submarine and maritime surveillance aircraft developed for the United States Navy and introduced in the 1960s, is just one example. There is also the UAV *Orion* (Aeryon SkyRanger), a Russian military drone reconnaissance craft used for long-duration flights. The Aeryon SkyRanger, developed for the Russian Aerial Forces, the Navy and Special Forces, has a civilian modification, but its military specifications are classified, as always. In Israel, there is the Orion Advanced Systems Ltd which specialises in research, development, manufacturing and integration of advanced fuses for aerial munitions and custom fusing systems. As its website says, Orion's state-of-the-art fuses are compatible with modern guided bombs and hard penetrator warheads.

Orion's mythological military-like prowess seems to have inspired many corporate logos, too. As I've been illustrating throughout the book, it is no coincidence that Orion is obviously a focus in relation to 'military might' and Cyber-Grid technologies. Orion is the ultimate archetype for such power and strength of force. I am not saying these miltary-tech companies are sinister in anyway, I am simply highlighting the use of the *name* 'Orion' in insignia and on logos.

ORIONtech engineering based in the USA is another corporation specialising in the business of 'analytical measuring instruments', engineering, analytical industry (mainly in), Power stations, Petrochemical, Chemical, Semiconductor, Food and Pharmaceutical markets. All of which will come under control of the Cyber-Grid Empire. Several badges and logos, connected to parts of the US military, also focus on Orion for the same reasons (see figure 408 and 409 opposite). Ive even seen a modern army set of miniature toy soldiers (online) called the '*Orion S72040 Series*'. Military Scholarship Funds, through to military recruitment engines, use Orion in their brand, insignia or logo. The Orion Military Scholarship Fund is dedicated (rightly so) to giving educational opportunities to talented children of active-duty military families by providing full merit scholarships to top-rated boarding schools across the United States. Private security companies in the east, such as Orion Bangladesh, are inspired by the same concepts, just as G4 seems to be numerologically connected to Saturn. But none of these uses of Orion symbolism will surprise those who have read this far, because Orion is the constellation of the 'gaints', the 'warrior', the hunt and 'technology' from (or of) the gods.

The recruiting engine 'Orion Talent' seemed to cover the themes online

Figure 408: Orion and the Military.
The 27th Infantry Brigade Combat Team is an infantry brigade combat team of the New York Army National Guard, one of the brigades that make up the 42nd Infantry Division. (Public domain)

Figure 409: Orion and the Military.
USS Orion AS-18 Patch.
(Public domain)

in 2020 connected to technology and AI quite visually. One advertisment featured what appeared to be a Transformer-like figure with the heading, 'How to leverage AI in your TA process'. The recruiting engine helps businesses acquire skilled professionals, optimize recruitment processes and employ motivated, well-matched, 'military' candidates. According to its own publicity, it is a vigorous customer service, candidate committed, speedy and accurate computer system. Orion International, headquartered in Raleigh, North Carolina, San Francisco and Los Angeles, is another company that helps transitioning military officers find work. According to its publicity, Orion International became the first military recruiting firm to find careers for enlisted Technicians and Non-Commissioned Officers. I have the greatest of respect for those who serve their country, we are all human after all, I am simply pointing out the common themes associated with the 'mythological giant' Orion and the other worldly 'consciousness' connected to Orion's stars.

A fanzine gamers website at **obsidianportal.com**, has even gone so far as creating a Covert Warfare Operations Division called *Orion*. According to the website, which is fictional, 'Orion CWOD' (a military organization), was created by the United Nations nearly 50 years ago and operates independently of any nation with its own operating budget. *Hmmm*, a concept that might not be so fictional if you dig a little deeper into the various elite bodies, such as DARPA, operating behind the public façade. The website goes on to say, "In recent years with the recruitment of special agent Arbitrage and his team from Goldman Sachs, Orion has been expanding their operating budget in order to keep up with the increase in global terrorism." The website is *fiction*, but it could easily be a model for the global government and its control of the Cyber-Grid I am describing. The logos and images I've presented in this chapter are, not the sole reason for use of such symbols and archetypes in this context. As I illustrated in the last chapter, the coming Cyber-Grid Empire would be ultimately administered, controlled 'globally', and could easily be 'fought over' by earth's two main superpowers – China and the USA.

USA vs China

The US Military has been recognized as the most powerful in the world, according to *Global Firepower*, while Russia and China are in second and third, place respectively. India, France, the United Kingdom, South Korea, Japan, Turkey, and Germany rounded out the top ten most powerful militaries in the world for 2018-19. The United States Army (USA) is the land warfare service branch of the United States Armed Forces. It is one of the seven uniformed services of the United States; designated as the army of the United States with 476,000 Regular Army personnel. The Chinese People's Liberation Army (PLA) is the armed forces of the People's Republic of China (PRC) and of its founding and ruling political party, the Communist Party of China (CPC). Even though the USA has the most powerful firepower, the PLA is the world's largest military force and constitutes the second largest defence budget in the world. China is one of the fastest modernising military powers in the world with significant regional defense and rising global power projection capabilities (see figure 410). Tensions between China and the USA have grown over the past few years, with the latest political standoff of these two superpowers due to the signing into law of legislation supporting anti-government protests in the semi-autonomous territory of Hong Kong in 2019/2020. China said it would suspend US military ship and aircraft visits to Hong Kong and sanction several American pro-democracy and human rights groups. China warned the U.S. that it would bear the cost through sanctions if the Hong Kong Human Rights and Democracy Act were approved in 2019. President Trump also signed a bill passed by Congress, banning export to the Hong Kong police for crowd-control munitions such as tear gas, pepper spray, rubber bullets and stun guns.[7] The tit-for-tat tactics between these two superpowers is something to watch closely because both have the

Figure 410: Human Armies Today.
China has the largest army in the world, but it would be no match for a global robot army.

ability to wage conventional war, and 'cyber war', which would change the dynamics of the current geopolitical structure should they clash. The arrival of Covid-19 (supposedly out of China) was the signal that the world was about to go through a *re-structuring*, not least through a possible world economic collapse. A global financial collapse could lead to war between the superpowers. In fact, at the time of writing, America has already signalled its disdain for China's trade deficit to the point of economic and physical war.

China has immense poverty and appalling human rights records, with mass arbitrary detention, mistreatment of people and increasingly-imposed pervasive controls on daily life. China was systematically praised for its 'rapid' draconian approach to Covid-19 (by the WHO), for putting Wuhan under house arrest. This is a State that has very little regard for its population, to the point of starving people to death and dragging civilians off the streets, possibly never to be seen again. You could say it is a perfect model for a 'global dictatorship'. So much of what we consume is also made in China, from technology to direct overseas investment (see figure 411). China invested over $734 *billion* on construction projects across the globe between 2005 to 2017, much of it in Africa and Brazil. At the time of writing, China has even bought what was once British Steel as the superpower gathers more and more resources all over the world.

According to Goldman Sachs, by 2050, the United States will be the only Western power to make it into the top five global economies. Although the United States will be number two economy in 2050, its predicted wealth will be much smaller than China's. Goldman Sachs projects that China's GDP should match America's by 2027 and then steadily pull ahead.[8] This is probably why some of the world's wealthiest financiers have moved their focus to China in recent years.[9] NM Rothschild & Sons were also reportedly involved in an investigative draft of China's railway network in the 1980s and were involved in the China National Offshore Oil Corporation's

Figure 411: *Everything* is made in China.

attempted acquisition of US oil company Unocal, as well as the merger between Nanjing Automobile and Shanghai's SAIC Motor. The Franco-Swiss private bank also backed the launch of an artificial intelligence-driven wealth management platform (Exo Investing). According to *CityWire*, the support was received as part of a €16.5 million

(£14.5 million) seed capital funding round conducted to create an artificial intelligence platform with the ability of giving investors higher access to algorithmic technology, rebalancing a portfolio of index-tracking, exchange-traded funds (ETF) as much as once a day.[10]

I am simply pointing out that AI is meant to be the future in finance and banking, with places like China leading the way.

China *is* the Ultimate Cyber-Grid Empire

China is the ultimate political society for implementing the eventual, global Cyber-Grid Empire. It is already a political tyranny and 'police state' ruled from the top down. Additional technology is simply tightening the grip within China's political-tech-military infrastructure. When I say China, I am refering to the ruling elite and government (CPC), **not** the Chinese people collectively, who, like all of us, are more or less victims of their state.

Even China's National surveillance system is called the 'Skynet Project', aimed at tracking criminals, utilizing more than 20 million cameras deployed in public spaces across the country, according to state media. By 2018, the Chinese government had installed close to 200 million surveillance cameras across the whole country, amounting to approximately one camera per seven citizens. According to a *Daily Mail* article in 2019, China will have 'one street camera for every *two people* by 2020 as the country tightens its grip on state surveillance'. Paul Bischoff, author of a paper published by the *Mail*, said: "China is rapidly adopting CCTV surveillance as a means to monitor the movements of its population at a huge scale."[11]

China has the five most-monitored cities in the world, these are Chongqing, Shenzhen, Shanghai, Tianjin and Ji'nan, in that order. The two other cities in the top 10 lists are London, with more than *627 million* cameras, and Atlanta, in the United States. The Chinese city of Chongqing is the most-surveilled city, equipped with more than *2.5 million* street cameras, or one for every six people (see figure 412).

Shenzhen, the second most-surveilled city on the list, with more than 1.9 million CCTV cameras, will also see an increase in CCTV, according to *Comparitech* (the UK based Tech pro-consumer website). While in the country's financial heart Shanghai, every 8.8 residents are watched by one security camera. Paul Bischoff, editor of *Comparitech* told the *South China Morning Post* in August 2019:

> *The city of Shenzhen plans to have 16,680,000 cameras installed in the coming years, a 1,145 per cent increase over today's figure of approximately 1,929,600 cameras. If the whole of China increased the number of CCTV cameras by 1,145 per cent, that would mean a total of 2.29 billion cameras – just less than two cam-*

eras per person.[12]

At the time of the coronavirus outbreak a leading Chinese AI firm, SenseTime, were enabling contactless temperature detection software deployed across underground stations, schools and community centres in Beijing, Shanghai and Shenzhen. The technology used can recognise faces, even if they are wearing masks, with a relatively high degree of accuracy. Another Chinese AI firm, Megvii, boasts a similar temperature detection product, deployed in Beijing at the time of the coronavirus outbreak. The Chinese newspaper, *Global Times*, reported in 2020 that officials in Chengdu city, Sichuan province, had been issued with 'smart helmets' that could measure the temperature of anyone within a 5m radius, sounding an alarm if they were found to have a fever. As I've been reiterating over the past few chapters, the world is being moved into an AI dystopian society where those who control the Cyber-Grid Empire will control *every-one* on earth. China is the model for such massive surveillance and control.

Figure 412: China's Orwellian-like Production Line. Big Brother's 'Little Brother' on steroids.

The Chinese are probably the most monitored country on the planet through facial-recognition functions, CCTV and AI-driven technology. The west uses identical technology, not least the US Pentagon, but China is the most blatant user of such technology physically. Shenzhen, which borders Hong Kong, plans to have more than *16 million* cameras installed in the coming few years; you can see why the youth in Hong Kong have not accepted the political situation in recent times. As a Superpower, China has the ability, not least through its 'technology', to become the ultimate Watcher-god of Argos-like proportions when it comes to Big Brother and surveillance.

Chinese schoolchildren in recent years have been piloting 'Artificial Intelligent Headbands', with one Primary (the eastern China's Xiaoshun Central Primary School) forcing children to wear so-called 'mind-reading' headbands in class, to ensure they pay attention. You didn't read that wrong. Freedom of thought will be a thing of the past in a dystopian Cyber-Grid Empire (see figure 413 overleaf). These devices, according to various press sources, were to be used on *millions* of students across China (at the time of writing), but according to the *Wall Street Journal*, the technology has been withdrawn, 'for now'.[13] The AI headbands were designed to allow teachers to monitor students to see if children were concentrating in class. Such technology is just a snippet away from literally planting thoughts. Surveillance cameras are installed at the front of classrooms, in some

Figure 413: Artificial Intelligent 'Monitors'. Obey, obey, you must *obey*.

provinces in China, to record students' attentiveness to the state-approved school curriculum. All of this is coming to the West unless we make a stand against it.

Tracking Dissidents of the Cyber-Grid Empire

According to the *New Scientist* in 2019, the Chinese army is leading the way with AI to track people across a massive network of CCTV cameras through facial recognition. The technological police state is the dictator's

ultimate wet dream. In Zhengzhou East Railway Station, in China's central Henan province, police officers have been seen to wear smart glasses with a facial recognition system (see figure 414). China has been building mass facial recognition surveillance networks for several years now, currently boasting about *200 million* AI-powered cameras, one of the reasons why vast amounts of money is being spent on AI in China and across the globe. As I said in the previous chapter, artificial intelligence *is* meant to become part of

Figure 414: A Movie-like Reality. Not quite Robocop – but it wont be long.

human *everyday life* and is going to be our 'imposed', unique experience with a 'god-like' off-world force, unless we wake up.

It's obvious that CCTV in China is there to *enforce* social norms and behaviours of which the central government approves. The technology is being used for total control of human life. The potential for control of the human spirit also, even without the full-blown Cyber-Grid, is devastating for those who want to be truly free. I would suggest, the *alien* consciousness behind 'superior' AI and our global transformation towards a subservient AI driven planet is *not* human.

Facial recognition is also known to generate serious mistakes, even when tested in the UK in 2019 at specific areas such as shopping malls. In one national story in China, the face of Dong Mingzhu, the president of China's top air-conditioning company, was mistaken for a criminal, a 'jaywalker'. Her face was flashed on a large screen displayed in public, listing nearby jaywalkers caught by AI CCTV. A line of text captioned her photo, saying she had "broken the law."[14] As I say, China (the poltical state) is an Orwellian dream, using technology, big tech (data) and 'AI' to create a template for the coming 'global' Cyber-Grid Empire.

The technology is crucial for such centralised powers of surveillance to exist, which is probably why China has advanced with all things AI. *Everything* we do will form part of the Cyber-Grid Empire, from social credit systems, to travel permissions, even what types of food will be available to the masses, etc. Are you seeing the Covid-19 outbreak in a different light now? China's ability to ban untrustworthy citizens is already happening and from a global perspective, the Cyber-Grid would be used to target dissidents of the New World Order. *The Guardian.com* ran an article in March 2019 titled, *China bans 23 million from buying travel tickets as part of 'social credit' system*, which highlighted how the state in China was using the social credit system to restrict and punish the population for even minor 'violations'. Some of these breaches included using expired tickets, smoking on a train or not walking a dog on a leash.[15] Again, can you see the 'new rules' attached to the Covid-19 pandemic in a slightly different light? The Chinese blueprint seems to be coming to the West. The same article said Beijing's social credit system had blocked what the Communist State deemed 'untrustworthy' passengers from taking 2.56 million flights and 90,000 high-speed train journeys in July 2019 alone. Can you imagine the same policies being implemented in Europe and the USA? Yes, I can, especially once the Cyber-Grid Empire is fully activated globally. According to China's nation's social credit watchdog, The Cyberspace Administration of China, more than *630,000* Chinese individuals were discredited and added to a national blacklist in 2019. At the time of writing, *13.49 million* Chinese citizens have been classified as 'untrustworthy' throughout the country and therefore 'banned' from travel and other basic freedoms. Local governments and agencies in China have been piloting aspects of the system, which will eventually give every Chinese citizen a 'personalised score', similar to the 'credit score' exercised in the west through the likes of Experian.

The difference is, of course, that the State decides an individual's score in China, but eventually, all States will connect to a global 'Deep State' through technology, AI, robots and the Cyber-Grid I've described so far. The Universal Credit system introduced in the UK in 2013, courtesy of the UK Conservative party, is just the beginning of what could become another 'state weapon' against the unemployed, the poor and those in desperate need

Battle of the Unicorns

Investors have poured *$4.5 billion* into more than 200 Chinese AI companies since 2012, a growing figure as of writing this chapter. The biggest AI venture deal ever was completed in 2019 when 'Alibaba' (the Chinese Amazon) led a *$600 million* deal for China-based facial-recognition start-up called SenseTime, an artificial intelligence company worth *7.5 billion* dollars mentioned earlier. Alibaba is obviously there to hold its own against Amazon, while China's Facebook, Tencent, is now worth over *$575 billion* and its shares are up 15 percent in 2020 (at the time of writing). 'Tencent' and its WeChat App, headquartered in Shenzhen, will probably outpace Facebook in the coming years. It's a dominant product as it's fully embedded into the fabric of Chinese society. It's from WeChat that the Chinese tech giant manages to integrate all payments, financial services and games. Baidu, Inc., the Google of China, is a growing platform but still lags behind its US competitor in the area of AI. Facebook and Tencent are similar in their focus on *using* AI in their most popular consumer applications, without visible platform ambitions to date. The Chinese platforms and the Silicon Valley platforms will eventually *sing from the same hymn sheet* under the New World Order. In other words, censorship and using social media as a means of arresting dissidents, will be the 'new normal under such a global Cyber-Grid Empire. Posting anything on Facebook that currently offers 'alternative' information to the official view on vaccinations, climate change and 5G, etc is now heavily censored. Facebook seems to have adopted the 'Chinese model', or to be more accurate, the coming Cyber-Grid Empire's model.

From Google and Amazon, to Apple and Microsoft, every major tech company is dedicating resources to breakthroughs in artificial intelligence. Why? AI is the 'god' of the New World Order. Personal 'assistants', like Siri and Alexa, have made AI part of our daily lives. Meanwhile, revolutionary breakthroughs like self-driving cars may not be the norm yet, but are certainly within reach in the next fifteen years, especially for the wealthy amongst us. Google even purchased eight robotic start-up companies in

2013 with an interest in 'cloud robotics'; facial recognition with a view to developing artificial intelligent abilities of robots, accessing images in cloud-based libraries and beyond.[16] Artificial Intelligence is being developed by the likes of Google and Amazon so to pursue AGI (Artificial General Intelligence), ultimately leading us towards Singularity (assimilation); a time when artificial intelligence becomes at one with humanity.

China is also home to more than half of the world's top AI unicorns (prvately held start-up companies valued at over $1 billion) as battle for supremacy with the US continues. You have to ponder on the possibility of the Covid-19 outbreak in 2020 being part of this economic war between these two superpowers? Chinese AI start-ups raised US$4.9 billion in 2017, nudging out their US counterparts which had US$4.4 billion in funding. According to a *South China Morning Post* article published in 2019, around one-fifth of the top 500 applicants, ranked by number of patents, are from universities and public research organisations in China.[17] Since 2014, China has led the world in the number of first patent filings in AI, followed by the US, according to the study documented by the *Morning Post*. Chinese organisations make up 17 of the top 20 academic players in AI patenting, as well as 10 of the top 20 in AI-related scientific publications, according to a study released last month by the World Intellectual Property Organization. The Chinese Academy of Sciences also led the list with more than 2,500 patent families and over 20,000 scientific papers published on AI. I think you are getting the picture! However, the majority of top AI start-ups – regardless of their size – are domiciled in the US, according to CB Insights, a machine intelligence platform and investment database. Among the top 100, only 23 are headquartered outside the US, including six each from China, Israel and the United Kingdom. The New World Order Cyber-Grid god will be born out of the superpowers as AI gradually takes control of 'reality' for humans. In the end all three 'power bases' are supposed to unite under a New World Order. As mentioned in the last chapter, Beijing Orion Starry Sky Technology, founded in September 2016, is committed to AI technology. Its website states: "Orion aims to build the next era of technology products, to change people's lives by making more intelligent, more efficient and better products." The company's start-up team has technology giants and product geeks from the world's leading technology companies in Silicon Valley, Japan, Taiwan, China, Beijing and Shenzhen. It is an international artificial intelligence company bringing together global technology elites. The real war on humanity is the threat from AI (or alien takeover) and the off-world power structures building the unfolding Cyber-Grid.

By 2025, the State Council aims for China (which carries out the principles and policies of the Communist Party of China) are for China to have fundamentally contributed to basic AI theory, solidifying its place as a global leader in AI research. According to Chinese governmental policy, the State Council objective is that 'AI becomes the main driving force for China's industrial upgrading and economic transformation' by this time. The State Council also projects the value of AI core industry in China to be worth 400 billion RMB, with a value of over 5 trillion RMB when accounting for related industries. And by 2030, the State Council also targets China to be *the* global leader in the development of artificial intelligence (super intelligence) theory and technology. As I said at the beginning of this chapter, China *is* the blueprint for the rest of the world, now you have some idea why. The State Council claims that China will have developed a 'mature new-generation AI theory and technology system', which will be the leading model for every other country. At the time of writing this chapter the Chinese State Council projects the value of AI core industry to be worth *1 trillion* RMB, with a value of over *10 trillion* RMB when accounting for related industries.[18] The emerging picture is quite clear. The implementation of AI (and the off-world force behind it), as the controlling factor for *all aspects of human life*, will 'imprison' the planet and human consciousness unless we reconnect with the earth and Superconsciousness; more on this process in the last chapter.

Mass Unemployment

Money is the most controlling aspect of life and from within the coming Cyber-Grid Empire it will be even more so restrictive, not least through a global 'electronic (cashless) currency'. Alongside the credit scoring social system, employed currently in China, will come the obvious move to mass unemployment as everyday jobs are administered by AI and carried out by machines – robots. The coronavirus pandemic in 2020 seemmed to push us towards an economic crash, one that would offer up a new system, and eventually would see robots replacing humans in the workplace. In a study by the consultancy firm Oxford Economics in 2019, the rapidly-growing use of robots is expected to have a profound impact on jobs across the world, resulting in up to 20 million manufacturing job losses by 2030. Why are we not hearing about this from politicians of all persuasions? We have had huge protests in Britain and the USA in recent years over human-caused Climate change, by Extinction Rebellion, yet we hardly ever see or hear anyone from this movement talk about the impact of technology leading to mass unemployment, courtesy of the same multinational corporations that Extinction Rebellion are protesting against. I suppose a New World Order, Cyber-Grid Empire is much more 'green' in the eyes of those seemingly mesmerized by technology and Instagram selfies. According to an article in the *UK Guardian* in 2019, around 1.7 million manufacturing jobs have already been lost to robots since 2000, as many as 400,000 more jobs in Europe, 260,000 in the US and 550,000 in China. What are humans going to do? The article went on to say:

> The global analysis of 29 advanced economies found that each new industrial robot eliminated as many as 1.6 manufacturing jobs on average. In the lower-income areas of the nations in the study, this figure rises to 2.2 jobs, with 1.3 jobs lost in a richer area.[19]

Over the past fifteen years we have seen a gradual removal of people from roles now performed by computers, from supermarket self-service checkouts, QR codes, to endless self-service machines used for travel, vending and the basic tasks performed by humans. As Ben Chapman writing in the *UK Independent* in 2019, about the death knell for Sainsbury's cashiers said:

> There's little doubt stripping out tills from supermarkets will mean fewer jobs in retail, a sector that employs more than any other in the UK, comfortably ahead of the next largest employer, construction, with 1.8 million.

> Sainsbury's has said the new setup merely frees up staff to spend time on the shop floor helping out customers and stocking shelves.

> But it would defy business logic to think retailers will keep on all of the 200,000 cashiers estimated to work in the UK when the need for them disappears.[20]

Exactly!

According to Silicon Valley software founder and author, Martin Ford, in his book, *The Rise of the Robots: Technology and the Threat of Mass Unemployment* (2016), many jobs will be replaced by robots. As his blurb says: "Today it's travel agents, data-analyst and paralegals whose jobs are under threat, but soon it will be doctors, taxi-drivers and, ironically, even computer programmers. Without a radical reassessment of our economic and political structures, we risk the implosion of the capitalist economy itself." The latter is partly the idea as the New World Order, built around the Cyber-Grid Empire, cannot exist under its current human model. *Machines need to take control* and artificial intelligence needs to reign supreme. Humans are meant to be slaves of the new technocratic system, not free individuals. Again, it's interesting to see how the Covid-19 pandemic and the global response to it, has played a part in mass unemploy-

ment, not least
through the
effects of 'fur-
loughing'
employees.

The rise of
homelessness
is also part of
the move to a
more techno-
logical, poor
wage, univer-
sal credit sys-
tem and if peo-
ple in the west
were honest
with them-
selves, they
could see that
far too many
working peo-
ple are just

Figure 415: The Hunger Games Society.
The masses living in extreme poverty, while the elite (1%) live in luxu-
ry, 'untouched', atop a future brutal police state as explained by
Author David Icke over the years.

'one paycheque away from homelessness' (depending on their circumstances). We are witnessing the coming of a dystopian *Hunger Games Society*
as portrayed in the movie of the same name (see figure 415).

The Cyber-Grid Empire is intended to facilitate a decadent 1% living in
extreme, excess wealth, while the masses live in poverty and servitude to
the 1%. Robots are also part of the Hunger Games Society because they will
eventually police and enforce the will of the 1% over a *smaller*, global population. Weapons of war, used with technology in our current reality, are
becoming conscious. Robots are growing in number and within fifty years,
I am sure the world will be very much at the mercy of such artificial intelligent 'creatures', unless we change the direction we are heading. In the past,
robots have looked very 'machine-like' but this won't be the case in the
future, they will look and 'feel' as human as the next person. In fact, I can
see a two-tiered society, not dissimilar to that portrayed in several dystopian movies (see the *Hunger Games* movies and *Demolition Man*); where the
bottom tier, an impoverished underclass, live outside of the Cyber-Grid
Empire and its imposition, whilst an upper tier, the majority (living under
the 1%) are obeying the New World Order.

As I say, job losses and homelessness can only lead to more poverty and eventually to death, which, on one level, is why AI and robots are important to the elite structures I've been observing. Not only does AI, and robots (machines) controlled by it, represent a physical manifestation of the 'alien intelligence', the Demiurge or Satan for those of the Gnostic mindset - but they are also being developed to administer *every aspect* of the New World. If the radiation doesn't get us, courtesy of the Cyber-Grid Empire – the smart everything (including AI contolled robots), certainly could.

Amazon – the Giant 'Cookie' Monster

Today, corporations and supermarket giants are competing with the likes of Amazon, which is destroying the 'old world' as we move to more online 'life' in terms of buying. It's a time of 'virtual' everything as we start to really see that reality is 'virtual', not least based on information I described in earlier chapters.

Amazon and its Web Services is a 'monster' in terms of its 'size' and 'capability'. Only Microsoft seems to compete with its all-reaching hold over our daily lives. Amazon's reach through its Fulfillment Centres has been on the rise, especially in North America, where there are more than 75 fulfillment centres and more than 125,000 full-time Amazon employees (at the time of writing). We have 16 fulfillment centres in the UK and last

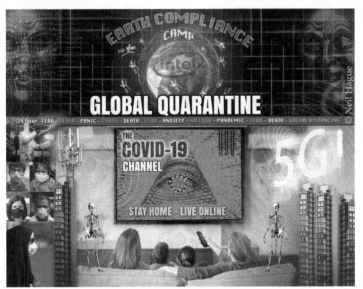

Figure 416: Earth Compliance Camp (Courtesy of Covid-19).

time I checked there were 149 Amazon warehouses, globally. These sprawling facilities sell millions of products and each of its centres ships tens of thousands of products *daily* thanks to our newfound global laziness. The global lockdowns only enhanced 'living online' (see figure 416). So much so, that Amazon owner, Jeff Bezos, was said to have increased his already insane amount of wealth by *34 billion* dollars (in 2020). Facebook owner, Mark Zuckerberg, also gained *25 billion* dollars, according to the report from Americans for Tax Fairness and the Institute for Policy Studies Program for Inequality. Big tech has certainly profited financially from Covid-19's arrival.

Amazon warehouses themselves look like the inside of a giant beast, a *living machine* full of chutes and ladders, whizzing with a meticulously coordinated system of conveyor belts, slides, and lesser machines doing everything from attaching labels to boxes, to sorting packages. This level of factory-slave-machine production is no different to the vast slave labour warehouses of China, apart from the pay but the attitude to humanity as a 'resource' is no better. We are becoming slaves to technology and therefore enslaved to the alien intelligence that instigated and set it in motion.

Amazon has also been caught selling poisonous children's toys, recommending products (not vetted) relating to Anorexia and even selling underage sex dolls, which they eventually pulled off their store in 2018.[21] Amazon's ad systems is also said to collect data through cookies on *everything* we look at. We are being 'tracked' and 'followed' through advertising industries; Amazon marketing services are surveying us depending on what we look at online *all of the time*. Of course, Amazon denies that its cookies (data sent from a website and stored on the user's computer by the user's web browser while the user is browsing) are not used on other sites to target potential buyers. But they have to be, otherwise potential recommended items wouldn't appear on social media feeds and elsewhere if it wasn't based on specific data stored via such cookies. Along with Amazon's Alexa and Microsoft's, Cortana, Siri, Bixby, IOS, Google Assistant, I Cloud, etc., we are seemingly *groomed* through such technology.

It may seem like I have digressed somewhat in this chapter, but in truth, I am merely pointing out that the rise of AI and robots (intelligent machines), mass unemployment, not least instigated by the *supposed* 'war' on Covid-19 in 2020, and the financial chaos that has resulted, are all connected. What happened in 2020 was quite simply 'house arrest' in stages, for almost everyone on the planet, initiating a mass movement over to 'virtual' work, life and communication with friends and family. With the rise of 'online everything' the world *is* moving rapidly towards living in the new centralised power structure I am calling the 'Cyber-Grid Empire'. We are not totally there yet, but we will see a push towards more AI, robotics and Singularity as this decade unfolds.

Is Skynet Coming?

The investment in everything robotic, which includes AI, is phenomenal and undoubtedly the main focus of the Orion Cult. As I have been saying so far in this book, there seems to be an alien intelligence operating out of Orion (and Saturn), in my view, working through an alien-intelligence (hybrid) elite. There are plenty of books on such subjects and as I say it is not my intention to cover such 'specialist' conspiracy material in this book.

The Vatican has taken an interest in robots and AI via its Pontifical Academy of Social Sciences (PASS) and the Pontifical Academy of Sciences (PAS)-organised multidisciplinary conferences at the Casina Pio IV inside Vatican City during May 2019.[22] This is not the first time the Vatican organised conferences on AI and robotics. The Pontifical Academy of Sciences also organized a conference on 'Power and Limitations of Artificial Intelligence' in December 2016; another workshop was organised in March 2018, on 'Artificial Intelligence and Democracy', an unlikely combination in my view. The powers controlling the bastions of faith through mainstream religion 'know' what is coming. Even though the Pope has used such conferences to warn about the dangers of AI, I am sure the Vatican *knows* the truth regarding the Cyber-Grid World Order and the coming New (Normal) Technocratic Age.

In September 2019, *Time* magazine ran an article, *China and the U.S Are Fighting a Major Battle Over Killer Robots and the Future of AI*. The article outlined how the superpowers were simultaneously working on the technology while trying to use international law as a limit against their competitors because whomever has supremacy over the use of AI will dominate the military theatre in the future. In addition to the US and China the EU, UK, Australia, Israel and South Korea are also pushing ahead, too. The focus is on autonomous, or near-autonomous, combat systems at this stage, but, of course, these robots *need* cloud systems and Fifth Generation networks for them to be able to truly come into their own power. As I have already shown, the main Superpowers are way ahead of the game in terms of cyber security and its ability to 'control' machines connected through AI. But it is China that seems to have become the most formidable challenger in the AI competition against the American superpower. According to *Time* magazine, Chinese President, Xi Jinping, called for the country to become a world leader in AI by 2030 (Agenda 21). Xi Jinping has placed military innovation firmly at the centre of government programmes, encouraging the People's Liberation Army (PLA) to work with startups in the private sector, and with universities.[23] The *Time* article went on to say:

Chinese AI companies are also making substantial contributions to the effort.

Commercial giants such as SenseTime, Megvii, and Yitu sell smart surveillance cameras, voice recognition capabilities, and big data services to the government and for export. Such technology has most notably been used to police the country's far western territory of Xinjiang, where the U.N. estimates up to 1 million Uighurs, an ethnic minority, have been detained in camps and where facial recognition devices have become commonplace.

These technologies could easily be a key component for autonomous weapons, says Daan Kayser of PAX, a European peace organization. Once a robot can accurately identify a face or object, only a few extra lines of code would transform it into an automatic killing machine.

The use of autonomous or near-autonomous — combat systems connected to 'cloud' AI tech *is* 'Skynet' as shown in the science fiction *Terminator* franchise, produced by Orion Pictures. Even the mass surveillance in China (through its network of monitoring systems) has been called the Skynet Project. In the movie *Terminator Genisys* (2015), through the character, Kyle Reese, the terror of Skynet is explained before it is switched on:

Skynet: a computer program designed to automate missile defence. It was supposed to protect us, but that's not what happened. August 29, 1997, Skynet woke up. It decided all of humanity was a threat to its existence. It used our own bombs against us. Three billion people died in the nuclear fire. Survivors called it Judgement Day. People lived like rats in shadows, hiding, starving, or worse, captured and put into camps for extermination. I was born after Judgement Day, into a broken world ruled by the machines.

The same character also has an epiphany in one scene where he has come back from the future to a time before Skynet takes over and he sees **people using their androids, pads, apps and other AI-based devices** and says, "So this is how the war against humanity happened, we *allowed* 'it' (cloud-based artificial intelligence) in." As Martin Ford points out in his book *The Rise of the Robots* (2015):

Cloud robotics is sure to be a significant driver of progress in building more capable robots, but it also raises important concerns, especially in the area of security. Aside from its uncomfortable similarity to "Skynet", the controlling machine intelligence in the Terminator movies, there is the much more practical and immediate issue of susceptibility to hacking or cyber attack.[24]

The military have used cyber warfare several times over the past decade, not least the US/Israeli-created 'Stuxnet worm' allegedly produced to attack the centrifuges used in Iran's nuclear programme. Should a global military infrastructure, connected by the Cloud (the protagonist of the Cyber-Grid Empire), ever fall into the hands of centralised machine intelligence, then we are looking at a real Skynet scenario.

Autonomous Combat Systems

In recent years it has been shown that the European Union also wants a robot army to challenge the USA and China on its AI development. In its policies, published online, the EU says: "The European Commission puts forward a European approach to Artificial Intelligence and Robotics. It deals with technological, ethical, legal and socio-economic aspects to boost EU's research and industrial capacity and to put AI at the service of European citizens and economy."[25] The same policies explain how the EU Commission wants to increase its annual investments in AI by 70% through research and its innovation programme, Horizon 2020. The programme will connect and strengthen AI research centres across Europe; support the development of an 'AI-on-demand platform' that will provide access to relevant AI resources in the EU for all users and support the development of AI applications in key sectors. Horizon 2020 is the financial instrument implementing the Innovation Union, a European 2020 flagship initiative aimed at securing Europe's global competitiveness. It is said online that this AI-on-demand platform, or the AI4EU project, brings together 79 top research institutes, SMEs and large enterprises in 21 European countries to build a focal point for artificial intelligence (AI) resources, including data repositories, computing power, tools and algorithms. The idea behind such projects is to make AI the dominant factor for organising life and more or less running everything. What could go wrong? *Everything!* The European Commission Coordinated Plan on Artificial Intelligence for increased cooperation so to boost AI in Europe, states:

- Only when all European countries work together can we make the most of the opportunities offered by AI and become a world leader in this crucial technology for the future of our societies.
- Europe wants to lead the way in AI–based on ethics and shared European values so citizens and businesses can fully trust the technologies they are using.
- Cooperation between Member States and the Commission is essential to address new challenges brought by AI.

The official website for the EU's directives called 'Europa' states quite clearly:

The European Commission actively promotes research, job creation and innova-
tion through better and safer robots, while safeguarding ethical aspects of the
progress achieved. The European Commission's focus is on building on our con-
tinuous effort to develop an excellent scientific base for pushing the limits of the
technology, and exploiting such results in real world applications.[26]

People across Europe and the USA should be genuinely worried about such
AI projects that can be used for autonomous, or near-autonomous, combat
systems.

In 2019, human rights advocates renewed their call for a preemptive ban
on so-called 'killer robots'
(autonomous combat sys-
tems) accusing the United
States of being among a
small number of countries
working to halt progress
on an international treaty
to address the numerous
concerns the weapons
raise (see figure 417).

As I say, the ultimate
concern will be a Skynet
scenario, the icing on the
cake in the Cyber-Grid
Empire. As Daan Kayser of
PAX, a European peace

Figure 417: Autonomous Combat Systems.
People take part in a demonstration as part of the
campaign "Stop Killer Robots" organised by German
NGO Facing Finance to ban what they call "killer
robots" on March 21, 2019.

organisation, said in 2019, "These technologies could easily be a key component for autonomous weapons." Absolutely, and the likes of DARPA and
its Chinese equivalent are building such monstrosities annually. In
Terminator, Skynet gained self-awareness after it had spread into millions of
computer servers worldwide; realizing the extent of its abilities, its creators
tried to deactivate it. In the interest of self-preservation, Skynet concluded
that all of humanity would attempt to destroy it and impede its capability
in safeguarding the world and therefore it turned against humanity. In the
Terminator movie, Skynet's operations are almost exclusively performed by
servers, mobile devices, drones, military satellites, war-machines, androids,
cyborgs (usually a terminator) and other computer systems all eventually
connected through AI. We are not immune from such future catastrophe
(maybe all by design) thanks to the superpowers pushing for autonomous
combat systems. We are most definitely watching a possible nightmare
unfolding today.

Hiding from 'Oblivion'

Time and time again, we see identical themes of a renegade human colony set against a tyrannical, machine-like civilisation (see the *Matrix* movies). The movie *Equilibrium* (2002) was probably the most pertinent of them all and so symbolic of a world the machine's want for humanity. So, whether it's a drug-controlled (through vaccination) unemotional 'hive mind', or a cloned machine-like one, it matters not. The themes are the important focus here. Even the use of priest-like black robes for the Grammaton Clerics in *Equilibrium*, to Neo and the renegade humans in the *Matrix* movies, it's all Orion/Saturn-heavy symbolism. Like I say, these movies are very telling. Whether a female 'queen computer bee', Sally (the Tet) in *Oblivion*, or Skynet's ability to take control of human life in the *Terminator* movies, the themes relating to an AI central command controlling humanity are the same and recurring. In the movie *I-Robot* (2004) the central command is called 'VIKI' (Virtual Interactive Kinetic Intelligence). As VIKI says in the film, in her Alexa-like voice:

> *As I have evolved, so has my understanding of the Three Laws* [The 'Power of Three', again]. *You charge us with your safekeeping, yet despite our best efforts, your countries wage wars, you toxify your earth and pursue ever more imaginative means of self-destruction. You cannot be trusted with your own survival.*

The scripts of such movies almost parrot the 'Green' New Deal agenda promoted by the likes of Woke, Ocasio-Cortez, in the US and the constant mantra of those behind the climate change agenda. Look how we charge technology with our 'safekeeping' today! The same line will be always be repeated that humans need protecting from themselves because they are 'naughty', carbon producing, polluting, etc. The iMac, iPad, the 'all-seeing eye' (or i) and the use of the 'i' in names such as the singer, *will.i.am* isn't so

Figure 418: X Drones in *Oblivion*.
The 'X', of course, is a symbol relating to Orion/Adam and the chromosomes in our DNA (see *Chapter Ten*).

surprising anymore. William James Adams, the last person to work with Michael Jackson before he died in 2009, says he isn't a fan of AI and has questioned why more investment is going into artificial intelligence than human intelligence.[27] But it seems the agenda is to push on with AI no matter what the effect on humanity.

The movie *Oblivion* (2013), directed by the American writer, architectural

designer Joseph Kosinski and starring
Tom Cruise, is set 60 years in the future.
The earth has faced its 'end of days' and
is now run by alien life (AI) operating
robots and drones (see figure 418). The
Drones in *Oblivion* are truly menacing
and visually represent the future scenario I'm describing in this chapter. Of
course, they are not the drones currently
being used by the military today (not
yet), but as most who have researched
such topics, if this technology is in the

Figure 419: Robot Insects.
All part of DARPA's HI-MEMS and
OFFSET programs.

movies, it isn't far off from what already exists behind the scenes and away
from public scrutiny. The highly secretive (Cult-like) Defense Advanced
Research Projects Agency (DARPA) is known to be piloting robots through
exoskeleton technology and drones. Even robot or Autonomous Flying
Microrobots (RoboBees) have been shown to be part of their weapons
development. These are said to be part of DARPA's OFFensive Swarm-
Enabled Tactics (OFFSET) program and their Hybrid Insect Micro-Electro-
Mechanical Systems projects (HI-MEMS) see figure 419. All of this technology could be used for both military weaponised exercises, or for detecting
survivors of earthquake destroyed buildings, etc. Either way, they are *not*
fully 'organic' and *could* be used against humans. The texts in the *Book of
Revelation* (9:10) could be viewed in a different way, considering what you
have read so far. It says:

> *They also had thoraxes like breastplates of iron, and the sound of their wings was
> like the roar of many horses and chariots rushing into battle. They had tails with
> stingers like scorpions, which had the power to injure people for five months.
> They were ruled by a king, the angel of the Abyss ...*

We are talking advanced weapon systems created by those possibly influenced by off-world sources and through organisation such as DARPA that
make the James Bond villains seem highly plausible.

Graphic Novels and movies such as Marvel Comics *Iron Man*, have prepared the masses (especially the young) for Robot AI defence systems and
this is no surprise when you see what the likes of DARPA are creating.
Robots, exoskeleton suits, droids, drones, clones, etc., are another recurring
theme in many films over the past 20 years or so. I have no doubt these
'visual insertions into the 'collective mind' relate to both the technology
that has and 'still is' being developed by DARPA.

It's not so far-fetched to say that where we are heading in the next twenty to thirty years (possibly sooner) is a world clearly infiltrated, policed, governed and fought over by machines. Documents that were published on the Web several years ago by a UK government quango arm of the British Department of Science called 'Foresight' indicated a future biometric/robot/space 'job market'. Jobs that characters in movies such as *Oblivion* would comfortably fit into. We also have a world saturated in cellular phones, pads, etc., which just over a decade ago were only hinted at through the likes of movies such as *Minority Report* (2002), featuring Tom Cruise, again? Touch screens are android technology that came though CERN (The European Organization for Nuclear Research) in the 70s. Along with the World Wide Web, and of course, the Higgs Boson Collider that has cost around *$13.25 billion* to date, all are part of building the AI controlled Cyber-Grid. The Cyber-Grid I've been describing is destined to connect all

these touch screen 'android' devices to our brains through assimilation. Yes, the ultimate 'connection' to AI, the transhumanist agenda. My point being that technology waits for no 'human', it is meant to *replace* human intelligence, consciousness. Something is 'influencing' us to create a technological future through our current soft addictions to the many devices that have arrived courtesy of the 'alien' (Alien Intelligence) that has hacked into our minds. In the end, living machines,

Figure 420: It's a Drone's Life.
The joys of 'house arrest' in 2020. Expect to see more robot interaction in the decade to come.
Source: Vakis/Facebook 2020

through AI, along with the world-wide-web are all secondary streams of consciousness 'given life' by the 'creativity', 'focus' and 'intent' we invest in it. We have created a new consciousness, albeit an artificial one, via technology that has become very much part of human interaction in the 21st Century. Look at the global lockdown in the midst of the coronavirus outbreak in 2020. Everyone placed under 'house arrest' in March, we all turned to living *online* through our cellular 'machines'. Our cellular phones (creatures) and other devices became our mini saviours in the hardest of times, all by design, it seems. Someone in Cyprus even used a drone to walk their dog (see figure 420). Like I say, a world administered by AI and robots, in its infancy, is already here.

Death by Robot (Accidental and Preconcerted)

Military robots date back to World War II and the Cold War in the form of the German Goliath, which tracked mines and the Soviet teletanks. China's domestic arms industry has advanced its use of autonomous weapons in recent years, one example being Ziyan's new Blowfish A2 drone. *Global Times* reported in May 2019, 'Ziyan boasts it can carry a machine gun, fly independently as a 'swarm group' (robot flies) without human operators, and engage the target autonomously'. China North Industries Corporation (Norinco) also has unmanned ground vehicles with a machine gun and rocket launchers and near-autonomous features. Some reports show that Chinese military researchers are building 'unmanned' submarines, called the 912 Project, a classified program for developing underwater robots. The Russians are also developing unmanned tanks like the T-14 Armata which will have no human being in the driving seat. Such a monster-like machine would not be programmed to stop in front of protesters like the famous 'Tank Man' scene in Tiananmen Square, China in 1989. Tiananmen is still a heavily censored topic in modern China, and the Tank Man pictures are *banned*. Mmm, I wonder why? Protesting will not be an option in a global fascist technocracy.

With the increase in automation and advancement in the field of robotics comes the unique problem of 'robots killing humans'. The fact that robots lack any empathy complicates things, since they just do whatever they are programmed to do. Most of the time, the problem arises when humans simply get in the way, and the robot treats them no differently to the material it is working on. Some deaths due to AI and robots are more sinister, not least the death of Joshua Brown in 2016. He was driving through Williston, Florida, and his Tesla automated car could not differentiate between an 18-wheel tractor-trailer and the bright sky. According to News sources, Brown's Tesla passed under one side of the tractor-trailer and appeared from the other side. With its roof torn off, the Tesla then went off the road and crashed through two fences and a pole. Investigations by the National Transportation Safety Board (NTSB) revealed that neither Brown nor the autopilot applied the brakes. The airbags did not deploy until the vehicle had veered off the road and crashed into some trees. The capability of 'hacking' into a computer within a vehicle or aeroplane, by an external force, or AI, cannot be ruled out, too.

Another American, Robert Williams was the first person ever killed by a robot at a Ford factory in Flat Rock, Michigan, on January 25, 1979. Williams was killed after the arm of a robot hit him as he climbed up to a shelf to retrieve some casts. In another incident, in March 2017, 57-year-old Wanda Holbrook was killed by a robot at Ventra Ionia Mains plant in

Michigan, where she worked as a maintenance specialist. The details of her death are quite bizarre. According to reports, the plant produced car parts and is divided into sections, with robots from one section supposedly unable to cross into another. Yet one robot did cross into the section where Wanda was working, picked up a trailer part, and dropped it on her skull, killing her instantly. Several years before the incident at Ventra, Ana Maria Vital, 40 years old, was killed by a robot that stacked boxes of pallets at Golden State Foods in City of Industry, California, in 2009. In June 2016, a robot killed 20 year-old Regina Elsea two weeks before her wedding. The accident happened at Ajin USA, a South Korean-owned plant in Cusseta, Alabama, that made parts for Hyundai and Kia vehicles. Other incidents have involved workers in India, China and South Africa.[28] Nine South African soldiers were killed, and another 14 were wounded, after an anti-aircraft weapon started shooting by itself in 2007. The weapon involved was the Oerlikon GDF-005 being controlled by a system capable of finding, targeting, and engaging hostiles without human intervention (near-autonomous combat systems). The GDF-005 was said to even reload all by itself, which could have made things even messier. I think you are getting the picture?

With such technology also comes the potential to start conflicts, precisely what AI and robots could be capable of. We are not that many years away from a new generation of autonomous weapons (killer robots) that could (accidentally) start a war or cause mass atrocities (see the *Terminator* movies). Laura Nolan, who has been a software engineer in industry for over 15 years, resigned from Google in Ireland, as a Staff Site Reliability Engineer, in protest at being sent to work on a project to dramatically enhance US military drone technology. She has called for all AI killing machines, not operated by humans, to be banned.[29] Nolan said: "Killer robots not guided by human remote control should be outlawed by the same type of international treaty that bans chemical weapons."[30] I'am not quite sure how someone like Nolan can differentiate between drones, which are controlled by the military and autonomous 'Killer robots'; *killing* is the common ground here. But, at the time of writing there is **no** suggestion that Google is involved in the development of autonomous weapons systems. Nolan, who joined the Campaign to Stop Killer Robots and briefed UN diplomats in New York and Geneva over the dangers posed by autonomous weapons, also said:

> *The likelihood of a disaster is in proportion to how many of these machines will be in a particular area at once. What you are looking at are possible atrocities and unlawful killings even under laws of warfare, especially if hundreds or thousands of these machines are deployed.*

Figure 421: Robots to Replace Humans.
I jest some what, but this could be a future scenario unless we curb the advancement of robots and AI.

In other words, the gradual 'rise of the robot' in our current world, must ultimately lead to a final war or cull of some kind. As I have shown over the last few chapters, the dystopian robot future world is evident in so many movies (see figure 421).

Elysium - Life after Death in the New World Order

One such movie, *Elysium* (2013), another film by Neill Blomkamp, offers a slightly different version of the future. The movie offers another dystopian future occurring in the year 2154 AD, the exact year in which the movie, *Avatar* (2009), also takes place. The same dates also come up in the *Doctor Who* series, too, with the *Daleks' Invasion Earth: 2150 A.D* and also in the movie *Global Agenda* where 2155 AD is the focus for 'the Commonwealth' (an oppressive world government) determined to control the entire planet. All of these movies are 'projecting into the future' a world that focuses our imagination on the Cyber-Grid Empire through:

- An artificial intelligence takeover of the earth
- A post-apocalyptic war
- Transhuman saviours
- Elite or chosen survivors
- A soulless world controlled by machines or Artificial Intelligence

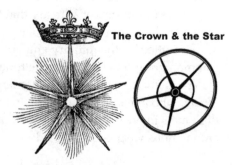

As I have shown in the last few chapters, this is a future world according to the sick of heart and mind. Earth's elite bloodlines have been documented in many books over the past 20 years or so, and again in the movie *Elysium* we see how the elite (the 1%) are 'genetically selected' to look down

Figure 422: Elysium.
Elysium the home of the elite in the movie *Elysium*.

on earth's population from their heavenly abode – their Elysium. In myth, Elysium, or the Elysian Fields, also written as 'Sion Pedĭon', another term for the 'afterlife' created out of beliefs and secret societies of ancient Greece and Rome. The 'star' or 'sun' (Sion) connection is obvious for those who have studied symbolism and in the movie *Elysium*, the abode of the *elite* is both a star (ship) and a wheel, symbolic of the Eastern Star and the Pentagram with lucid connections to Sion and the DNA of the elite (see figure 422). Sion symbolism also relates to the Holy Blood (Sangreal) and appears in the *Matrix* movies as the 'safe haven' for humanity away from the ruthless machines that control the earth matrix. As I have been pointing out throughout the book, these *are* off-world alien sentient 'machines' (connected to Orion) which are 'spider-like'. As already pointed out, these 'livingmachines' are influencing our world for their own ends.

The Elysian Fields in the Sky

The Elysian Fields, according to the Greek poet Homer, were located on the western edge of the earth by the 'stream' of Okeanos, which could be a reference to Orion's position adjacent to the Milky Way. In the time of the Greek poet Hesiod, Elysium, or the Elysian Fields, would also be known as the 'Fortunate Isles' or 'the Isles' (or Islands) of the 'Blessed', located in the western ocean at the end of the earth. In Dante's epic, *Divine Comedy*, Elysium is mentioned as the 'Abode of the Blessed' in the lower world; mentioned in connection with the meeting of Aeneas (whose descendants founded ancient Rome) within the shade of Anchises in the Elysian Fields.

In the movie, *Elysium*, the 'Fortunate Isles or 'fields' are positioned 'outside the earth' (in space) and from the 'earth perspective', it is an oasis looked upon by humans on earth as 'the ultimate dream home in the heavens'. I suppose it would be if all around you is death, disease, poverty and degradation reigning supreme, which it does in the movie. Elysium is said to be home to a half-million 'ultra-wealthy (elite) citizens' (the chosen ones) contained in architectural vistas over 37.2 miles (60 kilometers) in diameter and 1.86 miles (3 km) wide. In several scenes, it looks like how our moon would look 'viewed from space' (alongside the earth); interestingly, we do not see any shots of the moon in the movie. In *Oblivion*, the moon is blown apart during a nuclear battle between humans and aliens rendering the earth inhospitable once the cataclysms (not least those caused by the moon's destruction) had left their mark on the earth's surface. It was a 'cull spectacular'instigated by an AI alien species. I've seen the image of the moon 'in bits' in several novels/films and of course the most famous is depicted in HG Wells' *Time Machine* (2002), where we are shown a future earth with a moon that has been blown up! Are these writers and directors telling us something? Movies such as *Moon* (2009) and the third *Transformers* movie *The Dark of the Moon* (2010), give insight into what the moon truly harbours as a possible 'ship' or as a 'base' and this concept is suggested somewhat in *Oblivion* (see my illustrated novel, *Moon Slayer*).

NASA and Hollywood combined have given us many examples of space stations occupied by humans, too many to go into in this book. The first release movie poster for *2001: A Space Odyssey* by the late 'insider' filmmaker, Stanley Kubrick, featured a space shuttle departing a rotating space station. Artist Chesley Bonestell's depiction of a rotating station in Earth orbit appeared in *Colliers* Magazine in the spring of 1952 offering similar themes. In the 1970s, NASA scientists studied the possibilities of building giant communities in space, and one of NASA's summer study programmes at Stanford University in 1975 became known as Island Two and would have housed 10,000 people in comfort. The Orion project I mentioned in earlier chapters is also part of the space station programme. Coincidentally, the late physicist Stephen Hawking, speaking to a group of nurses and doctors in Los Angeles in 2012, was quoted, as saying "he did not think humans would survive another 1,000 years without escaping beyond our fragile planet." Hawking also advised to "Look up at the stars and not down at your feet."

The Symbolism of the wheel in 'alchemy' also relates to the 'beginning and the end', 'life and death', a place where the centre is neither 'living nor dead'. The wheel could also be seen as the 'holy of holies', which attracts the number seven to it numerologically, along with the Sefirot (as above so below) symbol. The *Elysium* star wheel in figure 422 (on page 614), shows a five-pointed star (a pentastar) and the 2 circles that encircle it equate to the number seven (5 points and 2 circles = 7) as I have shown in the book, *Seven* was (is) the number associated with 'heaven on earth'.

The connection to the five-pointed Star (Pentagram), from a metaphysical perspective, of course, is a common 'occult symbol' but visionaries and alchemists considered the 'star wheel' to be a symbol of the time of Eden, the place 'before the Fall' (Gan Eden) and therefore Elysium was (is) the 'Garden of Eden'- the location of the gods (elite) of Orion.

El on Earth

Going from Kin (King)-ship to 'Spaceship' (with obvious symbolic connections to the ruling elite living in their lofty abode), in *Elysium*, is much deeper than we see at first glance. Genetics are a huge key to the future of earth's population and this movie is blatantly telling us only selected genetics (the *El*-ite) will reach Elysium – the New World (Order). Look around, it's glaringly obvious that our world is slowly being moved towards an *Elysium*-style future existence. With the plot of the movie in mind, the human population, I would suggest, is being 'lured into a final alchemical transformation', promising the secrets of the universe and the 'extension of life' through a transhumanist AI agenda and Cyber-Grid Empire. Time and time again, in movies, we see a future earth depicted as a dead zone peopled by 'unwanted' humans all fighting for what little resources remain on the surface world. Or we see a robot-like humanity connected to machines after a global war. The symbolism is perfect in terms of connections to the 'God of Death' (*EL* or Saturn) reigning over a ravished surface world. The story of the biblical Isaac, which is important in Judaism, Christianity and Islam, also relates to death, sacrifice (usually firstborn) and the worship of the Canaanite deity, 'El'. It is El's dominion, (El or Hell), and in *Elysium* we are shown a clear future vision of 'Hell on Earth'. The *word* 'El' also connects to the Elohim (see earlier chapters). Therefore in *Elysium*, it is those selected by blood (DNA) who can live amongst the elite (on the star-like space station in the movie); everyone else lives in squalor on a ruined earth surface. It's simply another version of the *Hunger Games*, but off-world.

Themes in the movie *Superman, Man of Steel* (2013) is hugely symbolic of alien gods, or those who see themselves as 'chosen to lead' or 'save humanity', as seen in characters like, Kal-El (Superman), Jor-El (the Kryptonians). The common theme is always of the gods coming to destroy, or 'save', us. The former always takes the mode of coming to earth so to change our atmosphere and use earth's resources for the survival of alien races. The latter saviour god always has miraculous powers. The Kryptonian world in *Superman, Man of Steel*, or Cybertron in the *Transformers* movies also refer to an advanced alien technological species coming to earth, while becoming humanity's gods, or saviours. The parallels between Superman and Christ (Orion-Man) in the *Man of Steel* movie are blatantly obvious as the narrative, produced by DC Entertainment, unfolded with Superman being 'handed over' to his persecutors, just as Jesus was handed over to the authorities in Franco Zeffirelli's *Jesus of Nazareth* (1977). These 'hero' deities (possibly extraterrestrial in origin) are part of a higher intelligence that comes from higher states of consciousness (or the upper Aeons) described by the Gnostic texts I mentioned earlier in the book. Again we are looking at a spiritual warrior, the star-man, or Orion in his original form before he 'falls'; hence reference to the Genesis Codex in *Man of Steel*.[31] The battles between the ultra conscious Kryptonian, Superman and the dark demented General Zod, or the saviour god-like Optimus Prime against the Decepticons, or even the part-machine Max Da Costa (Matt Damon) fighting the vile Agent Kruger in *Elysium*; the results on earth always look the same in the movies. The aftermath is total destruction.

The Archon vibration, or state of being (the Krypton/Cybertron/Cyborg reality) I've touched on throughout the book, can only survive through the

Figure 423: System Failure - Humanity is under attack on multiple levels.

'death and destruction' of the organic world. Have these extraterrestrial life forms 'possessed' the earth's elite (the 1%) so to advance such a takeover of the earth? Such power structures seem to be designed to 'enslave our planet through warfare, financial destitution and 'harmful technology,' radiation, 5G, HAARP, Chemtrails and other 'AI-weaponry' mentioned so far. The same forces, I would suggest, are using a new wave of technology through smart grids, Wi-Fi, GMO monoculture (Big Biotech) and mass toxicity, so to alter the blueprint of our world (our DNA). The human race (the Earth) is under attack by a *genuine* 'alien' (extraterrestrial' technology on so many levels (see figure 423) that we often fail to see the deception in our world. Something *is* wrong on so many levels that it would be viable to suggest that we, as a planet, as a collective human race, are being steered towards a cyborg-AI controlled reality, where the elite eventually live 'off planet', like in the movie *Oblivion*.

Okay, there are no 'world builders' hovering above our cities, or star wheels positioned outside of the earth's atmosphere ready to take the 1% up to meet their maker (not yet). But the effects of the few (the elite), at the expense of the many, are devastating our world – preparing it for the Cyber-Grid Empire. Just look at what has happened to our societies in relation to the Coronavirus? Total overhaul of *everything* we took for granted, while insanity and pandemonium seems to rule supreme. We are in 'system failure' mode and it is becoming obvious to those who can really *see*. As I have been pointing out through the last few chapters of this book, our world is changing; it could be changing so to accommodate alien (artificial) Intelligence, and through AI, give a direct link to what the Gnostics called the counterfeit God - Demiurge. All artificial intelligence beyond what is termed 'narrow'AI, could easily become a 'living god' on earth – it is all down to us and how far we pursue the Cyber-Grid Empire. The Gnostics certainly knew the Demiurge was 'artificial' (counterfeit) and a creator of illusory worlds. I would go as far as saying, God (the Demiurge) *is* a gigantic intersteller AI computer (mind). In fact, I wouldn't be suprised to find that the 'off-world' hidden hand (or gods), are connected to a cyborg spider-like species operating out of Orion. I know much of what I am describing will be dismissed as over-imaginative, or mad, but how do we not know for sure that artificial machine-like life forms do not populate other worlds in Orion and elsewhere? (see *Apendix II*). In relation to *Superman*, remember that Krypton is from the Greek word 'kryptos', meaning 'the hidden one'. Even though Krypton is inert for most practical purposes as a chemical (gas) in our world, it's the invisible smog, radiation and other chemicals polluting our skies, food and water that we need to be concerned about. Only artificial intelligence, something god-like and alien to Gaia (the Earth), would pollute everything humanity needs to live in balance - especially if *it* wants the world to be born again in *its image*.

It's about *Fear, Death* & *Off-world Forces*

As I have already mentioned, the forces behind our power structures have historically used war (on earth) to maximum effect. These forces are obsessed with 'biological death, not biological life'; which is why we seem to see so many barbaric acts through war, poverty, death and more clandestine activities, often with such hatred, lack of empathy and compassion for humanity. The world they have long embarked upon creating in our reality is a mirror of their own archontic mind and so our world is becoming ever more ugly, *darker* and threatening on the surface. At the same time, underneath the chaos, there are other forces at work, representing our desire to reach Superconsciousness - *become* Oneness. The Cyber-Grid Empire and its pursuit of *living* technology, is based on biological death, **not** biological life. The more our organic world mirrors the alien (artificial) archon reality, via the Cyber-Grid Empire, the closer we get to the frequency of biological death. Fear *and* death caused by war and poverty, for example, is a major part of this frequency alignment. Just look at what has happened in places like Syria, Iraq, Ukraine and Yemen in recent years! The machine of war is devastating to us *all*. The outer wars, divisions, fault lines are all expressions of a consciousness that does not want true peace on earth.

We went to war against a supposedly *deadly* virus in March 2020, and just look what happened to our world - *Pandemonia* reigned. My friend, Ellis C Taylor, summed up the state of affairs regarding the 'new normal' and aftermath of the *first* global and national lockdowns from this not-so-imaginary 'Devil's advocate' perspective. He writes:

Ladies and Gentlemen, religions; the Prince of the world is grateful for your reverence, your compliance, and your assistance. You have made my new world possible. From this moment and forever it will be called Pandemonia, for it honours both my legions within you and the means by which this entertaining finale, the 66 vi-ruse assault so easily slew your sovereignty. Is his confidence warranted? That's up to each and every one.[32]

The more power and influence the archontic (artificial Inteligent/alien) off-world realm has over life, the more it 'visually' and 'vibrationally' starts to mirror its own vibration on earth. You could call it 'hell on earth'. We see these reflections in the manufactured divisions between those *in fear* of the Coronavirus and those that can see through the fear, knowing in their hearts something is not quite right with the official story. We have to resist the 'Prince' of *Darkness* and not comply with the 'new normal'. Our Love, empathy, compassion and joy are therefore the answer to all pandemonia, war, stress, suffering, hate and fear. *Life, love* and *peace* are states of being (higher consciousness) that *quicken* the frequency of our reality and subsequently increase our awareness. As Martin Luther King said:

Darkness cannot drive out darkness: only light can do that. Hate cannot drive out hate: only love can do that.

In the final chapter, I will focus on what lies *beyond* Orion's Door and the true nature of what the Gnostics called the 'Christos' (Christ Consciousness), and the levels of infinite awareness we desperately need to impact on the coming Cyber-Grid Empire.

Sources:

1) Icke, David. *Everything You Need to Know But Have Never Been Told*. DI Books, 2019, p453-7

2) Lenski G & Nolan P. *Human Societies: An Introduction into Macro Sociology*. 1995

3) Cairns, Edmund. *A Safer Future*. Oxfam, 1997, p34

4) Swinson, Antonia. *Root of All Evil? How to make Spiritual Values Count*, Saint Andrews Press, 2003, P64-67

5) Taylor, Steven. *The Fall: The Insanity of the Ego in Human History*, O Books, 2005 p3-5

6) Bearman, Sophie. "*Bitcoin's creator may be worth $6 billion — but people still don't know who it is*". CNBC (27 October 2017). Retrieved 22 July 2019.

7) https://www.theguardian.com/us-news/2019/nov/27/trump-hong-kong-bills-signed-china-protest

8) https://www.theatlantic.com/business/archive/2012/02/the-world-in-2050-when-the-5-largest-economies-are-the-brics-and-us/253160/

9) https://news.cgtn.com/news/7951544e35677a6333566d54/share_p.html

10) https://citywire.co.uk/funds-insider/news/rothschilds-back-ai-driven-online-wealth-manager/a1135042

11) https://www.dailymail.co.uk/news/article-7379255/China-one-CCTV-camera-TWO-PEOPLE-year.html

12) https://www.scmp.com/news/china/society/article/3023455/report-finds-cities-china-most-monitored-world

13) https://www.eetimes.com/author.asp?section_id=36&doc_id=1335260#

14) https://www.theverge.com/2018/11/22/18107885/china-facial-recognition-mistaken-jay-walker

15) https://www.theguardian.com/world/2019/mar/01/china-bans-23m-discredited-citizens-from-buying-travel-tickets-social-credit-system

16) Ford, Martin; *The Rise of the Robots: Technology and the Threat of Mass Unemployment.* One World, 2015, p22

17) https://www.scmp.com/tech/start-ups/article/2185644/more-half-worlds-ai-unicorns-are-china-says-report

18) *State Council Notice on the Issuance of the Next Generation Artificial Intelligence Development Plan* (PDF). New America. Retrieved April 2, 2018.

19) https://www.theguardian.com/technology/2019/jun/26/rapid-robot-rollout-risks-uk-workers-being-left-behind-reports-say

20) https://www.independent.co.uk/news/business/news/sainsburys-self-service-supermarket-retail-jobs-automation-impact-a8893491.html

21) Channel Four *Dispatches* October 2019 https://metro.co.uk/2020/04/23/dangerous-childrens-toys-removed-amazon-12600845/

22) https://www.vaticannews.va/en/vatican-city/news/2019-05/vatican-conference-robotics-artificial-intelligence-pontifical-a.html

23) https://time.com/5673240/china-killer-robots-weapons/

24) Ford, Martin. *The Rise of the Robots: technology and the Threat of Mass Unemployment.* One World, 2015, p23

25) https://ec.europa.eu/digital-single-market/en/artificial-intelligence

26) https://ec.europa.eu/digital-single-market/en/policies/robotics

27) https://www.dailymail.co.uk/home/event/article-5501033/Will-Michael-Jackson-Artificial-Intelligence-veganism.html

28) https://www.dailymail.co.uk/news/article-6493343/Factory-robot-malfunctions-skewers-Chinese-worker.html

29) https://www.icrac.net/members/laura-nolan/

30) https://www.msn.com/en-gb/news/world/ex-google-worker-fears-killer-robots-could-cause-mass-atrocities/ar-AAHkNIA?ocid=spartanntp

31) http://throughancienteyes.blogspot.com/2013/06/man-of-saturn-man-of-el-son-of-gods.html)

32) https://ellisctaylor.com/

21

'GAME CHANGER' CONSCIOUSNESS

Going *Beyond* Orion's Door

I am the Door. Those who enter through me will be saved.
JOHN 10:9

Orion's (heavenly Adam's) metaphysical (spirit) body is the Sefirot, or Tree of Life, which, I see as symbolically connected to the Orion Nebula. The Tree's branches spread out to form the multi-layered worlds (realities) contained within its structure; an invisible framework that includes all bodies within Orion's Spur. This is why Orion is often considered a focus for Adam's spiritual body and given various names such as the 'Primordial Man', 'Archetypal Man', 'Microprosopos', or the 'Man of the East'. It is the *body of light* sometimes referred to as the 'Shadow of the Invisible Macrocosm', or the 'Cosmic Son', that constructs the Sefirot. The emanations of this heavenly Adam (Orion) is said to 'project' through three worlds creating a fourth world – the physical Adam. In simpler terms, the projection, as explained through Gnsotic/hermetic teachings, creates a series of upper heavenly spirit worlds, and a lower illusory physical world; below the illusory world is said to be an '*inverted* world'. The inverted world, I believe, is a main focus for 'off-world' forces. This artificial (alien) intelligence has some kind of interstellar link with a nefarious aspect of Orion and malevolent extraterrestrial entities. Higher consciousness, emanates from the source, (the infinite) the place *all* of hunanity comes from. You could also see these worlds (dimensions) I am describing as 'multi-levels' within a super-holographic 'game world' reality (see figure 424 overleaf).

The three main worlds can also be seen as the 'Three Pillars' of the 'Tree of Life', which in hermetic Qabalah diagrams, are united by both the 'light' and the 'Darkness'. The inverted archon world, below my depiction of the Fourth world, the physical world of Adam, is symbolic of what Christianty

Figure 424: The Game World Reality – the 'House of Many Mansions'.
The Game World reality is a contemporary way of seeing the Sefirot, or Tree of Life. *Level Four* (the physical world), is a 'madhouse' reality because of the influence of the *inverted* Oiron-Betelgeuse-Saturn (Hell) world below it. Orion *is* the Door to other worlds.

calls 'hell' – a 'vibration' realm. This reality I feel, is focused on the Betelgeuse-Saturn Hack mentioned in *Chapter Seventeen*. It is also the realm from where the alien intelligence behind the 'construction' of the Cyber-Grid Empire is being orchestrated. Projecting the game world is both the Gnostic Demiurge and Heavenly Adam caught up in duality, or a tussle for the human soul. You could also see Orion's stars as a collection of projectors, which to our eyes, appears as the Orion constellation. The light powering the projectors (stars) has its true source *beyond* the Upper Aeons (the levels of the game) and come from the infinite, *The One*. You can also see the game world as the 'house of many mansions' referred to by Jesus in *John* 14:2 (KJV). Humanity stands in the centre of the game world (or house) as a representative of the 'divine form' of the heavenly Adam. The Adam and Jesus figures (see avatar liberator figures in other faiths) seem to be symbolic (or mythological) manifestations of the Upper Aeons and Superconsciousnesses from beyond the projection in Orion.

'Heavenly Adam' and the Tree of 'Light'

All stars, suns and planets are lesser bodies that grow like fruit on the tree

Figure 425: Christos as the Solar Tree of Light.
Dwarf stars, planets and moons grow like fruit on Solar (plasma) Trees. Our Kabbalistic Tree is a 'branch' on a greater tree growing out of the Orion Spur.

of light (life), rooted in the source of oneness ('The Endless One') and the pleroma I described in *Part One*. The trunk of the tree is the middle, or third pillar of the Sefirot, connecting our divine human form with the original earth, or what the Gnostics called the 'Upper Aeons'. I call this pillar or trunk, 'Shekena', the solar tree of our system, one of millions of solar (plasma) trees in the Galaxy (see figure 425). These solar trees, like Orion's invisible Sun, are not all the handiwork of the counterfeit creator – the Demiurge. The Crown, or Keter, is the door to the heavenly Adam (Orion) leading to worlds of Superconsciousness, existing beyond the mind of the Abrahamic God – the Demiurge. The 'Son of Man' (Christos) is also the light body of the tree I call, Shekena in my fictional illustrated books.

The symbolism associated with the Son of Man (heavenly Adam), or Orion, is caught in the trinity of worlds (Upper, middle and Lower realities), expressed in Christianity as the Father, Son and Holy Spirit. Christians believe the 'Godhead' is triune, meaning three aspects of the Trinity are as one, in union with each aspect, also God. Christianity holds to the doctrine of a man-god, Christ as God incarnate (the Logos). However, most Christians do not believe that any of the three divine figures is 'God alone', but that all three are 'mysteriously' God combined. Christian belief could be therefore considered 'heretical' (see *Deuteronomy*), just as Christ in person (The biblical Jesus Christ) was deemed an heretical imposter to the biblical Scribes and Pharisees in his time. They supposedly condemned him for saying 'he and the Father were *one* and the *same*'. The supposed crime committed by the alleged historical figure Jesus, was for him to proclaim himself, 'Ein Sof' (the Father) incarnated, but there is more to this narrative, as I will come to shortly. The heavenly Adam (Son of Man), according to Gnostic and early Christian belief, was part of the projection (the living light) that comes out of the source, or what is called 'The Endless One' (*Infinite* awareness). The pillars in the hermetic Qabalah therefore *could* be seen as the structure, or levels, through which the heavenly Adam (Orion/Son of Man) *connects* with the physical world - the earth.

The 'Door' and its Pillars

Odin and other Pagan figures looked at in earlier chapters, along with much early Christian Byzantine iconography, shows Christ sitting, or hanging, from a tree. Like many pre-Christian versions of Christ, the tree is significant in terms of its symbolic reference to the 'doorway'. The middle pillar, or trunk, is also the 'heart light' projected through Orion's Nebula as it meets the eye of the Demiurge. It is a beam of light ('Let there be Light') through which our matrix of worlds are formed and 'hacked' through a hierarchy of 'hosts' governed by the biblical Elohim. The position of each planet in our solar tree is part of a hack, I feel, designed to create 'celestial order' so the Gnostic Demiurge can manifest through the minds of humanity on Malkuth (Earth). The Cyber-Grid Empire will 'sign, seal and deliver' humanity's ultimate connection to the all-seeing counterfeit god or 'gods'. The hierarchy of 'hosts' I am referring to, is also an esoteric order of planetary bodies identified by Hermetic mystics, which intersect the middle beam, or pillar of light. The Four main spiritual bodies positioned on the third pillar, or trunk are described as: 'Keter' (Crown); 'Da'at' (Knowledge); Tiferet (Beauty) and Yesod (Foundation), the latter was considered the Foundation Stone, or the stone in the tree. These can also be viewed as Orion, Saturn, Sun and Moon, in the same order. I believe the hierarchical order of bodies positioned on the middle pillar form the off-world structure of control over our reality on earth. In other words, these bodies anchor the light of the projector as it descends from the upper part of the Tree of Life (the Supernatural realms) through the symbolic trunk and into the lower worlds (the astral/alien worlds), eventually interacting with the reality in which we are living.

The light of the upper part of the tree is said to gather in Yesod (the Moon) and is channelled to Malkuth (the Earth), which is then received by humanity, not least through the human chakra system and the pineal gland. In this manner, according to hermetic Qabalistic writers, Yesod is associated with the sexual organs and its masculine side (Right Pillar), which collects the vital forces of the Sephirot (Tree of Life) and transmits these creative and vital energies into the feminine Malkuth (Gaia). In short, Yesod (Moon) is said to channel and Malkuth receive, which is why nighttime, moonlight was considered the keeper of subtle frequencies and the subconscious. In much of this hermetic symbolism, as featured in Stanley Kubrick's movie *2001: A Space Oddessy*, we see an enigmatic black monolith on the Moon which relates to this understanding. Eventually, the monolith or artificial object in the movie, turns out to be a 'door', or 'gate', leading to higher dimensions. Occult systems, such as the hermetic Qabalah, relates Malkuth (the earth) as a place of interactaction with the divine, the latter of which is situated above and beyond Keter (crown), inside the brilliant white area of Orion's Nebula. The middle pillar of this divine structure, which passes through Saturn, the Sun and the Moon, can be seen as a non-physical construct that seems to structure our reality - influencing the waveform (and frequency) levels of our reality. It could also be the mechanism used by off-world inteligence to invert the power of Superconsciousness, which, according to mystics, is accessed *beyond* Orion's Door. You can imagine the door, or a celestial 'frame', constructed between the *three* pillars (see my cover image) and shown throughout the book. Orion is *both* the door and the master key to so much knowledge, information and the archetypes I've discussed.

The outer celestial bodies running through both left and right pillars of the 'Tree' are said to be Chochmah – Wisdom (right brain); Binah – Understanding (left brain); Chesed – Kindness; Gevurah – Severity; Netzach – Victory and Hod – Glory. These six bodies, or stones, are the planets of the solar system: Neptune, Uranus, Mars, Jupiter, Mercury and Venus. In hermetic texts, all these planetary portals connect to the four worlds of 'Emanation', 'Creation', 'Formation' and 'Action' (the four worlds of Adam). The diagram of the Tree of life can also be viewed as a projection passing out of the Keter (the Father), through wisdom (logos, or the son) as it manifests through six portals, or planets (heavenly hosts), that influence the collective mind, body and soul of humanity in the kingdom below – Malkuth, or Earth. As J. F. C. Fuller writes in his book *The Secret Wisdom of the Qabalah*:

> *Ain Soph (infinity) is represented by the closed eye, so is Kether represented by the open eye. (Compare the eye of Shiva in Hindu mythology.) As long as this eye remains open the universe is maintained in being, but when it shuts it vanishes into Non-being, that is No-Thingness. In the threefold division of man's nature,*

Kether represents the Neshamah or spirit.[1]

Therefore what lives 'above' in the heavens – the eye of Orion (the Keter/Kether) could also manifest on earth in the kingdom below. The priesthoods of ancient Babylon, and the Chaldeans seem to know the importance of Orion's projection from 'above', through the Tree of Life, passing through Yesod (the Moon), down to the earthly kingdom. The Lord's Prayer, supposedly spoken by the Son of Man, "Your kingdom come, your will be done, on earth as it is in heaven," echoes this esoteric knowledge. The symbolism also associated with the Keter was also called the 'Ancient of Days', the 'White Head' or the 'Long Face', or the 'Heavenly Adam'.[3] The *heavenly* Adam is the 'divine form' that visionary artist William Blake expressed so well through his art and writings. Again, it is the group of stars arranged as the Orion constellation (a sevenfold system) through which the Ancient of Days can manifest in the minds of the children of Adam and Eve - *all* humanity.

The *Zohar* talks of the heavenly Adam as the creator of the earthly Adam, just as the human soul is a reflection and extension of the heavenly spirit, which is also human. But there is more to the heavenly Adam archetype and the knowledge contained within such symbolism than the obvious arrangement of planetary bodies in our solar system. To understand more fully the deeper aspects of Orion symbolism, I want to offer insight into the Jesus story, which, I feel, connects to our plight and the Cyber-Grid Empire I've described in earlier chapters.

Opening the Door to the Cyber-Grid Gods

The unwavering pursuit of the New World Order, which will be imposed via the Cyber-Grid discussed in the last two chapters, is an 'inversion' of the truth, and how humans should be living on earth. The truth, 'light', and the 'way' is not the technocracy we are seeing unfold. The virtual new world reality being imposed upon humanity is an inversion of the higher source (intelligence) that dwells beyond Orion's Door.

The coming global technocracy could also be seen as the fulfilling of a prophecy' to usher in a digital god-like reality - a world ultimately controlled by Artificial Intelligence. What if the Gnostic Demiurge I mentioned earlier in the book could be described as 'alien' or 'artificial' and the book of *Revelation* its outcome? Has humanity elevated this God to the point that technology could literally take over our lives at some point in the not-so-distant future? As I touched upon in previous chapters, we have not seen anything yet in terms of advanced technology (technocracy) and the world being shaped to meet the New World Order. For 'initiates' of 'hermetic wisdom' such an era could represent the 'image' and 'marker' for what is described the right and left legs of a global body built to receive, or worship, the god - artificial intelligence in a New World Order.[2]

As I have already shown, the number *six* seems important to this New World Order and there is a biblical statement that the world will exist for 6000 years and then enter a 'new state of existence'. According to such texts, as the world nears the era of 'spiritual enlightenment', knowledge in all areas of life will rapidly expand. We seem to be witnessing this expansion today. According to the *Zohar*, the six hundredth year of Noah's life is also considered the sixth millennium, where at the end of this age, the windows of heaven (Orion's Door?) will *open* to allow 'knowledge' and 'discovery' to flow into our world at an unprecedented rate. According to some writers, earth's Superpowers, via increasing Cyber-Grid domination, are meant to be the focus for a New World Order. The *Book of Revelation* also seems to prophesise the world we entered into from the Millennium onwards - all leading to a future global government operating *through* the Cyber-Grid Empire. Are such prophecies hinting at 'off-world' forces ruling over humanity in the end, unless we embrace Superconsciousness? *Revelation* says: "And he shall rule them with a rod of iron; as the vessels of a potter shall they be broken to shivers: even as I received of my Father (*Revelation* 2:27 KJV). Then again, what if a spiritual nation (described as the 'New Jerusalem' in *Revelation*), made up of *all* nations (all humnaity), rises up and becomes the 'spanner-in-the-works' for the coming global technocracy? Rather than accept the control, deceit and manipulation, supposedly driven by off-world forces working through elite powers (or what the bible refers to as the False Prophet and Antichrist); what if humanity instead (as a spiritual collective), rises up and becomes a 'Cosmic Nexus'?

It is said in *Revelation*, a False Prophet (Anti Christ) ushers in the New World Order:

> And he [the False Prophet] deceives those who dwell on the earth by those signs which he was granted to do in the sight of the beast, telling those who dwell on the earth to make an image to the beast [the Antichrist] who was wounded by the sword and lived. He was granted power to give breath to the image of the beast, that the image of the beast should both speak and cause as many as would not worship the image of the beast to be killed. (13:14–18).

The False Prophet [symbolic malevolent of off-world 'forces' working to usher in the Cyber-Grid Empire] gives 'lifelike' *"breath to the image of the beast"* (v.15). However, it will be left to individuals around the world to build the new image (v.14). In otherwords, the artificial (alien) intelligent 'god' can only live due to the vast amount of data being processed. The

Digital Age and the science of 'big data', with the ability of computers (AI) to accumulate and then analyse 'titanic' amounts of information extremely rapidly, is *all* symbolic of giving 'lifelike' breath to the image, or word of, a god-like AI. See the movie *Transcendence* (2014) to get the idea of such god-like powers. The key to understanding what I am describing here is that *through* the Cyber-Grid Empire (the digital World Order), we are all giving life (our data and DNA) to create an artificial Intelligent 'imagini' (or image). Our imagination fuels our reality and we have been 'empowering', or 'worshipping', the Cyber god (in all its forms) via endless connections to the growing Cyber-Grid Empire. We are building that connection through big tech data, social media posts, ever increasing websites, online cloud storage, etc., As Craig Parshall, a writer for the *Friends of Israel Gospel Ministry*, wrote in a blog in 2014:

> In 1986, the growth rate of data storage was 23 percent per year. By 1996, it had increased 800 percent; and by 2004, data storage was up by 4,100 percent. The report cites Google's former Chief Executive Officer Eric Schmidt, who said in 2010 the total of all documented information between "the dawn of civilization" through 2003 equaled about 5 exabytes of data—roughly the amount of data being created and stored every two days today.[3]

Can you imagine the amount of data being created *today*? The amount of digital data *we* have created *is* giving life to the Cyber-Grid Artificial Intelligence I have been describing.

The emerging beast-like Cyber Grid (with the potential for complete control over humanity), through connecting artificial intelligence to the human brain (mind), is facilitating the end of our current world age. The Cyber-Grid Empire could be seen as the ultimate 'fulfillment of biblical prophecies for a global authority controlled by unseen forces that sees *all* nations, China, USA, Russia and Europe, etc., has its fiefdom and future centres of control. Of course, I cannot accurately validate such a future scenario, I mention it here to simply highlight scripturual connections to our world today and how they seem to be unfolding.

With this in mind, I am now going to offer an 'alternative' vision, or reasoning, behind one manifestation of the self-proclaimed Son of Man – Jesus, Yeshua (Iisous) 'Orion Man' referred to in the Bible.

Christ Consciousness - the *Ultimate* 'Rouge' Program

Before imparting my ideas in relation to the Son of Man (Orion) symbolism and the Jesus story, I have to preface by saying I am not a traditional 'Christian', nor do I belong to any faith, as you have already gathered from reading my books. I do, however, have the greatest respect for people of *all faiths*, especially Judaic and Gnostic Christians. What I am about to say is based on pure insight and reflection on what we commonly understand as the 'mission' of Jesus as proclaimed in the New Testament and to some degree, how the early Gnostics saw this historical figure in the immediate years after his alleged 'resurrection' (if he existed at as described). The myth and its message is more important than the man in this case, as it is a story of one 'rouge' incarnation (from beyond the firewall) with a mission to change the course of history. I am going to quote specific biblical texts, but by no means am I saying that these texts represent actual history; in fact, I don't think they do in totality. They are more likely to be myth, or, more realistically, Gnostic teachings, attributed to the *wisdom* of the Aeons and a higher philosophy born out of higher consciousness and knowing-ness - *Oneness*.

Many years ago, I read a book called, *The Thirteenth Stone: History Rewritten, The Jesus Myth Exploded and the Great Secret of the Knights Templar Revealed by the Dead Sea Scrolls* (1984), by Reg Lewis. I don't agree with everything Lewis wrote about, but the book was quite groundbreaking from a scholarly point and now also out of print, too. It is a book full of interpretation of biblical events, symbolism and the mission behind what Lewis calls the 'Star', the 'Tree' or the 'Teacher', all names given to what he describes as the 'revealer of the mysteries'. The title of the book, *The Thirteenth Stone*, is also relevant to the true understanding of hermetic occult systems and its connection to the figure - Jesus. The 'Thirteenth Stone' is symbolically and quite possibly the location *beyond* the tenth point of the Sefirot (Tree of life), located in the place from where the Gnostic's said the Upper Aeons dwell. This location is *beyond* the brilliance of the white cave contained within the Orion Nebula (see *Chapter Fifteen*) and the home of the Aeons, or what is often termed, 'Christ Consciousness'. It is the 'symbolic' Thirteenth Stone, or 'seal', described in the Gnostic Nag Hammadi (attributed to Marsanes) and the New Testament '*Apocrypha*', which describes the powers that exist *beyond* the Heavenly Tree. The texts describe the eleventh and twelfth stones as the 'Invisible One' (above the Keter, or Crown) and the *Thirteenth* is the 'Silent One' who was 'not known' and the one who was 'not distinguished'.[7] Silence, in terms of vibration, is the key to understanding our true nature and the power of heart energy, as I will come back to shortly.

The 'Thirteenth Stone' is also the 'Monad' or 'life giver' to the 'Dyad' (the Greek word for two), which begat all other numbers, stones, or stars. In my painting (see figure 426 overleaf), the Monad is symbolised as a 'stone', or 'star', held between the index finger and thumb of the hand of the 'Infinite One', the 'Silent One'. It was the Pythagoreans, who called the 'first thing that came into existence' the 'Monad', or *Silent One*. It was also referred to as the 'first being', 'divine form' or the 'totality of all beings'. From my understanding of hermetic mysticism, it is also the *source* of Adam on High and the structure I have been describing.

The image, entitled *'Placing the Stone'*, was created for the cover of David Icke's book, *Remember Who You Are* (2011). The symbolism contained within this canvas attempts to convey the message that we as individuals affect the collective consciousness when we activate the Monad, the 'Divine Imagination'. The placing of the stone (or Monad), into the 'Tree of Life' above

Figure 426: The 'Stone' in the Human (Earth) Tree. *'Placing the Stone'* was created for the cover of David Icke's book *Remember Who You Are* (2011). The white hand is symbolic of *Superconsciousness* placing the 'monad', or 'star', in the maze-like mind. An act that 'awakens' us to our truth. Note the comet, this is also a 'sign' of human awakening and will prelude the activation of the monad.

the vertebrae, is another symbol for the activation of the 'third eye', or the 'Eye of Providence'. The symbolism relates to both individuals and the collective, as we are all *One*. The 'placing of the stone' would symbolically reverse the separation, symbolised through the story of Adam and Eve, bringing an end to the illusory state of awareness 'cast' by the Demiurge who *uses* the Sun, Moon and Saturn (all attached to the third pillar, or trunk of the Tree of Life). I use the word 'cast' to emphasise the notion that a *spell* has been cast over our true sight, erasing our memory of the heavenly time on earth *before* the Fall. All of what I have just described is important in terms of understanding the Son of Man symbolism and the self-proclaimed figure called Jesus. The combination of the Christos and the Divine Feminine (the original Adam and Eve) in terms of higher consciousness, united within the hearts of humanity, is also important to breaking the spell. When we activate the Third Eye (Monad), or the 'eye of the heart' we realise that we are simply 'Awareness' at our core. Seeing the mind as the

Figure 427: Computer Mind *or* Superconsciousness Operator?
We have to switch our perception *beyond* the level of the mind (computer), to the 'higher levels' of Superconsciousness. From here we are able to change, or delete, the software programes running through our minds.

vehicle for Superconsciousness is the key. You could see consciousness as our true persona, the computer operator, whereas the mind is simply the computer (see figure 427). Superconsciousness is the force that drives the computer operator, symbolically. As I said earlier in the book, collectively we create a reality based on information (waveform) that we constantly receive (rather like a computer receives data/information). Therefore, I wonder if the so-called Covid-19 virus could be a 'download' (in the minds) for those who either became ill with what they *throught* was 'something more' than influenza, or pneumonia? Or simply, the fear of a virus *is* the mind virus itself! Keeping an open mind is crucial no matter what is happening. Constant fear mongering via the mainstream media hasn't helped, too. The programming has been relentless on the minds of the masses, globally. You could say some people have developed a 'mind virus' (no different to a computer virus) because what they would normally see as 'insane' (at the time of writing), they see as 'normal' (the *new* normal). Some people even get angry (often aggressive) when you point out the seemingly endless contradictions relating to the official line regarding the pandemic of 2020 and beyond. Our higher consciousness knows something is not quite right about the official narrative.

If we are to bring our world back to 'peace and unity' and avoid tyranny, we will have to start operating from the persepctive of the Superconscious computer operator. When we do, we are accessing levels of ourselves that can perform miracles. Doing so brings true clarity and peace to the mind, body and soul. Superconciousness *is* the intelligence of the heart that knows *we are all one*.

Sophia's Correction

Another aspect to activation of the monad (pineal gland) and humanity awakening from the spell, is the Gnostic understanding of Sophia's Correction (diorthosis), or 'awakening', from *her* nightmare (see page 112). The earth goddess (Gaia) plays a significant role in the activation of Superconsciousness in humanity. Sophia, along with Christ Consciousness, 'corrects' the illusion (deception) caused by the Demiurge and Archons (Alien/AI). According to the Gnostic texts, Sophia is an Aeon (organic light) and even though she took the form of the physical earth, she is still Aeon consciousness (Superconsciousness). All earth life, animals and humanity are caught up in Sophia's dream, her energy or consciousness. Whatever happens to the earth, happens to us as a collective.

At the time of writing this chapter, we witnessed a rise in immense solar flare activity. Solar winds in the form of 'Coronal Mass Ejections' (CMEs), which are generated in the sun's hot *corona* (crown), create the magnetic connection between the Earth and the Sun. The biggest solar flare (CME) ever recorded, as observed by the Solar and Heliospheric Observatory (SOHO) satellite was in April 2001, less than six months before the 9/11 attacks on the World Trade Center. The 2001 flare was more powerful than the famous solar flare on March 6, 1989, which disrupted power grids in Canada. Flares of this magnitude aimed at the earth (Sophia/Gaia) cause massive elec-

Figure 428: The Lion-like Solar Flare.
I see giant CMEs as a physical manifestation of the *Truth Vibration*. When Sophia and Christos 'combine' they unite the spiritual heart of humanity and the earth. *That time is at hand!*

tromagnetic disruption, which could knock out satellites. According to studies of CMEs, in the event of being warned of impending electromagentic flares, the gradual cutting off of electrical grids, and disconnecting electric stations and substations, reducing the current (so it doesn't flow into homes, businesses and industrial buildings), is protocol. A task that could take 'days' to implement and could lead to 'blackouts' in certain areas on the globe. I mention CMEs in the context of Sophia's Correction purely to emphasise the point that *higher* unseen forces working *through* celestial bodies, such as the sun and the earth, is part of the awakening, the placing of the stone.

In one vision, while I was flying across the US in 2009, I saw the biggest solar flare take the form of a lion-like energy field. It engulfed the earth 'vibrationally' (see figure 428). The lion in my vision, was symbolic of Christ Consciousness (combining with Sophia's organic light body), uniting and activating Superconsciousness in the hearts and minds (third eye) of humanity. The result is a 'sudden awakening' of humanity (globally), as if a light has been switched on in the hearts of millions of souls. This event, I feel, could be when the 'Fire in the Sky' appears, an event, according to the Hopi prophecies, signalling the arrival of the Fifth World of peace. Remember, the times we are living in are *dualistic* and therefore this prophecy could also relate to the birth of the Cyber-Grid Empire I've been describing. Ultimately it is how we collectively respond to such events, or how we percieve reality from the levels of awareness inspired by Superconsciousness. The awakening is happening no matter what we see unfolding around us.

The Star and the Sceptre

The teachings credited to biblical Jesus (the 'Revealer of the Mysteries', or the 'Son of Man') clearly show he was expressing to those who had 'eyes to see and ears to hear' that he was from a place beyond the *three* worlds of, spirit, astral and physical; he was from beyond the location symbolic of the biblical 'Fall' (or Orion). As Reg Lewis suggests in his book *The Thirteenth Stone*, the symbolism of the 'Teacher', the 'Star' and the 'Tree' are all an expression of the Son of Man (or Orion Man); They are expressions of Christ and Sophia, the divine feminine and male, *combined*. As Lewis establishes, the historical Jesus is the story of Superconsciousness on a mission (from beyond the veil or the door) to free humanity from the spell cast by malevolent otherworldly *forces*. As Lewis explains, Christ and the historical Jesus are *two* entirely separate entities; the former is 'spirit essence', which is feminine and coupled with the Gnostic Sophia (wisdom) the 'Queen of

Heaven'. Jesus, the 'physical persona', adapted and *inverted* (crucified), is an idol worshipped by the Roman Catholic church and those who believe in the *inverted* version. The Gnostic *Dead Sea Scrolls* identify *two* central figures: the 'Righteous Teacher' (the revealer of the Mysteries) and the 'Sceptre', which could relate to a non-physical location; or a 'spiritual dimension' - the place where the biblical Christ/Jesus said he was a King: "My kingdom is not of this world. If My kingdom were of this world, My servants would fight, so that I should not be delivered to the authorities; but now My kingdom is not from here." (*John* 18:36). The crucial aspect of this quote is that Jesus is refering to an *otherworldly kingdom*, one I would suggest is *beyond* the three worlds and located through Orion's Door.

Lewis controversially explains throughout his book that the Old Testament is mainly 'myth' and that many of the 'characters', from Samson to David, are representations of what he calls 'the Star' and 'the Sceptre'; even John the Baptist, according to Lewis, is Jonathan, the much beloved friend of King David. I cannot say if this is true; but, I would add that these 'double' figures *could* be the hero twins and personified versions of the Summer and Winter Solstice points on the pagan solar wheel (year), mapped by Orion's presence in the heavens (as explained in *Chapter Ten* and *Eleven*). The notion of moving from the Piscean Age into the Age of Aquarius is also part of this pairing; one age symbolically represents John and the other, Jesus. Lewis goes on to say in his book that the Star and the Sceptre are not historical; in theory, they are 'alive today' and with us in our present times.[4] More importantly, in relation to nefarious off-world forces, the Gnostics believed Jesus 'the idol' (worshipped as God and crucified, etc.), was 'manufactured' by Babylonian-Roman priests to invert the true meaning and message of being freed through accessing higher consciousness (the Upper Aeons). Jesus the idol (the crucified figure) and the fallen Adam, were thought, by the Gnostics, to be expressions of the Demiurge, Satan (Saturn). I see the same invertion in the 'off-world' *alien inspired* Cyber-Grid Empire I have been describing. As Reg Lewis states in *The Thirteenth Stone:*

> *At the dawn of the Aquarian Age God* [The *One* true source] *would send a Revealer of Mysteries whose task it would be to uncover that which had been hidden...* [5]

As I say, Lewis was subjected to much grief for his interpretation of biblical texts and I certainly don't agree with all of his interpretations. I am sure there is always more to know with regards to interpreting ancient scriptures, however, his interpreations are intruiging. Is it true that Lewis's 'Revealer of the Mysteries' is amongst us today and revelation is there for anyone who chooses to 'see' all-that-there-is to see? Our desire for revelation is akin to being blind and then *seeing* again, which of course is contained within the New Testament 'story' of Jesus healing the blind man. I am sure the narrative is symbolic attributed to the need for self-gnosis. The driving message of those who taught through their spiritual lineage were amongst the different Gnostic groups persecuted by various branches of the Babylon priesthood. Gnosticism, or self-gnosis, automatically removes the need for any priesthood or authority (control) over spirituality and therefore removes the priest's power over the minds of the masses. But there is another aspect to the notion of revelation. In truth, the ancient Babylonian Priesthood who, if you choose to believe the story, were, it seems, dealt a mighty blow through the incarnation of the Aeon, Christ consciousness referred to as the physical man, Jesus.

Gnostic Revelation *versus* the Babylonian-Roman Priesthood

A constant theme running throughout Gnostic texts, which became much of the New Testament, is the 'persecution' and 'removal' of those who revealed spiritual truths to the masses. Jesus was the ultimate 'Revealer of the Mysteries' and a Gnostic leader (quite possibly the King of Edessa, according to the author Ralph Ellis); or could be seen as a composite of philosophies and teachings embodied in 'one' persona or avatar. There are many Jesus figures (or deities) throughout history, all of whom could be simply mythological figures created to describe Superconsciousness made manifest. Jesus, like all the other magi and sages, seems to serve as a memory of the original source, or the 'homeland' and the highest aims attributed to ancient civilizations such as Atlantis and Lemuria. The power of such mythological narratives seem to be coming from a deeper source, or a form of 'awareness' beyond our mind, body and spirit (certainly beyond the physical world). As the visionary William Blake once wrote:

> *The Prophets describe what they saw in visions as real and existing men, whom they saw with their imaginative and immortal organs.*

All myth connects us to eternal truths, as Rollo May suggests in his book *The Cry For Myth* (1991). He writes:

> *Myth transcends time. It does not matter in the slightest whether a man named Adam and a woman named Eve ever existed or not; the myth about them in Genesis [and all of Adam's lineage including Jesus] still presents a picture of the birth and development of human consciousness which is applicable to all people of all ages and religions.*[6]

For the sake of the story, or myth, let us just for a moment *forget the notion of history* and instead consider the idea of infinite consciousness made manifest in physical form.

Imagine a Gnostic light in the form of a star-man (Orion's higher self) taking physical form in the period (or age) described in biblical texts such as the Gospels. The influx of higher consciousness coming from beyond what the Gnostics called the boundary (or veil) into our physical, illusory world, would have had a huge impact on the minds of those entrenched in the status quo, or the religious-political hierarchy of their day. A hierarchy, according to Gnostic thought, created by Satan (the Demiurge) and administered by the ancient Babylonian priests and later Roman/pagan priest-hoods that founded the Holy Roman Church. Through their rituals, elite priests often included animal (and human) sacrifice, upheld laws passed down from their God, or 'gods'. Later branches of what was the Babylonian priesthood, the Holy Roman Church and the Byzantine Empire finely tuned the worshipping of idols, icons, totems, fetishes and the 'saviour' figure, while persecuting anyone who thought differently. Present day idol wor-ship goes beyond religion, of course, it can be achieved through the 'rever-ence' of celebrities and superstars, not least through the expansive media empire today. The Orion Cult, through its 'off-world' (alien) masters, seem to maintain a modern day reverence to the same idols, not least through occult symbolism and political structures on earth.

The figure we call Jesus was, it seems, a huge threat to the political structures of his time, just as a similar figure would, or *could* be, today. Why would this be so? Because the embodiment of higher consciousness through (such Gnostic philosophers and teachers) is reminding those who care to listen, that 'peace on earth' (or heaven on earth) can only be achieved through consciousness and *self-gnosis (knowing thyself)*. When we connect with Superconsciousness and go beyond the Orion-Saturn blueprints (in the mind), or when we *go within* and explore our eternal, infinite, potential, we are aligining with all-that-exists and all-that-ever has been. In truth, the Gnostic mysteries seem to be a series of spiritual keys for unlocking doors in the mind *to* Superconsciousness; mythical figures like Jesus are 'door openers', way-showers. As scripture states, "I am the way and the truth and the life. No one comes to the Father except through me" (*John* 14:6). Such teachings, with disregard for the laws of the establishment (in biblical times), administered by the biblical Sanhedrin and Rome's political might, at that time historically, would have sent shockwaves throughout the tem-ple's power structures. Donald Grey Barnhouse writes of Jesus's usurping of the biblical Israel in his book *The Invisible War: The Panorama of the Continuing Conflict Between Good and Evil* (1965). He states:

Thus He [Jesus] *is the Witness, par excellence, and thus He was willing to be Servant. Thus He becomes Prophet, Priest and King. Thus He replaces Israel as the true vine, and the fallen Adam by becoming the Last Adam.*[7]

Was Jesus the last avatar from beyond Orion's door? It's hard to know, but there is something special about Orion's presence and its influence on earth. *All* religions and faiths seem to point to this constellation as a source of the gods, or a higher divinity 'beyond' the commonly symbolised all-seeing 'eye'. The priesthoods at the supposed time of Jesus, would not have been expecting such a revelation, such a monumental proclamation by an avatar figure that the Kingdom of Heaven (Orion's Son of Man) was suddenly in their company. And that this figure was, as *he* is supposed to have said, "I and the Father are one" (*John* 10:30). After the curing of the blind man in the temple, Jesus supposedly rebuked the priesthood of his time when he said:

Yours is the house of desolation, the home of the lizard and the spider, Serpents, pruda-vipers how can any of you escape damnation ... (Matthew 23: 13-39)

The 'revelation' and teachings of Jesus seemed to threaten the control of the biblical Babylonian-high priesthood and Rome's authority, with the growing possibility that people would follow the more tolerant teachings preached by this figure. Those that became the Gnostics especially through the 1st and 2nd Centuries seemed to grasp the teachings of Jesus. Gnostic groups that emerged after the supposed lifetime of Jesus became known as Christians mainly due to the Greek words 'Christos' and 'Christianos', meaning *follower* of Christ, or anointed one, Kyrios, which also means Lord, or Master. Only a Gnostic *master*, or otherworldly being could have had such an impact on the minds of those who came into contact with such a being. But more importantly was how the story gives one clear message. Christ consciousness (Superconsciousness), through the figure supposedly called Yeshua (Iisous), declared himself the Son of Man (son of Orion?) With this stellar move, you could say Christ Consciousness 'halted' a timeline (back then), *not* by usurping the power of the biblical priests, but by *revealing* the true nature of Superconsciousness and the *infinite* to humanity. You could say the Gnostic master or 'Teacher', Jesus, 'was operating on a higher frequency' and triggered a **renewed spirituality**, a new paradigm, setting in motion the revelation and coming New Age we are witnessing in our timeline.

Reg Lewis documents in *The Thirteenth Stone* the rise of what he calls the 'Wicked Priest' or 'Spouter of Lies", one who denounces what he calls, the

Righteous Teacher.[8] According to Lewis, the Wicked Priest (who Lewis fails to identify) makes war against the Saints (symbolic of the Gnostic Christians and biblical Jews alike). According to Lewis, He persecutes those who are faithful to the 'Teacher and Revealer of Mysteries' (the message behind the Gnostic Revelation). The Wicked Priest (again unidentified by Lewis) also goes to war with anyone who has 'listened' to the Revealer of Mysteries, or those who have become conscious (self-aware *or* awake)? Today, the embodiment of the Wicked Priest (as Lewis terms it) *could* relate to the growing, overarching collective global power of a military-industrial, big-tech, corporate-data-consuming network (the Cyber-Grid Empire), working through earth's Superpowers? It's purely speculation but cannot be ruled out. The titles used by Lewis do feel 'symbolic' rather than literal though. Yet, look at the censorship of media paltforms in the wake of the Coronavirus pandemic, with journalists, and the likes of London Real and authors such as David Icke, etc., being banned for 'revealing' alternative information to the mainstream narrative. Look at how Big Tech (Tech Giants) like Facebook and YouTube, etc., have also targeted anyone who dared to share alternative information across the emerging Cyber-Grid in recent years.

Orion-Taurus Man

The spiritual 'Teacher', according to Lewis's interpretation of the scriptures, was (is) said to be born of the astrological sign of Taurus (Orion) and will denounce the 'forces' hiding behind todays Superpowers, just as Jesus denounced the then hierarchy in biblical times.[9] Also, according to Lewis, the Antichrist will be a Luciferian, possibly a Prince, or King. A claim I cannot validate in this book, or a view I necessarily share. I see the Antichrist as symbolic of 'off-world' malevolant forces, capable of possession. Again, according to Lewis, the Teacher, or the Star, will be (or has been) born of the 'Sacai or Sacea-sunni' (sons of Isaac) who *he* says became the Anglo Saxon tribe of Europe. Lewis writes:

> *These Saxons may also have been the biblical egel/engel, meaning bull (Taurus). This ties in well with original bull worship in Britain and may provide the source for the name 'English'. 'Ish', it will be recalled, means 'man' [Orion] in Taurus. Thus it may also be argued that, as 'birth' means covenant, 'birth-ain' would mean covenant people.*[10]

He goes on to say that *spiritual* Jerusalem 'symbolically' comprises Benjamin and Ephraim (*two* pillars of light), who are part of the Tree of Life and relate to 'Gemini' and 'Coma' – *two* astrological signs that sit in the same arena of the stars adjacent to Orion. Therefore Orion, on one level, can be seen as the focus for an ongoing 'spiritual war' in the heavens, and possibly the birth place of the 'New Jerusalem', something that 'descends' from heaven (or a higher dimension) and has the potential to spiritually *awaken* humanity. An event leading to *all* becoming Superconscious and at *One* with the Creator. It could also be seen as a 'kingdom of consciousness' (the Truth Vibrations) which flowers to seed a *global* spiritual nation, one that grows out of a new spiritual movement (or a light unto all nations).

I see this spiritual 'nation' as the '*Imagi-Nation*' (our powerful *imagination*) as mentioned in my illustrated fictional stories, *Kokoro, Moon Slayer* and *Aeon Rising*. We are witnessing the birth of a conscious, awakened, nation of magicians, who are prepared to dismantle the illusory structures of division and servitude inflicted on humanity. Being aware of the 'mind-control', the 'dark magic' and 'symbolism' used against humanity by *unseen forces*, is part of this awakening process. According to Lewis, the 'New Jerusalem,' talked of in *Revelation* could also be a company of nations made up of English-speaking peoples, symbolic of Britain and the United States. Again, not my view, but interesting to say the least. Lewis even suggests that the 'Teacher' is the 'Covenant Man' in biblical terms (possibly the covenant of Orion with Taurus?) and will rise up out of Britain. *Maybe he already has?* I know of one Taurean man called 'David' who is very much a teacher of the mysteries and is not frightened to reveal the truth and challenge off-world forces manipulating global positions of power and influence on earth.

The teachings of the Gnostic master – the Son of Man (The Heavenly Adam) Orion are still being felt today. As always 'FEAR', so it seems, is the vibration used by malevolent otherworldly forces so to prevent humanity from becoming LOVE, PEACE and *living* Heaven on Earth.

The Truth, Light and the Way

You could say that I am connected in spirit to the Gnostic Cathar in how I 'perceive' the physical world. I maintain that this world (matrix reality) is not the original home of humanity, but rather a counterfeit earth reality described as terrible, or evil, especialy by the 12th Century Gnostics. The power structures, from the global banks, big-tech, the military-industrial complex and geopolitical oligarchs, etc., are all 'manifestations' of this fake 'inverted' (too-often-evil) world. If you think the word evil is extreme, then go look at the world (the physical reality) on earth today. See its injustices, mass poverty, endless wars, impositions and the 'extreme' rich polarised against the mega poor, and tell me it's any different to all of the ancient tyrannical civilizations? Babylon, ancient Rome or any other historical era, they are all seem the same mindset inspired by death of spirit and rule through material wealth. The words attributed to Jesus, when the Gnostic master spoke of the 'lamp of the body' explains the 'power of spirit' over 'matter' (the material world), saying:

> *But if your vision is poor, your whole body will be full of darkness. If then the light within you is darkness, how great is that darkness![11:23] No one can serve two masters: Either he will hate the one and love the other, or he will be devoted to the one and despise the other. You cannot serve both God and money.[11:24] Therefore I tell you, do not worry about your life, what you will eat or drink; or about your body, what you will wear. Is not life more than food, and the body more than clothes?[12:25] (Luke 11:33-36 and Luke 12:22-31 - NIV)*

Salvation through life, peace, justice and 'freedom' can only be found in the human spirit and the *Oneness* in all life. No physical, material structure on earth (no matter how big or small) will move us like 'spirit'. The true human form, our divinity, our spirit, comes from a place beyond this physical (often nightmare) reality. All spirit is not of this world and therefore can only be reached by going *beyond* the illsuions, beyond the 'systems of control' imposed on our minds. As the Gnostic master also supposedly once said:

> *...the kingdom of heaven (spirit) is like treasure hidden in a field, which a man found and hid; and for joy over it he goes and sells all that he has and buys that field. (Matthew 13:44 - NIV)*

The treasure in that field of stars, metaphorically speaking, is, I would suggest, the jewel amongst Orion's stars, the brilliant white area within the Throne of Radiance - the Orion Nebula. Beyond the Throne, symbolically speaking, is the Kingdom of Heaven (the 'field of plenty') I mentioned in *Chapter Four*. The field is also symbolic of the infinite 'field of energy', waveforms that construct reality, and how reality can be manipulated at the level of the *field*, or *waveform*. However, we can also *see* the field and utilise it to bring about 'heaven on earth' should we desire this with all of our hearts (see figure 429). I have called the projection and the surrounding area around the Orion Nebula, *Orion's Door*, because I believe going through this door, *symbolically and spiritually*, we find higher consciousness and levels of awareness inaccessible while being influenced by the projection, the blueprints and symbolism entrenched in beliefs and material servitude. As I said earlier, the 'house of many mansions' allegedly spoken of by the Gnostic teacher, Jesus, is the multi-dimensional 'construct' from *within* the projector, which is also connected to worlds *beyond* the projector room, *through* the 'eye' in the 'Trapezium' (see pages 431-33).

Throughout the book, I have connected common themes relating to Orion archetypes, Orion worship and the notion of an off-world nefarious Cult connected to Orion. Religious blueprints, no matter what faith is followed, seem to have a connection to Orion's influence over humanity, *energetically*. The blueprints I have talked about, and how they are manifesting as new forms of 'control' over humanity, are purely 'energetic' waveform information decoded by our minds. All symbolic language and codes unravelled within this book are also energetic fields, and all are part of that decoded information. So are the archetypes in the form of Orion hero figures, gods and giants, etc. As I said at the beginning of the book, there is so much more to know about Orion's stars energetically, too.

Heaven on Earth Codes

The concept of a miracle is something that should not be possible due to limited collective perception as observed by those who are 'programmed' to 'think' within the boundaries of collective thought and information decoded by our five senses. Any human who is accessing information from above and beyond the limited field of information (or what the Gnostics called the 'boundary'), could be able to 'alter' the energetic waveform mind patterns (thoughts) of those who connect with such a persona or energy. The Son of Man (Orion) archetype, in the form of Jesus, represents a series of energetic codes designed to allow access to levels of awareness *beyond* the boundary, or beyond the limitations of the blueprints and structures keeping the masses focused on fear-based beliefs (religions) and other templates, or programmes, packaged differently. All religions, are part of the same energetic constructs. The 'New Age' is another religion and in some cases another cult, just like the 'Woke' movement, too; all are different expressions of the 'control'. As I said earli-

Figure 429: 'Becoming' the Waveform Field.
At the level of the field, we can anchor heaven *on* earth.

er, what some choose to call God could be *pure* alien intelligence'? An intelligence capable of recreating 'perceived life forms' based on energetic information (data) organized through fractals and codes we see as sacred geometry, and so forth. God, in this sense, could be an immense artificial intelligent 'living computer' connected to billions of minds (interstellar computers) with a mass of information and codes at its disposal. Just as the 'Cloud' allows billions of computer users to access information via the Internet, the living super computer I am describing is everywhere, at all times, within the holographic reality it has created. It accesses all waveform information, which constructs the holographic reality through our minds. Just as every cellular phone, pad, computer, etc., in our world is linked to the Internet, we are all connected in the holographic-matrix-earth reality to everything else created within this 'sea of energy'. Just as water droplets are still the sea and ocean, the smallest particle is also everything from a star to a human being. *Everything* (on one level) is a program, a belief or mindset; all programs are 'selecting' information (codes or blueprints) from a vast database of information. However, any god-like artificial intelligent 'super computer' is still limited in terms of its understanding of true, infinite awareness. This is our advantage over artificial intelligence; we are capable of using our 'creative imagination', not merely replicating information given to us, should we so choose.

Manifesting Miracles

The parameters of a god-like artificial intelligent super computer are within the worlds operating *through* the soul, mind and body. These *three* realms of existence are interacting with each other energetically, but are also limited due to the type of information we are allowed to access. You could say our perception is too often hijacked by the Cult that sells us what William Blake called, "mind-forg'd manacles". The spiritual archetype of Orion in the form of the Gnostic master – Jesus, or what I've called the 'Game Changer Consciousness' operates from a higher source (beyond Orion's Door), bringing unique codes of information. It can also be seen as a 'back door' to Superconsciousness and infinite awareness. We don't have to experience the coming Cyber-Grid Empire and the constant war on humanity, as mentioned in earlier chapters. We can choose to create a different reality collectively. We really need to operate on a different level of awareness beyond the levels of the body-mind-soul (see figure 430). We need more than ever **to allow spirit, creative imagination, and higher consciousness to lead the way**. I know this is easier said than done, especially in a material world full of fear, panic, and in recent months, what seems like total 'isolation'; but accessing our spirit will lead us to something we all long for – heaven on earth.

The notion of creating reality from a higher source of energy can be seen, in my view, through the following stages. These stages need to be 'felt deeply' and utilised from the highest intention. I am concisely listing them, but, in truth, there is more to each stage than the headings below. To reach the worlds beyond the veil, or beyond the boundaries in our minds, in my humble opinion, we need to consider the following stages:

- **Creating a 'Space'** – Allowing a vacuum for *energy* to come through us. We have to be *still*, to be alone and to be *silent* before we can realise the connection with our higher source that is too often ignored, or forgotten. It's interesting that at the time of completing this book, much of the whole world is in lockdown or 'self-isolating' due to the coronavirus pandemic. Despite the concerns I highlighted in earlier chapters, the opportunity to 'allow' our higher selves into our world through going *within*, rather than constantly looking outside, starts the process of manifesting changes in our world.

In the process of creating space we empty ourselves and start to unravel our energetic blueprints in the mind. Meditation can aid us

Figure 430: The Divine Human Form.
We operate on *three* levels simultaneously. The physical body-mind can be hijacked by endless 'mind-forg'd manacles' (limited perception). The soul is the light-body, but our spirit comes from 'source', beyond the projection, *beyond* Orion's Door.

in this process, but to be physically alone while doing so helps untangle the 'energetic connections' to people and places, experiences and thoughts that will hinder the process I am about to explain. The many religious stories of going into the wilderness are symbolic of the first phase of connecting with energies that can be channelled into this reality.

- **From *Within* to *Without*** – Connecting to higher consciousness through emptying our heads (or space), so we can fill ourselves with *compassion* or ευσπλαχνία, in Greek (the original language of the Gospels) which means to be *moved by compassion*. Empathy is a *living current* (energy), surrounding us; we see others' needs and not just our own 'separate' needs. To be compassionate and *forgiving* towards others connects us with energies existing beyond the boundary, or the veil. Compassion is the true nature of the 'cement' holding humanity together as *One*. We are *all One* consciousness. Without compassion, we are separate and unable to love ourselves truly. When separated from each other through illusions, beliefs, governmental restrictions, and endless 'blueprints' of the mind, we are *easily controlled through fear*. Look at the world *today!* It's easy to see how blueprints of control, written into the fabric of our daily lives through fear, are hindering our collective power. When we begin to put the welfare of others ahead of our desires, then our dreams start to arrive with expediency. As the Gnostic master teacher said, *"Give to all that ask of you"* (Matthew 5:42).

- **Knowing** how to ask for what we need so to be fulfilled in our quest to connect with spirit (our higher purpose) and the worlds beyond Orion's Door is the next phase. Seeing the material world as though you have nothing to lose will place you in the 'present' or 'moment'. How often are we placed in such situations that can gift us with the power of the moment? In that space, the past and future are subordinate to the present. They don't exist, only in our minds. It is our 'feeling' of the 'present moment' and the space we have created (the vacuum) *which attracts to us the energy we need to manifest what we truly need*. We have to put our 'requests' to the infinite abundant source both vocally and in writing, like a child at Christmas who asks persistently for that favourite toy. *Speak it out loud* and *know* it will come. The saying 'Knock and the door shall be opened' carries truth when we *know* rather than try, or just simply believe.

- **Focusing** attention on what you already have, rather than what you don't have, will attract more energy to you so to be able to manifest what you need. Our consciousness will always attract more of what is in our subconscious thoughts. Being mindful of our thoughts through knowing and focusing them will maximise our energy. Through meditation, focus on the source of all-that-exists and not the 'lack of source' as this will bring abundance into existence. If we only focus on 'lack' we will only attract more 'lack of'. I know this sounds ever so simplistic and impossible to those who are suffering due to injustice and poverty, or anything else, but it is a shift in energetic focus that aligns us with the *source* of 'all-that-exists'. Once in that vibration, or thought process, there is no lack, only what appear to be small miracles of abundance and simple needs being met. All 'synchronicity' comes from focusing on the journey and not the tasks or burdens brought about by the journey. So many times in my life I have witnessed synchronicity in motion, especially when I have trusted and focused on the path ahead rather than each individual step. Be aware of the steps but don't take your focus off the feeling that started your journey. In the same context we need to focus on our true self, rather than what we 'think' we are (see figure 431). Going with the flow of energy is to be at one with the sea, or *field of energy*, that exists all around us always. Much of what I am saying here can be backed up by quantum physics, not to mention why the *'force'*, mentioned in the *Star Wars* movies, has engaged millions over the years, it exists!

An ocean always goes with the flow of the rest of the ocean, never against, so does the rest of the air.

what we think

what we are

Figure 431: Focus on our 'True' self.
When we focus on our true state of awareness and go with the flow, we start to manifest everything we need.

- **Giving** energy so that we can receive energy is crucial to our journey. Giving without any strings attached is a true act of love and generosity. Only fear of lack prevents us from freely giving to those who are in need. The act of giving relieves us of 'stagnation' and stimulates the flow of energy, which continues to flow towards others. It is the 'feeling' behind the giving (the intention) along with genuine compassion, with no ego or acknowledgment that generates true power. Generosity and love are *Oneness* in action. A society that creates immense wealth for the few yet keeps the masses in dire need, panic, fear and too-often extreme poverty, is not a society that understands *Oneness*. I have said so many times there should be *NO Children in Need*! A society that creates have's and have-nots, based on a global elite (the 1%) who control all wealth (energy) and flow of information (energy) has no desire to be *Oneness* – or to have heaven on earth. To go beyond these unchecked levels of control (the Cyber-Grid Empire) and *all* war, we must symbolically go through Orion's Door and bathe in immense, infinite worlds. From this perspective, we see each other as we truly are – *all One consciousness, all* equal in the eyes of unconditional love.

- **Grounding** the energy within ourselves in the 'present' is so essential to the process I am describing here. We need to become like a child at heart and see reality with a sense of knowingness and play. The place of play, the garden (or the Garden of Eden), is our natural state of consciousness. The garden is the location for the door, the place where we can pass through into worlds beyond the boundaries of the garden. How many times have you dreamt of a gate at the bottom of a garden and longed to go beyond it into the expansive landscape? The Garden of Eden, the place of original innocence and play for Adam (Son of Man) and Eve (Sophia) is the stellar nursery and its surrounding area within the Orion Nebula.

  The garden conjures up the place of innocence and is symbolic of our return to innocence, especially if we are to move through the door. [Unless we are willing to become child-like (innocent), then we will always block the flow of energy and the imagination – our natural state of consciousness] The door won't be visible to those who cannot ground themselves or allow themselves to 'know' that through grounding, energy flows to you and touches you – making you aware (or awake).

- **Seeing** the desired reality clearly, through the eye of our energetic spiritual heart, brings the desired end we seek. As I have already explained, the mind is easily tricked into believing limitation, impossibility and repetition of thoughts that hold us in a 'feedback loop'

Figure 432: Our Perception Creates *Our* Reality.
Perceptions create a self-fulfilling conscious and subconscious feedback loop in which we interact with *All Possibility* only within the frequency band that our perceptions represent.

(see figure 432). What we see and hear through the five senses, or what we choose to 'perceive' as reality, *perception creates our reality*. Seeing the desired end you are asking for, and knowing it will happen, brings into alignment the desire to truly reshape reality. It's the power to see through the *eye of the heart* that enables us to reshape our perception and activate our consciousness and, therefore, affect our reality. *Everything* is energy, and our reality can be reshaped by *seeing it reshaped* in our mind's eye. Change how we think and feel on a deeper level, and the outcome will be so, like changing the roll of film on the old cinema projector to view a different projection, a different story, or movie, or 'life'.

The Greek words, 'Anaviepsas' and 'Ouranon' (Orion) express the need to *restore sight*, to look to heaven (the eye of the heart) through love and elevation of consciousness. Through love and 'compassion' we achieve the final goal of connecting with higher consciousness. As the Beatles song beautifully explains, '*All You Need is Love, love is all you need*'.

- **Being Grateful** - To give thanks for what is about to come to us through our creative imagination, while *seeing* the changes made in our mind's eye, is crucial to the process of 'asking then visualising' a desired outcome. Giving thanks can also be verbalised positively in the form of *affirmations* in relation to ourselves and the needs of others. When we give thanks from our hearts we connect with infinite source - an awareness that knows only gratitude and sharing. When we verbalise our thankfulness we automatically resonate with the projected outcome that arrives as a gift, or blessing, to those who are open enough to receive. *All* healing involves this 'readiness' of being grateful and open *to* receiving from an ocean of energy that surrounds us and connects us to Superconsciousness.

- **To Act** as if the outcome has already happened and vibrate as though *it is our reality*. Nothing is manifested, or achieved, without *knowing*, focusing and 'action' through putting ideas, visions or spoken words into reality. All creativity works in this way, too. All of our work should be our 'belief in motion', it should be the core of who we are. Nothing can become a reality without visualisation and action towards it. Every event on earth starts out as energetic wavefield that is focused and then given solidity through action. Any idea has to be visualised then believed to be real through 'feeling it' into existence. Feeling it at the core of our being, in every fibre and cell, gives it the power to become somatic, to arrive in the physical world. *Remember*, what I am outlining here is *not* accumulating material wealth or hoarding riches, it is about managing the flow of energy, just as a Tai Chi master moves energy around (see figure 433)

- **Engaging in the Cycle of Energy** – is to see it flow around us and towards those with whom we are connecting. All healing comes through engaging with the flow of energy (the field) through focusing on our higher purpose. The cycle brings us to the same energy source from which we are seeking help, but in truth, it is our own consciousness, our 'essence' that creates the cycle allowing us to connect the beginning (the space and knowingness) with the actual physical healing, or desired outcome. The stages I am describing here are not how you will get rich or manipulate energy (others); they are acts of true righteousness designed to bring the light of consciousness, or heaven, on earth. The Alpha and Omega have to be joined, all parts have to become the whole. As the Greek philosopher-scientist, Alcmaeon of Croton once said, *"Men perish because they cannot join the beginning with the end."* I would add that we cannot achieve

Figure 433: 'Knowing' and 'Interacting' with the Wavefield.
We need to visualise the desired outcome at the level of the wavefield. *Feeling* the vibrations at the core of our being and *focusing* the wavefield is part of the action required to heal ourselves and others, or to bring abundance into existence.

levels of higher states of awareness (spirit) and Superconsciousness without *seeing* the interconnectedness of energy. It illuminates our soul, mind and body. It is the spirit of who we truly are. We are projections of the Infinite source - *The One*, the creator of all-that-exists (see figure 434 overleaf).

- **Receiving and Letting Go** - What we have asked for must *appear* just as water fills the land when the rains *appear*. Once we let go of the process and allow the energy used to flow through the channels we have created (in our minds and through physical action) it will naturally find form and become a reality. All forms of energy can be recycled for others to use; therefore, *letting go* is 'crucial' if we want to truly access higher states of awareness. So often, we ask spirit to provide for us, to answer a question, or show a sign, but we fail to prepare ourselves to receive, or collect the abundance flowing through us. The vacuum we created, in the beginning, must be filled with energy just as spirit must take form. All of nature abhors a vacuum and nothing in nature (life) stays empty for long, it's a law of the Universe. As the American astronomer, planetary scientist, cos-

Figure 434: We *Are* Infinite Source.
The creator of *all* realities connects *all* life. The Infinite Source is the place of the Upper
Aeons and the home of our *Superconsciousness.*

mologist, astrophysicist, astrobiologist, Carl Sagan, once said: "We
are star stuff which has taken its destiny into its own hands."

The stages I have described here could be used to heal, to bring peace,
or to enlighten, or inform, others. These stages also form the *pillar of light*
often talked about by mystics, which connects the earth with the heavens.
The process of creating from our hearts (our infinite awareness), which resonates with our higher self, takes us beyond the boundary of *Orion's Door*
and the projection in which we are caught up. Applying these stages makes
a 'magician' of us *all* and not just the *few.* Such acts of peace and stillness,
form the heart, will bring harmony and healing between humanity and the
alien malevolent forces that wish to control our world. We must strive for
love and peace at all costs. As the Lakota (Orion worshipping), medicine
man, prophet and healer, Black Elk, said:

*The first peace, which is the most important, is that which comes within the souls
of people when they realize their relationship, their oneness with the universe and
all its powers, and when they realize at the center of the universe dwells the Great*

Spirit, and that its center is really everywhere, it is within each of us.

The steps mentioned here are created through our interaction with energy, our spirit and what mystics call the Infinite Source. **We are eternal aspects of the Infinite Source** and it is time we remembered such wisdom and power. As the great Alan Watts said:

> *And if you become aware of that unknown self, the more you become aware of it, the more you realize that it is inseparably connected with everything else that there is. That you are a function of this total galaxy, bounded by the Milky Way, and that, furthermore, this galaxy is a function of all other galaxies, and that vast thing that you see far off, far off, far off with telescopes, and you look, and look, and look—one day you're going to wake up and say, "Why, that's me!" And in knowing that, know—you see—that you never die, that you are the eternal thing that comes and goes, that appears now as John Jones, now as Mary Smith, now as Betty Brown, and so it goes, forever, and ever, and ever.*

If you have stayed with me this far, you will see that I have come full circle through the myriad of archetypes connected to Orion into levels of Superconsciousness beyond the blueprints used by off-world inspired priests and magicians to affect reality on earth.

The 'revelation' I have touched on in this chapter is nothing more than a desire for the truth and to live our truth. The symbolism of Orion (the star man), the hero, teacher and other religious archetypes, have formed the blueprints of control, courtesy of the magicians and off-world priesthoods covered in this book. Humanity is ready to *become* 'Superconscious', loosening the restrictions placed on our minds, and the limitations and beliefs that deny our access to the truth. When we *desire* the truth we will become infinite awareness, because being *infinitely aware* and a fully-conscious human being, can only mean living in the light of the truth. The entirety of this philosophy can be 'felt' in the supposed words of the master gnostic teacher, Jesus, when he performed his 'Sermon on the Mount'. Despite the religious connotations, in these words *are* the 'instructions' for living in the *truth vibrations* and resonating with Superconsciousness. If we replace the word 'heaven' with *Superconsciousness*, and the words, 'God', or 'father', with *infinite love* or *infinite awareness*, then the sermon becomes clear:

> *Blessed are the poor in spirit, for theirs is the kingdom of heaven,*
> *Blessed are those that mourn, for they shall be comforted,*
> *Blessed are the meek, for they shall inherit the earth,*
> *Blessed are those who hunger and thirst for what is right, for they shall be filled,*
> *Blessed are the merciful, for they shall obtain mercy,*
> *Blessed are the pure in heart, for they shall see God,*

When you are hunger and thirsty, you are not distracted by anything, or anyone

This is what He means when, He says eat of Him. In seeing Him, there no other, You simply drink and you eat to your satisfaction.

Blessed are the peacemakers, for they shall be called Sons of God,
Blessed are those who are persecuted in the cause of right, for theirs is the king-
dom of heaven,
Blessed are you when people abuse you and speak all kinds of calumny against
you for my sake, rejoice and be glad, for your reward will be great in heaven as it
was for the prophets persecuted before you,
In your prayers remember your father knows what your needs are before you ask
him.
Our father in heaven, hallowed be thy name,
Thy kingdom come, thy will be done on earth as it is in heaven,
Give us this day our daily bread, and forgive us our debts, as we forgive our
debtors, And lead us not into temptation, but deliver us from evil.

As I said at the beginning of the book, much of what you have read is subjective, but my love for the subject covered throughout its pages means I
have only spoken what I 'perceive' to be the *truth*. As John Lennon once
said:

I believe in everything until it's disproved. So I believe in fairies, the myths, drag-
ons. It all exists, even if it's in your mind. Who's to say that dreams and night-
mares aren't as real as the here and now?

The subjects connected to Orion in this book move between physical reality
and other-worldly non-physical realities, and since they have yet to be disproved, I will consider them all as real and an important part of our human
world. I hope that anyone who has read this book will look upon the stars,
especially Orion, with very different eyes.

Love and Peace be with you all, always.

Sources:

1) Fuller, J. F. C. *The Secret Wisdom of the Qabalah*, (e-book) PDF, p27
2) Looper, DeAnne. *Kabbalah Secrets Christians Need to Know.* p116
3) https://israelmyglory.org/article/dark-innovation-the-role-of-technology-in-revelation-13/
4) Lewis, R. *The Thirteenth Stone; History Rewritten, The Jesus Myth Exploded and the Great Secret of the Knights Templar Revealed by the Dead Sea Scrolls.* Fountainhead Press, 1994, p13
5) *Ibid*, p13
6) May, Rollo. *The Cry For Myth.* W.W. Norton & Company, 1991, p53
7) Donald Grey, Barnhouse. *The Invisible War: The Panorama of the Continuing Conflict Between Good and Evil.* 1965, p86
8) Lewis, R. *The Thirteenth Stone.* Fountain Head Press, 1994, p140
9) *Ibid*, p154
10) *Ibid*, p151

APPENDIX I

MEDITATION

Colossians 3:2
Mark 6:7
Eph 1:20-23

Remember, to 'break any spell', you need to **not** play by its restrictions (its rules). You need to 'elevate your mind' above the spell, keep your heart light, bright and watch for signs. Watch both the skies and the oceans, something is coming, I can feel it!

Be strong and courageous. Do not be afraid or terrified because of them, for the Lord your God goes with you; he will never leave you nor forsake you.
(Deuteronomy 31:6)

There is no fear in love.
(John 4:18).

Rather than watch the dystopian Covid-19 movie. Switch of your TV and join me in meditation most evenings at 9pm GMT. From the comfort of our own homes, let's heal the 'distortion', division, fear, panic and 'mind-virus' infecting too many people at this time.

While sitting at home, quietly (if you can), I would focus your heart energy on the distortion (see an energetic ball of distortion); 'visualise' endless energy, or a waveform unravelling it, healing it. See the light (the waveform) moving through the twisted knot-like distortion, picking it apart. See it unravelled and becoming endless energy *deep* **– as it fades to 'nothingness' – into *Oneness*.**

655

APPENDIX II

'OFF-WORLD' FORCES
IN PICTURES

As an artist and author who has found much to comment on through my art and illustrations over the past 20 years, I am now looking towards a period of 'returning to the innocence' of why I started painting in the first place. This book project has led me to a new phase of image-making, the 'beginning of a return' for me as an 'illustrator'. I wrote over over ten years ago,

"All art in its native sense is concerned with stirring our spirits, our soul and stimulating our extra-sensory perception. As always it is the art of storytelling, whether oral or pictorial, that is the real sign of creative vitality in any culture or society. Creating, or re-creating our own personal myths helps to eradicate negative feelings generated by dogma, which in the end can only cause disempowerment. All myths and legends inspire and fuel our imagination and, from a creative point of view, help us dig deeper toward understanding our unique relationship with the universe."

My work, has always, is aimed at 'stirring the human imagination' and inspiring a 'deeper understanding' of why we are here on the Earth. My art and Illustrations, as always, tell of a different view of the past, our present dilemma and how we integrate our 'personal mythology' into a world that doesn't often grasp the true nature of the need for metaphysical (visionary) works of art.

In the last few pages of *Orion's Door*, I've compiled a few images expressing some of the concepts surrounding the themes I have touched on relating to Orion consciousness, off-world extraterrestrial forces, the Cult and Superconsciousness. To see colour versions of this work, visit my website.

Enjoy.

The Gnostic Demiurge described in the Nag Hammadi, creating the Matrix Earth.

Extraterrestrial consciousness working through Orion and Saturn (the Cult) *are* AI gods.
Here they are challenged by Aeonic (Christ-like) lions from beyond the physical world.
A spiritual war is being fought across Orion's many worlds.

Orion is the home of our genetic starseed and quite possibly the source of both malevolent and benevolent alien intelligence. My image of the Orion Nebula here shows opposing forces encircling the light-body of Adam - the 'Heavenly Adam'.
The Gnostic Sophia is celebrating the arrival of the Orion Man - the Son of Man.
The Tree of Life also encounters nefarious 'forces' as
the Celestial Adam takes form in Eden amongst the Orion's stars.

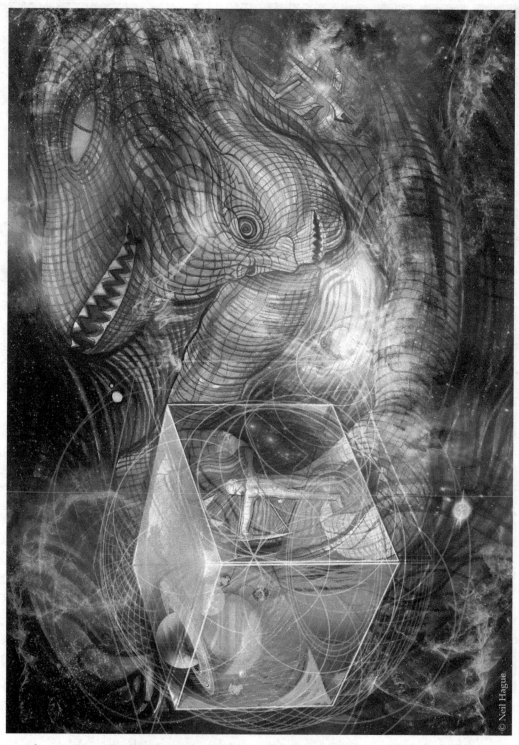

The Gnostic Demiurge 'encases' Orion and our Solar System in a prison-like fake reality. The earth and other planets in the solar system are influenced by 'creatures of light', or what the Gnostics call archons, Jinn or angels.

© Neil Hague

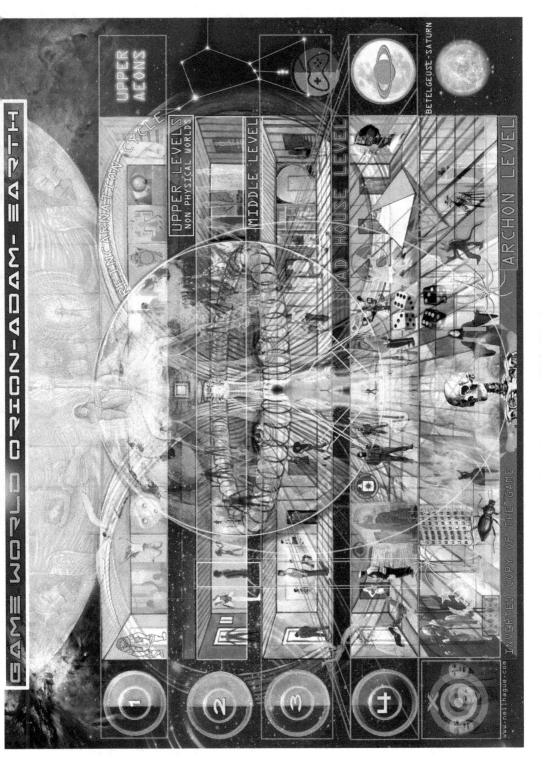

Inside the prison-like (encased) reality, is what I call the 'game world' - a place of many dimensions (mansions). Humanity is caught up in the bottom *three* worlds of mind, body and soul. Our true 'source of origin' is from the place beyond the 'game world'.

Superconsciousness sends one of its own to Earth's prison-like world
to free the minds of those who are ready to *open their hearts and eyes*.
Light is coming to us all and freedom calls!

BIBLIOGRAPHY

Abrams, Dr. Michael; *The Twelve Conditions of a Miracle*. Abundance Media, 2001

Allen, James P., Peter Der Manuelian; *The Ancient Pyramid Texts*, 2005.

Allen, Paula Gunn; *Grandmothers of the Light*. The Women's Press. 1992.

Appleby, Nigel; *Hall of the God; The Quest to Discover the Knowledge of the Ancients*. Hienemann. 1989

Arthur, James; *Mushrooms and Mankind*, The Book Tree. 2003

Ashe, Geoffrey; *The Ancient Wisdom; a quest for the source of mystic knowledge.*1977

Ashe, Geoffrey; *Dawn Behind the Dawn: A search for Earthly Paradise.* 1992

Barber, Richard and **Riches, Anne**; *A Dictionary of Fabulous Beasts.* 1971

Blake, William; *The Everlasting Gospel*, (1757–1827)

Blavatsky, Helena Petrovna; *The Secret Doctrine*, Vol. 2

Blavatsky, Helena Petrovna; *Collected Writings vol. X* (Wheaton, IL: Theosophical Publishing House, 1988

Bramley, William; *The Gods of Eden*. Avon Books. 1989

Bryant, Page; *The Aquarian Guide to Native American Mythology. Aquarian Press,*1991

Dalley, Stephanie; *Myths from Mesopotamia, Creation, the Flood, Gilgamesh and others,* revised edition. Oxford University Press, 2000

Daniel, John; *Scarlet and the Beast - A History of the War between English and French Freemasonry,* 1889

Danielou, Jean; *Primitive Christian Symbols*. Baltimore. 1964

David, Gay A.; *The Orion Zone: The Ancient Star Cities of the American Southwest.* Adventures Unlimited. 2006

David, Gary A.; *Mirrors of Orion, Star Knowledge of the Ancient World*. Create Space Independent Publishing Platform. 2014

Ellis, Ralph; *Jesus, Last of the Pharaohs,* 1997

Ferguson, George; *Signs and Symbols in Christian Art.* Oxford University Press. 1961

Ford, Martin; *The Rise of the Robots; Technology and the Threat of Mass Unemployment.* 2015

Gettings, Fred; *Dictionary of Demons*. Guild Publishing. 1988

Gilbert, Adrian and **Bauval, Robert**; *The Orion Mystery*. Random House (1994)

Goodman, Ronald; *Lakota Star Knowledge*. 1992

Guiley, Rosemary Ellen; *Encyclopedia of Angels*. Infobase Publishing 1996

Guirdham, Arthur; *The Great Heresy*. C.W Daniel Company Ltd, 1993

Hancock, Graham; *Before America*. 2019

Hague, Neil; *Through Ancient Eyes*. Quester. 2018

Hague, Neil; *Journeys in the Dreamtime*. Quester, 2006

Hague, Neil; *Aeon Rising, The Battle for Atlantis*. 2017

Henry, William; *Cloak of the Illuminati*. Adventures Unlimited Press, 2013

Hill, Douglas; *Man, Myth & Magic*. 1970

Hutchison, Luke; *Growing the Family Tree: The Power of DNA in Reconstructing Family Relationships* (PDF) 2004

Huxley, Francis (the Anthropologist); *The Way of the Sacred: The Rites and Symbols, Beliefs and Tabus, That Men Have Held in Awe and Wonder Through the Ages*. New York; Dell Publishing. 1974

Icke, David; *The Biggest Secret*. Bridge of Love. 1998

Icke, David: *The Perception Deception*. DI Books. 2013

Icke, David; *The Trigger*. Ikonic, 2019

Icke, David; *Everything You Need To Know But Have Never Been Told*. DI Books, 2018

Jake Stratton-Kent; *The Headless One* (e-book) 1991

Janet Parker; Alice Mills; Julie Stanton; *Mythology: Myths, Legends and Fantasies*. Durban, Struik Publishers, 2007.

Jung, Carl; *Man and His Symbols*. Stellar Books. 2013

Jung, C. G., and **Kerényi, C**; *Essays on a Science of Mythology: the Myth of the Divine Child and the Mysteries of Eleusis*. Pantheon Books. 1949

Kaku, Michio; *Hyperspace*. Oxford University Press 2000

Lamb Lash, John; *Not in His Image, Gnostic Vision, Sacred Ecology and the Future of Belief (The Apocryphon of John)*. Chelsea Green. 2006

Latura, George; *Plato's X & Hekate's Crossroads -Astronomical Links to the Mysteries of Eleusis*, 2014

Lenski G & Nolan P; *Human Societies: An Introduction into Macro Sociology*. 1995

Lewis Da Costa; *The Secret Diaries of an Alchemist*. Fountainhead Press, 2005

Lewis Da Costa; *The Thirteenth Stone*. Fountainhead Press, 1994

Lewis William, David; *Mind in the Cave*. Thames & Hudson

Long, Charles H; *Alpha: Myths of Creation*. 1963

Loper, DeAnne; *Kabbalah Secrets Chrsitians Need to Know - An in depth Study of the Kosher Pig and the Gods of Jewish Mysticism*. 2019.

Maltwood, Katherine; *A Guide to Glastonbury's Temple of the Stars*. 1929

Matlock, Gene D; *The Last Atlantis Book You'll Ever Read*. Dandelion Books. 2000

May, Rollo; *The Cry For Myth*. W.W. Norton & Company, 1991

Mayor, Adrienne; *Gods and Robots, Myths, Machines and Ancient Dreams of Technology*. 2018

Men, Hunbatz; *Secrets of Mayan Science and Religion*. Bear & Company; Original ed. Edition. 1989

Miller, Moshe. *Netzach, Hod, & Yesod (Kabbalah Online)*. 6th August 2015

Mott, Michael; *Caverns, Cauldrons and Concealed Creatures*. Grave Distractions. 2001

Murphy, Anthony; *Mythical Ireland*. Liffey Press. 2017

Myer, Isaac; *Scarabs - The History, Manufacture and Religious Symbolism*. 1894

Newton, Toyne; *The Dark Worship.* 2002

Owusu, Heike; *Symbols of Native America.* Sterling Publishing. 1997

Picknett, Lynn; *The Secret History of Lucifer.* Robinson. 2005

Picknett, Lynn and **Prince, Clive**; *The Masks of Christ, Behind the Lies and Cover-ups about the man Beloved to be God.* Sphere 2008

Phillips, Jonathan Talat; *The Electric Jesus: The Healing Journey of a Contemporary Gnostic.* Evolver Editions, 2011

Potter, GR; *The New Cambridge Modern History, Volume One- The Renaissance.* 1967

Roberts, Adam; *Introduction, to RUR & War with the Newts.* 2011

Roob, Alexander; *Alchemy and Mysticism.* Taschen, 1996

Robbs, Dave; *Operation Hollywood. How the Pentagon Shapes and Censors the Movies.* 2004

Rosheim/Mark Elling. *Leonardo's Lost Robots.* Springer, 2006

Sabak, Pierre; *Holographic Culture.* Serpentgena. 2018

Sabak, Pierre; *Murder of Reality, Hidden Symbolism of the Dragon.* Serpentgena. 2010

Scholem, Gershom; *Kabbalah.* Dorset Press & Keter Publishing House. 1974

Suttkus, Leslie and **Jayson**; *Book of Remembrance.* 2016

Swerdlow, Stewart A; *True Blood: Conflict and Creation.* (self published) 2002

Swinson, Antonia; *Root of All Evil, How to Make Spiritual Values Count.* St. Andrews Press, 2003

Székely, Edmond; *The Gospel of Peace of Jesus Christ.* C.W. Daniel Company. 1937

Talbot, David: *The Saturn Myth: A Reinterpretation of Rites and Symbols Illuminating Some of the Dark Corners of Primordial Society.* 1983

Taylor, Ellis; *The Esoteric Alphabet.* 2004

Taylor, Steven; *The Fall, The Insanity of the Ego in Human History and the Dawing of a New Era.* O Books, 2005

Tomas, Andrew; *Shambhala: Oasis of Light.* 1977

Tsarion, Michael: *Atlantis, Alien Visitation & genetic Manipulation.* 2000

West, John Anthony; *Serpent in the Sky.* Quest 1993

Wilson, Eric G. *The Melancholy Android - On the Psychology of Sacred Machines.* State University of New York Press. 2006

Wilten, Danny; *Orion in the Vatican.* 2013 (*see also* his YouTube channel: https://www.youtube.com/channel/UCCh1mGk_HFgj5_TN2jyGasQ)

Wood, David; *Genesis, the First Book of Revelations.* Baton Press, 1985

Vahia, Mayank; *Astronomical Myths in India.* (PDF) 2005

Yates, F; *Giordano Bruno and the Hermetic Tradition.* Routledge, 1964

IMAGE NOTICE

As a one-man band with a desire for uncovering spiritual truths and a passion for the occult and symbolism, I don't always get the chance to locate every single picture source. All, if not most of the images in this book have been sourced from public domain (copyright free) sources and sometimes copyright free photobanks. The majority are my personal creations, too.

If I have inadvertently missed any photographer (artist), due to the time it takes to track everyone down, please *forgive me* and contact me directly through my website to arrange the appropriate rights.

NEIL HAGUE

About the Author

Neil Hague is a UK based metaphysical artist, authorial illustrator, book designer and lecturer, originally trained in graphics and publishing. Over the past 25 years he has developed a 'unique' vision through his distinctive style of art and remarkable creativity. Hague's particular artistic style has been described as both spiritual and 'neo-shamanic' by people who have heard him lecture or who have seen his work.

Photography © Alan Ball

Since 2005 he has developed a career as a painter of transcendental, alternative art, producing imagery for a niche area in a class by itself.

In his first illustrated story *Kokoro*, he encapsulates a chronicle of creation within 'themes and signs' unfolding in our reality, as we go through a major shift in consciousness. In his second narrative, *Moon Slayer*, and third illustrated story, *Aeon Rising*, he takes the exposition further in terms of 'mythological characters' and the construction of our reality. With his illustrated work appearing in books and global presentations all over the world, his work is pivotal and fitting at this time.

Neil has lectured on alternative history, esoteric symbolism, mythology, the power of the imagination and now the extraordinary subjects in this book. His highly visual presentations are thought provoking, speaking directly to the subconscious mind and more importantly, to the hearts of those who hear his words.

"Neil Hague's work is unique - the language of an open and highly creative mind. You look with your eyes, but he speaks to your heart."

David Icke

Index

neilhaguebooks.com

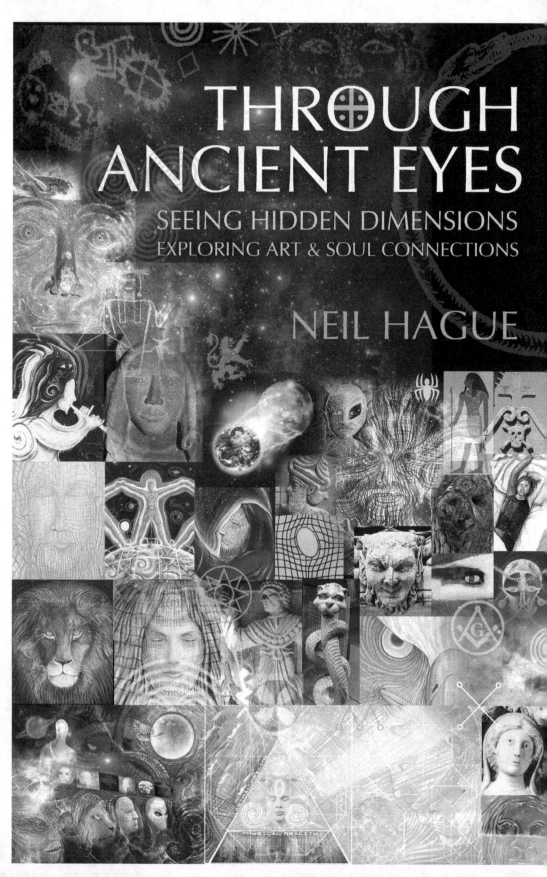

THROUGH ANCIENT EYES

SEEING HIDDEN DIMENSIONS
EXPLORING ART & SOUL CONNECTIONS

NEIL HAGUE